ROUTLEDGE LIBRARY EDITIONS: THE ECONOMY OF THE MIDDLE EAST

Volume 6

ARAB MONETARY INTEGRATION

ARAB MONETARY INTEGRATION
Issues and Prerequisites

Edited by
KHAIR EL-DIN HASEEB AND SAMIR MAKDISI

LONDON AND NEW YORK

First published in 1981

This edition first published in 2015
by Routledge
2 Park Square, Milton Park, Abingdon, Oxon, OX14 4RN

and by Routledge
711 Third Avenue, New York, NY 10017

Routledge is an imprint of the Taylor & Francis Group, an informa business

© 1981 Centre for Arab Unity Studies

All rights reserved. No part of this book may be reprinted or reproduced or utilised in any form or by any electronic, mechanical, or other means, now known or hereafter invented, including photocopying and recording, or in any information storage or retrieval system, without permission in writing from the publishers.

Trademark notice: Product or corporate names may be trademarks or registered trademarks, and are used only for identification and explanation without intent to infringe.

British Library Cataloguing in Publication Data
A catalogue record for this book is available from the British Library

ISBN: 978-1-138-78710-0 (Set)
eISBN: 978-1-315-74408-7 (Set)
ISBN: 978-1-138-81135-5 (Volume 6)
eISBN: 978-1-315-74531-2 (Volume 6)
Pb ISBN: 978-1-138-82004-3 (Volume 6)

Publisher's Note
The publisher has gone to great lengths to ensure the quality of this reprint but points out that some imperfections in the original copies may be apparent.

Disclaimer
The publisher has made every effort to trace copyright holders and would welcome correspondence from those they have been unable to trace.

Arab Monetary Integration

ISSUES AND PREREQUISITES

Edited by
KHAIR EL-DIN HASEEB
and
SAMIR MAKDISI

CROOM HELM
London & Canberra

© Centre for Arab Unity Studies
Croom Helm Ltd, 2-10 St John's Road London SW11

British Library Cataloguing in Publication Data

Arab monetary integration.
   1. Monetary unions — Congresses
   2. Money — Arab countries — Congresses
   I. Haseeb, K. II. Makdisi, S.A.
   332.4'566'09174927   HG3894

ISBN 0-7099-0712-5

Proceedings of a seminar held in Abu Dhabi, on 24-27 November 1980, organised by the Centre for Arab Unity Studies and the Arab Monetary Fund

Typesetting by Elephant Productions, London SE19

Printed and bound in Great Britain by
Biddles Ltd, Guildford and King's Lynn

CONTENTS

Preface

Part One: Monetary Integration and Monetary Co-Operation
1. On the Concepts, Objectives and Modalities of Monetary
   Integration *J. Williamson* — 11
   Comment *B. Dajani* — 28
   General Discussion — 31
2. The Relationship Between the International Monetary
   System and Regional Monetary Systems *R. Triffin* — 39
   Comment *J.W. Gunter* — 60
   General Discussion — 66

*Part Two: The Current Arab Monetary Situation and the Scope
Available for Arab Monetary Co-operation*
3. Analysis of the Financial Aspects of Arab Economic
   Co-operation and Opportunities for Monetary
   Co-operation *B. Dajani* — 73
   Comment *A. Al-Sagban* — 91
   General Discussion — 96
4. Trade and Exchange Regimes and the Exercise of Monetary
   Policy in the Arab Countries *K. Nashashibi* — 103
   Comment *S. Makdisi* — 125
   General Discussion — 138
5. The Arab Monetary Fund: Objectives and Performance
   A. Al-Sagban — 152
   Comment *M.L. Shoukair* — 187
   General Discussion — 194

*Part Three: Monetary Integration in Latin America, Europe
and West Africa*
6. Monetary Integration in Latin America *J.G. del Valle* — 205
   Comment *C.F. Diaz-Alejandro* — 225
   General Discussion — 228
7. The European Monetary System and European Monetary
   Integration *R. Masera and S. Rossi* — 233
   Comment *M. Sakbani* — 258
   General Discussion — 261

8. The Experience of the West African Monetary Union
   R. Bhatia ... 269
   Comment *A. Omrana* ... 286
   General Discussion ... 290

Part Four: Prospects for Arab Monetary Integration
9. The External Economic Positions of the Arab Countries and the Role of Financial Surpluses in Achieving Arab Monetary Integration *A.S. Ali* ... 299
   Comment *K. Nashashibi* ... 331
   General Discussion ... 337
10. Arab Monetary Integration: Benefits, Economic Obstacles and Modalities ... 346
    I. Costs and Benefits *A. Medio* ... 346
    II. Feasibility, Modalities and Selected Operational Issues
    M. Sakbani ... 356
    Comment *A.S. Ali* ... 376
    General Discussion ... 380
11. The Role of the Arab Monetary Fund in Achieving Arab Monetary Integration *F.A. Rasool* ... 390
    Comment *R. Sowellem* ... 414
    General Discussion ... 418
12. Basic Economic and Political Prerequisites for Achieving Arab Monetary Integration *F. Morsi* ... 422
    Comment *G. Corm* ... 448
    General Discussion ... 452

List of Participants ... 467

Index ... 470

PREFACE

The seminar 'Arab Monetary Integration: Issues and Prerequisites' was planned with three basic considerations in mind.

First, it was felt that the subject of Arab monetary integration, as part of overall Arab economic integration, had not received sufficient attention. A serious and objective examination of the various issues involved — benefits, costs, problems, feasibility — was deemed necessary for a clearer understanding of the processes and modalities associated with any move towards Arab monetary integration.

Secondly, it was decided that to accomplish this objective, the seminar should be conducted in an informal atmosphere, one that would permit the participants to engage freely in discussion of the issues before them. The choice of the issues to be examined did not, therefore, reflect any preconceived notions about Arab monetary integration. The aim was to stimulate an objective analysis of all aspects of monetary integration and of the measures which might be taken to strengthen Arab monetary co-operation.

Thirdly, it was believed that any discussion of Arab monetary integration would be greatly enhanced if it took into account the integration experiences of other regions of the world. It was agreed that these experiences could be highly instructive by way of defining the major issues involved. At the same time, it was recognised that each region has its own particular characteristics, traditions and aspirations and that the path towards integration finally chosen must reflect the realities of the region concerned.

The seminar was divided into four sessions. The first session took up the general concept of monetary integration and the relationships between regional and international monetary systems. The second was devoted to an analysis of the monetary conditions prevailing in the Arab countries and the scope available for Arab monetary co-operation. The third session focused on the monetary integration experiences of Latin America, Europe and West Africa, while the fourth and last session was given over to an examination of future prospects for Arab monetary integration, including the challenges and obstacles such a process is likely to face.

Altogether, twelve papers were presented, each one followed by prepared comments and a general discussion. The discussion of the seminar papers was generally animated and, in our opinion, proved highly useful in clarifying the issues under consideration. Unfortunately, limitations of space have made it necessary to condense several of the papers and,

Preface

in some cases, the written comments and discussions as well. In a few exceptional cases, whole sections have been deleted. In editing this material, we have endeavoured to preserve the essence of both the papers and the discussion; we can only hope we have been successful in this effort.

The seminar was planned by an advisory committee consisting, in addition to the editors, of K. Nashashibi, M. Sakbani and M.L. Shoukair. In its endeavour, the committee enjoyed the constant support of Jawad Hashim, president of the Arab Monetary Fund.

A number of individuals at both the Centre for Arab Unity Studies and the Arab Monetary Fund worked diligently in preparing for the seminar and, afterwards, in helping the editors to ready the proceedings for publication. While the list of names deserving of mention is too long for inclusion here, we cannot but acknowledge Ban Khayatt Saadeh's invaluable administrative assistance. Thanks are also due to Alison Brooks for translating many of the papers originally written in Arabic and for the editing of the English copy throughout.

K. Haseeb
S. Makdisi
Beirut

PART ONE

MONETARY INTEGRATION AND MONETARY
CO-OPERATION

1 ON THE CONCEPTS, OBJECTIVES AND MODALITIES OF MONETARY INTEGRATION

J. Williamson

Introduction

This paper is intended to survey the conceptual and theoretical aspects of monetary integration, including its relationship to economic integration. The following section of the paper deals with concepts: the concept of integration in economics, the concept of full monetary union and the various concepts of partial monetary integration that have received attention up to now. Section II considers the objectives of monetary integration and discusses what may be the key issue in choosing between full and partial monetary integration. Section III is devoted to surveying the modalities of monetary integration: first, of partial integration and then of the alternative strategies by which full monetary union might be achieved.

I. Concepts

The definitive discussion of the meaning of the concept of economic integration is that of Machlup[1] who argues that 'the idea of complete integration implies the *actual* utilization of all *potential* opportunities for the efficient division of labour'.[2] Within an integrated area, factors or goods are used or exchanged purely on the basis of the calculus of economic efficiency and, more specifically, without any discrimination or bias related to geographical origin or destination. This implies equality of prices for equivalent goods throughout the integrated region, with 'equality' of the means of production being defined in terms of perfect mobility and substitutability.[3] In sum, 'all inputs [have to be] considered eligible to compete for use in the production of all conceivable outputs, and all outputs are considered eligible to compete for allocations of all conceivable inputs. In this interrelatedness and interdependence among all economic activities I see the essence of general economic integration'.[4] Removal of obstacles to the movement of all kinds of labour, capital and products is viewed as a necessary but not necessarily sufficient condition for full integration, which may also require the establishment of institutions and common policies that will safeguard the perpetuation of non-discrimination and assure the absence of bias due to man-made geography.

Among the institutional arrangements that Machlup argues are essential if freedom of travel, migration, capital transfer and trade are to lead to high mobility (understood as high responsiveness to price incentives, rather than as large absolute exchanges) and thus to a high degree of integration, perhaps the most important is monetary integration. It would surely be difficult to challenge his argument:

> trade calls for payments, ... capital movements call for the exchangeability of different currencies and ... migrations ... call for chances to take possessions along and to remit earnings. Hence an international payments system that allows payments and foreign exchange transactions without restrictions or controls — in short, monetary integration — is an integral part of complete economic integration.[5]

To Machlup, the essence of monetary integration is this establishment of arrangements that facilitate foreign payments. The most thorough way of doing this is to replace separate national currencies by a common currency.

Machlup is in accord with most other writers in defining complete monetary integration, or monetary union, in terms of the establishment of a common currency. The only challenge to this practice of which I am aware is that launched by the Werner Report (1970), which treats full and irrevocable fixing of exchange rates as equivalent to the adoption of a common currency. Presumably the argument in favour of treating the two as equivalent is that, provided exchange rates really are irrevocably fixed, the private sector would be guilty of money illusion if it treated currencies differently just because they had different names and denominations. However, Corden[6] takes the lead in arguing that no promise that exchange rates were irrevocably fixed could be fully credible so long as separate currencies existed, since it would be too easy to revoke the promise if circumstances seemed to make such action expedient. Hence the private sector could not be made to believe that exchange rates were irrevocably fixed by any 'pseudo exchange-rate union', which would mean that speculative crises might still occur and capital mobility would still be impeded by risk aversion. Even if the promise of fixed exchange rates were never broken, the mere fact that the private sector lacked complete confidence in the promise's being kept would be sufficient to produce real economic effects. This reasoning now seems to be generally accepted and, accordingly, monetary union will be interpreted in this paper as the adoption of a single currency to serve throughout the area in question.

Monetary union has two important corollaries. The first is that, since the management of a currency must be someone's responsibility, monetary union implies the establishment of a central monetary authority.

Monetary Integration

This normally takes the form of a central bank. The second corollary is that, since exchange controls involve restrictions on the right to convert one money into another, there can be no exchange controls within a monetarily unified area.

Many discussions of monetary integration have been concerned with changes much less radical than the establishment of a single currency. It is convenient to refer to any form of joint monetary action by a group of countries with different currencies as 'partial monetary integration'.[7] The remainder of this section identifies and characterises seven forms of partial integration that have appeared in the literature and that seem to the author to be legitimately describable as 'monetary'.

A. Payments Union

A payments union is an arrangement whereby a number of countries with inconvertible currencies set up a multilateral clearing arrangement to handle payments for their reciprocal trade. Multilateral clearing ensures that payments due or made will be handled in the same way irrespective of who the trading partner is, thus eliminating the incentive to discriminate in trade as between the member countries of the payments union. The union may also furnish credit to cover a part of the net imbalances in one member's trade with other members. The first version of the Keynes plan for an International Clearing Union envisaged the post-war world organised in this way.[8] The major historical example of a payments union was the European Payments Union of 1950-8 (undoubtedly one of the most successful international economic institutions of all time), which is well discussed by one of its principal architects.[9]

B. Reserve-pooling

A reserve pool is an arrangement in which the members deposit some part of their reserves with an agent. The members acquire liquid claims on the agent, which continue to form a part of their reserves, while the agent holds liquid claims on third parties. So long as the payments imbalances of members are reasonably desynchronised, it is possible for the agent to extend credit within certain limits without jeopardising the liquidity of its members deposits (because of the customary principles of fractional reserve banking). This credit may be short term or medium term, automatic or subject to some form of discretionary control by the agent. Robert Triffin has been a leading advocate of reserve pooling.[10]

C. Exchange-rate Co-ordination

Exchange-rate co-ordination involves agreement among the member countries to pursue policies that will limit the extent to which the exchange rates between participants' currencies can diverge. Any such

14 *Monetary Integration*

action necessarily presupposes the establishment of some structure of 'central rates' between members' currencies and some obligation to restrict deviations from those central rates by means of intervention policies (i.e., by buying and selling some foreign currency in exchange for domestic money). Action of this sort has featured prominently in all plans for European monetary integration; it was the sole object of the 'snake' and is the principal object of the European Monetary System (EMS) that has superseded the 'snake'.[11]

D. Monetary Co-ordination

Various types of policy co-ordination (e.g., of taxes, fiscal policy, medium-term objectives) have sometimes been included under the heading of 'monetary integration' in European discussions, but the only one of these that seems to the author to have claim to inclusion is agreement as to the monetary policies that member countries will pursue. At one time, when Keynesianism was still the dominant intellectual orthodoxy, it was normal to think of agreed monetary policies in terms of the adoption of common (or concerted) interest rate targets. In recent years, with the rise of monetarism, it has become orthodox to think in terms of agreed targets for monetary aggregates of one sort or another. In countries with floating exchange rates, there is a choice between focusing on a target for some concept(s) of the money supply or a target for domestic credit expansion (DCE). In countries with pegged exchange rates, it is now widely accepted that monetary policy *means* domestic credit expansion and that a central feature of monetary co-ordination is the proscription of sterilisation: i.e., an undertaking that DCE will *not* be varied according to reserve changes.[12]

E. Parallel Currency

A parallel currency is a currency designed to serve the entire area in question as a supplement to, rather than a substitute for, the existing currencies. Such a currency is intended to serve the private sector rather than just to provide an accounting unit for the government sector, although it may of course do that as well. It has usually been envisaged that, at least initially, such a currency would find its first application in international roles, as a vehicle currency. The proposal was originated simultaneously and independently by Magnifico and Williamson[13] and by Woehrling.[14] A substantially modified and better known version is that known as the All Saints' Day Manifesto.[15]

F. Capital Market Integration

Just as integration in general refers to measures that increase the responsiveness with which goods or factors flow across boundaries in response to incentives, so capital market integration refers to steps

Monetary Integration

designed specifically to increase capital mobility. The most obvious of these is the abolition of exchange controls on capital flows within the area. Since the operations of financial intermediaries across national frontiers and the sale of financial obligations issued in one country to savers resident in another can be seriously impeded by differing national practices and regulations, capital market integration may also be promoted by the harmonisation of administrative requirements in financial matters.

G. Common Policies toward External Capital Flows

In addition to liberalising capital movements within the integration area, there are also possibilities for standardising policy regarding capital flows to or from the rest of the world. For example, it has sometimes been suggested that member countries should standardise their exchange controls *vis-à-vis* the rest of the world. Alternatively, member countries might harmonise their policies toward inward direct investment, as the Andean Group has done. A third possibility, which has been mentioned in the Arab context, is that of joint action to channel financial surpluses into investment outside the area.

II. Objectives

Machlup's discussion of monetary integration, cited above, treats it as a means to the end of economic integration. This is in the mainstream of economic thought, which has appraised monetary union overwhelmingly in terms of the economic benefits and costs involved, the principal benefit being identified as the elimination of obstacles to transactions between areas using different currencies. It is therefore natural to commence with a discussion of those obstacles that monetary union may hope to remove. They may conveniently be classified as exchange costs, exchange-rate risk and exchange controls.

Exchange costs are the real resource costs of converting one currency into another. They are reflected in the buy/sell spreads charged by banks for foreign exchange dealings, as well as in the inconvenience cost to the banks' customers. These costs are normally considered to be rather modest.

Exchange-rate risk is the risk that the exchange rate between two currencies will change in an unanticipated way during the interval between the decision to transact and the date of payment. This acts as a deterrent to transactions between risk-averse agents living in different currency areas. The risk can sometimes be avoided, however, by forward covering, where the transaction involved has a well-defined contract date and payment date and where there is an active forward market in the currency of both parties to the transaction. However, the force of this qualification is much more limited than is sometimes realised: forward cover entails additional costs (i.e., buy/sell spreads are wider in the forward market); by no means can all transactions be effectively hedged,[16] and few of the smaller currencies have well-developed forward markets, especially for longer maturities. It is also true that some exchange-rate changes, namely anticipated changes that serve to neutralise inflation differentials between countries, reduce rather than increase the risk involved in international transactions. However, there is now overwhelming empirical evidence that the variations of floating exchange rates cannot be primarily explained in this way and that they do indeed involve very significant volatility of real as well as nominal exchange rates. Finally, it has often been denied that exchange-rate uncertainty deters trade and other transactions. There have been several attempts to examine this subject empirically and until recently the evidence, at least so far as trade is concerned, seemed to support this position. However, three recent studies on the trade of developing countries[17] claim to have found evidence that the instability of the real exchange rate is a significant factor determining the volume of trade, thus providing some support for the traditional presumption that exchange-rate instability impedes integration.

Exchange controls are administrative regulations limiting or prohibiting certain foreign-exchange transactions. They necessarily discriminate against those who wish to undertake transactions between, as opposed to within currency areas and are thus inherently discriminatory and inimical to integration. Although exchange controls are seldom completely effective when the economic incentive to evade them is strong, there is no doubt that they can and often do impose serious obstacles to economic integration.

A secondary benefit that monetary integration may bring is a reduction in the social cost of providing money. One can presumably dismiss scale economies in the printing of bank notes as quantitatively trivial, but the same is not possible where the holding of liquid external reserves is concerned. For most countries — the exception being those low-absorption oil exporters that choose to hold substantial long-term investments in the form of short-term assets — there is a significant opportunity cost involved in increasing reserves. To the extent that payments imbalances within a monetary union or reserve pool are desynchronised, the member countries can achieve a higher level of security against reserve depletion or reduce their average reserve holdings for a given security level, or both.

Monetary union may also involve economic costs. The dominant economic cost is usually regarded as the reduction in policy autonomy in the constituent areas, which lose the opportunity of using exchange-rate changes to facilitate balance-of-payments adjustment and of using the inflation tax independently in order to secure command over real resources. Sharp differences of view between economists persist as to the significance of sacrificing the exchange-rate instrument. At one extreme lies the Keynesian-inspired analysis of Meade,[18] which assumes that at least some internal prices (of labour or of non-traded goods, perhaps) are fixed in nominal terms and derives the conclusion that exchange-rate changes provide a valuable non-distortional instrument for switching expenditures with the object of restoring internal and external balance. At the other extreme lies the 'global monetarist' view of the 1970s, which assumes that relative prices are determined exclusively by real forces (any possibility to the contrary being derided as 'money illusion'), and hence are not susceptible to influence by monetary actions like exchange-rate changes. If any devaluation is automatically, quickly and regularly neutralised by an acceleration of internal inflation, then obviously it can serve no useful purpose other than to allow a government to exploit the inflation tax without provoking a payments crisis. In between these two extreme views lies the eclectic position to which the author subscribes, which accepts that devaluation no longer provides a simple, mechanistic, reliable way of switching expenditures to correct a payments deficit but notes that there is also much evidence[19] that revaluation does not provide a simple, mechanistic, reliable way of controlling inflation either, as the global monetarist analysis would imply. Either devaluation or revaluation may, however, under appropriate circumstances, be a useful part of a comprehensive policy package seeking the best available combination of internal and external objectives. Those who hold this view regard loss of the exchange-rate instrument as a serious macroeconomic cost that has to be weighed against the microeconomic benefits of monetary union.

However, the issue of whether the economic benefits exceed the economic costs will also be influenced by political responses to economic pressures. For example, the author once conjectured that monetary union would tend to extend the reference groups whose wage levels influence the wage claims lodged in disadvantaged regions and thus result in those regions having their problems show up more in the form of unemployment and less in the form of low wages than occurs with independent currencies.[20] Because unemployment is a conspicuous form of social waste in a way that interregional wage disparities are not, it is plausible to suppose that political pressure would be generated for systematic fiscal transfers to the poorer areas. If that occurred, the net result could easily be a net interregional transfer of income leading to a more equitable distribution rather than a significant change in levels, which would presumably be judged a net benefit by those of an egalitarian disposition.

However, political value judgements must play a much more fundamental role than this in determining attitudes towards monetary integration. Naturally, economists have concentrated most of their attention on analysing the economic benefits and costs of forming a monetary union, but this should not blind one to the fact that there is also a fundamental political dimension to the question. A country with its own money issued by a central bank under its own control always has the power to finance a budget deficit by printing money, whereas a country without that power has to rely on selling its debt obligations in competition with other assets. It can use this power to command real resources without levying formal taxes, to fight economic depressions or to fight wars, and this is a power that governments typically do exploit *in extremis*. To abandon this power, this monetary sovereignty, is to accept a quite significant curtailment of the state's freedom of action in crisis situations; monetary sovereignty is a crucial component of national sovereignty. Whether surrender of this monetary sovereignty is judged a benefit or a cost is an eminently political question. Those of us who regard the nation state as a social institution that has acquired too much power for the good of mankind, and who believe that the pluralism of multinational decision-making generally places a useful constraint on national excesses, judge it to be a benefit. But I suspect that we are in a minority and that the main reason that the world has witnessed no major examples of full monetary union between countries is not the inconclusive nature of the debate on the economic benefits and costs, but rather the power of nationalism.

Unlike full monetary union, none of the forms of partial monetary integration identified in the previous section involves any decisive transfer of monetary sovereignty. The objectives that partial integration may promote vary with the form of integration in question.

The purpose of a *payments union* is to support trade liberalisation within an area that suffers from a chronic shortage of liquid international reserves. Such a shortage breeds pressures for bilateralism, since no country wishes to use precious reserves that could finance imports from hard-currency countries in order to finance a deficit with one of its weak-currency neighbours. Multilateral clearing ensures that additional exports have the same value, no matter for whom they are destined within the area covered by the clearing arrangement, and that additional imports have the same cost no matter what their source within the area. Such clearing arrangements thus eliminate the incentives for bilateralism — a trading pattern that is extremely disruptive of economic efficiency, seriously jeopardises the overall volume of trade and must in fact be close to the polar opposite of integration. In the rather special circumstances where it is appropriate, a payments union is clearly an instrument of integration in the fullest Machlupian sense.

A reserve pool is intended to economise on reserve holdings, as has already been explained.

Exchange-rate co-ordination is intended to reduce the exchange-rate risk encountered in intra-area transactions. Such a reduction in exchange-rate variability may also cut exchange costs. However, a reduction in exchange-rate variability achieved at the cost of an intensification of exchange controls may lead to a net decrease in integration. Machlup[21] vigorously attacks those who advocate or condone the use of exchange controls to defend pegged exchange rates, on the grounds that this involves accepting a major obstacle to integration in order to remove a minor obstacle.

There are two objectives that may be sought by *monetary co-ordination*. The first is that of promoting cyclical stabilisation. This factor is of potential importance where monetary policy has strong overspill effects on conjunctural conditions in other countries, as among the countries of the OECD (or, for that matter, among the countries members of the IMF). Even when that condition is satisfied, however, one also needs to be reasonably confident that more co-ordinated policies would in fact achieve greater stability before recommending such co-ordination. This is by no means axiomatic: given that policy acts only with a significant lag, it is entirely possible that a crude form of co-ordination requiring all countries to expand or contract simultaneously, depending on some collective decision, could increase instability. The OECD has in recent years become aware of this danger and has in consequence deliberately nurtured a degree of cyclical desynchronisation. The second possible objective is that of supporting a common exchange-rate policy *vis-à-vis* the rest of the world; more specifically, of enabling member countries to avoid intra-area changes in central rates. This demands that members base their monetary policies on a 'common'[22] rate of domestic credit expansion and agree not to sterilise reserve changes. Co-ordination takes the form of joint choice of the common rate of DCE.

The advantages of *capital market integration* are usually conceived of as (a) the resource-allocation benefits of allowing investment to occur where rates of return are highest rather than where savings are being effected; (b) the utility benefits, over certain time intervals, of being better able to smooth out the time stream of consumption when the income of individual regions is subjected to shocks of any sort; and (c) the portfolio-diversification benefits of allowing creditors to distribute their assets more widely. However, it has also been argued (in both Europe and Latin America) that these benefits are gained at the cost of a tendency to draw investment away from the weaker (i.e., poorer) members of the group, thus tightening the external constraint on economic policy in those countries and reducing their potential growth.

As in the case of full monetary union, therefore, one finds a conflict between the microeconomic advantages and the macroeconomic disadvantages of integration.

The objects sought by *common policies toward external capital flows* are as varied as the forms these policies may take. Similar exchange controls are regarded as a necessary complement to capital market integration; otherwise, residents in the countries with the tighter controls *vis-à-vis* the outside world would find it too easy to evade those controls by moving funds through the member countries with the looser controls. A common policy towards direct inward investment is envisaged as a defence against the members' competing to attract those investments which their customs union has rendered more attractive when made somewhere in particular in the region; it is feared that such competition could result in a disproportionate share of the benefits of the investment accruing to the investors, who are external to the region. Presumably the object of joint channelling of financial surpluses is to get better terms for external investments than would otherwise be possible, either by realising economies of scale (e.g., in the management of loans to developing countries) or by exercising a degree of monopolistic power on the world capital market.

III. Modalities

Several of the proposals for partial monetary integration have been advanced, at least in part, in the hope that they would be helpful steps in moving to full monetary union. It is therefore convenient to reverse the order of the previous two sections and to start by considering the modalities of partial integration. There are, of course, virtually no limits to what could be written about the modalities of monetary integration. The brief notes presented here are intended only to provide orientation; other papers at the seminar will no doubt treat some aspects of the subject in far greater detail.

A *payments union* requires establishment of a clearing house to which all intra-area transactions are reported by the central banks concerned. The clearing house periodically calculates the net balances due to or owed by each participant and arranges for settlement in reserves or credit or in some combination of the two. If the payments union has some funds at its disposal, it can make the terms on which surpluses are settled with the union somewhat harder (i.e., requiring a larger proportion of reserves) than those on which deficits are settled. A precondition for a payments union is that comprehensive exchange controls exist, so that all transactions are channelled through the central bank.

A *reserve pool* involves the choice or establishment of an institution to act as agent. Its duties are (a) to manage the reserve paid in by members; (b) to transfer reserves in accord with the decisions of the pool's creditors; and (c) to make loans to those deficit countries entitled to draw on the pool. The main problem lies in devising rules to limit the right to draw: without such limits, a reserve pool would virtually give a blank cheque to deficit countries to draw on the real resources of the surplus countries. This would create a temptation for members to adopt policies likely to generate deficits, especially if loans from the reserve pool carried a concessional interest rate. The problem has in the past been tackled in various ways: by laying down some fairly mechanical rules (as in the European Payments Union [EPU] or the low-conditionality facilities of the IMF); by having the institution managing the reserve pool lay down explicit policy conditions (as in high-conditionality drawings from the IMF); or by developing a strong consensus on policy obligations (as perhaps in the European Monetary System [EMS]).

The modalities of *exchange-rate co-ordination* depend on the structure of the exchange markets involved. Where currencies are traded in large volumes on competitive exchange markets with many transactors and a high degree of private capital mobility, so that exchange rates are determined by supply and demand, co-ordination takes the form of central bank intervention to limit deviations from the agreed central rates between the member currencies. This requires agreement on: (a) the structure of central rates; (b) the margins around the central rates that are to be defended by interventions; (c) the intervention medium; and, where intervention is in the members' own currencies; (d) the division of responsibility for intervention between the country whose currency is at the ceiling and the one whose currency is on the floor. Where, at the other extreme, there is no competitive exchange market but instead all transactions are undertaken at buying and selling rates posted by the central bank, exchange-rate co-ordination must take the form of ensuring that the rates posted by all participants remain constant relative to each other (unless, naturally, a deliberate decision to change the central rate is made). This requires that central rates be defined by all participants in terms of the same unit. It is highly convenient if this unit is also the intervention medium, so that intra-area exchange rates, which are the product of the buying rate posted by one country and the selling rate posted by another, are stabilised directly. Exchange-rate co-ordination may also involve limitations on national freedom to change the central rate, either in the form of restrictions on the size of the changes that may be made, as Thygesen[23] claims occurred informally in the later years of the 'snake', or in the form of a requirement that changes be mutually agreed by the participants (as in the EMS) or, alternatively, in the form of an agreed formula for determining central rate changes.

As with central rate changes, *monetary co-ordination* might be pursued either by discussion or by rule. Up to now, such co-ordination as has been attempted has been limited to the former and has been directed more towards the objective of conjunctural stabilisation than towards the support of a common exchange-rate policy. It might be more natural to adopt a formula if the principal objective were exchange-rate stabilisation. McKinnon[24] suggests that each country should be allowed a rate of domestic credit expansion adequate to satisfy the estimated increase in the demand for money balances due to real growth in the economy, assuming stability in terms of some appropriate price index. This would build in monetary pressure to stabilise exchange rates between the members with a common price trend of zero. In the event that member countries wished — or, perhaps more accurately, felt obliged — to accept different inflation rates, which would of course have to be reconciled by exchange-rate changes, the formula could be extended appropriately to allow for this. This might be done either by adding a target rate of inflation for each country or by constructing a feedback rule of partial monetary accommodation to the actual or forecast inflation rate. The idea in allowing accommodation of inflation is to avoid unexpectedly high inflation producing severe contractile pressures on the real economy, while the idea in making accommodation partial is to ensure that any inflation that does develop encounters monetary resistance. Thus the feedback rule would involve a term B p, with $0 < B < 1$. Finally, Williamson[25] has suggested that one could introduce considerations of conjunctural stabilisation and balance-of-payments adjustment into a DCE formula as well. The result would be a formula of the following character:

$$\text{DCM}/\text{M} = \alpha \hat{y} + \beta \hat{p} + YD + \delta(B - B^*)$$

where DCE = domestic credit expansion
M = money supply
α = estimated income elasticity of demand for money
$\hat{y}$ = estimated rate of growth in real income
β = coefficient measuring the extent to which inflation would be accommodated
$\hat{p}$ = target, actual or predicted inflation rate
D = estimated deflationary gap
B = current account surplus
B* = target current account balance.

The introduction of a *parallel currency* would raise two kinds of questions: how to determine its value, and how to determine its issue. The range of possible answers to the valuation question includes: valuing

Monetary Integration

it in terms of a unit external to the area (as the Arab monetary unit is defined in terms of the SDR); the same, but with the possibility of making discretionary changes in that value (for example, with the object of maintaining the value roughly constant in terms of the currencies of the area, or of pursuing payments balance for the area as a whole;[26] valuing it in terms of a basket of the currencies of the participants (as both the SDR and the European Currency Unit, or ECU, are now defined); or endowing it with a stable real value (for example, by increasing the units of each currency in the basket in proportion to measured inflation in each country, as proposed for the 'Europa' in the All Saints' Day Manifesto). The question of the issue of a parallel currency has been treated most extensively by Peeters et al. in Fratianni and Peeters.[27] In their scheme, the bank of a depositor who wished to switch his deposit into Europas would realise some of its assets, use the proceeds to buy a basket of currencies in proportions corresponding to the composition of the Europa (thus exerting exchange-market pressure to the extent that the demand to convert from national currencies into the Europa did not correspond to the proportional composition of the Europa) and exchange these with a 'Euro-agent', who would thus acquire claims on the European central banks and liabilities to the commercial banks. An alternative approach would be to allow the Euro-agent to accept the individual currencies, rather than a basket, at the prevailing exchange rates and to express its claims on national central banks in Europas rather than in national currencies: this would prevent the process of conversion from exerting pressure in the exchange markets. It is also worth noting that, in the event that the debtors as well as the creditors of the banks wished to convert their obligations into Europas, a simple process of redenomination, without the need for any actual transactions, would suffice.

The abolition of internal exchange controls, harmonisation of external exchange controls and standardisation of financial practices that are necessary for *capital market integration* raise issues of immensely complex detail rather than of principle. The negotiation of *common policies toward external capital flows* is bound to be far more difficult when the objective touches on areas of acute conflict of interest between the participants, such as the distribution of direct inward investment, than when the countries clearly share interests, for example in the efficient placement of investments in the rest of the world.

The move to *full monetary union* could conceivably be accomplished in a single major step, either by replacing all of the existing currencies simultaneously with a newly-created currency or by calling in all except one of the existing currencies and converting all financial claims into the remaining currency. However, all discussions of monetary union in recent years seem to have envisaged a gradual transition rather than this type of sudden change. Proposals for gradualist strategies have taken two general forms, giving pride of place to exchange-rate co-ordination and a parallel currency, in that order.

The Werner Report (1970) launched the idea of approaching monetary union gradually, through a series of successive stages in which the scope for intra-area exchange-rate changes would be progressively narrowed, until the final stage of irrevocably locked exchange rates was reached. In the first stage, the bands around parities within which rates were free to fluctuate were to be narrowed: this proposal was the origin of the European 'snake'. Subsequent stages were to see the circumscription, and ultimately the withdrawal, of the right to change parities, as well as further narrowing of the band, so that by 1980 the European currencies would have merged into one. The plan contained many other proposals, including reserve-pooling and much discussion of policy co-ordination, but its essence was the process of exchange-rate convergence.

The alternative approach envisages founding a new currency, destined ultimately to emerge as the single common currency, rather than seeking to melt the existing currencies into one. In the first instance, a parallel currency would be created. In one version of the proposal,[28] this would initially have been a vehicle currency intended to facilitate international transactions. It would have been extended to replace national currencies in their domestic roles only if and when there was a political decision that the European Community could safely dispense with internal exchange-rate changes. In the other version of the proposal (All Saints' Day), the parallel currency would have been freely accessible right from the start to anyone holding any of the European currencies. When over 50 per cent of the total European money supply had been voluntarily converted into Europas, the rest would have been called in through a compulsory conversion operation without any further political decision.

The other forms of partial monetary integration do not seem suited to playing an equally strategic role in a gradualist approach to monetary union. A payments union is essentially a way of escaping from the ills of a high level of financial fragmentation, rather than an instrument for achieving a high degree of integration. A reserve pool is a natural complement to exchange-rate co-ordination or the founding of a parallel currency, but it does not directly impinge on the private sector and is therefore peripheral to the key issue. Capital market integration and, perhaps, common policies toward external capital flows are natural candidates for early action because they promise benefits that are not seriously dependent on progress elsewhere, but they will never lead to full monetary union. The only other form of partial monetary integration that might be assigned a strategic role in a gradualist approach to monetary union is monetary co-ordination, inasmuch as the adoption of credible DCE targets consistent with the stability (or limited controlled changes) of exchange rates could be expected to provide a major reinforcement to exchange-rate co-ordination.

It is worth noting that there is disagreement as to whether the suppression of intra-area exchange-rate changes creates a case for an explicit redistributive mechanism through the fiscal system. The dispute runs more or less on monetarist/Keynesian lines. Those (monetarists) who maintain that markets can be relied on to clear as a result of price flexibility see the exchange-rate question as irrelevant: any case for redistrubution must, in their view, rest on the claims of social justice relative to resource endowment and be independent of monetary arrangements. Those (Keynesians) who doubt that wages are set in a way that produces any strong tendency to clear the labour market have seen a danger that monetary union will raise the real wage rate to unrealistic levels through demonstration effects in low-productivity regions and have concluded that a redistributive fiscal mechanism may be needed to ensure that all regions can expect to gain by the integration process.

IV. Concluding Remarks

The main themes of the preceding survey may be summarised as follows. In accordance with Machlup, 'economic integration' was defined as the full exploitation of all the potential benefits of specialisation within an area, and 'monetary integration' as the removal of all monetary obstacles to that state of affairs. Full monetary integration demands a single currency in use throughout the area in question. Analysis of the case for monetary union reveals an inconclusive trade-off between microeconomic benefits and macroeconomic costs. It is then suggested that the major explanation for the observable fact that there is a very strong tendency for nation states to create and preserve their own monies lies less in the economics of the matter than in its politics. This is because monetary union involves the sacrifice of monetary sovereignty, which is a crucial component of national sovereignty inasmuch as it has a powerful influence on the ability of the state to handle situations of extreme crisis.

The paper also distinguishes seven possible forms of partial monetary integration. None of these involves any decisive transfer of monetary sovereignty, and yet they may go a long way towards promoting monetary integration in the Machlupian sense. It is argued that the forms of partial integration of strategic importance in a programme aiming at gradual evolution to monetary union are exchange-rate co-ordination, the establishment of a parallel currency and also, perhaps, monetary co-ordination. However, any or all of these steps or, for that matter, of the other forms of partial integration may be possible and worthwhile in themselves, even in the absence of any expectation or desire to proceed to monetary union.

Notes

1. F. Machlup (ed.), *Economic Integration: Worldwide, Regional, Sectoral* (London: Macmillan, 1976), chap. 3, and *A History of Thought on Economic Integration* (London: Macmillan, 1977), chap. 2.

2. Ibid., p. 18.

3. My only reservation about Machlup's penetrating discussion is prompted by his assertion that 'equality of prices despite inequality of the marginal net value productivities — for example, due to lower efficiency or unfavourable location — is a typical form of discrimination, which may meet some standards of social justice but which definitely violates the principle of general economic integration'. (See Machlup, *A History of Thought on Economic Integration*, p. 19.) I would hesitate to describe that as derogating from the degree of integration (as opposed to the level of economic efficiency) provided that the policy being used to equalise prices is itself geographically non-discriminatory.

4. Ibid., p. 20.

5. Ibid.

6. W.M. Cordon, *Monetary Integration*, Princeton Essays in International Finance, no. 93 (Princeton: Princeton University Press, 1972).

7. I do, however, insist that this term be restricted to joint monetary action. 'Monetary integration' has sometimes been defined so widely as to embrace virtually any kind of fiscal or factor-market integration. (See Lamfalussy and Barre, in Machlup, *Economic Integration: Worldwide, Regional, Sectoral*, Section F.) This is surely an objectionable linguistic practice.

8. D. Moggridge (ed.), *The Collected Writings of John Maynard Keynes*, vol. 25: *Activities 1940-1944* (London: Macmillan, 1940), p. 33.

9. R. Triffin, *Europe and the Money Muddle* (New Haven, Conn.: Yale University Press, 1958).

10. Ibid.

11. N. Thygesen, 'The Emerging European Monetary System: Precursors, First Steps and Policy Options', in R. Triffin (ed.), *The Emerging European Monetary System* (Brussels: National Bank of Belgium, 1979).

12. R.I. McKinnon, 'On Securing a Common Monetary Policy in Europe', *Banca Nazionale del Lavoro Quarterly Review* (March 1973).

13. G. Magnifico and J. Williamson, *European Monetary Integration* (London: Federal Trust, 1972).

14. F. Woehrling, 'Pour une union monétaire européenne du 1973', *Chroniques d'Actualité* (February 1972).

15. T. Peeters *et al.*, 'The All Saints' Day Manifesto for European Monetary Union', *The Economist*, 1 November 1975, reprinted in M. Fratianni and T. Peeters (eds.), *One Money for Europe* (London: Macmillan, 1978).

16. Consider, for example, the case of a trader who has to submit a bid months before he knows whether he will win the contract; there is no market in forward currency conditional on his winning the contract in which he can cover himself at the time of making his bid. The case of a continuing trade relationship is better known. There are also the familiar problems of limited maturities.

17. On Colombia: C. Diaz Alejandro, *Foreign Trade Regimes and Economic Development: Colombia* (New York: National Bureau of Economic Research, 1976); on Brazil: D. Coes, *The Impact of Price Uncertainty: A Study of Brazilian Exchange-Rate Policy* (New York: Garland, 1979); and on several Asian countries: P. Rana, 'The Impact of Generalized Floating on Trade Flows and Reserve Needs of Selected Asian Countries', (PhD dissertation, 1979; to be published by Garland).

18. J.E. Meade, *The Theory of International Economic Policy*, vol. 1: *The Balance of Payments* (London: Oxford University Press, 1951).

19. Some outstanding examples of the failure to use the 'strong exchange rate option' to restrain inflation to levels that will preserve a sufficient degree of competitiveness are provided by Argentina (1979-80), Britain (1979-80), Denmark (1974-80), and Sweden (1974-6).

20. J. Williamson, in J. Vaizey (ed.), *Economic Sovereignty and Regional Policy* (Dublin: Gill and Macmillan, 1975).

21. Machlup, *A History of Thought on Economic Integration*, pp. 21-2.

22. The rates may differ slightly to accommodate different growth rates in real income and different income elasticities of demand for money. See the first term of the formula on p. 22.

23. N. Thygesen, 'The European Monetary System – An Approximate Implementation of the Crawling Peg?', a paper presented at the Conference on the Crawling Peg: Past Performance and Future Prospects, Rio de Janeiro, 1979.

24. R.I. McKinnon, 'On Securing a Common Monetary Policy in Europe'.

25. J. Williamson, 'International Monetary Reform: A Survey of the Options', Report to the Group of Twenty-Four, 1980 (mimeographed).

26. Magnifico and Williamson, *European Monetary Integration*.

27. Fratianni and Peeters (eds.), *One Money for Europe*.

28. Magnifico and Williamson, *European Monetary Integration*.

COMMENT

Burhan Dajani

The premise of Mr Williamson's paper is that complete economic integration represents a situation in which the full potential inherent in an efficient division of labour is realised. The underlying reasoning is that the free flow of goods and factors of production in an integrated area calls for monetary integration in order to facilitate payments, not only among the integrating countries but also with the outside world. As to the meaning of monetary integration, the paper stresses that it entails the creation of a common currency, the management of which has to be undertaken by a supra-national body.

However, the paper focuses on various forms of 'partial monetary integration', the latter denoting any joint monetary action by a group of countries with different currencies. It mentions seven forms of such integration: (i) a payments union; (ii) reserve-pooling; (iii) exchange-rate co-ordination; (iv) monetary co-ordination; (v) a parallel currency; (vi) capital market integration; and (vii) common policies toward external capital flows. Obviously, these forms tend to treat different aspects of monetary integration and the choice of one form over another would depend on the situation under consideration.

It is evident that the paper carefully analyses the objectives of these forms of partial monetary integration and the ways in which they could be implemented with the case of the European Common Market in mind. This is quite legitimate in view of the fact that the EEC is basically a customs union arrangement and the need for monetary integration (i.e., a common currency) would become pressing only were this arrangement elevated to the status of an economic union. However, the point that needs to be emphasised here is that much of the analysis presented in the paper has limited relevance to the Arab countries which are the focus of interest at this seminar.

To start with, the Arab countries are, by definition, developing countries and their economic integration ought to be approached not through mere trade liberalisation as is largely the case with the EEC, but through the co-ordination of their investment decisions in order to create complementary production structures from which trade flows would follow. This view is supported by numerous experiences of integration in the developing world and there is now a general presumption that the concept of integration ought to be applied on a selective basis, specifically to the areas which would generate an equitable ratio of benefits to costs for the participating countries. It is true that in such a situation partial monetary integration would be more relevant than full monetary integration, as the object would be to facilitate the exchange of a relatively limited number of goods in whose production the integrating countries specialise. But it can be argued that such 'agreed specialisation' in production, especially in the early stages, could be maintained without a supporting payments arrangement and that the settlement of payments arising from the exchange of goods could be made in accordance with existing national systems. Only when production lines organised on a regional basis start to multiply, does the need for monetary integration become pressing. This converges with the general view that inherent in the process of economic integration is a self-reinforcing mechanism such that if it does not generate pressures for further integration it will decline rapidly.

The situation of the Arab countries is that despite their underdevelopment, they are in a privileged financial position because of the oil industry. This industry not only generates financial surpluses for the oil-exporting countries, but also provides ample financial resources in various ways to the non-oil (or agricultural) countries. This has considerably eased the balance-of-payments problem in most of the non-oil countries and there is now ample opportunity to promote trade flows within the Arab region without monetary integration.

The need for monetary integration among the Arab countries will, however, become apparent as the process of economic integration gathers momentum. Moreover, there are strong arguments for monetary integration among the oil-producers in that it is in the interest of these countries to have a common currency which could be used as a unit of account to determine the price of oil exports, rather than having it determined by another currency which might be devalued. But, above all, monetary integration is advocated on the basis of the protection it would provide for the oil countries' financial reserves, allowing them to develop their common currency as a store of value. Obviously, this is conceivable only because there is a growing demand for oil in the international markets and its exportation would therefore not be hindered by the existence of a strong currency. Thus the incentives for a uniform currency in the Gulf lie not so much in integration as in the protection of their financial interests in international markets. Therefore, monetary integration may indeed be desirable among countries which have not yet started their economic integration process but enjoy common production patterns with the same international orientation.

This suggests that the cost-benefit analysis, as presented by Mr Williamson for evaluating the desirability of monetary integration, does not really apply to the case of the Arab oil countries. On the benefit side, one might note that since trade flows among the oil-producers are very limited at the present stage of their economic development, a common currency is not likely to produce benefits either by generating savings in exchange costs or by eliminating exchange-rate risk. In addition, the oil-producers do not maintain any significant trade restrictions nor do they exercise strict exchange controls. On the cost side, on the other hand, the creation of a common currency would entail the surrender of sovereignty in a strategic area, and this would be as undesirable for the Gulf States as for other countries. Nevertheless, it would seem that the benefits as cited in the previous paragraph, would outweigh whatever costs may be incurred.

If a wider currency union, involving not only the Gulf countries, but other Arab countries as well were contemplated, the incentive for it would lie in the establishment of a single investment area which ultimately could generate a customs union: the reverse of the process experienced by the EEC. There would first have to be a decision to facilitate investments. This might require modifying the relevant laws as well as offering incentives to investors.

GENERAL DISCUSSION

1. Mahmoud Sakbani

I would like to develop one point that Mr Dajani has touched upon. Monetary integration has been approached in the literature in terms of its feasibility within existing economic structures, notably current trade patterns, the degree of capital integration and the extent to which economic policies converge. While one cannot assess feasibility without reference to these factors, it is of great importance to emphasise the dynamic interaction between these factors and political decisions. In the Arab region, political factors have a profound effect on trade and on capital integration. The volume of exchange among various Arab countries fluctuates very considerably in response to political relationships. Consequently, the assessment of the economic characteristics should emphasise potential costs, benefits and changes in economic structures resulting from these political factors.

2. Mabid Ali Al-Jarhi

With regard to the different approaches to monetary integration elaborated in Mr Williamson's paper, there is a need for further systematic treatment of the taxonomic distinction between the two main strategies for monetary integration:

a. The co-ordination strategy, which calls for:

   (1) exchange-rate unification, entailing difficulties stemming from external factors (including the domination of foreign currencies) and internal political pressures; and
   (2) *ex ante* harmonisation of monetary policies which, to be successful, requires:
      (a) equally correct (or incorrect) real growth predictions;
      (b) the same (real) income elasticities of demand for money in member countries;
      (c) constant real exchange rates.

However, we cannot reasonably expect to attain any of these conditions.

b. The centralisation strategy, which includes the following options:

   (1) currency unification;

(2) free competition among currencies;
(3) a parallel currency.

The distinction between the two strategies is important, if we are to be guided towards some reasonable choice. In addition, further analysis and comparison between the different options available under each strategy would be especially enlightening.

3. Rainer S. Masera

Quoting Machlup, Mr Williamson maintains that, of all the institutional arrangements essential to the free movement and high actual mobility of labour, capital and goods, 'perhaps the most important is monetary integration'.

I have some reservations about the exclusive reliance on the concept of factor mobility and on purely economic calculations as the relevant criteria for the integration of economies mainly because I believe that other factors not immediately amenable to the pure interplay of competitive market forces play an important role: for the sake of my present argument, these can be subsumed under the term 'fiscal elements', e.g., expenditure on defence, education, social services and incentives to the industrial sector. To be considered on the revenue side are various taxes and their impact on the allocation of resources within any single economy.

However — and this is the first point I want to make — even if one does subscribe to Mr Williamson's logic, it does not follow that monetary integration is a necessary condition for mobility.

For instance, as was pointed out long ago by Milton Friedman, the requirements of a 'common market', which allows for all payments and foreign exchange transactions to take place without restrictions or controls, can be equally well satisfied, at least in principle, by a system of fully flexible exchange rates.

Without further elaboration on this point, let me come to the second question I want to raise, which deals with the argument made by Mr Williamson according to which abandonment of monetary sovereignty implies a severe curtailment of the state's freedom of action in crisis situations, because the state thus relinquishes the power to finance a budget deficit by printing money.

According to recent work on the integration of stock and flow analysis in terms of variable prices, the interpretation of the budget constraints on the government sector in both nominal and real terms clearly shows that inflation represents a tax on government debt, which is similar to ordinary taxation on income flows.

Monetary Integration

Correspondingly, the definition of the disposable income of the private sector economy must allow for (i) flow taxation on current incomes and transactions and (ii) stock taxation on external debt.

It thus follows that monetary integration does require that governments surrender their right to impose the inflation tax at different rates. This is a general point, i.e., its scope goes well beyond 'crisis situations'. In the medium term, I would maintain that this surrender is by no means a loss for the population as a whole, but in the short term the matter has to be carefully considered. In this context, it should be recalled, for instance, that the huge deficits of the public sector in the United Kingdom and in Italy during the 1970s largely disappear when allowance is made for the erosion of the real value of government debt.

The relevance of this point must also be seen with reference to the significance of sacrificing the exchange rate as an instrument for altering real wages.

Even if there is no 'money illusion' on the part of wage-earners in terms of ordinary income flows (or if full indexation obtains) so that real wage rates cannot be directly altered by an exchange-rate movement, the very change in the rate of inflation and the correspondent loss in purchasing power may well free resources from domestic absorption abroad. This need not be a once-and-for-all shock but, rather, a continuous process whereby what matters for depreciating currencies is the higher average rate of inflation.

If what I call 'fiscal illusion' obtains — whereby wage-earners do not require compensation for the loss in real net financial wealth stemming from inflation — exchange-rate depreciation can, in the short run, reduce the unemployment costs which would be encountered by letting the nominal stock of money adapt automatically to the contractile impulse stemming from the decline in the foreign component of the monetary base.

4. Robert Triffin

I shall confine myself to two observations regarding Mr Williamson's paper.

First, as long as convertibility is maintained, a mere payments union would seem — as he says — superfluous, unnecessary. This was the argument adduced by Britain in 1958 to kill the European Payments Union.

I strongly objected at that time to this abolition of the most successful monetary agreement in world history, to which the restoration of worldwide convertibility can largely be credited. The EPU, I argued, should be preserved in order to preserve convertibility itself against future mishaps that might lead to its collapse.

Events have clearly justified this misgiving. Britain, Europe and the world would have benefited immensely from the continuation of the EPU, the disappearance of which had soon to be palliated by the formation of the Group of Ten and, more recently, by the creation of the EMS.

Of course, convertibility would have spelled the elimination — or at least the substantial reduction — of automatic borrowing rights by deficit countries. But automatic lending or investment commitments by surplus countries should have been maintained and would have made possible both:

(a) the sterilisation of excessive surpluses with the inflationary dangers they entail; and
(b) the granting of stabilisation credits, under appropriate conditions, to deficit countries in need of assistance.

The EPU included, in this respect, some provisions which were superior to those of the present EMS and which should inspire the latter's future course.

I hope that this suggestion as to the usefulness of a payments union, even for countries with fully convertible currencies, might help remove a frequently-heard objection to a payments union among Arab countries, i.e., the fact that some have fully convertible currencies and others do not. An appropriately defined Arab payments union could encompass both groups of countries in its membership.

My second observation is that as long as an acceptable worldwide monetary unit is not established and does not fully displace present so-called parallel currencies, an Arab monetary unit should, to my mind, be defined — as is the ECU — as a basket of currencies reflecting the regional structure of the bulk of the Arab countries' international trade and other transactions.

To avoid unnecessary complications, however, minor divergences should be dismissed and a common unit of broad acceptability adopted. The main candidates in this respect are the SDR and the ECU. But each has its shortcomings from the Arab point of view. The SDR is too closely tied to the dollar and prospectively too weak in terms of the stronger currencies of Western Europe. The ECU is preferable from this point of view but has the disadvantage of totally excluding the dollar and the yen.

I would suggest offhand an Arab currency unit made up 50 per cent of SDRs and 50 per cent of ECUs, or maybe 40 per cent of SDRs, 40 per cent of ECUs and 20 per cent of a few major Arab currencies.

5. Rattan J. Bhatia

The monetary sovereignty argument, when discussing the cost of monetary integration, may be overplayed. First, if the necessary condition for integration, i.e., the co-ordination of interest rates and of the rate of monetary expansion, is observed within a union, there is little likelihood of undue cost differentials arising which would necessitate exchange-rate changes as between member countries. Secondly, if the union as a whole were to run into cost/price non-competitiveness, it could always change its exchange rate *vis-à-vis* the rest of the world.

A second comment I should like to make refers to the process by means of which a union may be achieved. Mr Williamson's argument was in favour of 'gradualism'. However, no matter what institutions are initially set up, there will have to be broad harmony between the co-operating states as to their basic sociopolitico-economic philosophy. I might cite here the break-up of the East African Community which occurred notwithstanding the existence of various prerequisites of integration, e.g., common parity, a payments union, short-term balance-of-payments credits, a regional investment bank and free trade.

6. Faika El-Refaie

Mr Williamson's discussion distinguishes between two options: complete monetary union and partial monetary integration. However, bearing in mind the differences in the political, economic and social structures of the countries with which we are dealing, the two options could be regarded as being complementary rather than alternative options. This is especially true in that some of the countries involved enjoy both the free movement of capital and labour and fully convertible currencies and are therefore candidates for monetary union (issuance of a common currency), while other countries suffer from substantial deficits in their balance of payments and have currencies which are inconvertible (exchange control).

In the light of these differences, one might consider dealing with the group in two parallel ways:

(a) by establishing a monetary union among suitable candidates (Saudi Arabia, UAE, Qatar, Bahrain, Kuwait and Oman); and
(b) by co-ordinating exchange rates with the other Arab countries.

With the ultimate goal of achieving economic integration over a longer period of time, say 20 years, this should of course be associated with a reserve pool and a central supra-national investment committee to ensure the proper channelling of financial resources within the area and to determine the bases for specialisation and for the division of labour.

7. Rafik Sowellem

First, I would like to express my disagreement with Mr Dajani's statement that the issues involved in monetary integration have little or no relevance to the economic integration of the Arab world, either at present or in the immediate future, and with his belief that these issues will become relevant only after the development of an adequate productive base in Arab countries sufficient to generate large trade flows. To my mind, this is similar to the question of which comes first, the chicken or the egg. How can we promote investment among Arab countries, and thus increase the productive base, and how can we promote the establishment of large-scale modern industries in such narrow fragmented markets, without simultaneously working for the removal of restrictions on trade and payments?

Secondly, I wonder if Mr Williamson would care to elaborate on two of his statements: the first is that a payments union is only relevant where member countries have inconvertible currencies; the second is that a precondition for a payments union is that comprehensive exchange controls exist in all member countries. I would agree with Mr Triffin that there are definite advanges to a payments union for all participants whether or not their currencies are inconvertible. Furthermore, I see no technical reason why the adoption of exchange controls should be a precondition for a country's membership in a payments union. The experience of all the existing unions clearly shows that this is unnecessary. The danger of such a statement lies in the fact that it would discourage potential members from joining such a union if they did not wish to adopt exchange controls.

8. John Wiliamson, in Response

I attempted to provide a comprehensive taxonomy of the issues that have arisen in the literature on monetary integration, but this very interesting discussion of my paper makes it quite clear that I failed. First, I neglected to recognise that one important objective of monetary integration may well be that of strengthening the ability of the integrating area to deal with the rest of the world. Mr Dajani has emphasised that this objective is paramount in the case of the Arab countries, and it has also been of some relevance to the European countries. Secondly, I failed to recognise that monetary union limits the ability of the member countries to exploit the inflation tax. As Mr Masera has said, many countries do use inflation more or less consciously to raise revenue, whereas under monetary union they would be obliged to limit their fiscal deficits to a level consistent with the bonds they could sell plus the amounts accruing from monetary expansion at the common rate.

I would also agree that in my discussion on exchange-rate co-ordination, I could have been more specific in recognising the importance of the choice of pivot currency, as Mr Al-Jarhi has urged. In the Arab context, this is surely a key issue, on which I, like Mr Triffin, have certain views which I hope to introduce into the discussion in due course.

I do, however, wish to defend what I wrote about the superfluity of a payments union under conditions of general convertibility against the criticism of Messrs Triffin and Sowellem. Multilateral clearing through a clearing house of the claims among a limited group of countries presupposes that the central banks are acquiring those claims in order to present them to the clearing house, whereas with general convertibility such claims are settled among commercial banks. When central banks intervene, it is in order to buy (sell) the intervention currency from (to) a commercial bank; the central bank never acquires any claim on the bilateral trade partner and therefore cannot present any claim to the clearing house — nor is there any need for it to do so. I accept that the specific statement in my paper cited by Mr Sowellem, to the effect that a precondition for a payments union is that comprehensive exchange controls exist, is incorrect; I think the true precondition is that the central bank be willing to accept claims on other members of the union and that traders in each country have some incentive to present such claims to the central bank. On reflection, it is clear that this does not require comprehensive exchange controls; but it is going too far to say that it is consistent with general convertibility and a competitive exchange market.

My final comment concerns Ms El-Rafaie's question as to the possibility of a two-tier approach, in which the surplus Gulf States would go straight to full monetary union while developing looser forms of partial monetary integration with the rest of the Arab world. I can see absolutely no technical objection to this. I would imagine that the major question is whether even countries as homogeneous as the Gulf surplus countries will be willing to sacrifice their monetary sovereignty. It is certainly true that some of the major reasons why countries traditionally value monetary sovereignty are conspicuously inapplicable in their case; one can hardly, for example, imagine the UAE or Saudi Arabia fearing that their war-making ability would be undermined by their inability to levy the inflation tax. I am not in a position to judge whether these analytical considerations will be sufficient to overcome the customary reluctance to make the major plunge represented by full monetary union. But if monetary union can be achieved among the Gulf States, this would in no way detract from the incentive to seek, or the possibility of achieving, partial integration over the wider area.

2 THE RELATIONSHIP BETWEEN THE INTERNATIONAL MONETARY SYSTEM AND REGIONAL MONETARY SYSTEMS[1]

Robert Triffin

Introduction

I plan to discuss:

1. The world monetary disorder in which we have been engulfed throughout the decade of the 1970s;
2. The chances for and timing of world reforms, too long postponed, and as vital and urgent today as ever before; and
3. The potentialities of regional monetary agreements, with particular reference to:
   (a) The European Monetary System, as the most advanced such agreement to date; and
   (b) Arab monetary agreements, still only incipient, but of the greatest interest to you.

I. The World Monetary Disorder

I need not rehash what you all know about the world monetary disorder of the last decade: an unholy alliance of recession and unemployment with the wildest inflation in world history, huge balance-of-payments disequilibria and fluctuating exchange rates, a monetary system in which reserve creation leads to the financing of the richer, more capitalised countries by the poorer, less capitalised ones, the abdication of any serious attempt at reform, either in Jamaica or in the second amendment to the Articles of Agreement of the International Monetary Fund, etc.

I have written abundantly on this gloomy picture over the last 20 years, beginning with my book *Gold and the Dollar Crisis* (Yale University Press, 1960). Those of you who would wish to refresh their memories in this respect might consult a few of my more recent articles.[2] Let me merely extract today from the flood of confusing statistics in which we are daily drowned a few figures which document the main conclusions of interest to you concerning the shortcomings of the present world monetary 'system', which should better be labelled a chaotic 'non-system'.

A. Extent and Sources of World Inflation in the 1970s

In order to place the developments of the 1970s in a broad historical perspective, I have included in the accompanying tables the estimates of world monetary reserves and reserve increases over the last 30 years, beginning in 1949. The reader may wish to focus his attention on the last four lines of Table 2.1, and the last two columns of Table 2.2.

The last lines of Table 2.1 show that world monetary reserves, measured in dollars at current exchange rates and market gold prices, have increased more than ten-fold in the last ten years. Think of what this means: ten times as much in ten years as in all previous years and centuries. They were still increasing in 1979 at an annual rate of 62 per cent, i.e., ten or fifteen times faster than the maximum conceivable growth of world trade and production in real, non-inflationary terms and much faster still than the actual growth of these activities in the recession that has characterised these years.

The sources of these wildly inflationary increases in world reserves are listed, in both tables, in decreasing order from most to least planned and acceptable. The last two columns of Table 2.2 show that:

1. The only source of reserve creation fully responsive to international concertation, namely SDR allocations and IMF credit, accounted for less than 2 per cent of world reserve increases over the last ten years and less than half of 1 per cent in 1979 (line I, 1);
2. The contribution of world gold, measured in volume at its old price of $ or SDR 35 per ounce, was slightly negative, owing primarily to IMF and US sales to the private market (line I, 2);
3. National central banks' foreign exchange purchases and retention — welcomed by some, but accepted only with increasing reluctance by others because of their inflationary impact on domestic monetary issues — have accounted for only 25 per cent (one-fourth) of global reserve increases over the last decade and fell in 1979 to little more than 6 per cent, down from 77 per cent in the 1960s (line I, 3);
4. By far the major source of reserve increases was obviously the least planned of all: 73 per cent (nearly three-fourths) of the global reserve increases of the last decade, and 93 per cent of the increases in 1979 originated in fluctuations of dollar exchange rates and gold prices (see line II, 1 and 2) totally deprecated by the monetary authorities theoretically in charge of the 'system'. Need I remind you how often governors of central banks, ministers of finance and even heads of states or governments used to proclaim that stability of exchange rates and gold prices — at $35 an ounce — would remain forever the intangible pillars of our international monetary system, whatever the other reforms admittedly needed for its

Table 2.1: Sources of International Monetary Reserves: 1949-79 (billions of US dollars)

	End of year					Ten-year increases			One-year increases
	1949	1959	1969	1978	1979	1950-9	1960-9	1970-9	1979
I. At $35 per ounce of gold	45.5	57.0	78.7	279.8	302.9	11.5	21.7	224.2	23.1
1. SDR allocations and IMF credit	0.2	0.8	4.4	18.8	20.5	0.6	3.6	16.1	1.7
2. World gold	34.3	40.0	41.2	39.9	39.3	5.7	1.2	-2.0	-0.6
3. Foreign exchange	11.0	16.1	33.0	221.1	243.1	5.2	16.9	210.1	22.0
II. Impact of fluctuations of:	-0.3	0.1	0.2	290.4	618.9	0.4	0.2	618.6	328.4
1. Dollar-SDR exchange rate	–	–	–	132.5	222.0	–	–	222.0	89.5
2. Gold-SDR market price	-0.3	0.1	0.2	157.9	396.8	0.4	0.2	396.6	239.0
III. Total gross reserves (I+II)	45.2	57.0	78.9	570.3	921.8	11.8	21.9	842.8	351.5
% growth rates:									
Over period:									
Measured in SDRs (I)						25	38	238	8.3
At $ market prices and exchange rates (III)						26	38	1068	62
Per year:									
Measured in SDRs (I)						2.3	3.3	13	8.3
At $ market prices and exchange rates (III)						2.3	3.3	28	62

Notes: 1. Sources of reserves and reserve growth are listed from the most to the least planned by the monetary authorities, ranging from SDR allocations and IMF credit, at one extreme, to gold price fluctuations at the other. 2. This breakdown by 'source' includes under 'world gold' and 'SDR allocations' reserves resulting from gold and SDR transfers to the IMF, included under 'Reserve Positions in Fund' in the IFS breakdown of reserves by 'composition'. Note also that the gold holdings of the EMCF (European Monetary Co-operation Fund) are listed in IFS under 'foreign exchange' (presumably in order to permit their breakdown by individual countries members of the European Community).

Source: International Monetary Fund, *International Financial Statistics* (IFS), vol. 33 no. 6 (June 1980), and International Monetary Fund, *Annual Yearbook 1979*, vol. 32.

Table 2.2: Sources of International Monetary Reserves: 1949-79 (percentage shares of world reserves or reserve increases)

	End of year					Ten-year increase			One-year increases
	1949	1959	1969	1978	1979	1950-9	1960-9	1970-9	1979
I. At $35 per ounce of gold	101	100	100	49	33	97	99	27	6.6
1. SDR allocations and IMF credit	0.4	1.5	5.6	3.3	2.2	5.4	16	1.9	0.4
2. World gold	76	70	52	7.0	4.3	48	5.6	–0.2	–0.2
3. Foreign exchange	24	28	42	39	26	44	77	25	6.3
II. Impact of fluctuations of:									
1. Dollar SDR exchange rate	–0.6	–0.1	0.3	51	67	3.1	0.7	73	93
	–	–	–	23	24	–	–	26	25
2. Gold-SDR market price	–0.6	–0.1	0.3	28	43	3.1	0.7	47	68

Notes and source: See Table 2.1.

International and Regional Monetary Systems 43

survival. Yet, the collapse of the gold-convertible dollar pillar of Bretton Woods is obviously the only major reform actually implemented so far; and the inflationary potential – still largely unrealised – of the multiplication of gold prices by a factor of nearly 20 (from $35 an ounce to $666.50 at the time of writing, September 1980) certainly does not promise us any 'light at the end of the tunnel' – to use another discredited slogan – within which gold prices and exchange rates continue to crawl, or jump, from day to day in a most unpredictable and deplorable fashion;
5. Even if we exclude gold from these calculations of world reserves and confine ourselves – as international financial statistics tables tend to do – to 'credit reserves' alone, their increase still amounts to $310 billion (828 per cent) over the last ten years, providing inflationary financing for balance-of-payments deficits that could never otherwise have been sustained on such a scale.

I might add that such financing, still under the theoretical control of the monetary authorities, has now paled into insignificance in comparison with the foreign credits extended to borrowers by the private market. The incomplete estimates published in the Annual Reports of the Bank for International Settlements show that over the last four years (1976-9) these have totalled $483 billion net of duplications ($792 million gross), i.e., nearly three times as much as the foreign credits extended by the monetary authorities and more than 50 times what these borrowers receive in the way of internationally planned credits (SDR allocations and IMF lending).

B. Regional Investment of Reserve Increases

The second major shortcoming of the system is now at the centre of the North-South debate and, particularly, of the Brandt Commission Report. This is the ludicrous distribution of these inflationary reserve increases between the richer, more capitalised industrial countries, on the one hand, and the less capitalised and poorer countries (with the exception now of some of the oil-exporting countries), on the other.

Year after year, the United Nations votes pious resolutions stressing as a goal the exportation of capital by the former countries to the latter, but in the area which should be most under the control of the authorities – i.e., the international monetary system – exactly the opposite occurs.

The reader is invited to turn to Table 2.3 and more especially to Table 2.4, which extracts from Table 2.3 some significant estimates of regional shares in world reserves (under line I) and of the contribution of 'borrowed' reserves to the gross reserves of the under-capitalised countries, the United States and the other industrial countries.

Table 2.3: Sources and Distribution of Gross and Net International Monetary Reserves at the End of 1979 (billions of dollars, at market prices)

	World	IMF	Countries	Industrial countries				Under-capitalised countries		
				United States	Other	Total		Total	Oil-exporting	Other
I. World gold, at market price in $	574	55	520[d]	135	312[e]	448		71	19	52
1. At $35 per ounce	39	3.7	36	9.3	21[e]	31		4.8	1.3	3.6
2. Impact of fluctuation of market price	535	51	484	126	291	417		66	17	49
II. Credit reserve assets	364	12	352	7.8	190	198		155	72	82
1. Foreign exchange	320	–	320	3.8	171	175		145	67	78
2. SDR holdings	18	1.1	16	2.7	9.6	12		4.2	1.4	2.8[g]
3. Reserve positions in IMF	26	11[a]	15	1.3	8.9	10		5.3	3.9	1.4
III. Credit reserve liabilities	364	15	348	183	152	335		14	1.0	13
1. Foreign exchange	320	–	320	179[f]	142[f]	320		–	–	–
2. SDR allocations	18	–	18	4.2	8.2	12		5.2	1.0	4.2
3. IMF credit	26	15[b]	11[a]	–	2.2	2.2		8.3	–	8.3
IV. Gross reserves (I+II)	938	66	872[d]	143	502	645		225	91	134
V. Net reserves (IV-III)	574	51[c]	525[d]	–39	350	310		212	90	122

Notes: [a] Use of IMF credit (gross). [b] Reserve positions in IMF. [c] Undistributed profits. [d] Exceeds sum of 'all countries' by $1.2 billion = SDR 85 million x 512 dollars per ounce, owing to discrepancy of 2.4 million ounces in IFS gold total. [e] Including EMCF gold holdings included in IFS total under 'foreign exchange'. [f] Including under 'other' about $17.5 billion in liabilities not identified by country in IMF, *Annual Report, 1980* ($2.6 billion of World Bank and IDA liabilities plus residual discrepancy), some of which may be US liabilities. Identified Eurodollar liabilities were estimated at $61 billion, of which $35.7 were identified in the Federal Reserve Bulletin as liabilities of foreign branches of US banks. [g] Misprint in June 1980 IFS which reports SDR holdings as SDR 2066 instead of 2123.

Source: Computed from international reserve tables in International Monetary Fund, *International Financial Statistics*, vol. 33, no. 6 (June 1980).

Table 2.4: Sources and Distribution of Gross and Net International Monetary Reserves at the End of 1979

	All countries	Under-capitalised countries	United States	Other industrial countries
I. Gross reserves[a]	100	16	26	58
1. Gold revaluation profits [a]	100	14	26	60
2. Credit reserve assets[a]	100	44	2.2	54
a. Foreign exchange[a]	100	45	1.2	55
b. SDR holdings[a]	100	25	17	58
c. Reserve positions in Fund[a]	100	34	8.1	58
II. Gross reserves[b]		100	100	100
1. Reserve liabilities[b]		6.0	128	30
a. Foreign exchange[b]		–	125	28
b. SDR allocations[b]		2.3	2.9	1.6
c. IMF credit[b]		3.7	–	0.4
2. Net reserves[b]		94	–28	70

Notes: [a] Reported as a percentage of the world figures for these items. [b] Reported as a percentage of gross reserves.
Source: See Table 2.3.

As of the end of 1979, credit reserves other than gold totalled about $350 billion. The less capitalised countries contributed (i.e., held as creditors) 44 per cent of the total, but received as borrowers only 4 per cent. The more capitalised, industrial countries contributed the other 56 per cent, but received as investments 96 per cent. The sharpest contrast is with the United States, which contributed little more than 2 per cent (less than $8 billion) of world credit reserves but received as investments more than 52 per cent ($182 billion) of the $350 billion total (see lines II and III of Table 2.3 and line I, 2 of Table 2.4).

Another way of looking at the same figures is to see what proportion of its gross reserves is derived by each group from 'borrowed' reserves. This is shown in line II, 1 of Table 2.4. In brief, at the end of 1979 borrowed reserves accounted for only 6 per cent of the less capitalised countries' gross reserves (1 per cent for the oil-exporting countries and 10 per cent for the others), while they represented 30 per cent of the gross reserves of industrial countries other than the United States and 128 per cent of those of the United States, whose net reserves were therefore negative.

Finally, being minor holders of gold reserves, the less capitalised countries benefited from less than 14 per cent of the huge gold revaluation profits of recent years ($66 billion out of a $484 billion total) as against 26 per cent for the United States and 60 per cent for the other industrial countries (see line I, 1 of Table 2.4 derived from line I, 2 of Table 2.3).

II. Chances for and Timing of Needed World Reforms

This brief review of the present system, or rather non-system, demonstrates a far more urgent need for reform of such an absurd method of reserve creation and investments than could be suspected from official pronouncements or even from the writings of academic economists. Most of the latter's publications in recent years — may I hazard 90 per cent as a rough 'guesstimate'? — have been devoted to the relative merits and demerits of fixed versus floating exchange rates and to the deflationary or inflationary impact of the oil price explosion. Important as they are, these two issues are less central to the functioning of the world monetary system than the proclivity towards flooding imparted to it by the use of one or several national reserve currencies — the pound in former days, then overwhelmingly the dollar and now also the Swiss franc, German mark, Japanese yen, etc. — as the main instruments for international settlements and reserve accumulation, both official and private.

The flooding of world reserves, politically irresistible under such a system, makes it absolutely impossible for either floating or fixed exchange rates to function satisfactorily. Moreover, it is the factor most responsible for the collapse of the gold-convertible dollar and of the Bretton Woods System in August 1971, more than two years before the explosion of oil prices in the fall of 1973. Indeed, the latter was impelled in part by a world inflation already well under way and not unrelated to the doubling of world monetary reserves in the short span of the previous three years (1970-2).

I need not dwell on my familiar prescription for world monetary reform, initially dismissed by the officials, then largely endorsed by them in the swan's song of the famous Committee of Twenty after long years of debate and negotiation and now buried — temporarily, I still hope! — in the second amendment of the IMF Articles of Agreement. Let me merely point out that the objections raised against my reform proposals by central bankers have been proved devastatingly wrong by the record summarised in the first section of this paper.

These bank officials used to denounce my proposals as wildly inflationary, because my proposed link between reserve creation and development financing would — they said — encourage the less developed countries to force excessive, inflationary issues of world reserves to increase such financing. They saw no such risk in dollar holdings which they regarded as perfectly liquid and convertible at will into gold, at an unchangeable price of $35 an ounce. (I could quote exact comments and famous names, but this would be unkind to men who were, and still are, my friends.)

The political and financial facts proved exactly the opposite: the LDCs had far less political influence in the IMF than the richer industrial countries. Even SDR creation — when belatedly accepted — was distributed primarily to the latter (70 per cent). The 100 or so less capitalised countries were allotted less than 30 per cent, i.e., little more than the United States alone (24 per cent).

Taken together, SDR allocations and IMF credits accounted for only 3 per cent of world monetary reserves at the end of 1979 while foreign exchange — invested only in a few of the richer countries — accounted for 37 per cent of these reserves and the rise of the dollar price of gold for another 56 per cent. (The remaining four per cent is represented by gold valued at its former price of $35 an ounce.)

One should hope that these facts are now sufficiently understood to revive the reform attempts aborted in Jamaica and in the second IMF amendment.

Yet several years are generally deemed likely — even by the most starry-eyed optimists — to elapse before meaningful worldwide reforms can be effectively negotiated and implemented. The only hope, in the meantime, is that the countries most dissatisfied with the shortcomings denounced above will pursue their efforts at regional agreements, both to minimise — to the extent possible — the inevitable damage caused by the present world system and to domonstrate to others the feasibility and advantages of reforms which need not wait for a unanimity which may be attainable only in the distant future.

III. Potentialities of Regional Monetary Agreements

My long career in international monetary economics has been devoted to the tireless pursuit of a two-fold objective whose components should be regarded, in fact, as inseparable and complementary, rather than as alternative courses of action: the adjustment of both worldwide and regional monetary institutions to the realities of economic and political interdependence in a shrinking world.[3]

Regional co-operation — and, one hopes, integration — must, however, be outward as well as inward-looking. The geographical scope of feasible so-called 'optimum currency areas' should entail co-operation and agreements, *de jure* or at least *de facto*, with the countries or areas of most importance to a country's foreign trade, services and capital transactions. Close agreements — aiming as high as full monetary union —

will of course be easier to negotiate among neighbouring countries linked together by long tradition as well as by economics. Such agreements have, for this reason, developed most spectacularly among the countries of the European Community since the last war and are now also developing between them and other Western European countries. Intra-European trade encompasses about two-thirds of Western Europe's trade, i.e., more than ten times its trade with the United States.

Similar agreements are less easy to negotiate among other countries wishing to build around commonly shared traditions and ideals but whose mutual trade constitutes only a minor share of their total foreign trade. This is the case for the countries of Latin America, of the Middle East and Africa and of Asia and the Far East. Co-operation for these countries, whether *de facto* or *de jure*, must inevitably encompass other countries or regional groups, including in most cases either Western Europe or the United States, or both.[4]

Table 2.5 clearly indicates that Western Europe constitutes, in this respect, a main pole of attraction for the countries of the Middle East. Their trade with one another represents only about 13 per cent of their total trade, 46 per cent of which is with Western Europe. This figure becomes 68 per cent (more than two-thirds) if one includes the broader group of countries[5] whose trade is also primarily Europe-oriented.

Before turning — briefly, only because of my unfamiliarity with the problems — to the potentialities for Arab monetary arrangements, it may therefore be of interest to summarise the experience of the European Monetary System (EMS) belatedly put into operation in 1979 and the high hopes placed by many of us on the development of its potential benefits for other countries as well as for its members.

A. *The European Monetary System and the ECU*

1. *The EMS Breakthrough*. The most hopeful sign of possible progress towards international monetary reform since the breakdown of Bretton Woods is indeed, in my opinion, the breakthrough finally achieved in March 1979 with the initiation of the EMS and the launching — however modest — of the ECU as a parallel world currency alongside the dollar.

Let me mention briefly three crucial features of the system which its promoters find most attractive.

(a) The system restores for the participating currencies the common denominator — or 'numeraire' — so sadly lacking in the reformed IMF Agreement. This common denominator is the ECU defined as a weighted basket of the participating currencies. Unsatisfactory as this definition may be, it is a more realistic benchmark for exchange-rate calculations and readjustments and for progress towards stability than the widely fluctuating dollar. This is because the trade, services

Table 2.5: **Regional Structure of Middle East Countries' Trade (percentages of total external trade)**

Foreign trade with	Total		Exports		Imports	
	1978	1979	1978	1979	1978	1979
I. Europe-oriented area	67	68	66	68	67	69
A. Western Europe	44	46	35	39	48	49
1. European Community	32	34	26	29	34	35
2. Other	12	12	9	10	14	13
B. Middle East	13	13	18	15	11	12
C. Other	10	10	14	13	8	8
1. Africa (excluding South Africa)	2	2	3	3	1	1
2. Communist countries	6	6	8	7	6	5
3. Australia, NZ, South Africa	2	3	2	3	2	2
II. Western hemisphere	13	14	11	12	13	15
A. United States	11	13	10	11	12	13
B. Canada	1	1	–	–	1	1
C. Latin America	1	–	1	1	1	1
III. Asia	10	10	15	14	8	8
A. Japan	5	5	6	6	5	4
B. Other	5	5	8	8	4	4
IV. Unspecified countries and special categories	10	8	8	6	11	8

Source: International Monetary Fund, *Direction of Trade Yearbook, 1980* (Washington D.C.: IMF, 1980), pp. 40-4.

and capital transactions of the countries of the European Community among themselves and with others — in Western Europe, the Middle East and Africa — likely to gravitate around the ECU, account for two-thirds to three-fourths of their total transactions and close to ten times their transactions with the United States.[6]

(b) One of the first consequences of this definition is to give, for the first time, an operational significance to the principle formulated in Article 107 of the Rome Treaty: 'Each member State shall treat its policy with regard to rates of exchange as a matter of common concern'. Since each country's official rate is defined in terms of the ECU, and since the ECU itself is defined as a weighted average of member currencies, it is impossible for the value of any one currency to move upward — or downward — in terms of this average without a compensatory depreciation — or appreciation — of all the other

participating currencies. Any readjustment of mutually agreed exchange rates can thus be effected only by mutual consent;
(c) Two other exchange-rate commitments are also central to the EMS agreement. The first is taken from the former 'snake' agreement: the monetary authorities of each country are committed to intervene in the exchange market — through sales or purchases of their own currency — in order to limit bilateral exchange-rate fluctuations between their currency and any other participating currency to a margin of 2.25 per cent (temporarily enlarged to 6 per cent for Italy). The second and totally novel one is to calculate for each currency a so-called 'divergence indicator' reflecting its market fluctuations in terms of the ECU *vis-à-vis* its officially agreed central ECU rate. When these fluctuations reach a certain percentage of the maximum divergence possible under the bilateral margins system, the monetary authorities of the issuing country are automatically presumed to take appropriate action (market interventions, internal monetary policy measures, other economic policy measures and/or readjustment of the central rate *vis-à-vis* the ECU). Short of taking such action, they are supposed at the very least to explain and discuss with their partners the ways in which the situation should be corrected. Thus, in total contrast with Bretton Woods and all other traditional monetary 'sovereignty' rules, consultations on desirable exchange-rate readjustments may be forced upon a reluctant country, rather than left exclusively to its own initiative;
(d) Beyond its 'numeraire' and 'divergence indicator' functions, the ECU also serves not only as a unit of account for an increasing number of Community transactions, but also as a means of settlement and reserve accumulation.

Central bank stabilisation interventions in the exchange market should be conducted, as far as possible, in member currencies rather than in dollars. Since, however, central banks do not in principle accumulate member currencies as reserves, such interventions require mutual credit operations between the two central banks concerned, the issuing bank of the strong currency accumulating claims against the issuing bank of the weak currency. Central banks grant each other through the European Monetary Co-operation Fund (EMCF) unlimited very short-term financing for their interventions and short-term monetary support, which can be supplemented further by medium-term financial assistance, granted by the EEC Council under appropriate conditions. These short- and medium-term arrangements now entail lending commitments totalling in theory 38.7 billion ECUs, not all of which, however, could be simultaneously utilised.

The borrower can exercise one of several options, or a combination

International and Regional Monetary Systems 51

thereof, when the reimbursement falls due. In case he wishes to settle in ECUs, he cannot force upon a reluctant creditor ECU settlements exceeding 50 per cent of the amount due. For any portion not settled in ECUs, the general rule — in the absence of any other agreement between the two parties — is to settle in reserve components in the same proportions as those in which the debtor central bank holds its reserves, excluding gold. In practice, therefore, the option is primarily between ECU and dollar repayments.

But how do central banks acquire such ECUs? They are credited in ECU accounts on the books of the EMCF against equivalent transfers[7] of gold and dollar reserves for amounts equal to 20 per cent of each country's gold and dollar assets. The conversion of these gold and dollar transfers into ECUs takes place at current market prices or (for gold) at the average of market prices over the preceding six months. From an initial total of about 26 billion ECUs, i.e., about $35 billion, these transfers amounted to 45 billion ECUs, equivalent to nearly $65 billion, at the end of August 1980.

The EMS baby is deemed by its parents to be reasonably healthy. Its growth to adulthood, however, will require additional and crucial agreements calling for a high degree of political vision and responsibility. I wish I could review here in particular the steps necessary to transform the EMCF into a European Monetary Fund, and, later, into the federal reserve system of a full-fledged monetary union. This, however, merits another paper.

Here I shall consider the external — rather than internal — problems confronting the EMS in the immediate and more distant future.

2. The ECU and the Dollar. One of the first and most urgent problems confronting non-member as well as member countries is the insertion of the EMS into the world monetary system and particularly the uneasy relationship between the ECU and the dollar in international settlements.

An important feature of the EMS in this respect is highly appreciated by European monetary authorities. This is the replacement — in principle, at least — of the dollar by Community currencies in intra-Community interventions in the exchange market and by the ECU in the settlement of mutual credits. There have, justifiably, been many complaints about the predominant use of the dollar in both of these transactions, as it can create strong, if unintended, upward or downward pressures on dollar exchange rates, irrespective of any development in the dollar's competitiveness in world trade, whenever Community countries' surpluses or deficits switch from eager to reluctant dollar-holders and vice versa.

The first months of operation of the EMS have been somewhat disappointing in this respect, dollar interventions having remained far larger than was intended. New measures are now under discussion to make possible a further reduction in the use of the dollar in market interventions and settlements. If successful, these measures should eliminate unneccessary pressures — upward or downward — excessive relaxation of which has proved, as noted above, to be the major generator of world inflation and continued balance-of-payments disequilibria for other countries as well as for the United States.

The use of the ECU outside the Community itself might, at first glance, seem more worrisome. As mentioned already, the ECU is likely to provide a powerful pole of attraction for other European, Middle Eastern and African countries, a major portion of whose total trade is with the Community. In fact, some of these countries are already looking to the ECU as a potential benchmark for their exchange-rate policies and stabilisation efforts. Switches from dollars to ECUs in private and official settlements and in reserve accumulation might become very tempting, if made possible by the EMS authorities or by the imaginative Eurocurrency and Eurobond sectors of the world economy. Such switches might depress dollar rates unduly on the exchange markets if they are not effected — as suggested below — with the future European Monetary Fund (EMF) instead.

Close, two-way co-operation between the EMS and the US authorities will be necessary, in any case, to prevent the further weakening of an already under-valued, over-competitive dollar. If this trend is allowed to proceed much further, it will inevitably trigger protectionist reactions abroad against so-called 'foreign exchange dumping' by the United States and, possibly, panicky reactions in the United States itself.

The fear of such a disastrous course of events is a powerful stimulus to co-operation between the US and Europe, and the EMS provides new and unprecedented instruments for making such co-operation more feasible and effective than in the past.

The first requirement in this respect will be the correction of the huge and growing US deficit of recent years and, indeed, the restoration of healthy surpluses in the balance of payments on current account. This, in turn, will require an even more determined and successful fight to reduce profligate American oil consumption and imports and a rate of domestic inflation there which is double or triple that of Germany, Japan, Belgium, the Netherlands or Austria, to say nothing of Switzerland. The clear affirmation of these policy objectives by the US Congress as well as by the Administration and their early implementation through concrete restraints on fiscal over-spending, excessive money creation, price and wage increases, oil consumption and imports should help restore confidence in the dollar and reverse bearish speculation in it by both Americans and foreigners.

Yet a total and lasting correction of the US deficit cannot be expected

International and Regional Monetary Systems

overnight. Corrective policies — including exchange-rate readjustments — produce their effects only slowly. The avoidance of an excessive depreciation of the dollar will still require considerable financing of foreign deficits for some time to come.

The US can, first of all, draw for this purpose on its own international reserves, estimated at $18 billion at the end of October 1979, but which would actually come close to $200 billion if gold holdings were revalued at the current market price of gold. This latter estimate is of course excessive, since gold prices would collapse in the event of massive sales from our reserves. It is nevertheless relevant as one of the many reassurances to prospective creditors as to our solvency and as an indication of our ability to transfer gold at market or close-to-market prices to foreign monetary authorities in settlement of their dollar claims.

Far more important, of course, is the willingness, amply demonstrated already, of foreign countries to participate in a joint defence of agreed dollar rates, including the readjustments — both upward and downward — that might be deemed appropriate, or unavoidable, before any stabilisation of the dollar *vis-à-vis* the other major currencies can be realistically envisaged, even as a presumptive goal, rather than a legally binding commitment. The radical policy changes announced and put into operation since November 1978 — and reinforced on 6 October 1979 — are essential in this respect.

First of all, the European countries have agreed to intervene massively in the exchange market, rather than leave such interventions almost exclusively to others. Secondly, they have agreed to reduce the inflationary impact of their borrowing abroad by borrowing in the financial market, rather than almost exclusively from central banks. Thirdly, they are now ready to denominate their foreign borrowings in the creditors' currencies as well as in their own, in order to make them more attractive and acceptable to prospective lenders deterred by the risk of exchange losses on a depreciating dollar. Fourthly, they are now willing to explore actively with their IMF partners the opening of so-called 'substitution accounts' in SDRs as a way to mop up some of the dollar overhang accumulated in the past.[8]

The EMS opens up new opportunities in all of these respects.

First of all, the adoption of the ECU as a parallel currency may soon enable the European countries to denominate some of their foreign borrowings in ECUs. Financially, this would expose them to smaller risks of exchange losses than alternative denominations in national currencies such as the mark or the Swiss franc. Politically, it would be a concrete and spectacular demonstration of their determination to support the new European Monetary System. It would also be far more acceptable than borrowings in any national currency other than the dollar; for this would open them up to the accusation, for instance, of making the dollar a satellite of the mark.

Secondly, a reinforced EMCF — and, later, a European Monetary Fund — should facilitate the effective concertation of joint intervention and management of European exchange rates *vis-à-vis* the dollar. It should also provide an additional mechanism for the 'substitution accounts' envisaged above. Reluctant dollar-holders could exchange them for ECUs if they wished, as well as for SDRs.

The *quid pro quo* of the ECU exchange guarantee granted by the US to the EMCF would be a substantial lowering of interest rates on European obligations and their consolidation into longer-term maturities. This consolidation *vis-à-vis* the EMCF would leave intact the 'liquid' character of the ECU claims held on it by the national central banks in exchange for their dollars, in so far as intra-EMS balance-of-payments disequilibria could be settled by mere book-keeping transfers of ECU balances from one member country to another. This liquid character would also be preserved for the financing of European deficits in relation to the United States — and other dollar-area countries — if our obligations toward the EMCF were expressed in the most appropriate form, i.e., in the form of 'consols' without any imperative repayment date. 'Consol' bonds paying interest to their holders, but repayable only at the initiative of the debtor — mostly through open market operations — used to be a most traditional and prestigious means of borrowing for the British government and — under the name of 'rentes perpetuelles' — for the French government as well. They could be made similarly popular and attractive today, especially if coupled with a 'contingent' repayment obligation in the event that present balance-of-payments disequilibria were reversed and Europe's creditors were again to incur substantial deficits in relation to the United States.

It would moreover express, operationally, an obvious and inescapable truth, i.e., that 'real' repayment of international credits can only be effected through the recovery of a surplus position by the debtor. All that financial arrangements can do, otherwise, is to reshuffle among the creditors the claims on a deficit country, but it is equally true that these creditors can only receive 'real' repayment for their claims by running deficits. I feel that the suggestions above would help dispel the financial fog clouding these transactions — and often misleading the transactors themselves into unfortunate and ineffective policy decisions — and adjust international lending practices to the facts of life.

Note also that the 'consols' accumulated by the EMCF — or a reformed IMF — should be negotiable in the market, under agreed conditions and whenever advisable, in order to mop up excessive, inflationary levels of liquidity.

3. Progress Towards Worldwide Reforms. Some people will still view regional monetary co-operation as the antithesis of worldwide monetary co-operation. I took the opposite view when I helped plan and negotiate the European Payments Union (EPU), which provided in the 1950s a most spectacular demonstration of the complementarity of these two approaches. The EPU did much more, indeed, than the IMF in those years to restore convertibility between the participating currencies and the dollar as well as the interconvertibility of these currencies themselves.

I am convinced that the success of the EMS experiment in achieving its basic objectives, and the indispensable co-operation between EMS and US authorities, might at long last break the deadlock which has, since Jamaica, undermined the determination shown in the past to restore a workable world monetary order. I hope I am not entirely alone in feeling that floating rates and the second amendment to the IMF Articles of Agreement should not mean that all previous proposals for IMF reform, ironed out over ten years of continuous, intensive negotiations, are relegated to the garbage can.[9] The revolutionary developments of recent years certainly require a modification of previous proposals for reform, in the sense not of emasculating them, but — particularly in the face of the fantastic explosion of private international credits — of enlarging them.

First and foremost, of course, should be the actual implementation of the often reiterated pious wish to substitute a reformed SDR for both the dollar and gold in international reserves and settlements. Estimates appearing in IFS[10] show how far we are from this goal: SDR allocations and IMF credits together accounted, at the end of 1979, for less than 3 per cent of world reserves as against 62 per cent for gold (valued at market prices) and 35 per cent for foreign exchange holdings. The mopping-up of outstanding gold and dollar holdings through 'substitution accounts' will be useless, however — and difficult to negotiate — if it is not complemented by those radical reforms to which it should be a mere prelude, i.e., those that will:

(i) limit the future expansion of the world reserve system to what is needed to make it an engine of world stability rather than of world inflation; and
(ii) attempt to earmark this growth for the financing of high-priority economic and social objectives commonly agreed, rather than for the haphazard financing of US or other reserve centres' deficits.

I would plead again, as a way to meet the first of these objectives, for a simple but only presumptive rule *à la* Milton Friedman: the IMF should be directed to expand its total lending and investment portfolio at a rate of 4 to 6 per cent a year, consistent with the reserve requirements of the non-inflationary growth of world trade and production.

Decision by two-thirds or three-fourths majority weighted vote should be required to authorise substantial departures from this presumptive target. For it to have the desired effect, moreover, the monetary authorities should invest all of their future surpluses in SDRs – re-baptised, of course, and made more attractive to members – and eschew any purchase of gold and foreign exchange, except for the minimum working balances in foreign currencies still needed for interventions in the market until SDRs are made available – as they should be – to commercial banks and even to other holders.[11] Particularly encouraging in this respect is the forward-looking 'Thoughts on an International Monetary Fund Based Fully on the SDR'[12] by the economic counsellor and director of the Research Department of the IMF: J.J. Polak.

As for the second objective, it would flow automatically from the fact that all reserve growth would become the result of agreed IMF decisions. These should include the type of operations financed by the Fund in the past – including those covered by the 'General Agreements to Borrow' – but to which would be added those now made possible by the substitution of SDRs for gold and foreign exchange reserves. These operations would not necessarily be limited – as is brilliantly explained by Professor Machlup[13] – to short-term lending. An expansion of IMF operations consistent with the first objective above should leave room for such operations. They might take the form of IMF investments in long-term bonds, or even consols, issued by various agencies such as the World Bank, its affiliates, other regional development banks, and even by other international agencies such as the World Health Organisation, etc.

B. Potentialities of Arab Monetary Agreements

The final part of my paper will be very brief and inadequate. I trust that this subject has been competently prepared for this meeting by other participants more knowledgeable than myself.

The experience of Latin America amply demonstrates that the full scope of feasible economic, financial and monetary co-operation can be reached only by decentralised agreements, i.e., whereby the agreements between certain countries (in Central America, for instance, or in the Caribbean or Andean areas) would be more extensive than those covering the whole of Latin America. Even in Western Europe, negotiations among the Community countries have been more successful than those between them and the EFTA (European Free Trade Association) countries, those within Benelux more than those within the Community as a whole and those within the Belgo-Luxemburg Monetary Union still more than those within Benelux. I suspect that the same will be true for the Arab countries, the nations of the Gulf, for instance, proving able to conclude closer integration agreements with each other – as the United Arab Emirates have already done – than with some of the more distant and heterogeneous countries grouped with them in the Arab Monetary Fund. The full-scale mergers — not surrenders — of national sovereignty indispensable to full economic and monetary union will, I hope, prove attractive and feasible, in the foreseeable future, to their statesmen and experts and also to public opinion.

Feasible aims for the Arab world in general will probably have to be more modest, at least for the years immediately ahead. They should nevertheless encompass — as for all countries:

(1) Arrangements for balance-of-payments financing help by the richer countries for the poorer, requiring inevitably:
(2) Some restraints on inflationary domestic policies; and
(3) Determined efforts to reduce avoidable exchange-rate fluctuations.

The most topical issue to be agreed, as soon as possible, among all those willing and able to do so, is obviously — as for the countries of the European Community — the development of a common 'exchange area' and a 'parallel currency' for their external transactions. This falls far short, of course, of the full monetary union that may or may not be sought some day, but which can only be achieved after this first, more modest step has proven successful.

Such an exchange area will, of course, have to handle its relations with other countries and exchange areas with which it conducts most of its trade, particularly the United States and Western Europe. The policies which it should try to develop in this respect would not be very different, in my opinion, from those recommended in subsection A above for the countries of the European Monetary System and the ECU will probably prove a major centre of gravity for any future Arab 'parallel currency'.

The richer oil-producing countries have already demonstrated their willingness to participate generously in the financing of poorer countries, outside as well as inside the Arab world. Contractual price and financing arrangements with the industrial countries also require enormous, trailblazing innovations. The respective roles of the SDR, the ECU or any Arab unit of exchange in these arrangements will have to be ironed out, but should provide to the creditors acceptable earnings and 'maintenance of value' guarantees.

I personally doubt, in this regard, that full 'purchasing power' guarantees could be realistically enforced for any length of time. Stability in relation to the strongest or at least the stablest exchange unit available may prove in practice to be the most that can be expected. The ECU offers, from this point of view, undoubted advantages in the immediate future and I continue to trust that worldwide monetary reform will some day make possible the universal acceptability of a worldwide exchange unit, i.e., of a vastly reformed and improved SDR.

Oil prices quoted in the agreed unit should be less volatile than in any other, national currency but could hardly escape adjustments in the light of supply and demand, guided by proper policies regarding the inevitable depletion of this scarce resource. But this problem lies far beyond the scope of this paper . . . and of my competence.

IV. Conclusion

The regional monetary reforms advocated above should not be regarded as mere stopgap measures, pending broader, worldwide agreements. They should be part and parcel of such agreements. A more decentralised — and viable — structure of monetary co-operation than that of the now defunct Bretton Woods arrangements has long been overdue. Such a structure would offer, to my mind, the three-fold advantage of:

1. Making possible the full exploitation of the wider potential for realistic co-operation and enforceable commitments that exists at the regional level as compared with the worldwide level;
2. Relieving the IMF of unnecessary responsibilities and enabling it to concentrate its time and attention on those which cannot be discharged as efficiently by regional groups; and
3. Making wholehearted participation in the IMF more feasible and attractive to disaffected countries, including many less developed countries[14] and, particularly, making effective participation possible and acceptable to the Communist countries, for whom the rules and norms derived from the less fully planned, so-called 'market-oriented' economies of the capitalistic world may often be inadvisable, inapplicable or even irrelevant in practice.

Notes

1. This paper draws heavily on my article, 'The Future of the International Monetary System', in *Banca Nazionale del Lavoro Quarterly Review* (March 1980); translated into French in *Revue de la Banque* (April 1980).
2. See, for example, Robert Triffin, 'Gold and the Dollar Crisis: Yesterday and Tomorrow', *Princeton Essays in International Finance* (December 1978) and 'Some Observations on the Geographical Structure of International Deficits and their Financing', *Pakistan Development Review* (Autumn 1979).
3. I hope some of my readers may be induced to glance at some of my former writings on this subject, particularly in Robert Triffin, *Europe and the Money Muddle* (New Haven, Conn.: Yale University Press, 1957; reprinted, West Port, Conn.: Greenwood Press, 1976), pp. 256-68; *Gold and the Dollar Crisis: The Future of Convertibility* (New Haven, Conn.: Yale University Press, 1960),

pp. 121-44; *The World Money Maze* (New Haven, Conn.: Yale University Press, 1966), pp. 375-543; and 'The Community and the Disruption of the World Monetary System', in *Banca Nazionale del Lavoro Quarterly Review* (March 1975), pp. 30-5.

4. 'The Future of the International Monetary System', *Banca Nazionale del Lavoro Quarterly Review*, Table 4, p. 55.

5. These are the Communist countries (69 per cent of whose trade is with Europe – as reported in the *Direction of Trade Yearbook*, which excludes their own mutual trade), Australia, New Zealand, South Africa and other Africa. See preceding footnote for further explanations and qualifications of these estimates.

6. One may argue that the somewhat larger shares of total trade contractually denominated in dollars are more relevant, but the choice of the dollar denomination in transactions with countries other than the US is itself an illogical residue of past habits, no longer justified today.

7. These 'transfers', however, are still for the moment reflected in renewable three-month swaps, leaving the exchange risks attending gold and dollars to the depositing central bank rather than sharing them through the EMCF.

8. Agreement on this technique, however, is likely to require a parallel agreement of some sort on the complementary proposal of the IMF Executive Directors and the Committee of Twenty on 'asset settlements'. See the remarks on this topic in M. Szaz, *The Emerging European Monetary System* (Louvain-la-Neuve, Belgium: IRES, 1979).

9. See Triffin, 'Gold and the Dollar Crisis: Yesterday and Tomorrow', particularly pp. 11 and 12.

10. *International Financial Statistics*, published by the IMF.

11. In the event that more substantial dollar accumulations are deemed necessary in a transition period, they should be deducted from the authorised IMF lending and investment operations.

12. Recently published by the IMF as No. 28 in its Pamphlet Series.

13. Particularly in 'The Cloakroom Rule of International Reserves: Reserve Creation and Resources Transfers', *Quarterly Journal of Economics*, vol. 79, no. 3 (August 1965).

14. Note also that it would contribute to the solution of the issue raised by the fact that the Fund system of 'weighted voting', even if reformed as desired by the LDCs, will still assure them, as well as other groups, only a minority of the total voting power.

COMMENT

John W. Gunter

Introduction

It is not my intention to review Mr Triffin's paper but, rather, to concentrate on current problems and trends. In this way I hope to complement his work.

I wish first to make some remarks on regional monetary systems and then I will turn to current trends in the international monetary system.

I. Regional Monetary Systems

There are sound economic reasons for the establishment of regional monetary systems as an essential part of economic co-operation among the states comprising a region. A regional system may be able to cope with some of the problems arising from failures of the international system and, as a minimum, the monetary relations among the member states can be isolated to some degree from the external disorder. Such defensive motivations may lead to action, whereas the mere promise of long-term benefits is not likely to do so.

The EMS fits this pattern. Although advocacy of the monetary integration of the European Community dates back to its establishment, no significant progress was made for over two decades. The immediate reason for the establishment of the EMS somewhat more than a year and a half ago was the depreciation of the dollar and its impact on exchange-rate stability among the European currencies. Now that the EMS exists, however, it promises to foster the economic integration of the Community that had been visualised at the outset.

The EMS is still in the early stages of development. As a mechanism for exchange-rate co-ordination, it has functioned very well in its first year and a half of existence, helped as it is by the US policy adopted in late 1978 for the purpose of strengthening the dollar.

From the viewpoint of the EMS, the important point is that it has not been faced with disequilibrating capital flows resulting from a weak dollar. If anything, the problems have been in the reverse direction.

The EMS is not yet in a position to move to its crucial second phase, when the European Monetary Fund is to be created and the ECU will take on a positive role as a reserve asset. This move in any meaningful form requires greater convergence of growth and inflation policies among the members of the EMS than has yet been achieved.

The crucial test for the EMS will be its ability over time to promote more effective adjustment of the payments positions of its members than could be achieved relying solely on the IMF framework. So long as adjustment is approached in terms of adopting policies that are consistent with the growth of multilateral trade, there is no inherent conflict between the EMS and the IMF. In fact, as Mr Triffin suggests, there is a 'wider potential for realistic co-operation and enforceable commitments on a regional basis than on a world scale'. The early experience of the EMS, while limited, is nevertheless encouraging in this respect.

What is the potential for regional monetary systems among the Arab countries? A number of observations can be made, as well as a few tentative conclusions:

(a) The Arab countries constitute a very heterogeneous group as economic units. This complicates the task of adopting compatible fiscal, monetary and foreign exchange policies;

(b) The possibilities for close monetary co-operation may, however, be great for some groups of Arab countries. The prime example is the group of countries around the Gulf, which have similar problems and much the same traditions;

(c) The approach to fostering the co-operative development of monetary policies among Arab countries might appropriately proceed along two lines. First, monetary policy problems could be discussed on a broad basis without seeking — at least initially — as close a co-ordination as would be expected within a regional monetary system. This loose kind of co-operation could well be carried out through the Arab Monetary Fund, which would need to become the pre-eminent expert on central banking policy in the Arab community. Such co-operation should improve the effectiveness of central banking policy throughout the area.

Secondly, monetary systems could be formulated by groups of Arab countries willing to seek a convergence of monetary policies.

There is nothing inconsistent about following these two approaches simultaneously. To provide a basis for Arab monetary co-operation, I suggest that an analysis should be made of the powers possessed by each Arab central bank with respect to monetary policy and of the actual practice of each in formulating and carrying out monetary policy.

II. Progress on International Reform

I wish to review progress on international monetary reform under several headings:

A. Exchange-rate stability;

B. Balance-of-payments adjustment;
C. The role of the SDR and the effectiveness of the IMF;
D. Reserves composition;
E. The SDR link.

A. Exchange-rate Stability

Since the adoption of the new dollar policy two years ago, the dollar has been generally stable within a fairly narrow range. Its effective (trade-weighted) rate has shown occasional bouts of weakness, but also periods of strength.

As between the dollar and the EMS, the key relationship is the DM/dollar rate. Its range of fluctuation has been between DM 1.72 and DM 1.95, or about 12 per cent. While fortuitous circumstances have contributed to the relative stability of the DM/dollar rate, greater concern with maintaining stability has also played a part.

The relatively stable relationship between the DM and the dollar, the effective functioning of the EMS and the strengthening of the Japanese yen in 1980 to a more appropriate level all suggest that an opportunity may be evolving to establish effective target zones for exchange-rate management. While exchange-rate flexibility continues to be necessary, a greater degree of stability is now feasible.

This improved stability in the short term would be based on co-ordination of intervention and monetary policies. Over the longer term the maintainance of stability is dependent on the convergence of growth and inflation rates among major industrial countries. The dollar cannot be considered 'out of the woods' until US inflation has been reduced to approach the levels prevailing in Germany and Japan and until more expansionary monetary policies are possible in the major industrial countries without fear of renewed inflation.

B. Balance-of-payments Adjustment

One of the most distressing features of recent monetary history is the extent to which countries have sought to avoid balance-of-payments adjustments by finding means of financing their deficits, particularly in the period following the oil price increases of 1973-4.

There is, however, growing international recognition of the need for adjustment and also an increased emphasis on symmetrical adjustment. Symmetrical adjustment is an unusually complex issue because the degree of adjustment available to the surplus oil-exporting countries is limited. It has become necessary for the international community to make provision for continuing surpluses for the oil-exporters in order to make possible an adequate level of oil production. Although fully satisfactory arrangements for financing the continuing substantial imbalance in international payments have not yet been established, the magnitude and nature of the problem are now perceived with reasonable clarity.

The prime responsibility for policy action lies, of course, with the United States where it could be said that progress in coping with excessive inflation has been slow.

Some developing countries which have relied excessively on financing their deficits through the banks are finding these sources drying up. They are now being forced in the direction of the IMF where credit has become available in larger amounts, but only with conditionality.

There remains the problem of low-income countries with little access to the banks which are heavily dependent on aid on concessional terms. With low incomes and inflexible economies, making the adjustments that qualify for IMF financing is inherently difficult. These countries cannot afford credit on market terms while they adjust; they need grants, a need that has grown greatly under current international economic conditions. Unfortunately, the supply of concessional aid has increased relatively little.

Perhaps the most important point to make about adjustment as it relates to reform is that the most that any international monetary system can do is to provide guidance as to when adjustment is needed and by whom and to put pressure on that party to initiate adjustment promptly. Actual adjustment programmes will remain politically difficult to formulate and implement.

No monetary system can function satisfactorily if key countries — the large industrial countries — are not behaving well. On the other hand, when the United States resolves its inflation problem, international monetary reform will appear much less difficult than it does today.

One of the most intriguing aspects of regional monetary systems is whether they will foster more effective adjustment by the members of the regional group than would otherwise occur. As suggested in the discussion of the EMS, this may well be true.

C. *The Role of the SDR and the Effectiveness of the IMF*

The IMF is in the process of making of the SDR a very attractive reserve asset. As of 1 January 1981, the SDR will become a five-currency basket, instead of comprising 16 currencies. This simplification greatly enhances the usefulness of the SDR for the denomination of market assets and liabilities. The SDR itself will also soon carry a market rate of interest and the existing limitations on its use are effectively withering away.

The crucial point in terms of reform is that the SDR, and the SDR assets created by the Fund as a consequence of its credit operations, are becoming reserve assets which are fully acceptable to central banks. The development of commercial markets in SDR assets will not be far behind.

Their use will, in fact, provide the opportunity for needed reserve diversification.

In recent years the IMF has struggled to become a more effective international institution. The second amendment of the Articles of Agreement, which came into effect in April 1978, has provided a firmer basis for exchange-rate surveillance while, as suggested earlier, exchange markets are becoming more orderly. But the Fund's financing activities have lagged. Once the oil facility created in 1974 was exhausted, the use of IMF resources declined. This occurred despite large financing needs and initiatives by the IMF to establish procedures whereby members were entitled to much larger drawings than ever before. The decline was partly due to the availability of credit from the commercial banks. Now that bank financing is less available and the magnitude of the deficits to be financed has grown so enormously, the need for an active IMF is widely recognised.

A major debate is underway over conditionality and, more specifically, over the extent to which the use of IMF credit will be supportive of adjustment. However conditionality evolves, it is to be hoped that the programmes being agreed to will lead to a substantial degree of adjustment. Otherwise, hopes for progress towards a satisfactory international monetary system may be dashed. The IMF will simply replace the commercial banks in providing finance and the discipline of an effective monetary system will still be lacking.

D. Reserve Composition

Mr Triffin has described the growth in reserves, emphasising appropriately the significance of the increase in holdings of reserve currencies. There are two current trends in reserve composition that require attention.

One relates to the diversification of currencies being used as reserve assets. Recently, Germany, Japan and Switzerland have made their currencies more easily available for reserve purposes than previously. As a consequence, a substantial part of the oil-related surplus is being placed in three of the strongest currencies. In the longer run, however, a wider use of the currencies in reserves may not be desirable.

The other trend is just getting underway as a result of the growth in IMF activity. The proportion of total reserves in the form of SDR assets may be expected to rise considerably and perhaps even sharply, even without the establishment of a substitution account.

E. The SDR Link

There are, as Mr Triffin has shown, some clear advantages in allocating SDRs disproportionately in favour of the developing countries, as these are the countries in need of financing. In this way, SDR allocations would perform a double service.

While discussions covering the SDR link are again being reviewed, it would be unrealistic to expect much to come out of this review. I would make three observations:

1. A link does not have the great potential today for financing development that had been envisaged in earlier discussions. In the meantime, the SDR has become a very different asset. At the outset the SDR carried an interest rate of 1.5 per cent, while it will soon carry a market rate. In the past, a country that utilised SDRs allocated to it paid only 1.5 per cent and did not have to repay the principal. Today, it still does not have to repay the principal, but it no longer enjoys the advantage of having to pay only a nominal interest rate.
2. To make effective a link providing for direct allocations to IMF members on a basis other than quotas would apparently require an amendment of the IMF Articles of Agreement — a long and increasingly difficult process.
3. It remains highly doubtful that the industrial countries will agree to anything more than an indirect link whereby some SDRs are allocated for support of IMF objectives, such as subsidy account to reduce the cost of using IMF resources by low-income countries. An indirect link can perhaps be established without amendment of the IMF Articles.

GENERAL DISCUSSION

1. Mabid Ali Al-Jarhi

In the interest of attempting better to understand the EMS, I would like to propose that it be viewed as a system of exchange-rate co-ordination coupled with an attempt, however incomplete, to establish the ECU as a parallel currency.

The policy of exchange-rate co-ordination has been attacked for three reasons:

(a) Interference in the foreign exchange market by one member imposes externalities on other members, least of which perhaps is the cost of neutralising the effect of such interference on domestic money supply;
(b) Provision of cheap credit to deficit countries could encourage inflation; and
(c) The evolution of the DM as a pivot currency could require other members, with relatively higher inflation rates than prevalent in Germany (e.g., Italy), to deflate at unacceptable rates. This would threaten the viability of the EMS.

Mr Triffin is therefore asked to compare this approach to co-ordination on the part of the EMS with a more centralised approach in the light of these criticisms.

2. Fouad Morsi

I would like to begin by saying that I agree with the valuable analysis of the international monetary system presented by Mr Triffin, particularly the idea that this system has led to the creation of a kind of reserve that, in his words, has 'resulted in the financing of the rich by the poor...' Mr Triffin has made it clear that fluctuations in the exchange rate of the dollar and in the price of gold are the main source of this increase in international reserves. The price of gold has increased around twenty-fold in the past six years.

One theme that is implied throughout the author's analysis is the particular responsibility of the dollar for the collapse of the international monetary system. This conception was inherent in the call for a European monetary system. The same conception might also be behind the position adopted by Mr Triffin on the question of establishing an

Arab monetary system. His position, however, is based on a specific phenomenon, the relative weakness of inter-Arab trade which, according to his estimates, represents only 13 per cent of total Arab trade (some estimates put it as low as 10 per cent); and the relative weakness of trade between the Arab countries and North and South America, which represents around 14 per cent of total Arab trade. By comparison, trade between the Arab countries and Western Europe represents around 46 per cent of total Arab trade, if not more. This fact serves as the basis for his suggestion that the dollar be excluded from the exchange market and from the settlement of debts between the Arab countries. At the same time, he advocates the creation of an Arab exchange area with a parallel currency for Arab external transactions, with the ECU being given the central role.

In response to this proposal, I would like to emphasise that the Arab countries should not abandon the dollar only to link their currencies to another foreign currency, even if it be the ECU. Arab currencies must be freed from all forms of dependency.

There is another issue that must be re-considered. While Mr Triffin wishes the Arab countries to move in the direction of greater monetary co-operation he recommends bilateral arrangements between the Arab states and urges the Gulf states to press on towards monetary integration, instead of co-operating with what he terms 'the more distant and heterogeneous countries' which are members of the Arab Monetary Fund.

Even though the Gulf countries are better suited and perhaps more ready than the other Arab countries to proceed with monetary integration, such a step will not markedly change monetary conditions in the Gulf unless it comes within the framework of overall Arab economic integration. This framework, in turn, is meaningless unless it is aimed at the comprehensive economic development of all the Arab states. Otherwise, what is the difference between creating a single Arab currency for the Gulf states and linking these states to the dollar, for example?

All the Gulf countries, generally speaking, are 'surplus' countries. The isolation of these countries from the other Arab countries, most of which are deficitory, may be technically justified in order to allow the former to move towards monetary integration; but such action is not justifiable in the broader economic sense and would certainly have harmful political consequences.

3. Robert Triffin, in Response

I am most grateful to all the contributors for raising important questions which have helped me to clarify my own thoughts and suggestions about essential, but controversial issues.

Let me stress first that I find no contradiction but, on the contrary, basic agreement between Mr Gunter and myself. Our papers complement each other. He stresses, realistically, the political obstacles to the speedy negotiation of agreements on the ideal solutions which my paper foresees. He is right and we must often resign ourselves to the second or third-best solution when it is the only one within immediate reach. But even in the short run, we should be guided by our ultimate objectives and warn the politicians that they will not be able to live for long with the compromises being made today.

I should add that the ambitious reforms which I proposed as early as 1959 were not deemed so unrealistic by responsible leaders since they were largely endorsed — after ten years of continuous scrutiny, debate and negotiation — by various groups, particularly the Executive Directors of the IMF and the Committee of Twenty (in its June 1974 report), before they were, unfortunately, put on ice in Jamaica and in the second amendment to the IMF Articles of Agreement.

I have learned from Jean Monnet that politics may be 'the art of the possible' for politicians, but for a true statesman politics is also the art of educating public opinion and making possible tomorrow the more ambitious, but indispensable reforms that are still unattainable today.

This fundamental truth underlies my answers to a number of specific questions raised by Mr Gunter and others.

For instance, the EMS has been able to rally the agreement of both European enthusiasts and obdurate nationalists, because the adoption of the ECU in international transactions does not yet displace national currencies in domestic payments. Mr Debré [then French Minister of Finance Michel Debré] would adamantly oppose a full monetary union replacing the French franc by the ECU in domestic transactions, but is delighted to see the ECU displace Eurodollars, Euromarks, etc., in transactions in which the French franc is not, and could not, be used today. Yet, the use of the ECU in the Eurocurrency market, now estimated by the Bank of International Settlements to involve more than $750 billion, will make it widely known to the public and facilitate, at a later stage, its gradual adoption in domestic payments, if and when the success of national policies and monetary co-ordination makes it possible for the weaker currencies to move towards the full European economic and monetary union repeatedly promised to their people by heads of states and governments at successive summit meetings. This is my answer to Mr Al-Jarhi's question about the 'parallel currency' approach versus the 'centralisation approach'. The former is a first step towards the latter.

Secondly, the ECU should not be regarded as a substitute for a reformed SDR, but as a step towards world monetary reform, demonstrating to the US authorities that the latter is feasible and that the near monopoly of the dollar as a world 'parallel currency' is a thing of the past. The ECU will grow as an alternative to the dollar until both the ECU and the dollar can be replaced — and not merely supplemented — by a reformed SDR in worldwide settlements and reserve accumulation by private as well as by official sectors of the world economy.

The new SDR formula will undoubtedly spur its use in the short run, but it will be some time before it can replace the dollar and the ECU, especially in view of the political suspicions resulting from the fact that the initial gold definition of the SDR was radically altered in favour of a paper dollar SDR in August 1971, and in favour of a currency basket in December of the same year. This was accomplished in a totally illegal fashion which by-passed the agreed rules for amendment of the IMF Articles of Agreement.

Thirdly, I agree with Mr Al-Jarhi that the fear of inflationary EMS credits has been an obstacle to the full acceptance of the ECU by conservative opinion. This fear seems to be confirmed by the 75 per cent increase in ECU issues over the short span of one and a half years, from March 1979 to September 1980. However, this increase had nothing to do with credits to members which represented at their peak — in September 1979 — less than 5 per cent of the total assets and liabilities of the FECOM and which had been totally repaid by March of 1980.

This inflationary increase is more than explained by the revaluation of the FECOM's gold assets. It should prompt the establishment of new guidelines for replacing the absurd legal traditions still governing the book-keeping gains and losses of central banks in their gold and foreign exchange holdings. Currency depreciation stemming from higher rates of inflation results in book-keeping profits which are, sooner or later, passed on to the State Treasury. This leads to further inflationary deficits triggering renewed currency depreciation, book-keeping profits, etc., in an endless vicious cycle, while currency appreciation in less inflationary countries results in book-keeping losses inducing monetary restraint, renewed currency appreciation, etc. It is high time to revise such an absurd system and to adopt the reforms which I successfully advocated, many years ago, for the banking systems of a number of Latin American countries. Such profits and losses should not be passed on to the State Treasury, but should be blocked in a revaluation account, so that they may offset each other, both at any point in time and over time.

This may prove as necessary tomorrow, in order to sterilise otherwise deflationary gold losses, as it is today in order to sterilise inflationary gold profits, for I do not believe in a full re-monetisation of gold, i.e., in the re-introduction of a gold standard under which countries would stabilise gold prices by committing themselves to purchase, at a fixed price, unlimited amounts of gold and to sell, at the same fixed price, unlimited amounts of gold, in exchange for their national currency. This idea is dead indeed, and will not be revived, but the gold holdings accumulated in the past should be mobilisable, at fluctuating market prices, to finance deficits in a country's international transactions. This is indeed the EMS solution.

Finally, I agree with many of my colleagues here on the need to exploit, as fully as possible, all negotiable possibilities for monetary co-operation among Arab countries as well as between them and other countries. The experience of Latin America as well as that of Europe amply demonstrates the complementarity of subregional, regional and worldwide agreements in this respect. It is likely that the Gulf countries may be able to move faster towards full monetary union than the Arab world as a whole. Let us encourage them to do so, so long as they keep in mind their ultimate goal and political objective and use their own strength and improved institutional machinery to help their weaker brothers financially, and permit them to accelerate their development, thus increasing their productive capacity, strengthening their national currencies and moving towards pan-Arab ecnomic and monetary union.

In conclusion, let us remember that when intelligent and well-intentioned people differ on their approach to needed reforms, it is often because their seemingly different approaches are complementary rather than contradictory. The European Payments Union proved, many years ago, that regional co-operation was not an alternative to worldwide convertibility, but rather a step in its direction. The improvement of policy co-ordination and institutional machinery on the national, subregional, regional and worldwide scales are all part and parcel of man's progress towards gaining greater control over his fate.

PART TWO

THE CURRENT ARAB MONETARY SITUATION AND
THE SCOPE AVAILABLE FOR ARAB MONETARY
CO-OPERATION

3 ANALYSIS OF THE FINANCIAL ASPECTS OF ARAB ECONOMIC CO-OPERATION AND OPPORTUNITIES FOR MONETARY CO-OPERATION[1]

Burhan Dajani

Monetary co-operation may be defined as the deliberate and orderly process of raising the financial relationships within a group of countries to a higher level. Some believe that economic co-operation becomes more feasible and more fruitful if, initially, it is focused on financial co-operation in general and the flow of capital in particular. This form of co-operation would not require the removal of trade and payments restrictions and would not even demand too much co-ordination of economic and monetary policy. Some even suggest that the free movement of capital should precede and pave the way for any liberalisation of trade or of the movement of factors of production.

Among the objective factors which now make financial and monetary co-operation among the Arab states an immediate imperative is the emergence in 1973 of the Arab oil countries as a world power and the subsequent channelling of a substantial portion of Arab monetary surpluses to the countries of the industrialised world. Before a sound assessment of the question of Arab monetary co-operation can be attempted, however, a number of definitions and classifications must be established and the different forms, techniques, functions and objectives of co-operation must be identified and differentiated.

1. Untied Funds

First of all, the distinction must be made between tied and untied funds. Untied frunds are blocks of ready assets that may be drawn upon under particular conditions for the purchase of goods and services. Withdrawals are effected according to the terms of the contracts which specify interest rates and details of debt service and repayment. From the purely economic standpoint, loan terms — particularly interest rates — are established on the basis of the terms prevailing on the market at the time loans are offered. In addition, individual loans may be adjusted depending on the credit rating of the borrower and the history of his previous transactions with the lender.

Some loans may be offered on terms that are more favourable than what can be obtained on the market. This is normal practice when governments contract loans from international financial institutions, specialised national institutions such as the US Import-Export Bank, government departments or agencies (as in treasury loans) or even the commercial money markets. In the latter instance, preferential terms can usually be obtained when loans are guaranteed by exceptionally credit-worthy parties.

Another distinction that must be made is that between 'commercial' money — available at market terms — and 'non-commercial' money which is available only through special channels. The terms of access to non-commercial funds may be clearly specified, as in the case of IMF loans, where each member country is assigned specific drawing rights, or in the case of payments union and agreements, where upper limits are established for automatic easy credit; beyond these limits, loans must be negotiated on a one-to-one basis.

Funds may also be transferred in the form of bank deposits. Banks of one country place term or demand deposits with banks of another country which run these funds through the normal banking channels. Such transactions of the world banking system are administered basically on the same principles as those described above and serve the same purposes. The terms of placement are adjusted on the basis of the domestic and/or external guarantees available. One example of this procedure in the Arab world is the deposit of funds in Egyptian banks by Kuwaiti and Saudi banks under the guarantees of their respective governments. This type of transaction occupies a middle position between commercial and non-commercial credit.

All debtors, of course, are expected to repay the principal and the interest on their loans through the agency of their bank, government or financial institution. The creditor-debtor relationship between nations, however, differs from that between private businesses; for example, unlike business establishments, governments are not liable to the provisions of commercial law or to bankruptcy or liquidation proceedings. In some instances where there is a creditor–debtor relationship between two states of unequal power, the stronger states have used their creditor position as a pretext for subjugating the debtor states or for intervening in their internal financial affairs. Some creditor states have used this position to seize and exercise financial control over debtor states in order to enforce and administer debt repayment. The Arab world was the victim of such practices during the Ottoman period when a group of creditor states set up a consortium to collect taxes and enforce the repayment of the Ottoman debt. Later, the Arab states which were carved out of the Ottoman Empire were obliged to repay the Ottoman debt in full. In the late nineteenth century, for example, a group of creditor nations took over the financial administration of the Egyptian government. As a result, Egypt lost control of the Suez Canal and was forced to repay the debt in full even after it achieved its independence.

Sanctions imposed on 'delinquent' debtor states — as in the cases described above — involve infringements of national sovereignty and violations of international rights. Such sanctions are far more serious than those imposed on individuals in similar circumstances. While these practices are no longer generally considered to be acceptable behaviour in international relations, strong creditors have other punitive measures at their disposal, with comparable effects. The punitive forms and measures may differ from those used in the past, but the results are the same.

Debtor countries, therefore, must make sure that the funds they borrow generate enough additional capital to cover the costs of repaying both the principal and all servicing costs. Many have argued that if the developing countries are to retain control over their own development processes, they need to secure funds with no strings attached. In other words, they require untied funds to tide them over the period of infancy through which all new projects must pass before actual production commences and to match the increased disbursements on new projects with equivalent stocks of goods, thus avoiding inflation and the disruption of the flow of resources. However, experience has shown that the developing countries' control over untied loans is limited. Large portions of the funds obtained in this manner have been either siphoned off through a number of common channels, e.g., expenditures on propaganda in support of the regime in power, spending on prestigious or 'show-case' projects, or lost through corruption at all levels. Political and social reasons are often advanced to justify such non-productive expenditures. In fact, however, many rulers in the developing countries are simply not concerned with what may happen after their term of office expires. Thus, they do not hesitate to take decisions that are bound to saddle their successors with difficult problems. They may even see this as an opportunity to promote the impression that things were 'better' when they were in office.

Thus the theory that untied financial assistance, i.e., outright grants, is an unqualified blessing to recipient countries would not seem to hold true. Considerable amounts of funds have in fact been transferred in this manner among the Arab countries. Massive grants have been made for the purpose of strengthening the Arab defence capability, i.e., to pay for the purchase of military equipment. It is not the lack of funds but the lack of a unified Arab will that has limited the impact of such expenditures. In any case, no study has yet been made of the ways grants of funds have been spent and the amounts that have been channelled into military purchases. What is clear is that most of these funds have found their way to the external trade sector, leaving only modest amounts for the financing of development projects. This has resulted in a temporary increase in consumption that has not been matched by a sustained increase in production. Accordingly, once these transfers are stopped, the inevitable bottlenecks will appear and the level of consumption will be forced down drastically.

The difficulties involved in the utilisation of untied capital flows, then, can be summarised as follows:

1. Commercial and semi-commercial capital flows must be matched by production increases that would contribute to the repayment of debt principal and charges.
2. Capital flows in the form of grants must also be matched by production increases sufficient to offset the consumption increases they generate.
3. If these capital flows are to achieve their objectives, the recipient countries must direct them towards productive projects.
4. Semi-commercial transfers, such as those effected by the Arab Monetary Fund or those once provided by the Gulf Fund in Support of Egypt require a continuing dialogue between recipient and donor in order to determine that the funds involved are put to productive use. The IMF and the World Bank monitor their transfers systematically through the annual consultations they carry out with member countries.

Although there are no available studies on the benefits which have resulted from capital flows in the Arab world, it is doubtful that these principles have been adequately observed by the Arab countries concerned.

The problem is that some recipient countries may not demonstrate with regard to these funds the necessary sense of obligation. Such an attitude could jeopardise the entire system of capital flows, especially since the donor countries do not impose serious checks and restraints. This is particularly true when the transaction is seen to transcend balance-of-payments considerations to involve the 'balance of total relationships and interests' between the recipient and donor countries. Accordingly, the most effective factor in the long-term consolidation of capital flows is the exercise of self-discipline founded on well-established principles and procedures that are consistently respected. Such a commitment, however, should be reinforced by granting donors the right to monitor economic conditions in recipient countries and the methods of disbursement of drawn funds. The question that remains is: who shall exercise this right and how?

There is a natural and understandable pressure on the capital surplus countries of the Arab world to increase the amount of capital they offer in different forms to the Arab countries that need it. The Arab oil countries have acted commendably to improve the terms of sale of their oil; thus they have earned the right to dispose of their oil revenues. On the other hand, the funds they have deposited in non-Arab countries are in danger of shrinking under the pressure of inflation. In fact, they are constantly exposed to the danger of expropriation or freezing, as happened recently in the case of Iran's deposits in foreign countries. It would be preferable to permit the Arab countries to benefit from these funds rather than leave them abroad to be exploited one way or another. The pressures on the capital-rich Arab countries for aid would produce better results, however, if they were accompanied by improved utilisation of the funds received. This would generate popular support for the transfer of funds from the capital-rich countries to the other Arab countries.

In the final analysis, Arab debtor countries will have to give the same consideration to all the funds they secure, whether the source is Arab, foreign or international. When breakdowns in self-discipline occur, the problems which subsequently arise in various areas generate adverse opinion in the creditor countries.

II. Methods of Drawing Untied Funds

Arab economists have devoted much thought to devising ways of increasing the volume of untied loans and grants among the Arab countries. This is usually what writers have in mind when they refer to the so-called 'Arab financial market'. Many methods have been proposed to promote this objective, including increased bank deposits, certificates of deposit and the floating of development bonds such as those recently issued by some Arab countries in both foreign and Gulf currencies.

It is widely contended that banks are in a favourable position to act as intermediaries in the distribution of capital and as monitors of the sound utilisation of funds. In fact, an examination of actual banking practice would reveal the following characteristics:

1. The flow of capital to banks in capital-poor Arab countries is no guarantee that the funds will be spent in those countries; some banks may find it necessary to export their funds to foreign banks operating in international money centres. They may have been induced to do this, however, partly in order to diversify their risks or because of the lack of well-prepared local projects.
2. A large proportion of these funds often goes to finance external trade. This is the pattern conventionally followed by Arab commercial banks. The Bank of Egypt, for example, has failed to recover its

role as an industrial promoter and Arab banks in general have avoided initiating projects or participating as joint owners, leaving this role to industrial, real estate and other specialised banks. In short, most untied funds end up financing the consumption, not the production, sectors. Commercial banks should be authorised to participate in the ownership of industrial projects with central bank liquidity backing.
3. Since international capital flows are transacted in convertible currencies, their continued flow will depend on the ability of the recipient economies to secure enough foreign exchange to cover the associated costs. Foreign exchange bottlenecks are in no one's interest, as they could disrupt the Arab financial market. If the development of this market is a desired objective, it must be recognised that this will depend on the Arab countries themselves — on their economic policies and on their ability to develop their production and export capabilities. No financial market is even conceivable in isolation from these considerations.
4. Arab financial institutions noted from the beginning that some debts received preferential consideration over others. Hence, they sought to establish joint Arab-foreign banks as a way of securing 'most favoured institution' treatment from debtors. Undoubtedly, the Arab partners in these joint enterprises would like to direct a greater proportion of their banks' funds towards the Arab markets. In addition to the above considerations, however, these joint banks have not received enough encouragement from Arab institutions which deposit with them, i.e., Arab central banks, Treasury departments and/or investment institutions.

In justifying this phenomenon it has been argued that depositors prefer to deal with the stronger and more diversified banks. The joint banks in question have tended to receive short-term individual and institutional deposits. Consequently, they have been in a poor position to handle transfers to Arab countries, particularly medium- and long-term loans for financing productive projects. These banks have directed their activities towards shorter-term loans in lower-risk countries. They are obliged to establish links with the world banking system in order to obtain Arab funds to which they might just as well have been granted direct access. In consequence they have tended to give greater support to import trade than to development activities.

Any attempt to organise the transfer of untied funds is bound to encounter the problem of the bilateral transfers that take place from the capital-rich to the deficitory countries of the Arab world. These are generally motivated by political considerations and their distribution is not subject to any control. They are usually concluded in response to *ad hoc* needs described as urgent, emergency or nationalist. The donor country exercises no control over the utilisation of its funds. Moreover, these bilateral funds are usually transferred to a multiplicity of parties in the recipient country, which may not always be subject to government control. To the extent that the funds reach government treasuries, they show up in the balances maintained in different accounts with central banks and other institutions outside the country. Such transfers may in fact account, to a large extent, for the improved foreign exchange positions of the governments and central banks of deficitory countries. Information regarding these transfers is not, therefore, likely to be made available to other parties by the donor and recipient governments. Unfortunately, this only complicates further the task of determining true monetary needs. It certainly does not help the institutions engaged in transfer activities to perform their function. Foreign exchange facilities, generally speaking, no longer constitute a major barrier to Arab economic development, except perhaps for the Sudan and Democratic Yemen. Rather, the monetary challenge currently facing the Arab countries as a whole is two-fold: in the short run, it consists in eliminating the remaining pockets of financial weakness indicated above, in the long run, it consists in creating the institutions and channels that will sustain a reasonable volume of monetary transfers amoung the Arab countries after the present period of financial affluence has passed.

As the specialised collective institution in this area, the AMF plays a major role in meeting the monetary requirements of the Arab countries. The situation described above, however, obstructs all efforts to apply carefully devised and executed monetary transfer schemes. Nevertheless, the AMF should receive greater consideration than it has in the past in any attempt to plan for future needs and institutional developments. The AMF should prove to be of valuable assistance in the effort to anticipate problems and developments. It should also provide an appropriate framework for identifying the required solutions.

The AMF is not alone, however, in the field of untied capital transfers. The Gulf Fund for the Support of Egypt is another, albeit unsuccessful, example. The different Arab development funds (excepting the Kuwait and the Abu Dhabi Funds) practise a combination of tied and untied transfer operations. Their transactions of untied transfers come under the category of bilateral transactions described above. Rational systems of monetary transfer in the future will undoubtedly seek to achieve a reasonable balance between bilateral and multilateral, open and secret, controlled and uncontrolled, and institutional and non-institutional transfers. At present the balance favours the second of each of these alternatives, thereby reducing the possibility for sound planning for the future.

III. The Role of Untied Transfers in Arab Economic Development

Reference has already been made to one effect that untied transfers have had on the economies of the Arab countries, namely, that they have removed the problem of the supply of foreign exchange as a constraining factor. Unfortunately, their positive effect on development virtually ends there. Rather than acting to stimulate the launching of new projects, they in fact reduce the pressure for such projects by providing easy access to consumer goods. Their greatest contribution to the development process is the improvement they have made possible in public works. On the other hand, by increasing the level of available credit, such transfers create additional inflationary pressures which are only partially offset by the imported goods they make available. This latter effect could, however, be an obstacle either because of the prevailing import system, as in the case of Syria and Iraq, or because of monopolistic practices, as in the case of the free trade countries. An ultimate balance between the costs and benefits of untied transfers may be impossible to achieve; the outcome will depend heavily on the ability to improve the utilisation of these funds and to resolve the problems they generate. What is certain, however, is that the easy access to money, coupled with the pressure to spend it quickly in the light of world inflation, has weakened the propensity to economise in spending and has encouraged instead the extravagant dissipation of available resources.

At the pan-Arab level, the flow of untied funds has had little effect on Arab economic integration, partly because no individual Arab country has demonstrated any unilateral commitment to such an objective. Moreover, these transfers do not necessarily favour joint projects or integrationist projects. While in theory it is possible to allocate a part of these transfers to such projects, their practical implementation presupposes a comprehensive view of economic integration as a framework for selecting projects. This requires collective Arab effort. Moreover, to date there is no evidence that any Arab capital-importing country has used even a portion of the funds it has procured to finance joint or integrationist projects.

While these transfers have had only a minor effect in terms of broadening the base for Arab economic integration, they have created a kind of interdependence which may induce some Arab countries to cultivate closer relations. They set up a creditor–debtor relationship between capital-exporting and capital-importing countries in the commercial transfer sector, in that the process of debt settlement requires increased import/export and financial dealings between creditor and debtor. The new relationship may also create an incentive for co-operation between the two parties in the areas of production integration and financial organisation. The effectiveness of this incentive will grow, moreover, as the commercial transfer sector becomes the preponderant one in exchange transactions. This shift will take place as the surplus oil money begins to dwindle and, eventually, to dry up. The strength of this incentive will also be a function of the nature and details of the relationship between creditor and debtor.

The relationships that have been generated by commercial and non-commercial, tied and untied capital transfers have created a favourable climate for Arab economic integration. The continuation of these transfers should assist considerably in the passage to more advanced stages of integration, provided they are preceded by carefully designed plans and carefully selected projects. Such progress, however, is bound to take place slowly. It is not likely to produce dramatic results – such as those achieved by the EEC, for example – for some time to come.

IV. Monetary Unification at the Regional and Pan-Arab Levels

Monetary unification has been a difficult and complicated issue ever since the gold standard was abandoned. The value of paper money is no longer based on the internal attributes of the currency itself, as was the case with gold money. It is rather determined by a combination of factors in the national economy relating to both demand and cost and is reflected, ultimately, in the purchasing power of the currency. The maintenance of relative currency stability is a major concern of government policy-makers. It is understandable, therefore, that countries are anxious to retain for themselves as much sovereign control of their currencies as possible. Any loss of monetary sovereignty may result in the loss of important social and economic options or in the obligation to adopt options that are unrelated to social and economic preferences. In fact, many governmental options are implemented through monetary policies and measures, and aspects of the social balance are affected by these policies in both the short and the long run.

A major dimension of this issue is the strong cause-and-effect relationship between monetary and political unity. Proponents of political unity therefore exhibit greater enthusiasm for monetary linkages while those who are wary of political unity tend to be opposed to such linkages. The doctrine of regional economic co-operation is based on the hypothesis that such co-operation widens the field of action of the participating countries without conflicting with or diminishing their sovereignty and independence. The doctrine of monetary linkages, on the other hand, assumes that political unity must either precede or follow monetary linkages. Hence, the decision in favour of monetary unity would seem to be intimately related to that in favour of political unity, the two decisions being mutually reinforcing. The limited Arab experience in this regard tends to support this view. When the League of Arab States was created in 1945, as representing the drive for Arab unity and as the instrument for directing relations among the Arab states towards this goal, among the first proposals to be submitted to it were two relating to the unification of all Arab currencies. They were submitted at a time when the Arab states did not yet have a deep understanding of the intricacies and mechanisms of paper money as practised by the dominant powers and their banking institutions. The breakdown of the Syrian-Lebanese economic union after the Second World War began with the dissolution of the monetary union between them. When the two countries took control of their respective currencies from the French-owned Bank of Syria and Lebanon, each adopted a different monetary policy, which soon created a disparity in the values of the two national currencies. In fact, Arab experience has shown that political unification is more easily attainable than monetary unification. For example, during the Syrian-Egyptian union of 1958-61 no steps were taken to unify the currencies of the two countries until February 1961, when the Syrian monetary system (the sounder of the two at the time) was modified, the better to resemble the Egyptian system. This step is considered to have marked the beginning of the breakdown of unity. Its failure indeed served to make the Arab countries even more hesitant concerning the issue of monetary unity.

The present Arab perplexity over monetary unification is the result of overlapping considerations of political unity and economic rationality. These involve both theoretical questions and considerations of Realpolitik, the latter giving rise to an unwarranted preoccupation with national sovereignty. Is it possible to isolate these considerations from one another and, if so, to what extent?

In recent years the subject of monetary unification has come up in relation to the proposed uniform Arab Gulf currency (the Gulf dinar) and as a revival of a proposal put forward several years ago by the then president of the Lebanese Bankers' Association, Pierre Eddé, who suggested the issuing of a uniform Arab currency backed by oil rather than by foreign currency or gold reserves, a suggestion which was not adopted at the time (see note 1, p. 90 below).

A. The Gulf Dinar

The call for the creation of a uniform Gulf dinar is usually backed up by sound economic arguments. The dinar would provide the Gulf states with a strong, stable currency capable of assuming a prominent place among the major world currencies. It would become the accepted currency for the financial transactions of the Gulf countries in the world monetary arena and would thereby shelter the funds of these countries from the periodic currency devaluations which are now affecting their currency deposits in foreign countries.

It is obviously in the interest of the Gulf countries that they conduct their international transactions in a currency whose value is subject to their control. The creation of a single Gulf currency would constitute a major step towards this goal. The Gulf countries acting collectively would be able to place deposits in Gulf dinar accounts in world banks on more favourable terms than would be obtainable by any one of them using its own currency. The same is true for the placement of loans of all types. Collective action would make these countries much better able to achieve the objectives to which each of them aspires separately. It would convert the Gulf into a stable and autonomous world financial centre.

Moreover, the Gulf countries would have nothing to lose, individually or collectively, from this measure. While all regional organisations today operate on the basis of a balance between profit and loss, the creation of a Gulf dinar would require no sacrifice from any party at the present stage in return for the opportunity to improve the terms under which they deposit their funds and place their loans.

The arguments put forward by opponents of the Gulf dinar are based on theoretical considerations concerning monetary linkages and on past Arab experiences as described above. None of these arguments is relevant, however, as they all apply to circumstances entirely different from those obtaining in the Gulf.

The most important difference is that it is possible to provide the value of the Gulf dinar with a 'real' backing — one even more solid than the gold standard. The value of gold-backed money was entirely dependent on the official price of gold which, after 1971, became subject to change. Eventually, gold was demonetised and its price determined by market forces. The dinar, on the other hand, can be given a value that has a much broader backing. It may be based either on a broad basket of currencies or a broad price index. Thus the 'real' backing of the Gulf dinar should dispense with the need for political backing. It will suffice for the authorities to refrain from taking measures inconsistent with its requirements. This should be possible for the duration of the oil era. Because the Gulf countries have no commodities for export at the present time other than oil, they need not utilise monetary policy for export promotion. Moreover, the governments concerned can apply domestic monetary policies without affecting the external value of their currencies. In fact, there are many mechanisms for doing this. What they need to do is to activate factors different from those activated in the industrialised countries enjoying a broad-based production pattern, but in order to achieve the same objective. This, of course, calls for some imagination and creativity and a determination not to rely on traditional methods or to adhere to models suited to other situations and circumstances. The Gulf states are, singly and collectively, capable of preserving the external value of the Gulf dinar, probably with no need for intra-Gulf transfers. If such transfers should become necessary, they would be confined to narrow and prearranged limits.

The monetary mechanism required for managing the Gulf dinar could be simplified and made to conform to the mechanisms already operating in the various member countries. A supreme monetary authority could be established to supervise the Gulf dinar, leaving monetary management in the hands of existing monetary institutions and central banks. This supreme body, however, should determine the size of the union's monetary reserves and maintain control over them. It is essential, however, that these reserves be adequate to meet foreign exchange needs. The monetary institutions of the member states would be left to manage their domestic money and to determine local monetary policy within prescribed limits in order to meet local needs as well as to adapt to seasonal circumstances and requirements. The paper currency might even bear the names of individual member countries along with that of the general issuing authority (e.g., 'Arab Gulf Monetary Authority – Kingdom of Saudi Arabia'). Of course, all this paper currency would have to become legal tender in all parts of the Gulf monetary zone. National monetary institutions would be under the obligation to exchange for convertible currencies any amount of the paper money circulated in other member countries. This would, of course, be achieved by means of clearing house procedures covering all the currencies in circulation. In brief, the monetary mechanism outlined above resembles that of the US Federal Reserve System, with modifications to accommodate the sovereign states of the Gulf area.

This mechanism naturally presupposes that the Gulf countries have at their disposal sufficient foreign currency to meet coverage, exchange and adjustment operations. If it was possible at one time for an Indian administration to issue a single currency for the entire region, there is no reason why an Arab Gulf administration should not be able to do so.

If the Gulf dinar is to be instituted, what should be the 'real' basis for its support? The answer to this question derives from the purpose of creating this dinar in the first place. That purpose is to shield the financial surpluses generated by oil production as much as possible from the impact of currency devaluation and inflation. Either of two possible standards might be used for fixing the 'real' value of the dinar: a currency basket (which might or might not be the SDR basket) or a price index. The first option would serve to reduce the impact of the depreciation of a single currency, whatever its importance (e.g., the US dollar), but it could not entirely absorb the impact, as the major currencies would have to remain part of any basket that might be considered. The first option would also make it possible to absorb the impact of inflation and gradual price increases, while under the second option, i.e., a price index, this would be only a theoretical possibility. On the other hand, while a currency based on a price index might help resolve the problems of creditor countries, it would at the same time complicate the position of debtor banks, governments, businesses and institutions.

The oil countries are certainly in need of new stores of value. The solution may be to have the recipients of funds in the industrialised countries issue bonds tied to a price index and to adopt a Gulf currency also tied to a price index. Some of the surplus funds might be converted into international currencies.

B. The Arab Dinar (Unification of Arab Currencies)

Would it be possible to extend the scope of this operation to include a wider area than the Gulf region? In fact, several obstacles stand in the way of such an extension. First of all, some of the countries whose inclusion in envisaged may not be able to maintain a sufficient level of foreign exchange to make possible the required convertibility. This obstacle could be overcome in the short run through the establishment of a reserve fund from which these countries could secure loans. As indicated above, the oil boom gave a number of Arab countries with payment deficits the opportunity to build up considerable foreign exchange balances. These countries would thus be capable of providing the necessary foreign exchange backing for the uniform dinar[2] in all but exceptional circumstances, when it might be necessary to borrow foreign exchange from the reserve fund. In this case, however, the deficit countries might become too heavily dependent on a foreign exchange policy whose effect would be to prevent them from making full use of their monetary reserves. In other words, they would be anxious to maintain a high proportion of foreign exchange in their monetary reserves, thus freezing funds that could be used for developmental purposes.

The major obstacle, however, arises from the conflicting objectives of the potential union members, which the same monetary policy would be expected to serve. The oil countries, which are essentially oil-exporters and commodity-importers, find it in their interest to maintain a high and stable value for their currency in order to raise the value of their exports and lower the value of their imports. The non-oil countries, however, have the opposite interest. As capital-importing countries, they have an interest in obtaining capital at a low price. As commodity-exporters, they have no interest in raising the value of their currency, as that would reduce their competitiveness — particularly since the oil countries do not accord them any customs privileges. In other words, their ability to continue to export their commodities to the oil countries depends to a great extent on the ability of all to reach agreement on a regional protective tariff policy within the context of a common market. The oil countries show great reluctance to enter into such arrangements given their present consumption needs. It may well be argued that these problems are capable of solution and that a uniform monetary system would provide collective benefits in the form of investment capital flows which would provide a strong support for the development effort. The establishment of a world monetary system is also in everyone's interest. While these arguments are compelling, they are all based on profit-loss calculations which the countries concerned seem reluctant to become involved in.

As has been mentioned, many countries also have political reservations about monetary unification. Were it not for these reservations, the Gulf dinar would already be a reality. It is regrettable that the same Gulf countries that once accepted a uniform Indian currency should now reject a uniform currency of their own. Whenever the possibility of monetary unification appears to draw near, certain parties intervene to adjust the foreign exchange parity of their currencies. This action tends to undermine the basis for monetary unification, i.e., the maintenance of the value of the uniform currency *vis-à-vis* foreign currencies. In practice, however, the measures taken have tended to have the opposite effect of that intended; for they demonstrate that the stability of the foreign exchange parities of local currencies is the norm and that deviations from this norm are exceptional and only occur as a result of interventionist policies.

In addition to these reservations at the regional level, many foreign powers are opposed to all attempts to standardise Gulf currencies; for they realise that the benefits that are bound to accrue to these countries will be realised at their expense. Some of these powers are not content to impose their currencies as the medium of exchange in the Gulf, but have gone so far as to try to impose their own conditions on all transactions, such as demanding the purchase of long-term, non-negotiable bonds at low interest. As long as the Gulf countries continue to operate on the basis of politico-military considerations instead of economic rationality, all ideas of reform — local or regional, sectoral or global — are bound to become entangled in these considerations. This problem should not, however, stand in the way of the clarification of issues and the formulation of theoretically sound and practicable methods and approaches that could be put into effect once appropriate circumstances prevailed.

V. Institutions for Financing Foreign Trade

It has been proposed that an Arab foreign trade bank and an Arab payments union be established to finance, monitor and prepare statistics on inter-Arab trade.

The idea behind the first proposal is that when Arab deficit countries need to finance their foreign trade through loans, they are obliged to resort to international credit facilities where they have to accept costly and sometimes exorbitant terms, depending on their financial situation at the time. An Arab bank, if established, would provide the Arab countries with the funds to finance their foreign trade at a lower cost and on easier terms.

It is not clear in these proposals whether the bank's capital is to be governmental, private or mixed. It should, in any event, have a predominantly public character in both its capital and its deposit structure, as it is intended to provide credit facilities on terms more favourable than market considerations would allow. Naturally, this bank, as proposed, would serve the interests of potential debtors more than those of potential creditors; for the latter, by definition, would be better served by obtaining the terms prevailing in the commercial markets. Thus the incentive here is not commercial gain; rather, these credit facilities would belong in the realm of assistance. Here lies the crux of the problem. As a 'collective' entity, the bank is not likely to suit many countries that prefer to grant assistance on a bilateral basis. Moreover, the favourable nature of its terms is bound to attract the great majority of foreign trade transactions. This means that the bank will require an enormous capital base and a continuous stream of deposits – conditions not likely to meet with the approval of the creditor countries, as they may be reluctant to find themselves committed to financing the totality of foreign trade in the form of assistance. This would indeed be a difficult proposition for them to accept. Moreover, the availability of easy money may induce countries to over-expand their foreign trade activities in relation to their economic capacity. This could result in the eventual cancellation of many of their debts and in the encouragement of a useless and indefensible rise in consumption. Finally, there is the fatal problem of indifference. Some debtor countries treat the funds they borrow as bad debts that do not deserve serious consideration. There are many such cases, where borrowed funds have been cast into the bottomless pit of foreign trade. This occurs both when direct untied loans are involved and when guarantees have been obtained for loans concluded with foreign parties.

Would it not be preferable to concentrate on the development of Arab and mixed banking institutions, giving them the responsibility for financing foreign trade on commercial terms? Such an arrangement would constitute a brake on extravagant importation and runaway consumption. Were Arab banking institutions to succeed in this area, they would become pillars of the Arab economy; on the other hand, if a foreign trade bank were to be created and then fail, it would become a source of bitterness that might endure for years.

The second proposal concerns the financing of inter-Arab trade. This problem has become less important than it seemed to be in the 1950s and 1960s, as the direction of most inter-Arab trade has tended to be from the non-oil countries (such as Lebanon, Jordan, Syria and the Sudan) to the oil countries. Trade moving in this direction is not exposed to monetary problems. Funds are available in abundant amounts and in convertible currencies and multilateral clearance and settlement problems are not involved.

Some trade also takes place among the non-oil countries themselves. This trade does not seem to present major problems either, in view of the present abundance of foreign currency and the favourable balance-of-payments positions at this time. Where problems exist, they are highly localised, as in the Sudan, and call for special treatment. Thus the need for an Arab payments union does not seem to be pressing at the moment. The greatest problems facing inter-Arab trade today arise from non-monetary obstacles: customs tariffs, the total or partial confinement of imports to the public sector, the refusal to consider inter-Arab trade as an aspect of domestic trade and, in some of the socialist countries, bans on the direct marketing of goods. The establishment of a payments union today would seem to be inadvisable. It might be wiser to concentrate on other matters while continuing to study the payments union project in greater depth so that it can be established at such a time as the volume of inter-Arab trade warrants it, views concerning its prospective establishment take new directions and the need for an effectively functioning payments union, and not just another formal institution, manifests itself.

On the other hand, the unique experiment undertaken by the Islamic Bank in financing specific commercial transactions within the Islamic world should be evaluated in terms of the Arab world. The AMF might be the organisation best suited to this task.

VI. Flows Tied to Specific Projects

I should like to conclude the paper by making some brief remarks concerning the flow of investment capital within the Arab world:

1. Investment activity remains weak, in comparison with both untied capital flows and investment opportunities in the Arab countries.

This state of affairs is due to the restrictive laws, policies and procedures prevailing in the capital-importing countries.
2. The capital-poor countries have devoted all their efforts to obtaining untied funds and to limiting the introduction of tied funds. However, this policy has not produced encouraging results. It has been shown how a major portion of these untied funds is being diverted to the consumer and services sectors. The only lasting effect of these funds has been the improvement in the infrastructures of some Arab countries made possible by increased public works.
3. If the transfers by expatriate workers are to be of a temporary nature, then a greater portion of these transfers should be allocated to investment so as to develop the economies of the labour-exporting countries to the point where they can reabsorb their workers when the time comes for them to return home. This calls for greater attention to development projects.
4. The encouragement of the flow of investment funds depends first and foremost on the policies pursued by the Arab governments and the incentives and security they can offer investors. Consequently, any country that truly desires to increase the inflow of investments can. do so. While bilateral and collective agreements are useful instruments, they are not needed to stimulate investment. For example, Arab investments in the United States and in other industrialised countries are not dependent on agreements with the host countries. They are made in accordance with the relevant laws of the country concerned. Lebanon before the war of 1975-6 provided an excellent example of the role a national policy could play in encouraging Arab (and foreign) investment.
5. Among the obstacles to investment is the slowness with which projects are identified, defined, studied and planned. This problem demands urgent attention at both the national and pan-Arab levels.
6. The expansion of the Arab market through the establishment of a genuine common market or the conclusion of a broad trade agreement would create new and dynamic investment opportunities.
7. There can be no objection to the policy of securing project loans; it is far preferable to borrowing untied funds and is essential when public works financing is the goal. In the case of productive projects, large and small, the choice has to be made in each instance between the loan and the auto-financing methods; contrary to what is believed, the loan method is not intrinsically superior to the auto-financing method.
8. Government-initiated joint enterprises are neither the only nor the most important form of joint investment. While these need to be expanded, so do joint investment opportunities of all forms and in all fields.

9. The participation of private and public investment sectors, enjoying genuine administrative autonomy and wide freedom of action, is essential to encouraging Arab capital investment in the Arab world.
10. Although it is more difficult to obtain investment capital than untied capital, investment capital has a greater and more enduring impact on the national economy than untied capital.

Notes

1. This paper, translated from the Arabic, is a substantially revised version of the one originally presented at the seminar. In particular, the author has condensed his discussion — highly detailed in the original version — of the various forms of Arab economic co-operation and the reasons for their limited effectiveness. While the comments made during the general discussion pertain more specifically to the original than to this revised version, they have nevertheless been retained as they relate directly to the issue of Arab monetary integration [eds.].

2. This capability, based on the relatively easy access to foreign exchange throughout the oil boom, may be what Pierre Eddé had in mind when he proposed oil as a monetary reserve, i.e., the unlimited ability to secure foreign exchange and distribute it widely among the Arab countries. It is interesting to note, in this connection, that until the war of 1975-6 Lebanon's monetary policy had aimed at consolidating and strengthening its currency partly through the maintenance of over 100 per cent backing in gold and foreign exchange reserves. The argument was that this was necessary if Lebanon was to play its role as a major financial centre. Although this policy went against the mainstream of economic thinking at the time, which held that using gold and foreign exchange reserves to back a currency 100 per cent represented an unjustified blocking of funds that could be used for development purposes, subsequent events showed that this policy was the appropriate one for Lebanon at the time.

COMMENT*

Abdul Aal Al-Sagban

I should like to begin my comments with some brief observations pertaining to the Arab Economic Unity Agreement which, as the author states, defined the ultimate goals to be achieved by organising Arab economic relations and which established a council to formulate projects and identify the phases leading to these goals.

The tasks laid down in the Agreement, however, have proved difficult to accomplish. With regard to trade, for example, the public sector in the countries with centrally-planned economies has played its 'planning' role by maintaining trade restrictions, while the countries with virtually no public sector have chosen completely to ignore their supposed devotion to 'economic freedom' whenever this has proved to be expedient. In the transport field, political disputes have continued to have disruptive effects.

The author refers to social problems which have arisen as a consequence of inter-Arab movements of labour. Imported workers are denied many rights by the recipient countries, particularly in comparison with their counterparts in the advanced industrial countries. For example, they are denied the opportunity of obtaining permanent residence in the host country, a situation which increases their uncertainty concerning future employment. On some occasions, they have even been subjected to arbitrary acts of discrimination. These are all problems which are in need of a solution. Iraq is an exception to this rule, however, because it has opened its doors to Arab labour to reside, obtain gainful employment and benefit from all the services of the state.

The author rightly believes that the integration of small national Arab markets into one regional market is the one inevitable means of fulfilling the basic conditions for industrial development, whether in terms of the geographical or qualitative expansion of the market, the identification of investment opportunities for Arab funds or the internalisation of technology and the co-ordination of industries. The author believes that while the Arab countries have succeeded in establishing joint Arab institutions such as the Arab League and the Council for Arab Economic Unity, they do not have a clear conception of the short- and long-term goals they wish to attain and lack a system of priorities concerning the issues to be discussed by the joint pan-Arab institutions. The definition of pan-Arab objectives remains a point of

* Translated from the Arabic.

contention among several different and competing schools of thought. This is why the author concludes that the pan-Arab goals of Arab economic co-operation are achieved spontaneously and inevitably from this co-operation without their being expressly sought.

Even if one agrees with the conclusions which the author draws from his analysis, it should be noted that the movement towards Arab unity is an historical movement which can be expected to suffer the same reserves but also to make the same advances as all historical movements.

The results achieved to date in the way of Arab co-operation in general, and Arab economic co-operation in particular, thus represent compromise solutions arising out of the struggle between the different schools of thought supporting the movement towards unity, on the one hand, and the forces of fragmentation and regionalism, on the other. The forces favouring fragmentation have found in the poverty of Arab thought and in the long domination of the Arab military over the destiny of this nation the right conditions for the training of their own army of intellectuals. These persons often argue that partitioning is logical and inevitable and that unity is an unrealistic aspiration and a diversion from the correct path. At the very least, they maintain that all calls for Arab unity are premature and unplanned. In a field survey conducted by the Centre for Arab Unity Studies, it was found that 22 per cent of those covered by the questionnaire did not believe in the existence of a single Arab world.

It would have been appropriate for the author to comment on the 'formalist movement', which has contributed to retarding joint Arab activity and to limiting its achievements by insisting on the reorganisation of the machinery required for joint Arab activity and its placement under the supervision and control of the Arab League. This has subjected Arab activity to (i) discussion of the 'form' before discussion of the goals; (ii) discussion of what should be achieved; and (iii) concern with perfecting the wording of new agreements rather than with the need to apply existing agreements above all else. Similarly, the author did not take up the differences between Arab schools of thought over the question of unity and their conflicting conceptions of joint Arab activity in its official context. I would have liked the author to refer, for example, to the regionalism and nationalism which still characterise the mentalities of those working in Arab organisations, and to how this weak pan-Arab orientation has led to a reduction in Arab economic co-operation, in substance if not in form. These are issues which are directly linked to the questions of national sovereignty and security of such concern to the existing political leadership.

It is only fair to say that there are many existing agreements and organisational arrangements which, if applied, could provide an appropriate starting point from which one could progress towards an Arab economic order and an Arab identity and nationality. This, in my view, is what Arab economic co-operation requires and not the additional interpretations, definitions and resolutions which are constantly being put forward.

The development of the objectives, programmes and organisation of joint Arab economic activity led in the 1960s to the agreements creating the Council of Arab Economic Unity and the Arab Fund for Economic and Social Development and, later, to the creation of the Arab Monetary Fund. The base of such activity has since broadened to include specialised institutions and consulting firms as well as co-ordination at the sectoral level. The challenge facing us therefore consists in putting into practice the means and objectives already in existence and not in creating new labels for joint Arab activity.

When discussing the relationship between Arab monetary co-operation and Arab economic co-operation, the author distinguishes between two approaches. The first is the strategic approach which views monetary integration as the apex of economic integration, its final objective being the establishment of a uniform Arab currency by means of the following three steps:

(a) Co-ordinating monetary policies;
(b) Stabilising exchange rates and ensuring the inter-convertibility of Arab currencies; and
(c) Facilitating multilateral settlements and creating an accounting unit (Arab dinar) whose value would be fixed in terms of a basket of Arab currencies.

In this context, the AMF represents the proper framework for efforts towards the strategic objective of achieving Arab monetary integration as a culmination to Arab economic integration. AMF objectives clearly include the three steps mentioned above. However, the author may have left the reader with the impression that he does not believe in the ability of the AMF to achieve these objectives; for when discussing the co-ordination of monetary policies, he refers to the co-ordination of monetary policies of the Arab central banks through the establishment of an Arab Monetary Council (tantamount to a union of Arab central banks) following the signing of an Arab Co-operation Agreement. As I have said, however, it is not by the creation of more Arab organisations and institutions that the problems facing joint Arab activity will be solved. The solution depends rather on the ability of those working towards Arab unity to bring it about through demo-cratic dialogue, whatever their differences over philosophical and organisational questions. My own views on this matter are put forward in my own paper, entitled 'The Arab Monetary Fund: Objectives and

Performance' (see pp. 152-86). It is my hope that our discussion of this matter will enable us to reach an objective evaluation of the proposals of some Arab writers for the creation of new organisations as an alternative to permitting existing organisations to achieve their planned objectives through means consistent with the flexible agreements which have created these organisations and with the prevailing Arab situation and the constraints it entails.

The second approach to monetary co-operation and its relationship to economic co-operation contradicts the first approach in that it proceeds from the thesis that financial integration leads to economic integration and not vice versa as the first approach would imply. This second approach assumes a steady and adequate flow of financial assets among the various countries, which would make funds available for coping with their balance-of-payments problems. Financial policy could, according to the author, play an effective role in correcting imbalances in economic performance from one country to another within the zone of economic integration.

The financial approach alone may indeed be sufficient for the achievement of serious steps towards economic co-operation. However, it will not lead to comprehensive economic integration culminating in unity unless it is accompanied by the political decision in favour of pan-Arab co-operation. Once this decision is made, then various activities can be envisaged, including either comprehensive or sectoral planning and sectoral or subsectoral implementation. Arab monetary co-operation is one aspect of economic integration which must develop in parallel with the other industrial, agricultural and commercial aspects of co-operation at the national, pan-Arab and international levels.

I am in complete agreement with the author's observations regarding tied and untied development aid and the need to monitor its utilisation. It should again be noted that Arab development aid should exhibit its own pan-Arab character as distinct from the philosophy governing world development aid which regards it as a compensation for the industrial countries' exploitation of the developing countries through international trade. On the basis of these specifically Arab nationalist considerations, an objective link is bound to emerge among the various political options taken by the Arab countries and among their corresponding positions with regard to defence matters and the volume and distribution of development aid. Such an objective link will manifest itself in the context of a clear Arab plan embodying an increasingly profound mutual commitment rooted in pan-Arab convictions.

I also share the author's view concerning the justification for establishing the Arab or Gulf dinar and the difficulties this entails. Whether one begins with the Gulf countries alone or with the Gulf in combination with other Arab countries capable of meeting the requirements for a uniform currency and willing to fulfil the relevant obligations out of pan-Arab conviction and economic interest, the essential condition is that this dinar should be Arab in character; for it is appropriate to strengthen pan-Arab expression, if only nominally, on the way to achieving such a strategic objective.

As for the author's remarks regarding Arab institutions for financing trade, I am more inclined towards the proposal mentioned in my own paper to the effect that the objective of settling payments should be combined with that of developing trade quantitatively and qualitatively and linking it to production planning. The financing of this activity should clearly be of a special nature and should include an appropriate volume of the grants and credit facilities which normally accompany development aid offered from a pan-Arab perspective. This approach need not preclude support for the author's recommendations regarding the development of Arab banking institutions, including mixed institutions, in order to finance foreign trade on commercial terms that would constitute a disincentive to lavish imports. I do not agree with the author, however, that this should be a substitute for the idea of an Arab foreign trade bank. Moreover, I believe, unlike the author, that the idea of facilitiating the settlement of payments should be combined with that of developing Arab foreign trade within one institutional body which should be linked with the AMF and considered one of its executive instruments in fulfilling the objectives assigned to it.

GENERAL DISCUSSION

1. Samir Makdisi

I would like here to refer to an important point raised by Mr Dajani, and commented upon by Mr Al-Sagban. The author's paper outlines two approaches to the process of monetary integration culminating in currency unification. But as presented, the two approaches appear to be contradictory. The first is that economic integration should proceed via the expansion of intra-regional trade and investments, paving the way for subsequent monetary integration. The second is that monetary integration — in particular, the free flow of capital resources and the development of integrated, financial markets — should be given particular emphasis in that it will itself pave the way for economic integration in the areas of trade and production.

It would seem to me that the issue being raised is not one of either/or. The two processes can be simultaneous and mutually reinforcing. Free transfers of capital resources within the integrated area, for example, and the development of regional financial markets would help to make the production process more efficient and would contribute to the expansion of intra-regional trade. Finally, greater integration in the areas of trade and production would call for closer monetary co-operation. The two processes — as indeed Mr Sagban has mentioned — should thus be viewed as simultaneously reinforcing and not as successive.

Perhaps Mr Dajani will elaborate on this point.

2. Mahmoud Sakbani

Many speakers seem to be equating monetary integration with currency unification. I would submit that currency unification is only one modality of monetary integration. From a technical point of view, a set of currencies with fixed exchange rates, full convertibility and freedom of movement is equivalent to a single currency. I am fully aware of the normative arguments that might be raised against this; however, the fact is that neither technically nor by definition is it acceptable to equate monetary integration with currency unification.

3. Mohammed Labib Shoukair

I shall confine myself to three questions which I would have liked the author to take up.

Mr Dajani has shown how the approaches towards achieving Arab economic co-operation which have been followd so far — at least with regard to trade and development — have been unsuccessful. He has offered a number of reasons for the failure of these approaches. To my mind, one of the most important reasons — not discussed by the author — is that the forms of trade co-operation proposed have not been accompanied by corresponding forms of monetary co-operation, covering, in particular, the settlement of payments between Arab countries. In addition to the 'real' aspect of trade reflected in the transfer of goods and services, there is also a monetary aspect which either facilitates or impedes this exchange and which concerns the settlement of payments. The practical problems raised by this matter of payments are many and complex, especially given the diversity of Arab monetary systems. As Mr Dajani knows, the 1953 trade agreement between the Arab countries was accompanied by another agreement pertaining to the transfer of capital and the settlement of payments. But whereas the trade agreement embodies specific commitments relating to trade flow, the payments agreement does not provide for similar commitments concerning capital flows and the settlement of payments. Is it not possible that this lack of monetary co-operation has led to the failure of trade co-operation?

Furthermore, at the theoretical level, there is at present serious debate over the impact that stabilising the cross-rates of Arab currencies would have on trade. And as Mr Dajani is an advocate of the development of trade as an approach to or a basis for Arab economic integration, I should like to ask him to comment on this issue. Does he favour flexible or fixed Arab cross-rates? Also, given the diversity of Arab exchange-rate systems, to what extent is it possible to achieve exchange-rate co-ordination?

4. Izzidin Ibrahim Hassan

As the author mentions, there were undoubtedly some positive aspects to the efforts at Arab economic co-operation in the 1970s. These were related to the Arab financial surpluses and the migration of Arab workers to oil-producing countries. However, this co-operation exhibited certain negative aspects as well. The migration of workers from the deficit countries created an acute imbalance in their labour markets. Wages rose sharply, especially in those fields in which manpower was relatively scarce. This, in turn, contributed to an increase in the levels of inflation in these countries. Furthermore, the migration from the deficit countries of large numbers of workers with basic skills could be one of the factors behind their slow economic growth and could possibly be the reason for the constant increase in their trade deficits.

A sound evaluation of the move towards Arab economic co-operation must take such negative aspects into consideration, along with the positive aspects.

5. Faika El-Refaie

I wish to comment on Mr Sakbani's idea that fixed exchange rates and convertibility constitute a perfect substitute for a common currency and that there is consequently no need for a common currency in order to achieve economic integration.

I disagree and I wish to refer to Mr Williamson's paper where it is indicated that the very fact that the fixed rates could be changed might induce the private sector to adopt inappropriate policies which would constitute an impediment to the most efficient allocation of resources. The recent breakdown of the parity rates between the Qatari riyal, the Bahraini dinar and the UAE dirham supports this point. A common currency should therefore be recommended to the Gulf countries rather than fixed exchange rates.

Secondly, the issue is not merely one of financial resources flowing from surplus to deficit countries. The free movement of capital may be accompanied by a poor allocation of real resources if such freedom is not associated with co-ordination of investment policies to achieve specialisation and an efficient division of labour, especially in that the Arab countries have a modest and under-diversified productive capability. A well-formulated long-term strategy for the Arab countries in the context of the world economy is needed and could be developed through the establishment of a supranational investment institution with a reserve pool to channel the financial surpluses towards the achievement of the planned objectives.

6. Khair El-Din Haseeb

The relationship between political will and Arab economic co-operation and the question of which should precede the other, i.e., whether we should start with political unification and follow it with economic unification or vice versa, have been much debated by Arab thinkers and decision-makers. In practice, the experience of the Arab world over the past 20 years clearly shows that there is a strong correlation between Arab political relations and the degree of Arab economic co-operation. If one examines developments in economic relations during the period 1958-68 between Iraq and Syria, Iraq and Jordan, Egypt and Syria, and Egypt and Saudi Arabia, one finds a puzzling and regrettable illustration of the strength of this correlation and of the irrationality of Arab economic decision-making when it becomes subordinated to political considerations.

Why has this taken place in spite of the obvious interest of the Arab peoples in economic co-operation? The answer is that they have not, except on rare occasions, had the opportunity of participating in vital decision-making, such responsibility remaining in the hands of the Arab regimes and their political leadership.

Expanded Arab economic relations would nevertheless be reflected in a greater degree of rationality prevailing in political decision-making with regard to Arab relations. The experience of the 1970s points in this direction. Although diplomatic relations were severed between Egypt and most of the Arab countries, the movements of Egyptian workers were not restricted. One can cite other examples where the deterioration of political relations — e.g., between Egypt and Libya, or Syria and Iraq — did not have adverse consequences for economic relations. This points to a more rational approach regarding these relations.

What can be done to improve the current situation? I should like to make three brief observations in this regard. First of all, the economic systems prevailing in the Arab countries are not as divergent as some have made them out to be. Oil resources have led to the growth of the public sector in the oil-producing countries, thereby bringing their systems closer to those of the public-sector oriented countries. Differences in Arab economic systems do not constitute, in my opinion, a major obstacle to co-operation. Given the necessary political will, practical measures for co-ordination among the different systems are certainly feasible.

Secondly, there is scope for rationalising joint Arab economic activities and for permitting them to be somewhat more independent of the influence of political factors. The adoption of more rational criteria in decisions relating to the management of joint Arab organisations, for example, would lead them to play a more efficient role in the area of joint economic activity.

Thirdly, the approach to co-operation should not, in my opinion, be focused on specific sectors. Instead it should cover various economic fronts especially in view of the interdependence of the different economic sectors.

Finally, I would like to remark that the relatively limited volume of inter-Arab trade should not in itself be regarded as necessarily retarding Arab economic co-operation. Viewed in a dynamic context, the potential for developing Arab production capacities provides important opportunities for increasing productivity, reducing costs and expanding inter-Arab trade. Indeed, Arab co-operation in the trade sphere would contribute to a more efficient use of potential Arab production capacities.

7. Burhan Dajani, in Response

A number of points have been raised. I shall respond to some of them, without necessarily following the order of their presentation in the discussion.

The first point is the observation made that the move towards economic integration in the trade sphere might have been impeded by the absence of a monetary agreement to complement the 1953 Arab Trade and Transit Agreement. What seems to support this view is the fact that the formulators of the latter agreement had themselves drawn up a parallel agreement, on the transfer of payments. As this agreement was not binding, however, and did not provide for an implementation mechanism, it was without effect.

I disagree with this view. Foreign trade will continue regardless of whether or not there is a formal mechanism for the settlement of payments arising from it. What actually happened was that some Arab countries, Egypt in particular, which practised exchange control were not willing to allocate a part of their foreign currency reserves for Arab trade. They preferred, as they claimed at that time, to use such reserves for the purchase of equipment, raw materials and basic necessities rather than for the purchase of Syrian or Lebanese agricultural commodities, for example.

I do not agree with those who claim that the Arab Trade and Transit Agreement and the attempt at integration through the trade sector failed. In fact, through this sector, a common market for agricultural products was created. The Arab countries, however, neglected the agricultural sector, thus weakening its capacity to produce export surpluses. Arab attention was focused at the time on industry and funds were accordingly diverted from agriculture to industry. Since the agricultural sector was geared to meet local needs rather than to provide exports, the export of agricultural commodities declined to the point where Arab countries were turning more and more to the outside world to secure their needs for wheat, milk, meat and poultry products. In fact, Egypt's need to import wheat was used in the early 1960s as a means of bringing pressure to bear on that country to pay heed to American policies. This became possible because Egypt's wheat needs were draining a significant portion of the country's foreign exchange earnings, which, in turn, obstructed economic development efforts.

Even in the industrial sector, industries were established almost exclusively on the principle of import substitution. As such, industry was oriented towards the local market and no Arab country was able to achieve a sufficient degree of specialisation in any given industry to produce a substantial surplus for export. This was true even in such traditional industries as textiles and clothing. Industrial planning has been inadequate, resulting in only modest industrial development. The number of factories has increased, but industry itself has not developed. Arab industry continues to depend on the outside world for its equipment and technology and the technological level of Arab products remains undeveloped.

The second point concerns the importance accorded by some to economic policies in the process of economic integration. I think that we should view Arab economic integration as an historical process which interacts with other processes active in the Arab world, be they political or social, internal or external. Consequently, I disagree with those of my colleagues who wish to approach integration from the purely economic and technological viewpoints. If this position is accepted, the contradiction to which some colleagues have referred, i.e., the two seemingly conflicting approaches to monetary integration, will be resolved. The two approaches are, first, that monetary integration is desirable in itself and could be a factor in helping to achieve economic integration and, secondly, that economic integration is a prerequisite for monetary integration. Actually, my position on this issue is based on practical experience. For example, at the present stage of Arab economic history, the Arab countries have huge financial reserves abroad. At the same time, efforts are being made to attract funds to the Arab world. This implies that there exists an issue independent of the question of integration, namely, how to induce the repatriation of Arab funds. The attraction and repatriation of Arab funds will not necessarily lead to Arab integration, but this is a matter which should be given special priority as Arab assets abroad will be subject to planned or unplanned reductions in their real value, e.g., through inflation, subscription to long-term bonds carrying low interest rates and the inability to place funds in safer and more profitable investments, not to mention outright seizure of assets (as in the recent case of Iran).

Accordingly, I advocate that steps be taken to re-transfer the largest possible portion of these funds as soon as possible, to be invested in the Arab national economies and used to promote Arab economic integration and render the Arab economies capable of facing the post-oil era.

I am aware of the possible consequences of re-transferring of these funds to the Arab countries; but I urge that these funds be brought back, regardless of the problems which may arise. Efforts should indeed by directed towards coping with the problems rather than delaying the transfer of funds.

Monetary integration may help to stimulate the re-transfer of Arab funds. As such, integration becomes desirable and useful in itself. It should not, however, be regarded as a necessary condition or prerequisite for the attraction of funds. If monetary integration can be used as a means for attracting Arab funds, and this is feasible as I have indicated in my paper, then we need not wait until the fulfilment of all the other conditions for monetary integration. If monetary integration is not used for this purpose, however, it will have to accompany general economic integration.

Another point that was raised was the need for a high-level Arab authority to handle all or some of the issues related to economic or monetary integration and to plan specialisation in production among the Arab countries. This is an excellent idea in theory. However, the Arab countries still prefer bilateral to multilateral action. They continue to adhere to the concept of national sovereignty. In fact, they have even tended to restrict the operations of certain regional Arab institutions, lest they become too successful. By contrast, institutions which do not interfere with decisions at the national level are favoured. I am nevertheless confident that once a dynamic, capable and determined leadership is available, much can be accomplished through existing institutions, such as the Council for Arab Economic Unity and the Economic and Social Council of the Arab League. Indeed, despite existing constraints, the Council of Arab Economic Unity has succeeded in promoting a number of important economic projects at the pan-Arab level.

4 TRADE AND EXCHANGE REGIMES AND THE EXERCISE OF MONETARY POLICY IN THE ARAB COUNTRIES

Karim Nashashibi

Introduction

Arab countries offer a wide diversity of production profiles and of ideological orientations. These have shaped their financial structures and the extent to which their economies have been open to their neighbours and to the outside world. Some, because of their oil wealth or their concentration on trade and services, have, on the strength of surpluses in their balance of payments, developed liberal trade and exchange regimes and a substantial financial sector. Others, whose production has been concentrated on primary commodities, mostly agricultural, have had to cope with such typical problems of underdevelopment as low export growth, inadequate savings and persistent deficits. These countries have tended to be more restrictive in their policies and to have less developed financial sectors. Cutting across both the surplus and the deficit countries are two different economic orientations, one which is essentially market-based and decentralised and the other in which the public sector dominates economic activity. These distinctions have been blurred to some extent since 1973 by the pressure for liberalisation generated by the rapid increase in oil wealth in the region and the resulting intra-regional movements of factors of production.

Among the first steps towards any attempt at realising economic integration among Arab countries will be exchange-rate policy co-ordination and its counterpart, monetary policy co-ordination. This paper will survey the disparities among the trade and exchange regimes of the Arab countries and examine their monetary policies. It is hoped that this may point to some of the problems which economic integration may face, as well as to the initial directions it may take. The discussion in the following two sections of trade regimes and monetary policies will be divided among three groups of countries: the oil-exporting countries, the market-oriented non-oil countries and the public-sector-oriented non-oil countries. Finally, in Section III, the paper will conclude by referring briefly to the implications of the present interaction among Arab countries and of their policies for Arab economic integration.

I. Trade and Exchange Regimes in the Arab Economies and the Openness of their Economies

A. Trade Regimes in Oil-exporting Countries

Trade regimes in Arab oil-exporting countries have generally been liberal since the early days of their petroleum discoveries. They share certain features such as full currency convertibility and relatively unrestricted capital movements.

The most liberal trade regimes among oil-exporting countries are in the Gulf region, e.g., Bahrain, Kuwait, Qatar, Saudi Arabia and the United Arab Emirates (UAE). In the case of the UAE and Kuwait, the combination of large oil revenues, low domestic absorptive capacity and a public expenditure pattern concentrated on infrastructure and the petrochemical industries, rather than on the domestic production of import substitutes, has resulted in large current account surpluses and no protective tariffs or restrictions on trade. In most of the Gulf countries, import licences are not required, and there are neither restrictions on the use of currency nor exchange controls on capital receipts or payments by either residents or non-residents. Where customs tariffs prevail, they tend to be imposed for revenue-raising purposes and are unusually low and uniform. While Saudi Arabia shares the liberal features of the smaller Gulf countries, it is also concerned with developing its agricultural base and its manufacturing sector. This has resulted in the imposition of protective tariffs, although these barely exceed 20 per cent. Fiscal policy instruments such as tax exemptions are also used to encourage the transfer of foreign technology and joint ventures in import-substitution sectors.

The emergence of huge current-account surpluses in search of foreign outlets has undoubtedly influenced the evolution of the foreign exchange markets of the oil-exporting countries. While the larger portion of the surplus funds has been diverted to the Eurodollar and other financial markets, there has also been a need to reduce the exchange risk by issuing financial papers denominated in local currencies. This offers the additional advantage to Gulf countries of diversifying their own economies by providing a service sector related to the export of their own surplus funds. The development of capital markets in these countries and the conversion of oil wealth into an expanding asset base abroad has made the unrestricted movements of capital in domestic and foreign currencies an essential feature of their exchange and monetary systems.

The major goal of the exchange rate policies pursued by the Gulf area oil-exporting countries is to maintain a large degree of stability between their currencies and the currencies of their major trading partners. The purpose of this stability is primarily to reduce the impact of foreign currency fluctuations on domestic prices and costs. However, stability has also become a desirable policy in support of the further development of regional capital markets. Since most of the oil revenues accruing to these countries are in United States dollars, it was only natural, initially, for the currencies of Bahrain, Kuwait, Qatar, Saudi Arabia and the UAE to be pegged to the dollar. However, with the weakening of the dollar after the mid-1970s, there was a switch of pegs to baskets of currencies, mostly to the SDR, substantial margins being maintained for fluctuations.[1] This resulted in an appreciation of the domestic currencies *vis-à-vis* the dollar by about 5 per cent between 1977 and 1979 and a remarkable stability in exchange rates among the Gulf countries (see Table 4.1).[2]

Three of the Gulf countries — Bahrain, Qatar and the UAE — attempted at first to co-ordinate their exchange-rate policies by fixing the cross-rates of their currencies to facilitate travel and business transactions. However, when Qatar revalued its currency upwards by 2 per cent *vis-à-vis* the dollar in May 1979 while Bahrain and the UAE maintained their exchange rates, the agreement was suspended with Qatar, and later between Bahrain and the UAE as well. In 1979, Bahrain and Kuwait also abolished tariffs between themselves, but in view of the limited amount of trade between the two countries, this measure was not to have a significant economic impact. In the case of Saudi Arabia, there have been modest attempts, kept within a 3 per cent margin, at using the exchange rate to stem domestic inflationary pressures originating abroad. More recently, there has been a tendency for the Kuwaiti dinar to depreciate *vis-à-vis* neighbouring currencies, as a result of some capital flight due to interest-rate differentials.

In the other Arab oil-exporting countries (Algeria, Iraq, Libya) trade regimes are less liberal than those of the Gulf region. This is not necessarily the result of balance-of-payments pressures. Rather, it is the deliberate policy of these countries to assign to the public sector a dominant role in all aspects of the economy.

All three countries impose quantitative restrictions on imports through a high degree of monopolisation of foreign trade by government trading agencies. Exchange controls on invisibles and capital transfers are enforced. With respect to exchange-rate policy, both Iraq and Libya have pegged their currencies to the dollar since 1973 and have maintained the same parity with the dollar. On the other hand, the currencies of both countries have sustained some depreciation *vis-à-vis* the currencies of their major credit partners. In the case of Algeria, exchange-rate stability has been sought through the pegging of the Algerian dinar to a basket of currencies representing the distribution of its import payments.

In Iraq and Libya, a strong balance-of-payments performance and

Table 4.1: Exchange Rates of Gulf Currencies, Expressed in Terms of the Kuwaiti Dinar (1974 = 100)

End of period	Dollars per Kuwaiti dinar	Bahrain dinars per Kuwaiti dinar	Qatar riyals per Kuwaiti dinar	UAE dirhams per Kuwaiti dinar	Saudi Arabian riyals per Kuwaiti dinar	SDRs per Kuwaiti dinar	Effective exchange rate of the Kuwaiti dinar[a]
1974	100.0	100.0	100.0	100.0	100.0	100.0	
1975	98.5	98.7	99.5	98.8	97.9	103.0	
1976	100.9	101.2	101.2	101.4	100.4	106.4	
1977	103.4	103.6	103.7	101.3	102.1	104.2	100.0
1978							
1st quarter	105.1	103.3	103.5	102.4	102.3	104.0	99.5
2nd quarter	105.5	103.6	103.6	102.8	102.3	104.2	98.6
3rd quarter	106.5	104.1	104.1	103.2	99.7	101.8	95.2
4th quarter	106.6	103.6	103.6	102.6	99.5	100.1	91.9
1979							
1st quarter	105.0	102.1	102.1	101.3	99.3	99.9	92.6
2nd quarter	105.0	102.1	99.6	100.2	99.8	99.6	92.8
3rd quarter	105.0	101.0	99.6	100.2	99.2	97.5	92.0
4th quarter	106.1	101.3	99.5	100.7	100.5	98.6	94.7

Note: [a] Import-weighted index, 1977 = 100. Movements above 100 reflect a depreciation of the variable currency.
Source: International Monetary Fund, *International Financial Statistics*, vol. 33, no. 9 (September 1980).

the accumulation of large foreign exchange reserves have introduced a high degree of flexibility into the controls on trade and payments.

Thus, the import programmes are often amended to allow for increased allocation to government agencies when the need arises. Similarly, restrictions on invisibles have been relaxed substantially in practice, while restrictions on capital movements have as their major purpose the channelling of foreign investment through joint ventures with the public sector and the regulation of the reinvestment of profits and the repatriation of capital.

B. Market-oriented Non-oil Countries

Market-oriented non-oil Arab countries can be classified into two groups, according to the degree of liberalism of their trade regimes.

The most liberal are Jordan, Lebanon and Yemen, all of which have generally enjoyed a strong balance-of-payments performance and accumulating reserves. Jordan and Yemen have pegged their currencies to the SDR and the dollar, respectively, while Lebanon's exchange rate is basically floating. Lebanon maintains a policy of complete freedom with respect to current and capital transfers. Import policies in the other two countries are essentially non-restrictive as import licences are granted liberally and foreign exchange is freely available. Protectionism is mostly manifested in the form of customs tariffs, although occasionally certain imports are restricted to encourage domestic production. While there are some formal controls on current payments for invisible and capital movements in Jordan and Yemen, in practice there is little control over them in an environment where the objective is essentially to attract workers' remittances, other unrequited transfers and capital flows. Laws regulating foreign investments are quite liberal and allow for the repatriation of capital on generous terms. Typically, as in the case of Jordan, profits may be remitted without limitation, while capital may be repatriated within a five-year period. Bank accounts denominated in foreign currencies are allowed, and there are no restrictions on transfers and payments in the domestic currency.

The other market-oriented non-oil Arab countries, whose balance-of-payments positions are much weaker, have pursued less liberal trade and payments policies. The persistent current account deficits of Mauritania, Morocco and Tunisia have resulted in quantitative controls on imports enforced through a licensing mechanism. In addition, there are margin requirements for import payments. Imports are typically classified into more or less restrictive categories according to whether they are of a developmental nature or non-essential and whether they compete with domestic production or not. The degree of restrictiveness varies with the overall availability of foreign exchange. It should be emphasised, however, that both Morocco and Tunisia face strict quotas imposed by the European Economic Community on their exports of textiles and other limitations on the exports of agricultural commodities. This has hampered export growth significantly, particularly over the last two years, and has contributed to their recent balance-of-payments difficulties. Exchange-rate policy in these three countries has been flexible, the exchange rate being kept in line with the fluctuations in a basket of currencies reflecting their major trading partners. Despite their balance-of-payments difficulties, they have been able to maintain this exchange-rate policy partly through restrictions on imports and partly through foreign borrowing. Like Algeria, Morocco offers a variable exchange-rate premium on its workers' remittances, so as to ensure parity between its currency and the French franc.

C. Public-sector-oriented Non-oil Countries

Trade regimes in Egypt, Somalia, Sudan, the Syrian Arab Republic and Democratic Yemen have been the most restrictive in the Arab world. Up to the advent of the oil boom, i.e., until the end of the 1960s, the trade regimes of these countries reflected the domination of their economies by the public sector, a weak balance-of-payments position and a very limited interaction with the neighbouring oil-exporting countries. In particular, the large movements of labour and managerial skills in the direction of the oil-exporters and the large capital flows in the opposite direction in the form of aid, direct investment and remittances, had not yet taken place. The public sector domination of internal and external trade, as well as of financial institutions, enabled the governments to exercise strict control over the quantity and commodity distribution of imports. Moreover, the large number of bilateral agreements which had been reached with the Socialist countries also determined the origin of imports and had an impact on resource allocation, the transfer of technology and other growth-related variables. Current payments on imports of commodities and invisibles, as well as capital movements, were subjected to strict exchange controls. Limitations were similarly imposed on travel abroad and employment in other countries, with the result that Egypt and Sudan, which both had surplus labour and agricultural resources, were isolated from their neighbours. This isolation was manifested in their balance of payments by the negligible amounts on account of workers' remittances, direct investment from abroad and even aid from Arab oil-exporting countries. Nor was there a strong trade link with other Arab countries, since their intra-regional exports accounted for less than 7 per cent of total exports for Egypt and about 10 per cent for Sudan.[3]

The allocation of foreign exchange among various claims was determined according to a set of government priorities usually defined by a foreign exchange budget. Typically, this regime was characterised by the emergence of 'free' exchange markets. The consumption pattern reflected a much greater degree of austerity than at present, as imports of consumer durables and luxuries were severely limited in order to release foreign exchange resources for imports of basic foodstuffs, raw materials and capital goods. On the other hand, this system retarded the growth of foreign-exchange earnings and reduced the overall availability of foreign-exchange resources. The undervaluation of foreign exchange penalised export activities, while the shortage in imported inputs hampered production and growth. Moreover, restrictions on capital movements and the repatriation of earnings, together with the perpetuation of unrealistic exchange rates, discouraged foreign private investment.

The dramatic expansion in oil wealth starting in the early 1970s generated a much greater degree of regional economic interaction than had existed previously, which in turn led to a liberalisation of exchange and trade regimes. Factors of production, namely labour and managerial skills, moved from the non-oil countries to the oil-exporting countries which, in turn, exported capital to the former. One of the first manifestations of the rise in oil revenues was a large increase in 1974 in official aid from the Arab oil-exporting countries to the non-oil countries.[4] This display of economic and political support, coupled with the explosion in demand for labour in the oil-exporting countries, encouraged the non-oil countries to allow their labour and management to seek more remunerative employment in the oil-exporting countries. This process created a growing pool of foreign exchange resources, accumulated by workers residing in the oil-exporting countries, part of which was repatriated, both for the maintenance of their families and for investment, mostly in real estate. The non-oil countries recognised that the large oil revenue surpluses would be in search of long-term investment and would be channelled to deficit countries in the form of private investment, bilateral aid and project aid through regional or national aid institutions. They also realised that, in order to attract remittances and private investment, as well as development aid from the market-oriented oil-exporting countries, i.e., in order to reap some of the oil wealth spillover, they would do well to foster a non-restrictive environment. All these factors prompted the national authorities to pursue more liberal exchange and trade policies. This process of liberalisation can be illustrated by the similar experiences of Egypt and Sudan, whose exchange and trade regimes were among the most restrictive in the area.

In Egypt and Sudan, trade and payments liberalisation was essentially promoted by two policy decisions which resulted in an effective depreciation of their currencies. The first was the creation of 'parallel' exchange markets and the second was the liberalisation of controls of

Table 4.2: Commodity Trade, Capital Inflows and Net Foreign Assets of the Non-oil Arab Countries for 1970 and 1979 (millions of dollars and percentages)

	Egypt[a]	Jordan	Lebanon	Mauritania	Morocco	Somalia	Sudan	Syrian[a] Arab Republic	Tunisia	Yemen	Democratic Yemen	Total
Exports												
1970	748	34	192	89	488	31	298	169	183	3	135	2368
1979	1354	402	705	147	1873	111	552	534	1766	2	221[b]	7640
Growth rate (%)	10.3	31.6	15.5	5.7	16.1	15.2	6.7	15.5	28.7	–	6.4[b]	13.9
Imports												
1970	787	184	653	56	684	45	288	361	306	32	200	3593
1979	3837	1962	2414	259	3678	287	1133	3006	2830	1393	544[c]	21343
Growth rate (%)	19.3	30.0	15.6	18.6	20.5	22.8	16.2	28.0	28.1	56.8	15.0[c]	22.0
Trade deficit												
1970	−25	−150	−461	33	−196	−14	−11	−158	−123	−30	−65	−1265
1979	−1997	−1560	−1709	112	−1806	−176	−575	−1685	−1065	−1392	−363[c]	−12325
Unrequited transfers												
1970	308	114	na	3[b]	73	13	0	10	58	na	52	631
1979	90	348[b]	na	230[b]	935	94	11	1739	332	1280	337	5396
Capital inflow												
1970	226	−1	na	21[b]	140	10	28	45	72	na	16	557
1979	1413	426[b]	na	76[b]	1409[b]	87	273	205	426	70	25	4410
Net foreign assets												
1970	−415	262	727[d]	–	120	16	−52	−28	16	na	66	709
1979	−3058	1234	3577	−52	445	50	−546	273	415	1443	193	3974

Notes: [a] Since Egypt and the Syrian Arab Republic are not exporters of oil, export and import data have been adjusted to exclude oil. [b] 1978. [c] 1971-9. [d] If gold reserves were valued at current prices, net foreign assets would amount to $9 billion.
Source: International Monetary Fund, *International Financial Statistics*.

imports financed from abroad. The main reason for establishing the parallel market was to encourage 'non-traditional' exports and to provide the private sector with a small volume of imports and invisibles. But, as had happened in the Syrian Arab Republic in the mid-1960s, the introduction of a parallel market became a powerful factor in relaxing the commitment to maintain an over-valued official rate of exchange for the national currency. The principle rationale for adopting this seemingly cumbersome approach to exchange-rate liberalisation, instead of simply devaluing the currency to its market value, was the fact that the currencies of both countries were vastly over-valued, by between 60 and 80 per cent. Therefore, a straight devaluation would have had an abrupt impact on prices, with potentially disruptive social and political consequences. Exchange-rate policy liberalisation in both countries was accompanied by the liberalisation of import policies.

The exchange and trade system in the Syrian Arab Republic has undergone a substantial liberalisation since 1973. A situation had developed whereby foreign exchange was being amply provided to the public sector, mostly at the official rate, but where demand in the private sector was not fully satisfied. Hence, an unofficial free market for foreign exchange emerged and rapidly expanded after 1977, as it appeared that regulations governing import payments would not be strictly enforced. Recent figures put the exchange rate in this market at about 10 per cent over the official exchange rate, while the volume of unofficial exchange market transactions is estimated to have reached one third of the total volume of imports.

D. The Impact of Trade Liberalisation on the Financial System

The policy changes in countries which were noted for their highly restrictive trade regimes created an environment more conducive to free enterprise and trade. These changes not only revitalised the private sector, but gave that sector a competitive advantage over the public sector by lending it access to scarce foreign exchange. This put governments under pressure to liberalise the regulations which governed the behaviour of the public sector, particularly its ability to set prices, seek imports from its own sources and engage in financial operations locally and abroad. This liberalisation of trade and exchange regimes brought about by the spread of oil wealth in the Arab world entailed the liberalisation of domestic economic processes, with a much greater role assigned to the price mechanism in the allocation of resources, a reduction in the monopoly power of government agencies and the revival of private investment and production.[5] However, the flood of consumer goods imported by expatriate workers — a concrete manifestation of the higher salaries earned abroad — further encouraged movements of labour and raised the population's expectations concerning its patterns of consumption.[6]

One major effect of trade liberalisation on the monetary system has been the marked expansion of the banking sector in a number of countries. In Egypt, for example, prior to 1974 there were only four commercial banks, all publicly-owned, which carried out government policy and specialised in various areas of public sector activity. The 'open door' policy and the foreign investment law of 1974 encouraged a number of foreign banks to set up their operations in Egypt. By the end of 1979, 38 banks had been established under this law, of which 25 were dealing primarily in foreign currencies. In Sudan, a similar process took place, though on a smaller scale. Since in most cases residents can hold bank accounts in foreign currencies, these currencies have had a direct impact on credit expansion in the country, as they can be converted readily into the domestic currency. Their becoming a part of the money supply adds another dimension to the conduct of monetary policy.[7] Since foreign currency deposits are mostly reinvested in the Eurodollar market, banks have been able to offer their depositors interest rates in line with international norms. These have directly conflicted with the interest rates offered on domestic currency deposits, which have traditionally been low. In Egypt, for instance, while interest rates on dollar time deposits were recently in the 12 to 13 per cent range, interest rates on domestic savings deposits have been 6 per cent, while rates on time deposits in domestic currency ranged up to 8.5 per cent for a five-year maturity. This has tended to create a strong disincentive to converting foreign currency to domestic currency, thus depriving the government of much of the remittance proceeds and raising the volume of deposits denominated in foreign currencies to one third that of total deposits. While the monetary authorities have endeavoured to reduce the distortions in relative rates by adjusting domestic rates upwards (they had been 5 and 6 per cent for savings and time deposits respectively up to 1978), the gap remains large and it will take a fundamental change in the domestic interest-rate structure to resolve this dichotomy.

The trend towards trade liberalisation has manifested itself in a rapid increase in imports. In the period 1970-9, imports for the Arab non-oil countries grew at an annual compound rate of 22 per cent, as against 19 per cent for the non-oil countries taken as a group. Countries maintaining more restrictive trade and exchange regimes, e.g., Egypt, the Syrian Arab Republic, Democratic Yemen and Sudan, experienced a smaller growth in imports than the Arab group as a whole. By contrast, exports during the same period grew generally at an annual compound rate of about 14 per cent, well below the average 20 per cent for the non-oil developing countries as a group.[8] It may be argued that the emigration of skilled workers abroad led to a decline in productivity at home, while driving wages upwards and raising the costs of production. The combination of these two factors may, at least in certain countries, have reduced the competitiveness of exports and dampened their growth. While countries maintaining the more restrictive regimes may have experienced lower rates of import growth than the Arab group average, their relatively weaker export performance has meant in practice both an increase in their dependence on imports, expressed as a percentage of gross domestic product (GDP) and a widening trade deficit.

This expansion in imports and the trade deficit has been made possible by a number of factors: the increase in service receipts (tourism, Suez Canal dues in the case of Egypt), some petroleum exports (Egypt and the Syrian Arab Republic), factor income from abroad (workers' and professionals' remittances), official unrequited transfers, such as foreign aid grants and support from Arab oil-exporting countries to the 'confrontation' states; foreign official project loans and cash loans; long-term borrowing from private institutions; and, finally, monetary movements, i.e., short-term borrowing and changes in reserves. Of these the most important single factor has been the rise in workers' remittances (see Table 4.3). As a result, the sharp increase in the trade deficit was not accompanied by a deterioration in the balance-of-payments position. If the net foreign assets of the banking system are taken as an indicator, the balance-of-payments positions of most non-oil-exporting countries have noticeably improved. Egypt and Sudan stand out as noteworthy exceptions, as the stagnation of exports resulted in a rapid rise of foreign indebtedness, despite the dramatic rise in remittances, particularly in Egypt.

II. The Exercise of Monetary Policy in Arab Countries

A. Monetary Policy in Oil-exporting Countries

Monetary development in oil-exporting countries is essentially determined by fiscal policy. Oil revenues, which range from 45 per cent of total government revenues in Algeria to over 90 per cent of government revenues in the Gulf countries, are converted into high levels of government[9] spending. Although part of this spending goes towards direct imports, particularly in development spending programmes, expenditure on imports barely exceeds one third of total spending. The bulk of public sector spending goes into wages and salaries and into domestic resources generating domestic liquidity. Public sector spending is also the prime determinant of aggregate demand (through the multiplier effect), stimulating private sector activity and private sector demand, which again is partly satisfied by imports, thereby exercising a contractile effect on the money supply. But public sector spending also stimulates

Table 4.3: Remittances from Expatriate Workers and Professionals in Major Labour-exporting Countries[a] (millions of dollars)

Country	1975	1976	1977	1978	1979
Algeria	423	456	388	436	453
Democratic Yemen	58	119	188	257	314
Egypt[b]	366	755	896	1761	2282
Jordan[c]	172	388	408	438	510
Morocco	489	499	574	657	944
Sudan[b]	140	160	130	240	270
Syrian Arab Republic[d]	99	140	243	231	290
Tunisia	161	364	511	538	589
Yemen	270	676	987	946	1025
Total	2178	3557	4425	5504	6677

Notes: [a] Data for Lebanon are not available. [b] Includes the country's own estimate of exchange imports which are financed by remittances. [c] These are gross remittances. There are small remittance outflows from foreign workers in Jordan. [d] Remittances effected through the Central Bank of Syria plus non-resident foreign exchange accounts with the Commercial Bank of Syria, mostly financed through remittances (1979 figure projected). Total remittances are much larger.
Source: International Monetary Fund, *Balance of Payments Yearbook 1980* (Washington D.C.: IMF, 1980).

supply directly, through investment in capital formation, and indirectly, by inducing the private sector to meet the demand for goods and services and confront the bottlenecks generated in the economy. Thus, in the short run, the expansion in the money supply corresponds to the public sector's net domestic spending (i.e., government expenditures on domestic resources minus government domestic revenues), offset to some extent by the counter-effect of the private sector balance-of-payments deficit.[10] In the longer run, supply capabilities expand through the development of the domestic resource base and through better import absorption in the economy, both of which relieve inflationary pressures. In this context, demand management policy has only one effective instrument for short-run stabilisation: the level of net domestic government spending. In most Arab oil-exporting countries, credit extended to the private sector is a small proportion of the liquidity generated by the government sector. But the more diversified the economy and the greater the proportion of the money stock represented by private sector credits, the more instruments the monetary authorities have at their disposal to stabilise aggregate demand. However, even in the more diversified oil-exporting economies, such as those of Algeria and Iraq, the 'private sector' is in fact largely taken up by ---' 'ic enterprises. Nevertheless, because oil revenues in these countries titute a smaller proportion of total government revenues and because a sizeable volume of domestic credit is directed to the non-governmental sector, their monetary authorities have more options available in restricting aggregate demand, and do not need to rely solely on cuts in government spending.

Developments in the oil-exporting countries during the 1975-7 period, i.e., in the wake of the large increase in oil revenues, illustrate the internal imbalances which can occur. The sharp rise in government expenditures immediately put great pressure on the availability of domestic resources in these countries and on their capacity to import. These cost-push pressures, coupled with a rapid rise in import prices during this period and the price rigidities which emerged from certain market imperfections, resulted in a sharp increase in the cost of living.[11] The restoration of internal balance necessitated a number of measures. While none of these measures was monetary, they proved together to be very effective in several oil-exporting countries: (a) a deceleration in the rate of growth of government spending; (b) a concerted effort to reduce supply bottlenecks, particularly in port facilities, and to facilitate imports; (c) the importation of foreign labour and managerial skills; and (d) a vigorous housing construction programme. As these measures took effect, with various delays ranging from one to two years, inflationary pressures abated and the oil economies settled into a pattern of lower growth in the non-oil GDP, but with a greatly improved capacity to import, to absorb investment and generally to respond to different patterns of expenditure (e.g., on domestic as opposed to foreign resources, on agriculture or on industry). Thus, there was a substantial decrease in the rate of monetary expansion in most oil-exporting countries after 1976 (see Table 4.4).

Table 4.4: Domestic Liquidity Expansion in Selected Oil-exporting Countries (percentages)

Country	1974	1975	1976	1977	1978	1979
Algeria	9	30	31	22	30	18
Iraq	43	39	21	17	43	n.a.
Kuwait[a]	16	37	44	28	24	16
Libya	40	20	25	26	12	35
Saudi Arabia	46	61	74	53	44	15
United Arab Emirates	n.a.	49	67	18	11	8

Note: [a] Fiscal years ending on 31 March of the following years for 1974 and 1975; years ending on 30 June thereafter.
Source: International Monetary Fund, *International Financial Statistics*, various issues.

While in the 1975-6 period monetary policy played virtually no role in coping with the excess demand and cost-push problems which the oil-exporting countries faced, it is more likely now to have an impact on the more diversified economic structure of these countries. With domestic market imperfections reduced by greater competition and a more effective price mechanism, there are greater possibilities for regulating demand management by means of a number of policy instruments such as the exchange rate, the interest rate and direct credit controls. Provided that imports are not hindered by transportation bottlenecks and their domestic market structure is relatively free of oligopolistic elements, a 3 to 4 per cent exchange-rate appreciation could significantly reduce exogenous inflationary pressures. Moreover, since the oil-exporting countries enjoy a higher than average degree of openness to the outside world by virtue of their large external trade and capital movements, domestic interest-rate policy becomes an important instrument in governing short-term capital flows. As was illustrated in the case of Egypt, a cleavage between domestic interest-rate policy and trends in Eurodollar rates can cause a demand for domestic credit in order to finance foreign currency holdings. This results in capital flight, pressure on the domestic currency and higher inflation, which further fuels the demand for foreign currency.[12] Lack of co-ordination between domestic interest rates and rates on Eurodollar deposits have caused some destabilising capital movements in some Gulf countries over the past two years. Yet, in most Gulf countries, domestic interest is not a prime monetary instrument in rationing credit, since most credit expansion stems from government spending; nor is it a development instrument in the sense of either inducing investment or allocating resources. Hence, there are no significant advantages to be had by insulating the domestic interest-rate structure from world fluctuations.

Control of credit is still in its rudimentary stages in the oil-producing countries and is mostly dependent on contacts with bank managers. Difficulties in control arise because of the type of credit extended and the differing means of credit. For instance, 80 per cent of credit outstanding in Kuwait is in the form of overdrafts. Hence, commercial banks cannot control credit by monitoring the use to which it is put. A shift in lending policy to a detailed specification of the utilisation of credit would improve overall credit control by monetary authorities and reduce the use of credit for speculative purposes. However, selective credit controls in a financial environment with no built-in checks, due to lack of records and financial supervision, would be at best limited to certain reputable creditors. Another major problem in credit control is the proliferation of credit sources. In most oil-exporting countries, commercial banks can be bypassed by resort to specialised credit institutions such as industrial banks and real estate banks. Money changers have also increased their retail banking activities substantially and are outside the control of monetary authorities. Finally, it is always possible to borrow from abroad, particularly from offshore banks which extend loans in the domestic currencies of the major oil-exporters. A case in point is the sizeable offshore market in Saudi Arabian riyal-denominated deposits and loans which has grown rapidly in Bahrain. The growth of this market was stimulated by the denomination, until recently, of all government contracts in riyals and by the incentives it offered to depositors, who could obtain higher returns on their funds than was possible in Saudi Arabia. To discourage this market from becoming a potentially large source of liquidity, which may add to inflationary pressures in Saudi Arabia, the government began in late 1979 to denominate its large contracts in foreign exchange. As an alternative to foreign borrowing, liquidity shortages are being alleviated in these countries by resort to the inter-bank market, a policy which can have adverse consequences, given the distorted distribution of deposits in favour of a few banks.[13] As open market operations are virtually non-existent, the monetary authorities regulate liquidity by shifting government deposits or through foreign exchange operations. However, the latter instrument has a direct effect on the exchange rate which may conflict with other objectives.

A necessary condition for the exercise of some measure of credit control, in view of the pitfalls mentioned above, is adequate banking control and supervision. This has become particularly important with the proliferation of banks in some oil-exporting countries (e.g., there are 52 banks in the UAE, and 61 banks in Bahrain, of which 42 are offshore), and the overall expansion of banking activities in the region. Monetary authorities have increasingly resorted to the use of such monetary instruments as reserve requirements and ratios of liabilities to capital and of advances to deposits, while monetary agencies in the Gulf countries have increasingly assumed the functions of central banks.

B. Monetary Policy in Market-oriented Economies

Among market-oriented non-oil economies in the Arab world, Jordan, Lebanon and Yemen have all benefited from substantial capital inflows from neighbouring countries. In addition to the official capital transfers from oil-exporting countries, the private sector has also been the recipient of foreign exchange in the form of remittances from foreign workers. These inflows, which have increased rapidly over the last decade, have had the same expansionary effect on domestic liquidity as oil revenues have had in the oil-exporting countries.

Official transfers are largely converted into government expenditures, including ambitious development programmes, but a portion also goes towards reserve accumulation. Workers' remittances also increase private liquidity and are directed towards housing construction and to satisfying other consumer demand. As in the oil-exporting countries, the private sector generates a balance-of-payments deficit which offsets to some extent the expansionary effect of government spending.

In Jordan, for example, the domestic budgetary deficit increased from $373 million in 1975 to $455 million in 1976.[14] By 1979, this deficit had reached $1 billion. Since most of these deficits were financed from abroad, there was no need to resort to borrowing from the Central Bank. Nevertheless, these increased government expenditures became the major component of aggregate demand and were primarily responsible for the considerable inflationary pressures generated in Jordan in 1975. Between 1975 and 1979, the money supply rose at an average annual compound rate of 28 per cent, while real output grew annually at about 9 per cent over the same period (see Table 4.5). The monetary authorities responded to the inflationary pressures by restricting credit to the private sector. Among the policy instruments used were an increase in the minimum reserve requirements for demand and time deposits, the introduction of a credit-to-deposit ratio, and the raising of interest rates. In 1977, there was a marked slowdown in the expansion of credit to the private sector, but it is likely that the slowdown was in response to a levelling off in the demand for housing rather than to a lack of liquidity. When the same restrictive measures were applied in 1979, bank credit to the private sector grew at a faster rate than it had done in 1978.

Table 4.5: Domestic Liquidity Expansion in Selected Non-oil Arab Countries (percentages)

Country	1974	1975	1976	1977	1978	1979
Egypt	30	21	26	20	20	31
Jordan	25	31	30	23	29	28
Morocco	31	20	19	20	18	14
Sudan	35	19	25	43	27	30
Syrian Arab Republic	46	26	24	28	27	30
Tunisia	28	22	16	13	20	17
Yemen	34	79	125	51	32	19

Source: International Monetary Fund, *International Financial Statistics*.

It should be emphasised that credit to the private sector is essentially the only factor in the money supply over which the monetary authorities have direct control. With respect to the prime determinant of monetary expansion, i.e., the level of net domestic government expenditure, there is little they can or want to do, given the legitimate desire of the policy-makers to translate foreign aid into capital accumulation. In their view, to the extent that the build-up of the capital stock can be justified economically, the claim it makes on domestic resources, with the resulting inflationary pressures in the short run, may be a small price to pay for a broader productive base and future growth. Additionally, governments have argued in favour of spreading the benefits of foreign aid by pursuing an income policy whereby budgetary subsidies are granted to basic consumer goods. This must be weighed against the inflationary pressures which such consumer expenditure would generate and the impact of inflation on income distribution.

Returning to the example of Jordan, another approach has been adopted — likely to have a greater impact in the long run — whereby efforts are being made by the monetary authorities to mobilise domestic liquidity by developing financial intermediaries, particularly a stock exchange, and new debt instruments. The latter include certificates of deposits (denominated in local currencies) and corporate bonds, as well as government development bonds. To the extent that these debt instruments are sold to the public rather than to the commercial banks, they absorb purchasing power diverted from consumption and release resources for capital formation. With the development of secondary markets, they may become an effective tool in the hands of the government for regulating the level of private liquidity.

Other market-oriented economies (e.g., those of Morocco and Tunisia) do not have the peculiar monetary problem of the accumulation of foreign assets which are translated into domestic liquidity. Hence, there is a better balance between the growth of domestic product and the growth of the money supply. In this framework, monetary policy can more effectively control the major sources of liquidity expansion but it must still accommodate the financing needs of the Treasury. In Tunisia, credit to the government is about one-fifth of total domestic credit, while in Morocco it accounts for a little more than half. To increase domestic liquidity, the central banks in these countries raise rediscount ceilings and manipulate the minimum reserve requirements. When sizeable government deficits emerge, these banks tend to limit credit to the private sector. But they have at their disposal better-developed money and treasury bill markets than in other deficit countries such as Egypt or Sudan (see below). In both Tunisia and Morocco, the government ensures that commercial banks participate in the financing of investment by requiring them to hold a proportion of their demand and time deposits in medium- and long-term bonds.[15] On occasion, the treasuries of both countries bypass the domestic banking system and borrow money abroad to finance their deficit.

C. Monetary Policy in the Public-sector-oriented Countries

Monetary policy in those countries dominated by the public sector has been traditionally relegated to playing a minor role by an environment of strict controls, central decision-making in the allocation of resources and reliance on fiscal measures to stabilise savings. In particular, in the absence of adequate mechanisms for the generation of savings, governments have relied on monetary expansion and the resulting inflation as a tax to claim resources from the public and promote capital accumulation. Once the level of domestic deficit financing is set, monetary policy is reduced to the administration of credit allocation among public sector firms and to the private sector. Where government-owned banks dominate the banking system, as in Egypt, Democratic Yemen, Sudan and the Syrian Arab Republic, this credit allocation is carried out through direct contacts between the central bank and the commercial banks. With the recent liberalisation of the economic environment towards a revitalisation of the private sector and the awareness that monetary stability is the essential factor in preserving social stability and in promoting growth, monetary policy has been given a more active role in the overall management of demand.

In most of these countries, credit ceilings have been established as the major instrument of control. An overall ceiling on credit to the private sector is divided up, usually on a monthly or quarterly basis, among existing banks.[16] However, the degree of compliance varies widely with the government's will to enforce the ceiling. Government-owned commercial banks have become part of the public sector decision-making establishment and can bypass the directives of the central banks by appealing directly to key government officials. Central bank penalties such as higher interest charges will have little significance in relation to higher profit margins realised in economies where market imperfection and distortions are widespread. Likewise, a number of public or semi-public enterprises can also exercise pressure to obtain credit, giving rise to competing claims on credit from different public sector agencies. In Sudan, the period from 1977 to 1979 was marked by a rapid increase in private sector[17] credit and frequent violations of the established ceilings. However, as the government resolved to reduce inflationary pressures, which had reached serious proportions, there was a much greater degree of ceiling enforcement and a substantial reduction in credit expansion. This was attained by moral suasion applied by the Central Bank, with the strong backing of the Ministry of Finance, and through a requirement that all loan applications above a certain value limit be submitted to the Central Bank for review.

While the revitalisation of the private sector in public-sector-oriented Arab countries has made monetary policy a more effective instrument of demand management, it is still the performance of the public sector and the size of development expenditures in relation to government domestic revenues which determine the degree of internal financial stability. Domestic resource mobilisation is hampered by the lack of adequate financial intermediation and the lack of incentives for savings. The absorption of excess liquidity can be achieved effectively through the sale of government bonds to the public at attractive interest rates, instead of borrowing from the Central Bank, and through the sale of debt instruments by private firms to investors.[18] Unfortunately, this type of financial intermediation in a number of Arab countries has so far been rudimentary and narrow, while financial assets have been relatively unliquid. The traditional policy of low interest rates originally introduced to encourage investment and subsequently maintained, partly to protect a relatively inefficient public sector, usually provides the saver with a negative real rate of return. When residents were allowed to keep foreign currency accounts in both Egypt and Sudan, the interest rates they were yielding were in sharp contrast to the interest paid on domestic currency deposits. It then becomes profitable for the saver, the exchange risk notwithstanding, to obtain a loan in domestic currency and convert it into a foreign exchange deposit. Moreover, while financial intermediation and the openness of the economy to the rest of the world have increased markedly over the past few years in countries such as Egypt, this has mainly benefited depositors by offering them higher yields on their assets and has been directed towards short-term trade financing. Relatively little has been channelled into long-term domestic investment in productive capacity. Yet, commercial banks hold over $1.8 billion in net foreign assets abroad, mostly invested in the Eurodollar market.[19] Presumably, these financial structural distortions are a manifestation of economies in transition in which the private sector is being revitalised, while the necessary institutional changes lag behind, giving the public sector time to adjust to a new competitive environment.

III. Arab Economic Integration and the Issue of Policy Co-ordination: A Brief Note

It is an axiom of economic policy that at least as many instruments are needed as there are policy objectives. If a certain rate of growth is pursued and the additional requirement is set that a certain rate of inflation is not to be exceeded, then the level of government spending, the interest rate, the exchange rate, official reserves and the level of labour migration may all need to be employed as policy instruments. However, if some of these instruments are turned into additional objectives, such as exchange-rate stability, low interest rates and the maintenance of the level of official reserves, policy-makers fall into a situation of conflicting objectives and insufficient instruments. There have been examples among Arab countries of such conflicting objectives. With the increase in the degree of 'openness' of the Arab economies to the rest of the world, there is need for greater responsiveness to international financial trends, most particularly in interest-rate policy. At the intra-regional level, exchange-rate policy co-ordination and the co-ordination of the domestic interest-rate structure, coupled with some agreement on domestic liquidity expansion, could constitute the first modest steps towards monetary integration. Although attempts at co-ordinating exchange-rate policies among Bahrain, Qatar and the UAE have so far been short-lived, the similarity in the trade regimes and institutional environments of these Gulf countries offers good prospects for effective policy co-ordination. This would ensure at least that their macroeconomic and exchange-rate policies did not work at cross purposes. Since the economies of these countries are wide open to outside shocks and are characterised by a high degree of capital mobility, their monetary authorities do not in any case enjoy much autonomy in formulating policy. Hence, such policy co-ordination would not result in any significant loss of sovereignty.

Arab countries might also reap substantial benefits by co-ordinating their policies with regard to labour movements. So far, labour has moved relatively freely among Arab countries but there is not enough information available to make it possible even to monitor such movements. Although significant social costs are incurred in both the labour-exporting and the recipient countries, little evidence has been gathered as to the magnitude of the economic impact. Suffice it to mention here the opportunity cost to the economy of the labour skills exported and the tax revenues lost to government budgets. A first step in assessing the costs and benefits of labour migration among Arab countries would be the exchange of information by those countries on the composition of the labour force which crosses their borders. Policy co-ordination could then make a start on a joint taxation approach to compensate labour-exporting countries for education and training costs.

With or without policy co-ordination among the Arab countries, the prospects for Arab economic integration would be strengthened if the non-oil countries could foster an institutional environment that would attract direct investment in productive enterprises by the oil-producing countries. From the point of view of the oil-exporting countries, a policy of exchange-rate stability and a moderate expansion of domestic liquidity would, given their substantial balance-of-payments surpluses, require an offsetting capital outflow, preferably in the form of long-term investments abroad and foreign aid.[20] The oil-exporting countries have in fact attempted to reduce their current account surpluses by increasing their local development expenditure and have tried to recycle their marginal surpluses into long-term investments which will generate a steady stream of income in the future, when oil resources are depleted. However, this policy of diversification of the countries' sources of wealth can only be gradual and will take time. Meanwhile, oil-exporting countries in the Gulf have accumulated reserves, mostly in short-term assets with rates of return substantially lower than the rate of the appreciation of petroleum prices over the past decade. In this respect, the monetary authorities, together with the investment companies which have increased in numbers and sophistication in the region, must devise a strategy for converting short term assets into more remunerative long-term investments which will aim at preserving the real value of their oil wealth. An attractive investment strategy may be to invest in other Arab countries, particularly in sectors which correspond to the consumption needs of the oil-exporting countries, such as the food-production sector. However, this requires a willingness to incur risks and the entrepreneurial ability to identify attractive ventures and to follow up the investment throughout its entire gestation period. Equally, the host country must offer, through a combination of competitiveness, accessibility and institutional factors, sufficiently attractive rates of return and the long-term stability to justify the risks incurred.

Notes

1. For the SDR, these margins are now 7.25 per cent on either side of the peg. Of the countries mentioned, Kuwait has pegged its currency to a basket of currencies in which the dollar has a heavier weight than in the SDR basket.

2. Exceptionally, there was a wave of speculation against the UAE dirham, leading to a weakening of the currency in the period from November 1976 to January 1977. This was arrested and reversed through strong intervention by the Currency Board at the end of January 1977.

3. Lee Preston and Karim Nashashibi, *Trade Patterns in the Middle East: Data for 1966* (American Enterprise Institute: 1970), Table II-2.

4. While the 'confrontation' states in the Arab—Israeli conflict received the largest share of aid, other Arab countries, such as Sudan, Democratic Yemen and Morocco, also received substantial help.

5. In Egypt, the prices of a number of products manufactured by the public sector were decontrolled in 1978 and 1979. The liberalisation of foreign trade and the greater availability of goods from competing sources also entailed a reduction in the share of foreign trade covered by bilateral payments agreements. While at the beginning of 1974 Egypt maintained bilateral payments agreements with 31 countries, by 1977 these had been reduced to 9.

6. The point was reached in a number of labour-exporting countries where basic craft skills became scarce. This necessarily had a negative impact on labour productivity.

7. There are good grounds for assuming that these deposits have a lower rate of circulation than other monetary liabilities, since their use in domestic transactions is much less.

8. International Monetary Fund, *International Financial Statistics*, vol. 33, no. 9 (September 1980).

9. The term 'government' is used here in the broader public sector sense.

10. The private sector in oil-producing countries is not a recipient of foreign exchange earnings, except for investment income. It generates a large balance-of-payments deficit resulting from the large import bill, the outflow of remittances and investment abroad.

11. For an account of fiscal policy in oil-exporting countries, see David R. Morgan, 'Fiscal Policy in Oil-Exporting Countries, 1972–1978', *International Monetary Fund Staff Papers*, no. 1 (March 1979).

12. An interesting attempt at stabilising domestic rates, while at the same time curtailing capital outflows whenever foreign interest rates rise, is the 'swap' facility used by the Bahraini Monetary Agency. Under this facility, the Agency sells Bahraini dinars for dollars against a forward repurchase. The forward rate is set so as to cover the interest rate differential between the desired domestic rate for dinar deposits and the actual dollar deposit interest rate. This facility worked well as long as the dollar was depreciating, but, as it stabilised, the outflow of funds from Bahrain towards other countries offering higher interest rates on foreign currency deposits increased.

13. This policy precipitated a banking crisis in the UAE in late 1976, when a reduction of government spending dried up the inter-bank market and put some smaller banks in difficulties. Lebanon has experienced similar problems.

14. Excluding foreign budgetary support. Data from Ministry of Finance, *Annual Budget* (Amman: Government of Jordan, 1976).

15. In Morocco, up to 30 per cent of total deposits must be held in treasury bonds. In Tunisia, banks must hold 18 per cent of their deposits in loans to the private sector and 25 per cent in long-term treasury bonds.

16. With the recent diversification of the banking sectors in Egypt and Sudan as a result of the entry of a number of foreign banks, absolute ceilings on credit have become difficult to establish. Consequently, Egypt has introduced a maximum loan/deposit ratio for new banks, while maintaining absolute ceilings for the others.

17. The private sector in Sudan is defined for monetary purposes as including public sector corporations.

18. Typically, private firms in developing non-oil Arab countries are under-capitalised and over-dependent on commercial bank credit. This often puts commercial banks in difficulties as their commitments in favour of manufacturing enterprises with weak productive and financial foundations become over-extended.

19. In contrast, net foreign assets of the Central Bank of Egypt were $4.2 billion. International Monetary Fund, *International Financial Statistics*, vol. 33, no. 4 (April 1980).

20. Oil output is taken as fixed and assumed not to be a policy variable.

COMMENT

Samir Makdisi

I propose to divide my comments on Mr Nashashibi's paper into two parts. The first part is intended to complement his paper by examining briefly certain aspects of the position and role of Arab financial intermediaries in the national economy. The second part pertains to a few major areas with which his paper deals.

1. Position and Role of Arab Financial Intermediaries

I shall begin with a survey of Arab financial systems and then proceed to discuss briefly the following three questions: (a) the financialisation of the Arab economies; (b) the role of the commercial banks and other financial institutions; and (c) alternative techniques for mobilising savings.[1]

a. Arab Financial Systems

The financial systems operating in the Arab world may be characterised as follows. First, they revolve essentially around the Central Bank and the commercial banks. The role of other financial institutions, while growing, remains relatively limited, with some Arab countries forging ahead of others in this area (e.g., Bahrain, Kuwait, Egypt, Jordan and Lebanon). In a few Arab countries (e.g., Sudan and Yemen), the non-bank financial sector is in the initial stages of development. On the basis of data for certain Arab countries (Egypt, Jordan, Morocco and Tunisia), it may be stated that the claims of non-commercial banking institutions do not comprise at present more than 10 per cent of total financial claims. In contrast, these ratios for the industrialised countries are generally much higher.

Secondly, while the commercial banking system encompasses the bulk of financial activities, there are important differences among Arab countries with regard to the position occupied by financial intermediaries in the national economy. If the ratio of financial claims to GNP is taken as one indicator of the participation of the financial system (in particular, the banking system) in the national economy, then the Arab countries can be divided into three categories. The first includes countries with relatively high ratios: Lebanon, Jordan, Egypt, the Syrian Arab Republic, Tunisia, Morocco and Algeria, although the ratios prevailing in some of these countries, e.g., Lebanon and Jordan, are much higher than those prevailing in other countries of this group.

The second category includes the countries with relatively low ratios, i.e., Iraq, Sudan and Yemen. The third category includes the oil-exporting countries: Libya, Saudi Arabia, Kuwait and the other Gulf states. These countries have relatively high ratios despite the fact that domestic financial activities in some of them are more limited than in other Arab countries. This is because a large portion of the accumulating oil revenue takes the form of financial claims on foreigners. Clearly, such ratios constitute only one indicator of the role played by the financial system in the national economy, but generally it may be stated that the higher this ratio, the greater the degree to which the domestic economy has been financialised.[2]

Thirdly, the degree to which decision-making in the banking sector is centralised or decentralised differs from one Arab country to another. In broad terms, two categories may be distinguished. The first includes countries where decision-making in the financial system is highly decentralised, the banking system comprising a number of competing banks which are largely privately managed (e.g., Lebanon, Jordan and the Gulf countries). The second category includes countries where the banking system has been nationalised and is managed under the direct supervision of the public sector (e.g., Iraq, the Syrian Arab Republic, Sudan and Algeria). Decision-making in these countries is much more centralised than in those of the first category. The degree of centralisation in decision-making has a direct bearing on the exercise of monetary policy: the higher the degree of centralisation, the greater the likelihood of effective compliance by the commercial banks and other financial institutions which prescribe monetary policy, i.e., the fewer the difficulties in the implementation of policy measures.

Fourthly, a number of Arab countries have forged ahead in developing their money and capital markets, notably Lebanon, Bahrain, Kuwait and Jordan. The Kuwaiti financial system has expanded rapidly, especially since 1974, i.e., after the initial oil price increases, and Bahrain has developed into an important offshore banking centre. All of these countries maintain a liberal exchange system, though the degree of freedom accorded to international economic transactions is greater in some countries than in others; for example, Lebanon does not maintain any restrictions whatsoever on current and capital transfers, whereas Jordan still retains a degree of control, particularly as far as transfers of capital by residents are concerned. The other oil-exporting countries (Iraq, Algeria and Libya) maintain controls and the public sector plays a dominant role in foreign trade. The same applies to certain other Arab countries, i.e., Democratic Yemen, the Syrian Arab Republic and Sudan. In contrast, Yemen maintains a liberal regime; to a lesser extent, so do Morocco and Tunisia, i.e., they maintain controls over certain categories of current capital payments. Egypt, which used to maintain strict controls, has tended to follow a more open policy in recent years.

It can thus be stated that a large number of the Arab economies are open to the world economy, as a result of the liberal exchange policies they maintain. Where the public sector dominates, however, the degree of openness is reduced. In general, Arab exchange regimes have been gradually liberalised, and, as is pointed out in Mr Nashashibi's paper, trade liberalisation in some of them has tended to stimulate banking operations.

Fifthly, the dramatic increase in oil revenues and the emergence of current account surpluses has fostered the creation of a number of regional (multinational) financial institutions, as well as national financial institutions with regional interests. I need not enumerate such institutions. Suffice it to say that they act as intermediaries for inter-Arab financial flows. The magnitude of such flows may not be as great as some observers might have wished, but the problem does relate partly to the inability of the non-oil Arab countries to attract sufficient funds for development purposes — or to absorb them, when they exist — and to the lack of an adequate network of regional financial links. Although these links are being established, their future development constitutes a major challenge for Arab financial planning.

b. Financialisation of the Arab Economies

The relationship of economic growth to the breadth and depth of financialisation of the national economy has been analysed in a number of studies.[3] The presumption underlying these analyses is that the development of the financial process helps to promote economic growth by giving rise to a more efficient system of mobilising savings and allocating them among investment outlets, within the context of overall national development plans and policy objectives. The purpose of this section is simply to give an idea of the degree of financialisation of the Arab economies.

Several criteria may be adopted to indicate the extent of financialisation of the national economy. For the purpose of these comments, and given the limitations of the available data, three ratios are utilised: total assets, domestic assets and deposits, each as a proportion of GNP or GDP, for two years: 1970 and the most recent year for which national income data are available (see Table 4.6). It might be added that these ratios should be treated as rough comparative indicators and in many cases do not reflect the actual state of financial development in individual countries as it concerns financial institutions or debt instruments.

With this reservation in mind, it can be observed from Table 4.6 that, for the majority of the countries included in it, the financialisation ratios increased during the 1970s. For a few countries, the increase was striking (e.g., Lebanon and Jordan).

Table 4.6: Financialisation Ratios for Arab Economies (percentages)

Country	Year	Total assets/ GNP	Domestic assets/ GDP	Total deposits/ GNP
Algeria	1970	60	54	34
	1977	82	66	33
Bahrain	1970	–	–	–
	1978	119	44	61
Egypt	1970	78	50	19
	1977	98	73	34
Iraq	1970	42	16 [a]	21
	1976	34	4 [a]	24
Jordan	1970	90	28	30
	1979	122	87	56
Kuwait	1970	82	14	46
	1977	75	32	36
Lebanon	1970	115	45	84
	1974	172	59	101
Libya	1970	56	7	28
	1977	49	19	17
Morocco	1970	45	32	22
	1978	62	58	26
Saudi Arabia	1970	45	10	22
	1978	122	7	20
Syrian Arab Republic	1970	70	52	18
	1978	67	60	20
Sudan	1970	29	24	9
	1976	43	40	12
Tunisia	1970	57	45	18
	1978	66	58	73
Yemen	1970	–	–	–
	1976	56	6	15

Notes: Assets are those of the banking system. However, data pertaining to assets of other financial institutions have been included when available. The valuation of foreign assets is that of the national authorities. [a] Claims of financial institutions other than deposit banks.
Source: Based on government sources and data in International Monetary Fund, *International Financial Statistics*, vol. 33, no. 9 (September 1980).

As observed earlier, three categories may be distinguished: (a) those with relatively high ratios (Lebanon, Jordan, Egypt, the Syrian Arab Republic, Tunisia and Morocco); (b) those with relatively low ratios (Iraq, Sudan and Yemen); and (c) those which are primarily oil exporters. Within each category, however, important variations exist. Concerning the first category, the highest ratios prevail in Lebanon and Jordan, which maintain liberal exchange systems, and especially in Lebanon, where the private sector, encouraged by the national authorities, has developed a highly active banking sector and money market. Jordan has also made important strides in recent years in developing its money and financial markets. The two countries, moreover, represent the smaller economies of the group. Jordan has tended in recent years to move in similar directions to those taken by Lebanon. This may partly explain why, for both countries, the divergence between the ratios for total assets and those for domestic assets is more marked than that for the remaining countries of the group, even though some of them have also been actively developing their domestic money and capital markets. It may tentatively be concluded, perhaps, that monetary or financial processes in Lebanon and Jordan have a greater influence on the national economy than in the other countries of the group.

As for the second category, one common characteristic is the particularly low ratio of deposits to GNP (ranging from 12 to 24 per cent in 1976). Iraq and Yemen also show very low ratios of domestic assets to GDP. In the case of Iraq, domestic claims by specialised banks on the private sector, though relatively limited, have in recent years been greater than the claims of the deposit banks. It would appear that substantial financialisation of the national economies of the countries in this category has yet to be achieved. However, where central planning has been adopted (e.g., in Iraq), it could act as a partial alternative to financial intermediation as a means of mobilising savings and channelling them into investment outlets.

As for the third category, which comprises the oil-exporting countries, the tremendous increase in oil revenues has led to relatively high ratios of total assets to GNP, largely the result of their accumulating foreign assets. This ratio is 75 per cent for Kuwait (1977), 119 per cent for Bahrain (1978) and 122 per cent for Saudi Arabia (1978). Given the special nature of these economies, and in the case of Saudi Arabia the still limited internal economic development, the gap between the total assets and domestic assets ratios would be expected to be wide indeed. The latter ratio stands, for the same years as indicated above, at 44 per cent for Bahrain, 32 per cent for Kuwait and as low as 7 per cent for Saudi Arabia. Bahrain's oil resources, and consequently its oil revenues, are much more limited than those of the other two countries. It is also a small, open economy which has developed into a trading and banking centre. These factors may help to explain its higher ratios for domestic assets and deposits. Kuwait has also made noticeable progress in developing its financial structure and markets, particularly, as already observed, since 1974, but its ratios for domestic assets and deposits remain low in comparison with a number of other Arab countries. Saudi Arabia clearly illustrates the case of an economy with a low degree of financialisation.[4]

c. The Role of Commercial Banks and Other Financial Institutions

Beyond the question of financialisation ratios, it has often been observed that the institutions and instruments available to the Arab financial markets need to be further developed. While this is true, considerable progress has already been made by certain Arab countries in this area. In addition to the commercial banks, most of the Arab countries have established specialised banks concerned with the provision of credit to various economic sectors. A few of these countries (particularly Kuwait, but also the UAE and Lebanon) have established investment banks or companies and in a few others (e.g., Sudan and Tunisia) savings institutions have been set up. In the case of Kuwait, investment institutions have been particularly active in mobilising private savings and channelling them to domestic and foreign outlets, or have acted as intermediaries for the placement of government funds abroad. While the particular aspects of the financial infrastructure which need to be developed may differ from one Arab country to another, the objective in each case should be to bring about a wider and more effective network of connections between the surplus and deficit units in the economy. This implies, among other things, the introduction of financial instruments tailored to the needs of actual and potential investors and the development of greater expertise in various specialised areas of financial operations. It also implies the establishment of active secondary markets and the pursuit by the government of policies which would help to create confidence in the new instruments. Beginnings in these directions have already been made in a number of Arab financial markets, e.g., the issuance of private and public bonds and government certificates (sometimes with rediscount facilities extended by the monetary authorities as a means of encouraging their use), the issuance of negotiable certificates of deposit, etc. Further, certain initial steps have been taken to establish secondary markets. In Kuwait, for example, the Arab Company for Trading Shares was created in 1977 to promote the secondary market in Kuwaiti dinar-denominated money market instruments. In Jordan, trading on the Amman Financial Market (established in 1978 to act as a stock exchange) has been expanded to include transactions in government development bonds. The Lebanese authorities are planning to create a discount house for the purpose of developing a secondary market, initially in government-issued bills.

With regard to the evaluation of Arab financial markets, two specific observations can be made.

First, the distinction between money and capital markets and between short-term and long-term financial operations is blurred, and, in any case, many observers argue that such a distinction is no longer as important as it might have been in the past. Many Arab banks now operate in both markets, as do certain other financial institutions, though the larger portion of their operations may be of a long-term nature. What matters is to enhance the ability of Arab financial institutions to change the nature of financial assets, i.e. to transform them from short-term debt instruments into long-term debt instruments more suited for the requirements of economic growth. This process has already begun in a number of Arab countries with the creation of various specialised institutions. In Kuwait, for example, the Credit and Savings Bank, one of three specialised banks, makes long-term loans at subsidised interest rates. The industrial Bank of Kuwait and the Kuwait Real Estate Bank have floated their own long-term bonds. Saudi Arabia now has specialised credit institutions which provide mostly long-term lending on concessionary terms. Similarly, specialised credit institutions in Jordan and Morocco have been active in providing long-term financing. Indeed, in recent years, credit extended by Moroccan specialised banks has comprised about 30 per cent of total domestic credit, a high ratio in comparison with the corresponding ratios prevailing in other Arab countries.

It is not the purpose of this brief survey to examine how this process can be further enhanced but rather to underscore the importance of developing national savings institutions with the objective of both broadening the financial infrastructure and strengthening the habit of national thrift. The reason for stressing this point is that the present availability of huge financial resources arising from oil receipts could lead to an undue reliance on 'readily' available resources. In the longer run (i.e., when the oil revenues are depleted), this reliance, by weakening the development of national savings, could prove detrimental to economic growth. This applies to both the oil exporters and the deficit Arab countries, which now tend to rely on the flow of funds from the oil-exporting countries.

The second observation that can be made is that in the oil-exporting countries, the monetary impact of government operations manifests itself through net domestic spending by the government. As illustrated in Mr Nashashibi's paper, this net spending has become the primary determinant of money supply. The increasing oil revenues have led to substantially higher levels of net government spending, augmenting the pressures on domestic resources.

The fact that oil revenues accrue, in the first instance, to the governments of these countries places them at the core of the development process at home and has permitted them substantially to influence regional developments as well. The dominant financial position enjoyed by these governments tends to curtail the role which the financial sector can play in the national economy. The government can determine, to a very large extent, whether its resources are to be invested via public sector bodies or indirectly via financial intermediaries, and, subject to the constraints of absorptive capacity, it decides the extent to which these resources are to be used locally, regionally and internationally.

The activities of banks and other financial institutions have thus become highly dependent upon governmental decisions with regard to economic activity and the allocation of national savings.

d. Alternative Techniques for Mobilising Savings and Channelling Investment

Traditionally, three alternative techniques are available: financial intermediation, central planning and the fiscal system.[5] While all three techniques are at their disposal, some Arab countries have come to rely on certain techniques more than on others. Their choice has, in large measure, been determined by the roles assigned to the public and private sectors in the national economy. In those economies where the public sector has become dominant, financial intermediation is of much less importance than in the other Arab economies, while central planning and the fiscal system are utilised heavily. In the oil-exporting countries, on the other hand, the fiscal system provides the dominant technique, by reason of the position occupied by the oil resources. In all the Arab countries, however, there remains substantial scope for developing the financial structure and the role of financial intermediaries in the national economy. The alternative techniques for mobilising savings can therefore be regarded at this stage as complementary rather than competitive. Given the limited development of the financial structure, policy planning could aim at the expansion of the financial markets and the improvement of the fiscal system, which in many countries is highly inefficient. Ultimate reliance on any one of the above alternatives is a matter for each country to decide in the light of both economic and non-economic considerations.

2. Exchange Regimes and Monetary Policy

The following comments are grouped in accordance with the three topics taken up in Mr Nashashibi's paper, namely (a) exchange-rate policy and the openness of the national economies (b) the exercise of monetary policy and (c) policy co-ordination.

a. Exchange-rate Policy and the Openness of the National Economies

The majority of the Arab economies – including the oil exporters – already maintain liberal exchange regimes, and the others are undergoing a process of liberalisation. Mr Nashashibi refers to three consequences of this liberalisation process. The first is the marked expansion in the banking sector in a number of Arab countries with, as its corollary, a growing divergence in the levels of interest prevailing at home and abroad. In a broader context, the greater openness of the national economies has rendered monetary management more complex. The second consequence is the increased import levels recorded by the non-oil Arab economies, financed in part by increased unrequited transfers. The third consequence of this process is that interactions with the world economy have tended to stimulate national financial markets.

At present, the Arab countries may be divided into five categories according to their exchange-rate policies. The first includes countries which peg their currencies to the SDR, namely Jordan and four oil-exporting countries: Bahrain, Qatar, Saudi Arabia and the UAE. Except for Jordan, they all maintain deviation margins of 7.25 per cent. The second category includes countries which peg their currencies to a basket of the currencies of their major trading partners, namely Kuwait and the North African countries of Algeria, Morocco and Tunisia. The third includes countries whose currencies are pegged to the dollar, namely Democratic Yemen, Iraq, Libya, Oman and Yemen. In the fourth category are countries which also peg their currency to the dollar but which maintain parallel exchange markets, namely Egypt, the Syrian Arab Republic and Sudan. The single member of the fifth category is Lebanon, whose exchange rate is market-oriented, with occasional intervention by the Central Bank in order to maintain orderly exchange conditions.

Concerning these categories three observations can be made. The first is that many Arab countries desire to maintain relative exchange-rate stability by pegging their currencies to a basket, either their own basket or the SDR basket, rather than to single currencies. The second observation is that relative cross-rate stability has been maintained within each of two subgroups of the Arab countries, namely the group of countries whose currencies are pegged to the dollar and the oil-exporting countries whose currencies are pegged to the SDR. With respect to the the oil-exporting countries, these relatively stable cross-rates have been maintained, as mentioned in Mr Nashashibi's paper, despite the permissible 7.25 per cent margins. Thirdly, to the extent that the basket of currencies of major trading partners is not too unlike the basket making up the SDR, it can tentatively be stated that the two broad movements among the Arab currencies are represented by those pegged to the dollar, on the one hand, and those pegged to the SDR, on the other.

Since the majority of the Arab countries maintain liberal exchange regimes, the exchange rates of their currencies are not dependent on indirect support exercised through various controls over payments. One can only assume that the rates linking national currencies to the dollar or to a basket of currencies have been correctly judged to be realistic and are therefore defensible.

This is clearly not the case with respect to the Arab countries which maintain parallel markets. They are still, in fact, in transition towards the stage of maintaining realistic rates. The same may perhaps be said of those Arab countries which maintain relatively strict controls on outward payments. However, in all these countries, the public sector dominates the economy. One issue which arises, therefore, is how to define a 'liberal' regime in such circumstances, so that proper comparisons can be made and a realistic assessment of exchange-rate policy attempted. What criteria should one adopt for the purpose of comparing the different Arab exchange and trade regimes, including their exchange-rate policies? When one speaks of possible integration and thus of the need for some policy co-ordination, such an issue is bound to arise.

A related question is whether it is desirable to move towards stable cross-rates among the Arab currencies, as an initial step towards closer monetary integration, i.e., even before other monetary co-ordination measures have been instituted. The Latin American and African experiences are perhaps instructive in this regard, as is the experience of the Gulf countries.

b. The Exercise of Monetary Policy

Mr Nashashibi discusses the exercise of monetary policy in the Arab economies according the three subgroups: (a) the oil-exporting economies, (b) the market-oriented economies and (c) the public-sector-oriented economies.

Monetary developments in the oil-exporting countries are basically determined by fiscal policy. In the short run, the level of net government spending is the basic instrument of demand management. However, with the gradual diversification of the economic structure, it should be increasingly possible to regulate demand by means of additional instruments, such as exchange-rate policy, interest-rate policy and credit controls. In this connection, Mr Nashashibi mentions [p. 116] that the appreciation of the national currency could be an effective anti-inflationary measure. This is true. But exchange-rate policy may seek other major short-term and longer-term objectives. To what extent, therefore, can the exchange rate be used as a deliberate anti-inflationary measure?

The divergence between domestic interest rates and those prevailing abroad has been cited as an important factor governing short-term capital flows. This has created problems for some of the Arab countries, but while in some of them greater co-ordination between the levels prevailing at home and abroad may be possible, in certain other Arab economies, i.e. non-oil market-oriented economies, this may prove to be a difficult task, especially if the central bank discount rate is not an effective instrument. Under these circumstances, the monetary authorities can influence the level of interest rates indirectly by influencing the level of domestic liquidity. The objective of the interest-rate policy, in this case, may not be compatible with other policy objectives. This is a complex problem which must be examined with respect to each Arab country, so that an assessment can be made as to how effective the interest rate is as an instrument of control at the disposal of the authorities.

In market-oriented economies, credit to the private sector, as well as government deficits, influences monetary developments. Typically, reserve requirements, other ratios and credit ceilings have been used to regulate credit flows. Mr Nashashibi has emphasised that it is only private sector credit which is susceptible to control by the monetary authorities, and that little can be done about government spending [p. 118]. However, it would seem that this is not equally applicable to all the market-oriented economies since it would depend partly upon the degree of autonomy which the monetary authorities enjoyed in pursuing their policies. Is monetary policy in these countries simply one of accommodating the financial needs of the government? Or is it possible for the government to reach agreement with the central bank concerning the extent to which budgetary deficits can be covered by bank credit, particularly if the contemplated deficit is not geared towards the build-up of the capital stock? Such agreements could become part of policy co-ordination in individual Arab countries. Perhaps Mr Nashashibi can shed some light on this issue.

In public-sector-oriented economies, monetary policy basically accommodates the level of domestic finance as set by the government. But, as is pointed out by Mr Nashashibi [p. 120], the recent liberalisation of these economies has assigned to monetary policy a potentially more active role in demand management. Credit ceilings have, for example, been used to regulate credit to the private sector. None the less, the level of government expenditure, and particularly development expenditure, is what determines the degree of monetary stability. A major issue here is that financial markets do not as yet play a significant role in mobilising savings, since they are in the early stages of their development. But, as has been indicated, in public sector economies, the fiscal system and central planning have acted as alternatives to financial intermediation for mobilising savings and channelling them into investment outlets. While there is substantial scope for developing the financial markets, this has to be considered alongside the desire of the authorities to retain control over the savings/investment process. Many of the required savings will have to be generated in the public sector itself. Similarly, the effective way to control financial instability is to exercise control over the level of government spending. Still, the role of financial intermediation may be allowed to develop, particularly if public sector enterprises and bodies are engaged in the financial market alongside private entities. It is therefore correct to emphasise the development of these markets as an important policy objective.

Again, Mr Nashashibi might be invited to comment on what steps can be taken in this regard.

c. Policy Co-ordination

At the national level, one major problem, as illustrated in Mr Nashashibi's paper, is to reconcile various policy objectives. In a broad sense, the desire for accelerated development spending must be reconciled with the desire to maintain relative monetary stability in open economies. An example of a more specific problem is the reconciliation of the interest-rate levels prevailing at home and abroad. The ability to cope with this issue may differ from one Arab country to another. The greater the role of market forces in the economy, the more difficult it will be for the authorities to reconcile these levels. Given various political factors and considerations, how readily can the reconciliation of these objectives be achieved? What steps can be envisaged? Should the monetary authorities be accorded greater or complete autonomy in their area of decision-making?

At the regional level, one major issue pertains to the reconciliation of exchange-rate policy and policies governing domestic liquidity. Again, given existing differences in the management of the Arab economies, their varying degrees of openness and differences in the effectiveness of monetary policies, how can the Arab economies, in practice, move in the direction of policy co-ordination, assuming that such a move is desirable as part of the integration process? Should the Arab countries try first to create similar foreign exchange regimes and financial environments? Does the importance of policy co-ordination depend upon the type of economic integration being envisaged?

A proper understanding of these issues is important if one is to map out the course which Arab monetary integration should take as part of overall economic integration.

Notes

1. A fourth aspect pertains to Arab financial institutions concerned with Arab development. This subject, however, is dealt with in other conference papers.
2. It has been observed that, whereas economic development is accompanied by a rising financialisation ratio, it tends eventually to level off. See R.W. Goldsmith, *Financial Structure and Development* (New Haven, Conn: Yale University Press, 1969), p. 44.
3. See R.W. Goldsmith, *Financial Structure and Development* and E.S. Shaw, *Financial Deepening and Economic Development* (Oxford: Oxford University Press, 1973).
4. A comparison with the financial ratios prevailing in the industrialised countries of the West reveals that the domestic assets ratios in these countries generally tend to be much higher than in the Arab (and other developing) countries. This is mainly attributable to their more developed financial structures, particularly with regard to financial institutions other than commercial banks. These countries also tend to have higher ratios of total assets to GNP.
5. Inflation is an additional technique whereby savings are diverted from the consumer to the business sector, as a consequence of the inflationary process.

GENERAL DISCUSSION

1. Mohammed Labib Shoukair

I would like to pose four questions to the author. First, Mr Nashashibi seems to believe that if the Arab countries are to achieve any integration at all, they must all reconvert their economies to the market system. Therefore, in the case of an economy where the public sector has a role of a certain importance, that role would have to be eliminated or substantially reduced prior to any integration. Is this impression correct or am I mistaken?

Secondly, even if one assumes that the author recognises two types of economies in the Arab world, those which are basically market economies and those characterised by substantial government intervention, how does this affect the process of integration? How will this process take place? This is really the point we expected the author to raise in his paper, because integration in the Arab region poses the same monetary problems as in other regions, as well as the additional problem of disparate economic systems.

Thirdly, the author would appear to believe that the free exchange system is the only system that should be adopted. This is the point of view of the International Monetary Fund and one which has provoked controversy in several quarters. Given the author's advocacy of free exchange and expansion, what bearing does this have on the subject of development in these countries? Does Mr Nashashibi indeed give priority to development and, at the same time, advocate complete freedom of exchange, thereby permitting foreign trade to determine the course of economic development? Does he believe that development can occur in the context of a free exchange system?

Fourthly, the author suggests that the more banks there are in a particular country, then the sounder will be the economy. He refers to one Arab country which up to 1974 had only four banks but now has 38 foreign banks, not to mention its Arab banks, and prides itself on this development. Does Mr Nashashibi believe that the number of banks is in itself a factor in development? Further, would the opening in a developing country of a large number of foreign banks, linked to foreign countries, serve the objective of development or of achieving even a modicum of freedom and independence? Or might not such a situation increase dependency, which in turn would affect the pattern of development in ways which were detrimental to the process of Arab monetary integration?

2. Fouad Morsi

In reading Mr Nashashibi's paper, I felt that it amounted to an undeclared defence of IMF policies with respect to the so-called 'developing' countries, and especially the countries of the Arab region.

Criticisms of IMF policies abound. For example, in the Arusha Document, issued at a meeting held there in June and July of 1980, it was pointed out that IMF policies suffer from three defects: first, they are not scientific; secondly, they are not objective; and, thirdly, they are far from being neutral.

I shall therefore confine my remarks to the country I know best, which is Egypt. As I see it, the trouble with the IMF approach to the economic problems of various countries is that it is essentially monetary, whereby quantitative monetary and financial measures are applied in order to arrive in the end at a kind of monetary balance. In applying this approach, the IMF follows a formal, linear course. It is indeed quite possible to achieve monetary balance without regard for or even at the expense of development considerations, whether economic or social. It is precisely for this reason that we prefer, in the case of Egypt, a structural approach to the treatment of its problems.

When Egypt was facing pressing development problems in the early 1960s, the IMF described its development plan as being too ambitious. The policy recommended by the IMF for coping with these development problems, which Egypt finally adopted in the 1970s, can be summarised as follows:

(a) *Balancing the public budget.* This was to be done both by curbing public spending and by increasing government revenues. In practice, this meant cutting back on development expenditure and abolishing price supports for staple commodities, while burdening the workers with taxes; for with progressive tax exemptions for foreign capital and even for local capital, the government no longer had any other recourse than to levy both indirect and direct taxes on the income of government and public sector employees;

(b) *Adjusting the balance of payments.* This was to be done by limiting imports and expanding exports. Whenever the government appeared incapable of taking this friendly advice, the ready IMF solution was to recommend devaluation of the Egyptian pound, which it considered overvalued. In view of the well-known inflexibility of Egyptian imports and exports, the only effect devaluation had was to increase the outside world's claims against Egypt;

(c) *Balancing costs and prices.* This meant that the products of the public sector itself should be valued according to their real cost; hence, prices should fully express this cost. It meant, in short, that the public sector had to give up its two-fold function within society, a function which was at once economic and social. Behind many of the products or services which it provided was an effort to achieve legitimate social objectives. It is true that the public sector's being prevented in the past from selling its products according to their real cost meant that it was forfeiting the generation of profits which could eventually have been invested in development projects. But the profits being generated now are not being invested in development.

In short, in order to achieve monetary balance, development objectives, both economic and social, have to be sacrificed. Such an approach leads, in fact, to a dead end. We all recall how these policies pushed Egypt to the brink of civil war in January 1977 and, in practice, led to a nearly exclusive reliance on private enterprise and foreign aid. Whereas the inflation rate in 1970 did not exceed 5 per cent by the highest estimate, it had reached, by 1979, between 40 and 50 per cent. Foreign debt, which stood at £1.2 billion in 1970, increased to more than £14 billion in 1979. And all this has been accompanied by widening social disparities.

3. Adel Hussein

It appears to me that the author, in his defence of current practices, is guilty of certain biases which affect the validity of the conclusions he draws. His bias against the policies previously followed leads him to claim that the primary reason for the increase in monetary surpluses is the liberal policies pursued by the Arab countries, whereas the real reason for this phenomenon is the rise in oil prices. These surpluses should have been accompanied by adjustments in the economic, financial and monetary policies of the surplus countries for the purpose of facilitating investments within the Arab region. However, the policy adjustments which occurred were not in this direction; the 'open door' policies practised by the Arab countries have been essentially directed towards the North. Such policies — currently being followed by oil-producing countries and non-oil countries alike — indicate that the IMF has succeeded in implementing its policies. Mr Nashashibi's paper can be commended for making clear the extent of the success achieved.

The open door to the North has manifested itself *inter alia* in increased Arab imports from the Western industrialised countries and not in any increase in inter-Arab trade. The expansion of imports from the industrialised countries, thanks to the 'open door' policy IMF-style, brought Egypt's balance of payments to the point of collapse and overwhelmed the economy with bank debts, especially between 1974 and 1976. While Mr Nashashibi concedes that this type of economic

Trade and Exchange Regimes in the Arab Countries 141

liberalisation has not led the way to an increase in inter-Arab trade, he observes that active movements of capital and labour have taken place across Arab borders. However, Gulf financial flows have always moved in accordance with outside decisions. Mr Dajani spoke about tied and untied flows, meaning by the latter that they were not restricted to specific projects. In practice, all untied flows are influenced by IMF decisions regarding their volume, type and timing. Untied loans are provided by the Arab development fund within the framework of financing agreements worked out with the World Bank.

This leads, in fact, to the question of Arab financial surpluses as a whole. The basic problem here does not lie in the fact that the bulk of the surpluses is invested abroad but rather in the fact that they are subject to direct outside management and that, consequently, the Arab countries have no control over them. If the movement of Arab surpluses within and outside the Arab region is subject to foreign control, then we must ask whether it is in the interest of those who control Arab financial movements that Arab funds should be used to foster economic and monetary integration and national unification. The answer must be in the negative; for the interests of foreign groups or powers conflict with the objective of integrating the oil region with the rest of the Arab economy, and they will not hesitate to use force, if need be, to prevent the achievement of that objective.

There is no question but what an independent national will is a primary prerequisite of economic integration and financial and monetary policy unification.

4. Rattan Bhatia

The harmonisation of exchange rates may be a difficult issue for any prospective Arab monetary union if the exchange policy is to serve different objectives for different member countries. On the other hand, if it is to serve the same objective, it would appear that the needs of the weakest country, or group of countries, will have to be the main consideration in determining exchange-rate policy. In practice, this means that the policy will have to be geared to the balance-of-payments needs of the non-oil countries, with consumer subsidies providing the counter-inflationary instrument in the oil-producing countries.

The alternative exchange-rate policy in such a union, i.e., one conforming to the needs of the oil-producing countries, would have undesirable consequences. I have in mind such consequences as (a) a progressive weakening of the non-oil sector within such a union and (b) progressively larger subsidy transfers from the oil-producing to the non-oil countries of the union, subsidies which would not necessarily be of the most suitable nature or even confined to the productive sectors.

5. John Williamson

I, too, would like to discuss exchange-rate policy. I have, it is true, said that convertibility plus a concerted exchange-rate policy is not equivalent to the establishment of a single currency, and I stand by my statement; but this does not for one moment imply that I would deny the value of a move to a concerted exchange-rate policy. On the contrary, I believe this is an action that could be taken in the short run; what I wish to do is to consider the form that such action should take.

It is important here to distinguish between the two dimensions of exchange-rate policy that I have already mentioned: the question of what to peg to and the question of changing the peg. Prior to the floating of the currencies of the industrialised countries in 1973, the Arab world (with the exception of Lebanon) was in practice a fixed exchange-rate area. Since 1973, it has not been. Some nine or ten Arab currencies are pegged to the dollar, others to the SDR and still others to their own individual currency baskets, while the Lebanese currency still floats. What this means in practice is that over 75 per cent of inter-Arab exchange rates (the cross-rates between Arab currencies) are liable to change — not as a result of some deliberate Arab decision that an exchange-rate change is desirable, but rather as an accidental by-product of exchange-rate changes in the industrialised countries' currencies. In so far as exchange-rate stability is a supporting factor in stimulating trade (and I cite evidence to this effect in my own paper), the elimination of this arbitrary volatility in Arab cross-rates is clearly desirable. What is needed to this end is the adoption of a common peg for all the Arab currencies.

The other dimension of exchange-rate policy is the flexibility offered by deliberate changes in the peg. The case for suppressing this form of flexibility seems to me far less compelling; indeed, about the last thing one should seek to harmonise are inflation rates, given the pressures that arise to harmonise them upwards. Very slow changes in central rates could eliminate those pressures to which Mr Bhatia has referred. There is no inconsistency whatsoever between retaining this form of deliberate flexibility and suppressing the random volatility that results from the present diversity of pegging practices.

The key question is what the common peg should be. There is not as yet any agreement as to what should be the ultimate criterion in choosing such a peg: whether its purpose should be to minimise the variability of the balance of trade, of real income, of employment, of the terms of trade, of the distribution of income or of the allocation of resources. All these criteria have been suggested in the recent literature on this subject. However, this ambiguity is perhaps not too crucial, since, with the exception of the terms of trade — which ought not, in my view, to be used as a criterion[1] — all of them seem to indicate the desirability of seeking to stabilise some element in the real exchange rate. The question arises as to just which concept is appropriate. Should one use straight trade weights or 'elasticity weights' (i.e., trade weights that give a proportionately larger role to the more price-elastic trade flows)? Should the trade flows include imports, exports, both, or some part of both, etc?

While care must be taken in adopting any given concept, the results of the three existing empirical studies[2] of the implications of alternative pegging practices for Arab currencies are sufficiently striking to merit attention. Each of these studies finds that, for every Arab currency covered, over every period studied (with just one exception in about 80 observations), a peg to the SDR would have resulted in less variability in the nominal exchange rate (in some cases import-weighted, in other cases trade-weighted) than a peg to the dollar. In every case, except that of Morocco which pegged its currency to its own basket of currencies, an SDR peg would also have been better than the peg actually used. These results are sufficiently pronounced to suggest that, of the obvious candidates for the choice of a common peg for the Arab currencies, the SDR would almost certainly prove the most satisfactory.

There are, however, disadvantages in using a basket rather than a currency as a peg: notably, the country's inability to intervene directly in the unit in terms of which it is pegging, and the lack of a forward market that would enable its traders to cover trade denominated in third currencies. So long as the SDR remains no more than a basket unit of account and an official reserve asset, these are serious arguments against adopting the SDR as a common peg. But need the SDR remain a non-currency? Arab financial power could, for example, be deployed to establish the SDR as an actively-traded currency in the offshore (Eurocurrency) markets. A decision could be taken to denominate the oil price in SDRs and to demand payment in (Euro-) SDRs. Such action could within months create an active Euro-SDR market adequate to support intervention directly in SDRs and thus to permit the pegging to the SDR, not just of the Arab currencies but also of those of other developing countries which currently face the same dilemma as that faced by the Arabs but lack a similar opportunity to reform the system through their own initiative.

6. Shakour Shaalan

Mr Morsi has raised some serious questions concerning the policy advice of the IMF to developing countries and has characterised it as being generally 'catastrophic'. He identifies five essential areas to which the Fund has directed its attention and takes Egypt as a case in point. First, he states that the Fund has attempted to influence the economic philosophies of certain countries, with the basic aim of moving them away from a philosophy of central control in order to make their economies more market-oriented. Secondly, the IMF, in its policy recommendations, aims at what he terms monetary equilibrium. Thirdly, and closely related to this, is the Fund's so-called obsession with attaining a balanced budget. Fourthly, balance-of-payments equilibrium, according to the Fund, is a desired objective to be attained by changes in the exchange rate. Lastly, undue emphasis is placed by the Fund on adjusting cost/price relationships, particularly in the public economic sector. Mr Morsi concludes, referring to the case of Egypt, that the Fund's policy recommendations contributed to a sharp increase in the inflation rate, rising foreign indebtedness and the food riots of January 1977.

I wish to correct these misconceptions. It may be best to start with Mr Morsi's conclusions about accelerating inflation and rising foreign indebtedness in Egypt and outline their main causes. In a country that has, over an extended period of time, experienced a high rate of monetary expansion rising to 30-40 per cent annually, essentially brought about by mounting budget deficits due to rising government expenditures, caused in turn, in large part, by the pricing policies of public sector enterprises, it would seem to me that policy action should address these issues. This is where both the Egyptian authorities and the Fund are in full agreement. The Fund does not impose specific recommendations as to which expenditures to cut or which particular prices to increase. This is left entirely to the country concerned and will depend on the social objectives the authorities wish to pursue. The Fund does not aim at achieving a balanced budget, rather it attempts to reduce total monetary expansion to a level which is non-inflationary and which will support a viable investment programme. Egypt has pursued an active development policy; for this policy to be sustainable, it needs to be accompanied by policies aimed at mobilising domestic savings, in particular public sector savings. As to the balance of payments, the Fund does not aim at attaining a balance-of-payments equilibrium. The IMF fully realises that developing countries, by the very nature of their economies, are likely to have a deficit on current account, which is financed by capital inflows. True, in an inflationary situation the exchange rate may constitute an important policy tool for influencing the level of exports and imports and for promoting viable investments.

I do not wish to elaborate on the causes of the 1977 riots in Egypt. Suffice it to say that these were not caused by IMF policy prescriptions. I am not in a position to elaborate further on this point.

Let me conclude by noting that when any country has, over a long period of time, engaged in economic mismanagement, the necessary corrective medicine cannot be altogether pleasant in the short run. The Fund has recently realised that the process of adjustment may take longer to correct than had previously been anticipated. Accordingly, recent policy has aimed at approaching the adjustment question in a more gradual way and at supporting adjustment policies by providing significantly more financial resources.

7. Mabid Al-Jarhi

Mr Nashashibi calls for exchange-rate and monetary policy co-ordination as among the first steps towards monetary integration. As for monetary policy, he specifically mentions the co-ordination of the domestic interest-rate structure, coupled with some agreement on domestic liquidity expansion.

Monetary policy co-ordination has been mentioned in the economic literature as a means to equalise rates of inflation and hence to stabilise exchange rates. However, as I have pointed out in previous comments, the effectiveness of this approach is highly questionable. Exchange-rate policy co-ordination, in particular, is likely to be ineffective owing to a number of drawbacks, including the following:

(a) The automatic *ex ante* consistency of price targets (exchange rates) and quantity targets (money stocks) cannot be ensured;
(b) Since participating countries retain the power to exercise their own discretion, as well as the instruments necessary for this, there is no mechanism which would automatically prevent them from violating the co-ordination rules;
(c) There is no means of ensuring the automatic renewal of co-ordination agreements;
(d) There is no automatic process through which the discretion of the individual countries is reduced over time.

Such an approach cannot, therefore, ensure the predictability of exchange rates. However, monetary and exchange-rate policy co-ordination might be desirable if it aimed at the more modest objective of rationalising market structures, with a view to reducing the costs of transactions in intra-regional trade.

8. Karim Nashashibi, in response

I feel that Mr Morsi's comments on the role of the IMF in developing countries are largely outside the scope of my paper and have been answered by Mr Shaalan. I shall therefore confine myself to questions asked by other participants, starting with those of Mr Makdisi.

He raises the question as to how one can define a liberal trade regime in the Arab context, where the public sector often dominates economic processes. My answer would be that one can have a large public sector or public involvement in all facets of the economy and, at the same time, maintain a liberal regime. Liberalism as it relates to Arab economic integration essentially means having a set of trade, payments and price policies consistent with the operations of a mechanism governed by the profit motive and thus capable of providing the necessary incentives for the development of trade and private capital flows among Arab countries. This implies the maintenance of a realistic exchange rate and the provision of facilities for import payments, debts and transfers of earnings. Mr Makdisi then asks whether it is desirable to move towards 'stable relationships' among Arab currencies as an initial step towards closer monetary integration. As I point out in my paper, the relationships among the Gulf currencies have been quite stable and whatever instability has arisen is attributable either to differentials in interest rates or to the excessive injection of liquidity into the economy by government spending. Hence, stable exchange-rate relationships depend to a large extent on the consistency of the use of the exchange-rate instrument with the use of other policy instruments. On the other hand, if economic integration is contemplated among countries which exhibit sharp differences with respect to trade restrictions and economic orientation, then such differences would have to be reduced before integration could be attempted in any meaningful sense. The evolution of the European Economic Community and the fact that various countries were permitted to join it only after they agreed to bring their policies into line with Community objectives offers a useful lesson in this respect.

I have pointed out that the use of exchange-rate policy as an anti-inflationary instrument can be quite effective in the Gulf countries because they have very little import substitution and hardly any exports other than oil. Therefore, the appreciation of the national currency does not reduce the competitiveness of these sectors. On the other hand, in the non-oil countries or in the oil-exporting countries with a more diversified resource base, exchange-rate policy must take into account potential effects on the various sectors of the economy, including potential exports and import substitutes. In such countries, its applicability as an anti-inflationary instrument would be much more restricted.

Mr Makdisi points out that the extent to which government spending can be controlled by the monetary authorities depends on their degree of autonomy. In my experience in the Arab world, I have found very little central bank autonomy, even in the market-oriented economies. In some countries, the central bank has been reduced to acting as an executive arm of the Ministry of Finance. In other countries, particularly those with a large and dynamic private sector, the central bank has become a useful intermediary between the government and the private sector. It conveys to the government the pressures it perceives in the market, serves as an adviser to the government and, in some cases, even initiates policy. At the same time, the central bank relays government policies to the private sector. Nevertheless, in all cases the government does exercise ultimate authority over the policies pursued by the central bank.

Mr Makdisi brings up the very important issue of ways and means of mobilising savings in the economy. In particular, he stresses that in public-sector-oriented economies, the fiscal system and the planning mechanism have been viewed as alternatives to the development of financial intermediation. The question really is whether such alternatives have been adequate in mobilising savings in these countries. My experience with public-sector-oriented economies in the Arab world has been that public enterprises have been mostly recording losses, while the government shoulders the burden of investment. This fundamental imbalance has caused inflationary pressures and frustrated investment plans, and I would strongly agree with Mr Makdisi that financial intermediation must be fostered as a policy objective to mobilise domestic resources in both public and private-sector-oriented economies. The promotion of such an objective does require, however, an economic environment which inspires in the private sector the necessary confidence and which offers it incentives to invest its resources. This brings us to Mr Makdisi's last question, namely should Arab countries try to create similar conditions in their foreign-exchange regimes and financial environments prior to attempting economic integration? I think I have replied to this question in my earlier answers. To summarise, let me say that the process of economic integration cannot be sustained solely by political will. Meaningful economic integration can only be attempted if it is firmly based on the mutual economic benefits to be reaped by the countries involved. Trade regimes must be compatible, in order to encourage the flow of trade, labour, remittances and capital. Economic behaviour must be sufficiently liberal to allow for the exploitation of new opportunities and to reap the benefits of integration.

Mr Shoukair notes my reference to the growth of banking in Egypt and wonders whether the proliferation in the number of banks is in itself a good thing. Certainly, it is not the number of banks but the degree of financialisation of the economy that is important, as well as the ability of the banking system to channel private savings into investment. In this respect, I feel that the problem with Egyptian banking has been its failure over the past few years to channel the large foreign-exchange deposits at the banks' disposal into productive domestic investment. Mr Shoukair also asks whether the implication of my paper is that we should move towards market-oriented economies where the price system predominates in order to ensure economic integration. In a related question, he asks whether development would still be possible if a public-sector-oriented economy were to shift towards a free enterprise system. It is perfectly possible to have economic integration between two centrally planned economies, as has happened to some extent among the Comecon countries. It would be built upon a planned division of labour in the productive structure and the co-ordination of the countries' policies. However, in the Arab context, the increased interaction which has developed among the Arab economies over the past decade has mostly been based upon the free movement of labour and the large aid flows emanating from countries committed to the free enterprise system. A number of public-sector-oriented economies have accommodated their exchange-rate policies and payment regulations to encourage this interaction. Looking ahead, the great potential benefits of Arab economic integration lie in the possibilities which would open up for movements of private and public capital from some surplus countries to deficit countries. This movement of capital would be based in the surplus countries on a sober evaluation of alternative investments, profitability and income flows in the long term, as well as on various geo-political considerations. Hence, there must be, in the recipient country, an economic environment which is conducive to profitability and the establishment of long-term confidence. This does imply a certain degree of encouragement of free enterprise. It can be consistent, however, with the public ownership of large subsectors of the economy, as long as these are responsive to the market mechanism and profit incentives. A reorientation of public-sector-dominated economies towards a larger role for the market mechanism should not be detrimental to the development process, as Mr Shoukair claims. As I mentioned before, the record of public enterprises in the Arab world has been poor. While governments may want to retain the initiative in large productive investment, the subjection of such public enterprises to the market mechanism and the profit motive would tend to improve their efficiency and profitability and would increase public savings and lead to greater development.

9. Rainer S. Masera[3]

I would like to comment briefly on the question of a commen currency, which I consider to be a general point relevant to any process of monetary integration and thus applicable to Latin American and Arab countries alike. The question has indeed been raised by Mr Williamson with reference to the Arab countries.

If I have understood Mr Williamson correctly, he suggests that, even if the question of monetary unification and thus of irrevocably fixed exchange rates among Arab countries cannot realistically be regarded as an immediate goal, there might still be important advantages for all Arab countries in the adoption of a common (adjustable) peg. He goes on to argue that the SDR may be a good basket to peg to, as shown by recent studies based on the so-called 'optimal peg' approach. He concedes that the SDR is not, properly speaking, a currency, which implies obvious disadvantages compared with pegging to a true international currency, but he goes on to conclude that the financial strength of the Arab countries is such as to make it possible for them to impose the SDR as a parallel currency in international financial transactions.

I would now like to raise two general points concerning this important subject and then pose a question to Mr Williamson. First of all, if my understanding of the available literature is correct, whatever criterion is selected, the new peg approach implies each country's finding an 'optimal' peg in relation to the particular structure of its economy. It thus follows that the process would lead to different results (baskets) for each country. If account is taken of the disparate economic conditions and structures of the 21 Arab countries, I doubt whether a common external peg such as the SDR would satisfy the optimisation requirements for all of them. Allowance must also be made for differences in the financial structures of the various Arab countries.

My second point concerns the two alternative methods for defining the basket, one defining it in terms of internal and the other in terms of external currencies. The SDR basket does not include any Arab currencies. Therefore, if the objective is to achieve a higher degree of short-term stability and long-term cohesion among the integrating currencies rather than between them and external currencies, consideration should be given to pegging to a basket of the currencies of the integrating area. This is indeed the European experience with the ECU basket. Let me stress that this approach would clearly require some complementary arrangements which would make it possible to pursue common policies *vis-à-vis* major external currencies.

My question for Mr Williamson concerns the very definition of the SDR basket to which he refers: does he have in mind the old or the new basket? Here, one cannot but note the disadvantages of pegging to a basket whose definition can be altered following decisions in which the integrating countries do not even have a voice, let alone a majority voice.

10. Mahmoud Sakbani

I would like to make one brief remark regarding the pegging arrangement. Mr Masera argues that optimising a pegging arrangement will depend on the economic structures of the countries concerned. While this is true in principle, its importance should be evaluated in terms of the interdependence of these structures and the objective function performed by the monetary authority.

For the Arab region, intra-union pegging would be effected in terms of the Arab dinar, which is a basket of the Arab currencies. Given the present volume of trade, this should not raise serious problems.

As for the outside world, obviously the common Arab currency or the jointly-pegged individual ones would peg, in turn, to a basket of foreign currencies, because they would float against the outside world.

As to how to select the basket, this would depend on the objective function performed by the monetary authority.

Statistical tests show, surprisingly, that the performance of the SDR as compared with a basket of currencies of major trading partners is quite acceptable if the objective is to stabilise the payments position. I shall elaborate on this point in my own paper.

11. John Williamson

I too would like to offer some answers to the three questions raised by Mr Masera, to supplement Mr Sakbani's comments.

First, is there a contradiction between seeking a common basket and using the literature on how to select an optimal basket for an individual country? It is true, of course, that the 'optimal basket' will differ for each country; hence, if each country insists on using its individually optimal basket, there will be no common peg. There must be a trade-off between having the *best* peg, from the standpoint of minimising the variability of the real exchange rate, and having a *common* peg, defined in terms of a unit in which one can intervene. The evidence I referred to earlier suggests that the sacrifice entailed in discounting the minimum variance objective and adopting a common SDR peg would be minimal, but this is of course an empirical proposition.

Secondly, should the basket to which one pegs be a basket of currencies external or internal to the region? The fundamental analytical point here is whether one wishes the jointly-pegged currencies of the area to float or to peg *vis-à-vis* the rest of the world. An ECU composed of the European currencies is appropriate because the objective of the European countries is to peg among themselves but to float against the dollar and the yen. It appears, however, that with the exception of the Lebanese pound, the Arab currencies are at present in no condition to float, because of the under-development of the Arab financial markets; even if they were, the fact that some 85 per cent of imports originate outside the area casts doubt on the desirability of floating against the rest of the world. The purpose of the basket is therefore that of defining where to intervene against external currencies, not against other Arab currencies; for that purpose it must be composed of currencies external to the region. (As a matter of fact, the addition of Arab currencies to the basket would be entirely cosmetic so long as the purpose of the basket was to peg against the outside world.)

Thirdly, can one legitimately conclude anything about the desirability of an SDR peg on the basis of past studies, given that the SDR basket is about to be reduced from sixteen to five currencies? Since all available empirical calculations are based on the sixteen-currency basket, the change introduces yet another ambiguity into these comparisons. On the other hand, the five major currencies which are to make up the new basket constituted over two-thirds of the old basket and the five-currency basket will thus tend to reproduce the big basket. It would appear, therefore, that past studies can still be reasonably useful as a basis for judging the merits of an SDR peg.

Notes

1. The use of the terms of trade as a criterion is mistaken, not because terms of trade are unimportant but because (a) small countries cannot affect their terms of trade, and (b) countries which *can* affect their terms of trade should seek to optimise them rather than to stabilise them, which is necessarily a different thing.

2. See Gerakis and Roncesvalles, 'Alternative Exchange Regimes for Middle Eastern Countries: The Numerical Aspects', *International Monetary Fund*, DM75/96, 1975. Crockett and Nsouli, 'Exchange-rate Policies for Developing Countries', *Journal of Development Studies* (January 1977); and the ongoing research of Brodsky and Sampson in UNCTAD.

3. This and the following two comments pertaining to exchange-rate policy were made subsequent to the author's response to the discussion of his paper [eds.].

5 THE ARAB MONETARY FUND: OBJECTIVES AND PERFORMANCE*

Abdul Aal Al-Sagban

Introduction

This paper sets out to discuss and analyse the objectives of the Arab Monetary Fund (AMF) and to assess its performance to date in achieving them. It is divided into three sections. The first and main section deals with the objectives of the AMF, first in the Arab sphere, then in the international sphere and, finally, in the organisational sphere. Section II provides a brief comparative analysis of the AMF and the IMF, while Section III contains concluding remarks.

Before the AMF objectives are analysed in detail, a brief reference to the AMF set-up may be appropriate. The Fund was established in 1975, after lengthy and arduous discussions among governors of Arab central banks,[1] and began operations in April 1977. Its capital was set at 250 million Arab accounting dinars (AAD), the equivalent of SDR 750 million. Fifty-two per cent of the Fund's capital has been paid up, 50 per cent of this in convertible currencies and the remaining 2 per cent in national currencies. In furtherance of its objectives, the Fund may borrow up to twice the value of its capital from international financial markets.

The AMF now stands alongside other Arab organisations which aim at furthering efforts towards Arab economic integration, most notably the Arab Fund for Economic and Social Development and the Council of Arab Economic Unity, all three organisations operating within the framework of the Arab League and in accordance with the League's strategy for joint Arab activity.

I. The Objectives of the Arab Monetary Fund

Article IV of the AMF Agreement states the objectives of the Fund as follows:

(a) To correct the balance-of-payments disequilibria of member states;
(b) To stabilise the exchange rates of Arab currencies, to bring about their inter-convertibility and to strive to eliminate current payments

---

* Translated from the Arabic.

restrictions among Arab countries;
(c) To firmly fix policies and procedures with regard to Arab monetary co-operation as a means of accelerating Arab economic integration and economic development in the member states;
(d) To offer advice, where required, with respect to policies for investing the monetary resources of the member states abroad in such a way as to preserve the real value of these resources and promote their growth;
(e) To develop the Arab money markets;
(f) To study ways of expanding the use of the Arab accounting dinar and of creating the conditions for the establishment of a uniform Arab currency;
(g) To co-ordinate the positions of the member states with regard to international monetary and economic issues so as to serve their common interests while helping to solve world monetary problems;
(h) To settle current payments among member states with a view to increasing the flow of trade.

Article VIII of the Agreement refers to another objective when it states that the Fund shall provide technical assistance and other monetary and financial services to those member states which conclude economic agreements aimed at reaching monetary unity among them as a stage in the process of achieving the Fund's objectives.

Article V of the Agreement includes a reference to devices for implementing these objectives, starting from the premise that there is more than one way to achieve any single objective. In this regard, the article refers *inter alia* to the following devices:

(a) Offering short- and medium-term credit facilities to member states to help them finance their global balance-of-payments deficits resulting from the exchange of goods and services, currency conversions and capital and financial transfers;
(b) Issuing securities to member states to reinforce their borrowings from other sources to finance global balance-of-payments deficits;
(c) Mediating in loan issues on the Arab and world financial markets on behalf of the member states and with their guarantees;
(d) Co-ordinating the monetary policies of the member states and developing co-operation among their monetary authorities;
(e) Liberalising and developing trade relations and the settlement of current payments resulting from them and encouraging the flow of capital among the member states;
(f) Opening a special account and allocating for it a sufficient portion of the Fund's resources, paid in member states' currencies, to be

used as credit facilities for the settlement of current payments among the member states in accordance with the rules and regulations decided by the Board of Governors;
(g) Managing any monies entrusted to it by one or more member states for the benefit of other Arab or non-Arab parties in conformity with the Fund's objectives. The Fund shall, by agreement with the member state or states concerned, make the necessary arrangements for managing these moneys and shall open special accounts for this purpose;
(h) Holding regular consultations with the member states concerning the state of their economies and the policies they should follow to help achieve the objectives of the AMF and those of the states themselves;
(i) Conducting studies aimed at furthering the Fund's objectives;
(j) Providing technical assistance to the monetary and banking bodies of the member states.

Article VI refers to co-operation among member states and between them and the Fund, such co-operation itself representing one means of achieving the objectives of the Fund. The article states that each country should strive, in particular, to:

(i) Reduce its restrictions on current payments with regard to other member states as well as restrictions on capital and revenue transfers, with a view to eventually eliminating all restrictions;
(ii) Achieve the necessary degree of co-ordination in its economic policies, especially its financial and monetary policies so as to serve the interests of economic integration.

A. AMF Objectives in the Arab Sphere

Overall economic integration is the road to comprehensive economic and social development on a regional level. Hence the central objective of the AMF as a regional organisation consists in laying the monetary foundations for Arab economic integration and promoting rapid economic development in all the Arab countries.

Promoting rapid economic development is a two-pronged objective within the framework of the movement towards Arab economic integration. First of all, for any Arab country to be prepared to make a positive contribution to Arab economic integration, it must first have achieved a sufficient degree of economic development so as to have economic interests worth defending and products worth exchanging. The AMF can play an effective role in promoting the rapid economic development of every Arab country in the framework of an integrationist orientation.

Secondly, there is the need to promote economic integration in every Arab country in order to put an end to the destructive rivalry resulting from like economies and the lack of the information necessary for adopting integration-oriented planning decisions. The philosophy of the AMF is founded on accelerating such an orientation.

In any case, the AMF Agreement does not leave these overall objectives to random interpretation and vague generalities but rather links them to specific goals in the monetary sphere. The monetary goals are clearly defined in terms of what would best serve the objectives of integration and development. These clearly defined goals will be discussed one by one.

1. Correcting Balance-of-payments Disorders. The authors of the AMF Agreement resolved from the beginning to deal with both types of balance-of-payments disorders – surpluses and deficits – since such disorders signify either a malfunction in the economic performance of the member states or an insufficiency of means at their disposal.

a. Balance-of-payments surpluses. The AMF Agreement stipulates the means for implementing the objective of correcting balance-of-payments surpluses in paragraphs H, I and J of Article V. These are the paragraphs which discuss the holding of regular consultations with the member states concerning the economic and political conditions they face, carrying out studies to further the Fund's objectives and providing technical assistance to the monetary and banking bodies of the member states.

The various devices provided for in the articles of the AMF Agreement should be considered jointly. Consultation, as a device, is linked to the devices cited for co-ordinating the monetary policies of the member states, developing co-operation among their monetary authorities and encouraging the flow of capital among the member states. These are the devices provided for successively in paragraph D of Article V, paragraph B of Article VI, paragraph E of Article V and paragraph A of Article VI. Moreover, the Fund retains the right to pursue any means it may find appropriate, in order to play an effective role in correcting these kinds of disorders. The choice of any particular method or methods for dealing with balance-of-payments surpluses is to be determined by the AMF in the light of existing circumstances and its practical experience in dealing with the issues of Arab economic development.

One might imagine that the AMF would encounter certain difficulties in its regional dealings, especially in the early stages of its activity, given the phenomenon of surplus assets in some member countries. However, when this issue is considered in the regional context of overall

Arab economic and social development, the possibilities and scope for dealing with this imbalance are enhanced; for in this context, real support can be offered for the economies of the Arab countries generally and of the surplus countries in particular.

Nevertheless, some doubts have been expressed about the willingness and ability of the Fund to deal effectively with balance-of-payments surpluses because the surplus in the Arab countries is the result of oil exports and not of the exportation of manufactured goods or agricultural produce as is the case for the industrial countries.[2] It is difficult for the oil countries to reduce the volume of their oil operations, for instance, because oil is bound up with the world economy and its energy needs. It is equally difficult to ask that these countries revalue their currencies upwards in order to reduce the surplus in their exports by increasing the value of these exports, because oil exports are not paid for in their national currencies.[3] Some have claimed that the mention of this objective of reducing surpluses is meant to give the impression that the Fund is serving the interests of the deficit and surplus countries to the same extent.[4] In any discussion along these lines, it should be said that there has been no deliberate attempt to 'give an impression' since all discussions have been frank about the fact that the role of the AMF in dealing with payments surpluses is to provide balance by co-ordinating monetary policies, encouraging the transfer of capital and offering regular consultation.

In this regard, it should be pointed out that the means to which the drafters of the Agreement refer are those traditional means available to any international community where the role of its monetary institutions is restricted, as in the case of the AMF, to one of providing assistance and does not extend to integration and unification. If the countries making up the Arab nation are seen as a whole, their surplus appears small and temporary. Indeed, this surplus only exists by virtue of the fragmentation imposed on the Arab nation. The fact is that there would be no surplus if these resources were directed into Arab development goals in accordance with a pan-Arab plan some aspects of which would, in the early stages, be mandatory and others merely recommended.

But one can only agree with the authors of the AMF Agreement that the AMF may appear incapable of dealing effectively and directly with this objective. It should rather seek, in the early stages, to achieve other objectives which would treat the surplus problem indirectly. The fact is that the intention of the Agreement and of its authors was clear with regard to the remedy for a balance-of-payments surplus in that their discussions focused on methods for recycling these funds to the Arab nation and creating the proper climate for channelling them from the surplus countries to the deficit countries. With this understanding and on this premise, the AMF was entrusted with developing financial markets as one of the objectives of Arab economic integration, i.e., the integration of investment.

In any case, it is not yet feasible for the Fund, still in its early stages, to enter into the process of correcting this imbalance by means of consultations or by co-ordinating policies. Nevertheless, it is making an effort, as we shall see, to carry out studies on the prospects for developing the Arab financial markets and hastening the creation of a climate for the flow of funds between the Arab countries which would contribute just as much to achieving one aspect of this objective.

b. Balance-of-payments deficits. There is no doubt that balance-of-payments deficits represent the Achilles heel of most developing economies, including those of the Arab countries. Indeed there is a cause and effect relationship between this problem and the process of social and economic development itself.

The deficit problem has become more acute in most of the Arab countries since the first serious steps towards setting up the AMF were taken in 1975. In the period 1975-9, the total current account deficit for all the Arab deficit countries reached $33.409 billion. In 1979, the financial reserves of some of these countries represented an amount equivalent to only 14.1 per cent of their imports, i.e., in some cases the equivalent of only a month and a half's worth of imports and for other countries the equivalent of less than two weeks' worth.[5]

As a result of this situation, the indebtedness of these countries has increased. Total credit extended to them rose from $27.565 billion in 1975 to $65.935 billion in 1979. Amounts actually drawn on this credit rose from $15.221 billion in 1975 to $44.61 billion in 1979. In that year, debt servicing cost these countries about $6.568 billion or 6 per cent of the value of their aggregate GDP, up from 2.6 per cent in 1975. It represented 29 per cent of the value of commodities exported in 1979, up from 12 per cent in 1975.[6]

In the light of these facts and of the anticipated consequences, helping the deficitory Arab countries cope with their balance-of-payments deficits occupies a central place among the objectives of the AMF. This help is provided through the extension of short- and medium-term credit facilities to member states to finance their global balance-of-payments deficits, i.e., those resulting from the flow of goods and services, financial transfers and capital movements (Article V, para. A). The Fund thus participates in the financing of global deficits and not regional deficits. There are two reasons for this: first, the difficulty of defining the regional deficit; and secondly, the limited volume of inter-Arab trade.

However, this has in no way diminished the need for the Fund to play an active role in encouraging Arab trade and in settling commercial payments among Arab countries. Indeed, it has encouraged the Fund to concern itself with preferential trade relations in such a way as to permit their development both quantitatively and qualitatively.[7]

(1) The sources of AMF credit facilities

The primary source of the Fund's credit facilities consists of its capital holdings and general reserves plus what may accrue from other reserves, from the loans and facilities which it may receive and from any other resources decided on by the Board of Governors.

As stated previously, 52 per cent of the Fund's capital has been paid up, a figure equivalent to AAD 124 million, of which two per cent is in local currencies. The countries concerned still have to produce 48 per cent of the capital, AAD 64.9 million remaining due from the financially strong countries and AAD 61.3 million from the deficit countries.

By 31 December 1979, the overall total of AMF reserves had reached AAD 5.315 million of which AAD 1.5 million was in the General Reserve Fund, AAD 2.0 million in the Technical Assistance Reserve Fund and AAD 1.815 million in the reserve fund set aside for currency differentials. Thus the grand total of paid-up capital plus reserves at the end of 1979 was AAD 135.315 million. Nevertheless, the Fund appears to feel, along with a number of experts and economists, that these resources are inadequate. Their limited volume has discouraged member states from having recourse to the Fund and has led to the limitation of its capacity to deal positively with economic fluctuations in general and monetary ones in particular, which function it was meant to perform. The Fund has conducted studies showing that a minimum of one billion AAD is required to achieve its objectives as follows: to cover the increasing needs of the financially weak Arab countries; to strengthen the capacity of capital-importing countries to cope with the debt burden; to increase the capacity of the Fund to encourage Arab commercial transactions and to lay the foundations for Arab monetary integration; and to maintain an acceptable relative balance between the shareholdings in the IMF and those in the AMF. This requires the Fund to augment its capital to AAD 1.052 billion (a 400 per cent increase in its capital); it must also require that the unpaid portion of its present capital be paid up during 1981.[8]

However, the Fund's credit sources are not restricted to its capital holdings; another source is borrowing. We have already pointed out that the Fund may borrow up to double the value of its capital and reserves combined. Taking this into account, if the remainder of the capital were actually paid up, the Fund would be able to borrow AAD 500 million. If we suppose that it could collect a sum of AAD 100 million from its reserves and from the revenues from the Arab Development Decade, it would be able to borrow AAD 200 million, and by these means it would achieve a total of AAD 1.052 billion without augmenting its capital.[9] Other studies point out, however, that the goal of doubling the GNP of the non-oil Arab countries, with the exception of Egypt, will lead to a deficit in their balance of payments over the period 1981-90 estimated at about $60 billion. Table 5.1 has been compiled on the basis of a projected decrease in the imports of these countries, as a proportion of GNP, from 30 per cent at the beginning of this period to 29.5 per cent at the end, and on the assumption of an increase in exports whereby, as a proportion of GNP, they would rise from less than 20 per cent at the beginning of the period to 25 per cent by the end.[10]

Table 5.1: Projected Balance of Trade of Non-oil Arab Countries (1981-90)[11] (millions of dollars)

Year	Imports	Exports	Balance-of-trade deficit
1981	17,023	11,371	5,653
1982	18,245	12,461	5,784
1983	19,554	13,656	5,898
1984	20,958	14,964	5,994
1985	22,462	16,399	6,063
1986	24,174	17,970	6,104
1987	25,802	19,693	6,109
1988	27,654	21,580	6,074
1989	29,639	23,648	5,991
1990	31,766	25,915	5,851
Total	237,277	177,657	59,521

Source: Government publications.

It is assumed that a positive investment climate would increase the flow of capital into these countries and thus help to cover their anticipated balance-of-payments deficits.

The Agreement limits the loans the Fund may extend to member countries to an amount equivalent to three times the country's paid-up capital subscription. This may be increased to four times the paid-up subscription by a three-fourths majority vote under the terms of paragraph B of Article 21 of the Agreement.[12] In addition, the member country may borrow the equivalent of up to 100 per cent of its paid-up subscription to deal with an urgent situation resulting either from a drop in the value of exports of goods and services or from a large increase in the value of agricultural imports due to bad harvests, in accordance with the standards set by the Fund. Services were included along with goods in this regard in view of the lessons learned from the experience of the IMF in applying its policies.

The Agreement does not confine itself to capital and reserves as sources for the Fund's facilities. Rather it adds to these a parallel facility which consists in issuing the guarantees provided for in paragraph B of Article V of the Agreement. Article XXIV of the Agreement sets the same limits and conditions on the Fund's facilities when they take the form of guarantees as it does on the loan amounts. Therefore, combining loans and guarantees, a member country may borrow from the AMF, within a 12-month period, the equivalent of up to four times its paid-up subscription. This may be increased to eight times the paid-up subscription in the event of an exceptional drop in the value of exports or a large increase in the value of food imports.

Whereas it is often possible to obtain loans at low interest rates on the international market place, guarantees are somewhat more difficult to secure. If these guarantees were easy for member countries to obtain, they would not need to resort to the Fund. Thus the role of the Fund is to make it easier for countries to obtain such guarantees, especially since the international financial markets do not generally lend to countries in need except after obtaining a 'green light' from the IMF. The AMF is expected to play the same role, at least in relation to Arab countries borrowing in the international markets.

Notwithstanding this state of affairs, the Fund's Board of Directors has interpreted these guarantees as constituting a substitute for loans and members are therefore prohibited from benefiting from both at the same time. Such an interpretation is surely at variance with both the letter and spirit of the text of the Agreement and also with the discussions on this point which took place at the preparatory meetings. It might be well to recall the stipulation contained in Article XVIII to the effect that the maximum indebtedness of the Fund, including the sums borrowed and the guarantees issued, is 100 per cent of its declared capital and general reserves combined, meaning that the guarantees constitute a source of credit in addition to the facilities generated from its capital holdings and not a substitute for them.

Paragraph C of Article V refers to a third facility for assisting member states: intervention on behalf of member states in loan issues on the Arab and international financial markets with the states providing the guarantees. The implication of the text is clearly that the Fund's loans and guarantees for member countries may not suffice. In this case, the member may be compelled to seek additional loans from the financial markets and the Fund offers its intervention as a device for strengthening confidence in the ability of the member to repay the loan. However, the Agreement explicitly stipulates that its role is confined to intervention and does not extend to providing guarantees, because the member country is the one responsible for providing the guarantee. This provision can be commended for the fact that such intervention helps the Fund to achieve two other major objectives: the development of the Arab financial markets and the development of the resources of the member states made possible through the experience the Fund acquires in managing loans in the international financial markets.

Finally, the Agreement refers to a source no less important than those previously indicated for financing member states' balance-of-payments deficits, namely that mentioned in paragraph G of Article V which refers to the competence of the Fund to manage any monies which a member country may entrust to it, in the interest of other Arab or non-Arab parties and in accordance with the objectives of the Fund.

This paragraph takes on a special significance today in the light of the premises on which the Arab Development Decade has been based and of the strategy of joint Arab activity. It is also significant in view of the lessons learned from the IMF's management of its Oil Facility and Compensatory Facilities and the management by the Arab Fund for Economic and Social Development, in co-operation with OAPEC, of oil facilities entrusted to it by the Arab countries in 1975 for the benefit of Arab oil-importing countries.

The role the AMF can play in this regard is not confined to co-operation with Arab parties, but rather extends to include co-operation with non-Arab parties. This co-operation might involve harmonising the flow of resources from the Fund with the flow from international institutions and preventing the international institutions from obstinately imposing credit terms which either restrict the freedom of Arab and other countries to draw up their own integration-oriented economic and social policies or compromise their independence.

The AMF is thus expected to assume tasks on a geographical scale which goes beyond the expanse of the Arab nation. Relevant here is the effective role which Arab resources have played and continue to play in supporting the activities of the IMF, the World Bank and similar institutions. These include the national Arab development funds whose activities extend to non-Arab countries, the Arab development banks, which are taking on an international character, the Arab commercial banks and the Islamic Bank. Such an international role is based on the identity of interests shared by members of the developing world to which the Arab countries belong.

All the ideas presented here are expressed in Article XXVI of the AMF Agreement which was drafted by the General Secretariat of the Council of Arab Economic Unity and which reads as follows:[13] 'One or more members may request the Fund's assistance in investing capital in other specified Arab or non-Arab countries or in extending loans and credit facilities on their behalf to those countries.' In these cases the Fund, by agreement with the member or members, makes the necessary arrangements for such loans or facilities.

(2) The Fund's credit facilities and the terms attached to them

After defining the sources of the Fund's facilities the Agreement establishes the conditions under which a member may use these facilities. These conditions were determined at a time when the credit terms offered by the IMF were considered by many Arab countries to be too stringent. As an illustration of this, it might be pointed out that the total sum of money granted by the IMF to the Arab deficit countries to date, i.e. in 35 years of lending, does not exceed SDR 1.8 billion, representing 75 per cent of the Arab countries' paid-up shares. This figure drops to 31 per cent of the shares if we look at the net drawings made on these facilities.[14] Actually, the Arab countries make use of the IMF primarily for investment and supplementary financing and also use the Trust Fund.

Given these circumstances and taking advantage of the lessons inherent in the experience of the IMF, the authors of the AMF Agreement decided to impose less stringent credit terms.

(a) Loan ceilings. An early draft of the Agreement had stipulated that loans over any 12-month period should be limited to an amount equivalent to twice the member's paid-up subscription and that no single loan might exceed four times the paid-up subscription. The Board of Directors might increase these loan ceilings by a two-thirds majority vote with no restrictions on the amount of the increase.

However, the meeting held by the governors of Arab central banks with financial experts on 14 October 1975 re-examined this subject and lowered the ceiling for a single loan to three times the paid-up subscription with the possibility of increasing it to four times. Opinion leaned towards giving the Board of Directors the right to increase these amounts but the hardliners succeeded in vesting the authority to decide increases in the Board of Governors rather than in the Board of Directors.[15]

(b) Loan payment periods. From the beginning, the aim of the AMF has been to extend short- and medium-term loans as long-term loans are handled by the Arab Fund for Economic and Social Development, the Arab development funds and joint ventures. Although it had been proposed that loans be extended for up to ten years,[16] the Agreement set an upper limit of seven years for repaying loans.

(c) Interest rates on loans. During the preliminary discussions, it was proposed that the Fund should charge moderate interest rates on its loans and exempt automatic loans from interest. Indeed, the discussions at the joint meeting with experts on 14 October 1975 referred to interest rates of ½, ¾ and 1 per cent.[17] However, as indicated in subparagraph (a), the Board of Directors did not follow these proposals when making its final decisions.

(d) Types of loans. The Agreement distinguishes between three types of loans:

(i) Automatic loans up to an amount equivalent to 75 per cent of the country's paid-up capital subscription and granted to finance global deficits under normal circumstances;
(ii) Support loans granted to support a financial programme, which the Fund and the member shall agree upon for a period determined by the Board of Directors, aimed at coping with a temporary balance-of-payments deficit;
(iii) Extended loans granted in the case of a substantial deficit resulting from a structural imbalance in the member country's economy, aimed at bringing about an appropriate solution to the member's problems. This type of loan is to be used in accordance with the timetable of the corrective programme agreed upon.

Despite the stipulation in the Agreement that the global deficit to be financed with the help of the Fund may be the result of the flight of capital, paragraph B of Article XX takes a cautious position on this matter when it states that the Fund's resources are to be granted for the purpose of coping with the flight of capital only in exceptional cases.[18]

(3) Application of the Fund's policies

The Fund formed at the very outset a joint team of experts in loan management and research to prepare special studies relating to lending. These studies formed the basis for the decisions of the Board of Directors with regard to its lending policy.[19] Of the basic principles embodied in this policy, the most important are perhaps the need for balance between the credit facilities offered by the Fund and its financial position and the principle of equal opportunity in making these facilities available.[20]

According to the figures available, it would seem that in relation to their quotas in the two institutions, the financially poor Arab countries have borrowed proportionately more from the AMF than from the IMF.

Of course, IMF loans under ordinary circumstances will necessarily be larger than those of the AMF, by virtue of the high level of capital participation of the Arab countries concerned, the many lending options at its disposal and the fact that loans from all the credit sources of the IMF may reach 455 per cent of a country's share in the Fund, or 405 per cent if we exclude the financing facilities of the Reserve Fund. However, the capabilities of the IMF in this regard have become limited due to the halt in the concessional outflows from the Trust Fund and the beginning of their reimbursement period, the abolition of the Oil Facility and the difficulties involved in obtaining auxiliary financing.[21]

This situation imposes an additional role on the AMF, i.e., that it turn to financing the balance-of-payments deficits of the member countries. However, capital participation in the AMF is still limited, for several reasons:
— The small amount of its capital, the modest degree of participation by the smaller countries and the link between loan ceilings and paid-up shares. We have already mentioned that not more than 52 per cent of the shares have so far been paid up.
— The conservative policy of the Board of Directors of the AMF and its desire to preserve a balance in the Fund's resources, a factor which has resulted in fixing the ceiling for loans at 200 per cent of the paid-up subscription instead of the 400 or 500 per cent stipulated in the Agreement.
— The virtual elimination of the guarantee facilities because the Board of Directors has chosen, perhaps on the basis of its conservative policy, to interpret these facilities as a substitute for loans and not a supplement to them, which effectively deprives members of additional possibilities.
— The lack of any flow into the Fund of additional private resources to meet the burdens stemming from the impact of oil price increases after 1975 on the Arab oil-importing countries. An inflow of such resources had been expected in accordance with the agreed principles of Arab regional co-operation. The remedy for this problem facing the Arab oil-importing countries should not be left to world financial policies laid down for the purpose of dealing with such cases in relation to all countries.
— Delays in paying up the remainder of the Fund's capital and the stipulation by the Board of Governors creating a link between the loan repayment period and the Fund's use, in its lending policies, of specific proportions of its capital representing not less than 50 per cent of the paid-up shares. The fact is that the remedy for this demands a rapid repayment of capital and early consideration of the possibility of augmenting it. The Fund's capabilities must also be given free reign with regard to lending on the Arab and international markets and must be objectively strengthened through the creation of new options for aiding the poorer Arab countries. At the same time, the conservative policies of the Board of Directors must be reconsidered, whether with regard to loan ceilings or to the proper degree of relaxation of the guarantee and interest rate terms.

(a) Interest rates. The Fund's Board of Directors has imposed an interest rate of 3.75 per cent on automatic loans. This rate is compounded annually by 0.5 per cent to make it 4.75 per cent in the third year. Similarly, the interest rate for extended loans starts at 5.2 per cent in the first year and reaches 7 per cent by the seventh year.

Actually, this state of affairs represents a considerable departure from the original conception of the authors of the AMF Agreement. In fact, early discussions had moved in the direction of making automatic loans altogether interest-free except for the administrative fees deducted at the outset and estimated by the Fund at 0.25 per cent. These fees might have been regarded as an annual duty in exchange for the management of automatic loans. The interest rates on extended loans are also high, especially given the fact that these loans come out of the Fund's capital and are for modest amounts (due to the small percentage of paid-up shares) and also given the fact that the loan ceilings have been reduced. One might think that such interest rates came about as a result of borrowing activities by the AMF in the financial markets for the purpose of re-lending to the member countries and were therefore meant to finance the high net interest rates which the Fund had to pay in these markets. However, this was not the case.

(b) Loan repayment period. The AMF Board of Directors ultimately settled on a policy of limiting loan repayment periods to three years for automatic loans, five years for support loans and seven years for structural deficit loans. The repayment period for support loans should rightly be extended to seven years when these are coupled with structural deficit loans while the period for automatic loans should be extended to five years when such loans are coupled with support loans only and to seven years when coupled with structural deficit loans. We have already mentioned that the move to set the repayment periods for loans at ten years was rejected during the preparatory sessions despite the support for this idea from certain experts. One is inclined to agree with this decision because a ten-year repayment period might have led to a certain laxity in the application of corrective policies, the effectiveness of the Fund and the balancing of resources.

(4) Difficulties encountered by the Fund in the application of its credit policies

Personal interviews conducted by the writer with certain AMF officials early in 1980 revealed a recurring problem facing the Fund, namely, the need to dispatch teams to assist in the collection of the data required before loans can be granted. This is necessary despite the fact that most of this information has usually been gathered already by the IMF. Moreover, some officials in the countries applying for loans find it unacceptable that the AMF should require of them the same information as the IMF when one considers the difference in the size of loans provided by the two funds. Consequently, it is difficult for the AMF to agree on corrective policies with the borrower states. However, such a situation was to be expected given the experience of the IMF in this regard. That experience has shown that 'many states are reluctant to accept this kind of interference in their internal affairs in view of the political, social and economic repercussions involved. Consequently, the Fund does not venture to implement such a program except under special and exceptional circumstances if the states do not agree to it, unless they happen to be in direct need of the loan in order to check a deteriorating situation...'[22] In fact, the difficulty of obtaining the data needed to decide whether and on what terms to provide a loan need not lead to this conclusion. Furthermore, the size of the loan is not the decisive factor in the acceptance or rejection of corrective policies. Indeed, many states refuse such intervention even on the part of the IMF. Examples of this are abundant in the Arab region.

The next difficulty that the AMF may encounter in performing its functions is related to its credit terms. This is because any conditions which the AMF imposes over and above those of the IMF represent an added burden for the borrower country and undermine the supposed easy terms offered by the AMF. On the other hand, if the AMF contents itself with imposing the same conditions as the IMF, it is feared that the criticisms levelled against that organisation will be withdrawn and aimed at the AMF. These assumptions do not, however, take into account the possibility that the conditions of the AMF could be less restrictive than those of the IMF. In addition, the conditions set by the AMF may reflect pan-Arab considerations, which cannot be claimed to constitute an additional burden; for such conditions have a specific counter-value, namely AMF loans. Furthermore, the Arab Fund may decide to provide credit facilities without requiring that all the conditions of the IMF be met or that they be applied to the letter. In addition, the partial overlapping of the conditions of the two funds need not prevent the AMF from maintaining overall easier terms.

The third difficulty facing the Fund stems from its limited credit facilities, as described earlier. AMF executives have suggested three solutions for this problem:

(a) Increasing the loan ceilings: It is clear that this solution is of limited value in view of the relative scarcity of the Fund's resources and because this would upset the financial balance in the AMF and might result in its eventual dissolution;

(b) Augmenting the Fund's capital: We have already mentioned that this would require first, that all the capital be paid up and, secondly, a liberalisation of the policies of the Board of Directors. Thirdly, it would require a review of the whole question of the Fund's credit facilities in light of the organisation's experience to date.

In the view of the Fund executives, there are three possibilities for augmenting the Fund's capital:[23]

(i) The Fund's agreeing to finance a greater proportion of the deficits of the poorer Arab countries on the condition that they increase their shares. It would be natural, in this case, for these deficit countries to increase their shares. But this, as the Fund executives add, would mean that the deficit countries would be bearing the responsibility of financing their own balance-of-payment deficits. It would also increase the borrowing costs and thus the burden on the deficit countries;

(ii) Increasing the shares of the surplus countries which would increase the Fund's resources. However, this would not address the question of the size of the facilities available to the other countries if the borrowing equation were not changed and assuming the link were retained between the size of the facilities and the paid-up shares;

(iii) Implementing an across-the-board increase in the shares. While this would be more acceptable, it would pose the same difficulty for the poorer Arab states, i.e., that of finding the money to pay for their shares in the Fund's capital.

In our opinion, this last possibility represents the soundest solution for increasing the capital of the Fund, irrespective of the size of the increase or its timing. The Arab states must find a suitable way to enable the deficit states to pay up their shares. This is imperative, even at the price of implementing a corrective programme, in order to further the process of Arab economic integration and to benefit Arab states collectively and individually.

(c) Creating new options for the Fund's credit facilities: In this connection, the following possibilities might be mentioned:

(i) Compensating the Fund for lending at nominal rates of interest whatever it borrows at market interest rates from the Arab or international financial markets or directly from a government. The interest-rate differential might be financed by means of a fixed investment by the Fund, from a reserve fund created solely for this purpose or from an annual amount to be allocated by the surplus states at each annual meeting of the Board of Governors and in accordance with an estimated budget drawn up by the Fund;

(ii) Qualitative and quantitative development of inter-Arab trade by means of resources allocated by the wealthy Arab states. The details relating thereto would be worked out in consultation with the Council of Arab Economic Unity and in conjunction with the progress made toward the implementation of decisions relating to the Arab Common Market;

(iii) An Oil Facility with details to be worked out in co-operation with the OAPEC countries;

(iv) A scheme related to the Arab Development Decade, with details to be arranged in co-operation with the Economic Council and the Arab Development Fund in accordance with the recommendations of a summit meeting held for this purpose;
(v) A scheme related to pan-Arab defence with details to be arranged in co-operation with the Joint Defence Council in accordance with a plan which would necessarily lead to the achievement of pan-Arab liberation goals and which would offer facilities commensurate with the obligations undertaken.

Whatever the method suggested for confronting this difficulty, it is the writer's opinion that this aspect of the Fund's activities has been given more than its due share of attention, more than that given to other aspects of Arab monetary integration. This should not be the case since there is a relationship between Arab monetary integration in particular and the deficit financing of certain Arab states in general. For the achievement of the former would generate the solution to the latter, whereas the accomplishment of the latter will lead only to an Arab 'rapprochement' which might be merely temporary and self-serving. We shall refer to this point later.

Another difficulty is the conditions imposed on automatic loans, whose maturity is limited to three years and whose renewal is prohibited unless the indebtedness of the borrower member country falls below 75 per cent of its paid-up share. In fact, these conditions are the result of policies adopted by the Fund and are nowhere stipulated as such in the official text of the Agreement. We have already mentioned that the maturity of such loans should be increased beyond three years when they are coupled with support loans or extended loans. The renewal of the loan could be made possible upon its repayment, given the special nature of the loan. The AMF would be wise to adopt this change as it would offer a means of accommodating the Arab states which are financially incapable of paying up their shares in the Fund's capital. It is in this context that the suggestion was made previously to exempt such loans from interest and simply to collect an annual commission to cover administrative costs.

In fact, these obstacles could be removed either by the Board of Directors or by the Board of Governors. That they have not been reflects, in the writer's opinion, another facet of the conservative policies of the Board of Directors, policies which demand thorough reconsideration in the light of the variables affecting the administration of the Fund.

The AMF Annual Report for 1979 refers (beginning on p. 38) to the continued relaxation of credit terms introduced by the Board of Directors. This leads one to believe that the Board of Directors will find in the studies presented at this seminar great scope for a reconsideration of its policies specifically related to lending and to the Fund's achievement of its objectives in a balanced manner.

At any rate, one should not assume that the AMF is the only source of support for balance-of-payments deficits. In this regard, the 1979 AMF Annual Report mentions that the size of remittances by Arab nationals working outside their countries decreased from $6 billion in 1974 to $3.5 billion in 1978. This figure includes private transfers to Egypt, Yemen, the Syrian Arab Republic, Jordan and Sudan, but not those to Lebanon and occupied Palestine. This total figure drops to approximately $2 billion if the transfers to Egypt are excluded (approximately $1.5 billion).[24]

In addition, Arab monetary co-operation has developed substantially with respect to balance-of-payments support for the poorer Arab countries by means of increased deposits by the central banks and monetary institutions of the Arab oil-producing countries with similar banks and institutions in the non-oil Arab countries. Support has also been offered in the form of guarantees by Arab oil-producing countries on behalf of non-oil Arab countries in the international money markets. However, there is no need to dwell here on facts that will be presented by other participants in this seminar, e.g., figures pertaining to Arab aid to Arab countries, which are quite readily available.

Irrespective of the method suggested for managing the resources of the Arab Development Decade or those to be allocated towards achieving the strategic tasks of the joint Arab effort, these resources can only constitute a positive factor with regard to balance-of-payments support. This, in turn, will reduce the pressure on the AMF and will enable it to concentrate on achieving its own objectives and furthering Arab monetary integration.

2. Financial Integration. Considerable attention has been paid in Arab economic publications to Arab financial markets as one means of achieving the objectives of ambitious development plans; for most Arab economists consider that the establishment of an Arab financial market would mean the achievement of Arab economic integration as it relates to financing economic development.[25]

The development of Arab financial markets is indeed closely linked to economic development, since these markets facilitate the transfer of capital, provide suitable avenues for its optimum investment and strengthen the ties between the economy of the Arab world and the international economy. Furthermore, the commissions and profits earned in the financial market for services rendered by residents to non-residents represent invisible exports and are no less important than export earnings in their positive effect on the balance of payments.

170 *The Arab Monetary Fund*

They also reduce the amounts paid by the Arab economies for these services.

However, the immediate objective which the Fund hopes to realise through its specialisation in the development of Arab financial markets is the recycling of Arab funds from the international market to the Arab market, the development of the Arab market itself and an easing of the pressure exerted on it by balance-of-payments problems. The AMF governors have been careful to emphasise this objective and it was also stressed in a memorandum published by the General Secretariat of the Council of Arab Economic Unity and in discussion among financial experts both at the February 1975 meetings in Baghdad and at all their subsequent meetings. Paragraph E of Article IV of the AMF Agreement refers explicitly to this objective. Article V emphasises the role of the Fund in encouraging the free flow of capital between the member states. It also provides for the stabilisation of Arab currencies, their inter-convertibility and the elimination of payments restrictions (to which reference will be made under the discussion of the Fund's goal of monetary integration). The AMF will undoubtedly find rare opportunities for innovation in the achievement of this objective in harmony and co-ordination with other joint Arab organisations.

In an effort to initiate moves towards financial integration, the Fund has drawn up a strategy for developing the Arab financial markets over the coming three years. This plan contains five basic points:[26]

(a) Reliance on two forms of action in providing technical aid and participating in the creation and consolidation of local Arab financial markets. The first, direct action, would concentrate on making it possible for the AMF to participate in the establishment of local brokerage houses so as to reinforce existing primary and secondary markets or those which might be established in the future in the member countries;

The second, indirect action, would involve the preparation of detailed studies on the condition of financial and money markets in each Arab country. These studies would determine what is required to strengthen the activity of these markets and also determine their needs in the way of technical assistance. They would also consider what type of aid should be provided, whether experts or consultants should be provided, for example, or whether scholarships and training grants would be more appropriate.

(b) The preparation of special studies in order to evaluate the prospects for linking Arab financial markets, especially in view of current regulations in the Arab countries regarding the issuance, registration and trading of securities, discussion of the findings of these studies and the presentation of appropriate recommendations.

(c) Efforts towards activating a regional Arab securities market within the limits allowed under the AMF Agreement. The Fund would thus issue securities for its own account and underwrite or guarantee securities issued by member states. This would enable the Fund to influence supply and demand in the financial market on the regional level.
(d) Helping to improve the investment climate in the member states by taking part in the preparation of an Arab agreement on investment and by supporting efforts towards its implementation and follow-up, as well as evaluating the results of its application on a regular basis.
(e) Efforts to develop the role of Arab banks and financial institutions in both the international and regional spheres, in order to encourage the investment of surplus Arab funds and as a source of short- and medium-term credit for Arab borrowers.

The fact is that, as will be discussed below, other Arab institutions have not as yet abandoned their activities in this domain, activities which the AMF, as a specialised institution, is perhaps better suited to perform. However, the Fund continues to co-operate with other institutions;[27] in this respect, it prepared and submitted a memorandum to the September 1980 Jeddah meeting of the governors of Arab central banks. In it, the Fund outlined the areas where action was indicated in the light of previous technical studies. In particular, the memorandum recommended: bolstering the capital and reserves of Arab banks; issuing certificates of deposit; lending at moving interest rates; investing in international bonds issued in Arab currencies; issuing bank acceptances; making public offerings to finance public debt; and developing local Arab legislation relating thereto.

3. Arab Monetary Integration. The Fund's objective in this area is two-fold: (a) to stabilise the cross-rates of Arab currencies and to bring about their inter-convertibility;[28] (b) to investigate possible means of expanding the use of the Arab accounting dinar, thereby laying the groundwork for the establishment of a common Arab currency.

It could be said that inter-convertibility of Arab currencies represents the first stage towards the creation of a uniform Arab currency. More important is the fact that in the context of the existing international monetary system with its floating currencies, regional efforts have already proved effective in protecting the exchange rates of the currencies of regional groups and maintaining their inter-convertibility. This has been demonstated by the success of the European Monetary System and by the role of the European Currency Unit (ECU) within it. This system, with its European Monetary Co-operation Fund, entails the right of intervention to correct exchange-rate deviations when such deviations exceed 2.5 per cent of the fixed value of a country's currency within the currency basket of the European Common Market.[29] It is also true that regional co-operation has become the primary means of achieving currency stability.

Nevertheless, doubts about the ability of the Fund to achieve inter-Arab exchange-rate stability have been raised. Fawzi Al-Qaisi has maintained that the stability of exchange rates depends on the international transactions of the Arab countries rather than on inter-Arab transactions, and that the pegging of Arab currencies to different currency blocs would make the achievement of this objective difficult.[30] He does not, however, rule out the possibility of pegging all the Arab currencies to the Arab accounting dinar which would ensure the maintenance of inter-Arab exchange-rate stability. The Fund would then provide loans to deficitory countries in order to help them stabilise their exchange rates. Balance-of-payments support would, in other words, be the means for stabilising Arab currencies. Consequently, to judge the Fund's capacity to achieve this objective, one must look at its capacity to provide sufficient support for purposes of currency stabilisation. This is a question the Fund should examine.

As for inter-Arab currency convertibility and the removal of exchange controls, this would seem to be possible for those countries which follow a free enterprise system and also, with some effort, for those countries which pursue central planning, provided the Fund achieves sufficient progress towards co-ordinating the monetary and financial policies of the member states.

At present, nine Arab countries peg their currencies to the US dollar.[31] Four Arab countries use the dollar as a basis for fixing the daily exchange rates of their currencies and change these in accordance with specific indicators with respect to the parity of the dollar *vis-à-vis* the SDR.[32] One Arab country has pegged its currency to its own special basket of major currencies.[33] Another group of Arab states has adopted a special basket, in which the French franc weighs heavily, as a basis for fixing the value of its currency.[34] One country has chosen to peg its currency to the SDR.[35] Finally, another country has chosen to maintain a floating rate.[36]

What must be achieved, however, is the objective of establishing a uniform Arab currency as stipulated in paragraph F of Article IV of the AMF Agreement, though this is perhaps one of the most controversial objectives of the AMF. The establishment of a uniform Arab currency constitutes a legitimate pan-Arab aspiration whose justification is the same as that for the establishment of a national currency by any state.

In addition to the pan-Arab considerations behind this move, the creation of a uniform Arab currency is dictated by the nature of prevailing international monetary conditions and the collapse of the Bretton Woods system. Economic thinking in the monetary field generally concedes that regional monetary systems such as the EMS can play an effective role in the stabilisation of the international monetary system by stabilising the currencies of its own members and by making it possible to recycle surpluses and use them to finance agreed objectives. It is therefore logical to envisage a positive role for an Arab monetary system and a uniform Arab currency which would complement the role of the major currencies in providing international liquidity and the reduction of destabilising elements in the monetary sphere.

It would be beyond the scope of this paper to go into a discussion of the meaning of monetary unification. Whether this would mean a uniform currency issued by a single authority which would replace all other Arab currencies, how the various Arab central banks would participate in a uniform currency system on the basis of specific technico-economic arrangements and standardised monetary regulations, the question of permitting free convertibility among the local currencies, all these questions would have to be addressed in such a discussion.[37] Our concern here, on the other hand, is simply to point out that this is neither an impossible task to accomplish, nor an easy one.

Some of the difficulties standing in the way of currency unification are: the different bases used for valuing the Arab currencies; the monetary and financial dependency of the Arab states; differences in monetary and financial policies; the absence of Arab financial markets through which Arab capital could easily flow into investment channels; disparities among the exchange rates of Arab currencies; the absence of inter-convertibility among them and their non-convertibility into foreign currencies; and the numerous restrictions imposed on current payments and capital transfers.

The AMF Agreement is to be credited for having set out explicit recommendations for dealing with these issues. Furthermore, it has sanctioned the concept of the Arab accounting dinar and defined it as being equivalent to three SDRs. The AMF, however, has yet to initiate the required steps which would achieve the unification of Arab currencies.

Undoubtedly, its success in this area will depend on its success in achieving exchange-rate stability and inter-convertibility among the Arab currencies. We have seen that the Fund is still in the early stages of tackling this goal. In this connection, the author agrees with Fawzi Al-Qaisi's view that the hard realities of the situation should not discourage the Fund from studying the means of expanding the use of the Arab accounting dinar as this would gradually lead to the creation of a common monetary base from which further steps towards monetary union could be launched.

4. Trade Integration. The goal of integrating trade and developing trade flows between the Arab countries is closely related to the Fund's objectives. We have already mentioned that the Arab Common Market Resolution stipulated that reciprocal payments agreements were to constitute a transitional solution pending the establishment of the Arab Monetary Fund. Some Arab countries originally believed that the development of trade should be a basic goal of the AMF and that the Fund's role should be confined to the financing of deficits arising from inter-Arab trade and not global deficits.[38] However, subsequent discussions revealed the difficulty of implementing this, on the one hand, and its inadequacy as an AMF objective, on the other. Consequently, it was decided that the volume of a member's trade would be a basic criterion which the Fund would take into account when granting loans (subparagraph A6 of Article XX). In addition, loans granted by the Fund for financing deficits arising from inter-Arab trade would be subject to easier conditions than those imposed in financing a global balance-of-payments deficit. This preferential treatment excluded only oil exchanges since the object of the Fund was to encourage trade outside the oil sector.

While the provisions of the Agreement in their totality serve this goal, direct reference to this objective appears under two headings, namely: 'Removal of Restrictions on Current Payments' and 'Settlement of Current Payments'.

a. Removal of restrictions on current payments. Exchange controls of varying degrees exist in most of the Arab countries,[39] some for historical reasons, some for monetary reasons and others for social reasons. No matter what the reasons behind them, their existence has the effect of impeding trade and of inhibiting moves towards economic integration. In fact some Arab countries have used these restrictions as a pretext to delay meeting certain of their obligations.

At the same time, some of these restrictions may be inevitable for those countries suffering from chronic balance-of-payments deficits related to their development effort, their national defence commitments or, perhaps, to the failure of the development effort itself. It is the responsibility not only of the individual countries but also of various Arab organisations to create favourable conditions for economic development. To this end, paragraph E of Article V of the AMF Agreement provides for the liberalisation and development of trade and current payments between member states, while paragraph A of Article VI provides for co-operation between these states and the Fund in 'reducing restrictions on current payments between member states ...

with the object of removing them altogether, as a means of achieving the Fund's objective of eliminating payments restrictions'.

This issue will need to be dealt with gradually, given the fact that some Arab member states have free enterprise economies while others have adopted a socialist system. What must also be considered are the resources available to the Fund for dealing with balance-of-payments disorders and the progress of the Fund in achieving its other objectives such as developing Arab financial markets and fostering Arab trade as part of a policy of collective self-reliance as opposed to 'local self-sufficiency'.

b. Settling payments. No doubt, any arrangements designed to promote regional trade require a definite system for settling payments. Paragraph H of Article IV of the Agreement stipulates that it is within the competence of the Fund to 'settle those current payments between member states which would strengthen trade activity'. Paragraph F of Article V clearly states the method by which the Fund is to realise this: 'The Fund should allocate a sufficient share of its resources, contributed in member states' currencies, to provide the necessary credit facilities for settling current payments between members in accordance with the rules and regulations which may be set down by the Board of Governors within the framework of a special account opened by the Fund for this purpose'.

This implies the establishment of arrangements by which the Fund would extend credit facilities to its members equal to their debit balance resulting from transactions with other members. This should not be difficult to accomplish and such arrangements would help limit the harmful effects of the bilateral character of Arab trade, enhance inter-Arab trade and encourage a relaxation of trade restrictions among the member states.

However, the agreement provides that only 2 per cent of the countries' shares shall be paid in national currencies, which means that the capital provided by this arrangement would be less than AAD 7.5 million even if the capital of the Fund were fully paid up. In our opinion, one of the reasons why the AMF has faltered is because the facilities it offers are less extensive than those provided for in some bilateral payments agreements between Arab states.

The Fund's objective of providing support for current payments can be achieved and will clearly be of benefit as long as two provisions are included in the arrangements relating to it:

(i) Resources allocated for this purpose must be increased to match not simply the present volume of Arab trade but also the future volume of this trade anticipated within the framework of a programme for

Arab economic integration which would ensure the broadening of the production base to meet the exchange needs of the member states;

(ii) A specialised body[40] would perform this function with the methods, responsibilities and scope normally associated with import-export banks, so that the matter would not stop at the settlement of payments in the conventional sense. Rather, it would extend to the development and diversification of trade and to the terms of related guarantees, institutions and arrangements aimed at creating and reinforcing the infrastructure for the development of inter-Arab trade in each country. It would also extend to: developing institutions for commercial services in the government and business sectors; increasing the volume of trade in those commodities already being traded and introducing new products for trade; providing multichannel marketing both within the Arab world and abroad; developing methods and means for import operations; and providing manpower training. The organisation of payments settlement between Arab states in a manner which would contribute effectively to the development of Arab trade would necessarily be based on a combination of three known institutional arrangements. These are the settlement of payments, import-export banks and regional centres for the development of trade. All these fall within the scope of AMF activities.

B. AMF Objectives in the International Sphere

Paragraph G of Article IV of the AMF Agreement stipulates that the Fund shall 'co-ordinate the views of member states on international monetary and economic issues in a way which emphasizes their common interests and contributes to the solution of world monetary problems'. This stipulation had the unanimous support of the bank governors and financial experts who took part in drafting the Agreement at the various meetings and preparatory sessions.

Attention might be drawn here to some of the points which were constantly referred to during discussions of these international issues:

(i) The Arab countries have a definite interest in setting up a new, equitable and stable monetary system and it would be only fair for them to be given a greater say in taking decisions connected with setting up this system;

(ii) Such a system must provide for a balanced role for the regional groupings and currencies in order to prevent any single currency from dominating international liquidity. Therefore, the Arab world, while seeking a role which would be in accordance with the development of its economic strength, calls for a serious rearrangement of the roles accorded to different economic forces in exerting a decisive influence on the international monetary system, in the light of (i) changes which have taken place in the centres of greatest economic progress within the group controlling the present system; and (ii) the need to curb the control by one or two countries over fundamental decisions affecting the system and over international liquidity. Furthermore, the voting strength of the United States must be reconsidered. Similarly, regional currency systems, including the European and the Arab systems, must play a more important role in providing international liquidity;

(iii) The current monetary system is one which gives expression to Western economic interests. If it is to take on a truly universal character, then its organisation must be altered in a way which would attract the participation of countries of the Socialist bloc and of Switzerland. This is so because the responsibility of the international monetary system is a comprehensive one by virtue of the universal nature of economic relationships, the increase in the degree of interdependence and the fact that world prosperity is organically bound up with the positive development of this interdependence.

The AMF was designed to act as a forum and an institution through which the Arab countries could crystallise their attitudes with regard to international issues so as to contribute to their solution. So far, although the Fund has exhibited some positive signs in this regard, it is still a long way from the full assumption of this role. This may not be attributable to the Fund as much as to the fact that some Arab countries have not yet enabled their regional organisations to do their job in the way laid down by their charters.

C. AMF Objectives in the Organisational Sphere

The establishment of the AMF completed the series of organisations necessary for Arab economic integration by providing specialisation in the monetary aspects of such integration. Just as the IMF works alongside the International Bank for Reconstruction and Development (IBRD) and the General Agreement on Tariffs and Trade (GATT) organisation,[41] so must the AMF work alongside and in co-ordination with the Council of Arab Economic Unity (and the Arab Common Market arising out of it),[42] the Arab Fund for Economic and Social Development (AFESD) and the other joint Arab organisations, within the framework of a joint Arab economic strategy.

While the joint Arab organisations currently operating are of a fundamentally comprehensive nature, this is not yet the case with the Council of Arab Economic Unity Agreement and the Arab Common Market. However, from the very outset, the Fund has been a natural outcome of the activity of the Council of Arab Economic Unity and the objective of its plan is tied up with the decision to create the Arab Common Market. Future developments will undoubtedly see the materialisation of this comprehensiveness with regard to the Arab Economic Unity Agreement and the Arab Common Market because the scientific approach to the problem of Arab economic integration confirms one truth and one alone. This is that Arab economic integration begins at a higher stage than that of co-operation. It is to the co-operation stage and the conventions established during that stage that certain Arab departments and officials would like blindly to adhere contrary to the very purpose of common Arab activity.

In any case, paragraph I of Article XXX of the AMF Agreement stipulates that 'the Board of Governors shall co-operate in drawing up its policies ... with the Economic and Social Council, the Council of Arab Economic Unity and the Arab Fund for Economic and Social Development'. One might say that the governors could have set down this article at the beginning without reference to the Economic and Social Council or the AFESD on the strength of Article VII of the Agreement which stipulates that the Fund 'shall co-operate with all similar Arab institutions in realizing its objectives. It shall also co-operate with similar international organizations when necessary'. Nevertheless it was decided to add both the Economic and Social Council and the AFESD along with the Council of Arab Economic Unity on the day the Agreement was signed.[43]

What is crucial is that the AMF plays a fundamental role among the institutions of Arab economic integration. It must be enabled to perform this role as the organisation which co-ordinates both the monetary policies of the Arab countries and their international positions *vis-à-vis* the world monetary situation. In addition, the Fund should be empowered to fulfil all the objectives assigned to it.

The Fund has also aspired, as its reports indicate, to take the initiative in drawing up specific programmes of action aimed at the co-ordination of Arab organisations generally and of the Council of Arab Economic Unity, the Economic and Social Council and the AFESD in particular. Nevertheless, one notes that the Economic and Social Council has continued to perform two functions over which it was clearly decided that jurisdiction be given to the AMF, i.e., the meetings of central bank governors and the development of the Arab financial and monetary market. We can only emphasise here that both of these functions should henceforth be conducted under the auspices of the AMF.

II. The AMF and the IMF

It is not surprising that the ways and means of regional co-operation resemble those of co-operation in the international arena.

The AMF is an institution for regional monetary co-operation which is performing its own role and at the same time reinforcing the role and activities of the IMF, in the economic sphere generally and in the monetary sphere in particular. As it happens, every member of the AMF is also a member of the IMF, though a given Arab state could, in theory, be a member of one and not of the other. Nevertheless, this overlapping in the membership of the two organisations makes co-operation between them all the more necessary.

It could be said that the IMF has four main objectives, namely:

1. The establishment of an international monetary system under whose auspices currency exchange would take place in conformity with previously agreed rates, with a degree of flexibility within limits known to the Fund or by agreement with it. This objective was amended following acceptance of the principle of floating exchange rates at the international level.
2. Removing currency restrictions after a transitional period and establishing a multilateral, international system for payments.
3. Working towards the elimination of balance-of-payments disorders. This could be achieved by: making international financing available to members to meet unforeseen or temporary balance-of-payments deficits; dealing with the surplus countries by authorising other countries to impose restrictions on them without having either to ask the Fund's permission or to call on the surplus country itself to change the exchange rate of its currency.
4. The establishment of a permanent institution within whose framework international co-operation could take place in the monetary field.

The same sort of objectives were also decided upon in the AMF Agreement whereby the AMF also strives to: deal with balance-of-payments disorders; minimise restrictions on payments with a view to eliminating them altogether; stabilise the exchange rates of Arab currencies and make them inter-convertible; set up a system for settling payments among Arab countries; and establish an institution for monetary co-operation among Arab countries. Although the two funds follow different methods and technical arrangements and do not enjoy the same executive capabilities in terms of achieving their objectives, such differences do not affect the essence of the resemblance. Nevertheless, there do remain a number of differences between the two funds.

The AMF is striving towards an ultimate objective, namely union. In other words, it is the prerogative of the AMF to prepare the way for the creation of a uniform Arab currency and work for Arab unity in the monetary field. For this reason, the preamble to the Agreement clearly stipulates the signatories' 'desire to establish the monetary components of Arab economic integration'. Then, Article VIII of the AMF Agreement stipulates that 'the Fund shall provide technical services and assistance in the monetary and financial spheres to member states which conclude agreements with a view to attaining monetary unity among themselves as one of the stages in achieving the Fund's objectives'. While the concepts of integration, monetary union and unity are related to each other as stages in a succession, any one of them constitues a higher stage than the co-operation stage within which the IMF is still operating. The integration and monetary union referred to in the AMF Agreement are no more than stages in the process of realising the Fund's higher objectives, nothing ranks higher than integration or union except full unification.

The difference between the two funds is also apparent in the conditions under which they were established.

The establishment and organisation of the IMF came about in response to an American conception of monetary issues which had been formed by the monetary situation between the world wars, in general, and by the problems and consequences of the Great Depression of the 1930s, in particular. This was a time when protectionism and nationalism were widespread and when there was a good deal of competitive currency devaluation. At the same time, a policy of forming rival economic blocs was being generally applied in the absence of any mechanism for international co-operation, while the American view regarding appropriate solutions to these problems was gaining currency. The AMF, on the other hand, was set up to complete an existing series of institutions for Arab economic integration, to draw up suitable solutions to the problems of member states in the monetary field and to form an Arab bloc capable of protecting the Arab countries from the dangers of international monetary problems and focusing the efforts of these states on solving world monetary problems. The AMF is an organisation with defined aims and objectives which are not necessarily those of the IMF. Likewise, the methods of the AMF and the market it comprises do not exactly match the methods of the IMF or the market associated with it.

The Bretton Woods Agreement depended on the existence of the International Bank for Reconstruction and Development as a vehicle for the transfer of development resources by providing long-term credit on easy terms. As such, it was clear from the start that the funds of the IMF were unavailable for development financing or for reconstruction following the Second World War and that their use was to be confined to the financing of extraordinary or temporary deficits through the granting of short-term loans. In contrast to this, the AMF Agreement assigned to the AMF the responsibility for developing Arab financial markets and laid down as one of its basic objectives the fostering of economic development in the Arab states. In outlining the means at the Fund's disposal, the Agreement explicitly provided for the possibility of the Fund's acting as an intermediary in the international and Arab markets. The text did not stipulate that the purpose of this intermediary role should be the financing of the global balance-of-payments deficit, as it did with respect to the issuance of guarantees. The text firmly related the issuance of guarantees to the objective of financing the global deficit. Nevertheless, the concept of relating deficit financing to the development process is, in itself, far in advance of the concept behind the IMF.

Differentiating between the IMF and the AMF in another respect, we find that membership in the former was restricted initially to countries with very similar economic systems, while membership in the AMF was expanded to include all Arab countries irrespective of the substantial differences in their economic systems.

The drafting of the Bretton Woods Agreement represented the victory of the ideas of a single country with superior economic power in a clear contest between two draft proposals. One was presented by the British economist Keynes, who represented the point of view of the debtor countries, and the other was put forward by Harry White, representing the American point of view. In the AMF, on the other hand, all the preparatory work and the discussions were oriented towards defending the interests of all Arab countries without differentiating between the surplus and deficit countries. In fact the representatives of the deficit countries were those most concerned about preventing the AMF from being a credit institution only; they wanted the Fund to be an institution that would achieve the objectives of monetary integration and unification, inspired by the vision of a future Arab monetary system. This point is verified by the fact that participation in the capital of the Fund was determined according to two criteria: the ability to contribute and the extent of the need to utilise the resources of the fund. The Arab countries with the least financial capability were free to subscribe to any number of shares they desired. This is very different from the way subscriptions in the IMF were determined, whereby trade volume, GNP size and political considerations were used to set the size of shareholdings so as to ensure that certain countries would maintain a controlling interest. This was reflected in the 73 per cent voting power secured by the big industrial countries and the 28 per cent secured by the developing countries. This state of affairs persisted from the time the Bretton Woods Agreement came into effect up to the adoption of the Smithsonian Agreement, which reduced the former percentage to 68 per cent and raised the latter to less than 33 per cent. By comparison, the voting power of the wealthier countries in the AMF amounts to 52 per cent compared with 48 per cent for the poorer countries. This comparison should require no further elaboration.[44]

In another connection and to further illustrate the differences between the AMF and the IMF, it could be said that the AMF's goal of developing Arab trade amounts to an explicit contravention of the principle of international free trade for which the IMF works. Nevertheless, it represents a step forward on the road to economic development for a group of countries through self-reliance in the context of legitimate regional arrangements and national aspirations which can only be welcomed and respected.

III. Concluding Remarks

The nature of the AMF, its goals and its performance have been the subject of this paper. Reference to many other matters has necessarily been omitted. Some of these matters are important: for example, the Fund's success, despite the short period during which it has operated, in preserving and developing its resources. This has increased confidence in its ability to assume possible future responsibilities. Another important factor is the Fund's experience in both the Arab and international arenas and its flexibility in dealing with the obstacles encountered in both. In addition, it should be noted that some of the difficulties which have been encountered in the organisational sphere can gradually be resolved. Perhaps future developments in the reorganisation of the machinery and organisations for joint Arab action will bring about suitable solutions which will enable the Fund to perform its role as an Arab institution within whose framework Arab monetary policies, whether related to Arab or international questions, can best be decided.

However, one might mention here a point which has often been made by those who have followed the progress of the Fund and of Arab monetary co-operation, if from a somewhat narrow perspective. This often-repeated point pertains to the limited sources for the Fund's credit facilities and the resulting reluctance of the member states to deal with the Fund. In fact, the AMF was designed to deal with the monetary aspects of Arab economic integration and not merely to finance members' global balance-of-payments deficits. Such deficit financing is only one of the Fund's many roles and should not overshadow the others. The attempt by other Arab organisations to duplicate the Fund's functions most probably stems from their over-emphasising the objective of deficit financing and the sources of this financing at the expense of all other objectives.

The Arab Fund is a pioneering regional experiment and represents the foremost institution of joint Arab action with respect to definition of goals and flexibility of means. The present stage through which the economies of the Arab nation are passing requires the Fund to move in several directions in a balanced manner. The problem of increasing the sources of the Fund's credit facilities is one which the realities of the situation will determine just as they determined the amount of the Fund's capital. This was set at AAD 250 million, after all, while Arab action had previously failed to implement a payments union whose capital was no more than AAD 51 million.

Irrespective of precisely what is understood by monetary cooperation, monetary integration or monetary union among the Arab states, all fall within the objectives and means of the AMF. The AMF should tackle its mission with more programmes and meetings with Arab monetary authorities. These meetings should be conducted within a framework of close co-ordination with those responsible for economic policy in the member states.

At such meetings, discussion should be mainly devoted to setting well-defined programmes for the achievement of Arab monetary integration within the framework of the AMF. No other topic should supersede this. Let us, as a part of a movement in Arab thinking which is in tune with international experience, remind the Arab governments of the documents they have signed and ask them to fulfil their commitments. Let us hear from them their suggestions for ensuring the successful application of these agreements instead of becoming preoccupied with the wording of this or that phrase or the drafting of some objective or other. This preoccupation with details is something to which some of our dear colleagues are extremely prone, thereby providing suitable pretexts for those who wish to water down agreements or delay their execution.

Notes

1. For details of these discussions, see the recommendations and resolutions of the meeting of governors of the Arab central banks, Baghdad, 22-24 February 1975, in Council of Arab Economic Unity, General Secretariat, *Arab Monetary Fund: Minutes and Proceedings of the Meetings Preparatory to the Agreement* (Cairo: Council for Arab Economic Unity, 1977). (In Arabic.)

2. Fawzi Al-Qaisi, 'The Arab Monetary Fund: its Objectives and Importance', *Majallat al-Iqtisadi al-'Arabi*, vol. 1, no. 3 (July 1977), p. 11 (in Arabic).

3. Ibid., p. 12.

4. Ibid., p. 12.

5. For further details concerning the AMF capital augmentation, see the AMF memorandum presented at the special AMF meeting in Tunis, September 1980. It divides the deficit countries into two categories:

Category A: This category includes countries with moderate deficits or limited surpluses and which have therefore succeeded in keeping their indebtedness within acceptable limits. They are: Jordan, Bahrain, Algeria, Oman, Lebanon and Yemen;

Category B: This category comprises those countries which have been experiencing rising deficits in their payments balances and includes all the other Arab countries with the exception of the surplus countries (the UAE, Saudi Arabia, Iraq, Qatar, Kuwait and Libya).

6. Ibid.

7. See the Council of Arab Economic Unity memorandum in Council for Arab Economic Unity, General Secretariat, *Arab Monetary Fund: Minutes and Proceedings of the Meetings Preparatory to the Agreement*, with special reference to the discussion in vol. 1, pp. 361-459.

8. See the Council of Arab Economic Unity memorandum, ibid., p. 26. It would appear that the Fund has based its estimate on the assumption that the additional expenditure on development would be within the limits of $1.5 billion. We will return to a discussion of this point later.

9. Further reference will be made to the reductions in borrowing costs that can occur when financially weak countries utilise the Fund's facilities in this way.

10. Based on a study prepared by Sabbah Kajahji, Sinan Shubaibi and Ali Murza, Iraq, July 1980 (mimeographed).

11. In addition to what accrues from development contracts, the anticipated sources of this capital flow are the regional development funds, the Arab and Islamic funds and the joint Arab companies whose combined capital amounts to about $12 billion. This could be doubled if there were opportunities for investment and for collective or bilateral Arab aid, in addition to revenues from development contracts and those related to international and non-Arab government institutions (provided these are not tied to terms inconsistent with the objectives of Arab development or the political independence of the Arab countries).

12. The Agreement stipulates that loans extended to member states may not exceed twice the paid-up subscription over a 12-month period.

13. See Council of Arab Economic Unity, General Secretariat, *Arab Monetary Fund: Minutes and Proceedings of the Meetings Preparatory to the Agreement*, vol. 1, p. 134 and pp. 171-2.

14. See the Arab Monetary Fund memorandum presented at the special AMF meeting in Tunis, September 1980.

15. Council of Arab Economic Unity, General Secretariat, *Arab Monetary Fund: Minutes and Proceedings of the Meetings Preparatory to the Agreement*, vol. 1, pp. 591-8.

16. Ibid., vol. 2, pp. 795-805.

17. See the discussion on providing low interest rates, particularly where deficits resulting from inter-Arab transactions are involved. Ibid., pp. 836-58.

18. For a clear account of the reasons and thinking behind this stipulation, see the discussions in Council of Arab Economic Unity, General Secretariat, *Arab Monetary Fund: Minutes and Proceedings of the Meetings Preparatory to the Agreement*, particularly pp. 572-82, p. 793 and pp. 818-22.

19. See AMF, *Arab Monetary Fund, Annual Report 1977* (Abu Dhabi: Arab-British Chamber of Commerce, n.d.), p. 7.

20. See AMF, *Arab Monetary Fund, Annual Report 1978* (Abu Dhabi: Arab-British Chamber of Commerce, n.d.), p. 17.

21. See the Arab Monetary Fund memorandum presented at the special AMF meeting in Tunis, September 1980, p. 13.

22. Al-Qaisi, 'The Arab Monetary Fund: Its Objectives and Importance.'

23. For further details and complete coverage of this topic, see the Arab Monetary Fund memorandum presented at the special AMF meeting in Tunis, September 1980, pp. 26-35.

24. AMF, *Arab Monetary Fund, Annual Report 1979*, pp. 30-1.

25. Council of Arab Economic Unity, General Secretariat, 'Arab Financial Markets: their Present and Past', *Majallat al-Waḥda al-Iqtiṣādiya al-'Arabiya*, vol. 2, no. 3 (April 1976), (in Arabic).

26. Ibid., pp. 46-9.

27. The latest developments in the progress of the Arab financial market in other areas were taken up at the meeting of governors of Arab central banks in Jeddah on 3-4 September 1980. At that meeting, the AMF memorandum was discussed and the recommendations of the Technical Committee, on which the memorandum was based, were approved. The Union of Arab Banks was assigned the responsibility for preparing a survey of banking institutions and joint Arab-foreign banks in the Arab countries for the purpose of identifying the problems and obstacles they face. The findings of the survey were to be relayed to the AMF which would then prepare the necessary studies relating thereto for submission to the Board of Governors at its next meeting.

28. Paragraph B of Article IV of the AMF Agreement.

29. For additional merits of regional monetary arrangements see: Robert Triffin, 'The Future of the International Monetary System', in *Banca Nazionale del Lavoro Quarterly Review* (March 1980); translated into French in *Revue de la Banque* (April 1980).

30. See Al-Qaisi, 'The Arab Monetary Fund: Its Objectives and Importance'.

31. Sudan, the Syrian Arab Republic, Somalia, Iraq, Oman, Libya, Egypt, Yemen and Democratic Yemen.

32. UAE, Bahrain, Qatar and Saudi Arabia.

33. Kuwait.

34. Algeria, Mauritania, Morocco and Tunisia.

35. Jordan.

36. Lebanon.

37. For details refer to Mohammed Labib Shoukair, *Economic Relations Between the Arab Countries* (Cairo: Manshūrāt M'ahad al-Dirāsāt al-'Arabiya al-'Aliya, 1958), pp. 285-6 (in Arabic).

38. Refer to the remarks made by the governor of the Libyan Central Bank and the ideas and solutions raised during the preparatory meetings with respect to this topic in Council of Arab Economic Unity, General Secretariat, *Arab Monetary Fund: Minutes and Proceedings of the Meetings Preparatory to the Agreement*.

39. Twelve Arab states presently maintain some form of exchange control. Some have planned economies, others suffer from deficits and a third group exhibits both these characteristics. States which do not maintain exchange controls are Bahrain, Kuwait, Lebanon, Oman, Qatar, Saudi Arabia, the UAE and Yemen.

40. A study was prepared by the General Secretariat of the Council of Arab Economic Unity at the end of 1977 in connection with the establishment of such a bank based on a resolution adopted by the Council at that time.

41. It was assumed that the Havana Charter, which set up the International Trade Organisation in 1947, would complement the Bretton Woods Agreement, but the process of establishing this organisation was obstructed and the inter-

national community became convinced of the American solution in this sphere. This was the solution that formed the basis for the General Agreement on Tariffs and Trade (GATT).

42. The Council of Arab Economic Unity Agreement comprises 13 out of a total of 22 Arab countries. The Common Market Resolution comprises 6 countries.

43. For details on this matter, see the account of the different sessions of financial experts and bank governors in Council for Arab Economic Unity, General Secretariat, *Arab Monetary Fund: Minutes and Proceedings of the Meetings Preparatory to the Agreement* and the proceedings of the special meeting of the governors of the Arab central banks in Rabat, 19-20 November 1975.

44. Algeria, Bahrain, Democratic Yemen, Egypt, Mauritania, Morocco, Palestine, Somalia, Sudan, the Syrian Arab Republic, Tunisia and Yemen were considered poorer only by virtue of their balance-of-payments positions.

COMMENT*

Mohammed Labib Shoukair

I would first like to concur with two basic observations which Mr Al-Sagban makes in his paper. These constitute the point of departure for my comments.

The first observation is that in any collective activity on an international or regional scale, political will plays a crucial role not only in the establishment of the agreements through which such collective activity is organised but also, and especially, in how these agreements are applied and the extent to which this collective activity is supported, developed and reinforced. I do not wish to dwell on the role of political will in its various aspects as it relates to the role of the Arab Monetary Fund. I will simply say that the stronger the political will exhibited, the more forceful and effective will be the Fund's work, the more varied and numerous its facets and the better the opportunity for it to achieve all of the wide-ranging objectives provided for in the Agreement by which it was created.

It should be noted that the AMF has not remained idle in this regard but has been trying with all the means at its disposal to contribute to creating the required political will and steering it in the direction of supporting joint Arab economic activity generally. The AMF and other Arab organisations still have a long way to go, however, in this regard.

The second observation I would like to make is that joint Arab economic activity currently reflects a constant duplication of effort. This is not the place to examine the reasons for this or the factors which have led to this phenomenon; these are known to all and can be found in other experiences of regional economic co-operation as well, both in Europe and in Latin America. What matters is that this duplication should be eliminated in order to put an end to the contradictions and inconsistencies resulting from a situation where several organisations are responsible for the same activity. Here again the outcome depends, in the end, on the emergence of the political determination necessary to eliminate this redundancy. Mr Al-Sagban is among those who have attempted to eliminate existing duplication. The same is true of the AMF which submitted a study to the relevant parties outlining the reasons for this duplication and suggesting ways to overcome it. Unfortunately, however, it continues to prevail and a substantial effort is still required to put an end to it.

* Translated from the Arabic.

In the light of these two remarks, I can now begin to focus on some of the points on which I agree with Mr Al-Sagban in terms of their importance to the Fund's activity.

1. I am in complete agreement with him that the Fund's objectives as stipulated in the Agreement make it an institution for Arab monetary integration working in the service of both Arab economic integration and the Arab economic development process.

We can easily infer from the Agreement the philosophy behind it, namely that some of the necessary means for achieving the objectives must be utilised immediately, or in the short run, due to the urgency of the problems with which they are meant to deal and because they can be readily activated from a technical point of view. The other means and objectives require for their implementation a longer period of time.

Despite the clarity of this distinction in the Agreement, the Fund has, since its creation, been dealing with all of the objectives and means, from the standpoint of its activity, as if they were equally pressing. For this reason, it has taken with respect to each of them steps which reflect this attitude, according to the nature of each of these means and objectives and the effort and phases required to put them into force.

2. I am also in complete agreement with Mr Al-Sagban that, as concerns the Fund's activity in correcting payments imbalances, the text which refers to the Fund's giving support for such imbalances by offering guarantees to the member countries should be interpreted to mean that these guarantees be subject to the same limits as apply to loans, i.e., 300 per cent (which may go up to 400 per cent) of the member's capital subscription. Furthermore, they should be offered as a supplement to the loans which the Fund grants to the member within the same limits. In fact, one of the first papers discussed at the AMF after it commenced its activities was one submitted by Mr Al-Imam which took the view that guarantees should be understood in this sense.

However, we shall see that, even if there were agreement on this interpretation, there is an economic factor which might compel us seriously to examine its application, namely its impact on the Fund's ability to borrow directly from the financial markets in order to cope with the needs of the member countries.

3. I also agree with him that the Fund's role cannot be confined merely to granting credit facilities to support the payments balances of the member countries. It also has a role in fostering the development process in the member countries: a part of its activity must be directed towards assisting these countries in their development as per Article V of the Agreement which makes one of the means available to the Fund the arranging and guaranteeing of loans to the member countries from the financial markets. Since the Article does not stipulate that the purpose of these loans should be to support payments balances, they

may be used for development purposes. Moreover, arranging for these loans on the Arab markets would be one way of contributing to the support and development of these markets themselves and of achieving greater cohesion among them.

4. Similarly, I agree with Mr Al-Sagban's proposal for opening up new outlets for the Fund's facilities. It is by means of these expanded outlets that the Fund can assist and support the payments balances of the member countries. Possibilities include an oil facility; a facility whereby the Fund would be compensated for the low interest rates at which it must lend provided that this would be financed out of an amount which the surplus countries would allocate annually in support of Arab solidarity; a facility for promoting the development of trade among the member countries, and a facility for coping with the effects of pan-Arab defence expenditures on the balance of payments.

5. Nor do we differ over the importance of the Fund's international role and the role it must play in the area of co-ordinating the position of the Arab countries in relation to international monetary, financial and economic issues. The AMF has acted forcefully in the international sphere. For example, in July 1980 it sponsored a seminar jointly with UNCTAD [United Nations Conference on Trade and Development] whose aim was to unify the positions of the developing countries *vis-à-vis* the international monetary system and various monetary issues. This included a clarification of the oil issue as it has developed since the 1973-4 price increases and, in particular, the non-responsibility of the oil countries for the inflationary pressures prevailing in the industrialised nations which may be attributable to many factors too numerous to discuss here. One of the Fund's objectives in holding this seminar was to clarify this issue and to prevent any split in the positions of the Arab and other Third World countries. I think the document which came out of that seminar is an indication of the great success achieved by the Fund in this regard.

The Fund has also succeeded in convincing Arab countries to express their positions on these international issues as a unified group at the annual meetings of the IMF and the IBRD. The Fund is responsible for the preparation of the position paper jointly with the AFESD and in consultation with the member countries. While the co-ordination of the Arab position on international monetary, financial and economic issues no doubt requires something farther-reaching than this, it is nevertheless a starting point from which we will gradually move on to more important measures.

6. As concerns the meetings of the governors of the Arab central banks, I agree with Mr Al-Sagban that these meetings were supposed to take place under the sole auspices of the AMF. Duplication of effort still prevails, however, and the current practice of holding the meetings

in co-operation with one or more other parties is preferable to their not being held at all. Such meetings contribute to the process of coordinating the positions of the Arab monetary authorities on international monetary, financial and economic issues. It is the AMF, in any case, which should submit the studies and make the necessary recommendations in this connection. There is no harm in the Fund's calling meetings jointly with other parties, as long as it has the responsibility, in the end, for drawing up the required technical studies. Future developments in this regard will depend on the extent to which the current duplication of effort is eliminated.

7. I also agree with Mr Al-Sagban as to the importance of the Fund's role in promoting the development and integration of the Arab financial markets. Far from overlooking this issue, the Fund has devoted considerable effort to studying ways of achieving this objective, as one step towards monetary and financial co-operation and the achievement of partial Arab monetary integration. However, this subject entails many problems which require extensive study. The AMF has consulted many experts and held numerous discussions on this matter with economists, including Mr Al-Sagban himself. The results of these consultations will be submitted to the AMF Board of Governors so that it may take the necessary decisions in this regard.

9. Thus, the AMF has acted to achieve its objectives and has not confined its operations merely to the granting of credit facilities as might have been inferred from the remarks of some of the partipants in this seminar and from Mr Al-Sagban's paper.

10. To the extent that the AMF has indeed been particularly concerned with its lending activities, this can be explained by a number of factors.

(a) The Fund has found that a large number of member countries are suffering from increasingly serious balance-of-payments deficits. If this matter had not been dealt with, it would have forced the Arab countries concerned to look for financial aid abroad. This would only have increased the degree of their foreign dependency, whereas one of the Fund's objectives is to attract these countries to Arab financial sources with the aim of drawing them into the process of Arab monetary integration.

(b) There are also technical factors which have created the impression that the Fund is more concerned with its lending activity than with the issue of monetary integration. These include the fact that the question of monetary integration is inseparable from other aspects of economic integration, e.g., trade, services and the transfer of capital. The Fund has found it necessary to participate with the other Arab organisations responsible for these aspects of economic integration in laying down the appropriate bases and arrangements for expanding inter-Arab trade and capital transfers. These organisations include the Council of Arab Economic Unity and the Economic and Social Council of the Arab League. The Fund was involved in drawing up a new draft agreement for the protection of capital transfers among the Arab countries which was approved by all the Arab countries at the September 1980 meeting of the Economic and Social Council in Tunis. The Fund considers this agreement an important step in developing Arab financial markets.

11. In addition, the achievement of monetary integration is not, from a technical viewpoint, as easy as it may appear. First of all, what is generally meant by monetary integration? Messrs Williamson and Triffin list more than nine definitions of monetary integration. Which of these should we adopt? It was precisely because the AMF found itself faced with such a choice among various approaches that it decided to hold this seminar in co-operation with the Centre for Arab Unity Studies. This seminar therefore represents a major effort by the Fund – and a continuation of its many efforts in the three years since its creation – to define the concept of monetary integration by which the Fund should be guided in its future endeavours.

If we assume that we must adopt one of the modes of partial monetary integration discussed at this seminar, which mode should it be? Then, if we agree on a particular mode of partial integration, how can we achieve it and apply it, given the current pegging of Arab currencies to international currencies?

A proposal prepared by the AMF for settling payments between Arab countries is now completed and will be presented shortly to representatives of the Arab central banks, then to the governors of these banks preliminary to its submission to the AMF Board of Governors. A recent academic seminar, attended by economic experts from various countries, discussed experiences around the world with regard to the settling of payments in order that the Fund might benefit from these experiences in making its proposals. Clearly, then, the monetary integration objective has been from the outset as important a part of the Fund's activity as its lending operations, even if for a number of reasons the AMF has not made it a point to publicise these activities.

12. I now arrive at the points on which I am afraid I differ with Mr Al-Sagban. They pertain to the resources required to provide balance-of-payments support for member countries.

The Fund has always felt that its resources were less than sufficient for the needs of the deficit countries. Mr Al-Sagban himself refers in his paper to the many obstacles facing the Fund in its lending activity on behalf of the member countries. For example, the share-holdings of the deficit countries in the Fund's capital are relatively meagre, a fact which limits their ability to borrow from the Fund, as the amounts available to them depend on the size of their capital subscription (300 per cent of their subscription which may be increased to 400 per cent by decision of the Board of Governors plus an additional 100 per cent in the case of compensatory loans, which are granted in order to deal with an urgent export deficit or an urgent increase in agricultural imports). Thus the deficit countries find that it is hardly worth the trouble to apply for loans from the AMF with all the procedures and follow-up involved, in order to obtain such limited amounts compared with their deficit financing needs and compared with what they can secure from the IMF.

To remedy this situation, the AMF has made a number of proposals: first, that the deficit countries increase their share-holdings in the Fund, even if they have to pay for the additional shares through a loan from the AMF for the amount of the increase; this will enable the AMF to increase its lending to these countries. Secondly: that the link between the size of the share and the size of the loan no longer be maintained in the rigid way currently provided for under the Agreement. These two proposals were presented to the Board of Governors meeting in a special session in Tunis in September 1980 and are included in a document submitted to the Arab Summit Conference to be held this month [November 1980] in Amman. Thirdly, the Fund's capital should be augmented. This proposal did not originate with the Fund but rather was included in a resolution passed by the Conference of Ministers of Foreign and Economic Affairs in Amman in July 1980 which requested that the AMF prepare a study concerning the proposed increase. In a memorandum which it submitted to the Board of Governors at its special September 1980 meeting in Tunis, the AMF proposed that its capital be augmented to a little over AAD 1,000 million.

Mr Al-Sagban states that the AMF may be over-emphasising the issue of capital augmentation. He points out that the Fund's capital is AAD 250 million with the unpaid part (half of the shares) still due. The Fund could always borrow from the international financial markets within the limits defined by the Agreement, i.e., at the rate of 200 per cent of its capital. So let us say it borrows AAD 500 million. Its resources would then amount to AAD 750 million. Add to this AAD 100 million from its reserves and any amounts allotted to it from the Arab Development Decade. The Fund could also borrow up to twice the amount of its reserves, i.e., AAD 200 million, bringing the total of the AMF's resources to AAD 1,050 million. This would bring us up to the amount of the proposed AMF increase in its capital, but without having to wait for such an increase to take effect.

It might be possible to accept this solution if it were not for a certain number of considerations which must be clarified and discussed:

(i) First of all, it is not reasonable for a modern institution such as the AMF to rely on borrowing in order to obtain three-quarters of its resources.

(ii) Secondly, assuming for the sake of argument that this were reasonable, the prevailing interest rates at which the Fund would have to borrow may be very high. This means that the Fund would not be able to carry out what Mr Al-Sagban considers so necessary, namely the extension of loans at low interest rates not to exceed 4.5 to 5 per cent.

(iii) Mr Al-Sagban might nevertheless respond that, as he proposes in his paper, the wealthy Arab countries would pay the AMF certain annual amounts as compensation for the difference between the high interest rates at which it borrows on the market and the low interest rates at which it lends to its members.

This brings us to the question of whether or not the wealthy Arab countries would accept this proposal. In fact, the issue here becomes one of choice and preference. Will the wealthy countries prefer this solution or will they prefer to augment the Fund's capital by means of increasing the shares they hold?

There is nothing, as I see it, which would actually prevent the AMF from accepting the first solution were the wealthy countries to accept it as well. In practice, they have opted to consider increasing the Fund's capital. A serious problem will, of course, arise if they do not accept either of the two solutions. For the deficit countries will then continue to suffer from serious deficits without being able to obtain from the AMF the necessary financial assistance.

13. I do share Mr Al-Sagban's view regarding the question of guarantees. In his opinion guarantees made to the member countries should be subject to the same limits as apply to loans: i.e., 300 per cent to be increased to 400 per cent by decision of the Board of Governors, plus 100 per cent in the case of compensatory loans. He notes, however, that if this were applied without an accompanying increase in the Fund's capital, the AMF would not easily be able to borrow the equivalent of 200 per cent of its capital. The guarantees represent in the end potential debts for the AMF in the event that the member countries borrowing from the international market are unable to meet their obligations. Therefore, potential lenders could be expected to take such guarantees into account when the AMF applied for loans on the financial markets, i.e., they would want to ensure that the total of the Fund's guarantees and its borrowings did not exceed 200 per cent of its capital. This reasoning reinforces, in my opinion, the need to augment the Fund's capital.

GENERAL DISCUSSION

1. Amer J. Khayatt

Both Mr Al-Sagban's paper and Mr Shoukair's commentary raise some basic questions concerning the role of political will in achieving integration. Political will is, in my opinion, an important factor which merits emphasis.

Many of the seminar papers basically revolve around establishing the need for monetary integration and finding an appropriate theoretical foundation for it. In dealing with this issue the authors of these papers have adopted three basic approaches: the first involves a discussion of available means and alternatives, indicating for each alternative its positive and negative aspects; the second approach attempts to record the experiences of all the countries that have pursued policies of economic co-ordination with the objective of achieving partial or comprehensive integration; the third approach evaluates Arab attempts to achieve some form of Arab co-ordination and participation in joint projects and economic institutions, which could ultimately lead to the realisation of the goal of economic integration. The positive and negative aspects of these efforts are discussed so as to be taken into account in future efforts towards integration.

Despite the wealth of materials and the intensive analysis found in these papers, the general trend has been to get bogged down in the details before the necessary general framework has been established. Such a framework is, however, necessary as a reference point for any discussion of details.

The most important feature of this framework must be the existence of the political will to introduce a qualitative change into existing monetary relations so as to achieve a minimum level of integration in the monetary field. Even though it may seem elementary, I feel that we must emphasise this point so that the true relationship between this political will and the objective sought may be properly understood. The contention here is that it is the exercise of political will that will determine the extent to which the goal of economic integration is realised, rather than the mere existence of theoretical and practical means for achieving this goal.

Arab economic integration cannot be discussed except in the context of the theory and philosophy of Arab unity. This issue is not one of the mechanics of a given situation but rather one of organic and integrated relationships. This means, for example, that the desired economic and monetary integration cannot be achieved by merely balancing the interests of the states concerned in the hope that such a balance may lead automatically to integration. In fact, the opposite is true; for no step can be considered as a positive move promoting economic integration unless it is linked to a comprehensive integrationist theory. In addition to the political will, which must be present, there must also be an integration of our conceptions of Arab unity and of the goals of the Arab nation with all their political, social and economic implications.

These are some of the basic questions which I believe should serve as a general framework within which the details, experiences and models discussed at this seminar should be placed.

2. Rifaat El Mahgoub

I would like to confine my comments to two points raised in Mr Al-Sagban's paper.

The first is that monetary integration should serve economic integration. The second point is that economic integration in the developing countries should, in turn, serve economic development and economic independence.

The first point requires, as far as I can see, that every stage of economic integration should be accompanied by a corresponding stage of monetary integration. This should take place in such a way as to prevent the latter from lagging behind the former, or from outpacing it (which would, in any case, be difficult to imagine). In this connection let me point out that policies which provide for fixed exchange rates between the currencies of countries involved in integration may be disruptive to these countries' economies, especially in the long run, because such rates could have repercussions with regard to economic development to a degree not reflected in their domestic purchasing power. While the inter-convertibility of these currencies could be detrimental to the stronger currencies, protecting them, which would include sacrificing their convertibility into external currencies, would also be very costly.

Furthermore, contrary to what was claimed in some papers presented at the seminar, a uniform Arab currency (or a uniform Gulf currency) would not guarantee the protection of Arab financial surpluses as long as these are invested in other monetary zones. Consequently, we should not think that the mere creation of a uniform Arab currency is in itself a sufficient safeguard for Arab financial interests. I was pleased to hear from Mr Shoukair that the AMF is concerned with studying all aspects of the problem of currency integration. I merely wish to draw the attention of the researchers to these dangers.

As for the second point, it would be difficult, not to say unwise, to base the economic integration process solely on the present international division of labour and economic capability because this would perpetuate certain unsatisfactory forms of Arab economic development. This approach may be suitable for the integration of the advanced Western capitalist world with the under-developed world or for integrating Wester Europe, where each country has achieved an advanced stage of economic development. However, on its own, it may not be an appropriate model for the Arab world, whose economic integration, in addition to advancing the interests of the Arab world as a whole, should also advance the legitimate economic aspirations of the individual Arab countries.

I noticed that the recommendation adopted by the February 1975 Conference of Governors of Arab Central Banks, in Baghdad, called on the AMF to endeavour to bring about the balanced economic development of all member states and to seek to promote Arab economic integration. The contradiction between the principle of balanced development for each Arab state and the principle of economic integration (which means balanced development at the level of the Arab world as a whole) is obvious. When I referred back to the AMF Agreement, I discovered that it had avoided this contradiction by specifying economic development without describing it as 'balanced'. I would like to hear Mr Al-Sagban's view on this issue, since Arab economic integration (which means balanced development at the level of the Arab nation), requires the acceptance of the concept of unbalanced development (development poles) at the level of the individual Arab states.

3. Robert Triffin

I shall comment only on the question of capital contributions to the AMF, raised by both Mr Al-Sagban and Mr Shoukair.

Most of you would agree, I am sure, that these contributions are still too modest and that their distribution among member countries is erratic to the point of sheer absurdity.

Could both of these shortcomings be remedied if the national contributions were made in the form of deposits with the AMF of a uniform percentage of each member country's gross international reserves, in exchange for a reserve deposit account in appropriately defined Arab dinars (possibly 20 per cent initially, as in the EMS today)? This would relate the comparative contribution of each country to its financial capacity. And it would not entail the sacrifice of any country's national reserves if it were provided that the depositing country could draw on its AMF reserve account to finance any payments deficit with other members and to finance some agreed proportion (20 per cent) of its deficits with non-member countries. Such reserve deposits would then be as liquid as present exchange reserves in sterling, dollars or other foreign currencies, and would carry better exchange-rate guarantees. The only difference is that they would be jointly managed and invested for commonly agreed objectives, rather than left — as now — to the discretion of foreign banks and treasuries. Most of these investments would have to be retained in major foreign money markets, but joint investments would give the depositors more bargaining strength in the negotiation of interest rates and exchange-rate guarantees.

More important, of course, is the fact that some of the reserves now held abroad could be used by the AMF to help finance, under appropriate conditions, the deficits of its own members, particularly those most in need of development capital. And this need not, of course, be confined to its members alone. It may be deemed desirable also to help other under-capitalised countries, and even, at times, industrial countries in temporary deficit.

This would curtail to some extent the role of financial intermediation conferred by the present system on the foreign money markets into which Arab reserve investments are now channelled to an excessive degree, forcing Arab countries and others to seek their own borrowings in these markets, and thereby permitting the latter to accumulate unnecessary financial profits and undue political power.

I am aware of the many difficulties raised by such a suggestion but cannot deal adequately with them in this brief comment. I suggest that you follow attentively the debates now taking place among the experts and officials of the countries of the European Community, preparatory to the second stage of the European Monetary System, i.e., the creation of a European Monetary Fund, initially planned for March 1981, but postponed now until after the presidential elections in France [May 1981].

You might also wish, for the theoretical basis of this proposal, to glance at my 1967 proposal to the United Nations Economic Commission for Asia and the Far East.

4. Abdul Wahid Al-Makhzoumi

Mr Al-Sagban supports the establishment of an Arab import-export bank devoted to the expansion of trade among the Arab countries and considers that such a bank would complement the Fund in the pursuance of one of the objectives provided for in its Agreement, i.e., the settlement of current payments among the member states so as to enhance their mutual trade. At the same time, however, we find that he opposes an organisational procedure which, far from conflicting with the purposes of the Fund, is in fact consistent with one of its objectives (Article IV, paragraph G) and would contribute to its achievement. I am referring to the periodic meetings of the governors of Arab central banks and monetary institutions, an established practice to which Mr Al-Sagban takes objection. These meetings, in which the AMF could play its own role, could indeed offer the Fund an excellent opportunity for the effective fulfilment of its responsibilities.

5. Mahmoud Sakbani

Mr Al-Sagban has been taken to task for advocating monetary integration before the foundations necessary for its success have been laid. It has been argued that monetary integration by and of itself will fail.

If I understand Mr Al-Sagban correctly, he advocates monetary integration as an instrument of economic integration or at least in parallel with it. He must then have in mind that fiscal redistributive measures, security market integration and net resource transfers to the poorer subregions, would all go hand in hand with monetary integration. If this is so, it would seem that the arguments made against him are unjustified.

6. Abdul W. Khayyata

I would like to propose for consideration some possible means of increasing the resources of the AMF:

(a) The Fund might resort to the international markets for short-, medium- and long-term loans, bonds and certificates of deposit, as certain international institutions have done;

(b) Interest rates paid on monies raised in the international markets should be taken into account in the Fund's lending policies so as to ensure a balance between cost and benefit. It may be worthwhile to remember in this context that the availability of credit is at least as important as its cost and may take precedence over it. The application of the market mechanism with respect to interest rates could restore realism to the operations of the AMF;

(c) Furthermore, the application of a rate of interest reflecting the real cost of money would provide the AMF with additional reserves. Such reserves would strengthen the financial picture in the long run, particularly given the fact that the AMF has no obligation to distribute dividends. In order to maintain the low interest rates applied at present, the Fund could institute a two-tier interest-rate structure: a low rate for a portion which is X multiple of the quota and another rate for the remainder, above that level, where the real cost of money would be passed on to the borrower.

(d) The volume of guarantees that the AMF can extend to help member countries raise financing from various sources should be reconsidered. It has been said that the AMF cannot extend guarantees which total more than its own capital. In other words, the thinking in the AMF seems to be based on a 1-to-1 ratio between guarantees and resources. Indeed this self-imposed 1:1 ratio seems too low and could easily be raised internally, e.g., the AMF could act on the basis of a 1:2 ratio.

(e) The flow of resources into the Fund is of course greatly influenced by the regularity of loan repayments by borrowers. If and when the AMF enters the international arena, it should be confident that its commitments to the international markets are matched by firm repayment schedules.

These suggestions are not meant as alternatives to the capital increase under consideration by the AMF. They are rather to be construed as supplementary means of increasing its resources.

7. Mabid Ali Al-Jarhi

Concerning the question of the AMF's raising loans on the international markets, I would like to cite an interesting suggestion from Mr Faik Abdul-Rasool's paper (see below, pp. 390-413) to the effect that the wealthy member countries should offer loans to the AMF on the same concessionary terms they offer the IMF, especially since these countries have influence and voting power in the AMF which they do not enjoy in the IMF.

Moreover, I must admit that I cannot find in economic theory anything to support Mr Rifaat El-Mahgoub's contention that for every stage in economic integration there exists a parallel stage of monetary integration.

8. Abdul Aal Al-Sagban, in Response

Without going into the details of the proposals which have been made I shall begin with the issue of increasing the Fund's capital. There is nothing in my paper to suggest that I am against augmenting this capital. A recommendation to this effect is indeed contained in a document entitled 'Strategy for Joint Arab Economic Activity' presented in November 1980 to the Arab Summit Conference in Amman. What I do want to emphasise is that neither the question of the balance-of-payments deficit nor that of the Fund's role depends fundamentally on increasing the Fund's capital by this or that amount. The estimated figure for the combined Arab balance-of-payments deficit is $60 billion, not counting Egypt or Algeria which, if included, would bring the total deficit to over $100 billion. This means, among other things, that no increase, no matter how great, in the Fund's capital would be enough in itself to cope with this problem. The solution lies in co-ordinating the Arab economies and planning their development orientation. The problem faced by the AMF is one of formulating work programmes for member countries whereby they commit themselves to the Fund's objectives with regard to monetary integration.

This brings us to the question of the Fund's ambitions. What I said is that the Fund has a number of objectives, some deferred and some immediate. The focus has been exclusively on the immediate objectives whereas what should be considered is how to develop inter-Arab programmes which would reconcile particular stages of economic integration with a degree of monetary integration appropriate to those stages.

I shall not get into the arguments which Mr Al-Jarhi presented, but logic dictates that the means is inextricably bound to the end sought. The end is Arab economic integration. It is therefore inconceivable that there could be a leap forward in monetary integration which would not be matched by a similar integration in the industrial, commercial, agricultural and planning spheres. It is really in this sense that a balanced course for joint Arab economic activity is being advocated.

The excellent proposal made by Mr Triffin on the subject of deposits might be perfectly acceptable were it not for the fact that the project submitted by the Council of Arab Economic Unity carried two stipulations: first, that the Arab countries should deposit reserves with the Fund; and secondly, that these should amount to 20 per cent of their total monetary reserves so as to constitute a guarantee, on the one hand, and economic support for the Fund's resources and for its entry into the international market, on the other. However, this was found to be premature. If the Arab countries are prepared to support the Fund, thre is no need to introduce a new mechanism into the Fund's operations at this early stage. By the same token, the stipulation to the effect that the AMF should cycle certain funds to the Arab surplus countries if they so request was excluded from the Council's project. The Fund's activity has been confined to monetary resources and has not covered other areas. If requested by the Arab countries, the Fund may, however, intervene. Mr Triffin's proposal still stands, however, and I do not think there is anything in the AMF Agreement which would contradict it. That agreement states that the Fund may, by decision of the Board of Governors, pursue 'any other means' to achieve its objectives. The Fund's objectives include coping with balance-of-payments deficits. So it could well resort to the special fund or the deposit idea, among others.

What is actually required, given the existence of a planned development orientation, is that certain Arab monetary reserves be used to stabilise the Arab currencies and contribute to achieving their interconvertibility. The technical difficulties become negligible once we fully realise that there is no danger in undertaking such measures. I say this, of course, because it does not signify the relinquishment of sovereignty. The Fund, it would seem to me, should concentrate not so much on increasing its capital or on offering credit facilities to the member countries as on inducing members to increase their efforts towards achieving economic integration. In this way, we might expect that Mr Triffin's idea would achieve a great deal and we could go along with it. Nevertheless, I would like to add that while lending, as Mr Khayata has said, could serve the Fund's objectives, the value of the Fund does not lie in its being a mere financial institution but rather in its being the Arab Monetary Fund. Those who advocate the Fund's entry into the market as a borrower are the Arab countries with surpluses which lend their money on the international financial markets. However, credit facilities in the form of capital would certainly come under less pressure with regard to corrective policies than credit facilities acquired through borrowing. We are all aware of the issue which has been posed to the effect that the Arab countries will have to decide whether they would prefer to offer about 200 million dollars a year to finance the differential between the high interest rates at which the Fund must borrow on the market and the low interest rates it charges its members, or whether they would rather increase the Fund's capital to the extent they regard as appropriate. This becomes a question of priorities and standards but this does not mean, as some may have mistakenly thought, that I advocate borrowing as a substitute for increasing the Fund's resources. It is simply that, in my opinion, the Fund will not produce maximum results nor will it succeed in its mission unless it exhibits an appropriate balance in all its objectives and in the means for achieving them. In this connection, I might cite paragraph I of Article V of the AMF Agreement which provides that the Fund 'shall manage any monies entrusted to it by one or more member states for the benefit of other Arab or non-Arab parties in conformity with the Fund's objectives, and shall, by agreement with the member country or countries concerned, make the necessary arrangements for their management'. This idea, in order to be programmed and implemented, must go beyond balance-of-payments deficit problems to include the Arab role in the international sphere. Why do the Arab countries offer their resources as monetary facilities for the IMF to manage rather than having them managed by the AMF? This question relates directly to the role and objectives of the Fund, both of which are in need of further clarification.

I am not sure whether I have managed to come closer to Mr Shukair's view on the matter of loans. I can nevertheless assure him that I am fully aware of all the Fund's accomplishments and think they should be publicised even if the Fund is reluctant to do so. The AMF is in reality one of the pillars of Arab economic integration. No integration can be achieved without the planned provision of long-term or short-term financing: hence the central role of the AMF in this regard. Further integration, I should like to add, cannot be achieved unless there is an authority capable of making binding decisions.

As concerns Mr Al-Makhzoumi's comment, I have not called for an Arab import-export bank. Whatever measures I have proposed were to be considered in the context of the AMF itself. As to the meetings of the governors of Arab central banks, while they may not be devoid of any benefit, it is important that they not become institutionalised at a time when a further expansion in Arab institutions is uncalled for.

I shall conclude by saying that I agree with many of the points raised by Messrs Sakbani, Al-Jarhi and Khayata.

PART THREE

MONETARY INTEGRATION IN LATIN AMERICA,
EUROPE AND WEST AFRICA

6 MONETARY INTEGRATION IN LATIN AMERICA

Jorge Gonzalez del Valle

Introduction

When monetary integration was first becoming a relatively dynamic factor of regional economic policy in Latin America in the early 1960s, a broader movement towards overall economic integration was already in full swing. In both the Central American Common Market and the Latin American Free Trade Area, which together involve 16 countries representing up to 96 per cent of Latin America's GNP, the bases for substantial liberalisation of trade and industrial complementarity among the participating countries had been formally agreed.[1] The fact that both integration schemes were initially successful and encouraged the expectation of further achievements in the field of economic union was doubtless instrumental in giving the central banks the strong support they needed to pursue monetary integration with broad powers of discretion.

It should also be noted that, due mainly to a tradition established in the 1930s, the Latin American central banks enjoy substantial political and administrative independence and thus were not required to follow any rigid policy directives concerning the financial aspects of economic integration. Moreover, the formal integration treaties did not explicitly contemplate the forms of monetary co-operation required to support trade liberalisation or industrial complementarity.

Inter-bank relations were of course already well established in the early 1960s, but they were confined mainly to the few large foreign banks with branches in several Latin American countries which settled their international accounts through New York and London. Branches of Latin American commercial banks and inter-bank bilateral payments arrangements were rare and limited. While this was in part the result of the numerous and wide-ranging exchange-control systems which remained after the Second World War, the fact that the volume of intra-regional trade and investment was small and unstable must have further discouraged any serious attempt to compete with the large foreign banks, some of them long established in Latin America, which already had a well-developed network of international banking services.

Economic integration did not emerge in Latin America merely as an isolated attempt to reap the advantages of geographical proximity or to renew the ideals of political unity which had been vainly tested in the nineteenth century. It was rather the result of a generalised conviction that economic development was possible only if export capacity could be expanded, which in turn would require a deliberate process of industrialisation and access to wider markets. Economic integration was expected to accelerate this process — which also involves a high degree of import substitution — particularly in the case of those small countries which could only industrialise through protected custom unions.

This major thrust of regional economic policy would necessarily require the support of appropriate financial and monetary institutions. As regards the financial means as such, all integration schemes in Latin America were accompanied by the creation of regional development banks, which have now reached maturity.[2] On the monetary side, however, the merging of national monetary systems has proceeded in different ways and with different degrees of intensity from one subregion to another. None of the subregional arrangements has reached the stage of a monetary union since the process of integration is far from attaining the ideal of economic union in all cases. But the existing clearing and credit arrangements combine, in one way or another, different elements which are addressed to the objective of fuller monetary integration.

I. Clearing and Payments Arrangements

There are at present three clearing and payments arrangements in Latin America: the Central American Clearing House, the payments system of the Latin American Free Trade Association (LAFTA) and the Caribbean Community Multilateral Clearing Facility. They were established in 1961, 1965 and 1977, respectively. All are designed to facilitate private and official monetary transfers among participants on a multilateral basis, but their specific objectives and operational features vary to a considerable degree since each clearing system is adapted to the requirements and possibilities of the corresponding subregional integration scheme.

A. Objectives and Purposes

The fundamental difference among the three clearing systems in this respect is that whereas the Central American Clearing House[3] explicitly contemplates the use of the national currencies of the five participating countries — which have five different parities — for the settling of payments among themselves, the other two clearing systems operate on the basis of the dominant international currency only, i.e., the US dollar.

As will be explained below, this major difference in the objectives of monetary co-operation stems from the fact that the Central American

Clearing House was initially conceived of as the first step in the creation of a monetary union which would eventually do away with separate national currencies. This approach to monetary integration was possible in the case of Central America because of a long tradition of fixed parities and of basic freedom of exchange, whereas the more numerous and larger South American countries of LAFTA could not reasonably be expected to undertake the sudden adoption of fixed exchange rates and/or the elimination of exchange controls merely to improve the efficiency of intra-regional payments.[4] Moreover, this was not necessary since the monetary requirements of a multilateral free trade agreement are obviously simpler than those of a common market or a customs union.

The explicit objectives of the three Latin American clearing arrangements are to facilitate the settlement of overall reciprocal foreign exchange positions among the participating countries on a multilateral basis, to reduce the cost of monetary transfers elegible for clearing and to minimise the use of official foreign exchange reserves for the settlement of intra-regional balances. These objectives are achieved through direct central bank interchanges of reciprocal holdings of foreign exchange claims (bank notes, cheques, money orders, etc.), which are then reported to a central agent for multilateral clearance and settlement. This normally involves interim financing by the creditor central banks, which must be repaid at short fixed intervals (up to six months) and which earns interest at mutually agreed rates.

B. Major Features of Existing Arrangements

The Latin American clearing arrangements have evolved over the years in directions intended to enhance both the macroeconomic advantages of the regional payments systems and the administrative efficiency of multinational transfers and to reduce the financial costs to the users. In this way both the Central American and the LAFTA arrangements have reached what may be considered a high degree of development, whereas the Caribbean scheme is gradually perfecting its procedures.[5] The operational features which warrant emphasis in this context are those related to interim financing, the degree of multilateralisation of clearings, the eligibility of transactions, the unit of account and the form of final settlement.

1. Interim Financing. The basic approach to interim financing has consisted in restricting the credit required to finance debtor positions arising from payments clearances to amounts and payment periods compatible with the overall volume of transactions between the parties involved, provided such financing is used neither as regular export credit nor as global balance-of-payments support. The specific amounts and maturities are, of course, subject to negotiation and may not in all cases correspond to the concept of predictable reversibility of net balances according to which an ideal clearing system would operate.

In the case of the Central American Clearing House interim financing is limited to a six-month uniform line of credit granted by each participant to the others taken as a group, whereas in the LAFTA system the amount of credit is agreed bilaterally by each pair of participants in accordance with the volume of their trade and payments, while the maximum payment period is four months. On the other hand, in the Caribbean clearing facility the amounts of credit granted and received by each participant vary according to such factors as reciprocal trade and the foreign exchange reserves of the participating countries.

In principle, interim financing in the three clearing systems is intended to avoid the waste involved in too frequent settlements of bilateral or multilateral accounts and is therefore considered to be a temporary investment of foreign exchange by the creditor central banks. These short-term investments are fully convertible into usable international currencies (mainly the dollar), earn interest at reasonable commercial rates and are not subject to automatic refinancing. The three arrangements provide for immediate collection of any outstanding balance in excess of the line of credit agreed by the creditor central banks, though they are free to grant additional credit at any time during the period between the established settlement dates.

2. Degree of Multilateralisation. Both the Central American and the Caribbean clearing arrangements are fully multilateral, in the sense that all clearing operations and the final settlement of accounts are automatically centralised in the hands of a financial agent (one of the participants) which determines the net debtor or creditor position of each participant *vis-à-vis* the others taken as a group. This means that all transactions of the clearing system are subject to uniform rules with regard to eligibility, type of documentation, reconfirmation procedures, etc.

The LAFTA payments system also operates on a multilateral basis at that point where the individual net position of each participant can be determined as a result of the combined clearance of the different bilateral agreements. It is true that these agreements are subject to rules of eligibility and documentation which may differ for each pair of participants, depending on the foreign exchange regulations applied in the countries concerned. Nevertheless, the bilateral agreements of the LAFTA system have been largely standardised such that settlement dates, interest rates on net claims and procedures for the payment of outstanding balances are now uniform.

The lack of full multilateralisation in the LAFTA payments system is understandable if account is taken of the fact that it involves the central banks of 12 countries with widely different GNP levels, financial structures, reciprocal trade patterns and foreign exchange policies. While this diversity may make bilateral agreements on interim credit and eligibility for clearance necessary, it should be possible from the technical point of view to design a multilateral arrangement with individual credit quotas and well-harmonised rules of documentation.

3. Eligibility of Transactions. A common feature of the three Latin American clearing systems is that the utilisation of their facilities is, in principle, voluntary. This means that both the private and the public sectors of the participating countries have the option either to use such facilities or to make foreign exchange payments through conventional international channels, except when exchange controls involving currency prescription are applied in the country of the transferor. One would naturally expect all official transfers to be made through the multilateral clearing systems while private transfers would be better served, in terms both of cost and of expediency, by regional clearings.

Although the broad objective of the three clearing arrangements is to encompass all current and capital balance-of-payments transactions whatever financial instruments are used to effect them, in practice the participating central banks are frequently called upon to impose eligibility restrictions. This may be due to the requirements of exchange control regulations or simply to the temporary needs of foreign exchange policies. From this point of view the bilateral agreements on which the LAFTA payments system is based seem to provide more flexibility than would a global multilateral arrangement, especially if restrictions have to be applied on a country-by-country basis.

In the case of the Central American Clearing House, all balance-of-payments transactions are eligible, provided the instrument of payment is expressed in the national currency of the transferor; the only exceptions are transactions subject to the relatively lax exchange controls which have occasionally been applied by some participating countries.[6] In the case of the Caribbean Community, the Board of Directors of the Multilateral Clearing Facility is empowered to prescribe eligible transactions other than sales and purchases of Caribbean Community currencies by commercial banks covering transactions approved by each participant; in principle this also means a basically liberal policy of eligibility.

The flexibility provided by the bilateral payments agreements of the LAFTA system makes possible a wide range of eligibility rules. LAFTA countries which tend to employ liberal regulations with regard to payments abroad — constituting at present a majority of the membership — would be expected to relax or eliminate any restrictions in their bilateral agreements, thus approaching the stage of universal eligibility which is desirable in any multilateral clearing system.

4. Unit of Account and Settlements. Convertibility of net claims arising from multilateral clearing is an essential element in any arrangement of this kind. It may be recalled that international opposition to the creation of regional payments unions in the 1950s was based on the fear that they might involve the accumulation of inconvertible balances, which would run counter to one of the major objectives of the International Monetary Fund. This view induced the Latin American countries to design payments arrangements that would be guided by the principle of limited, short-term and fully convertible interim financing, as explained above.

Both the Central American and the Caribbean systems employ a specific unit of account for the valuation of clearing operations and the outstanding balances — expressed in national currencies — arising therefrom. In the first case an *ad hoc* unit of account called the 'Central American peso', at par with the dollar, has been adopted, while in the second case, all accounts are directly denominated in dollars. The parities of all the national currencies of the participants *vis-à-vis* the unit of account correspond to the 'central rate' of such currencies as listed with the IMF. In the LAFTA system no unit of account is required since all documents, instruments and book-keeping are expressed exclusively in dollars.

In practice, all settlements in the three clearing systems are carried out directly in dollars, this being, for obvious reasons, the major international reserve asset in Latin America. But in order to maintain the value of the creditors' claims between settlement dates, whatever may be the alteration in the external value of the national currencies of the debtors, both the Caribbean and the Central American clearing arrangements incorporate provisions for immediate notification to the central agent of any change in the central rate of the currency involved and for prompt revaluation of the other participants' holdings in that currency and of in-transit items. These provisions, plus the strict compliance with the settlement rules, represent the essential convertibility guarantees referred to above.

So far no problems have been reported concerning inability to meet the settlement and/or convertibility conditions of the clearing systems, though over the past 20 years occasional balance-of-payments emergencies have arisen due to war, natural disasters or economic distress. It is probable that in such cases additional monetary arrangements have been activated to assist the participant concerned in order to avoid the suspension of the basic provisions of the multilateral payments system. As explained below, most Latin American central banks have entered into multilateral credit agreements to finance balance-of-payments disequilibria, but it is also well known that many of these central banks have arranged bilateral credit facilities which are presumably more flexible than the multilateral ones.

C. Economic and Financial Advantages

Multilateral clearing arrangements are supposed to be closely linked with the expansion of trade among developing countries, especially if such countries are engaged in broader integration programmes. It is still a subject of debate whether trade expansion is a precondition of successful clearing arrangements, but there is at least some evidence that once multilateral payments flow efficiently in a given geographical area, international trade and investment can be fostered therein.

As was explained earlier, in Latin America the creation of clearing systems followed without much delay the establishment of integration schemes which explicitly contemplated the development of common markets, customs unions or free trade areas. There was thus a high degree of coincidence between the commercial and financial aspects of integration, making it very difficult to identify the determining factor in the relationship between these two aspects. In fact, this may be no more than an academic question since trade and payments within a given group of countries are merely a reflection of objective conditions conducive to economic co-operation in general.

There is little doubt that the mere existence of banking facilities that allow residents of a given country to make payments abroad without having to bear the financial costs involved in foreign exchange operations — exchange commissions, market spreads and interest accrued for delays in settlement — provides considerable encouragement for both capital and current international transactions, including trade. This economic result should be further enhanced in those multilateral clearing arrangements which either require or permit payments in the resident's national currency since in most cases transfers can be made without bank intervention. The relative importance of the reduction of such financial costs at the macroeconomic level is, of course, a matter which largely depends on the volume of intra-regional payments and on the efficiency of the multilateral clearing mechanism.

In Latin America the prevailing opinion is that the three subregional clearing systems have effectively supported the expansion of trade and investment, though no reliable estimate of the incidence of reduction of financial costs can be made. There is, however, another factor which has probably had a more direct impact on the volume of intra-regional payments: the relaxation or elimination of exchange controls, which had sometimes been applied exclusively to intra-regional transactions, has obviously had the effect of fostering closer relations among the economic sectors of the participating countries.

In the last analysis, of course, the expansion of intra-regional trade and investment in Latin America has been the result of both the development of real resources and capabilities and the positive effect of specific integration policies in the commercial and industrial spheres. The reduction of trade tariffs, the elimination of non-tariff restrictions and agreements on joint investments and multinational enterprises, including those dealing with industrial complementarity, have unquestionably increased the volume of trade and payments in the three integration areas of Latin America. Hence it would appear that the clearing arrangements have played a supplemental, albeit very important, role in this larger process.

From the viewpoint of a more rational use of official foreign exchange reserves, the macroeconomic advantages associated with the operation of multilateral clearing facilities can be readily appreciated. The fact that the banking systems of the participating countries do not have to hold substantial balances of foreign exchange to finance outgoing payments, and that their central banks may compensate them with incoming payments or interim financing from the other participants, is obviously an important contribution to orderly foreign exchange and balance-of-payments policies. Here again, the effective economic impact of this advantage depends on the ratio of intra-regional payments to the total volume of external transfers; it is estimated that in the three Latin American integration areas this ratio now ranges, on the average, between 20 and 30 per cent. Moreover, it is also estimated that the amount of foreign exchange required to finance net settlements in these clearing systems has been reduced, on the average, to between 3 and 10 per cent of the total value of all transactions cleared.

II. Credit Arrangements for Balance-of-payments Support

In the late 1960s most Latin American central bankers realised that, notwithstanding the rapid development of the multilateral clearing systems, further monetary co-operation was needed to sustain the trend towards trade and payments liberalisation which was essential for the development of both the Central American Common Market and LAFTA. It became clear that participating countries which faced serious balance-of-payments disequilibria could hardly be expected to accelerate the abolition of remaining exchange controls and trade restrictions, especially if such disequilibria were in one way or another associated with the adaptation to the requirements of economic integration.

Accordingly, there now exist in Latin America three different multilateral credit arrangements: the Central American Monetary Stabilisation Fund, the Financial Assistance Agreement of the Latin American Free Trade Association (the 'Santo Domingo Agreement') and the Andean Reserve Fund. The first two arrangements were established in 1969 and the Andean Fund in 1978.[7] Their scope, specific objectives and operational techniques differ considerably, as will be explained below.

A. Collective Management of Reserves

Even before the establishment of the existing credit agreements, the idea of pooling the foreign exchange reserves of the Latin American countries in order to foster regional monetary co-operation was explored by their central banks, but it understandably ran into the opposition of some major holders of reserves who, among other things, objected to the lack of clearly-defined economic purposes such as balance-of-payments assistance, external debt refinancing, or the substitution of foreign-controlled export–import credit. No feasible proposals in this regard were ever discussed, for reasons related, perhaps, to the incipient development of overall economic integration, the ever-present fear of inconvertibility and the sharp disparities in the balance-of-payments and reserve positions of the Latin American countries.

Nevertheless, this idea was further analysed by the Central American central banks under the influence of the rapid development of the Clearing House and the expectation that the favourable trends exhibited by the Common Market would eventually justify serious consideration of a monetary union. The fact that these central banks had in 1964 established a Central American Monetary Council to guide the process of financial integration and co-ordinate national monetary policies also helped, since this forum provided the knowledge and the analytical means better to understand on a regional scale the relationship between integration and the external sector, as well as the relationship between reserve management and balance-of-payments financing.

The Central American Monetary Stabilisation Fund essentially combines the idea of joint management of reserves with a recognition of the increasingly important interaction between economic integration and the balance of payments. In principle, the members of this Fund – i.e., the same central banks which participate in the Clearing House – have agreed to place equal amounts of their official reserves under the authority of the Monetary Council exclusively for the purpose of financing stablisation loans to members facing balance-of-payments difficulties. If no stabilisation loans are required, the fund temporarily invests these reserves amounts in the international markets. At the beginning, the amount held by the Fund represented barely one per cent of the combined gross international reserves of the members, but by 1980 this ratio had risen to nearly 7 per cent. However, due to the differences in individual reserve positions, for one of the members the paid-up contribution to the Fund represents as much as 40 per cent of its gross reserves while for two other members this ratio ranges between 13 and 15 per cent.

The Andean Reserve Fund is broadly based on the same principles as the Central American scheme, except that in addition to holding the members' contributions in foreign exchange and engaging in supplemental external borrowing, the Andean Fund is empowered to accept foreign exchange deposits, to issue its own bonds and to act as trustee in foreign exchange operations of interest to its members. Moreover, although its main objective is to use the contributions of members directly to finance stabilisation loans required by members facing balance-of-payments difficulties, the Andean Reserve Fund may also offer guarantees to members who borrow externally for the same purpose, and invest some of its financial resources in securities issued by the Andean Finance Corporation and in bankers' acceptances, bonds and other securities issued in the member countries.[8]

The Andean Reserve Fund represents a credit agreement which partially encompasses the membership of LAFTA since five (Bolivia, Colombia, Ecuador, Peru and Venezuela) of the eleven member countries of the latter participate. This reflects the fact that, without withdrawing from the looser and more general trade agreements of LAFTA, these five countries established in 1969 a subregional integration scheme (the Cartagena Treaty) which goes beyond trade liberalisation and may eventually evolve into a common market or a customs union, including an industrial complementarity programme which is already in progress. In this context, while the central banks of the Andean group do not yet see the need for a clearing arrangement and a supplementary facility different from the LAFTA payments system and the 'Santo Domingo Agreement', they have apparently felt that an accelerated process of monetary integration is required in connection with the collective management of reserves for the purpose of mutual balance-of-payments assistance.

At present the agreed foreign exchange contributions to the Andean Reserve Fund represent only 2.5 per cent of the combined gross reserve holdings of members, but for one of them the ratio is as high as 25 per cent. It should also be noted that the actual proportion of members' international reserves managed by the Fund may increase considerably if the latter is able to encourage voluntary deposits from the banking systems of the Andean countries or to arrange the placement of its own bonds denominated in foreign currencies.

B. Balance-of-payments Assistance

Whereas both the Central American Monetary Stabilisation Fund and the Andean Reserve Fund are concerned with financing the global balance-of-payments deficits of the participating countries, the LAFTA Financial Assistance Agreement[9] is specifically designed to assist members to refinance sizeable net debtor positions arising from the operations of the LAFTA clearing system. This refinancing, however, is not automatic and can only be granted if the borrowing member is suffering simultaneously from a global balance-of-payments deficit and a 'weak' international reserve position.

The LAFTA Financial Assistance Agreement does not require permanent financial resources but relies on contingent lines of credit agreed among the participants, the amounts of which are related in turn to the participants' quotas in the IMF. A participant's access to the facility is now limited to 300 per cent of its own credit line, but must not exceed 30 per cent of the aggregate amount of the facility's credit lines. Furthermore, all drawings must be repaid within one year. Consequently, the fundamental objective of the 'Santo Domingo Agreement' is to provide short-term assistance to those participants whose overall reserve position is likely to be seriously affected as a result of intra-regional payments.

At the request of several participants, the 'Santo Domingo Agreement' is now being re-examined with a view to expanding the scope and flexibility of its financial facilities, especially with regard to incorporating the principle of global balance-of-payments adjustments in place of the much narrower concept of intra-regional deficits. This will probably require the consideration of longer-term financing and of some procedure for applying policy performance conditions to borrowers, which in turn might require permanent financial resources and appropriate surveillance rules. The final shape of this reform of the present LAFTA Financial Assistance scheme may not be known until 1981.

On the other hand, both the Central American Monetary Stabilisation Fund and the Andean Reserve Fund have inevitably adopted specific rules and conditions for the use of their financial resources. First, while members have access to medium-term loans for global balance-of-payments purposes in amounts equivalent to several times their foreign exchange contributions, they must prove that they are both willing and able to implement stabilisation policies to correct the external disequilibria within a reasonable period of time. Secondly, conditionality as regards policy performance increases in proportion to the amount and the maturity of such stabilisation loans. Thirdly, policy performance, including, in principle, compliance with regional integration obligations, is subject to collective surveillance by the Fund's participants.

The main difference between the policies of the Central American and the Andean Funds concern the maximum maturity of stabilisation loans and the simultaneous or previous use of the facilities of the IMF. Whereas the Central American Fund can extend loans for up to seven years and does not require the borrower to have resorted to or to intend to resort to the IMF, the loans granted by the Andean Fund may not exceed three years and, in practice, must be supplemented by the use of the IMF facilities.

There are also, of course, differences in the actual experience of the two funds which stem mainly from the nine-year span that separates their respective dates of establishment. The older Central American Fund has so far granted six loans to four of its five members for an aggregate amount equivalent to approximately four times it own resources, which means that it has had to resort heavily to external borrowing. It has thus had ample opportunities to acquaint itself with diverse balance-of-payments problems and the application of a variety of stabilisation policies and techniques. The Andean Reserve Fund, on the other hand, has so far granted only one short-term stabilisation loan for an amount which represents a small portion of its own resources.

C. Other Credit Arrangements

In addition to the institutional credit agreements referred to above, the Latin American central banks have experimented in recent years with certain *ad hoc* arrangements which at bottom represent joint investments of a portion of their official international reserves to help some of them overcome serious balance-of-payments difficulties. These have been mainly temporary arrangements designed either to supplement existing credit arrangements or to deal with special cases which could not otherwise be taken care of.

An outstanding arrangement of this type is the collective 'financial co-operation agreement' concluded in 1973 between the central banks of Latin America and Spain in order to help a Latin American country which the previous year had suffered a natural disaster with serious economic consequences, including substantial balance-of-payments deficits associated with reconstruction. The financial assistance took the form of voluntary, one-year foreign exchange deposits, renewable for up to five years, with the central bank of that country. The size of each participating country's deposit was proportional to its quota in the IMF. This arrangement was activated three more times in 1975 and 1979.

In a broader context, it should be noted that the operations of the

Central American Monetary Stabilisation Fund have been facilitated by three important loans arranged with the central banks of Mexico, Venezuela and Colombia. A common feature of these loans is that the monies are made available exclusively at the request of the Fund — thus precluding any bilateral link with the Fund member in need of the loan — to finance stabilisation loans approved by the Fund in accordance with its own procedures and conditionality rules.

From another point of view, the Latin American Export Bank (BLADEX) has actively invited deposits in foreign exchange from the central banks of the region, offering them interest rates at least as high as those of the Euromarket. At present up to 13 central banks in the region hold deposits with BLADEX for an aggregate amount representing approximately 67 per cent of BLADEX's total deposits and 42 per cent of its total assets. In the last analysis these operations are another way of pooling intra-regional foreign exchange reserves for balance-of-payments support since the main activity of BLADEX is the financing of Latin American exports through the rediscount of credit granted by the exporting country.

Finally, information available to the author indicates that it is likely that some of the *ad hoc* credit arrangements described above will be institutionalised to reinforce the facilities of both the Central American Clearing House and LAFTA. In the first place, it is almost certain that before the end of 1980 the Central American Clearing House will be supplemented by a mechanism (further explained below) designed to refinance persistent debtor positions through medium-term loans from BLADEX. Secondly, one of the alternative proposals now being considered to improve the LAFTA Financial Assistance Agreement is to incorporate into it a permanent mechanism for voluntary foreign exchange deposits similar to that of the 'financial co-operation agreement' referred to above.

III. The Special Case of Central America

There are several reasons for the earlier and perhaps more substantial progress made by the Central American countries towards monetary integration in the Latin American context: the relatively small size of their economies, their tradition of close political relations, the simpler structure of their banking and financial systems and, possibly, their deeper conviction that economic integration is in the long run the only reasonable hope for the survival of small and medium-sized countries. After almost 20 years of rich experiences in this field, the Central American area now has a comprehensive set of multilateral institutions and arrangements which in fact represent the basic elements of a payments union.

The formal aspects of this approach to monetary integration are explicitly contained in the Central American Monetary Agreement of 1974, which reinforces and harmonises the aims, activities and operations of the Monetary Council, the Clearing House and the Monetary Stabilisation Fund, and further provides for the establishment of supplementary arrangements that might be deemed necessary to improve the coherence and effectiveness of the monetary integration framework as a whole. A brief review of these interconnected elements would seem appropriate if the significance of the Central American experience is to be properly evaluated.

A. *The Monetary Council*

The five central banks of Central America are represented in this Council exclusively by their governors, thus ensuring that its decisions are effectively carried out. The Council is responsible for the overall guidance of the monetary integration process, the general management of both the Clearing House and the Stabilisation Fund, the periodic review of the economic performance and prospects of the region and of the member countries, and the adoption of ways and means to co-ordinate the members' financial policies. The Council is assisted by committees which deal with specific issues related to monetary, exchange and financial policies and to legal integration matters.

The Monetary Council has exerted considerable influence in other important integration areas, such as commercial, fiscal and development policies, through joint meetings with the corresponding national officials at the ministerial level. This has considerably enhanced its role in the general integration strategy while at the same time preserving the political and administrative independence of the national central banks. The Council has also been responsible for the application of regional policies with regard to the members' relations with international financial institutions, in particular the IMF.

In guiding the region through the gradual stages of monetary co-operation and integration, the Monetary Council is inevitably influenced by the changing political conditions of the area, which have sometimes seriously jeopardised the overall integration process. The relative political independence of the central banks, however, has contributed to the preservation of the main achievements at the regional level. There are some striking examples of this in the history of the Monetary Council: the Council has continued to meet and both the Clearing House and the Stabilisation Fund to operate despite a declared war between two members in 1969, a serious breakdown of the integration treaties in 1972 and a violent, radical change in the institutional organisation of the state in another member country in 1979.

B. The Clearing House

In addition to being a fully multilateral payments system, the fact that the Central American Clearing House is required to deal exclusively in the national currencies of the members makes it an outstanding example of monetary integration. This requirement goes beyond the mere replacement of the conventional international currency when making intra-regional payments; it represents a limited but significant internationalisation of the national currencies thus creating a monetary area which, despite the present diversity of currency parities, could be the cornerstone of an eventual monetary union in Central America.

It should be noted, moreover, that the Clearing House has not remained isolated within such a monetary area. Since 1965 the Monetary Council has selectively promoted links with other Latin American countries having intensive trade and investment relations with Central America. It has so far concluded two clearing and payments arrangements of this type with the central banks of Mexico and Colombia. The Central American central banks participate collectively in these arrangements through the Clearing House, which is also charged with the administration of the clearing and settlement operations. While Mexico and Colombia are Central America's principal trading partners in the region, similar arrangements are nevertheless possible with the central banks of Venezuela, Brazil and the Dominican Republic, which are rapidly becoming important trading partners.

The performance of the Central American Clearing House may be illustrated by some figures related to intra-regional trade, payments and international reserves. It is estimated that in 1979 intra-regional trade represented about 25 per cent of total export trade. However, the volume of transactions cleared considerably exceeded the recorded value of visible trade, thus reflecting a sizeable volume of capital and service operations. In any event, the combined value of settlements in dollars did not exceed 5 per cent of the aggregate value of transactions channelled through the Clearing House.

C. The Stabilisation Fund

It has already been noted that the Central American Monetary Stabilisation Fund performs an important role in helping the member countries to avoid foreign exchange policies which might have an adverse effect on the integration process, such as exchange controls or exchange-rate devaluation. While in this sense the purposes of the Central American Fund coincide with those of the IMF, there are nevertheless important differences in their respective approaches to balance-of-payments adjustment.

In the first place, since it is not required that the borrowing member make prior or simultaneous use of the IMF facilities, the Central American Fund is free to apply independent criteria with regard to the scope and the specific characteristics of stabilisation policies. From the very beginning, Central American economic experts and central bankers chose to look upon the adjustment process as combining conditions of both global demand and global supply. They concluded, accordingly, that the process could not be effectively influenced by a purely mechanical monetarist policy and therefore required not convulsive shock treatments, but rather a smooth, medium-term, multi-policy strategy. It is well known that the IMF has been recently moving towards this kind of approach, especially in connection with its so-called 'extended facility'.

In the second place, instead of applying rigid rules concerning the amount and maturity of its stabilisation loans, the Central American Fund adopted at the outset a blend of quantitative and qualitative criteria to assess the particular needs of the borrowing member. For one thing, the size of the actual or prospective balance-of-payments deficit is a prime consideration, together with a realistic estimate of the borrower's ability to secure other international financing, including IMF resources, for the same purpose. Moreover, the Central American Monetary Council may approve loans with maturities of one, five or seven years, depending on the expected duration of the balance-of-payments disequilibria involved after making allowances for the probable effects of the proposed stabilisation policies.

D. Supplementary Financing

Late in 1979 the Central American Monetary Council approved the establishment of a new financial facility which could effectively fill the institutional gap that existed between the Clearing House and the Stabilisation Fund with regard to the refinancing of debtor balances in intra-regional clearing operations. In normal times, all outstanding debtor balances are paid on the agreed settlement dates and if a debtor member faces difficulties due to a global balance-of-payments deficit and a weak international reserve position, it can always borrow from the Stabilisation Fund. Since 1978, however, intra-regional financial conditions have been far from normal due to an unfortunate combination of civil war in one country, economic instability in another and political disturbances in still another two countries. As a consequence, some debtor positions in the Clearing House have been abnormally high and persistent and most members have already exhausted their access to the Stabilisation Fund. Moreover, although the Central American Monetary Agreement provided for voluntary refinancing of debtor positions by the creditor members, this has become increasingly difficult for the same reasons. In any event, the Monetary Council has shown a clear preference for multilateral arrangements whenever bilateral operations, however useful they may be on a temporary basis, seem likely to become permanent features of the monetary co-operation programme.

Available unofficial information indicates that the Monetary Council is in the process of arranging a medium-term, multilateral line of credit with the Latin American Export Bank which would allow central banks with sizeable debtor positions in the Clearing House to obtain short-term credits in foreign exchange to finance their intra-regional settlements. Alternatively, the creditor central banks could rediscount through BLADEX certain portions of the balances outstanding, provided the debtors were willing to document them in an appropriate form and bear the costs of rediscounting.[10]

This supplementary financial facility, together with the Clearing House and the Stabilisation Fund, will move the Central American monetary integration framework much closer to the form of a payments union with limited credit automacity. Although this is still far from an ideal monetary union, there is no doubt that the combination of these three elements, plus the existence of a high-level authority charged with increasingly important responsibilities concerning the harmonisation of national financial policies, will go far to consolidate monetary integration in Central America and to enhance the prospects for still further progress.

IV. Concluding Remarks

In general terms, monetary integration in Latin America has evolved over the past 20 years in two stages: in the 1960s, clearing arrangements to support intra-regional trade expansion were encouraged so long as they did not entail risks of inconvertibility associated with the frustrated payments union schemes proposed during the previous decade. Then, in the 1970s, credit agreements for mutual balance-of-payments assistance were concluded, thus requiring closer and stronger relations among the parties concerned. The 1980s appear to have started with a critical re-examination of such agreements which may set in motion a third stage of bolder and more imaginative achievements in monetary integration.

Although Latin America was certainly better prepared than other Third World areas to embark on regional monetary co-operation, given the global economic integration programme adopted as early as 1960 and 1961, the importance of this factor should not be exaggerated. In the first place, actual performance in both Central and South America is still far from attaining the ambitious targets of full customs unions, common markets and free trade areas contemplated in the original treaties.[11] Secondly, such treaties did not explicitly contemplate monetary integration as a supporting or supplementary element of overall economic integration, thus leaving national sensibilities on the so-called 'monetary sovereignty' question largely unruffled. Thirdly, although economic integration has inevitably meant a process of trade liberalisation, the participating countries have not been required to forsake exchange restrictions or unilateral exchange-rate policies.

On the other hand, it is evident that the integration process is the driving force behind the extraordinary expansion of intra-regional trade and investment that has taken place in Latin America, which in turn supports the expansion of reciprocal payments and deepens the interdependence of national monetary systems as well as the common interest in each member's balance-of-payments well-being. This development is thus the main source of monetary co-operation in Latin America, which may take different forms and be achieved through different procedures, depending on the actual needs, possibilities and limitations of the participants.

For several reasons, the Central American experience appears to be richer and more varied than that of the other Latin American integration areas. The combination of such elements as a clearing system, a balance-of-payments stabilisation facility and a short-term debt refinancing mechanism, all co-ordinated under a regional authority, clearly foreshadows a payments union or future monetary union. This goes far beyond the provisions of the 1960 integration treaty and is a realistic reflection of a rare case in which central bank traditions and self-confidence overshadow voluble political circumstances which have not, in recent times, been conducive to regional integration in general.

The evolution of monetary co-operation within the LAFTA, Andean and Caribbean groups has more closely followed the actual development of economic integration in these regions. The Andean Reserve Fund probably represents the most advanced concept of monetary integration among the four existing multilateral arrangements in these regions, but the current revision of the LAFTA Financial Assistance Agreement may also lead to a more comprehensive and updated credit arrangement for balance-of-payments support. Moreover, it is possible that the Caribbean Community will find it useful or necessary to supplement its Clearing Facility with a new credit agreement.

These considerations bring to mind the question of integrating the existing multilateral monetary arrangements and agreements into a Latin American system, or at least linking them together in order to enhance their combined usefulness. An overall Latin American system would not appear feasible due to the significant differences among the three integration areas with regard to their specific objectives, stages of development and political limitations; but a network of functional links is certainly possible — at least from the technical point of view — and might yield considerable advantages for all the countries concerned. As noted above, the Central American Clearing House is already linked to the national financial systems of Mexico and Colombia; these links could be extended to other LAFTA and Caribbean Community countries on the same selective basis.

In principle, the linkage of subregional clearing systems should not present insurmountable problems. Inter-system agreements on settlement dates, multilateral interim financing and interest rates on outstanding balances would have to be adopted; but other operational details, such as eligibility of transactions, documentation procedures, etc., could be left to the discretion of the transferor's central bank. Similarly, credit arrangements for the limited refinancing of debtor positions could be adopted along the lines of either the present LAFTA Financial Assistance Agreement or the proposed supplementary facility of the Central American Clearing House.

On the other hand, direct links between the two existing global balance-of-payments support agreements cannot be established as long as they remain legally restricted to the member countries of the respective integration areas, and links between them and the prospective LAFTA global credit agreement would very much depend on the final structure and scope of the latter. However, informal and indirect links among the three agreements could be established by means of both the reciprocal investment of unused resources and the standardisation of major credit conditions and policy performance requirements. These rather simple actions would materially open the way for a better quality of monetary integration in Latin America.

A final word should perhaps be said about the role of monetary co-operation in relations between Latin America and the rest of the Third World. On the basis of the experiences described in these pages, Latin America stands a good chance of leading the way towards even more comprehensive, dynamic and efficient forms of multilateral monetary co-operation among developing countries. However, to be effective, this leadership requires the fulfilment of at least two basic conditions: that monetary policies in the Third World be made increasingly interdependent with economic and social development policies, and that no effort — political or intellectual — be spared to bring about a fundamental reform of the international monetary system which would make possible, among other things, the effective participation of the less developed countries.

Notes

1. The Treaty for Central American Economic Integration entered into force on 13 December 1960 and the Treaty of the Latin American Free Trade Association became effective on 1 June 1961. The latter was replaced on 12 August 1980 by the Treaty of the Association for Latin American Economic Integration which, however, did not contemplate important modifications in the integration approach.

2. These are: the Inter-American Development Bank, the Central American Bank for Economic Integration, the Caribbean Development Bank and the Andean Development Corporation. The Latin American Export Bank, established in 1979, may also be considered in this category of institutions.

3. Its members are the central banks of Costa Rica, El Salvador, Guatemala, Honduras and Nicaragua.

4. The members of the LAFTA payments system are the central banks of Argentina, Bolivia, Brazil, Chile, Colombia, the Dominican Republic, Ecuador, Mexico, Paraguay, Peru, Uruguay and Venezuela.

5. The members of the Caribbean Community's clearing facility are the central banks of Barbados, Belize, Guyana, Jamaica, Trinidad and Tobago and the East Caribbean Currency Authority.

6. As a matter of tradition rather than law, when a Central American country is forced to impose exchange controls, these are not applied to the other members of the Common Market except to avoid speculative capital flights.

7. It is known that the members of the Caribbean Community are now considering the feasibility of a credit agreement to supplement their Multilateral Clearing Facility.

8. This operational flexibility is due to the fact that the Andean Reserve Fund is a legal entity under an international treaty, whereas the Central American Monetary Stabilisation Fund is based on an agreement among the central bank members only.

9. The Central Bank of the Dominican Republic also participates in this arrangement.

10. Although there appeared to be broad agreement on the main features of this line of credit, details on guarantees, documentation and operational procedures were still being worked out at the time of writing.

11. The Andean Group and the Caribbean Community, being considerably younger, and probably more realistic, would appear to have a better chance of success.

COMMENT

Carlos F. Diaz-Alejandro

What follow are some reflections motivated by Mr del Valle's stimulating and informative paper.

'Monetary integration' covers several dimensions and steps, each having a different impact on economic welfare. Clearing and payments arrangements reduce costs to a modest extent and are likely to be instructive. Among countries without a history of close financial links these arrangements are sensible 'import substitution projects', where the imports being substituted are services previously provided by foreign financial institutions. The establishment and maintenance of these arrangements would appear to be fairly straightforward, while the benefits for all participants are obvious. No very bold steps would seem to be necessary. By themselves, however, these new institutional mechanisms are unlikely to play more than a modest role in encouraging trade and financial links among the participating countries.

Credit arrangements for balance-of-payments support, whether they include the pooling of reserves or 'safety-net' provisions, involve a deeper commitment to interdependence and a greater trust of one's partners. One may note that neither these arrangements nor those involving special clearing and payments mechanisms *have* to be undertaken together with other integration steps, such as a lowering of tariffs. But they could provide additional impetus for the integration of commercial policy. One of the barriers to customs unions is the fear that a lowering of tariffs will yield balance-of-payments deficits; arrangements for financing possible deficits could play an important supportive role, not unlike that of trade adjustment assistance. Safety-net arrangements among like-minded countries could be more generous on the 'conditionality' of the loans that the IMF. And the pooling of reserves could lead to significant economies in the demand for reserves as well as more advantageous earnings from their investment.

On the whole, neither the pooling of reserves nor the special arrangements for balance-of-payments support have gone beyond very prudent first steps in Latin America. The Central American Fund appears bolder than the Andean Fund, whose loans '... must be supplemented by the use of the IMF facilities' [p. 216]. Such a contrast is consistent with the general picture of greater advances in Central American commercial integration mechanisms, compared with other Latin American integration efforts which have been in a more or less continuous state of crisis throughout the 1970s.

The culmination of monetary integration would, of course, be a thoroughgoing monetary union with a common currency (or permanently fixed exchange rates among the members of the union) and common credit, monetary and financial policies. Latin American countries as a whole have had a very diversified history of inflation, so it would be Utopian (or worse) to expect the region to leap directly into a monetary union. One would think that the Central American countries, with their long tradition of fixed exchange rates and reasonable price stability, might have approached a complete monetary union at a faster pace. Perhaps these countries did not want to yield the option of changing their minds on fixed exchange rates or were unwilling to co-ordinate their monetary policies. Or perhaps they simply decided that a monetary union in itself would add little of substance to effective commercial and financial integration. It would be interesting to hear further comments from Mr del Valle on the obstacles to Central American monetary union.

The tone of the preceding remarks on monetary integration, and on Latin American integration more generally, has been somewhat skeptical and pessimistic. The proportion of all Latin American imports originating within the region rose only modestly from 1962-8 to 1972-8: from 13.7 per cent to 14.1 per cent.[1] One might also note that the proportion of Latin American imports originating in the Middle East, Asia and Africa rose between these two periods from 3.0 per cent to 10.4 per cent, mainly as a result of the increase in oil prices.

On the other hand, the aggregate figures for intra-Latin American trade conceal certain important accomplishments. They contain a high share of all Latin American manufactured exports, for example. It is unclear to what extent these exports are the result of specific integration mechanisms, or whether they are the consequence of other variables, such as general export promotion and trade liberalisation policies, or improvements in the intra-Latin American infrastructure, such as in transport and communications. One might also note that official trade figures do not include the large volume of smuggling carried out at the borders of many countries of the region which involves many locally-produced goods.

Looking back on the 1960s and the early 1970s, it can be argued that international economic conditions were not conducive to integration efforts by the less developed countries (LDCs). Markets in industrialised countries were expanding fast and were reasonably open to LDC exports. But this situation began to change in the late 1970s, and the outlook for the industrialised countries in the 1980s is one of mediocre economic growth accompanied by protectionist pressures. Under these conditions it would seem prudent for LDCs to take a fresh look at their mechanisms for economic integration. Third World growth *could* be maintained even under international conditions such as those prevailing in the 1930s; note that Brazil registered very impressive industrial expansion during the 1930s. Economic integration among LDCs could accelerate such growth and make it more efficient.

What should be the role of monetary integration in these renewed efforts at 'collective self-reliance'? As noted earlier, clearing and payments arrangements, as well as generous credit mechanisms for balance-of-payments support could encourage trade expansion. Unless they are accompanied by direct efforts in the trade area, however, such as tariff reductions and joint ventures in new projects, they are unlikely to achieve much; I doubt that one can achieve real integration by pulling on a monetary string. In the Latin American context, in particular, any attempt to achieve complete monetary union would still appear to be premature. Enlarging somewhat the concept of monetary integration, one can see a greater role in the 1980s for medium- and long-term credit arrangements for encouraging inter-LDC trade in capital and other goods, and the establishment of LDC joint ventures.

Before closing, I would like to point out some institutional developments in connection with the Latin American integration efforts of the last few years. More flexible mechanisms have been sought, such as the Latin American Economic System (SELA). Using SELA as a kind of umbrella, several joint ventures have been launched by groups of countries. Other *ad hoc* schemes centre on river basins, such as those of the Amazon and the Plate. While these are important efforts, I remain convinced that old-fashioned integration instruments, such as the reduction of tariffs and the relaxation of other trade restrictions, could play a powerful role in accelerating integration among the Latin American countries.

Note

1. See Inter-American Development Bank, *Economic and Social Progress in Latin America, 1979 Report,* Table II-4, p. 47.

GENERAL DISCUSSION

1. Samir Makdisi

Mr del Valle's paper is instructive as regards the problems which developing countries face when trying to move towards closer economic and monetary integration, especially in areas where one finds heterogeneous economic and exchange regimes.

I should like to pose two specific questions concerning Latin America which I believe are of relevance to other areas as well. The first relates to exchange-rate policies. What rules or criteria apply concerning rate adjustments? Unlike the Central American countries, the LAFTA group maintains heterogeneous exchange regimes. Has this heterogeneity contributed significantly to the weakening of the integration process in LAFTA noted in the author's paper?

The second question pertains to balance-of-payments assistance. In the case of the LAFTA group, this assistance is judged in the light of intra-regional transactions and not in the context of overall economic transactions. How important have intra-regional deficits been in comparison with overall balance-of-payments deficits? What are the reasons for retaining this feature of balance-of-payments financing in LAFTA, in contrast to the Central American Common Market where balance-of-payments assistance is related to global balance-of-payments deficits?

2. Mohammed Labib Shoukair

There is no doubt but what much can be gained from studying the Latin American experience and deriving from it guidelines for developing the process of Arab monetary integration. We shall of course have to take into account the differences between the two regions when devising our own approach to monetary integration. I would like, in this connection, to ask Mr del Valle to suggest the steps which he believes are necessary to begin the process of Arab monetary integration in the light of the Latin American experience and his knowledge of the Arab world.

3. Mabid Ali Al-Jarhi

I am particularly impressed with the fact that in the Central American Payments Union, domestic currencies are used by traders to settle their payments. This effectively renders domestic currencies inter-convertible, at least for the purpose of intra-regional trade.

This particular feature of the Central American Payments Union is in my opinion applicable to the Arab situation and should be insisted upon. I would be interested to hear Mr del Valle's opinion as well as that of other participants in this regard.

It would also be helpful to have some comments on the possibility of transforming, perhaps gradually, a clearing house into a regional central bank, particularly the practical steps that might be taken in this regard.

The point made by Mr Diaz-Alejandro concerning the prospects for LDC exports to industrialised countries is of special interest, since he calls for an interregional approach to monetary integration between developing countries. I am sure that Mr del Valle's long experience would enable him to assess the prospects for such an undertaking.

4. Jorge Gonzalez del Valle, in Response

The relevance of the Latin American experience to monetary integration in the Arab world has partly to do with the time lag between the experiences of the two developing areas. One has to keep in mind that the Arab countries have been attempting to bring about co-operation and integration among themselves for less than 30 years, whereas the Latin American experience covers 160 years and we are still trying to devise ways to move closer together for the common good. Remembering this fact should help us to be a little more patient and to maintain realistic expectations with regard to monetary integration.

Concerning Mr Makdisi's question on the harmonisation of exchange-rate policies in the Central American Common Market after the 1971 dollar crisis, it must be noted that the central banks of the five member countries, acting through the Central American Monetary Council, did explore at that time different options, including the pegging of their currencies to the SDR. Various external policy objectives were evaluated. The consensus was that a revaluation *vis-à-vis* the dollar would not yield any real economic advantage, especially since neither the overall payments positions of the five countries nor their terms of trade were favourable at that time.

It was therefore decided to maintain the same parities *vis-à-vis* the dollar through the new system of 'central rates' established by the IMF at the end of 1971. This was the least damaging alternative under the circumstances. Tradition and the overwhelming importance of Central America's economic relations with the United States also had much influence on this decision.

It should be noted, in passing, that under the new Article IV of the IMF Agreement, 16 countries in Latin America have continued to peg their 'central rates' to the dollar, whereas the other seven (Argentina, Bolivia, Brazil, Colombia, Mexico, Peru and Uruguay) have adopted a policy of independent, though regulated, floating of their exchange rates.

Mr Makdisi also inquired as to the reasons for the LAFTA credit arrangement's not being a fully-fledged, global balance-of-payments support arrangement similar to the Andean Reserve Fund or the Central American Stabilisation Fund.

In this connection, not all Latin American monetary authorities share the view that a credit arrangement of this type is needed. However, as I stated in my paper, the LAFTA central banks (five of which already participate in the Andean Fund) are finally moving in this direction. At present, two proposals for the modification of the restricted, intra-regionally directed 'Santo Domingo Agreement' are being considered: one of them would operate as a general purpose 'safety net' and the other would be limited to balance-of-payments support in cases of natural disaster only. An agreement on the new arrangement should be reached in early 1981.

Mr Al-Jarhi asked about the possibility of an eventual Latin American monetary arrangement. There is indeed a chance that if LAFTA's central banks agree next year on an appropriate balance-of-payments 'safety net', it may attract the interest of both the Central American and the Caribbean countries and thus become the basis for a future global monetary arrangement. I do not know what might then become of the Andean Reserve Fund and the Central American Monetary Stabilisation Fund, but I suspect that such a system might signal the beginning of a process which would eventually consolidate all existing clearing and credit arrangements.

It should also be noted that the idea has been expressed in recent years that the Latin American countries are ready to consider the establishment of a Latin American Monetary Fund. This could also be seen as a way to consolidate or merge existing arrangements. No specific proposals have been made in this regard, but those who have suggested the idea seem to have in mind an ambitious scheme to pool all the international reserves of the participants, to centralise balance-of-payments support and to undertake a collective approach to external debt refinancing.

Mr Al-Jarhi also inquired as to the reasons for the failure of the Central American countries to establish a regional central bank since the national currencies are used already in making intra-regional payments through the Clearing House.

The answer is that a central bank would have been the obvious outcome of a monetary union, but this required certain political conditions which were not present. A monetary union would have required the merger of the present national central banks or the creation of a new one to replace them. However, the war between two member countries in 1969 seriously affected all Common Market policies and no new institutions have developed since then. The peace treaty between these two countries was signed just last month [October 1980], but other political and economic developments of recent years are now affecting the whole integration programme. In short, it may take some time to resume any monetary integration initiatives.

I deeply appreciate Mr Shoukair's confidence in asking me what I think should be done to foster monetary integration in the Arab world on the basis of my very limited observations during two previous visits to Abu Dhabi.

I hope I do not sound presumptuous if I answer that the Arab Monetary Fund is working now on precisely those two aspects which I think should constitute the next steps in the whole monetary integration process. One is the proposal to establish within the AMF a clearing or settlements arrangement for intra-regional payments, which I understand has recently been revised by a group of experts and is now in final form. I had the opportunity to take a look at the proposal and think that it is very sound and realistic. In fact, I feel it may become the best clearing arrangement in the Third World since it is based on a thorough review of existing techniques and practices.

The second aspect concerns AMF lending policies. At a recent meeting of Third World regional credit organisations in Bogota, Colombia, I suggested that the whole range of conditionality rules of both the Arab Monetary Fund and the Andean Reserve Fund should be revised as they were too heavily dominated by the conditionality of the IMF, which was already being liberalised. After the announcement made by the Managing Director of the IMF at the Board of Governor's Annual Meeting in Washington last September [1980], which confirmed such liberalisation, it is now simply essential that the conditionality of the AMF be revised. I further suggested that borrowing by members could also be encouraged by establishing 'windows' or special facilities, by means of existing legal prerogatives, which is something the IMF has also done in recent years.

I am grateful to Mr Diaz-Alejandro for his amplification of my paper through the addition of some very important comments on overall Latin American integration developments and prospects. In particular, I agree with him about the importance of the Latin American Economic System (SELA) and the contribution it may eventually make to enlarging the scope of economic integration in general. I know of several joint economic activities now being promoted by SELA which in fact reflect regional or subregional integration projects, e.g., fertilisers, petrochemicals, shipping, fishing, commodity commercialisation, etc.

I am pleased to hear Mr Diaz-Alejandro's optimistic view of monetary integration in the future. I would hope that the Central American countries will find a way to solve present problems and be ready to move forward again, especially if they have to continue to rely on existing arrangements as much as they have done in recent years. On a larger scale, I think that the impending decision to establish a new, general purpose credit arrangement within LAFTA may also foster the achievement of a global monetary integration.

7 THE EUROPEAN MONETARY SYSTEM AND EUROPEAN MONETARY INTEGRATION

Rainer S. Masera and Salvatore Rossi

I. The Construction of the European Monetary System

A. *The Three Components of the European Monetary System*

The European Monetary System (EMS) will first be analysed in the light of the objectives which were outlined when the system was conceived and which stressed its role as a decisive element contributing to the cohesion of the Community and to the process of European integration. It shall later be seen that this ambitious original plan has suffered a partial setback, largely as a consequence of the renewed inflationary push and of payments imbalances which are mainly attributable to the second oil shock.

The resolutions of the EEC Council meetings in Bremen (7 July 1978) and in Brussels (5 December 1978) show the determination to set up a scheme for achieving closer monetary co-operation which would lead to a zone of monetary stability in Europe. The efforts to relaunch the process of monetary and economic union — which presupposed a 'co-ordinated approach in all areas of economic policy' — were to take place along three main lines: (a) exchange-rate agreements; (b) reciprocal credit mechanisms, to be consolidated with the creation of the European Monetary Fund, and (c) measures in favour of the less prosperous member states.

The leitmotiv of the new approach to European monetary integration proposed at the Bremen meeting was the emphasis placed on the synergism of these three lines along which action should be taken simultaneously, as a means of overcoming the difficulties encountered by earlier plans. The construction of a European monetary system was thus conceived of as an evolving process in which — and this was its novel aspect — reciprocal commitments must be put into effect simultaneously in the three areas just mentioned. (As shall be seen, this aspect was not entirely followed up at Brussels.)

More specifically, in connection with exchange rates it was stressed that these commitments would have to reconcile the discipline imposed by the system with the divergences still existing in the Community, particularly as regarded inflation differentials: the symmetry of the adjustment process was to be the basic goal of the system, which should exhibit neither an inflationary nor a deflationary bias.

As for the European Monetary Fund (EMF), while it was recognised that it would be impossible to set up such an institution immediately, its main features were nevertheless broadly outlined so that it might, within two years, begin functioning as a European central bank, albeit on a small scale. On the other hand, it was also recognised that if the European exchange-rate agreements were to be implemented, it would have to be possible to rely on the main credit mechanisms provided for at Bremen as soon as they came into operation.

Finally, on consideration of the measures in favour of the less prosperous member states, it became apparent that their importance derived not so much from the immediate impact of the redistributive mechanisms in their favour which the EMS would activate as from the fact that the EEC budget would play a major role in the process of European integration and that this would involve, in the medium term, a thorough review of the functioning and implications of EEC policies with regard to the redistribution of resources.

B. The Exchange-rate Mechanism

1. The 'Snake' and the Basket: from Bremen to Brussels. According to the annex to the communiqué issued at the conclusion of the Bremen meeting, the principle behind the European exchange-rate agreements was that the ECU would be at the centre of the system. The two conflicting interpretations of this principle which were proposed during the technical consultations which followed the Bremen meeting were based on two very different models which, for the sake of simplicity, may be called the 'French' (basket) model and the 'German' (snake) model, as they were supported by the representatives of these countries, respectively.

According to the 'French' model, the ECU was equated with the EUA (European Unit of Account) a unit of the basket type, consisting of fixed quantities of the Community currencies. This ECU would have been both the 'denominator' (numéraire) of the system and the unit in relation to which the pivot rates, the fluctuation margins and hence the obligations to intervene on the exchange market would be defined. The main features of this system can be summarised as follows:

(a) Generally, a currency — the so-called 'deviating' currency — reaches the upper/lower margin without any other currency's being situated at the opposite margin. In principle, the deviating country, whether a deficit or a surplus country is under obligation to assume unilateral adjustment commitments. If the deviating country intervenes in EEC currencies, 'involuntary' debit (or credit) positions are created among the countries whose currencies are used;

(b) The fixing of a given percentage fluctuation margin does not make it possible to establish the levels which the bilateral exchange rates will record each time the ECU margin is reached. Indeed, while it is theoretically possible to calculate the maximum bilateral rates — which would imply a bilateral margin twice as large as that of the ECU[1] — it is extremely unlikely in practice that the relative positions of each currency will be such as to permit this;

(c) the weight of each currency is different and may vary over time (downwards in the case of depreciating currencies and upwards in the case of appreciating ones). It follows that the currencies exercise different powers of attraction in relation to the basket itself, which leads to static and dynamic symmetries in the functioning of the system. Specifically, given the same ECU margin (m) for all the currencies in the basket, the actual fluctuation margin allowed each currency in terms of its bilateral spread *vis-à-vis* all the other currencies (m_b) is directly proportional to its weight ($m_b = \frac{m}{1-\pi_i} > m$).[2] An extreme case occurs when one currency assumes the dominant weight ($> 1/2$); in this event, the currency cannot reach the upper or lower margin because it would first force another currency to overshoot the opposite margin;

(d) A change in the bilateral exchange rates *vis-à-vis* a single currency (for instance, the divergent one) leads to a revision of all the central exchange rates *vis-à-vis* the ECU and a redistribution of the weights of all the currencies.

The 'German' interpretation of the Annex was based on a completely different model. According to this approach the ECU-related central rates at the date of enactment of the European exchange-rate agreements would only serve to establish a grid of bilateral exchange parities, against which the intervention margins, also only bilateral, would be fixed. The grid and the intervention points would be maintained until a change in the pivot rates occurred. The system proposed was, therefore, substantially a new and enlarged version of the 'snake', in which only the definition of the reference unit changed.[3]

Technical analyses soon made it clear that neither of the two contrasting models could win broad consensus. Not only did the 'pure' ECU = EUA model show several theoretical shortcomings but its implementation would create serious problems. Apart from any other consideration, the members of the 'snake' were extremely reluctant to adopt a system which had no concrete points of reference to offer the market. Indeed, its indeterminate nature, which would become more marked and more serious when diversified margins were adopted for the currencies floating at that time, made the system unacceptable to them.

On the other hand, the 'German' model proved to be merely a revival of the 'snake', and not very appealing to the countries which had abandoned that agreement. The main objection to the system was the declared lack of a really symmetrical distribution of the burdens of adjustment: a loss of reserves, since these are necessarily limited, forces a country to adopt corrective measures much earlier than in the opposite case of a balance-of-payments surplus.

2. The Reconciliation Formula Adopted at Brussels. The model for the functioning of the European exchange-rate agreements — finally adopted in Brussels after many serious disagreements and the near breakdown of negotiations during the meetings of the technical committees — is basically a compromise between various proposals.[4] The reconciliation formula is based on three principles:

(a) The ECU, defined as an EUA-based basket, is the 'denominator' of the system. The upper and lower intervention points are, however, established on a bilateral basis, according to the grid-type mechanism previously described;

(b) The divergence margin of the individual currencies from the ECU basket is the basis for determining the degree of divergence from the European pivot. The 'divergence threshold' is also calculated for each currency in such a way as to eliminate the influence of the differences in weight on the probability of reaching the threshold;

(c) When the bilateral margins are reached, interventions on the exchange markets are compulsory and unlimited, in accordance with the general regulations governing the 'snake'. On the other hand, when a currency crosses the divergence threshold, this results in a presumption that the authorities concerned will take action in the form of measures such as: 'diversified' intervention, domestic economic policy measures, changes in central rates and other economic policy measures.

The European exchange-rate agreements do not, therefore, stipulate any obligation to adopt corrective measures once the divergence threshold has been crossed, since the authorities concerned may abstain from intervention until a bilateral margin has been reached, giving their reasons for doing so during the 'concertation among central banks' or during consultations within the Monetary Committee, the Co-ordination Committee or the Council of Ministers of Finance.

The philosophy behind the model for the operation of the EMS — taken as a set of actions designed to bring about greater harmonisation and coherence in the policies pursued by the member countries and bodies of the Community — is based on the belief that the present degree of coherence and integration of the economies of EEC members is not sufficient to justify relinquishing the exchange rate as an instrument for adjusting external disequilibria. On the other hand, it is recognised that in open, integrated and indexed economies, exchange-rate changes cannot on their own constitute a satisfactory tool of adjustment and that a high and variable rate of inflation precludes the achievement of sustained real growth.

Under these circumstances, it has been agreed that 'prompt and discreet' adjustments of the central exchange rates, though made 'by mutual agreement according to a common procedure in which all the countries participating in the exchange-rate mechanism and the Commission take part', will be a basic feature of the system.

C. Credit Mechanisms

1. The Indications Contained in the Annex to the Bremen Communiqué.
It may be useful to begin this section by again referring to the technical annex to the communiqué issued at the conclusion of the Bremen meeting of the EEC Council, this time as it concerns credit mechanisms.

It was the Council's intention to make the ECU the means of settlement between central banks. To this end, two ECU-denominated accounts were to be created. In the first account would be recorded the ECUs representing assets of the central banks, freely available and issued against a deposit of gold and US dollars. The initial deposit would amount to 20 per cent of the central banks' stocks of these assets, subject to a mechanism whereby subsequent increases (declines) in the central banks' dollar reserves would give rise to new deposits (withdrawals) for the creation (liquidation) of ECUs in accounts with the Fund, to maintain the proportion of 20 per cent.

In the second account would be recorded the ECUs issued against the deposit of national currencies. The total amount of ECUs in the second account would be the same as in the first. The utilisation of ECUs in the second account would, however, be subject to conditions which would vary according to the size and maturity of the loan, though short-term credits (up to one year) would in any case be 'substantial'.

Two years, at the most, after the start of the system the agreements and institutions would be consolidated in a European Monetary Fund (EMF), which would specifically replace the European Monetary Co-operation Fund (EMCF).

2. From Bremen to Brussels. As with the European exchange-rate agreements, a conflict arose in the course of the technical evaluation which followed the Bremen meeting between two very different views concerning the form and extent of the credit mechanisms to be created in support of the new agreements. Equally divergent were opinions on the desired features of the EMF.

The basic point of contention concerning the creation of ECUs against the contribution of reserves was the economic and legal nature of the 'deposit'. In some quarters it was maintained that the contract in question should be in the form of a swap, at a pre-set exchange rate, periodically adjustable, between the central banks and the EMCF.

Naturally a contract of this type would not involve any transfer of reserves, and, in substance, would take place only on the books. More specifically, the EMCF would have no control over the utilisation of the assets deposited, for the individual central banks could in fact continue to manage these. It is obvious, moreover, that the funds 'deposited' with the EMCF could not be regarded as a Community asset, arising from the pledge by member countries to make reserves available to the Community, and could not be used to guarantee any loans made by the EMCF outside the system. Finally, it would be impossible to assign to the EMCF an active role in any operations on the foreign exchange markets as part of the policy worked out with the central banks which aimed, in particular, at co-ordinated intervention in respect of non-participating currencies. To some this approach seemed unduly restrictive, even in the initial stage, since it made the creation of ECU reserves basically an exercise in 'Community windowdressing' whose principal economic effect was to make possible the activation of gold holdings.

The points of view conflicted even more with regard to the issuance of ECUs against national currencies. On the one hand, it was maintained that the system outlined at Bremen would imply changing the structure of short-term monetary support so as to make credits available through the actual creation of ECUs with the EMCF, and not through the traditional forms of credit between central banks. This would lead, in particular, to the abolition of the creditor quotas adopted under the system then in existence and would give the ECU a highly innovatory content. The objection to this approach was principally that it would not be technically and legally possible to create a mechanism in time to go into operation at the starting date of the EMS, but also concerned the implications raised by the volume of ECUs which a single central bank might be forced to accumulate owing to the absence of acceptability limits.

Opinions also varied as to the amount of credit which was to be made available under the system. The Bremen Annex stated that the total should be comparable to that for the creation of ECU reserves. Indeed, since 20 per cent of the gross reserves held by the European central banks amounted to about 25 billion ECUs, many felt that the total amount of credit should be the same. This point of view was not, however, shared by all.

3. The Agreements Reached in Brussels and Basle. From a conceptual point of view, the agreements reached in Brussels and later defined in Basle, during the meetings there on 13 March 1979 of the EEC Governors and of the EMCF Board of Directors, represent a basically conservative solution. In the quantification of the credit subsidies, however, they came close to satisfying the most fervent proponents of increases. The compromise consisted, therefore, in keeping the forms of credit available under the 'snake' unchanged as far as possible from an economic and legal angle, while considerably increasing their amount. The EMS credit system is based on the following main points:

4. Very Short-term Credit Facilities. As in the 'snake', so that intervention can be effected in EEC currencies, atutomatic, unconditional and unlimited very short-term credit facilities are available. Settlements must be made within 45 days[5] following the end of the month of intervention. However, this period may be prolonged for another three months for amounts not exceeding the size of the debtor's quota under the short-term monetary support agreement (see below). Technically, the facilities are granted by each central bank to each of the other participating banks; they take the form of spot sales (purchases) of Community currencies against the crediting (debiting) of accounts denominated in ECUs, effected at the ECU rates recorded by the EEC Commission on the day on which the interventions are made. The debtor and creditor interest rates applying to very short-term credit facilities are the average of the official discount rates of all the EEC banks, weighted in accordance with the weights of their respective currencies as derived from the ruling ECU central rates.[6]

b. The creation of ECU accounts against the contribution of reserves and the settlement of very short-term financing operations. The resolution passed by the EEC Council at the Brussels meeting made explicit provision for the creation of ECUs against reserves in order to make possible the settlement of debts arising from the utilisation of very short-term credit facilities. 'To serve as a means of settlement, an initial supply of ECUs shall be provided by the EMCF against the deposit of 20 per cent of the gold and 20 per cent of the dollar reserves currently held by the central banks. This operation shall take the form of specified, revolving swap arrangements. By periodical review and by an appropriate procedure it shall be ensured that each central bank maintains a deposit of at least 20 per cent of these reserves with the EMCF.'[7]

It should, however, be noted that in defining the legal aspects and the operation of settlement transactions the Committee of Governors introduced some restrictions on the use of ECU holdings as a means of repayment. Specifically, when a financing operation falls due, settlement must be effected[8] entirely or in part by transferring ECUs, with the proviso that a creditor central bank may refuse to accept settlement in ECUs for an amount exceeding 50 per cent of its claim. The balance must be settled by means of sales of other reserve components in accordance with the composition of the debtor central bank's reserves as at the end of the month preceding the settlement.[9]

The gold and dollar contributions to the EMCF are in the form of legal contracts for three-month revolving swaps. In particular, the governors decided to establish the value of the reserve components transferred to the EMCF as follows:

(i) For the gold portion, the average of the prices, converted into ECUs, recorded at the London fixings during the previous six months, but not exceeding the average price of two fixings on the penultimate working day of the period.
(ii) For the dollar portion, the market rate two working days prior to the valuation date.

As regards the earnings on the ECU balances, it decided that the central banks whose ECU assets were less than their forward sales of ECUs to the EMCF (as part of the swap operations) would pay interest to the EMCF on the difference between these two aggregates. In the case of central banks whose ECU assets exceeded their forward sales, the EMCF would pay them interest on the difference between these two aggregates.[10]

c. Short- and medium-term credit mechanisms. As mentioned previously, the Brussels Resolution did not provide for the creation of ECUs against national currencies; on the other hand, the existing credit mechanisms were maintained for the initial phase of the EMS, though the amount of effectively available credit was increased from ECU 10 billion to ECU 25 billion. Of this amount, ECU 14 billion was allocated for short-term monetary support and ECU 11 billion for medium-term financial assistance.

Effectively available credit may be defined as the maximum amount of credit which can be utilised by the system at a given moment.

(i) Short-term monetary support

The agreement pertaining to short-term monetary support was concluded by the EEC central banks on 9 February 1970. It was first extended in January 1973 to include the three new members of the Community and again extended and amended in March 1974 and February 1977. Decisions in its regard are taken by the EEC Committee of Governors. The short-term monetary support agreement provides financial assistance for the financing of temporary balance-of-payments deficits. Initially, no conditions are attached to the assistance, though consultations take place within the Committee of Governors. Specifically, when monetary support is granted, the Committee of Governors examines the monetary situation and the monetary policy of the beneficiary country. Support is initially granted for a period of three months and may be renewed twice for periods of three months, so that the maximum duration is nine months.[11]

The credit mechanism is based on the co-existence of debtor quotas (ceilings on borrowing) and creditor quotas (ceilings on lending) for each central bank: the creditor quotas are double the amount of the debtor quotas. The system also provided for 'extensions' on both the debtor and creditor side: more specifically, as a rule each central bank may obtain support up to the amount of its debtor quota plus the extension[12] and, conversely, a central bank may in theory be called upon to contribute its creditor quota plus the entire extension.

(ii) Medium-term financial assistance

This mechanism was created by the EEC Council resolution of 22 March 1971 and later amended twice, first to extend it to new Community members and then, in December 1977, to double its amount. Further to the Brussels Resolution, the Council passed a resolution on 21 December 1978 raising the total amount of effectively available credit to ECU 11 billion and modifying the limits on the amount of support to be financed by each country.

The decision to accord medium-term financial assistance does not rest with the Committee of Governors but is taken by a weighted majority of the Council, upon the recommendation of the EEC Commission and following consultation with the Monetary Committee. The mechanism provides for the granting of medium-term (2-5 years) financing to any country within the Community which 'must overcome difficulties or a serious threat of difficulties in its balance of payments'. In principle, a country may not receive financial assistance amounting to more than 50 per cent of its total creditor quota.

It must be stressed that, unlike the very short-term and the short-term credit facilities, medium-term financial assistance is subject to conditions: when granting reciprocal financial assistance the Council establishes the commitments which the beneficiary country must undertake in order to restore internal and external equilibrium (taking into account the Community's quantitative guidelines for medium-term economic policies) and fixes the amount and the terms of credit, especially the payment period and rate of interest.

In principle, the financing will be provided by all the participating creditor countries in proportion to their respective quotas. However, the Council may exempt a member country which is experiencing or is likely to experience balance-of-payments difficulties and/or a persistent decline in its foreign exchange reserves from participation in the financing of support. In addition, in accordance with the decision of the Council, the member country which experiences balance-of-payments difficulties may mobilise its claim in one or more of the following manners: (a) the transfer of its claim within the system; (b) the refinancing of its contribution outside the system; (c) the premature repayment of its claim by the debtor country. The position of the country which has been exempted from participation and whose claim has been mobilised will be evaluated by the Monetary Committee, which, if the situation later permits, will request the country to participate in the financing of support.

The Council may demand the premature repayment of the support by the beneficiary country if the conditions which justified the granting of medium-term financial assistance no longer obtain.

D. Measures in Favour of the Less Prosperous Member States

At the conclusion of the EEC Council meeting at Bremen, the president presented the technical annex on the EMS which was to serve as a guideline for the Committee of Governors and the Monetary Committee, relating it to the measures in favour of the less prosperous member states in the following terms: 'The EEC Council has discussed the attached scheme for the creation of closer monetary co-operation (EMS) leading to a zone of monetary stability in Europe. The Council regards such a zone as a highly desirable objective. The Council envisages a durable and effective scheme. Parallel studies will be made of the steps which must be taken to strengthen the economies of the less prosperous member countries within the context of this scheme: these steps are essential if the zone of monetary stability is to be successful.'

The economic logic behind this approach was based on the consideration that gradual monetary integration and the related gradual loss of freedom to manœuvre the monetary and credit aggregates (and, as a corollary, interest rates) must be offset by the creation of supranational fiscal instruments. Even for countries substantially open, with integrated and directly or indirectly indexed economies, such as the member states of the Community, the relinquishment of domestic management of monetary and exchange-rate policies implies certain sacrifices when inflationary impulses — namely, the cost of labour and the public deficit — are not convergent.

In order to create a scheme for monetary integration that is capable of evolving towards a real currency area, an automatic 'solution' must be found to national balance-of-payments difficulties. If this is to be done without turning these difficulties into 'regional' ones and increasing the problems of domestic employment and growth besetting the tendentially deficit areas,[13] there must be available flexible and selective fiscal instruments with a redistributive effect.

Recently, the so-called MacDougall Report[14] has provided authoritative confirmation that it would be possible gradually to channel the EEC budget into the regional redistribution of resources by ensuring that a minimum 'critical' size is attained.

The European Monetary System   243

The fact that some countries have proved extremely unwilling to review the theoretical and practical aspects of the present perverse effects of the Community budget caused by the common agricultural policy has made it very difficult to consider the complex problems posed by the measures in favour of the less prosperous member states within a single and consistent framework.

Although the results obtained in Italy and Ireland, the two less prosperous states adhering to the EMS exchange-rate agreements, do have some quantitative significance,[15] they are not such as to demonstrate the kind of clear progress all along the line which had been envisaged in Bremen and which would have consisted in making a gradual but extensive revision of the Community budget.

II. The First 17 Months of EMS Operations

A review of the first 17 months of EMS operations and of certain features of the system can be conveniently broken down into five periods, on the basis of the evolution of the ECU vis-à-vis the dollar (see Figures 7.1 a and b).

Figure 7.1a: Movement of Major Extra-EEC Currencies vis-à-vis the ECU on the Basis of Quotations as at 13 March 1979

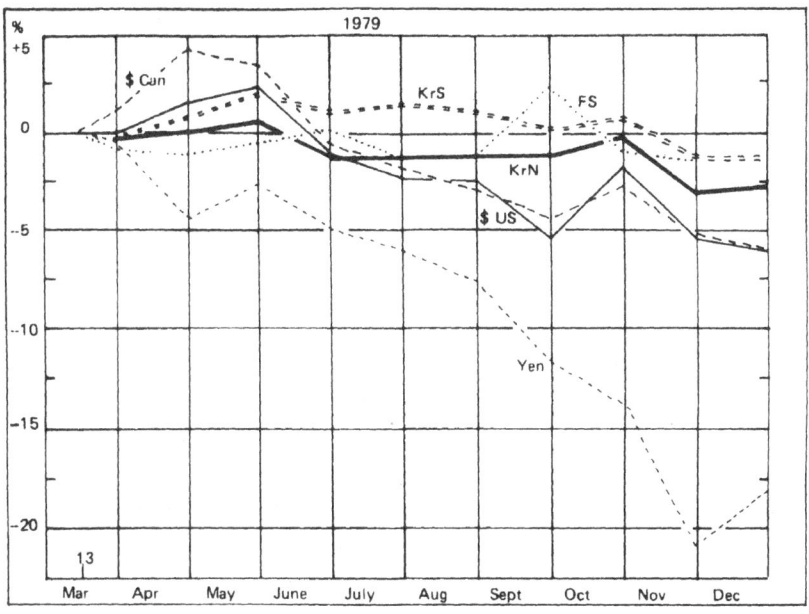

Figure 7.1b

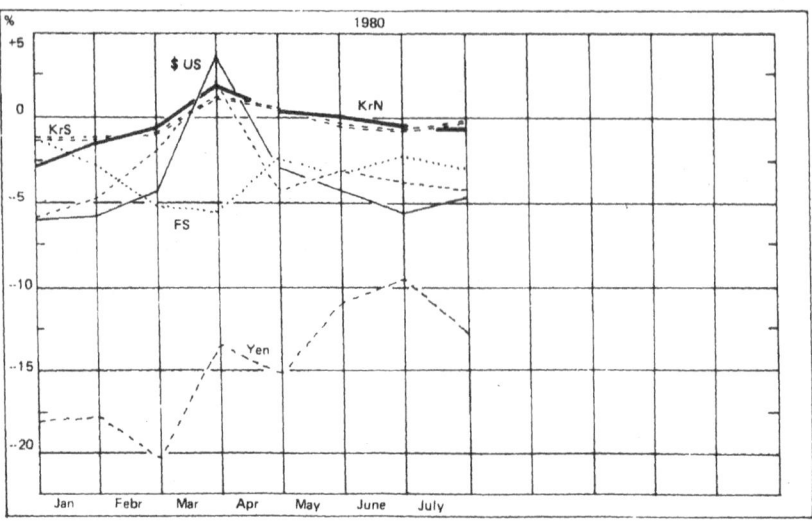

A. The first phase of the system covers the period from 13 March to 31 May 1979. This period was characterised by the relative strength of the dollar against the ECU and against the DM, in particular, and by bilateral tensions within the EMS between the Danish kroner and the Belgian franc. During these months, substantial intra-marginal interventions took place. In particular, while the Banco d'Italia was buying dollars to prevent what was regarded as an excessive appreciation of the lira, the Bundesbank was intervening in the opposite sense, to prevent a depreciation of the DM, which would have exacerbated the problem of domestic inflation; such interventions on the part of the Bundesbank continued also in May, when the DM first crossed the zero line of the divergence indicator and subsequently (23 May) reached the maximum 2.25 per cent *vis-à-vis* the Belgian franc (see Figures 7.2a and 7.3a).

B. The second phase of the system covers the period from 1 June to 23 September 1979 when the first realignment of central rates took place in Brussels. During this period, characterised by the progressive decline of the dollar, the DM stood permanently at or very near the 2.25 per cent spread *vis-à-vis* the Belgian franc and the Danish kroner and the interventions at the bilateral margins acquired significant proportions. Furthermore, monetary policy measures were introduced by various central banks to combat inflation or defend their own currencies. In the main, these measures consisted in raising interest

Figure 7.2a: Movements within the EMS Parity Grid

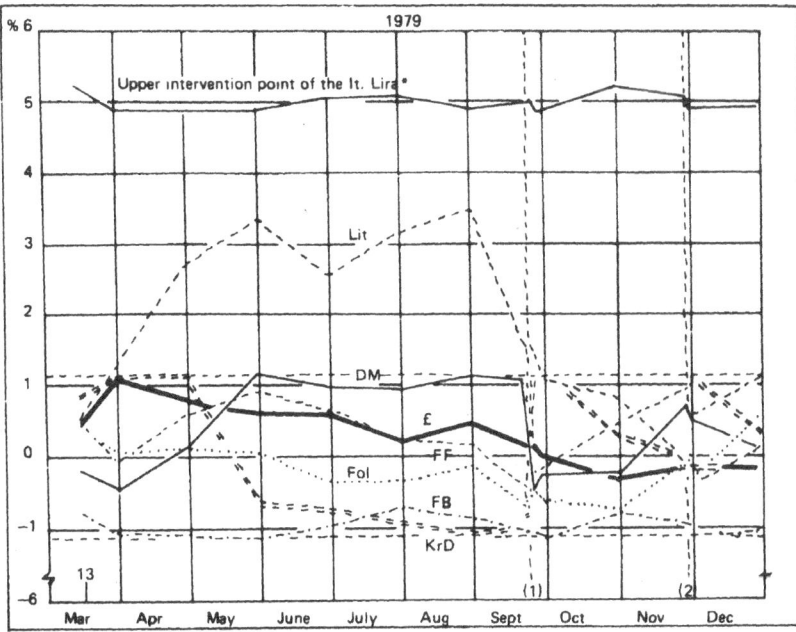

Figure 7.2b

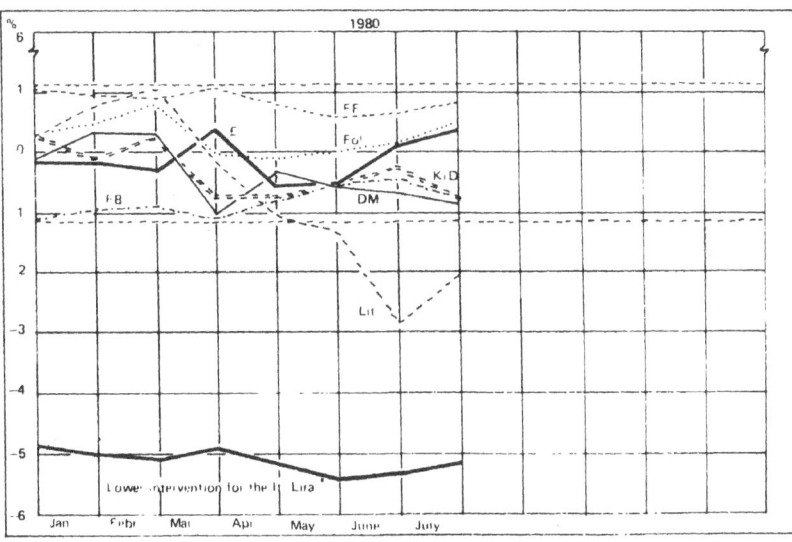

(*) The upper (lower) intervention point of the Italian lira represents the maximum theoretical spread *vis-à-vis* the weakest (strongest) currency in the narrow band (∓2.25 per cent) (1) First realignment of EMS central rates, effective from 24 September 1979 (2) Second realignment of EMS central rates, effective from 30 November 1979

Figure 7.3a: Movement of the Divergence Indicator

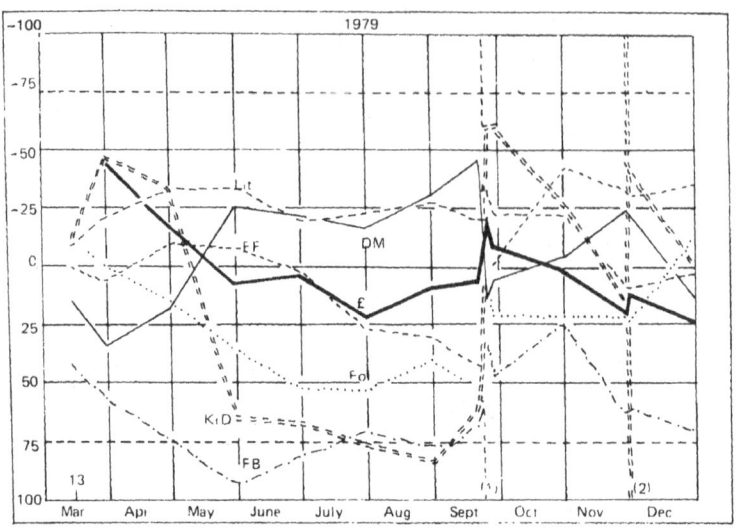

Figure 7.3b

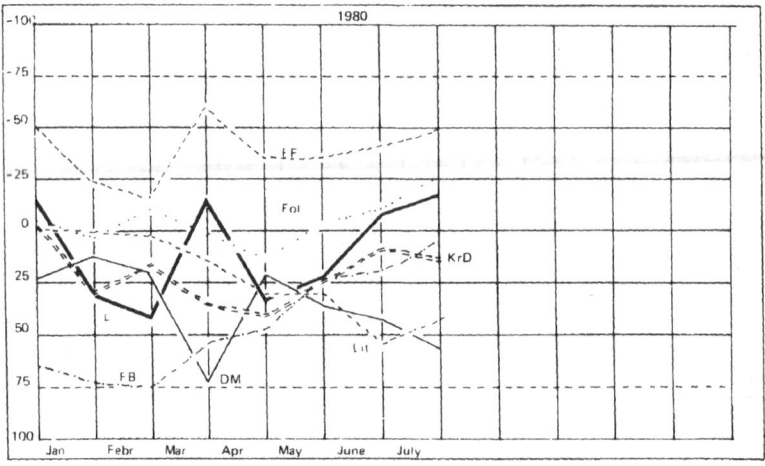

The indicator of divergence measures the position of each currency participating in the European exchange-rate mechanism in relation to its ECU central rate. The maximum divergence spread is the maximum percentage amount by which the market quotation of the ECU in terms of any currency may appreciate (depreciate) vis-à-vis the ECU central rate. It is expressed as ± 100; the divergence 'threshold' is ± 75. The calculations are made on the basis of actual market quotations corrected for the movements of the lira and the pound outside the narrow (2.25 per cent) margins. A + (−) sign denotes an appreciation (depreciation) of the ECU vis-à-vis the currency in question, i.e., a weak (strong) currency. (1) First realignment of EMS central rates, effective from 24 September 1979 (2) Second realignment of EMS central rates, effective from 30 November 1979.

rates: the escalation which took place during the period (see Tables 7.1a and b) was no doubt influenced by the increase in interest rates in Germany — whose currency was, as will be recalled, at the top of the narrow-margin band — prompted by the desire to counter the inflationary impact of the energy price rise.[16] The fall in the dollar over this period also implied significant — but varying — movements in nominal (and real) exchange rates. This was one of the factors which was taken into account during the (difficult) negotiations in Brussels on 23 September 1979, in the course of which the German monetary authorities made it clear that the combination of intra-EEC tensions and dollar weakness were entailing too heavy a cost in terms of domestic stability. It was therefore decided to effect a realignment of central rates, consisting in a revaluation of the DM by 5 per cent against the Danish kroner and by 2 per cent against all the other participating currencies.

C. The third period runs from the Brussels realignment to December 1979. In this phase, too, the dollar trend was of paramount importance. The agreements reached by the German authorities, Secretary Miller and President Volcker in Hamburg were followed by the measures announced by the US Federal Reserve Board (FED) on 6 October, which made it possible to stop the decline of the dollar. Short-term tensions within the EMS subsided, although stabilisation of exchange rates continued to be achieved by means of sizeable intra-marginal interventions, mainly in dollars and in order to support that currency.

The increasing weakness of the Danish kroner in November brought about another realignment of the central rates consisting of a devaluation of that currency by 4.76 per cent against all the other participating currencies.

Interest rates during this period continued their upward trend in nominal terms: in particular the Bundesbank again increased its discount rate, from 5 per cent to 6 per cent on 1 November 1979.

D. The fourth phase of the system covers the period from 1 January to 31 March 1980. During this period, exchange market developments were influenced mainly by the continuous and rapid rise in US interest rates. The dollar, which had been fairly stable in January, began to improve after the US discount rate was raised in mid-February (by one percentage point) and appreciated strongly in March, chiefly as a result of the upward movement in short-term interest rates (the prime rate was raised in rapid steps to 19.5 per cent), stimulated by the monetary and credit measures which were part of an official anti-inflation programme.

The currencies participating in the EMS subsequently underwent

248 *The European Monetary System*

Table 7.1: Discount Rates (end of period) (percentages)

Countries	1979										1980				
	March	April	May	June	July	August	September	October	November	December	January	February	March	April	May
Belgium	6.00	6.00	8.00	9.00	9.00	9.00	9.00	10.00	10.00	10.50	10.50	12.00	14.00	14.00	14.00
Denmark	8.00	8.00	8.00	9.00	9.00	11.00	11.00	11.00	11.00	11.00	11.00	13.00	13.00	13.00	13.00
France	9.50	9.50	9.50	9.50	9.50	9.50	9.50	9.50	9.50	9.50	9.50	9.50	9.50	9.50	9.50
Germany	4.00	4.00	4.00	4.00	5.00	5.00	5.00	5.00	6.00	6.00	6.00	7.00	7.00	7.00	7.50
Ireland	11.85	11.85	11.85	13.70	13.70	13.70	13.70	13.70	13.70	16.40	16.40	16.40	16.85	16.85	16.85
Italy	10.50	10.50	10.50	10.50	10.50	10.50	10.50	12.00	12.00	15.00	15.00	15.00	15.00	15.00	15.00
Netherlands	6.50	6.50	7.00	7.00	8.00	8.00	8.00	8.00	9.50	9.50	9.50	9.50	9.50	9.50	10.00
UK	13.00	12.00	12.00	14.00	14.00	14.00	14.00	14.00	17.00	17.00	17.00	17.00	17.00	17.00	17.00
United States	9.50	9.50	9.50	9.50	10.00	10.50	11.00	12.00	12.00	12.00	12.00	13.00	13.00	13.00	12.00
Japan	3.50	4.25	4.25	4.25	5.25	5.25	5.25	5.25	6.25	6.25	6.25	7.25	9.00	9.00	9.00
Switzerland	1.00	1.00	1.00	1.00	1.00	1.00	1.00	1.00	2.00	2.00	2.00	3.00	3.00	3.00	3.00

Source: International Monetary Fund, *International Financial Statistics*.

Table 7.2: Money Market Rates (end of period) (percentages)

Countries	1979										1980				
	March	April	May	June	July	August	September	October	November	December	January	February	March	April	May
Belgium	8.05	8.05	9.16	9.75	12.00	12.00	12.50	14.10	14.35	14.45	14.50	15.00	17.50	17.00	15.75
Denmark	13.50	13.50	13.80	14.80	14.80	14.90	16.70	16.80	17.00	17.00	17.00	18.90	19.00	19.10	19.10
France	7.12	7.00	8.62	9.19	10.69	11.37	11.62	12.50	12.37	12.62	12.19	13.62	13.69	12.56	12.37
Germany	5.35	5.75	6.40	6.65	6.95	7.45	7.90	9.75	9.50	8.70	8.85	9.50	9.80	9.97	10.20
Ireland	14.50	14.37	14.25	18.50	17.87	17.62	17.62	17.50	17.75	18.12	18.00	18.37	19.12	18.75	17.66
Italy	11.50	11.50	11.50	11.44	11.62	11.62	11.62	12.75	13.62	17.12	17.75	17.62	17.87	16.50	17.12
Netherlands	7.25	7.50	9.12	8.50	9.62	9.62	9.87	10.75	14.75	13.00	11.37	12.87	11.25	10.37	11.25
UK	12.19	11.62	11.75	14.00	14.19	14.12	14.06	14.75	16.81	17.00	17.75	18.31	18.12	17.12	17.00
United States	9.99	9.64	10.15	9.94	10.20	11.26	11.95	14.72	12.90	13.70	13.49	15.45	16.44	13.70	7.90
Japan	5.05	5.01	5.21	5.29	5.61	6.41	7.12	6.97	8.14	8.01	8.02	9.86	12.68	12.12	12.53
Switzerland	0.67	1.62	2.12	2.00	1.62	2.12	1.62	3.62	4.50	6.12	6.00	5.25	7.37	6.37	5.62

Source: *World Financial Markets*.

significant fluctuations — both the Danish kroner and the Deutschmark began to slide towards the lower limit of the fluctuation band, in opposition to the French franc, which by the end of March was alone at the top of the system (see Figure 7.2b).

It should be noted that during this phase of dollar strength the measures taken by the German authorities to support their currency (raising the discount rate, selling dollars on the exchange market) did not succeed in preventing the depreciation of the mark because of the considerable outflow of short-term funds stemming from the rapid widening of the interest-rate differential in favour of the dollar. Such a situation, unlike that of May 1979, allowed the divergence indicators of the weak currencies (particularly the Belgian franc) to move well away from the lower threshold (see Figure 7.3b) and enabled the central banks responsible for these currencies to reduce the frequency of their interventions on the exchange markets.

E. During the fifth phase of the system, lasting up to July 1980, the most significant development was the sharp decline of the dollar against almost all the other currencies. The upward movement of the dollar recorded since the middle of February was quickly reversed at the beginning of April and the US currency continued to weaken for almost all the remainder of the period. This was due, in the main, to a very steep decline in US interest rates — signalling the onset of recession — against a backdrop of continuing high inflation. This dollar trend allowed the EMS to relax its controls; the spread between the currencies observing the 2.25 per cent margin narrowed considerably and the divergence indicators moved well away from both the upper and the lower thresholds (except for the Italian lira, which showed a marked weakness, especially in June, but did not reach either its divergence threshold or its intervention limit).

In conclusion, looking at the entire 17-month period, one may note that the evolution of the EMS has been characterised mainly by the relative stability of the nominal exchange rates, while the real exchange rates — that is the competitive positions — have shown significant variations. Such a situation requires that a serious attempt be made to reduce the divergences within the Community in the key inflationary factors, namely labour costs, productivity and public finance trends. Indeed, if the inflation differentials persist or widen further, the system will run the risk of evolving towards some kind of crawling peg scheme, weakening its ability to lead to European monetary integration.[17]

Moreover, three relevant features of the system may be noted in the light of the experience gained during the period under review. First of all, the frequent recourse to intra-marginal interventions, both in EEC currencies and in outside currencies, warrants mentioning.[18] Until the end of 1979, the ratio of these interventions to those effected at the margin limits was about ten to one. This fact undoubtedly reflects a high degree of co-operation and concertation among central banks to prevent tension and to ensure orderly market conditions. Admittedly, however, these interventions may alter the signals to be derived from a 'pure' divergence-indicator system, whereby interventions on the exchange market should only begin after the threshold of divergence has been reached.

Another point concerns the relative importance of dollar and Community currency interventions: total gross interventions within the EMS in 1979 can be put at about $70 billion, over three-quarters of which were in dollars (the remaining quarter representing mainly interventions in EEC currencies by the FED). These simple figures highlight the need for a co-ordinated approach to dollar policy, which shall be discussed in Part IV below.

As to the interventions on the exchange markets, it should be noted in passing that those effected in EEC currencies were covered largely by spot settlement; indeed, while some recourse was had to very short-term financing, no use was made of short-term monetary support or medium-term financial assistance.

Finally, during these months the workings of the divergence indicator were characterised by an anomaly, which was pointed out in the technical discussions preceding the inauguration of the EMS and then confirmed by experience: sometimes the bilateral margin between two currencies was reached before the indicator singled out one of these currencies as the divergent one.[19] For instance, the ECU 'alarm-bell' began ringing for the Belgian franc a month after this currency had reached the lower limit of the fluctuation band, in opposition to the Danish kroner.

III. The Prospects for the EMS

A. The Creation of the European Monetary Fund and the Role of the ECU in the Final Phase of the EMS

As stated earlier, it was decided at the Brussels meeting of the EEC Council to consolidate the existing credit mechanism in a European Monetary Fund, within two years following the inauguration of the EMS.

Even if the final resolution did not restate the guidelines issued in Bremen for the establishment of this Fund, it nevertheless confirmed that the establishment of the EMF should achieve the following basic objectives: (i) full utilisation of the ECU as a reserve asset and means of settlement; (ii) improved co-ordination of exchange-rate policies, with regard to both Community and outside currencies, and of monetary policies; and (iii) promotion of the convergence and stability of the member countries' economies.

The political, legal and economic debate over the EMF persists. Although technical studies are being made by the Monetary Committee and the Committee of Governors, at the time of writing it seems unlikely that the Fund will have begun to operate by March 1981, as per the original plan. This will depend on the complexity of the problems to be faced, as well as on changes in the overall economic situation as a consequence of the second oil shock.

From the analyses developed so far, a number of general principles have emerged, in particular the need for parallel progress in monetary and economic integration. Furthermore, as a corollary to this, an evolutionary approach should be adopted, so that the development of the EMF will be in line with the conditions and progress made in economic, monetary and financial integration within the Community.

Moreover, three main options have been identified with regard to the role and structure of the future European Monetary Fund. It could be conceived of as:

1. An institution basically similar to the EMCF;
2. An institution along the lines of a regional 'IMF-World Bank'; or
3. An embryonic central bank.

The first approach — which might be termed 'minimalist' — would essentially limit the Fund to the accounting role currently played by the EMCF, without, in particular, according it any direct responsibility for exchange-market interventions or for the formulation of guidelines for monetary policy co-ordination. With respect to the present functions of the EMCF, the concept of the new Fund might, according to this approach, be extended to include at the most the direct administration of the short-term monetary support facility (credit-granting by the Fund would have to be from its own sources or from funds borrowed in each case from the central banks). Moreover, the present system of revolving swaps of ECUs against extra-Community reserve assets might be prolonged indefinitely with the Fund empowered to manage the remaining reserves.

According to the 'regional IMF-World Bank' approach, the Fund would acquire powers largely of an economic nature and would also deal with structural problems. It would take over direct responsibility for administering the short-term monetary support and the medium-term financial assistance facilities (using, as in the former case, its own resources or borrowed funds), under a system of quotas and drawing rights like that operated by the IMF. Credits would, in principle, be conditional, particularly in the case of medium-term assistance, with the terms taking the form of formal commitments by the debtor country. The Fund would also either take over or, at least, work in close contact with, the European Investment Bank (EIB).

The third approach would also give the Fund a stronger and more autonomous role than that of the EMCF. It is like the second approach, but oriented towards creating the embryo of a Federal Central Bank. First and foremost, the Fund would be given responsibility for administering the short-term monetary support facility. It could also take over the administration of the very short-term facility (which would remain automatic and unconditional) and keep the accounts for the medium-term financial assistance facility so as to have a complete and homogeneous picture of member countries' credit positions. The Fund would, like the EMCF, issue ECUs against contributions of reserve assets by the member central banks, but these contributions would take a definitive form (sales or, say, capital contributions), so that ownership of the reserves and responsibility for their management would pass to the EMS. Furthermore, the Fund could also issue ECUs against contributions of national currencies. It should eventually have operational powers greater than those of the EMCF; in particular, it might support the co-ordination of national monetary policies by intervening in the money markets.

Obviously, the choice to be made among these three options will have important repercussions for the process of monetary integration in Europe. From this point of view, it seems clear that only a 'central bank' approach would be able to ensure the further development of this process, in accordance with the spirit and the letter of the Bremen resolution.

An approach of this kind requires that particular attention be paid to the mechanisms for creating ECUs, which should no longer be essentially an accounting entry.

First of all, as to the issuance of ECUs against contributions of reserve assets, it would seem that, in the final phase of the system, a mechanism should be created providing for a true partial pooling of reserves. Moreover, another source for the creation of ECUs should be activated, based on payments in national currencies.

In this connection, the debate on the reform of the international monetary system which took place among Triffin, Meade, Bernstein and others in the early 1960s[20] should provide some inspiration. As early as 1957, for instance, J.E. Meade maintained, with regard to the establishment of a monetary fund on a European scale, that it should be an institution 'into which all members paid certain amounts of their own currencies and possibly also of their reserves of gold and dollars . . .'

Such a view is still valid and a mechanism of this kind, already provided for at the EEC Council meeting in Bremen, should be considered an essential part of the theoretical framework of the EMS.

As regards the operational features of this mechanism, the following model, in accordance with the guidelines issued in Bremen, might be envisaged: the Community countries would obtain, against payments in national currencies (entered under the Fund's assets), ECU deposits (which would be liabilities of the Fund); these deposits would not be freely available, but regarded rather as tied time deposits. The country wishing to use its deposit would have to submit to adjustment rules and the ECUs would be released in tranches depending on results. However, once these ECUs were released, they would have all the same powers and features as those created against contributions of reserve assets and would represent, in particular, a complete instrument for settlement among the central banks of the Community.

Naturally, according to this model, the Fund's liabilities, i.e., the ECU deposits held by the central banks, would become the active means of settlement for the system.

The model just described tends to stress the 'central bank' functions of the new Fund and provides the institutional basis for making it the nucleus of the European central bank, when the stage of true monetary unification is reached.

B. The EMS as the Framework for the International Monetary System

1. The Relationship to the Dollar. There are several reasons why Community countries may have, in principle, different ideas about the appropriate or sustainable rate of exchange between their own currencies and the dollar. In the first place, a given performance by the dollar will not have, *ceteris paribus*, the same impact on the competitiveness of all European currencies, due to the varying importance of US trade for each country.

Furthermore, the real exchange rate desired will vary from country to country depending on the ultimate economic objectives being pursued. Countries which are primarily concerned with the implications of exchange-rate movements for internal price stability will prefer, at least within certain limits, a high exchange-rate for their own currencies against the dollar, while those which are more concerned with maintaining competitiveness will prefer a low exchange rate against the dollar.

In the light of these circumstances, policies *vis-à-vis* the dollar held to be suitable by EMS member countries may prove to be incompatible with the exchange-rate agreements of the system. Indeed, it is impossible for two members of the EMS to pursue independent dollar policies for long; sooner or later such policies will clash with EMS obligations, at which point either one of the two countries will have to modify its dollar policy or there will have to be a realignment of central rates within the system.

Therefore, it follows that the European exchange-rate agreements should be complemented by the operational definition of co-ordination procedures in exchange-rate matters with regard to outside currencies, especially the dollar. This is particularly important in an international context, such as the present one, in which the American authorities' policy of benign neglect has been replaced by one of active interest in the external value of the dollar. The setting of a (moving) fluctuation band between the ECU and the dollar should be agreed upon between the European central banks and the FED. In the medium-term, EEC co-ordination could come within the ambit of the EMF and take the form of direct interventions in ECUs, were the European 'scudo' to circulate as a parallel currency.

More generally, it should be noted that the operative configuration of the EMS is considerably different from the forms, explicitly based on real exchange-rate trends, which were proposed following the crisis of the Werner approach[21] and the failure of the Marjolin and Tindemans[22] Reports.

On the other hand, it is clearly impossible to ignore the movement of real exchange rates, if there is to be no risk of the EMS causing distortions in the productive process instead of contributing to balanced growth and the proper allocation of resources within the Community. For this reason, it might be worth introducing, in addition to the existing exchange-rate agreements, certain 'rules of the game' for the real exchange-rates as well. These rules should promote the convergence of nominal exchange rates and the lowering of inflation rates. The definition of these rules should involve the commitment of the economic authorities, employers and unions. In analytical terms, this would require the definition of 'permitted' margins with regard to real exchange rates, as well; when these were exceeded, adjustments could be made in the ECU exchange rate, though within certain previously agreed limits, set, for example, every year.

It is obvious that these limits would have to be fixed with due regard for certain expected trends in the exchange rates of extra-Community currencies, and revised if these developed otherwise.

2. The Question of Recycling. One of the main focuses of the debate on the future development of the EMS is the desirability of developing the use of the ECU outside the European Community. Discussions in this regard have most recently centred on relations between the Community and the oil-exporting countries.

The conclusions of the EEC Council meeting held at Luxemburg in April 1980 state that: 'The council paid particular attention to the growing deficit in the developing countries' balance of payments, the extent of the petroleum-producing countries' surpluses, the volume of international liquidity and the effects which these factors in combination might have on the stability of the international economic and financial system and on trade. The Council took the view that to deal with these problems it would be necessary to step up co-operation in appropriate forms between States and with the relevant international institutions'. In this connection a question arises as to the extent to which the Community as a whole could be involved in the recycling process, even through its financial institutions, and what forms this involvement might take.

Indeed, there is general agreement as to the desirability of supplementing the market recycling of OPEC surpluses by the involvement of official institutions in this process. Many in Europe believe that the EEC should play a larger role in this regard, not only by means of direct bilateral transactions with the OPEC countries but also by means of new initiatives, e.g., promoting the use of the ECU in relations with the OPEC countries.

It must be stressed, however, that there is no easy way to activate a truly multilateral recycling process based on the ECU unless certain fundamental prerequisites are met: (i) the use of the ECU as an independent reserve asset and an effective means of settling intra-EEC payments and (ii) the strengthening of Community institutions, in particular the creation of the EMF to replace the EMCF. Moreover, whatever recycling scheme involving the ECU is formulated, it should not incorporate, either implicitly or explicitly, substitution account features in respect of dollar holdings.

The SDR substitution account was frozen because of the difficulty of satisfactorily apportioning the burden of possible losses between the United States and other countries. It is inappropriate for the world payments system that an account of this type should be created without an active role being played by the United States. Doubts were expressed about the substitution account, as proposed in Hamburg, mainly because the United States seemed to play an insufficient role: its complete exclusion is decidedly undesirable.

In the light of the foregoing remarks, it would seem that, before attempting to give the EEC a role as protagonist in the official recycling of surpluses, the trend towards developing an approach to the final phase of the EMS should be reinforced.

Notes

1. For example, a margin of $1\frac{1}{8}$ per cent *vis-à-vis* the ECU makes possible, at any given moment, a maximum bilateral margin between two currencies of 2¼ per cent. This was the percentage adopted in the 'snake'; however, it may also be

obtained from margins of $\pm 1\frac{1}{8}$ per cent *vis-à-vis* the EMUA (European Monetary Unit of Account) — the conventional unit of reference in that system.

2. For example, a $1\frac{1}{8}$ per cent margin *vis-à-vis* the ECU would have permitted the German mark to appreciate by 1.55 per cent against all the other currencies at the weights of 28 June 1974 and by 1.68 per cent at the weights of 12 March 1979; the corresponding values for the punt would have been 1.142 and 1.138 per cent.

3. For a description of the 'snake', see the *Bundesbank Bulletin* (January 1973). To assist the reader, the main features of this system can be summarised as follows: (1) the system automatically designates the intervention currencies (currencies in opposition); (2) since the currencies are not weighted, the system allows all of them to fluctuate bilaterally to the same extent; (3) the system is not affected by the non-participation of some currencies; (4) changes in the pivot rates may be unilateral only; and (5) the system does not indicate which currency is deviating from the average when two currencies are in opposition.

4. P. Baffi, 'Il Sistema monetario europeo e la partecipazione dell'Italia', *Thema*, no. 2 (1978).

5. In the 'snake' the term was 30 days.

6. The technical details of the very short-term credit facilities and of the other three credit mechanisms established by the EEC Committee of Governors and the Board of Governors of the EMCF have been published by the EMCF.

7. The resolution adopted at the Brussels meeting establishes (implicitly) that a member country which does not participate in the exchange-rate mechanism (as in the case for the United Kingdom) may not obtain very short-term support but allows (explicitly) that country to obtain ECUs against the deposit of reserves.

8. In so far as it has not been effected directly through sales of holdings in the creditor's currency.

9. These provisions are without prejudice to other forms of settlement agreed between creditor and debtor central banks. It should also be noted in this connection that the composition of reserves is determined on the basis of the assets denominated in convertible currencies and SDRs. Gold holdings may be used if the price proposed by the debtor central bank is accepted by the creditor central bank.

10. As in the case of the very short-term credit facility, the rate of interest is equal to the weighted average of the discount rates. The amount of interest is calculated on the basis of the average daily balances.

11. The option to renew for a further three months after the initial six was decided in Brussels. The decision conforms with the guidelines established in Bremen for backing up the European exchange-rate agreements with substantial credits for a period of one year (on average 2 + 3 months for the very short-term credit facilities and 3 + 3 + 3 months for the short-term monetary support, or a total of 14 months).

12. As a rule no central bank may be granted more than one-half of the extension, but this limit may be waived if the governors consider that the special situation and the particular needs of the country applying for support warrant it.

13. See, for example, H. Myrdal, *Economic Theory and Underdeveloped Regions* (London: 1967).

14. D. MacDougall, *Report on the Study Group on the Role of Public Finance in European Integration* (Brussels: Commission of the European Community, 1973).

15. Community loans primarily intended to finance projects and programmes relating to infrastructures have been made available for a period of five years and for a maximum amount of one billion EUAs per year, with a subsidised interest rate of 3 per cent (the net earnings from this interest are divided into yearly

quotas of 200 million EUAs, for five years). While the United Kingdom remains outside the European exchange-rate agreements, these facilities are granted to Italy (2/3) and to Ireland (1/3).

16. It may be recalled in this context that the timing of the domestic impact of the international increase in these prices varied considerably among the EEC countries. While certain countries delayed and resisted the process, other countries (notably Germany) immediately allowed the rise to be felt domestically. Thus, in Germany, the 'fuel and electricity' item in the consumer price index in August 1979 showed a 27 per cent increase with respect to the previous year. The corresponding rise in the Netherlands, France and Italy, for instance, was 5.6 per cent, 17 per cent and 18 per cent, respectively.

17. This risk was clearly pointed out by N. Thygesen, 'The Emerging European Monetary System', a paper presented at the Seminar on the EMS, Louvain, 1979, and R.S. Masera, 'The Operation of the EMS: A European View', *Economica Internazionale* (November 1979).

18. Note in this connection that intra-marginal interventions in EEC currencies were exceptional under the 'snake' rules.

19. For a mathematical treatment of this point, see R. Masera, *Studi sull unificazione monetaria e lo SME* (Bologna: Il Mulino, 1979), and S. Rossi, 'Un approccio analitico al problema degli indicatori di divergenza nello SME', Banca D'Italia, 1979 (mimeographed).

20. See, for example, E.M. Bernstein, 'A Partial Program for Internal Monetary Reserves', *Quarterly Review and Investment Survey of Model*, no. 4 (1963); J.E. Meade, 'The Balance of Payments Problems of a European Free Trade Area', *Economic Journal*, vol. 67 (1957), and R. Triffin, *Our International Monetary System: Yesterday, Today and Tomorrow* (New York: Random House, 1968).

21. See P. Werner, 'Report to the Council and the Commission on the Realization by Stages of Economic and Monetary Union in the Community', *Bulletin of the European Communities*, no. 11, supplement (1970).

22. R. Marjolin, *Report of the Study Group 'Economic and Monetary Union 1980'* (Brussels: Commission of the European Community, 1975), and L. Tindemans, 'L'Union Européene, rapport au Conseil Européen', *Bulletin of the European Communities*, no. 1, supplement (1976). See also the Duisenberg plan in Duisenberg, 'Declaration Concerning the Strengthening of the Community's Internal Cohesion of Economic and Financial Matters', *Bulletin of the European Communities*, no 7/8 (1976), p. 3, and the *Optica Report, Inflation and Exchange Rates: Evidence and Policy Guidelines for the European Community* (Brussels: 1977).

COMMENT

Mahmoud Sakbani

My comments, while referring to the paper before us, also aim at bringing out some key issues with regard to the EMS, which bear directly on the working of a would-be Arab Monetary Union. Many of the operational policy issues raised in my own paper could be profitably elaborated in relation to the EMS and the European experience.

Regarding the EMS exchange-rate arrangement, Messrs Masera and Rossi (hereinafter M-R) clearly elucidate the differences between the so-called 'French' and 'German' interpretations of the role of the ECU. Their exposition might have benefited, however, from the use of specific figures, especially to illustrate the relationship between the change in the relative weight of a currency and its intervention limits [pp. 234-5]. Moreover, it would seem to me that it is somewhat unfair to characterise the French ECU interpretation as operationally unclear and to stop there. The M-R paper might have enlightened us by devoting some space to the question of establishing central ECU rates and reference rates, actual deviations from which (whether arising from interventions in ECUs or from mere exchange-rate adjustments) would provide a basis for adjusting the central rates. This question is extremely important to any discussion of transforming the SDR into an intervention currency. I know that Mr Williamson once suggested that the Ethier-Bloomfield reference rate proposal be considered in this context. I am sure that the Monetary Committee in Brussels has addressed this question. With their 'Italian connection' M-R may be able to bring us up to date on this and in the process say something positive about the French interpretation.

The surprising record of exchange-rate stability of the EMS is positive evidence that political commitment at the highest level can produce a zone of exchange-rate stability. However, it would be foolhardy to conclude that the EMS exchange-rate alignment will continue to hold in the future if the present divergence in inflation rates and fiscal policies persists. Therefore, I should like to qualify the success of the EMS by making the following three points:

(a) Some of the prospective differences in inflation rates were discounted before the central rates were set together.
(b) It so happens that countries with high inflation rates (Italy and France) have enjoyed strong balance-of-payments positions, while the positions of the low inflation countries, notably Germany,

have been weak.
(c) EMS members have been quite willing to adjust the central rates when stresses developed and have done so without encountering political difficulties.

The other point raised in the M-R paper which requires further elaboration is the relationship between the dollar the the EMS. One can perhaps claim that the EMS has had an easy time with the dollar. If the dollar were to weaken in the future, or go through turbulent periods, the stronger EMS currencies would experience substantial upward pressures. This would strain the whole grid arrangement in the EMS. To my knowledge there are no clear guidelines for establishing a common dollar policy in the EMS and this could become a very serious problem.

I turn now to the credit arrangements. The two-year deadline for the second stage of the transformation of the EMCF into the EMF is still binding. The very short-term support facilities do not give me concern. But once one moves up to the medium-term facilities, there is a host of issues that the EMS has to face up to. M-R refer to the fact that it has not yet been decided to offer ECUs against national currencies. This is a very important point. Not only are the character and future of the ECU at stake, but so is the future role of the EMF itself. If ECUs can be issued against transfers of national currencies, the stock of official liquidity will be affected. The EMF will then act at best as a supranational central bank exercising what may be called a residual banking role. The question is how this evolution from a reserve pool to a supranational authority will be guided. Will the EMF develop by taking over various aspects of monetary authority or by becoming a kind of IMF for Europe, in some cases imposing consultations – if not its will – on members? These are issues which the European states have not yet thrashed out.

Finally, let me turn to the future of the EMF as a vehicle for the transfer of resources from the rich to the poor areas. M-R rightly emphasise the importance of this issue and point out that it has been unfairly neglected.

My own paper emphasises this issue for the Arab countries and I venture to think that M-R would concur with this reasoning: a union between the poor and the rich is impossible without redistributive measures. In a union, one cannot merely lump together all the welfare functions of the individual countries; a new welfare function, allowing gains and losses along a whole line of variables, is more in the spirit of a union. The role of fiscal co-ordination and of the community budget in this area is crucial. I am afraid this issue has not yet been adequately addressed.

One last point about the EMS. If the ECU becomes a reserve asset or is transformed over time into an acutal currency, it will certainly affect the investment portfolios of the Arab countries and international portfolios in general. This raises several questions:

(a) Will the ECU become a new asset, alternative to the dollar? Will Europe form a monetary bloc around the ECU?
(b) What will be the impact of the ECU on the SDR?
(c) ECU holdings are permitted to private holders. Will this development have a destabilising effect on capital movements?

GENERAL DISCUSSION

1. Alfredo Medio

I have gained much from reading the Masera and Rossi paper, particularly as it concerns the structure and characteristics of the European Monetary System. I have learned rather little, however, about one crucial question which is not only of interest to Europe but of general interest as well, namely: is the European Monetary System a good thing and if so, for whom, for which countries?

The problem might be discussed by taking, as an example, the case of Italy and West Germany. Transactions between these two countries have been characterised by the fact that, over the years, Italian production costs, if valued at fixed exchange rates, have tended to rise in relation to German production costs. This can only lead to payments imbalances, with Italy running a current account deficit and Germany running a surplus. Joining a fixed exchange-rate scheme like the EMS means, for Italy, the surrender of a basic instrument of adjustment, i.e., the variation of the price of its products as a whole relative to the price of German products. If these cost-price disequilibria are not eliminated, a situation will soon arise in which, if Germany cannot be persuaded to accept a higher inflation rate, Italy will have to devalue its currency (or withdraw from the system).

True, alternative adjustment mechanisms are contemplated in the EMS. But funds for regional aid are hardly sufficient to mitigate or eliminate fundamental disequilibria. Schemes for fiscal redistribution might also be conceived and implemented, but, for the time being, progress in this area is very limited.

Short-term credit facilities are abundant but, as Mr Masera has reminded us, they are meant to correct temporary, essentially reversible disequilibria, not fundamental imbalances.

In this situation, what remains is the hope that, once Italy has entered the system in the name of the political ideal of a Greater Europe, its government will somehow be able to find and enforce an agreement among the various social groups whose conflicting interests are at the root of inflation. I doubt whether such hope is well founded.

2. Mabid Ali Al-Jarhi

The Masera and Rossi paper states that the EMS is a system based on a scheme for exchange-rate stabilisation and on a unit of account, the

ECU, which it is hoped will play a more dominant role in the future.

The paper correctly states that the stabilisation of exchange rates has been accomplished mainly through market intervention rather than through policy co-ordination. Perhaps policy co-ordination has been ruled out because of the failure of the only attempt by the EEC to harmonise the rates of domestic monetary expansion, represented by the October 1972 resolution of the Council of Ministers which was never applied.

The question of exchange-rate stabilisation through market intervention warrants a more critical examination, not only in the light of the enormous costs associated with such interventions but also in view of its inefficiency, given the volume of the resources which have to be mobilised for this purpose. A particular disadvantage of this system is that the need to stabilise in relation to the dollar has meant that because of that currency's continuous decline, market intervention has been accompanied by a transfer of resources from Europe to the United States.

The paper raises the issue of the composition of the ECU. This composition is reflected in the magnitude of intervention in the dollar market. In this respect, the question may be raised as to whether a purely European ECU is possible or whether a dollar content is mandatory. While the large volume of Euro-American trade justifies a dollar content, there is still the question of whether stabilisation *vis-à-vis* the dollar can be separated from intra-European exchange-rate stabilisation, i.e., whether a common European dollar policy is needed.

I would also wonder whether it might not be advisable to move further in the direction of a parallel currency by strengthening the ECU, in order gradually to replace the current scheme of market intervention with another scheme. However, if the authors are less ambitious in this regard and are content with the creation of a European reserve asset, then I would appreciate their elaborating on how the current system of exchange-rate stabilisation might be improved.

3. Robert Triffin

I have learned much from Mr Masera's incisive explanation of the political compromises which toned down the more ambitious and logical provisions of the Bremen outline in order to reach concrete agreement in negotiations on the EMS. I fully agree with him and with Mr Rossi on the urgent need to come closer to the initial plan proposed by President Giscard d'Estaing and Chancellor Schmidt which was aimed at enabling the EMS to make its full contribution to the reordering of the European and of the world monetary systems.

The success of the first year and a half of EMS operations is undoubtedly due in large part, as noted by Mr Sakbani and others, to favourable external circumstances which cannot be expected to last for long. Indeed, the EMS has not yet altered as radically as had been hoped some of the more dangerous, crisis-prone features of the pre-EMS system of European settlements.

The EMCF machinery operates only for marginal interventions on the exchange market, i.e., those interventions which are compulsory when bilateral rates reach their floor and ceiling between two currencies. But such interventions are only a fraction of total central bank interventions, most of which are intra-marginal and presumably still effected overwhelmingly in dollars, as in the past.

Secondly, the EMS financing of these marginal interventions has been extremely modest. No recourse has ever been had either to short-term or to medium-term credits and the small amounts of very short-term credits that have been used were fully repaid — overwhelmingly in marks — by March of this year [1980]. No credits whatsoever have been extended since then in monthly settlements and the interventions recorded with the EMCF have been small or even nil in recent months.

Finally, the ECU settlements themselves are tantamount to gold and dollar transfers. The main change — and it is of course very significant — is that the EMS has promoted a much fuller use of gold transfers and at rates approximating market rates. Large gold transfers have thus been effected by means of ECU transfers, and have been more than offset for the paying countries, according to published reserve figures, by the spectacular increase in gold prices.

A major step forward will be the use of the ECU by the private sector — particularly commercial banks — as well as by the central banks. This is, of course, a prerequisite for the use of the ECU itself in exchange market interventions, since ECUs cannot be used by central banks in these operations if the private sector is not allowed to buy — nor therefore able to sell — ECUs in exchange for national currencies.

Some time ago, I organised in Louvain-la-Neuve a debate on this topic to which were invited representatives of the major commercial banks, potential lenders and borrowers, insurance companies, central banks and academics. The proceedings have now been published and widely distributed by the Kredietbank of Brussels and will serve as a basis for another meeting early next year [1981] in Rome, which will be attended by representatives of more than 100 banks. A wide interest has been manifested in the prospective use of the ECU as an alternative to Eurodollars, Euromarks and other Eurocurrencies in a market now estimated by the Bank for International Settlements (BIS) and Morgan Guarantee to total more than $700 billion in assets and liabilities of European commercial banks.

The use of the ECU in bond flotations has already begun and will grow rapidly as a result of the recent Luxemburg decision to denominate Community borrowings in ECUs rather than in dollars, marks, etc.

The popularisation of the ECU with the public may also result from the creation of travellers' cheques in ECUs, also under study at the moment.

Central bankers have at least accorded what Mr de Strijcker, governor of the National Bank of Belgium, calls 'benevolent attention' to these developments, and their views and actions will be as crucial to the success of the ECU as they have been to all major monetary reforms in history. Let us remember that the most important monetary reform in history — for better or worse — was the substitution of paper money for gold and silver coins, in the century preceding the First World War. This was not achieved by governments — the French 'assignats' failed miserably — but by commercial and central banks, still private in those days. Governments remained for years unaware of the profound changes implied thereby in the functioning of their national monetary systems. As recently as the late 1940s, some European central banks still objected to the inclusion of 'checking deposits' in the money supply statistics published by the IMF.

Another essential step, still to be achieved, will be to make the transfers of gold and dollar reserves in exchange for ECUs permanent. The present 'swap' system means that exchange-rate risks continue to be assumed by individual central banks and this obviously precludes the concerted interventions in the exchange market — particularly the dollar market — for which a 'communitisation' of these risks is an obvious prerequisite.

I might refer some of the discussants to my paper as regards the potential and essential contribution of the EMS to the defence of agreed rates between the ECU and foreign currencies, particularly the dollar.

My answer to Mr Al-Jarhi in this respect is that the rate of the ECU *vis-à-vis* the dollar — and other currencies — should be dealt with jointly, by the Community, whereby a system could be devised for the joint floating — or later stabilisation? — of the Community currencies *vis-à-vis* the dollar. This means that, during the transition towards full monetary union, the exchange rates of member currencies *vis-à-vis* the dollar may still have to be readjusted occasionally, but that these readjustments will have to take place through changes in the exchange rates of member currencies *vis-à-vis* the ECU.

4. Rainer S. Masera, in Response

Let me start by assuring Mr Sakbani that no prejudice was intended, from the Italian side at least, in my analysis of an ECU-based intervention system. While the original proposal was to my mind unworkable, the Community has gone a long way towards avoiding its shortcomings, while preserving the attractive features implicit in the concept of unilateral intervention. The final choice was, however, a political one. I would like to note, in passing, that countries of the EEC have subscribed to a common agreement whereby they do not invest their foreign exchange in the Euromarkets.

I come next to the question related to the use of the ECU as a parallel currency. While I think this might have certain advantages, I also believe that such a role can be envisaged only once the EMF has been created and is able to supervise the process of creating high-powered ECUs.

Mr Medio would have liked an assessment as to whether the process of European monetary integration is a 'good thing' or not. The answer to this cost-benefit problem is clearly beyond the scope of this paper. Let me add that I find the question somewhat naive since a proper answer would depend on many considerations entailing value judgements.

I wish, however, to take up in more theoretical terms the better-defined question on the role of exchange rates in the adjustment process. I have already questioned the view according to which exchange rates play no role at all in the adjustment process. As I have stressed, however, their importance in highly open, integrated and indexed economies does not lie principally in the traditional argument which says that exchange rates alter relative prices as between tradeables and non-tradeables, and between real wages and profits. To my mind, the more important line of response is based on the recognition of the non-neutrality of money, even leaving aside the fixed-price character of the goods and labour markets but allowing for the operation of the government sector. Once a correct integration of stock and flow analyses is made in a variable-price context, it is easy to see that inflation, by reducing the real value of the government debt, represents a source of taxation, which reduces real disposable income and, in particular, the total real wage bill.

It is my contention that the existence of a short-run Phillips-curve type of relationship between the rate of inflation and unemployment can be explained on the basis of 'fiscal illusion', whereby wage-earners do not realise that the loss in real net financial wealth stemming from the inflationary consequences of the monetary-base financing of government deficits effectively reduces their disposable income by more than what is apparent in terms of wage flows. Thus the compensatory adjustments in terms of nominal wages — even in the limiting (unrealistic) case represented by 100 per cent wage indexation — need not represent a full compensation for the losses deriving from inflation: hence the reduction in the true wage bill.

Note in this respect that in certain high-inflation European countries — notably Italy — a significant part of overall government expenditure takes the form of direct transfers to the corporate sector. The inconsistency between 'autonomous' wage costs and labour productivity at given employment levels is thus initially offset by means of 'compensatory' government intervention, which reduces the 'overall' unit cost of labour to enterprises.

If, however, given an insufficient elasticity in total explicit fiscal revenues, a structural (current account) government deficit builds up, recourse to monetary-base financing sooner or later becomes imperative. In this situation, the tax from inflation on government debt effectively reduces — in real terms — the government deficit. In this indirect way, the gap in nominal (explicit) tax revenues is bridged by means of the inflation tax, which lowers the true real wage bill, since it falls ultimately on the household sector.

I have questioned the wisdom of inferring from a rigidity in perceived real wages the ineffectiveness of exchange-rate changes in adjusting inflation. My own analysis is, however, consistent with the view that inflation is not reconcilable with full employment and steady growth in the medium term. The curve relating inflation and unemployment over the long run may well be positively sloped: this conclusion follows however mainly from (i) consideration of the negative impact on investment generated by the higher uncertainty as to relative prices and as to the posture of economic policies, necessarily associated with high but variable inflation rates and (ii) recognition of the 'social function' of prices and the consequent cost of adapting the economy to high inflation.

The different degrees of imbalance and rigidity which exist in the sectoral and regional wage-productivity relationships and in the public sector financial impulses — and which have been exacerbated, also to varying degrees, by the structural changes in some key relative prices, notably that of energy — result in very different potential inflationary pressures in the EEC countries. True enough, these potential impulses could not become actual without an elastic money (liquidity) supply in high inflation countries, as suggested by the relative stability of the real demand for liquid assets in all EEC countries.

I have tried to indicate that, under these circumstances, any attempt to impede inflation based merely on monetary constraint would result for some EEC countries in very high unemployment costs (mainly due to the rigidities in the labour market), quite apart from the consideration that in many countries this scheme would simply not be feasible, owing to the limited degree of autonomy of their central banks.

Under these circumstances, while it would not be sensible to ask (let alone force) relatively low-inflation countries to adopt policies leading to increased domestic inflation, it does not appear desirable either to require weak-currency countries to pursue deflationary policies by simply pegging the exchange rates of their currencies to strong currencies.

If this approach is accepted, three main consequences suggest themselves: (i) the control of inflationary impulses originating upstream of monetary flows must be undertaken simultaneously with a programme of exchange-rate integration, with a view to moving gradually towards monetary unification; (ii) the convergence in overall economic and structural policies may well imply certain short-term costs in the high-inflation countries, which are also characterised by relatively low income levels. To this end, as has been shown by the MacDougall Commission (1977), a certain increase in the overall Community budget and, above all, a restructuring of expenditures making it possible to cope with cyclical and regional problems is required; and (iii) the strategy for implementing the EEC exchange-rate agreements must allow for the problem posed by movements in extra-Community currencies. I come here to the very important question raised by Mr Al-Jarhi. This question related directly to the well-known 'n^{th} currency' question. Pursuit of independent relationships with regard to non-EEC currencies tends to impose immediate strains on bilateral EEC relations. On the other hand, (a) the objective importance of movements *vis-à-vis* non-EEC currencies in external transactions varies from one European country to another and (b) the relationships desired may also differ according to the relative short-term importance attached to the fight against inflation and unemployment by the monetary authorities, especially in the case of exogenous price shocks. With regard to this latter issue, the considerations developed above are thus clearly applicable. These general questions are, of course, especially relevant when account is taken, on the one hand, of the key role of the dollar as an intervention currency within the EEC and, on the other, of the process of diversification of international reserves, which can lead to strains in the dollar-DM exchange rate, as confirmed by the direct monitoring of this rate carried out by the US authorities since 1 November 1973.

5. John Williamson*

Since the geometric mean is the latest cause to which I have been converted — just last week! — I find it difficult to resist a brief comment. This may sound like an obscure cause, but it turns out to be a rather important point. Mr Masera's problem with the lira's getting itself underweighted in the ECU basket, for example, would not have arisen had the ECU been defined as a logarithmic basket, i.e., on the basis of the geometric mean.

What I wish to suggest is that the inability of the market to replicate a logarithmic basket need not necessarily be an argument against it. It is often said that there is no real motivation for an investor to hold SDRs or ECUs, in view of the ease of replicating an equivalent portfolio. Conversely, eliminating the possibility of building up an equivalent portfolio might in itself provide an incentive to hold the asset.

---

* This comment was made subsequent to the author's response to the discussion of his paper [eds.].

8 THE EXPERIENCE OF THE WEST AFRICAN MONETARY UNION

Rattan Bhatia

I. Organisational Background

The origins of the West African Monetary Union (WAMU) go back to 1955, when the right of currency issue in the then French West African Federation was transferred from a private commercial bank to a new publicly-owned institution: l'Institute d'Emission de L'Afrique Occidentale Française et du Togo. In 1959 the name of the institution was changed to Banque Centrale des Etats de l'Afrique Occidentale (BCEAO) to identify it as a central bank. However, it was not until 1962, when the treaty establishing the WAMU was signed, providing for a common currency and a common central bank that the BCEAO began to operate as a central bank. The 1962 statutes remained virtually unchanged until October 1974 when they were substantially modified to better reflect the conditions prevailing in the Union. During this period, membership in the Union was gradually reduced from an original nine countries to the six remaining today: Benin, Ivory Coast, Niger, Senegal, Togo and Upper Volta (Guinea, Mali and Mauritania had withdrawn).

Under the 1962 statutes, the BCEAO entered into a co-operation agreement with France; it held its external reserves in an Operation Account with the French Treasury and France guaranteed unlimited convertibility of the CFA franc into the French franc.

Although the BCEAO issued a common currency and held members' foreign reserves in a common pool, it maintained separate accounts for each member and in practice operated individual operation accounts with respect to foreign assets for each member country. The Bank's headquarters were in Paris but it maintained branches in each member country. At the apex of the administrative pyramid was the Council of Ministers, but overall management was entrusted to a Central Board of Directors consisting of two directors from each member country and a number of members from France equal to the sum of the directors from the other countries. The day-to-day management was the responsibility of a Director General who, until the new statutes came into effect, was always a Frenchman appointed by the Board.

The national branches of the BCEAO were managed by national directors. In each member country the credit and monetary decisions taken by the Central Board of Directors were implemented by a five-member National Monetary Committee (NMC) appointed by the respective governments and including the two national representatives on the Central Board of Directors. Within the limits of the global ceiling fixed by the Board for each six-month period, the NMC in each member country set individual re-discount ceilings for banks and re-discount limits for enterprises, though the statutes also stipulated that the ceilings could be reviewed by the Board at the request of the NMC.

During 1974 and 1975 the WAMU was restructured and the changes were institutionalised by a set of new statutory documents comprising (i) a treaty among the WAMU countries, including new statutes for the BCEAO and (ii) agreements with France governing economic co-operation and access to the Operation Account, which lay down the principles for diversifying the foreign assets of the BCEAO and provided for an exchange guarantee on the part of France (based on the SDR-French franc rate) to cover BCEAO deposits in the Operation Account held with the French Treasury.

Under the new statutes, administrative power has been reallocated among various levels and bodies. The highest political bodies are the Conference of Heads of State and the Council of Ministers whose decisions must be unanimous. The central banking operations, on the other hand, are managed by the governor and the directors of the BCEAO. The Conference of Heads of State meets at least once a year and decides on matters relating to membership in the Union and on all matters left unresolved by the Council of Ministers. This latter body, made up of two ministers (including the Minister of Finance) from each member country, is responsible for the formulation of broad monetary guidelines and for overseeing banking co-ordination within the Union. The governor of the BCEAO, who is now a national of a member country, is appointed for a six-year term and is the chairman of the Board of Directors which is composed of 14 members, with two representatives from each member country and from France. The headquarters of the Bank have been shifted to Dakar. Major changes, described in Section IV below, were also made in the operations of the Bank to provide for more decentralisation and flexibility in the conduct of its monetary policy.

The political and economic conditions in the WAMU member countries have also undergone considerable changes. As late as 1962, when the WAMU was created, the member countries were economically and financially dependent upon France. Most of their exports went to France under preferential arrangements, France represented a large source of official capital inflows and more than two-thirds of imports originated in France. Since then, this dependency has steadily and significantly diminished. With membership in international financial institutions and associate membership in the European Economic Community, the countries of the Union have been opened to financial, trade and capital inputs from outside the franc zone. Furthermore, the domestic economies of member countries have developed differently over the period and the authorities have pursued specific, and often different, policies, especially in the fiscal and development areas, in pursuit of their respective national objectives. Notwithstanding these and other developments, the essential character of the Monetary Union has remained unchanged, save for the important modifications introduced in late 1974 under the revised 1973 statutes of the BCEAO.

The currency issued by the BCEAO, the CFA franc, has a fixed exchange rate *vis-à-vis* the French franc of CFAF 1.00 = FF 0.02. This rate has remained unchanged since 1948 and has, accordingly, moved *pari passu* with that of the French franc *vis-à-vis* other currencies.

II. Economic Backgound

When the BCEAO was formally created in 1963, its members were essentially less developed countries in which agriculture predominated. Thus, in the six countries which are currently members, the contribution of agriculture to total GDP was approximately 40 per cent and the sector was even more important in its contribution to domestic employment and total exports. The ratio of savings to GDP approximated 15 per cent, while that of investment to GDP was 16 to 17 per cent. As members of the French franc zone, these countries had liberal trade and payments regimes, with the ratio of their total external trade to GDP standing at about 40 per cent at the time of the creation of the WAMU. More than two-thirds of their trade, however, was with France and less than 5 per cent among themselves.

The lack of a significant volume of trade among the countries that formed the WAMU reflected the similarity of their production structures, whereby they were producing competitive rather than complementary products and raw materials, destined for processing and consumption in countries, mainly France, outside the Union. Thus, both the Ivory Coast and Togo produced and exported significant amounts of cocoa; Dahomey, Togo and the Ivory Coast exported palm kernels and palm products; and Senegal and Niger were heavily dependent on exports of groundnuts. Moreover, France (and later the EEC) provided a unique inducement for these countries to export to France (and later to the EEC) in the form of preferential prices (i.e., prices above world market prices). In 1963, the additional revenue made possible by these preferential prices was estimated for the six countries at CFAF 10.2 billion, an amount equivalent to 10 per cent of the total value of their exports.

The WAMU was also established at a time when there was little direct financial exchange among the member countries. While it is not possible to estimate the volume of non-monetary capital movements within the BCEAO countries at the time of the creation of the WAMU, these movements are generally considered to have been negligible. The absence of intra-Union financial flows reflected both the lack of adequate savings by member countries and the financial structure of the Union. Almost all the financial and banking institutions had their head offices in France and the movement of funds in and out of a member country occurred almost invariably via France. Even transactions between two branches of the same bank in two different countries were channelled through the head office in Paris.

Thus, at the time of the formal establishment of the WAMU, the member countries were still at an underdeveloped stage of monetisation, with a similar degree of financial and economic development, and had similar requirements with regard to the conduct of monetary policy. Under these circumstances, one of the major tasks facing the monetary authorities was to supplement private financial savings with the resources of the central bank in order to meet the credit requirements of the member countries with a view to facilitating their trade and development. The almost identical structure of the WAMU economies and their correspondingly similar financial requirements made it possible for the authorities to accomplish this task within the framework of a 'uniform' monetary policy, with the uniformity taking the extreme form of issuing and maintaining a single currency, assuring the circulation and transfer of the currency among member countries, pursuing a relatively liberal credit policy with an identical interest-rate structure throughout the Union and maintaining free convertibility of the currency into French francs.

With these limited targets for policy-makers, the range of instruments at the disposal of the monetary authorities was also limited to the re-discount ceilings, the liquidity ratio and the interest rate. The job of the BCEAO was facilitated by statutory limits on bank credit to governments (initially equivalent to 10 per cent of fiscal revenues) and, more importantly, by the French government's unlimited guarantee of convertibility. The former was intended to minimise the danger to monetary stability represented by excessive government borrowing while the latter aimed at enabling the monetary authorities to conduct their day-to-day credit policies without the constraints which would normally stem from their balance-of-payments position. Nevertheless, the statutes of the BCEAO included certain automatic monetary brakes to be applied in the event of persistent balance-of-payments difficulties which might be experienced by the Union as a whole or by individual member countries.

No special provisions were incorporated into the WAMU treaty to foster economic integration by encouraging intra-Union mobility of factors of production or by some central allocation of investments among Union members to foster complementary investments. In theory, there was of course free movement of labour and capital among the member countries. But for most member countries the only surplus labour at their disposal was unskilled so that, apart from the border mobility of labour encouraged by historical and tribal traditions, there could be little mobility of complementary labour. Similarly, there was the possibility of capital movement between member countries but, again, since each of these countries had a shortage of savings, significant intra-Union mobility of capital could not be expected. Thus, intra-Union mobility with regard to both labour and capital was lacking.

Of course, France (and later the EEC) invested large sums of capital in the member countries of the WAMU. Had a conscious policy of economic integration been followed, economic complementarity might have been advanced by the selection of corresponding investment projects in member countries. However, this was not the case. Most public investment was in the development of either traditional agriculture or small manufacturing industries designed to meet local needs rather than to satisfy the needs of other markets of the Union.

III. The WAMU in Practice

The experience of the WAMU may be divided into two periods, one preceding and the other following the institution of the new BCEAO statutes in late 1974.

As mentioned earlier, the similarity and the relatively underdeveloped state of the economic structures in the member countries left the monetary authorities with little more than the simple task of regulating liquidity in these countries. The statutes of the BCEAO did not stipulate that it was to pursue any particular objectives. Thus, no explicit mention was made in the old statutes of monetary and price stability, adequate development or even the balance of payments. Rather, the statutes appeared to indicate concern with maintaining the 'liquidity' of the BCEAO by legally requiring it to introduce corrective measures when the ratio of its foreign assets to its short-term liabilities fell below 20 per cent for 30 consecutive days, with more specific measures to be taken when this ratio fell to 10 per cent for 30 consecutive days. It would appear that the main concern of the drafters of the BCEAO statutes was the balance-of-payments situation, though the

French government's formal guarantee of convertibility made this consideration of less than primary importance.

Under these circumstances, the BCEAO tended to concentrate on ensuring an appropriate supply of liquidity in the economy. During this period, the BCEAO regarded itself as a major source of supplementary resources for the commercial banks (and through them for the economy), on the presumption that the resources likely to be available to commercial banks through the normal process of intermediation would be insufficient to meet the demand for credit. Thus, the BCEAO played the role of 'co-financer' rather than, as is the case with central banks, of lender of last resort.

The role of co-financer was discharged by the BCEAO primarily through its policy of re-discount ceilings. Such ceilings were fixed separately for each member country and, within each country, separately for each bank and for each major enterprise. Separate ceilings were also fixed for short-term (up to six months) and medium-term credit. In general, these re-discount ceilings tended to be generous and flexible and were seldom attained. Furthermore, the Bank provided these funds relatively cheaply by actively pursuing a policy of low and stable interest rates (which remained unchanged, with the re-discount rate at 3.5 per cent throughout the period).

This policy of supplementing the resources of commercial banks at relatively low interest rates served the limited objective of convertibility and transferability quite well so long as the basic hypothesis of a uniform shortage of financial savings in each member country was valid. However, beginning in early 1970, the validity of this hypothesis became questionable. The income elasticity of total deposits with the commercial banks tended to be greater than that of the demand for re-discounts, suggesting that the inflow of deposits into the banking system was sufficient to finance the additional demand for re-discountable credit. This tendency might have been interpreted by the monetary authorities as a signal that it was time for commercial banks to begin relying increasingly on their own resources and to reduce recourse to the re-discount facilities of the BCEAO. But the BCEAO did not alter its policy course and continued to pursue a relaxed credit policy, leading to an undesirably high degree of credit expansion in the years prior to the 1975 reform.

However, even if the BCEAO had attempted to change its policy course, its instruments of policy under the old rules might have proved to be inadequate. The control of the money supply, through the use of re-discount ceilings alone, is possible only in the case of closed economies and not with open economies such as represented by the WAMU countries at that time. To the extent that the balance of payments of the WAMU was almost entirely determined by the production and price of exports, the role of monetary policy as a determinant of money supply was already severely circumscribed and the limited range of policy instruments utilised by the BCEAO confined this role even further. Although changes in the monetary liabilities of the BCEAO have been the primary determinant of the money supply (accounting for 86 per cent of the increase during the years 1963 through 1974), the impact of changes in net foreign assets has also been important. In the context of radical changes in external resources, the inadequacy of the monetary arrangements for controlling credit was most clearly illustrated by the developments of 1974 (described below).

In a separate study[1] examining the role of the BCEAO's re-discount policy as a means of influencing credit developments, it is shown that during the period 1963-4 the actual accrual of deposits with commercial banks exceeded the need for re-discountable credit as the income elasticity of total deposits (1.91) significantly exceeded the income elasticity of the demand for rediscountrable credit (1.65). Furthermore, a significant part (about 40 per cent) of the increase in deposits came in the form of time deposits. An analysis of the determinants of re-discount ceilings employed by the BCEAO also shows that the latter tended to leave with the commercial banks nearly half of the increase in time deposits, to be devoted to the financing of non-rediscountable credit, an operation largely outside its own purview. Also, these time deposits were not subject to the liquidity ratio requirement which was one of the policy instruments under the pre-1974 statutes. In view of the low interest ceilings on re-discountable credit, the commercial banks were reluctant to use their own resources to extend such credit and instead expanded non-rediscountable credit, which the BCEAO was unable to control. Thus, in 1974, when the increase in non-rediscountable credit accounted for more than half of total credit expansion, the credit multiplier (influenced by changes in such behavioural ratios as the ratio of currency to money supply, the ratio of time deposits to total deposits and the cash reserve ratio) nearly tripled (from six in 1973 to 18 in 1974). The BCEAO could offset this only by changing the monetary base, which it did. However, this measure succeeded in offsetting only about 25 per cent of the increase in credit caused by the change in the credit multiplier. A further reduction in the monetary base, by a decrease in the re-discount ceiling, would have 'crowded out' the priority sectors (which borrowed at low, preferential rates). Nor could an adjustment of the liquidity ratio, which stood at 78 per cent in 1974, have helped; an increase of five percentage points in the liquidity ratio would have reduced the rate of increase in credit (48 per cent) by only one percentage point. Thus no practical use of the credit policy instruments available at that time could have significantly altered the exceptional rate of credit expansion recorded in 1974.

An important feature of monetary policy during this period was the prevalence of low and stable interest rates. Thus, throughout the period 1963-73, the re-discount rate of the BCEAO was maintained at 3.5 per cent, the lending rates for seasonal credit at between 4 and 5.25 per cent and maximum savings deposit rates at 4.5 per cent. This policy came to be questioned by outsiders as being inimical to savings, while providing little incentive for investment. However, at least in the initial stages, the policy was a logical extension of the perceived role of the BCEAO as co-financer, where the objective of the policy-makers was not to discourage the demand for credit but to supplement the supply. Moreover, there was some confusion in the minds of the critics as to the nominal and real interest rates. Implicit in the concern over a low interest-rate policy is the assumption that low interest rates imply negative real rates and discourage savings. An examination of the relevant data for the BCEAO countries reveals, surprisingly, that savers were in fact offered a positive real rate at least until 1972, after which year the inflation rate tended to exceed the interest rate. It could still, of course, be argued that the monetary authorities did not provide enough of an incentive to encourage savings and that a policy of higher interest rates would have been more appropriate. But no significant evidence has been offered to support the assumed positive relationship between the saving ratio and the real interest rates in the BCEAO countries. Even the relationship between financial savings and interest rates is only partially confirmed by the data for the BCEAO countries.

Thus, at least until the early 1970s, development considerations could not necessarily be said to support a policy of high interest rates. However, as individual countries within the Union tended, especially in the 1970s, to experience periods of significant surpluses in financial savings, which were invested outside the WAMU in response to higher interest rates, the Union experienced a capital outflow which could not be considered desirable. This, combined with a significant acceleration in inflation which rendered interest rates negative, called for a revision of the traditional policy of low interest rates — a revision encompassed in the 1975 reform of the BCEAO.

IV. The Revised Statutes

The restructuring of the West African Monetary Union that came into effect in October 1974 was designed to redress the deficiencies in the workings of the monetary policy pursued during the previous decade and to address itself to the questions of economic development and economic integration. To these ends, the BCEAO was provided with a wider range of policy instruments, which would enable it to increase the efficacy and flexibility of its monetary policy, both across the Union and at the national level. Furthermore, the West African Development Bank was established, with half of its capital provided by the BCEAO and the other half in the form of equal contributions by member states.

The new statutes and the decisions subsequently taken by the Conference of Heads of State and the Council of Ministers provided for: (a) a new procedure for controlling credit expansion; (b) the harmonisation of interest rates with international markets; (c) the establishment of an inter-bank money market managed by the BCEAO; and (d) the limiting of the liquid assets which the banks could hold outside the Union to minimum working balances.

One of the objectives of the new statutes was to decentralise decision-making with regard to credit expansion with a view to allowing each member state to pursue a credit policy adapted to its particular needs, though still within the global requirements of the Union. The newly-created National Credit Committees in each state were similar to the National Monetary Committees under the previous statutes in that the chairman of each committee, the Minister of Finance, would propose to the Board of Directors of the BCEAO the total amount of credit to be extended for each 12-month period.[2] The Board would decide on the ceiling, taking into account the economic conditions prevailing in each country and the overall policy objectives of the WAMU. There was, however, a major difference in application, in that a greater degree of latitude was left to the National Credit Committees in determining the use and distribution of credit. Furthermore, under the previous system, specific re-discount ceilings prescribed for individual enterprises gave the impression of an automatic right of access to re-discounting facilities. Under the new statutes, while an overall re-discount ceiling for the country was retained, specific ceilings for banks and particular enterprises were abolished. In addition to its increased discretion in deciding which sectors would be offered re-discount facilities, the BCEAO was able to influence the distribution of credit by providing re-discount facilities at a preferential rate for certain specific activities, thus responding to the requirements of seasonal farming, small- and medium-sized national enterprises and small-scale construction activity.[3] Moreover, the BCEAO was empowered to direct banks to allocate a certain proportion of their working capital for the financing of certain national enterprises. The new statutes also authorised the BCEAO to impose reserve requirements with a view to controlling credit expansion during periods when the banks might be excessively liquid.[4]

One major change in relation to the previous system was that the overall credit ceiling for a member country included both the private and the government sectors. Accordingly, the private sector had access only to the balance of credit remaining after the requirements of the government had been met, subject of course to the limit on credit extended to the government sector, set at 20 per cent of the previous year's revenues. However, as in the previous system, the 20 per cent limit, though covering only the credit for the banking systems, included in practice borrowing from virtually all domestic sources, due to the lack of any means for tapping the non-bank sector. Therefore, for any government running a deficit beyond the 20 per cent limit, the tendency was to resort to foreign financing.

Another key objective of the new statutes was to foster the use of capital within the region. Several measures were brought to bear upon this objective. First, an interest-rate policy more in line with conditions in the international markets was pursued with the basic re-discount rate initially being increased to 8 per cent. Secondly, an inter-bank money market managed by the BCEAO was established to channel funds from one country to another. Thirdly, to avoid any leakages, banks and financial institutions were not permitted to maintain abroad more liquid assets than were required as working balances.

The concern with external sector developments was no more explicit in the new statutes than it had been under the old statutes. It was reflected, however, in the requirement that decisions regarding general credit conditions be taken by unanimous vote whenever the foreign reserves of the BCEAO fell to an average of less than 20 per cent of the Bank's short-term liabilities for more than three consecutive months.

Thus, the new statutes were a move in the right direction in so far as they provided more adequate instruments for the control of domestic liquidity and greater flexibility in the application of monetary policy at the national level. At the same time, they stressed the importance of promoting economic development and of utilising funds within the region.

V. The Experience Under the Modified Statutes

Notwithstanding the modified statutes, the BCEAO has continued to rely primarily on re-discount ceilings as its instrument of monetary management. In addition, selective use has been made of the prior approval of the BCEAO for bank credits exceeding certain prescribed limits. The money market, through which the BCEAO has redistributed liquidity within the Union, has also developed.

From a strictly monetary point of view, while developments in the

WAMU region since 1975 (as indicated in Table 8.1) show a mixed picture, it must be emphasised that these developments have been heavily influenced by several exogenous factors, including the substantial increase in oil prices, world inflationary conditions in general and the commodity price boom in the mid-1970s. It would seem that the rate of domestic credit expansion has accelerated in the post-reform period, as has the rate of inflation, while current account deficits have increased as a percentage of GDP. At the same time, the economies of these countries are growing at very modest rates. The exceptions are the Ivory Coast and Niger, but even in these countries real GDP is growing at a considerably slower rate than domestic liquidity. There is little evidence that the BCEAO has been able to control credit expansion within the limits initially fixed, and its failure to do so does not appear so far to have induced the authorities to employ other instruments of credit policy to manage liquidity.

Table 8.1: Selected Data on the BCEAO Countries (percentages)

	1975	1976	1977	1978	Average 1975-8
1. *Rate of increase in real GDP*					
Benin	−1.0	4.3	3.8	5.5	3.7
Ivory Coast	7.0	12.5	4.7	10.6	8.7
Niger	0.6	20.6	13.0	8.0	10.5
Senegal	7.9	7.3	0.1	−10.1	1.3
Togo	0.5	3.8	1.7	10.0	4.0
Upper Volta	0.1	−0.1	2.5	3.1	
2. *Rate of inflation* [a]					
Benin	6	11	8	5	8
Ivory Coast	15	44	37	21	29
Niger	9	24	24	10	17
Senegal	32	1	12	3	15
Togo	18	12	23	1	16
Upper Volta	19	−8	33	30	19
3. *Rate of increase in domestic credit*					
Benin	11.4	0.5	5.3	28.0	11.3
Ivory Coast	29.8	38.5	42.8	11.2	30.6
Niger	23.5	−4.8	0.1	160.4	49.8
Senegal	20.0	25.9	18.8	31.1	24.0
Togo	89.1	28.2	39.1	24.4	45.2
Upper Volta	173.3	42.7	49.3	35.5	75.2

Table 8.1: continued

	1975	1976	1977	1978	Average 1975-8
4. Rate of increase in broad money (M2)					
Benin	72.7	−3.9	13.7	12.0	
Ivory Coast	9.5	42.8	49.8	10.9	
Niger	9.8	31.1	28.7	44.1	
Senegal	11.4	32.0	15.2	21.3	
Togo	−7.1	45.7	16.7	35.1	
Upper Volta	38.7	29.8	12.7	19.5	
5. Net foreign assets of the banking system					
Benin	5.3	6.6	6.3	0.2	
Ivory Coast	2.3	−2.6	35.8	44.2	
Niger	11.0	18.7	23.4	20.0	
Senegal	−10.3	−10.7	−12.9	−31.8	
Togo	5.8	12.7	4.3	9.9	
Upper Volta	15.9	12.6	5.9	−1.3	
6. Current account deficit					
Benin	−21.9	−25.3	−28.2	−31.4	
Ivory Coast	−89.9	−64.1	−53.6	−165.2	
Niger	−31.5	−19.0	−23.1	−31.0	
Senegal	−30.5	−41.5	−35.9	−76.0	
Togo	−24.4	−13.5	−29.1	−66.6	
Upper Volta	−29.8	−25.1	−37.6	−40.4	
7. Current account deficit as percentage of nominal GDP					
Benin	19.4	19.4	19.3	19.4	19.4
Ivory Coast	10.8	5.8	3.5	9.5	7.4
Niger	21.1	9.2	8.2	8.3	11.7
Senegal	7.4	9.1	7.5	16.8	10.2
Togo	19.8	10.1	17.7	38.5	21.5
Upper Volta	26.0	20.5	25.5	24.4	24.1

[a]. Measured by the consumer price index, except in the case of Benin where the GDP deflator was used.

A major change during this period relates to the establishment of the inter-bank money market. Interest rates were raised initially, with the discount rate increased to 8 per cent. While this rise reflected the interest rates in the international markets at that time, a gap subsequently developed when interest rates in the international market rose sharply to exceed 10 per cent, without Union-wide rates following suit.

Ironically, whereas during the pre-1975 period of cheap money the real rate of return for savers had been generally positive, in the post-reform period this rate has proved to be negative. The effect of this development on the growth of savings and financial savings has yet to be assessed. However, the savings and investment gap (defined as the equivalent of the current account deficit in the balance of payments) widened to represent almost one-quarter of the GDP for such countries as Upper Volta and 10 per cent of the GDP for Senegal. The effect on capital outflows from the WAMU region has been limited, however, to the extent that under the new statutes there is a strict limit on the amount of liquid funds that banks can keep abroad.

The relatively low interest rates maintained in the inter-bank market have been reflected in an excess demand for funds. During 1977, only 64 per cent of the funds demanded on the inter-bank market were supplied. This figure dropped to 37 per cent in 1978. The use of the inter-bank market has been heavily concentrated in the Ivory Coast and Senegal which, in 1977 and 1978, accounted together for an average of nearly 80 per cent of total transactions. The overall level of transactions on the inter-bank market has remained relatively low, the value of those occurring between WAMU member countries being very modest. Such intra-Union transactions, which amounted to an average of about 30 per cent of all transactions on the inter-bank market in 1977 and 1978, probably reflect a conscious policy on the part of the BCAEO to channel funds among member countries as all member countries (with the exception of Togo) face an excess demand situation. In the Ivory Coast in particular, only 50 per cent of the funds demanded were supplied in 1977 and this figure dropped to 25 per cent in 1978.

To sum up, the four-year period from 1975 through 1978 was characterised by relatively slow rates of real growth in the region, high rates of expansion in domestic liquidity, strong inflationary pressures and growing imbalances in the current accounts of the countries concerned. To the extent that developments in the various countries differed substantially and to the extent that the volume of intra-regional transactions did not increase appreciably, the period 1975-8 cannot be viewed as one in which a palpable move towards economic integration in the region was achieved. While this reflects in part the exogenous influences undergone by these countries during this period, it also reflects the inability of their common monetary policies to cope with the emerging problems. This inability is partly related, in turn, to the authorities' insistence on the continued utilisation of the traditional instrument for controlling domestic liquidity, i.e., re-discount ceilings. More importantly, however, it stems from the nature of the emerging problems, which are unlikely to be manageable by means of monetary policy instruments alone, especially if there is insistence on broad uniformity in their application.

A brief general comment on this latter point may be in order. In general, one would expect that as the economic structures of member countries were unified, common monetary policies would become more relevant and applicable. However, in the case of the WAMU, common monetary policies have been applied to a maximum since the establishment of the Union, while little effort has been made to foster economic integration. The economic structures of individual countries have in fact remained virtually segregated, and different inflationary and structural problems have emerged. These require broader and more comprehensive corrective measures which might be more easily borne were there more scope in the selection and application of monetary measures adapted to the particular problems of individual member countries. In short, the growing discrepancy between the continued application of a broadly uniform monetary policy, on the one hand, and the widening disparities in the structural and financial imbalances of member countries on the other, is beginning to generate certain problems in the Union which would appear to warrant immediate attention.

It is doubtful that the promotion of economic integration can be neglected for long in the search for a medium-term solution which would at the same time strengthen the existing monetary union. On the other hand, some flexibility will have to be introduced into the exercise of internal and external monetary policies, including greater selectivity in their application to specific member countries and, probably, compensatory measures at the national level to overcome some of the inconveniences created by the common constraints inherent in a monetary union.

VI. The General Implications of Monetary Integration for Economic Integration

The purpose of this section is briefly to outline the implications of the experience of the West African Monetary Union for Arab countries wishing to set up a monetary union as an initial step towards global economic integration. In this regard, it must be borne in mind that the economic characteristics of the WAMU member countries differ substantially from those of the countries belonging to the Arab Monetary Fund. The WAMU member countries share a number of characteristics. They have essentially similar production structures, producing competitive primary commodities for export, mainly to the industrialised countries. Reflecting this, intra-regional trade is less than 5 per cent of total WAMU trade. The per capita incomes of the WAMU countries are relatively close, though they have begun to diverge. All these countries have an adequate supply of indigenous labour and all show current account deficits. The characteristics of the Arab countries are, by contrast, more varied. The production profiles of the Arab countries are more diverse; different countries are at markedly different stages of industrialisation. A number of the Arab countries are oil producers which rely heavily on oil as a source of export proceeds, while others export mainly agricultural and light manufactured goods. Reflecting the differences in their production profiles, their intra-regional trade represents about 10 per cent of their total trade (excluding oil). Their labour endowments and their per capita incomes are also considerably different. Some of the Arab countries face a shortage and others a surplus of indigenous labour. Furthermore, as a reflection of these differences, the current account positions of the Arab countries vary considerably, with some recording large surpluses and others large deficits. As such, it would appear that, in general, the Arab countries exhibit economic characteristics which are more complementary in nature than those of the WAMU member countries. Nevertheless, there are some lessons that can be drawn from the experience of the West African Monetary Union in setting up an Arab Monetary Union — particularly if the Monetary Union is to be viewed as a prelude to economic integration.

However, before these lessons are discussed, the meaning of economic integration should be clarified. The process of economic integration involves the elimination of national barriers to economic transactions between countries, with a view to achieving a free flow of goods, capital and labour within a region. The benefits that are supposed to accrue to the region stem mainly from improved resource-allocation and the potential for economies of scale offered by the establishment of industries in the member countries designed to meet the demands of the region. In the final analysis, the process of economic integration should be reflected in the growing complementarity of the production profiles of the countries in a region and a consequent rise in intra-regional transactions.

It is evident from the existence of the WAMU that a monetary union can be set up, and can function effectively, without having as its objective economic integration. Its functioning can be confined to the 'co-ordination' of monetary policy among the member countries without its specifically fostering economic integration. Accordingly, in setting up a monetary union, it is of the utmost importance clearly to spell out the objectives of the union. If it is regarded as a first step towards full economic integration, due attention should be paid to endowing the Union with policy instruments and institutions which can be used to provide adequate investment incentives designed to generate complementary production structures in the member countries. In particular, it would be advisable to complement the establishment of a monetary union with that of a regional development bank and a regional planning organisation which could work closely to promote economic integration.

Another lesson to be drawn from the West African experience is the need to secure a sort of financial belt around the region included in a monetary union, in order to avoid the outward flow of capital funds, and to combine this with appropriate interest-rate policies. This would work towards the development of an efficient capital market within the region which would contribute to the promotion of investment and economic growth. To some extent, as pointed out earlier, the revised statutes of the West African Monetary Union represent a move in this direction since they limit the amount of capital that banks can place outside the region, establish a regional intra-bank money market and provide for greater flexibility in the pursuit of interest-rate policies. This avoids, to some extent, the 'costs' associated with closely linking domestic interest-rate policy to the international capital markets.

One of the most difficult tasks faced by any monetary union is the reconciliation of the financial policies pursued in each member country with what may be considered the overall policy orientation for the region. The harmonisation of economic policies is essential if one is to prevent the emergence of pressures within the union resulting from financial imbalances in the member countries. If the imbalances become too large, countries may be tempted to impose restrictions which may have adverse effects on the process of economic integration. In this connection, it is worth noting that in so far as the exchange-rate instrument cannot be used at the level of the individual country or is not permitted flexibility in a monetary union, member countries faced with external disequilibria will have to resort to a more intensive use of domestic financial policies to bring about adjustment.

Notes

1. Rattan J. Bhatia and Paul A. Acquah, 'Monetary Instruments and Policies in the BCEAO Countries, 1962-74 – An Analysis', *International Monetary Fund DM series*, DM/77/52.

2. Under the previous statutes, a credit ceiling was proposed for each six-month period.

3. This was, partly at least, an incidental result of the new move away from the pre-1974 cheap money policy. These preferential rates were designed to alternate the effects of a high interest-rate policy on the preferred sectors.

4. It should be noted that, under the pre-1974 statutes, banks could be required to maintain deposits with the BCEAO, but that this policy instrument

was not used. In addition, the liquidity ratio specified under the previous statutes had proved ineffective in controlling the expansion of credit by the banking system; it was abolished under the new statutes.

COMMENT

Abderrahim Omrana

Introduction

Mr Bhatia first summarises the historical background of the West African Monetary Union, outlining its organisational development. He then assesses the financial and monetary policy in the Union and relates this to certain domestic and international developments. In so doing, he is able to pinpoint certain areas of weakness in the Union. He then makes a number of constructive suggestions, not only for the countries of West Africa but for the Arab countries as well. The lessons which the author draws from the West African experience, and with which he concludes his analysis, would seem to suggest that no agreement in the monetary field can hold unless it is comprehensive, integrative and flexible and unless it fits within the framework of uniform economic and financial planning.

My comments will be limited to an assessment of WAMU in the light of its relationship to the outside world, with special emphasis on the treaty linking the Union to France and its implications for the financial and economic policy of the Union as well as for its future development.

I think this point concerning relations with France is extremely important. Mr Bhatia has dealt with it very briefly and without analysing its dimensions and consequences. In order that my remarks may complement his analysis, I have found it necessary, therefore, to return to this point and at the same time, to analyse the Union's monetary policy. In this way, I also hope to show the lessons which the Arab countries as a group may draw from the West African experience in establishing an effective monetary union.

With regard to relations with France, it is important to understand the functioning of the Operation Account. The treaty with France states as follows: 'The BCEAO shall pay into the Operation Account the disposable funds that can be raised outside its zone of issue ... with certain exceptions' (Art. 2). In the event of a shortage of disposable funds in the account, the French Treasury may, in accordance with the provisions of Art. 5 of the treaty, grant overdrafts. Article 7 stipulates the conditions of payment of the debit or credit balances of the account. This mechanism is intended to provide certain advantages to each of the two parties. It might be relevant here to sum up these advantages before taking a critical look at them.

For France, there are two principal advantages to this system. First of all, when French exports to the WAMU countries are less than its imports from these countries, the system enables France to settle its debt resulting from the deficit in its balance of trade *vis-à-vis* these countries through a mere registration of credit in favour of its partners. Without such a mechanism, France would either have to sell to these countries more of its goods and services or draw on its gold and foreign exchange reserves in order to settle its debt.

Secondly, when exports of the WAMU countries to countries outside the franc zone exceed their imports from the same countries, the foreign exchange earnings of the WAMU countries also benefit France.

The advantages to this system for the WAMU countries, on the other hand, can be summarised as follows:

On the exchange front: these states may obtain from abroad any amount of foreign exchange without restriction and beyond their foreign exchange earning capacity;
On the monetary front: the CFA franc indirectly enjoys the same guarantee as the French franc;
On the investment front: the monetary guarantee inspires the confidence of investors, thus helping to attract foreign capital.

How real are these advantages? One can appraise this system, as it operates, in two areas: foreign exchange and investment.

(i) Foreign Exchange

Theoretically speaking, members of the Union may acquire as much foreign exchange as they wish, merely be debiting the Operation Account. However, such a guarantee is not a real one; in fact the pooling of the foreign exchange acquired by member states from abroad makes it possible to offset the deficits of some member countries with the surpluses of the others. Therefore, France is only obliged to grant advances in the Operation Account to members of the Union when the member states *as a whole* register a deficit *vis-à-vis* the rest of the world. Such a situation arises so rarely as to render this monetary guarantee hypothetical.

Furthermore, provisions exist to prevent such a situation from occurring: when the ratio of foreign assets to short-term liabilities falls below a floor of 20 per cent, the Board of Directors is called upon to take appropriate measures. The actual evolution of this ratio shows that the 20 per cent floor is far from being reached, which means that this restriction prevents the BCEAO from utilising the full credit potential at its disposal, in particular for the purpose of financing medium-term credit. The movement of this ratio also suggests that the policy of the BCEAO is dictated more by variations in the volume of external assets than by the needs of the members' national economies.

It would appear from the foregoing that it is only for a guarantee against a potential risk and not a real one that the Union member states have imposed upon themselves a certain discipline as signified by the following:

The definition of a parity which may not be appropriate to the economic situation of certain member states;

Free transfers of capital, which implies the absence of exchange controls on transfers towards France; and

The free circulation of goods between Union members and France, for trade regulations do not apply to their reciprocal trade. This means that trade is strongly polarised in the direction of France (despite a certain recent reorientation of this trade towards the European Economic Community).

(ii) Investment Promotion

One might think that, because of the free convertibility of their currency and the constant parity of the CFA franc with the French franc, the WAMU countries would offer the most favourable conditions for attracting investments. However, statistics show that such investments are insufficient and some members of the Union, like Senegal, are currently suffering from a shortage of both public and private investment.

Foreign investors are not attracted solely by stability, monetary guarantees and the absence of exchange controls but also by more decisive factors such as the availability of natural resources and the profitability of their exploitation. For this reason, a few countries in Latin America, e.g., Brazil, have been able to attract large sums of investment capital despite persistent inflationary pressures and permanent budget deficits. In the context of Africa, the Ivory Coast is a case in point.

What lessons can the Arab countries draw from the experiences of West Africa in the area of monetary integration?

It would appear that one can rule out the possibility of their adopting the West African system *in toto*. The reasons for this are, first of all, political; for it is unlikely that the Arab countries would agree to peg their common currency to a dominant foreign currency. Secondly, from a purely economic point of view, the mechanisms of the Operation Account exhibit a number of disadvantages, as we have seen.

The members of the West African Monetary Union, aware of these deficiencies and taking into consideration developments both in the international monetary arena and in their own economies, have adjusted these mechanisms in order to secure for the BCEAO greater autonomy in the management of their external assets and a more dynamic role in the development of their economies.

Thus, since 1974, the BCEAO has been permitted to limit its assets held in the Operation Account to 65 per cent of its total assets; these assets earn interest. The remaining 35 per cent are denominated in foreign exchange and either deposited in a current account kept with the Bank for International Settlements or with foreign central banks or used to purchase bonds maturing within two years.

Moreover, the French Treasury is under obligation to compensate the BCEAO for any depreciation of its assets denominated in French francs by means of an exchange guarantee mechanism with regard to assets held in the Operation Account.

The lessons to be drawn from the West African experience can be reduced to, first, an observation and then a conclusion:

1. The example of WAMU offers evidence that monetary union is possible without economic union. The Union has much to its credit: it has held up through some difficult times and is quite efficiently managed; its members have not suffered from lack of liquidity and have moreover recorded respectable growth rates, acceptable rates of inflation and a reorientation of trade flows in directions more in line with their interests. It would be difficult for these countries to dissociate themselves from the French franc without jeopardising their unity and undermining the confidence of investors. What is essential is that they try to derive continually more advantages from the French monetary guarantee, a mechanism which must work entirely to the advantage of the Union.

2. The Arab world must try to succeed where West Africa has failed, namely, in promoting economic co-operation for common development. The Arab countries enjoy certain distinct advantages compared with the WAMU countries: capital, a larger and more highly skilled labour force and abundant resources. A monetary union among these countries is not, in my opinion, of the highest priority, but it could be developed as part of a strategy aimed at economic union. After all, monetary union is not an end in itself. Its purpose is to support intra-regional trade and development. The fact is that the volume of inter-Arab trade is still very modest.

The Arab Monetary Fund presently represents no more than a step towards monetary union (see definitions of forms of monetary union by Machlup and Williamson). It should develop further so as to become a real development bank for the Arab world. (Of course, this would pose problems with regard to resources and options.) As for the creation of a common Arab currency, I think it is an objective for future generations. Would it not be well, in the meantime, to fix the exchange rates of the Arab currencies in relation to each other and to create a payments union and a common unit of account?

GENERAL DISCUSSION

1. Mohammed Labib Shoukair

There are three particularly interesting aspects to the West African experience. First, the monetary union has attained an advanced stage despite the lack of any attempt to bring about economic integration; though this experience appears to be unique, it can be explained, as I shall demonstrate below. Secondly, France plays an important and special role in the monetary union. And thirdly, the monetary union has not encouraged the development of trade among the member countries.

The West African experience thus demonstrates that it is possible for a monetary union to work and to endure for almost twenty years without there being close links among the member countries. What, then, is their interest in such a union? The union has certainly been of benefit to France, as explained by Mr Bhatia and Mr Omrana, for it has ensured the total linkage of the West African countries' economies to its own. In fact, this system merely represents a modification of the older franc zone, with France continuing to exercise the same economic dominance as in the past. By contrast, the benefits to the West African economies from the monetary union are far from obvious; for they have not achieved any measure of joint economic development. My conclusion from this would be that monetary integration cannot be realised unless it is based either on close internal links among the economies of the countries concerned, or on close links with an external economy, leading to the reinforcement of the state of dependency of the member states *vis-à-vis* the dominant country, as in the case of West Africa. However, bearing in mind the lesson derived from the West African experience, I do not believe that monetary integration should be implemented unless it is accompanied by economic integration. Both processes should be effected simultaneously, especially if dependence on dominant foreign economies is to be avoided or at least minimised. I would like to hear Mr Bhatia's views regarding the ability of the West African union to continue if France were to withdraw from the picture.

2. Mabid Ali Al-Jarhi

The most interesting conclusion contained in Mr Bhatia's paper is that a monetary union can be established without reference to the stage of economic integration which has been achieved. Yet, the failure of the West African Monetary Union to further economic integration requires further explanation. In any case, it should be stressed that propositions attempting forcibly to relate monetary integration to the level of economic integration cannot be supported by the current state of economic knowledge and would moreover seem to defy common sense.

I would like to offer as a partial explanation of the failure of WAMU to become a vehicle for economic integration the following factors:

(a) The limited role of the BCEAO as a central bank, especially its failure to act as a lender of last resort;
(b) The generally low endowment of both capital and labour in the member countries which has limited the usefulness of these factors, however mobile they may be, as vehicles for economic integration;
(c) Some of the rules embodied in WAMU have been designed to make the French guarantee of CFA franc convertibility as harmless to France as possible.

We can therefore suggest two corollaries:

(a) That WAMU could be modified to serve the purpose of economic integration;
(b) That, with certain modifications, such a monetary union should be more successful in the Arab world, given the resources already available in the region.

3. Izzadin Ibrahim Hassan

Mr Williamson quotes Machlup as saying that 'monetary integration is an integral part of complete economic integration'. Considering the situation in West Africa, it would seem that we have indeed a monetary union without economic integration. Could it be that what we have in West Africa is not really a monetary union? Or is it that Machlup's definition has failed the test of experience?

4. Jorge Gonzalez del Valle

While I share the surprise of some of my colleagues at the 'discovery' of a case of monetary integration which is clearly *not* associated with any economic integration programme, I would like to point out a similar case. This is the case of the Caribbean Clearing Arrangement which involves four Latin American countries (to be joined by two more soon-to-be independent nations). Despite the fact that very little progress had been achieved in the economic integration of the CARICOM area, the central banks and currency boards of these countries decided in 1977 to go ahead with the clearing arrangement on an experimental basis. This arrangement has since been renewed three times and is soon to become permanent. Moreover, the Caribbean monetary authorities are now seriously considering a supplementary credit arrangement to cope with global balance-of-payments deficits. This clearly shows that monetary integration is deliberately being pursued in the Caribbean even though it is not supported, for the time being, by any substantial developments in the direction of economic integration.

5. Karim Nashashibi

In his paper on the West African Monetary Union, Mr Bhatia clearly shows that monetary integration is an empty shell unless it is given some content in the way of policies designed to improve the division of labour and economic complementarity and thus to promote economic integration. Under the standard definition, complementarity means a flow of benefits in both directions, as would pertain between Denmark and Sweden, for example, where you have different comparative advantages in financial resources than might be found between two Arab countries. In the Arab world, complementarity is sometimes understood as a movement of labour in one direction and of capital in the other. These two views are, in my opinion, compatible since the standard definition does not capture the longer-term dimension of complementarity whereby, for example, the investment of oil surpluses in projects such as large agricultural estates would eventually be of direct benefit to the oil-producing countries, not only economically but also strategically. I would appreciate hearing Mr Bhatia's view as to whether this type of complementarity is sustainable.

In this context, I would like to mention that we have, up to now, spoken somewhat vaguely about Arab economic integration and Arab monetary integration. As we approach the last hours of our seminar, we must give some concrete content to our thoughts on this matter and ask: what will be the role of oil surplus funds in this integration? What are the objectives of Arab monetary integration?

6. Isselmou Ould Boye

Permit me to make one very brief comment. My country, Mauritania, was the first to leave the West African Union, though it was a founding member. The reason is that the Union tended to place constraints on Mauritania's developmental capabilities.

7. John Williamson

I feel I have to say a word in defence of Fritz Machlup, whose position I endorsed yesterday.

To say that monetary integration is an essential part of economic integration is not the logical equivalent of saying that monetary integration implies economic integration. Therefore, at the level of logic, I do not think one can challenge Machlup. On the other hand, we both take the position that monetary integration is justified in large part because it promotes economic integration; if the experience of Africa shows that it has done no such thing, that is important evidence undermining the case for monetary integration. But how well established is the conclusion that monetary integration has done nothing to promote economic integration? The countries in question exhibit little natural complementarity; nor has there been any attempt at a concerted programme of import substitution. Therefore, the fact that the volume of intra-Union trade is low proves little. Much has been made of the fact established in Mr Bhatia's paper that this intra-Union trade has declined over time (proportionately), but even this is not decisive, because what we really need is a comparison between what actually happened and what would have happened in the absence of the monetary union. Perhaps we could make a more sophisticated calculation that would throw light on this question by comparing the evolution of trade among the six countries that remained within the Union with that between those six and the three that withdrew? Has any such comparison been made? Similarly, has there been any serious attempt to use the comparative experiences of these two groups to estimate the extent of trade diversion towards France resulting from the rigid peg to the French franc? Any information on this question would be valuable in illuminating one of the reasons that has been pointed to for the desirability of pegging to a basket rather than to the currency of a single industrial country.

8. Rattan J. Bhatia, in Response

In my response I do not wish to be either an attacker or a defender of the role of France in the West African Monetary Union; I think this is neither necessary nor desirable. I am rather looking at the experience of the union as an economic entity and at its overall relevance to the subject of this seminar. As another introductory remark, let us not confuse the lack of economic integration in the Union with economic stagnation. Actually, the WAMU member countries have, in general, achieved very satisfactory records in terms of growth rates, price performance and the balance-of-payments. If one were to compare the performance of the WAMU with other countries in a similar economic position, one would conclude that the WAMU countries have at least not done any worse than they and have in fact probably done significantly better. I might mention, in particular, the performance of the Ivory Coast.

As for the role of France, it exhibits both positive and negative aspects. Among the former may be mentioned the convertibility guarantee which has had a significantly positive impact both in terms of maintaining the confidence of investors and in terms of economic and technical assistance. Among the negative aspects may perhaps be mentioned the encouragement provided for the maintenance and development of bilateral trade and financial flows between individual member countries and France, rather than among the member countries.

This brings me to the question raised as to what would be the effect on the Union of an eventual removal of the French convertibility guarantee. This would doubtless have an immediate and traumatic effect, especially on foreign private investment. However, the long-term consequences cannot be predicted, as the rules of the game would have changed. Whether the chances of economic integration would increase, I do not know.

While I did, in the conclusion of my paper, point out the difficulties that have surfaced in the operation of the Union, I nevertheless believe that these can be surmounted, and the Union maintained, if attention is paid to the underlying structural and institutional improvements needed in the light of past developments and the experience gained so far.

Mr Al-Jarhi has tried to extract from my paper the reasons which could explain the failure to make progress on economic integration. But he appears to have misunderstood the role of the BCEAO. I do not think the BCEAO 'failed' to act as a lender of last resort, in fact, the re-discount ceilings of the BCEAO were overly generous. In my opinion, an important reason for the lack of progress on economic integration was the complete openness of the Union, which encouraged transactions with the outside world and discouraged (though not deliberately) the strengthening of intra-Union links. I have in mind the required infrastructure which could strengthen these links.

As regards Mr Nashashibi's question, i.e., whether the kind of complementarity represented by an exchange of labour for capital between Arab countries is sustainable in the long run, I believe that such an exchange is sustainable, so long as the required surpluses exist. Of course, these exchanges would need to be undertaken at the going market prices. But let me also say that the creation of a monetary union is not necessary for such exchanges to take place. A considerably more convincing case will need to be made for a monetary union.

PART FOUR

PROSPECTS FOR ARAB MONETARY INTEGRATION

9 THE EXTERNAL ECONOMIC AND MONETARY POSITIONS OF THE ARAB COUNTRIES AND THE ROLE OF FINANCIAL SURPLUSES IN PROMOTING ARAB MONETARY INTEGRATION*

Abdul Munim Al-Sayyed Ali

Introduction

The aim of this paper is four-fold: (a) to examine the flow of trade and of economic resources in general among the Arab countries; (b) to assess their balance-of-payments positions; (c) to examine the flow of financial resources among them; and (d) to consider the role of financial surpluses in helping to achieve closer Arab monetary integration.

I. Inter-Arab Trade Flows

Three general observations can be made regarding the foreign trade sector in the Arab economies.

First, foreign trade represents a significant part of national income.[1] In 1976, the ratio of exports to GNP in the oil-exporting countries (excluding Algeria) ranged from 59 to 100 per cent, while in Democratic Yemen the ratio was 47 per cent. In eight other countries,[2] it ranged from 14 to 34 per cent. Only in the four remaining countries[3] was the ratio less than 10 per cent. In the same year, the ratio of imports to GNP ranged from 16 to 100 per cent, the latter ratio applying to Bahrain. The ratio of total foreign trade to GNP ranged from 30 per cent in the case of Yemen to 140 per cent for Democratic Yemen. Moreover the degree of dependence of the Arab economies on foreign trade has been increasing substantially, especially since 1963.[4] This has primarily been the result of continuing economic development, especially in the oil-producing countries. It is also partly the result of increases in the prices of exports and imports, particularly imports of manufactured goods from industrialised Europe.

Secondly, the exports of most Arab countries comprise either agricultural products or raw materials of one or two types.[5] In 1975, for example, agricultural products and raw materials of agricultural or mineral origin represented between 50 and 100 per cent of the total exports of each country. In the oil-exporting countries, oil exports represented the bulk of total exports. In the same year, imports of

---

* Translated from the Arabic.

Table 9.1: Arab Foreign Trade in Relation to Gross Domestic Product in 1976

Country	Exports	Imports	GDP	Exports	Imports	Total Foreign Trade
	In millions of dollars			As a percentage of GDP		
1 – Algeria	5333	5338	15760	33.8	33.9	67.7
2 – Bahrain	1386	1668	1360	101.9	122.6	224.6
3 – Democratic Yemen	177	335	374	47.3	89.6	136.9
4 – Djibouti	16	114	187	8.6	61.0	69.5
5 – Egypt	1522	3808	16031	9.5	23.8	33.2
6 – Iraq	9272	3470	15777	58.8	22.0	80.8
7 – Jordan	209	1022	1170	17.9	87.4	105.2
8 – Kuwait	9830	3324	12080	81.4	27.5	108.9
9 – Lebanon [a]	497	1224	2830	17.6	43.3	60.8
10 – Libya	8441	2198	17017	49.6	12.9	62.5
11 – Mauritania	178	180	522	34.1	34.5	68.6
12 – Morocco	1262	2618	9219	13.7	28.4	42.1
13 – Oman	1578	1102	2390	66.0	46.1	112.1
14 – Qatar	2210	775	3460	63.9	22.4	86.3
15 – Saudi Arabia	36125	8694	52900	68.3	16.4	84.7
16 – Somalia	85	162	566	15.0	28.6	43.6
17 – Sudan	554	980	6005	9.2	16.3	25.5
18 – Syrian Arab Republic	1065	1986	6170	17.3	32.2	49.4
19 – Tunisia	788	1529	4418	17.8	34.6	52.4
20 – United Arab Emirates	8543	3327	11060	77.2	30.1	107.3
21 – Yemen	8	410	1390	0.6	29.5	30.1

[a] The figures for Lebanon are for 1973.

Sources: United Nations, Department of International Economic and Social Affairs, Statistical Office, *Statistical Yearbook 1978* (New York: UN, 1979), pp. 446-9; Organization of the Petroleum-Exporting Countries, Statistics Unit, *Annual Statistical Bulletin 1977* (Vienna: OPEC, 1978), pp. 1, 3-5; United Nations, Economic Commission for Western Asia, 'Gross Domestic Product at Current Market Prices for the Arab World' (unpublished tables). Taken from: Mahmoud El-Homsi, *Arab Development Plans: Integrative and Non-integrative Aspects of their Orientation* (Beirut: Centre for Arab Unity Studies, 1980), Table 2-2, p. 53 (in Arabic).

manufactured goods and foodstuffs represented more than 50 per cent of total imports for most Arab countries.

Thirdly, inter-Arab trade as a proportion of total Arab foreign trade has actually declined. Thus, although in absolute terms the value of inter-Arab trade rose from $1,276 million in 1960 to more than $7,656 million in 1977, in relative terms the ratio of inter-Arab trade to total

Table 9.2: Changes in the Value of Foreign Trade as a Percentage of GNP in the Arab Countries for the Period 1963-6

Country	As a percentage of national income for 1963-8	As a percentage of GNP in 1970	As a percentage of GDP in 1976
1 – Algeria	68.1	53.0	67.7
2 – Bahrain	–	434.2	224.6
3 – Democratic Yemen	–	248.0	136.9
4 – Djibouti	–	–	69.5
5 – Egypt	15.6	22.5	33.2
6 – Iraq	32.5	52.1	80.8
7 – Jordan	20.3	38.2	105.2
8 – Kuwait	50.8	88.6	108.9
9 – Lebanon	28.2	47.5	60.8[a]
10 – Libya	46.3	85.4	62.5
11 – Mauritania	–	–	68.6
12 – Morocco	24.5	32.6	42.1
13 – Oman	–	117.5	112.1
14 – Qatar	–	177.0	86.3
15 – Saudi Arabia	–	95.8	84.7
16 – Somalia	–	–	43.6
17 – Sudan	15.6	33.4	25.5
18 – Syrian Arab Republic	19.0	32.0	49.4
19 – Tunisia	20.0	38.4	52.4
20 – United Arab Emirates	–	154.2	107.3
21 – Yemen	–	12.1	30.1

[a] This figure is for 1973.
Sources: For 1963-8: Mohammad Abdul-Moneim Afar, *Proceedings of the Meeting of the Union of Arab Economists, Damascus, 1971*, p. 626 (in Arabic); for 1970: United Nations Industrial Development Organization, *Comparative Study of Development Plans of Arab States*, annex, Table 8, p. 259; United Nations, Department of International Economic and Social Affairs, Statistical Office, *Statistical Yearbook 1977*, pp. 470-3; for 1976: Table 9.1. Taken from: El-Homsi, *Arab Development Plans: Integrative and Non-integrative Aspects of their Orientation*, Table 2-3, p. 55.

Arab trade declined from about 10 per cent to about 5 per cent over the same period. This is because, while inter-Arab trade increased sixfold, Arab trade outside the Arab region increased twelve-fold, from $12,352 million in 1960 to $151,039 million in 1977.[6] The ratio of inter-Arab exports to total exports fell from about 21 per cent in 1960 to about 4 per cent in 1977. The ratio of inter-Arab imports to total imports declined from about 7 per cent to slightly more than 6 per cent during the same period.

These are clear indications that, despite the Arab Economic Unity

Table 9.3a: Commodity Composition of the Foreign Trade of Arab Countries. Structure of Arab Exports: Percentage Shares for the Main Categories of Exports

Country	Year	Total value (millions of dollars)	All food items	Agricultural raw materials	Fuels	Ores and metals	Manufactured goods	Chemical products	Other manufactured goods	Machinery and equipment	Unallocated
Standard International Trade Classification (SITC)			0+1+22+4	2 less (22+27+28)	3	27+28+67+68	5 to 8 less (67+68)	5	(6+8) less (67+68)	7	
1 Algeria	1970	1008.8	19.98	0.51	70.54	5.05	3.92	0.36	1.93	1.63	0.00
	1975	4294.5	4.08	0.12	92.38	2.04	1.38	0.14	0.48	0.75	0.00
2 Bahrain	1972	323.1	3.93	0.07	72.61	0.96	22.31	6.25	11.85	4.20	0.11
	1975	1147.1	1.51	0.06	75.01	8.79	14.61	6.70	5.03	2.89	0.02
3 Democratic Yemen	1968	109.9	5.35	5.77	74.67	0.29	1.80	0.00	1.50	0.31	12.12
4 Djibouti	1974	19.8	89.07	5.07	0.69	1.32	3.57	0.00	1.96	1.61	0.28
	1975	16.0	71.21	2.90	10.31	2.42	2.91	0.11	1.12	1.68	10.25
5 Egypt	1970	761.7	21.28	46.26	4.78	1.61	26.07	1.97	23.30	0.79	0.01
	1975	1401.9	17.41	38.54	9.45	2.39	32.19	4.43	26.71	1.05	0.02
6 Iraq	1970	1099.8	2.96	1.20	94.06	0.28	0.95	0.11	0.83	0.02	0.55
	1975	8433.1	0.53	0.16	99.06	0.03	0.22	0.16	0.05	0.01	0.00
7 Jordan	1970	26.1	57.42	2.06	0.02	24.32	16.18	2.84	10.05	3.28	0.00
	1975	125.6	28.95	0.52	0.70	49.91	19.91	4.85	13.90	1.16	0.01
8 Kuwait	1970	1901.4	1.00	0.07	94.00	0.20	4.64	2.93	0.57	1.15	0.09
	1975	9186.0	0.36	0.08	91.53	0.37	7.66	4.56	1.09	2.01	0.01

Table 9.3a: continued

Country	Year	Total value (millions of dollars)	Main categories of exports (%)					of which			Unallocated
			All food items	Agricultural raw materials	Fuels	Ores and metals	Manufactured goods	Chemical products	Other manufactured goods	Machinery and equipment	
Standard International Trade Classification (SITC)			0+1+22+4	2 less (22+27+28)	3	27+28+67+68	5 to 8 less (67+68)	5	(6+8) less (67+68)	7	
9 Lebanon	1970	197.8	29.99	5.96	0.14	6.95	56.97	7.60	29.95	19.43	0.00
	1973	502.5	21.13	5.51	0.47	5.55	66.31	7.73	33.03	25.54	1.03
10 Libya	1970	2357.1	0.01	0.03	99.92	0.05	0.00	0.00	0.00	0.00	0.00
	1975	6834.7	0.00	0.01	99.99	0.00	0.00	0.00	0.00	0.00	0.00
11 Mauritania	1970	88.8	8.29	2.48	0.07	88.32	0.84	0.00	0.49	0.36	0.00
	1975	174.3	8.20	0.53	0.70	90.08	0.41	0.02	0.36	0.03	0.08
12 Morocco	1970	487.9	51.79	5.52	0.38	32.64	9.65	2.17	6.99	0.50	0.02
	1975	1543.0	25.05	2.14	0.92	59.40	12.45	2.29	9.73	0.43	0.04
13 Oman	1971	221.1	0.47	0.00	99.53	0.00	0.00	0.00	0.00	0.00	0.00
	1975	1436.5	0.22	0.00	99.78	0.00	0.00	0.00	0.00	0.00	0.00
14 Qatar	1972	449.1	0.64	0.06	96.64	0.08	2.28	0.06	0.07	2.14	0.30
	1975	1809.2	0.11	0.01	97.17	0.03	2.67	2.15	0.04	0.48	0.00
15 Saudi Arabia	1970	2423.7	0.09	0.00	99.75	0.05	0.10	0.04	0.05	0.00	0.01
	1975	29668.9	0.09	0.00	99.32	0.02	0.58	0.02	0.33	0.23	0.00
16 Somalia	1970	31.4	85.50	8.19	0.00	0.12	4.87	0.01	0.78	4.08	1.31
	1975	88.6	90.30	6.47	0.02	0.01	2.94	0.00	0.31	2.62	0.26

Table 9.3a: continued

Country	Year	Total value (millions of dollars)	Main categories of exports (%)					of which			Unallocated
			All food items	Agricultural raw materials	Fuels	Ores and metals	Manufactured goods	Chemical products	Other manufactured goods	Machinery and equipment	
Standard International Trade Classification (SITC)			0+1+22+4	2 less (22+27+28)	3	27+28+67+68	5 to 8 less (67+68)	5	(6+8) less (67+68)	7	
17 Sudan	1970	291.8	24.55	74.62	0.36	0.39	0.07	0.03	0.04	0.00	0.01
	1975	424.0	42.45	53.09	3.62	0.59	0.13	0.10	0.03	0.00	0.11
18 Syrian Arab Republic	1970	203.0	27.36	44.52	16.74	0.11	10.86	0.56	9.81	0.49	0.42
	1975	930.0	5.25	15.00	70.31	1.67	7.77	0.22	6.50	1.04	0.00
19 Tunisia	1970	182.5	29.90	4.68	27.23	23.73	14.38	9.60	4.36	0.43	0.00
	1975	856.2	19.21	1.56	43.60	16.24	19.40	9.41	8.94	1.05	0.00
20 United Arab Emirates	1971	935.3	0.59	0.06	96.39	2.46	0.47	0.05	0.10	0.32	0.02
	1975	6695.7	0.53	0.08	97.74	0.44	0.87	0.10	0.36	0.41	0.34
21 Yemen	1970	2.8	55.15	35.12	0.00	9.52	0.17	0.00	0.17	0.00	0.04
	1975	10.9	26.25	66.49	0.00	0.45	6.76	1.83	4.63	0.30	0.06
Total (in millions of dollars)	1970[a]	13122.9	1007.7	742.7	10302.1	402.2	643.1	142.5	384.1	116.4	24.8
	1975[b]	75688.6	1618.7	1033.3	68903.7	1616.1	2474.9	792.3	1153.6	528.0	45.7
Percentage shares	1970[a]	100.0	7.7	5.7	78.5	3.1	4.9	1.1	2.9	0.9	0.2
	1975[b]	100.0	2.1	1.4	91.0	2.1	3.3	1.0	1.5	0.7	0.1

[a] The figures here are approximate values for the following reasons: (i) Data for 1970 were not always available; consequently, data for other years were used as follows: PDRY: 1968; UAE and Oman: 1971; Bahrain and Qatar: 1972; Djibouti: 1974. (ii) Export values for each commodity group in each country have been obtained by means of the percentages shown in the table. These values were then used to calculate the total for each group and its share in the grand total. [b] These are approximate estimates for the following reasons: (i) Data for 1975 were not always available; consequently, data for other years were used as follows: PDRY: 1968; Lebanon: 1973. (ii) See (ii) under note a.

Source: United Nations, *Handbook of International Trade and Development Statistics 1979*, (New York: UN, 1979), pp. 152-94. Taken from: El-Homsi, *Arab Development Plans: Integrative and Non-integrative Aspects of their Orientation*, table 2-4, pp. 58-9.

External Economic and Monetary Positions 305

Table 9.3b: Commodity Composition of the Foreign Trade of Arab Countries. Structure of Arab Imports [a]: Percentage Shares for the Main Categories of Imports

Country	Year	Total value (millions of dollars)	All food items	Agricultural raw materials	Fuels	Ores and metals	Manufactured goods	Chemical products	Other manufactured goods	Machinery and equipment	Unallocated
Standard International Trade Classification (SITC)			0+1+22+4	2 less (22+27+28)	3	27+28+67+68	5 to 8 less (67+68)	5	(6+8) less (67+68)	7	
1 – Algeria	1970	1256.8	12.75	3.86	2.12	13.61	66.82	8.12	22.24	36.46	0.85
	1975	5974.1	21.70	2.08	1.70	10.87	63.64	6.68	17.02	39.94	0.00
2 – Bahrain	1972	377.5	10.94	0.61	40.34	4.62	43.40	3.80	21.15	18.45	0.10
	1975	1158.2	6.43	0.53	50.82	3.41	38.80	3.68	16.35	18.77	0.02
3 – Democratic Yemen	1968	202.7	13.32	2.50	32.39	0.00	9.37	0.00	7.43	1.94	42.42
4 – Egypt	1970	786.6	23.22	8.31	9.39	9.13	49.93	12.97	10.40	26.56	0.01
	1975	3933.7	35.92	5.48	6.93	8.48	43.18	13.18	9.54	20.46	0.02
5 – Iraq	1970	508.6	17.71	3.91	0.09	13.05	63.58	9.13	25.61	28.84	1.66
	1975	4204.6	17.51	2.84	0.28	17.07	62.22	5.88	15.33	41.01	0.08
6 – Jordan	1970	184.5	31.04	3.04	5.67	7.12	46.55	6.11	23.53	16.91	6.58
	1975	730.8	22.40	1.99	10.64	5.57	58.03	5.21	21.06	31.76	1.37
7 – Kuwait	1970	625.1	19.79	1.09	0.71	4.92	73.32	4.64	32.82	35.86	0.17
	1975	2388.2	17.07	0.73	0.59	4.87	76.13	3.87	26.64	45.62	0.61
8 – Lebanon	1970	567.5	25.07	6.28	5.92	8.40	54.32	9.02	25.40	19.90	0.01
	1973	1224.5	18.23	6.38	4.79	9.49	61.03	9.36	26.26	25.40	0.08

Table 9.3b: continued

Country	Year	Total value (millions of dollars)	Main categories of imports (%)					of which			Unallocated
			All food items	Agricultural raw materials	Fuels	Ores and metals	Manufactured goods	Chemical products	Other manufactured goods	Machinery and equipment	
Standard International Trade Classification (SITC)			0+1+22+4	2 less (22+27+28)	3	27+28+67+68	5 to 8 less (67+68)	5	(6+8) less (67+68)	7	
9 – Libya	1970	554.4	22.59	1.42	3.18	7.36	65.45	5.76	30.04	29.65	0.00
	1975	3542.5	17.13	1.95	1.94	9.65	69.33	3.72	31.34	34.27	0.00
10 – Mauritania	1970	55.9	23.41	0.80	7.74	4.70	63.32	6.46	18.95	37.92	0.02
	1972	85.2	22.63	0.63	6.15	5.05	65.28	5.21	18.23	41.84	0.26
11 – Morocco	1970	684.3	20.66	8.14	5.46	10.07	55.65	8.47	15.52	31.66	0.02
	1975	2547.3	29.61	4.74	10.85	7.21	47.56	8.10	10.71	28.74	0.03
12 – Oman	1971	33.1	39.31	1.91	6.93	0.85	49.63	4.19	20.41	25.04	1.38
	1975	670.5	13.30	2.23	4.67	6.64	67.73	3.89	22.44	41.40	5.44
13 – Qatar	1970	67.9	24.08	2.02	1.90	13.11	58.21	4.24	23.16	30.80	0.69
	1975	409.8	13.92	1.17	0.92	8.16	75.11	4.38	19.43	51.30	0.72
14 – Saudi Arabia	1970	692.1	30.90	2.15	1.12	5.83	57.86	5.11	20.02	32.73	2.14
	1975	4141.2	15.64	1.45	0.69	5.42	76.66	4.85	30.76	41.05	0.15
15 – Somalia	1970	45.1	33.68	5.48	6.29	3.12	51.13	6.75	27.86	16.52	0.30
	1975	154.7	26.01	2.93	6.16	3.65	61.00	6.80	22.50	31.70	0.25

Table 9.3b: continued

Country	Year	Total value (millions of dollars)	All food items	Agricultural raw materials	Fuels	Ores and metals	Manufactured goods				Unallocated
								Chemical products	of which Other manufactured goods	Machinery and equipment	
Standard International Trade Classification (SITC)			0+1+22+4	2 less (22+27+28)	3	27+28+67+68	5 to 8 less (67+68)	5	(6+8) less (67+68)	7	Unallocated
16 – Sudan	1970	311.1	21.27	2.29	8.40	4.93	62.33	10.53	25.23	26.57	0.78
	1975	957.0	18.67	0.91	3.69	5.68	70.65	12.52	26.10	32.03	0.40
17 – Syrian Arab Republic	1970	350.0	28.59	5.71	8.02	9.96	47.60	9.53	19.93	18.14	0.11
	1975	1669.1	21.38	3.10	6.51	11.58	57.23	11.69	16.74	28.79	0.20
18 – Tunisia	1970	304.6	27.86	5.50	4.84	8.59	53.17	7.41	19.52	26.24	0.05
	1975	1417.8	18.72	3.21	10.40	7.58	60.08	7.96	19.67	32.45	0.01
19 – Yemen	1971	37.0	43.78	1.31	4.57	3.47	42.48	5.09	23.54	13.85	4.39
	1975	293.9	45.42	0.11	5.04	3.03	46.26	5.59	25.07	15.60	0.14
Total (millions of dollars)	1970[b]	7644.8	1630.1	317.0	511.6	659.2	4387.9	583.2	1652.7	2152.2	139.5
	1975[c]	35705.8	7490.7	961.3	1920.7	3215.4	21947.6	2494.5	7171.9	12280.5	170.7
Percentage shares	1970[b]	100.0	21.3	4.1	6.7	8.6	57.4	7.6	21.6	28.2	1.8
	1975[c]	100.0	21.0	2.7	5.4	9.0	61.5	7.0	20.1	34.4	0.5

[a] Excluding UAE and Djibouti for lack of data. [b] These are approximate estimates for the following reasons: (i) Data for 1970 were not available for all Arab countries. Consequently, in some cases data for other years were used, as follows: PDRY: 1968, Oman and North Yemen: 1971, Bahrain: 1972. (ii) Import values for each commodity group in each country have been obtained by means of the percentages shown in the table. These values were then used to calculate the total for each group and its share in the grand total. [c] These are approximate estimates for the following reasons: (i) Data for 1975 were not available for all Arab countries. Consequently, in some cases data for other years were used, as follows: PDRY: 1968, Mauritania: 1972, Lebanon: 1973. (ii) See (ii) under note [b].

Source: United Nations, *Handbook of International Trade and Development Statistics 1979*, (New York: UN, 1979), pp. 152-94. Taken from: El-Homsi, *Arab Development Plans. Integrative and Non-integrative Aspects of their Orientation*, table 2-4, pp. 58-9.

Table 9.4: Inter-Arab Trade and its Importance Relative to the Overall Trade of the Arab World, 1960 and 1977 (millions of dollars)

Country	1960 Exports	1960 Imports	1977 Exports	1977 Imports
1 – Algeria	–	–	–	–
2 – Bahrain	–	–	250.3	17.6
3 – Democratic Yemen	2.0	9.4	19.0	66.0
4 – Djibouti	–	–	–	–
5 – Egypt	56.3	55.1	150.3	134.7
6 – Iraq	7.5	1.5	36.2[a]	67.1
7 – Jordan	5.9	24.1	114.8	230.2
8 – Kuwait	281.9	422.1	871.5	118.2
9 – Lebanon	0.1	47.6	665.0	–
10 – Libya	1.4	5.4	–	–
11 – Mauritania	–	–	–	–
12 – Morocco	3.3	1.2	33.1	204.8
13 – Oman	–	–	3.3	160.8
14 – Qatar	–	–	–	124.0
15 – Saudi Arabia	173.0	74.6	1490.0	1879.0
16 – Somalia	–	–	–	–
17 – Sudan	0.1	–	–	–
18 – Syrian Arab Republic	50.6	39.8	138.1	396.4
19 – Tunisia	10.4	2.9	48.5	8.7
20 – United Arab Emirates	–	–	–	314.0
21 – Yemen	–	–	1.3	123.3
(1) Total flow between Arab countries	592.5[e]	683.8[e]	3811.4[b]	3844.8[c]
(2) Total trade of Arab countries	2763.6[e]	9589.6[e]	91393.6[d]	59635.4[d]
Ratio of (1) to (2)	21.4%	7.1%	4.10%	6.4%

[a] Excluding oil. [b] Includes 13 Arab countries: Bahrain, Democratic Yemen, Egypt, Iraq, Jordan, Kuwait, Lebanon, Morocco, Oman, Saudi Arabia, Syrian Arab Republic, Tunisia and Yemen. [c] Includes 14 Arab countries: Bahrain, Democratic Yemen, Egypt, Iraq, Jordan, Kuwait, Morocco, Oman, Qatar, Saudi Arabia, Syrian Arab Republic, Tunisia, United Arab Emirates and Yemen. [d] Includes 20 Arab countries (all those listed in the table). [e] Includes 12 Arab countries: Democratic Yemen, Egypt, Iraq, Jordan, Kuwait, Lebanon, Libya, Morocco, Saudi Arabia, Sudan, Syrian Arab Republic and Tunisia.
Source: Federation of Arab Chambers of Commerce, Industry and Agriculture. Taken from El-Homsi, *Arab Development Plans: Integrative and Non-integrative Aspects of their Orientation*, Table 2-5, p. 62.

Agreement, the Arab Customs Union, a number of joint ventures, bilateral trade agreements, and the existence of free trade zones, the Arab economies are not sufficiently open to each other and that trade links between them have actually weakened. In the view of the author, this reflects first of all the failure of the arrangements just mentioned.

One of the drawbacks of the Arab Economic Unity Agreement is that it does not provide for a transitional period during which the policies of the participating countries can be co-ordinated. Instead, it allows participating countries to conclude bilateral trade agreements with non-participating countries, as well as to grant preferential treatment to them. Also, decisions under the Agreement are non-binding and are treated as mere recommendations. In practice, little has been achieved concerning the free movement of goods and factors of production among the Arab countries.

The Arab Common Market has done very little to redress this situation. Free movement is provided only for goods. Movements of capital and labour are still restricted. Members of the Common Market are permitted to extend preferential treatment to non-members, and thus members and non-members are placed on an equal footing. Moreover, the choice of commodities to be placed on the tax exemption list is effected haphazardly. This has encouraged applications for further exemptions, without any consideration being given to the economic interests of the group. The Agreement has also failed to standardise customs duties among the member countries.

The low volume of inter-Arab trade also reflects important differences in Arab trade regimes. Thus, while in some countries, foreign trade is exclusively a public sector activity, in others public sector control is minimal. Under some regimes, foreign exchange is strictly controlled, whereas under others it is a free market operation; and, while some countries apply export promotion and import control measures, others do not follow these policies.[7]

Moreover, despite numerous conferences, bilateral agreements, etc., the foreign trade policies of each Arab country remain fixed along narrow nationalistic lines. As a result, any move towards Arab economic integration will be governed to a large extent by political considerations. It should, however, be noted that the present nationalistic political orientation is only one among many reasons responsible for the lack of progress towards Arab economic unity. The substantial differences among Arab economic, social and political systems have also vitiated efforts to achieve the proclaimed objectives of the Arab Economic Unity Treaty. These differences have often led to the pursuit of conflicting economic and development policies by individual Arab countries. Therefore, successful economic integration will require fundamental changes in the economic structures of the Arab countries and co-ordination of their economic, trade, financial, monetary and development policies, all of which can be achieved only through an independent political will to achieve Arab unity.[8]

II. The Balance-of-payments Positions of the Arab Countries[9]

It is customary to classify the Arab countries into two categories: those with surpluses in their balance of payments and those with deficits. The first category comprises mainly the oil-producing countries, while the second category is made up principally of the non-oil-producing countries.

Table 9.5: Current Account Balances of the Arab Countries for the Years 1970-7 (millions of dollars)

Country and year	Trade balance	Net services	Net private transfers	Current account balance (A)	Net government transfers	Current account balance (B)
	(1)	(2)	(3)	(4)=(1)+(2)+(3)	(5)	(6)=(4)+(5)
Algeria						
1970	−65.0	−324.0	251.0	−138.0	12.0	−126.0
1971	−173.5	−264.8	284.8	−153.5	196.6	43.1
1972	−96.6	−329.0	288.8	−136.8	13.0	−123.8
1973	−308.8	−515.0	416.1	−407.7	−35.8	443.5
1974	934.5	−744.4	395.7	585.7	−425.7	160.0
1975	−1010.2	−1075.7	437.1	−1648.8	−12.1	−1660.9
1976	509.1	−1854.2	475.7	−869.4	−13.9	−883.3
1977	−272.0	−2374.7	343.3	−2303.5	−17.5	−2321.0
Democratic Yemen						
1970	−35.6	−25.4	52.1	−8.9	–	−8.9
1971	−47.8	−7.6	43.8	−11.6	1.0	−10.6
1972	−39.6	−15.9	27.1	−28.3	–	−28.3
1973	−67.1	−17.4	32.9	−51.6	0.5	−51.1
1974	−128.2	−13.8	41.1	−100.9	0.6	−100.3
1975	..	..	..	..	..	..
1976	..	..	..	..	..	..
1977	..	..	..	..	..	..
Egypt						
1970	−267.0	−195.0	4.0	−485.0	304.0	−154.0
1971	−280.8	−204.6	11.0	−474.4	267.8	−206.6
1972	−357.2	−108.6	5.4	−460.3	289.9	−170.4
1973	−429.2	−134.7	6.0	−557.9	635.4	77.5
1974	−1242.3	−120.2	42.1	−1320.5	993.4	−327.1
1975	−2373.7	−99.5	89.8	−2383.4	985.9	−1397.5
1976	−2232.8	715.8	86.6	−1430.4	623.4	−807.0
1977	−2128.4	869.8	60.7	−1197.9	384.1	−813.8

Table 9.5: continued

Country and year	Trade balance (1)	Net services (2)	Net private transfers (3)	Current account balance (A) (4)=(1)+(2)+(3)	Net government transfers (5)	Current account balance (B) (6)=(4)+(5)
Iraq						
1970	635.0	−536.0	1.0	100.0	1.0	101.0
1971	914.7	−724.2	3.0	193.6	1.0	193.6
1972	697.0	−154.2	2.2	545.0	1.1	546.1
1973	1354.3	−543.6	1.2	811.8	−10.7	801.1
1974	4226.1	−1372.2	2.4	2856.3	−236.9	2619.4
1975	4139.0	−1169.3	1.2	2971.0	−265.9	2705.1
1976	..	..	..	..	..	..
1977	..	..	..	..	..	..
Jordan						
1970	−129.7	0.7	4.4	126.0	109.4	−16.6
1971	−158.4	−3.8	3.1	−159.0	99.4	−59.6
1972	−189.6	1.9	6.5	−181.1	184.7	3.6
1973	−219.1	33.6	10.6	−174.9	186.2	11.3
1974	−277.1	15.4	7.1	−254.6	263.5	8.9
1975	−496.0	125.3	5.7	−365.0	432.0	67.0
1976	−700.9	402.2	11.3	−287.4	369.3	81.9
1977	−976.2	488.0	−3.6	−491.8	507.4	15.6
Kuwait						
1970	..	..	..	..	..	..
1971	..	..	..	..	..	..
1972	..	..	..	..	..	..
1973	..	..	..	..	..	..
1974	..	..	..	..	..	..
1975	6082.9	876.6	−275.6	6683.9	−792.8	5891.1
1976	6378.7	1130.2	−315.2	7193.8	−222.8	6971.0
1977	5796.7	835.9	−370.1	6263.6	−806.8	5456.8
Libya						
1970	1723.0	−920.0	−45.0	758.0	−113.0	645.0
1971	1784.3	−862.6	−48.1	873.6	−90.3	873.3
1972	1179.1	−787.2	−52.1	339.8	−102.1	237.7
1973	1516.4	−1250.5	−44.1	221.7	−156.2	65.5
1974	3467.2	−1429.9	−137.1	1900.2	−68.6	−1968.8
1975	1993.6	−1866.1	−37.6	−95.9	−163.9	−259.8
1976	4470.3	−1854.1	−36.9	2579.2	−144.3	2434.9
1977	5169.8	−2073.6	−39.7	3056.6	−151.8	2904.8

312 *External Economic and Monetary Positions*

Table 9.5: continued

Country and year	Trade balance (1)	Net services (2)	Net private transfers (3)	Current account balance (A) (4)=(1)+(2)+(3)	Net government transfers (5)	Current account balance (B) (6)=(4)+(5)
Mauritania						
1970	25.2	−32.7	−5.3	−12.8	7.9	−4.9
1971	..	..	..	..	..	..
1972	..	..	..	..	..	..
1973	11.7	−28.3	−14.3	−30.9	45.2	14.3
1974	20.4	−29.8	−12.7	−22.1	69.4	47.3
1975	−41.0	−84.3	−20.6	−145.9	79.3	−66.6
1976	−90.3	−117.7	−26.1	−234.1	149.9	−84.2
1977	−124.3	−85.3	−26.3	−236.0	113.8	−122.2
Morocco						
1970	−137.0	−60.0	69.0	−128.0	4.0	−124.0
1971	−137.4	−31.1	106.3	−62.2	3.0	−59.2
1972	−67.3	−22.8	137.9	47.8	−	47.8
1973	−124.0	−23.9	237.2	89.4	7.2	96.6
1974	−14.4	−115.5	323.5	222.5	6.0	228.5
1975	−734.6	−306.0	512.4	−528.2	−4.9	−533.1
1976	−1031.0	−842.8	527.6	−1346.2	−23.1	−1369.3
1977	−1537.6	−879.1	574.4	−1842.3	−29.2	−1871.5
Saudi Arabia						
1970	1260.0	−925.0	−183.0	152.0	−81.0	71.0
1971	2639.8	−1454.3	−207.6	977.9	−68.2	909.7
1972	3053.0	−1155.2	−267.1	1630.7	−157.4	1473.3
1973	5427.8	−2344.1	−392.2	2701.4	−498.3	2203.1
1974	26378.7	−1838.8	−518.3	24021.5	−1015.0	1406.5
1975	21151.7	−3240.6	−852.3	17058.8	−3127.6	13931.2
1976	25070.4	−6741.1	−1473.2	17126.1	−3328.5	13797.6
1977	25729.8	−7546.9	−1503.8	16679.2	−3886.7	12792.5˙
Somalia						
1970	−9.3	−9.3	0.7	−17.9	12.2	−5.7
1971	−11.4	−7.1	2.1	−16.3	17.2	0.9
1972	−6.3	−17.9	1.8	−22.4	15.2	−7.2
1973	−40.4	−26.9	2.7	−64.6	25.9	−38.7
1974	−69.8	−33.6	3.5	−99.9	48.2	−51.7
1975	−52.5	−49.8	1.9	−100.3	100.3	0.0
1976	−72.0	−38.0	1.2	−108.9	39.7	−69.2
1977	−107.8	−33.3	2.2	−138.8	105.9	−32.9

Table 9.5: continued

Country and year	Trade balance (1)	Net services (2)	Net private transfers (3)	Current account balance (A) (4)=(1)+(2)+(3)	Net government transfers (5)	Current account balance (B) (6)=(4)+(5)
Sudan						
1970	16.1	−58.3	−1.2	−43.4	1.5	−41.9
1971	15.4	−55.2	−0.9	−40.6	−1.4	−42.0
1972	8.0	−66.8	0.7	−58.2	6.3	−51.9
1973	106.7	−83.7	3.9	26.9	−1.7	−25.2
1974	−157.3	−139.0	2.5	−293.8	18.4	−275.4
1975	−331.3	−144.4	−0.4	−476.1	45.9	−430.2
1976	−36.4	−148.5	−0.1	−185.0	20.3	−164.7
1977	16.6	−107.6	−0.1	−92.1	20.4	−71.7
Syrian Arab Republic						
1970	−136.0	56.0	7.0	−73.0	3.0	−70.0
1971	−185.6	98.3	8.0	−79.2	21.1	−58.1
1972	−146.6	91.2	39.1	−16.3	44.5	28.2
1973	−212.2	150.2	37.0	−25.0	363.6	338.6
1974	−256.2	−37.3	44.5	−248.9	416.1	167.2
1975	−495.4	−117.8	52.2	−560.9	654.4	93.5
1976	−1036.8	−190.5	53.1	−1174.1	401.8	−772.3
1977	−1528.3	135.4	92.2	−1300.6	1136.0	−164.6
Tunisia						
1970	−105.0	−6.0	27.0	−84.0	31.0	−53.0
1971	−120.4	56.2	49.1	−15.0	21.1	6.1
1972	−140.1	50.0	59.7	−30.4	26.1	−4.3
1973	−206.2	14.3	93.0	−98.9	38.1	−60.8
1974	−119.1	15.6	111.8	8.4	20.4	28.8
1975	−452.9	95.9	136.0	−221.0	37.6	−183.4
1976	−620.0	53.1	130.5	−436.4	48.5	−387.9
1977	−812.6	78.2	156.4	−577.9	44.4	−533.5

Table 9.5: continued

Country and year	Trade balance (1)	Net services (2)	Net private transfers (3)	Current account balance (A) (4)=(1)+(2)+(3)	Net government transfers (5)	Current account balance (B) (6)=(4)+(5)
Yemen						
1970	..	..	..	..	..	..
1971	..	..	..	..	..	..
1972	..	..	..	..	..	..
1973	..	..	..	..	..	..
1974	−181.8	−12.2	135.5	−58.6	53.3	−5.3
1975	−232.3	−25.7	271.6	13.6	116.9	130.5
1976	−461.8	−21.2	677.7	194.7	102.8	297.5
1977	−705.2	−62.6	948.3	180.5	119.9	300.4

Note: A dash (−) indicates that the amount is nil or negligible; two dots (..) indicate that the data are not available or are not separately reported.
Source: UNCTAD, *Handbook of International Trade and Development Statistics, 1979*, pp. 332-82.

Beginning with the first category, this group enjoys high purchasing power, high ability to import and large accumulated foreign currency reserves at both the government and the private level. Their most striking characteristic is, however, their large current account surpluses. In 1979, the surpluses in the current accounts of four Arab oil-producing countries alone, Saudi Arabia, Kuwait, the UAE and Qatar, amounted to an estimated $36 billion.[10]

The countries in the second category, those with current account deficits, export primarily agricultural products and raw materials of agricultural origin, and their economies are already strongly dependent on the Western countries. Savings and investments in these countries are at relatively low levels, whereas they are in need of large investments to build their infrastructures, pay for imports, especially of capital goods and intermediate products, and support their chronic balance-of-payments deficits.[11] They frequently resort to short-term loans from Western money markets to meet balance-of-payments deficits and development expenditures. Even some of the oil-producing countries, notably Iraq (in 1975) and Algeria (often) rely on this source.[12]

In 1973, the aggregate external debt of ten Arab countries reached $12 billion. Debt service reached an amount equivalent to about 3 per cent of the value of total exports for Iraq, and 35 per cent for Egypt.[13]

In 1977, the foreign debt of 12 Arab countries amounted to more than $27 billion. In that year, the ratio of foreign debt to GNP was 4 per cent for Iraq, 42.5 per cent for Algeria, 69 per cent for Egypt and 93 per cent for Somalia. If the two oil producers, Iraq and Algeria, are excluded, the foreign indebtedness of the rest, which are the original deficit countries, would amount to over $18 billion.[14] This represents more than 41 per cent of the combined GNP of the countries concerned in 1977. In the same year, debt service was equivalent to 22.8 per cent of the value of total exports for Egypt, 15.5 per cent for Algeria, 10.9 and 10.7 per cent for Morocco and Somalia, respectively, and 8.7 and 8.8 per cent for Sudan and Tunisia, respectively. In the remaining countries the percentage was smaller.[15]

While some of the surplus funds of the first category do flow to the deficit countries in the second category, as shall be seen below, most of these funds flow to the West. Specifically, these surpluses are either held in the current deposit accounts of international banks and financial institutions or invested in foreign government securities, real estate, and industrial, agricultural and tourist ventures. They are placed mainly in the Western European countries, particularly the countries of the European Economic Community, the United States and Japan.[16] Arab investments in international markets amounted to about $43 billion in 1979,[17] while their total accumulated investments in these markets through that year amounted to about $209 billion. In other words, these industrialised countries secure Arab oil for their energy needs and then receive the money paid for this energy back again, either as payments for their exports to the Arab countries or in the form of Arab investments on their territory.

There are many reasons for Arab surpluses seeking investment in the Western monetary and financial markets, among which are the limited capacity of local economies to absorb all the oil revenues, the lack of investment guarantees in the Arab countries, conflicting political systems and the lack of well-studied economic projects.[18] Ironically, however, the risks involved in investing Arab funds abroad are no less serious, and indeed can be more serious, than those involved in investment locally. To begin with, there are, in addition to the commercial risks, potential political risks. These include possible expropriation and the freezing of funds. Foremost among the commercial risks, on the other hand, one can cite exchange-rate fluctuations, which now beset all Western currencies, and particularly the serious decline in the value of the dollar. Moreover, a large portion of the surpluses has already become 'sunk investment', i.e., committed to fixed liabilities. These surpluses cannot be retrieved easily or without substantial loss.

Thus we have seen that while costs incurred by Arab countries are

Table 9.6: Balance of Payments and Debt Service in Selected Arab Countries

Country	Current account balance prior to payment of interest on public foreign debt (millions of dollars)		Interest paid on public foreign debt (millions of dollars)		Debt service			
					As a percentage of GNP		As a percentage of exports of goods and services	
	1970	1977	1970	1977	1970	1977	1970	1977
Algeria	−116	−1935	10	387	0.8	5.3	3.2	15.5
Democratic Yemen	−9	−92	—	—	—	—	—	—
Egypt	−116	−529	38	285	4.1	8.8	28.7	22.8
Iraq	110	1209	9	13	0.9	0.6	2.2	1.1
Jordan	−15	30	2	16	0.7	1.7	3.6	3.2
Kuwait	—	5483	—	—	—	—	—	—
Lebanon	—	−23	1	2	0.2	—	0.5	0.7
Libya	245	2905	—	—	—	—	—	—
Morocco	−101	−1743	23	129	1.8	2.4	7.7	10.9
Saudi Arabia	71	12791	—	—	—	—	—	—
Somalia	−6	−31	—	2	0.5	2.6	2.1	10.7
Sudan	−30	−443	12	25	1.2	1.5	10.1	8.7
Syrian Arab Republic	−64	−137	6	27	2.1	1.4	10.8	6.7
Tunisia	−36	−476	17	59	4.4	3.1	17.1	8.8
Yemen	—	3.3	—	1	—	—	—	—

Source: IBRD, *Annual Report on World Development 1979* (Washington: IBRD, 1979), Table 13 (in Arabic).

Table 9.7: Public Foreign Debt in Selected Arab Countries for 1977

Country	Public foreign debt		
	In millions of dollars	As a percentage of GNP	As a percentage of exports of goods and services
Algeria	8165	42.5	15.5
Democratic Yemen	291	50.3	–
Egypt	8099	69.2	22.8
Iraq	761	4.0	1.1
Jordan	645	29.4	3.2
Lebanon	39	–	0.7
Morocco	3469	36.0	10.9
Somalia	401	92.6	10.7
Sudan	1732	35.4	8.7
Syrian Arab Republic	1528	20.7	6.7
Tunisia	1942	39.9	8.8
Yemen	147	14.6	0.2
Total	27219	–	–

Source: IBRD, *Report on World Development 1979*, Table 15, pp. 38 and 39, Table 13, pp. 34 and 35.

substantial indeed, relative to both GNP and to total exports, large Arab surpluses are being transferred and accumulated abroad for lack of local opportunities.

III. The Flow of Financial Resources among Arab Countries

The question arises now as to the magnitude of the flow of financial resources between the surplus and the deficit Arab countries[19] and the extent to which these flows have been adequate to meet the balance-of-payments deficits in the latter countries and to support their socio-economic development. There are three indicators of the flow of financial resources from the surplus to the deficit Arab countries: first, government and private transfers; secondly, government and private loans and loans extended by various Arab development funds; and, thirdly, loans from the Arab Monetary Fund (AMF). However, the special nature of AMF loans has to be borne in mind.

For the period 1970-7, five Arab surplus countries show a large increase in net government transfers abroad, especially after 1974.[20] Most of these transfers have been earmarked for the Arab deficit countries, particularly for those classified as 'confrontation' states in the struggle against the Zionist entity. Iraq, Saudi Arabia and Kuwait figure prominently among the five with the largest transfers showing in the current account of their balance of payments.

The net private transfers abroad of the oil-producing countries also represented a considerable sum over the same period. This is particularly true for Saudi Arabia, Libya and Kuwait. For Saudi Arabia alone, these transfers amounted to about $1.5 billion in 1976 and again in 1977. If private transfers are added to government transfers, the figure for each of these two years will, for Saudi Arabia alone, be in the range of $5 billion. These transfers have undoubtedly mitigated the balance-of-payments deficits of the recipient countries. Nevertheless, the sums transferred represent only a small fraction of the total deficit of the non-oil Arab countries.

With regard to the second indicator, development loans, in the period 1970 to 1977, seven countries — Iraq, Algeria, Kuwait, Saudi Arabia, Qatar, Libya and the UAE — supplied together loans amounting to $26.8 billion for development purposes. A considerable portion of these claims went to the non-oil Arab countries.[21] They were channelled either directly through bilateral agreements or by Arab development funds. Total loans by six of these funds amounted to about $4.6 billion between 1962 and 1977. Up to 1979, allocations were as shown in Table 9.11. Roughly $4.2 billion of this amount was granted during the period 1975-7. This indicates a large increase in the funds' allocations after the substantial increase in oil revenues beginning in 1973.

Until 1976-7, between 53 and 100 per cent of the loans granted by the Arab funds went to 15 Arab countries. After this period, loan facilities were extended to non-Arab developing countries as well. As a result, the share of the non-oil Arab countries in the total loans by the funds declined to not more than 50 per cent. The loans which were granted for the development of socio-economic infrastructures, agriculture and industry, were made subject to minimal conditions.[22]

The volume of the loans granted by Arab development funds began to decline in the first half of 1978. Various reasons have been given for this decline. The loanable funds of these institutions, it is claimed, were in most cases committed to operations and projects of a long-term nature. Furthermore, the institutions did not entertain the idea of borrowing, whether in local or international markets.[23]

In any case, the loans made available by these Arab development funds do not represent more than a small part of the non-oil Arab countries' development needs. Moreover, the flow of private loans from the surplus to the deficit Arab countries is very meagre, a fact which stems from the inadequacy of the present set-up and from differences in the economic, financial and monetary policies of the Arab countries.

Finally, let us examine the role of the Arab Monetary Fund and its contribution towards improving the financial situation in the deficit

Table 9.8: Current Account Balance and Monetary Surplus for Kuwait, Qatar, Saudi Arabia and UAE, 1973-9[a] (billions of dollars)

	1973	1974	1975	1976	1977	1978	1979[a]
Exports	14	49	45	56	62	60	95
of which: oil and gas	13	48	44	55	60	58	93
Imports	4	7	11	17	24	30	35
Trade balance	10	42	34	39	38	30	60
Service payments and net official and private transfers	−4	−4	−10	−13	−17	−20	−24
Current account balance	6	38	24	26	21	10	36

[a] Figures for 1979 are estimates.
Source: Bank of England, *Quarterly Bulletin* (June 1980), p. 154, Table A.

Table 9.9: Current Account Balance and Monetary Surplus Available for Investment in Oil-exporting Countries, 1973–9[a] (billions of dollars)

	1973	1974	1975	1976	1977	1978	1979[a]
Exports	41	123	113	138	154	148	225
of which: oil and gas	37	116	107	130	144	138	213
Imports	22	39	59	74	89	104	105
Trade balance	19	84	54	64	65	44	120
Service payments and private transfers (net)	–12	–15	–22	–26	–36	–43	–43
Net government transfers	–1	–2	–3	–3	–2	–2	–3
Current account balance	6	67	29	35	–27	–1	74
Net external loans from banks	—	–12	4	10	11	18	8
Miscellaneous adjustments	—	—	3	–6	—	–2	3
Monetary surplus available for investment	—	55	36	39	38	19	79

[a] Figures for 1979 are estimates.
Source: Bank of England, *Quarterly Bulletin* (June 1980), p. 154.

Table 9.10: Net Loans Granted by the Arab Oil Countries to the Developing Countries and to Multilateral Agencies 1970–7 (millions of dollars)

	Algeria	Iraq	Kuwait	Libya	Qatar	Saudi Arabia	United Arab Emirates	Total
1) Concessional								
1970	1.0	2.0	130.0	63.0	–	155.0	–	
1973	25.4	11.1	345.2	214.6	93.7	304.9	288.6	
1974	46.9	422.9	621.5	147.0	185.2	1029.1	510.6	
1975	40.7	218.4	975.3	261.1	333.9	1997.4	1046.1	
1976	53.6	231.7	614.3	93.6	195.0	2407.1	1060.2	
1977	46.7	53.4	1441.8	109.4	117.6	2373.0	1261.8	
2) Non-concessional								
1970	–	–	10.2	229.0	0.1	–2.5	–	
1973	4.4	–	210.5	189.2	–	30.0	–	
1974	4.5	17.3	564.6	116.2	32.7	593.0	238.8	
1975	1.5	36.0	735.9	101.7	27.8	469.3	160.5	
1976	13.0	23.0	1260.4	269.6	45.3	410.2	84.3	
1977	28.8	63.1	475.7	161.3	73.5	369.7	175.2	
3) Total (1+2)								
1970	1.0	2.0	140.2	292.0	0.1	152.5	–	587.8
1973	29.8	11.1	555.7	403.8	93.7	334.9	288.6	1717.6
1974	51.4	440.2	1186.1	263.2	217.9	1622.1	749.4	4530.3
1975	42.2	254.4	1711.2	362.8	366.7	2466.7	1206.6	6410.6
1976	66.6	254.7	1874.7	363.2	240.3	2817.3	1144.5	6761.3
1977	75.5	116.5	1917.5	270.7	196.1	2742.7	1437.0	6756.0
Total	266.5	1078.9	7385.4	1955.7	1114.8	10136.2	4826.1	26763.6

OPEC countries (the Arab countries listed plus Nigeria, Venezuela and Iran only)   32121.2
Ratio of Arab oil countries to total OPEC countries   83.32%

Source: UNCTAD, Handbook of International Trade and Development Statistics, 1979.

Table 9.11: Allocation of Development Loans to 1979 (millions of dollars)

	Loan commitments	Number of loans	Number of recipient countries
National funds			
Abu Dhabi Fund for Arab Economic Development	406.0	45	24
Development Fund of Saudi Arabia	1,586.0	54	29
Kuwait Fund for Arab Economic Development	1,560.0	114	40
Regional funds			
Arab Bank for Development in Africa	209.6	29	21
Arab Development Fund	1,018.0	48	14
Islamic Bank	74.0	12	11

Source: International Monetary Fund, *International Monetary Fund Survey*, vol. 8, no. 3 (5 February 1979), pp. 36 and 37.

Table 9.12: Distribution of AMF Loans as of 30 November 1980

Recipient country	Type of loan	Date of loan	Amount (AAD)	Amount (SDR)
Egypt	Automatic (1)	14/7/78	4,687,500	14,062,500
Sudan	Automatic (1)	16/8/78	1,875,000	5,625,000
Mauritania	Automatic (1)	17/1/79	750,000	2,250,000
Morocco	Automatic (1)	6/2/79	1,875,000	5,625,000
Syria	Automatic (1)	19/4/79	750,000	2,250,000
Sudan	Automatic (2)	29/9/79	1,875,000	5,625,000
Sudan	Extended	18/10/79	11,250,000	33,750,000
Mauritania	Automatic (2)	26/2/80	750,000	2,250,000
Mauritania	Ordinary	28/4/80	4,500,000	13,500,000
Somalia	Automatic (1)	14/6/80	1,500,000	4,500,000
Sudan	Compensatory	10/11/80	5,000,000	15,000,000
			34,812,500	104,437,500

Source: Arab Monetary Fund

Arab countries. The AMF annual report for 1979 shows that its total loans for that year exceeded AAD 23 million.[24] The distribution of AMF loans since its creation in 1977 is shown in Table 9.12. These figures indicate that the role played by the AMF has been rather limited. This may be largely explained by the newness of the institution and its relatively small capital base.

Another indication of the inadequacy of the present flow of loans among Arab countries is the increase in the loans which are extended by international financial houses, to Arab governments and to the private sectors both. Between 1971 and 1978, these totalled about $16.5 billion, excluding those concluded outside the banking system. If it is borne in mind that the flow of Arab financial surpluses to the United States, Europe and Japan in 1978 was between $145 and $150 billion,[25] and if these sums are compared with total Arab loans to the same markets, it will be clear how unsatisfactory the present state of affairs is.

Not only is the volume of surpluses utilised in the interest of the Arab countries inadequate but the procedures imposed for obtaining such funds are highly complicated. An Arab country can more easily borrow Arab funds through intermediaries and financial houses abroad than directly through Arab financial institutions. The explanation given for this anomalous situation is that Arab financial markets are generally weak or limited, the existing financial infrastructure is inadequate, and the policies pursued by the various Arab countries are conflicting, notwithstanding the efforts made by various Arab organisations to develop them.

Two conclusions can be drawn thus far. First, despite the large financial resources available to the Arab surplus countries, the flow of funds between the surplus and the deficit countries has been inadequate. Secondly, the main countries to benefit from the Arab surpluses have so far been the United States, the West European countries and Japan. These countries receive back what they pay out for crude oil through payments for their exports, and by attracting Arab surplus funds. One can really speak of two flows out of the Arab region: the flow of oil, followed by the flow of surplus funds. Thus, to all intents and purposes, it is Western financial institutions (private and public) which have benefited from the recycling of the Arab surplus funds.

IV. The Role of Financial Surpluses in Achieving Arab Monetary Unity

In the light of the preceding discussion, the following conclusions concerning the Arab economies may be made:

(a) The economies of both the oil-producing and the non-oil-producing Arab countries are in a state of dependency;
(b) The volume of inter-Arab trade relative to the region's trade with the rest of the world has declined;
(c) While the balance-of-payments positions of the oil-producing countries, and especially the Gulf countries, are strong, the situation in other Arab countries is unsatisfactory. Except for Lebanon, which is a special case, and Yemen, whose position has been affected by the large private and public transfers in its current account, little improvement has taken place in the external positions of the non-oil-producing Arab countries in the past two decades;
(d) The oil-producing countries enjoy substantial financial surpluses which are at present directed towards the financial markets of the Western industrialised countries. The proportion of these surpluses channelled to the deficit Arab countries is minimal.

The question which now arises is: to what extent can the Arab surplus funds be instrumental in realising Arab monetary integration? Would monetary integration be a cause or a consequence of Arab economic unity and if the surplus funds cannot help to achieve monetary integration, what other forms of monetary co-operation can they help to bring about?

Individual Arab economists and national and regional institutions all agree that the establishment of monetary integration, i.e., complete monetary unity including all Arab countries, is premature at this stage. The reasons given are the wide disparities in Arab economic, financial, monetary and development policies on the one hand, and the absence of the necessary political will, on the other.[26] Given these obstacles, it is the view of a number of Arab economists, including the author, that monetary union can only come as the culmination of the process of economic integration. By economic integration is meant the abolition of tariff and quota restrictions leading to free trade and free capital movements. This, in turn, would make possible the full inter-convertibility of the Arab currencies and eventually the creation of a common currency. When that day comes, moreover, monetary integration should mean more than the mere creation of a unified Arab currency. It should mean consistent and co-ordinated economic policies and the existence of a supreme body responsible for drawing up and implementing those policies. It should pave the way, once economic unity is achieved, for the full political unity of the Arab countries.[27]

Since monetary integration, as has been explained, should come as the culmination of the process of economic integration, and since the latter process is, by its very nature, a gradual one, the existence of

Arab surpluses cannot be expected, for the time being, to constitute an incentive to overall Arab monetary integration. The question remains: could not these surplus funds help to bring about a certain degree of Arab monetary co-operation? The answer is in the affirmative, for the following reasons:

First, the Arab surpluses could be used to provide short-term loans to support the balance-of-payments deficits of the non-oil Arab countries. This support can and must be effected by the AMF through the expansion of its lending operations. However, before this can be done, more funds must first be made available to the AMF. The AMF should advance these loans for two types of balance-of-payments deficit: temporary deficits and chronic deficits. Short-term loans should only be provided to meet the former. For the latter, medium-terms loans should be provided. Countries should also be requested to revise their economic structures and to reform their trade, monetary and fiscal policies to redress any imbalances. Loans through the AMF should be preferred to direct loans or bilateral arrangements among the Arab countries. This would help to orient the Arab countries towards common action with a view to achieving eventual monetary and economic unity.[28]

Secondly, the surplus countries should provide long-term loans and grants to support the deficit countries. This could be done either directly between the governments concerned or through development funds. However, these latter institutions should be reorganised, with a view to establishing a central development-financing institution to replace the present multiplicity of development funds. The management of the surplus funds should be made the responsibility of this central body, so that it could allocate the funds centrally to meet the needs of the deficit countries. The funds would be used to achieve balanced and consistent Arab development aiming at Arab economic integration in the long run. Perhaps the most appropriate candidate for this position is the Arab Fund for Social and Economic Development. This fund could be turned into a central development bank with large financial resources and high-level expertise.[29] Since oil revenues and hence Arab oil surpluses are government-owned, it would be easy for the governments concerned to direct their surpluses through national, regional and international institutions to support the development efforts of the Arab countries. By the same token, governments should be able to facilitate the movement of the surpluses within the region. Of course, the security of the funds and their earnings, as well as their convertibility into other currencies — or into a central currency when available — should be guaranteed. Thus government assurances and participation by Arab commercial banks are two important prerequisites for facilitating the flow of surplus funds between the Arab countries.

This would help to establish what could be termed an Arab money and financial market, despite prevailing differences in economic, social and political systems.

Would this require the stabilisation of the cross-rates of Arab currencies and the establishment of an Arab monetary zone? And could this take place at the level of the Arab region as a whole, or would it require multiple Arab monetary centres?

The existence of surpluses and deficits among the Arab countries would render the establishment of a monetary zone governing all Arab countries somewhat difficult, first because the exchange rates of the deficit countries tend to be unstable. Secondly, the economic, monetary and financial policies of the Arab countries are widely different. Thirdly, most of the countries concerned suffer from balance-of-payments deficits. And finally, the fixing of exchange-rates would require a large common reserve fund, which is not likely to be established in the near future, for a variety of reasons.

The role that can be played by the AMF is also limited. For the AMF can pursue only its declared objectives. These are (a) to stabilise the cross-rates of Arab currencies; (b) to establish the inter-convertibility of Arab currencies; and (c) to abolish restrictions on current payments among the member countries. In performing its duties, the AMF is severely handicapped by the limited funds available to it relative to the large deficits incurred by the member states.

It has thus far been established that the Arab monetary surpluses, while they cannot at this early stage play a role in fostering overall Arab monetary integration, can nevertheless be utilised to promote monetary co-operation. The question arises as to whether, in addition to this, these surpluses might not be a factor in making monetary integration possible in one region of the Arab world, i.e., the Arab Gulf region.

Some Arab economists believe such a monetary zone is possible.[30] Thanks to their surpluses, which are managed directly by their governments, the Gulf countries, they maintain, are in a strong financial position. Furthermore they do not expect any instability in their balance of payments. Moreover, the economic structures of these countries tend to be similar. All this should encourage them to fix the cross-rates of their currencies.[31]

A prospective Gulf monetary zone should properly comprise all the Gulf countries, including Iraq and Saudi Arabia. These countries are all oil exporters and some have good developmental potential. They could benefit, therefore, from large inflows of capital, while the region could also become the supplier of capital to the rest of the Arab world.

However, while the establishment of a monetary zone and a common currency in the Gulf region is possible, certain economic and non-economic prerequisites must first be met. Measures would have to be taken to create the following conditions: first, the free movement within the zone of all factors of production, e.g., capital and labour; secondly, the full inter-convertibility of the member countries' currencies; thirdly, fixed cross-rates among the currencies concerned, or rates allowing for fluctuations within a narrow margin which would be gradually reduced, the end result being a uniform currency which could be used as a means of exchange, provide a store of value, and serve as legal tender; fourthly, a joint higher council whose decisions would transcend political borders and which would be responsible for making decisions in the economic, financial and monetary spheres, as well as applying them in a consistent and co-ordinated manner to all countries; and fifthly, the establishment of a central monetary body.

The adoption of these measures would require a political decision by member countries, whereby they would make certain concessions with regard to their sovereignty in decision-making in the field of economic, financial and monetary policies. These concessions would be necessary in order to establish fixed exchange rates, leading to the introduction of a common currency.

The concept of a common currency should be distinguished from that of a common accounting unit, e.g. the Arab accounting dinar. The latter does not need a material base. It is a theoretical or formal concept used to measure values. The former requires a strong material base, i.e., a diversified production pattern, a strong and large economy, and abundant foreign and local assets. This should create a large internal and external demand for it, for the purposes of valuation, exchange and savings, resulting in a sufficient supply of the common currency to meet the rising demand in terms of volume, value and strength. Its supply, however, should be elastic enough to meet any expansion in the demand for it inside or outside the economy. Such a growing demand will strengthen the currency in the foreign exchange market and help to stabilise its exchange rate. Then it will be possible to use the unified currency both locally and internationally. It will be universally accepted as a measure of value, as a means of exchange and as a foreign reserve asset.

A common currency would be developed gradually and would coexist with the local currencies while the public became accustomed to its use. Gradually, the amount of the common currency in circulation would be increased until it eventually replaced the local currencies.[32] The common currency would be used by the public to pay government taxes and by public and private financial institutions in their transactions and in valuing their assets and liabilities. Arab central banks, as well as banking institutions in general, would issue securities denominated in the common currency, and governments would do the same. This in turn would help to establish an Arab securities market within the framework of the new common Arab monetary unit.

The common currency would be issued by a central federal bank (similar to the US Federal Reserve Bank). The Arab central banks would become active members in this bank, and contribute to it part of their foreign currency holdings. They would also contribute part of their local currency holdings, against which the federal bank could issue the new common currency. The governments of the countries concerned would be the first to accept the new currency in payment of taxes and liabilities. The commercial banks would include it in their reserves, as a means of creating a short-term money market, and for financial issues with long maturities. When the public gradually began to accept these short- and long-term assets, the federal bank would be in a position to use the securities in its open market operations in the monetary zone. This would facilitate the movement of capital and surplus funds among the countries, which would, in turn, help to establish a financial market at the federal regional level. The federal bank would employ all the aforementioned means to support the local currencies. It would do this in accordance with instructions laid down by a committee composed of local central banks, which would be similar to the Open Market Committee of the US Federal Reserve Bank.

After a period of time, and as the new currency became widely circulated, the federal bank would be able to replace the various local currencies by the new common currency. However, it would still be necessary gradually to co-ordinate monetary policies, on the one hand, and financial, economic and development policies, on the other.

The five prerequisites for monetary co-operation listed earlier have not yet been met by the Gulf countries. The other — and all-important — prerequisite is the existence of the political will to integrate. The history of the Arab region provides several illustrations of the importance of political will. The Gulf countries, as well as the Arab countries in general, were, during the Ottoman period, relatively unified monetarily. There were also, during the British and French colonial era, numerous partially unified monetary zones. Yet, as soon as a measure of political independence was achieved, these unified economic, monetary and financial systems broke up.[33] Later, the United Arab Republic of Syria and Egypt failed to institute monetary unity. While this failure can be partly attributed to economic factors,[34] the major obstacles were political.

In conclusion, then, without the fulfilment of these conditions, both economic and political, it is pointless to talk about a Gulf monetary zone. The attainment of all or most of these conditions, on the other hand, and particularly the political ones, would help to achieve a significant degree of monetary integration in the Gulf and thus lead the way to the eventual monetary integration of all Arab countries.

Notes

1. See Table 9.1.
2. Algeria, Jordan, Lebanon, Mauritania, Morocco, Somalia, the Syrian Arab Republic and Tunisia.
3. Djibouti, Egypt, Sudan and Yemen.
4. See Table 9.2.
5. See Table 9.3a.
6. These figures do not include all Arab countries. See Table 9.4.
7. See Abdul Hamid Brahimi, *Arab Economic Integration and Future Prospects* (Beirut: Centre for Arab Unity Studies, 1980), pp. 136-40 (in Arabic).
8. See Brahimi, *Arab Economic Integration and Future Prospects* pp. 211-29, and, on Arab economic dependency and its consequences, Mahmoud El-Homsi, *Arab Development Plans: Integrative and Non-Integrative Aspects of their Orientation* (Beirut: Centre for Arab Unity Studies, 1980), pp. 52-68 (in Arabic).
9. See Table 9.5 for the current account balances of the countries concerned during the period 1970-8.
10. See Table 9.8. Also, for a detailed study of the balance of payments of oil-producing countries, see Abdul Munim El-Sayyed Ali, *Studies in the Economics of Arab Oil* (Cairo: League of Arab States, Institute for Research and Arabic Studies, 1979), pp. 194-203, and 211-14 (in Arabic).
11. Compare Tables 9.3a and 9.3b regarding differences in the exports and imports of various Arab countries during 1970 and 1975.
12. Algeria, although it is an oil-producing country, registered current account deficits in 1970 and 1977, amounting to $116 million and $1,935 million, respectively. It also frequently borrows to meet development expenditures and external debts. See Table 9.6.
13. See Ali, *Studies in the Economics of Arab Oil*, pp. 240 and 241.
14. See Table 9.7.
15. Ibid.
16. See *International Monetary Fund Survey*, vol. 9, no. 13 (7 July 1980), p. 212 and Bank of England, *Quarterly Bulletin* (June 1980), pp. 154-9.
17. Bank of England, ibid.
18. See the League of Arab States, Arab League Educational, Cultural and Scientific Organisation, Institute for Research and Arabic Studies, *Utilization of Arab Oil Revenues through the End of the Seventies* (Cairo: League of Arab States, Institute for Research and Arabic Studies, 1977), pp. 194-6 (in Arabic).
19. For a detailed discussion of the financial flows between the surplus and the deficit countries, see Ali, *Studies in the Economics of Arab Oil*, pp. 216-41; The League of Arab States, Institute for Research and Arabic Studies, *Utilization of Arab Oil Revenues through the End of the Seventies*, pp. 37-53, 103-21 and 139-70, and Mahmoud Abdul Fadhil, *Oil and Arab Unity: The Effect of Oil on the Future of Unity and Arab Economic Relations* (Beirut: Centre for Arab Unity Studies, 1979) (in Arabic).
20. See Table 9.5.
21. See Table 9.10.
22. IMF, *International Monetary Fund Survey*, vol. 8, no. 3 (5 February 1979), pp. 36 and 37.
23. Total funds granted to developing countries (inclusive of Arab countries)

by six of these Arab development funds (including the Iraqi Fund for Development but excluding the OPEC Special Fund) amounted to about $1,240 million in 1978, and about $1,005 million in 1979. See *Bulletin of the Organization of Arab Petroleum Exporting Countries*, vol. 5, no. 3 (March 1979), pp. 17 and 18 and vol. 6, no. 2 (February 1980), pp. 16 and 17 (in Arabic).

24. One AAD = three SDRs.

25. These figures are based on percentages of totals for all OPEC countries appearing in *Bulletin of the Organization of Petroleum Exporting Countries*, p. 18.

26. See some of the suggestions made in Organisation of Arab Petroleum Exporting Countries, *The Arab Accounting Dinar, Studies and Opinions* (Kuwait: OAPEC, 1979) (in Arabic); Suleiman Hamid Al-Muntheri, *Arab Monetary Cooperation: Scope and Possibilities* (Cairo: League of Arab States, Institute for Research and Arabic Studies, 1978) (in Arabic); Hisham Mitwalli, *Research on Syrian Arab Economies* (Damascus: Ministry of Culture, 1974), pp. 227-67 (in Arabic), and Brahimi, *Arab Economic Integration: Future Prospects*, pp. 107 and 108, 194-204, and especially 378-82 (in Arabic).

27. P. Coffey and J.R. Presley, *European Monetary Integration* (London: Macmillan, 1979), p. 1.

28. See Ali, *Studies in the Economics of Arab Oil*, pp. 262-9.

29. Ibid.

30. See Salim El-Hoss, 'The Gulf Dinar: Concept and Application', a lecture delivered before the Kuwait Chamber of Industry and Commerce, February 1975, in *The Arab Accounting Dinar* (Kuwait: Organization of Arab Petroleum Exporting Countries, [n.d.]), pp. 127-53.

31. Ibid., pp. 136 and 137.

32. E. Magnifico, *European Monetary Unification* (London: Macmillan, 1973), and H.G. Grubel, *The International Monetary System*, 3rd edn. (Harmondsworth: Penguin Books, 1977), pp. 212 and 213.

33. For causes and subsequent developments, see Alfred G. Masri, *The Arab Common Market: A Study in Inter-Arab Trading Relations, 1920-1967*, translated into Arabic by Salib Boutros (Cairo: Dar al Ma-aref, 1975), chap. 3.

34. See M.S. Nabulsi, 'Problems of Integrating the Monetary Systems of Egypt and Syria under the U.A.R. Regime, 1958-1961', *Middle East Economic Papers* (Beirut: The American University of Beirut, 1964).

COMMENT

Karim Nashashibi

One of the strongest arguments in favour of establishing some form of economic integration among countries in a region is that it makes it possible to reap the benefits of the better division of labour and higher efficiency which can result from the dismantling of tariff barriers and the establishment of a common market. Much has already been gained by the vast movements of labour and capital within the Arab world. An analysis of trade flows among the Arab countries over the past two or three decades and of the impact of the oil boom on non-oil intraregional trade can cast much light on the cost/benefit implications of Arab economic integration. Would the establishment of an Arab common market be trade-diverting or trade-creating? And, given the large increase in the demand for imports in Arab countries in the wake of the rise in oil revenues, what is the potential for expanding trade flows among Arab countries? Mr Ali addresses himself to the question of trade flows among Arab countries, but as this is only one of four areas he deals with in his paper, he does not devote too much space to it and relies mostly on the results obtained by Mahmoud El-Homsi in his book on Arab development plans.

I would like, in commenting on the section of Mr Ali's paper dealing with trade, to develop some of the issues which he raises and try to set out some orders of magnitude. From the outset, I should mention that in analysing trade flows among Arab countries in relation to Arab economic integration, it is more useful to focus on those exports which stem from the productive capacity of these countries and on the imports which compete with or supplement this productive capacity. Hence, one must exclude oil from exports and imports, as well as other depletable minerals such as phosphates and iron ore. Since oil accounts for about 90 per cent of all Arab exports and for over 50 per cent of inter-Arab imports, it distorts all trade percentages. It also distorts time series relating to trade because of its disproportionate increase in unit value over the past decade.

In relating the value of foreign trade to GDP, Mr Ali states that the degree of dependence of the Arab economies on foreign trade has increased substantially, especially since 1963. However, he does not distinguish between exports and imports or between oil-exporting and non-oil-exporting countries.

With respect to the exports of the non-oil countries, there is evidence that these as a percentage of GDP have actually been declining for some of the major agricultural exporters, such as Egypt, Sudan and the Syrian Arab Republic. Morocco's exports/GDP ratio declined during the 1960s but seems to have remained constant in the 1970s. The ratios for Jordan and Tunisia, on the other hand, have increased steadily. Nevertheless on average, one may say that exports from non-oil-exporting Arab countries have tended to decline as a proportion of GDP. The imports of these non-oil countries on the other hand, have tended to rise as a proportion of GDP, hence the increase in their trade deficits as a proportion of GDP and in the financing of those deficits.

For the oil-producing countries, it stands to reason that the imports/GDP ratio has declined for those with low absorptive capacity, simply because imports could not possible rise proportionately to the rise in oil revenues. The residual share of their GDP would be made up of factor income going abroad, capital investments abroad and accumulating reserves. This is confirmed in Table 9.2 in the case of Saudi Arabia, Libya, Oman, Qatar and the UAE.

With respect to trends in inter-Arab trade, Mr Ali observes that the ratios of both inter-Arab exports and inter-Arab imports to total exports and imports, respectively, declined between 1960 and 1977. He then concludes that trade links among Arab countries have weakened and that this reflects the failure of the Arab Customs Union and other Arab bilateral and multilateral arrangements. But, as he has included the oil trade in these percentages, a ready answer emerges to explain these declines. The oil component in inter-Arab trade has risen at a slower rate than either exports of oil to the rest of the world or imports from the rest of the world. This is explained by the fact that half of the Arab countries are oil-producers, while some which were major importers of oil have become exporters of oil. For this reason, during the 1950s and 1960s, imports of Arab oil by non-oil Arab countries declined as a proportion of inter-Arab imports. While this relative decline may not have continued during the 1970s, owing to the disproportionate rise in oil prices, the underlying downward trend was such that the actual rise was less than the rise in Arab oil exports as a proportion of total Arab exports. Hence, since oil accounts for about half of total inter-Arab trade, other things being equal, inter-Arab trade as a proportion of both total exports and total imports can only have declined.

Interesting questions arise, however, when oil imports and exports are excluded from inter-Arab trade and from total imports and exports. Has the share of intra-regional exports, excluding oil, declined as a share of total regional exports, excluding oil? Unfortunately, the data presented in the paper do not provide an answer to this question. Some time ago, I constructed trade matrices for 1958 and 1966 in order to study trade patterns in the Middle East and found that the ratio of inter-Arab exports to all exports, excluding oil, was about 15 per cent and had not changed significantly between those two years.[1] However, events have changed dramatically since then, and particularly since the advent of the oil boom. My guess would be that the ratio of inter-Arab exports to total Arab exports has increased as a spillover from the large movements of labour and professional skills among the Arab countries, the liberalisation of payments procedures and the improvements in transportation. While a cursory look at the trade data for Egypt, Jordan, Sudan and the Syrian Arab Republic tends to confirm this view, it would be worthwhile to carry out this analysis systematically for all Arab countries.

On the import side, I found that intra-regional imports as a percentage of total imports, excluding oil again, declined from 7.2 per cent to 5.3 per cent between 1958 and 1966. In the wake of the oil boom, I would suspect that a further decline in market shares has taken place, given the considerable increase in the demand for imports of capital goods and those consumer goods with a high income demand elasticity, i.e., manufactures, consumer durables and the more expensive range of food products such as meat and processed foods. But, as Mr Ali has pointed out, the composition of Arab exports is mostly concentrated in foods and agricultural raw materials, although the share of manufactured exports has been rising. If oil were excluded from Arab imports for 1975, as shown in Table 9.3b, food would account for about 22 per cent, agricultural raw materials 3 per cent and manufactures 65 per cent. Thus, the profile of Arab exports does not compare well with the high income demand pattern of Arab countries. Moreover, in the field of those simple manufactures which Arab countries have been able to develop, I doubt whether their production can compete with that of other developing countries with cheap labour available (e.g., China, Taiwan, India and Korea), given the rapid rises in wages in Arab countries and the possibility of some decline in productivity. Under these circumstances, a customs union would be trade-diverting and might reduce regional welfare.

The economic performance of the large exporters among the deficit-prone Arab countries suggests that the decline in the ratio of non-oil inter-Arab imports to total non-oil imports may reflect a weakening in their export capabilities rather than a change in the pattern of demand or lack of competitiveness. For example, the erosion of the export surplus that has accompanied the rise in domestic consumption in some of these countries is partly the result of low growth in their exportable output, often due to the mismanagement of export incentives such as the exchange rate. Weaknesses in the supply structure of major Arab exporters, the low growth of output and distortions in prices and incentives are, to my mind, the real impediments to the growth of inter-Arab trade rather than the differences in trade regimes, political differences or the lack of progress in the implementation of the Arab Economic Unity Agreement, all mentioned by Mr Ali. Were such impediments to be removed and were Arab countries to become export-oriented, the potential for the expansion of intra-Arab trade would be great indeed. Arab exporters would benefit from some advantages in transport costs, but mostly from a taste preference for their food items and textiles.

Moving to the issue of Arab economic integration, Mr Ali examines the balance-of-payments disparities between surplus and deficit countries and remarks that most Arab oil surpluses are invested in the Western financial markets. He deplores the fact that only a minor portion of the surpluses is directed to the deficit Arab countries in the form of bilateral aid, regional aid (through the AMF and the Arab Fund for Economic and Social Development) and direct investment. He finds these flows inadequate and suggests that the surpluses of oil-exporting countries should be used to cover the deficits of the non-oil countries. In his view, this would be the role of oil surpluses in promoting Arab economic integration. But this approach is one-sided, as it does not also regard the oil surpluses from the point of view of the oil-exporting countries. Aid cannot be open-ended and the oil exporters have the responsibility of converting a depletable asset — which must have recorded one of the highest rates of appreciation of any asset in history over the past decade — into an alternative asset base which approaches petroleum in its relative mix of rate of return and risk. Hence, once the level of aid to Arab and other developing countries is determined — and it has been considerable by United Nations standards — the bulk of the financial surpluses will have to gravitate towards the highest rates of return. It is therefore understandable that a large part of these surpluses is invested in the Eurodollar market or in long-term assets in industrialised countries. To the extent that deficit Arab countries want to capture a larger share of these surpluses, they must strive towards fostering the economic environment and the institutional set-up in such a way as to make direct foreign investment attractive on commercial grounds. But this process itself goes beyond the resource-generating capacities of the poorer Arab countries and would require considerable aid, both financial and technical.

To foster direct investments in the non-oil Arab countries and to broaden their own distribution of assets, oil-producing countries can help the deficit countries to promote the necessary structural and institutional changes which would encourage a better growth performance and generate the economic dynamism which is the first thing investors look for. In this respect, I would agree with Mr Ali that there must be better co-ordination among governments and among regional and national aid organisations in order to increase the effectiveness of aid. I would add two things. First, there is a need for greater consistency in the flow of aid to the non-oil countries which would permit them to plan more effectively. The experience of a number of non-oil countries has shown that bilateral aid flows have indeed been erratic. Secondly, too much aid is concentrated on projects, while the surrounding economic environment is often ignored. More emphasis needs to be placed on programme aid whereby institutional rigidities, sectoral malfunctions and structural weaknesses are dealt with directly. Ultimately, any increase in direct investment in the productive capacity of these countries will to a large extent depend on such changes.

As I argued in my own paper, I feel that the emergence of large surpluses in the oil-producing countries has already played a fundamental role in promoting greater Arab economic interaction. The demand for labour in the oil-producing countries, the increase in aid and direct investment and the liberalisation of travel, trade and exchange regimes which followed upon the oil boom have reduced the institutional disparities among Arab countries and increased their openness to one another and to the rest of the world. In this connection, Mr Ali deplores the fact that labour movements are still being restricted. Surely these movements are already quite substantial and any restrictions on them being imposed by the oil-producing countries are intended to preserve some measure of social balance. The importation of labour is a policy instrument for the oil-producing countries, helping them to reduce inflationary pressures and to promote growth in the non-oil GDP, but it also has a social cost.

With regard to the promotion of Arab economic integration, I feel that Mr Ali places too much stress on the political aspects. Given compatible political systems in two countries, only a clear perception of the economic benefits which would accrue to both can induce them to give up some of their sovereignty and share economic objectives. Thus, the most fruitful patterns of economic integration, i.e., between deficit and surplus Arab countries which offer some degree of complementarity, will also be the most difficult to achieve. Only a sustained improvement in the economic performance of the deficit countries can pave the way for integration. By contrast, the smaller Gulf countries appear from the outset to be well suited for some form of economic co-operation among themselves, particularly in the field of exchange-rate co-ordination. Unfortunately, Mr Ali does not discuss the costs and benefits of such co-ordination. Obviously, there would be advantages as a result of reducing exchange-rate fluctuations in these countries and co-ordinating the interest-rate structures. This would promote stability in capital movements and exchange-rate behaviour. But might these not be the only advantages? Trade among these countries is very limited and so is their degree of complementarity. Therefore, would it make sense for them to go beyond simple policy co-ordination? Only a detailed analysis of these economies and their interaction could provide some answers. I feel that such an analysis should be the starting point for any consideration of economic integration. For no matter how much political good will there may be in support of promoting the objectives of economic integration, unless it is anchored in firm economic foundations it is bound to be short-lived.

Note

1. See Lee Preston and Karim Nashashibi, *Trade Patterns in the Middle East* (New York: American Enterprises Institute, 1970).

GENERAL DISCUSSION

1. Shaker Moussa Issa

In referring to the Gulf region as a possible area for monetary integration, the author mentions the similarity of the economic structures of the oil-producing countries concerned, the existence of financial surpluses and so forth. I would like to add that the countries of this region have long been aware of these factors and have begun to examine various aspects of monetary unity at the meetings held every six months among the governors of these countries' central banks and the directors of their monetary institutions. These aspects include the question of creating a common monetary unit, i.e., issuing a Gulf dinar. The idea of beginning with the creation of a monetary unit at the level of the Gulf countries represents no more than a preliminary step, a first phase which must be undertaken in order to create the incentive for the achievement of monetary unity at the pan-Arab level. Such an attempt would not be likely to succeed if it were not accompanied by moves on the part of the other Arab countries — whether oil-producing or non-oil-producing — to complement and support it. Mr Nashashibi rightly mentions the process of co-ordinating the flow of aid from the oil-producing to the non-oil-producing countries. This process should, however, be carried out within the framework of the institutions or organisations which would have to be set up in the Arab world and linked with the proposed monetary unit in the Gulf.

Another point I would like to make pertains to the importance of the role of trade in the monetary integration process. I agree that this is vital, but the objective reality of the economic structures of production in the Gulf countries and elsewhere must also be borne in mind, as well as the meagre possibilities for trade between them, given the small quantities and limited range of goods available. It is crucial that the proposed monetary unity or integration be linked to the economic development process and the modification of the productive structures in favour of the industrial sector, for this will expand the horizons for trade among the Arab countries. In this connection, the Gulf countries have also initiated, as part of a policy of diversifying their sources of income, the establishment of a Centre for Industrial Consultancy Studies. This centre has begun to carry out studies of industrial projects and their possible location and is moreover investigating prospective sources of financing for such projects within the Gulf region. As is well known, the narrowness of the Gulf market also creates the need to link this market with the overall Arab market and consequently to find new outlets for goods and increase the volume of Arab trade.

Mr Nashashibi has mentioned his study of trade matrices among the Arab countries (user-producer tables). I remember in this regard the work I carried out in this area with Mr El-Imam during our study of such trade matrices for the Iraqi economy and the importance of singling out imports and distinguishing between the complementary and the competitive imports used in all branches of the economy. However, the global outcome of trade relations among the Arab economies is of little importance at the present time, although it will gain in importance in the future when these relations are based on the possibility of developing productive capabilities, especially those related to the industrial sector. Major changes could then be expected in the level of exports and imports among the Arab economies. Co-ordination within the present framework of the industrial development process could play an effective role in this regard.

2. Jorge Gonzalez del Valle

I am impressed by Mr Ali's frankness in approaching the question of the recycling of surplus funds to help to finance the balance-of-payments deficits of the non-oil Arab countries. This question goes beyond the technical aspects of monetary integration as such to take in the broader issue of financial integration which should be of interest to all attending this seminar.

I would like to refer to the approach to the intra-regional recycling of funds being followed in Latin America, though our problem is of a rather smaller magnitude and the solution is still only a partial one. We have surplus countries whose earnings derive mainly from oil exports (Venezuela, Ecuador and Trinidad and Tobago) other countries whose earnings stem mainly from exports of coffee (Columbia and Guatemala), and one country – Argentina – whose earnings derive from meat and cereal exports. In order to recycle a portion of these surpluses to the several Latin American countries which face heavy deficits, a joint international bank was established in 1978. This is the Latin American Export Bank (BLADEX), which operates in the Eurocurrency markets in Panama and is owned jointly by Latin American governments, central banks, domestic commercial banks and the international banks operating in Panama.

The recycling by BLADEX takes two forms: (a) it offers on the open market bankers' acceptances which originate from non-oil-exporting countries, thus providing the surplus countries with an opportunity to invest their foreign exchange; and (b) it accepts foreign-exchange deposits from the central banks of surplus countries. It may also be noted that BLADEX has received deposits from the Inter-American Development Bank and the OPEC Special Fund.

In this way, the usual objection to recycling, which is that surplus countries have to invest their reserves in Eurocurrency markets and cannot engage in the provision of open-ended aid to deficit countries, has been met. Through BLADEX, we in the Latin American region follow a businesslike, banking approach, but there is a very important difference in that it is *our* bank, we manage it and we guide its policies in such a way as to support our broad financial integration objectives.

3. Mabid Al-Jarhi

I have first one comment to make concerning regional Arab trade, which is in support of Mr Nashashibi's remarks. Mr Ali says that this trade represented about 10 per cent of all Arab trade in 1960, then dropped to about 5 per cent in 1977. As Mr Nashashibi points out, this percentage drop is attributable to the inclusion of oil in the calculations. If oil is excluded, it will be found that regional Arab exports represent more than one-third of all Arab exports.

It is the author's belief that conditions are not ripe at this time for Arab monetary integration, owing to the disparate economic policies pursued by the Arab countries and the absence of political will. I think, however, that it is the lack of political will which should be singled out, and not the disparities in economic policies; these can be dealt with through monetary integration and do not necessarily have to be eliminated before such integration is begun.

I find, therefore, that the five 'pre-conditions' which the author lays down would better be termed 'components' of integration and not conditions for it. It is generally granted that monetary integration includes currency convertibility and stable exchange rates, and that for monetary union to work, there must be a central monetary and financial institution. Must there also be, however, an organisation with global economic prerogatives? Would it be necessary to provide complete freedom of movement for the factors of production or might not the free movement of goods, combined with a partial freedom for the factors of production, be sufficient? I think the question is whether we really have to consider monetary integration to be the culmination of economic integration or merely a part of that integration. Finally, I agree completely with the author's proposal concerning a parallel currency. It is one of the alternatives available within the strategy of currency unification. Mr Ali is thus calling for Arab monetary integration before economic integration is completed and is proposing that it be achieved gradually, beginning with a parallel currency.

It would undoubtedly be appropriate to begin with the Gulf states or even with some other group within the Arab world. This would serve the objective of overall Arab monetary integration. But it is perhaps not advisable to begin with subgroups if it is at all possible to include all the Arab countries within a single monetary union, which would come into existence gradually, as the author suggests.

4. Adel Hussein

Monetary integration is part of a broader process of political integration. Therefore, monetary integration among the Gulf states, which may appear to be perfectly feasible form a technical standpoint, would in fact be extremely difficult to achieve, owing to various internal factors, but more particularly external ones, which would tend to work against it. It might be added that the economic benefits which would accrue from such monetary integration — should it occur — are less than obvious, whether seen in terms of its relevance to the integration of production or in terms of facilitating trade between these small countries. Thus, it would be more logical to think in terms of the monetary integration of all the Gulf countries or in terms of integration within the framework of the 'Greater Gulf', including Saudi Arabia and Iraq. This proposal would entail greater technical difficulties, but these could always be coped with (given the fact that all these countries enjoy surpluses to one degree or another). Monetary integration within this wider framework could be linked in particular to integrated developmental efforts and could constitute the cornerstone of a regional monetary order, which could in turn influence the international monetary order in such a way as to benefit all the Arab countries. Implicit in all this, however, is the existence of a nucleus of unified political authority amongst the Gulf states. I would emphasise here that the main task of the naval fleets massed in the Gulf is to prevent just such an eventuality.

Monetary integration should be discussed in terms of the political context in which it can be achieved rather than in terms of what is technically feasible. Since the Gulf states do not have, either individually or as a group, the political capacity required to achieve integration, a combination of Gulf and non-Gulf Arab countries should be considered as a politically more feasible approach to monetary integration.

In my opinion, three possible patterns of integration in the Arab world should be considered: integration among non-oil-producing countries; integration among oil-producing countries; and integration between oil-producing and non-oil-producing countries. I think that the last mentioned would be the most complex pattern, although it is feasible, given the necessary political will and technical capability.

Any monetary integration (envisaged on the basis of any of the three patterns mentioned) should always remain organically linked to the ultimate objective of setting up an Arab monetary order which would encompass all Arab countries.

5. Mohamed Mahmoud El-Imam

I would like to deal with the issue of surpluses and their movement. One might raise the question as to what forces govern the movement of resources. Present movements of labour and capital among the Arab countries reflect market forces, and are not the consequence of integration policies. Labour moves under the impetus of wage differentials. It has so far been employed in the services and public works sectors which are financed out of the budgets of the host countries. Once activity concentrates on the productive sectors needed to replace the oil sector, due care should be given to the question of productivity. Similarly, if capital movements are left to market forces only, they will be guided by rates of return. Given the unprecedented levels of interest on investment prevailing in world markets during times of persistent inflation, it is all the more difficult for the deficit countries to compete with these markets in attracting capital inflows.

What is needed at present is not the mere removal of the obstacles facing the mobility of economic factors; it is strong and rapid action to develop a solid and interdependent production structure at the regional level. This can only be brought about by comprehensive regional planning. These considerations apply equally to any proposed monetary union among the Gulf countries.

In this connection, I would like to mention that Mr Ali (like Mr Al-Sagban) focuses his attention on movements of capital through official channels (funds and governments). How does he assess the role of Arab financial markets?

6. Rattan Bhatia

I believe the concept of the investment of surplus funds should be clarified. This investment may be an investment in financial assets, or in real assets or projects. As far as the Arab region is concerned, I would assume that we are referring to project investment by surplus oil-producing countries in the deficit Arab countries. To the extent that such new investment will require additional imports from outside the Arab region, the overall balance-of-payments surplus of the entire region will decline. What surplus remains will, of course, have to be invested outside the region in financial and other assets. Some among us have referred to developing financial assets within a proposed Arab monetary union in order to invest these surpluses. However, this cannot be a substitute for investing the financial surpluses in outside markets, so long as it is assumed that the proposed union will, after having met the investment requirements of the region, register annual overall balance-of-payments surpluses. The only change will be that the original owners of those surpluses will hold 'domestic' (i.e., regional) financial assets, while some other economic entity within the proposed union will invest the proceeds in the international financial markets.

7. Monammed Labib Shoukair

I have three main remarks to make: the first is that the author focuses on monetary integration among the Gulf countries and fails to pay sufficient attention to overall Arab monetary integration. The author should have dwelt more on this matter; for if it is assumed that monetary integration within the Gulf region is made possible by the similarity of conditions in these countries, then the real problem becomes that of how to achieve such integration for the Arab countries as a whole, given the disparities in their economic systems. In order to facilitate the process of Arab integration, it might be necessary first to bring about a greater degree of economic interaction among the Arab countries through, for example, the establishment of joint production enterprises with the participation of capital from both the Gulf countries (or the oil-producing countries in general) and the non-oil-producing countries. This would initiate the process of monetary integration between these two groups of countries. Unfortunately, the joint enterprises which have been established up to now do not fit this description.

My second remark pertains to the author's contention that economic integration is necessary for monetary integration. During this seminar, two distinct positions seem to have crystallised concerning this matter. The first is that economic and monetary integration are closely linked; the second is that the two processes need not be linked. While this latter position may be correct with regard to the more advanced countries where economic policies favour a market-oriented economy and the volume of intra-regional trade is high, it is not so with regard to the developing economies. For monetary integration to succeed for these economies, there will, as I have already stated, have to be increased interaction among them.

Thirdly and finally, I am in complete agreement with the author about the possibility of utilising a parallel currency as a way of setting in motion the process of monetary integration. As for Mr Nashashibi's comment that the increase in Gulf trade with Korea and China is due to wage and output factors and not to trade regimes, as suggested by Mr Ali, I would draw attention to the increasing ratio of Asian to Arab migration in the Gulf countries and to the fact that trade is concentrated in the hands of Asians. This may explain why imports from Korea and Japan have been increasing at a faster rate than those from the Arab countries; thus, the problem is also political and social.

8. Isselmou Ould Boye

I believe that one of the factors blocking monetary integration is the preference of the Arab surplus countries for foreign markets, despite the fact that the risks are greater in the foreign than in the Arab markets. As far as I can see, monetary integration is a purely political matter. I really wonder whether it is possible to do anything in this regard until we are convinced of the need to invest Arab surplus capital in Arab countries, not out of altruism, but by reason of our common interests.

The same applies to private capital, but this problem is less serious, because, in most cases, private capital defers to and follows public policy. I would add that the Arab Common Market has largely failed to fulfil its obligation to supervise the efforts being made by financial institutions. It has in fact confined itself to traditional domains, such as the abolition of customs duties. But of what use is it for Mauritania to abolish duties on Egyptian goods as long as these goods never come and as long as the Mauritanian importer is incapable of purchasing them?

Why is there no system similar to the French system for guaranteeing and encouraging trade by providing credit facilities to importers and exporters? This should be looked into and, in addition, attention should be given to regulating Arab financial markets and familiarising Arab businessmen with their operations.

Another problem relates to the limitations of the Arab financial markets. These limitations are such that, even if there were a desire to direct Arab surpluses into Arab markets, these surpluses would in practice end up in the Western markets. Hence, it is imperative that Arab financial markets should be developed.

9. Abdul Munim Al-Sayyed Ali, in Response

In response to the comments made by Mr Nashashibi, I do not see how extending foreign trade statistics to include oil as an exported or imported material leads to distortions in the various percentages, either among the Arab countries themselves or between them and the outside world. On the contrary, given the importance of oil to the Arab economies, this product must enter into the calculations of the volume of foreign trade. In any case, I do not believe the figures mentioned in my paper would change much even with oil excluded.

I agree with Mr Nashashibi that the low export capacity of the Arab countries has helped to maintain a low level of trade among them. I also agree with him about the effect of structural factors in this regard. Political factors and disparities in social systems nevertheless remain important reasons for the low volume of inter-Arab trade.

As for the financial surpluses, I did not propose that they be used to cover the balance-of-payments deficits of the non-oil-producing countries; what I said was that it has become necessary for the surpluses to contribute to this and that the deficit countries should begin to reconsider their distorted economic structures and to change the environment within which their economies operate. The surplus countries should help the deficit countries to make these changes. I agree with Mr Nashashibi's observations concerning the need to co-ordinate financial aid policies and the importance of programming this aid.

I also agree completely with Mr Issa's remark concerning the need for the deficit countries to set up joint institutions and to establish integrated industries, as well as the need for co-ordination among Arab financial institutions.

I see no harm and indeed much to gain in following Latin America's example by setting up an export bank in which the central and commercial banks and other institutions participate. Its purpose would be to recycle the financial surpluses of the member states, to centralise the investment of these surpluses and, at the same time, to provide assistance to the deficit countries of the region.

I have stressed in my paper the importance of political will in achieving monetary integration. In this regard, I agree with Mr Hussein. I have therefore focused on monetary integration in the Gulf, though I do not believe this can be achieved at present, given the diversity of social and political systems in the region, of economic policies generally and of monetary and financial policies in particular.

I fully agree with Mr Shoukair concerning the fostering of economic interaction among the Arab countries as a means of achieving first economic and then monetary integration. I also agree with him that economic integration must precede monetary integration in the developing countries. In the advanced countries, as he points out, this may not be the case. It is indeed a mistake to apply any economic theory indiscriminately just because it happens to be applicable to the advanced economies. There may be other theories, such as the classical theory, which are more applicable than Keynesian theory to the developing countries. The same is true of the experience of monetary integration and the theory behind it in the advanced countries: that experience cannot be applied completely to the developing countries, because conditions differ in the two groups of countries. The main problem for the Arab countries is of a political character, and this implies the need for political will, without which neither economic nor monetary integration can ever take place.

10 ARAB MONETARY INTEGRATION: BENEFITS, ECONOMIC OBSTACLES AND MODALITIES

Alfredo Medio and M. Sakbani

I: Costs and Benefits (A. Medio)

The ultimate purpose of this two-part paper is presumably to establish whether monetary integration among Arab countries is desirable and, if so, the ways and means by which it can be achieved.

To answer this question, it is necessary, on the one hand, to clarify the general criteria according to which the desirability of such integration may be assessed and, on the other hand, to investigate whether these criteria apply to the countries under discussion.

As the author has not had the opportunity to gain a sufficiently deep knowledge of the economies of Arab countries, no attempt will be made in this first part of the paper to develop the second aspect of the question. Rather, a concise presentation will be provided of the main theoretical points put forward in the recent literature on monetary integration.

Nor will any attempt be made to answer the question: what is the appropriate domain for a currency area? Rather, the presentation will begin with national economies, and consideration will be given to the more limited but presumably more relevant question of how to determine the desirability of unifying the exchange rate of a given set of countries *vis-à-vis* the outside world.[1] In this respect, the alternative to a unified exchange rate will not be taken to be freely floating rates — i.e., rates fully fixed by market forces — but, more realistically, either adjustable or 'managed' floating rates.

The question under discussion cannot be answered on purely economic grounds, as it involves rather intricate welfare questions and bears on a number of contentious national as well as social issues. It is, however, essential that administrators, with whom eventually the decision will lie, should be fully aware of certain technical implications of policy measures. This has been the main purpose of the extensive literature on optimum currency areas and monetary integration, the main issues of which will now be considered.

Participating in a fixed exchange-rate area involves certain rather obvious costs, as well as certain less obvious benefits, the magnitude of which is affected by a number of economic and institutional factors.

A. Costs

The principal cost for a country joining a fixed exchange-rate area is the *loss of a basic policy instrument* to deal with fundamental external disequilibria. The latter may be defined as situations in which the cost-price relationships in a country *vis-à-vis* its trading partners are such that any attempt to reach the levels of real output and employment that are domestically desirable would lead to imbalances in external payments.

Disequilibria of this kind may be due to a once-and-for-all shift in costs, particularly in wage costs, or in demand conditions. More importantly, they may be due to cumulative differences in the rates of growth of productivity and wages. The latter, in their turn, depend on the strength of the labour unions and national attitudes towards unemployment and inflation.

Although it is doubtful whether the exchange rate alone can be an adequate instrument of international adjustment, recent historical experience seems to suggest that it will remain a necessary instrument as long as it is easier to change real incomes through alternations of prices than through alternations of money incomes.

When such adjustment is precluded by adherence to a fixed exchange-rate area, the presence of persistent cost-price disequilibria must lead either to deficit members tolerating higher unemployment levels and/ or to surplus members tolerating higher inflation rates than would have been the case with flexible exchange rates. The distribution of the burden of adjustment between deficit and surplus members depends on a number of factors, among which is their ability, respectively, to run down reserves (or to borrow) and to finance the accumulation of reserves, which, in turn, depends on the co-ordinated overall policy of the union. Moreover, this need not be a zero-sum game. The structure of the Phillips curves of the individual countries may be such that the inverse relationships between unemployment and price inflation in the union as a whole may be less favourable than if the members had retained their right to adjust their exchange rates.[2]

Participation in a currency union also means the *surrender of the power to alter national money supply*. When equilibrium interest rates are fixed internationally, the attempt of a participating country to increase the supply of internal money by open market operations leads to downward pressures on the domestic interest rate, and consequently, to increased purchases of foreign financial assets by private individuals. The newly created domestic money is thereby placed anew with the foreign-exchange authorities. The only result is the depletion of reserves.

If the additional supply consists of outside money, which implies an addition to the net stock of financial assets in the economy, there will be an increase in expenditures and imports. This will lead to a balance-of-trade deficit which will drain additional financial assets out of the system. Once again, the stock of assets cannot be increased permanently under a system of fixed exchange rates.

Of course, the conclusions drawn here must be altered when the economic size of a country is such that the equilibrium interest rate prevailing internationally is not independent of its domestic monetary policy. These conclusions must also be changed when the hypothesis of perfect capital mobility does not hold and controls on capital movements are introduced so that the interest rates may be permanently different in different countries, even independently of expectation of exchange-rate variations.

To conclude this brief assessment of the costs associated with exchange-rate fixity, it must also be mentioned that the imposition of constraints on the choice between inflation and unemployment, on the one hand, and on the mixture of monetary and fiscal policy, on the other, implies a loss of welfare, independently of the presence of random disturbances of equilibrium.[3]

Alternative adjustment instruments. In a currency union, the role of the exchange rate in pursuing adjustment must be taken over by alternative instruments. Broadly speaking, these may be divided into market-based and government-based policies.[4]

Market-based policies largely result in *labour migration* from the depressed areas to the more capital-rich and dynamic ones. This reallocation of labour and the consequent changes in labour market conditions might also affect the relative strength of wage demand and working habits in the two areas, so as to bring them into line with relative productivity. As recent history has shown, this may be a very costly strategy, both economically and socially. Moreover, the transfer of labour induced by unemployment is not necessarily justified from a structural point of view and cannot be reversed easily or without extra costs to workers and to society in general.

As far as government-based alternative adjustment policies are concerned, they may be divided into two categories, namely fiscal redistribution and regional policies.

Fiscal redistribution, however desirable on other grounds, is not necessarily helpful in mitigating external disequilibria. Indeed, there is no guarantee that relative prosperity among the countries of the union will be correlated with relative payments strength. When it is not (as, for example, when external imbalances are due to divergences in relative cost pressures), certain countries' tax-payers may be asked to finance fiscal transfers across the border, not for the sake of distributional equity but for the sake of exchange-rate agreement.[5]

Regional policy, designed to assist depressed areas is in principle a more helpful instrument for correcting external disequilibria. Difficulties may arise here also. Regional subsidisation is likely to meet greater political opposition internationally than domestically. Moreover, it may have distributionally adverse effects to the extent that subsidies benefit the more affluent groups in depressed areas or they replace (rather than supplement) domestic regional subsidies.

B. Benefits

The main costs of exchange-rate unification, as well as some of the alternative adjustment instruments, having thus been sketched, the main real or presumed advantages of such a policy can now be considered. It should be noted that *ex ante* advantages will be considered, i.e., advantages expected before a country actually joins a currency union. It is indeed widely agreed among economists that after a common currency (or an irrevocably fixed exchange rate) has been used for some time, habits and expectations are formed which make withdrawal impossible or extremely costly.

Generally speaking, *the value of a currency as a medium of exchange and as a store of value* is greater, the larger the area in which that currency circulates. This also applies to some extent in the case of exchange-rate unification. Whether it has significant practical importance and what the minimum critical economic size of a country must be to secure the monetary value of its currency are questions which cannot be answered *a priori*.

A second category of advantages relates to *capital flows*.

First of all, the establishment of a fixed exchange-rate area should eliminate speculative flows among participating countries and the costs associated with their control. It might also reduce speculative flows between the currency area and the outside world. However, internal speculation might not be eliminated and might even increase when exchange-rate fixity is not certain (or is not believed to be so). The experience of the Bretton Woods agreements suggests that a system in which exchange rates are altered reluctantly and only by judiciously chosen large amounts provides the best basis for successful speculation.

Secondly, the establishment of a fixed exchange-rate area would also increase *capital mobility* within the area. This is not necessarily an advantage, however, especially in the presence of persistent disequilibria. This point is referred to again below.

Some authors believe that exchange-rate unification stimulates *intra-union trade* by reducing the risks involved. This point is not uncontroversial, however. Most of the pure exchange risks in international transactions may be hedged, provided that a large and efficient exchange market exists in the area. On the other hand, the risks associated with investment in trade industries depend on the ability of the integrated area to correct cost-price imbalances quickly. From this point of view, therefore, whether intra-union trade is stimulated or discouraged will depend on whether or not the process of adjustment is smoother and quicker as a consequence of the establishment of fixed exchange rates. As has been seen, it may not be.

Certain other benefits of a common currency (or of a fixed exchange-rate regime) can be grouped under the label: *monetary efficiency*. Mundell enumerates these as reserve saving, reduction in the cost of financial management, risk-pooling, intermediation, information saving and innovation.[6]

It has been noted, however,[7] that some of these benefits, and in particular reserve saving, are likely to be limited in the early stages of a monetary union when actual reserve-pooling is limited. It must also be observed that reserve-pooling and mutual credit arrangements may well be established without any movement towards a currency union, as the Latin American experience suggests.[8]

Some authors consider most important the potential benefits deriving from the effects of the establishment of a fixed exchange area on *governmental functions*. In particular, it is believed that monetary integration is likely to accelerate fiscal integration.[9] Whether fiscal integration is likely to be advantageous to the countries concerned is not clear, however. At any rate, the European experience seems to suggest that progress in this area may prove exceedingly difficult.

C. Factors Affecting the Costs and Benefits of Fixed Exchange Rates

Whether the advantages of fixed exchange rates will outweigh the cost related to the loss of the exchange-rate instrument depends on a series of factors, the analysis of which has provided the basis for establishing the criteria for an optimum currency area, the most important of which will be discussed next.

1. Labour Mobility. This point has been stressed, particularly by Mundell.[10] Although Mundell's original argument is formulated in terms of factor mobility, the emphasis is on the mobility of labour. Flexible exchange rates among national currencies — Mundell argues — may eliminate disequilibria in external payments, only if factor (labour) mobility is high internally and low internationally. If, however, the area under consideration is divided into regions within which only mobility is high and which do not correspond to national boundaries, flexible rates cannot bring about adjustment unless currencies are reorganised along regional lines.

This argument needs some qualification, however. If labour intensities in the industries of the regions among which migration takes place are different, labour mobility may not be sufficient to eliminate payment imbalances. As Kenen has noted,[11] 'rather special patterns of consumer demand and methods of production may be needed in each region if a simple labour movement and the corresponding locus of demand are to end an imbalance in two regions' labour markets and also to equilibrate the trade flow between them'.

In other words, perfect inter-regional mobility requires perfect occupational mobility, which in turn requires the homogeneity of labour or identical skills in the industries affected. Strictly speaking, Mundell's condition for the optimality of currency areas applies only to single-product regions.

As these regions would inevitably be very small, the benefit derived from labour mobility would be more than offset by its cost in terms of the utility of the currency as a medium of exchange and store of value. Clearly, a compromise must be reached between these two conflicting requirements.

In his analysis, Mundell adopts the classic Ricardian dichotomy between the perfect mobility and the perfect immobility of factors of production — and in particular of labour — the only difference being that Mundell takes into account the fact that areas of perfect mobility may not coincide with national boundaries.

In reality, however, there is a continuum of different degrees of labour mobility both internally and internationally. The crucial question is whether such a mobility may be taken as the cornerstone of the equilibrating process among, as well as within, trading areas.

2. Capital Mobility. As far as capital mobility is concerned, it is not even certain whether this will reduce the costs associated with exchange-rate fixity.

Payments disequilibria among participating countries are followed by corresponding changes in output, profits and employment — all of which will presumable rise in the surplus countries and decline in the deficit countries.

What happens to the interest rates in the two types of countries depends on the response of investment and savings to the changes in the level of activity: they will rise if investment increases more (or declines less) than savings and vice versa.

Since capital flows will move towards areas with higher interest rates, they may well constitute a destabilising, rather than a stabilising factor. In this case, a higher capital mobility would make adjustment with a fixed exchange rate more difficult, not easier. The likelihood that capital mobility will be a destabilising influence is greater if surplus countries attempt to use monetary policy for internal rather than external stability. In such a case, they will raise their interest rates to check inflationary pressures, which will in turn stimulate capital inflows (which they will try to sterilise), thereby making deficit countries' external positions even worse.[12]

3. Product Diversification. Peter Kenen[13] has argued that nations with high product diversification can tolerate fixed exchange rates better than those with less diversified national economies.

There are various reasons for this, all of them deriving from the law of large numbers or, to express it otherwise, from the 'insurance principle'. First of all, if shifts in demand and supply conditions are random, then the more varied a country's commodity exports, the less they will be affected by each shift. Secondly, the greater the variety of export goods, the smaller will be the changes in investment induced by changes in the demand for these exports. Thirdly, the more diversified a national economy, the smaller will be the effect on domestic employment of any drop in the demand for its principal exports.

The main argument against Kenen's conclusions is that the output of a large economic region with a relatively small foreign trade sector is likely to be highly diversified. According to the product-diversification criterion, this region should prefer a fixed exchange-rate regime and pursue external balance by means of monetary and fiscal policies. But this would lead to 'the tail wagging the dog', i.e., wide variations in domestic demand and employment would be required to correct relatively minor external imbalances, which is clearly not an optimal solution.[14]

Moreover, the validity of Kenen's point is restricted to disequilibria of a microeconomic type, e.g., arising from changes in demand as between the products of different participating countries. However, when imbalances are of a macroeconomic type – e.g., when they are due to cost-push factors affecting all sectors alike – the need for adjustment will be equally great, whether product similarity among countries is high or low.[15]

4. The 'Openness' of an Economy. The 'openness' of a country's economy – conveniently measured – may affect the costs and benefits associated with the establishment of a fixed exchange-rate area in a number of ways.

First of all, there is the criterion suggested by McKinnon,[16] and based on the ratio of tradeable goods (goods whose price is fixed in terms of an outside currency) to total production. According to his criterion, which, it has been noted, may conflict with the one based on product diversification, the greater the 'openness' of a country's economy, the smaller will be the cost of (or the greater the gain from) exchange-rate fixity.

It is true that a higher degree of trade integration is likely to lead to greater disequilibria. However, disequilibria of any given size will be adjusted by means of corrections in domestic demand. The greater the 'openness' of the economy, the smaller the necessary corrections.

This conclusion can be derived from application of the foreign trade multiplier with constant prices. Indeed, the more open the economy (the greater the propensity to import), the smaller will be the variation in income and employment needed to correct a given external imbalance, and the less will therefore be the cost of keeping the exchange rate fixed.

On the other hand, in a relatively open economy (openness meaning here the ratio between tradeable goods and GNP), variations in the exchange rate will lead to greater price instability. In this respect, therefore, countries with high trade interpenetration will find it beneficial to form a fixed exchange-rate area.

It has been observed[17] that McKinnon's conclusion depends crucially on the implicit assumption that conditions in the external world as a whole are relatively stable. If this is not the case, a flexible exchange rate should be used to attempt to insulate a country's economy from external macroeconomic disturbances.

The ratio of tradeable to non-tradeable goods affects the desirability of joining a currency union in yet another way.[18] The liquidity properties of money depend primarily on the stability of its value in terms of a range of goods which is representative of the pattern of expenditure of the owners of wealth. Consider a small country characterised by a high ratio of tradeables to non-tradeables. If there is no inflation, the domestic currency will have a stable value in terms of non-tradeables, whereas its value in terms of tradeables will depend on the exchange rate *vis-à-vis* the foreign currency. In these circumstances, and with the existence of trade disturbances, flexible exchange rates may lead to a severe impairment of the liquidity of the domestic currency. Domestic owners of financial wealth may feel that the purchasing power of their assets is not sufficiently guaranteed in terms of the range of commodities they deem to be representative, and consequently they will attempt to buy foreign assets. Similarly, purchases of domestic assets by foreigners will be discouraged, even though the domestic rate of return may be higher than the outside rate. This will result in capital outflows which are not justified by consideration of the real characteristics of the country under consideration, but simply by the insufficient monetary quality of its currency. In this case, other things being equal, a small 'open' country would be well advised to seek monetary integration with other countries in order to form a currency area sufficiently large to ensure that variations in the exchange rate of the common currency will not impair its liquidity.

Finally, the degree of openness of an economy also affects the presence of 'money illusion', which will be discussed next.

5. Money Illusion. This is a crucial factor. We have already seen that the effectiveness of exchange-rate alterations in correcting external imbalances largely depends on the existence of 'money illusion', defined as people's readier acceptance of reductions in real income brought about by price increases than of the same reductions brought about by reducing their money income.

In open economies, characterised by a high import-GNP ratio, exchange-rate variations will entail corresponding changes in the level of prices and thereby in real incomes. In particular, whenever money wage changes are tied to a price index including imports, the exchange rate may become ineffective as an instrument for correcting external imbalances.

As Fleming[19] has observed, however, the indexation of wages seldom operates instantaneously and only partially offsets the effects of exchange-rate adjustment. In the opinion of this author, money illusion may well be relevant the other way around. Since national currencies have a strong tendency to retain their functions as a means of exchange and a standard of value, especially where wage settlements and payments are concerned, once a common currency is set up, it may be very difficult to revoke it, even if its establishment has proved to be a mistake.

6. Similarity in Rates of Inflation. This factor has been less prominent in the literature on the subject but it has great importance for assessing the desirability of establishing a fixed-rate area. Most of the criteria discussed in the literature on optimum currency areas assume that external disturbances arise principally from microeconomic sources, e.g., changes in demand and supply conditions in specific industries. Recent historical experience suggests, however, that this may not be the case and that payments disequilibria may most often be determined by macroeconomic factors, most importantly by inflation and inadequate demand management policies.

In this respect, it is essential to ascertain the ultimate causes of divergences in inflation rates. If the latter are mainly determined by deep-rooted differences in national employment goals, pressures from trade unions, the degree of monopoly exercised by producers or productivity trends, the maintenance of a fixed exchange rate may prove unfeasible or exceedingly costly. Some authors believe that participation in a currency union may itself be a powerful instrument for correcting the price trends of the most inflation-prone members of the union. This argument has been used, for example, in the recent discussions preceding Italy's adherence to the European monetary system. It is doubtful, however, whether national governments which were not able to implement anti-inflationary policies before joining the union could persuade their electorates to tolerate the cost of the operation, simply in order to maintain the agreed rate of exchange.

7. Degree of Policy Integration. This criterion represents a generalisation of some of the issues related to the inflation rate criterion. The main idea is that policy attitudes and policy co-ordination, rather than economic characteristics, are relevant to the decision on the desirability of a fixed exchange-rate area.

The practical relevance of this criterion was brought to the fore during the discussions concerning the European Monetary System. Two schools of thought confronted one another on this issue. The first one, whose members were labelled 'economists', maintained that monetary integration could usefully be implemented only when certain economic pre-conditions (the most important of which have already been discussed here) obtained. The second school, whose supporters were called 'monetarists', favoured an early monetary integration in the belief that this would force policy co-ordination.

The author has already expressed his doubts concerning the political soundness of the thinking of the 'monetary' school. From the economic point of view, however, it is not clear whether policy co-ordination would necessarily help to mitigate payments diseqilibria, thus making the loss of the exchange-rate instrument less costly.

Some of the main difficulties in this area have already been touched upon in the discussion of alternative adjustments. It may be added here that centralisation measures in the field of monetary and banking policy might worsen rather than mitigate payments disequilibria among participating countries. If the union's hypothetical central bank pursued the uniformisation of short-term interest rates throughout the area, this would increase the mobility of factors of production among countries. But, as is known, increased capital mobility might exacerbate rather than reduce the disequilibria, while greater labour mobility, although it could favour equilibrium from a payments point of view, might be undesirable.

D. Conclusion

In concluding this discussion, I should like to add a few brief and very tentative remarks, in order to relate the general issue of the costs and benefits of monetary integration to the more specific question of the desirability of such integration for the Arab countries.

First of all, if these countries are considered as a whole, it appears rather unlikely that the establishment of a fixed exchange rate — let alone a common currency — would be desirable or even conceivable, in view of the extreme diversity of their economies and of their social and political structures.

Moreover, most Arab countries, like most developing countries, trade far more intensively with the industrialised countries than with each other, so that fixing the exchange rates among their own currencies would not produce the advantages of trade and price stability.

The only factor working for monetary integration is perhaps labour mobility, which is substantial among Arab countries, owing to religious and cultural motives, as well as to economic incentives.

I agree with Mr Triffin that for the years immediately ahead more modest policy objectives should be pursued, with a view to strengthening balance-of-payments financing arrangements, reducing inflation differentials and mitigating exchange-rate fluctuations.

The situation looks different, however, if one concentrates on smaller groups of countries with common problems and characteristics. I am thinking, in particular, of the surplus, oil-exporting Arab countries.

These countries might seriously consider the possibility of establishing a common currency, in a more or less gradual manner. The potential advantages of such a measure would lie not so much in the trade as in the financial area. In particular, monetary integration might bring about substantial benefits in terms of reductions in the cost of financial management, information saving and innovation.

Moreover, a common currency characterised by stability of purchasing power over such a sought-after commodity as oil, might prove an attractive financial asset and — I am again making reference to Mr Triffin's paper — it could play a significant role worldwide, alongside other 'super-currencies' like the United States dollar and the European ECU.

II. Feasibility, Modalities and Selected Operational Issues: Introduction (M. Sakbani)

This part of the paper falls into three main sections. Section A outlines the rationale of monetary integration with particular emphasis on its instrumentality for economic integration in the Arab world. The approach followed in this section emphasises the politico-economic calculus of feasibility in a dynamic setting in contrast to the traditional approach of the literature on optimum currency areas with its heavy emphasis on static microeconomic analyses.

In Section B the various modalities of monetary integration are surveyed and a detailed discussion is offered of the major operational issues which arise in monetary unions.

In Section C a brief analytical treatment of market integration is given.

A. A Framework for Arab Monetary Integration

1. Economic Integration and Monetary Integration. When a group of countries seeks to achieve economic integration, each country in effect seeks to substitute a large economic domain, that of the group, for its own small domain. The economic advantages of scale, resource diversity, complementarity of needs and, above all, the furtherance of economic viability and well-being, provide substance and justification for such endeavours. However, economic integration does not consist merely in amalgamating resources and widening horizons; rather, it consists in forging new structures of relationships with new institutional modalities within which economic activities can take place. Hence, economic integration implies a transition from one state of economic sovereignty to another and, hence, the basic decision at stake is a political one.

In its full sense, economic integration seeks, in the words of Fritz Machlup, to achieve actual utilisation of all potential opportunities for the efficient division of labour.[20] Factors and goods move freely within the domain of integration. Ultimately they should enter production and consumption at the levels where their marginal product and/or marginal utility per unit marginal cost are equal to their respective prices and maintain that ratio in time. Throughout the domain, equal goods and services fetch the same prices. In this optimal setting, efficiency is maximised and the welfare of all is enhanced.

It is obvious that free mobility of all factors of production and of all goods and services is the necessary condition for economic integration. However, inasmuch as real flows generate symmetrical monetary flows, the integration of the markets for factors, goods and services, i.e., the real markets, is bound up with the integration of the currency and security markets. Moreover, since products and factors are exchanged for money, the integration of the currency and security markets brings about a high degree of integration of the real markets; two goods can substitute for each other if each of them can substitute for currencies or securities traded in an integrated market.[21]

2. A Minimal Concept of Monetary Integration. The various modalities of monetary integration define a range of choices running from a currency area at one extreme to a monetary union at the other. These modalities will be discussed in detail in Section B of this paper. It suffices here to define monetary integration in minimal terms. At a minimum, the integrated area should have one currency or several freely convertible currencies tied together by fixed exchange-rates and enjoying unfettered movement within the area. Moreover, the supply of the currency or currencies must be fixed by a union rule, or lodged in a union authority. The ability of commercial banks to create money must be brought under the union authority, e.g., a currency board, vested with full authority over high-powered money.

While this minimal definition might be found wanting by many economists, it does none the less identify fixed exchange rates and free capital movement as primary steps towards monetary integration. This is perhaps why discussion of monetary integration within the EEC gave primacy to exchange-rate fixity and intervention rules in the establishment of the European Monetary System (EMS). The Werner Report of 1970 was one of the first such reports to couch monetary integration in multiple currency terms.

3. Monetary Integration: Feasibility, Benefits and Costs.

a. The feasibility question. The question of the feasibility of monetary integration has been approached in the literature in the context of the viability of fixed exchange rates for a currency area. According to Mundell[22] factor mobility, especially labour mobility, in a certain region can, within a range of labour intensity of production, eliminate payments imbalances more effectively than exchange-rate adjustments. McKinnon[23] chooses the degree of openness of the economies — defined as the ratio of tradeables to GNP — and the absence of money illusion as indicators of the cost-benefit ratio in monetary integration; the greater the openness of the economy, in the absence of money illusion, the greater will be the gains from fixed exchange rates in terms of price stability. Kenen[24] argues that the greater the product diversification of a country, the less exchange-rate changes are effective and the more fiscal and monetary adjustment policies become relevant for payments equilibrium. Ingram[25] and Scitovsky[26] emphasise that capital mobility is a more decisive adjustment mechanism than exchange rates if it obtains in a given area. Fleming[27] and Haberler[28] lay stress on similarity in inflation policies and the argument is carried further by Whitman[29] and cast in terms of belonging to a 'policy area'. According to these arguments, a group of countries can gain from a fixed exchange-rate zone if they have similar policies or belong to a co-ordinated policy area.

The feasibility criteria, especially the latter two, were given prominence in the debate on the viability (and advisability) of the EMS. Many EMS proponents subscribed to a global monetarist view or to an extreme neo-Keynesian view (see below): these two views converge in arguing the inefficacy of exchange rates as an adjustment mechanism and lay stock in the instrumentality function of the EMS for European integration. Two comments on this literature are in order:

(1) The dominant approach in the literature on optimum currency areas is microeconomic in character. Furthermore, this approach

assumes in general a stable external environment and employs partial equilibrium analysis to trace the impact of one disturbance at a time. As Cordon[30] argues, if micro-disturbances are external, flexible exchange rates are better for an open economy. Hence, this approach is of little relevance to a world where external disturbances dominate and where important divergences among countries stem from differences in social preference with respect to socially deep-rooted problems like inflation and wage trends. While this literature is interesting, it is hardly serviceable from the point of view of policy;

(2) The traditional theory usually emphasises actual rather than potential characteristics, costs and benefits and is therefore static in nature.

This last point is of great importance to any discussion of monetary integration in the Arab region. If the examination of the structural and economic characteristics of the Arab states yields at this time a rather sceptical, if not negative, judgement regarding the feasibility of Arab monetary integration, if does not follow that these states should not undertake the necessary structural transformation and policy co-ordination to bring about a favourable configuration for a monetary union. The crucial question is whether the economic benefits of a potential Arab monetary union are great enough to create the political will necessary to bring about a viable union in the Arab region. The move towards an Arab monetary union would of necessity be a process of gradual convergence in such crucial areas as general economic policy, inflation policy, monetary and banking structures and wage differentials.

Cultural, historical and political bonds are at least as important as economic factors in determining the eventual success or failure of monetary integration. Hence, it can be claimed that the drive towards an Arab monetary union would be reinforced by the deeply-imbedded cultural similarities and the common historical aspirations of the Arab peoples as well as all other factors making for Arab cohesiveness.

However, the political will to bring about Arab economic integration and its corollary, monetary integration, has to derive substance from objective factors present or potential. Moreover, it has to contend with two debilitating factors. The first is that the Arab countries do not have the same form of economic organisation. Some are market-based and at varying levels of market development, while others — a substantial minority — are, in principle, planned economies. If the decision were made by the latter to join a region-wide monetary union, they would have to accept intra-union freedom of movement of capital and labour and allow the functioning of integrated security markets. This would significantly erode their centralised control over their own economies and, in my opinion, would work against the attainment of a high degree of socialisation of those economies. The second factor is the long record of failure, of ill-prepared union schemes and lightly-made commitments to economic and political integration in the Arab region, a record which discourages the formation of effective political will. Nevertheless, rational, positive analysis reveals a strong basis for Arab economic integration. Moreover, to the extent that the public sector is highly involved in economic life in the various Arab countries (regardless of the orientation of their economic systems) there is considerable scope for *dirigisme* at the operational level, despite initial preferences for different systems.

One may wonder why it is argued here that the economic system most suitable for Arab monetary integration may be a market system rather than a centralised one. One can point out, without expressing a personal preference, three compelling reasons:

(1) An Arab monetary union must capitalise on the particular historical circumstances of the Arab region at this juncture. Specifically, it must aim at channelling a large measure of the exceptional oil surpluses of the region into real, productive investments within the region. This is best done by safeguarding the property rights of the surplus owners in a market system;

(2) The non-market alternative involves unification of political structures and authority, which would appear to be nearly impossible in the foreseeable future;

(3) The market model offers the only viable alternative to the Western markets where the surpluses are now invested.

As for the objective factors contributing to political will, it goes without saying that these will ultimately depend on the Arab polity. Nevertheless, in deliberating this question, the following observations are of specific relevance:

(1) From the point of view of the capital surplus of the Arab oil producers, an Arab monetary area would offer a potentially large and politically secure capital market for investment. Moreover, to the extent that free mobility opens up to savers all the investment possibilities of the Arab region, real investment as opposed to financial placement would reduce their accumulation of financial paper assets;

(2) The political security of Arab foreign placements is dependent upon the continuation of the present configuration of energy interests among the developed countries. Once the oil era is over, the risk to the accumulated stocks of financial investments abroad might increase considerably;

(3) In the context of a monetary union, the economic interests of potential Arab creditors are secured by the stability and freedom of movement indispensable to such a union. To the extent that the net borrowers among the union members have a continual interest in financing their development requirements from a highly developed,

secure and active capital market, the configuration of interests is symmetrical and stable;

(4) The most troublesome problem in monetary unions is usually the transfer of wealth to the poorer regions of the union. This usually comes about either by the rich subregions continually financing the current account of the poorer subregions or by fiscal redistributive measures in favour of the poorer areas. In the Arab context, the poorer areas are the capital-deficient regions with a high absorptive capacity and rich potential. Hence, given the aid policy dispositions of the surplus countries so far and their stake in securing future equities across the region, redistributive transfers and transfers of wealth might be less problematic in this than in other regions;

(5) As was argued above, once monetary integration is viewed as a process in time, an initial period for co-ordination might overcome some of the existing divergences. It should be recalled that such co-ordination among the Arab countries might lead them to constitute what Marina V.N. Whitman calls 'a policy area'.[31] Moreover, the strong impact which political disputes have been observed to have on inter-Arab trade and inter-Arab financial relationships significantly diminishes the weight of *ex-post* objective arguments against monetary integration.

In evaluating the feasibility of Arab monetary integration, its instrumentality function should be accorded due recognition. As was shown above, monetary assets integrate through exchange in the goods and services markets. Of all the instrumentalities of economic integration, monetary integration, as defined here, is one of the most effective.[32]

This function was not sufficiently appreciated in the early writings on optimum currency areas.[33] Along with other political aspects of monetary integration, the instrumentality function took a back seat to purely economic and structural aspects in indicating where to draw the lines around a currency area. When the issue was raised with respect to the EMS, some economists, notably F. Hirsch, took a negative view of it.[34] Yet it cannot be denied on the basis of the record that the unfolding EMS is bringing about an increased co-ordination among its members and raising issues whose settlement is crucial for the future evolution of European economic integration.

In closing this discussion it should be pointed out that the instrumentality function could be valuable in the Arab context. It is well known that the drive towards Arab political and economic integration has lacked sufficient and stable institutional modalities. Perhaps monetary integration can provide this drive with some new and economically powerful institutional forms.

b. The benefits and costs of monetary integration: a comment. It is beyond the scope of this paper to offer a systematic review of the costs and benefits of monetary integration. However, for the Arab region some specific comments are in order:

(1) In the event of Arab monetary integration, the Arab states should experience a reduction in their foreign reserve holdings, due not only to reserve pooling but also to a decrease in their joint imports from abroad — made possible by the intra-regional capacity for import substitution — and to a reduction in the aggregate prudential reserve-import ratio. Given the strong capital position of many Arab countries, the reserve-import ratios they observe could be significantly reduced in the context of a wider trade area;

(2) Monetary integration in the Arab region would be a harbinger of security market integration. The gain from generalised market integration in the Arab region would be particularly significant from the point of view of regional investment of Arab financial surpluses;

(3) The experience of the last few years under the system of managed exchange rates qualifies the weight that would have to be accorded to the loss of exchange rates as a policy instrument. In determining short-term exchange rates, in particular, the role of capital markets has been decisive. The tendency of these markets to overshoot and undershoot is already well known and has served to undermine the adjustment role of exchange rates. With a very high degree of inter-Arab labour mobility, it is doubtful that Arab governments could, given the present political constraints, use exchange rates to reduce real wages;

(4) It is argued by Fleming and others[35] that full capital integration would attract capital to the more prosperous subregions. The high labour mobility in the Arab world, in conjunction with the fact that the less prosperous Arab regions would enjoy comparative advantages in locating productive investment, turns this argument completely around;

(5) The establishment of an Arab monetary union would forge a collective economic identity for dealing with the outside world. This would have collateral advantages in terms of bargaining power and security which hardly require elaboration.

In conclusion, it should be stressed that the gains and losses associated with monetary integration remain to a large extent unquantifiable and interdependent. Nevertheless, the European experience up to now in no way justifies pessimism.[36] In fact, the EMS has worked surprisingly well and without severe strains. There is no doubt that the loss of exchange rates as a policy tool robs governments of an instrument for adjusting real incomes through money illusion. However, the evidence on the efficacy of exchange rates as an adjustment mechanism remains mixed.

B. Modalities and Operational Aspects

1. Modalities of Monetary Integration. An operationally useful distinction may be made between four integration modalities: (a) currency areas; (b) currency unions; (c) monetary areas; (d) monetary unions.

Currency areas satisfy our minimal definition of monetary integration. They involve arrangements for a fixed parity grid together with the associated money-supply strictures mentioned earlier. Currency unions add to this a common foreign-exchange policy. By implication they would necessarily entail a union reserve pool and a common inflation policy.

The monetary arrangements in (c) and (d) involve banking and money market controls. A monetary area is one where in addition to all the prerogatives of the union under (a) and (b), different kinds of money (money, near money, bank deposits, etc.) are freely exchanged in integrated money markets.[37] Finally, monetary unions are the most advanced form of monetary integration. Besides all the elements of (a), (b) and (c), they involve a common banking policy. In other words, they would imply a uniform banking structure throughout the union. Hence, financial intermediaries of all types would operate on a union-wide basis.

These four modalities of monetary integration set forth above do not include payments unions. A payments union groups together countries with inconvertible currencies for the purpose of settling payments among the members. Under certain conditions, a payments union might extend credit in convertible currencies to a member state. In the author's judgement, payments unions are mere payments arrangements. They do not involve the transformation of monetary assets into new forms, nor do they make members' currencies perfectly substitutable. They also lack a crucial element, namely an effective monetary authority. That they may result in a measure of policy co-ordination is relevant from the point of view of economic co-ordination rather than from that of monetary integration. Therefore, they will not be considered among the integration modalities.

All types of monetary arrangement involve a degree of monetary authority lodged in the hands of the union. Whereas this authority is least in the case of currency areas, monetary unions involve the virtual transfer of full monetary sovereignty to the union. Each of the four types of arrangements mentioned raises crucial operational and policy issues, depending on its nature. There follows here an examination of the major issues raised by the most advanced form: monetary unions.

2. Major Policy Issues

a. Phasing Arab monetary integration. There are no analytical principles to be invoked in phasing an Arab monetary union. Essentially, phasing should be judged by pragmatic considerations such as the convergence of monetary policies. In the author's opinion, there should be three phases to a monetary union. After the agreement to set up an Arab monetary union was signed, an initial period would be fixed for the co-ordination of economic, monetary, fiscal and banking policies. Once the agreement entered into force, interim arrangements with regard to exchange rates, the reserve pool operation and income and employment policies would go into effect. Simultaneously, the legal and institutional modalities for a single Arab security and currency market would be worked out and budgetary procedures streamlined in the various countries. The last phase would usher the union itself into being. No attempt is made here to prescribe a timetable for these operations as this is a purely pragmatic question.

b. The domain of Arab monetary integration. It is sensible to advocate unions among Arab states of similar economic configuration. Such unions are pragmatically desirable and facilitate the task of co-ordination. However, monetary unions are not an end in themselves; they serve a practical purpose and their desirability depends essentially on the goals sought. Viewed this way, schemes for integrating the Arab Gulf countries or the Arab surplus countries first would sacrifice purpose to expedience. The two compelling reasons for Arab monetary and economic integration at this historical juncture are to invest the Arab oil surpluses — to the extent possible and with due regard for international responsibility — within the Arab region, thereby solving the payments problems of the surplus countries, and to transform and develop the economies of the Arab countries. For this reason it is the author's considered opinion that schemes involving only the Arab oil surplus producers do not have a great deal to recommend them.

c. Currency unification. The prevailing view among economists is that monetary integration implies a common currency. This could be a combination of various national currencies reduced to interrelated fractions of each other, or even a foreign currency declared to be legal tender in the union.

The unification of the currency may proceed gradually or in one step. The basic considerations in deciding the form of the new currency and the speed and manner with which to phase it are the readiness of the public to accept it and the convenience of the new unit as a medium of exchange.

It would also be possible to keep the old national currencies as they were but to tie them together through a grid of fixed exchange rates. In this way, these currencies would be perfectly substitutable for each other. As long as they were freely convertible and freely transferable throughout the union, they would be technically equivalent to one currency. This view is supported by many economists such as Mundell and P.R. Allen.[38] However, other economists, notably W.M. Cordon, take issue with it. According to Cordon, exchange rates cannot be fixed irrevocably without the convergence of the other basic economic factors. Hence, exchange-rate fixity is always regarded as suspect by the private sector whose motivation to speculate is therefore likely to persist.[39]

In the event that old national currencies continued to circulate, their future supply would have to be controlled by the union authorities. Naturally, the new union currency could and perhaps should circulate side by side with the old national currencies. The acceptance by the public of the old currencies derives from deep psychological and historical habits and it would be some time before a new parallel currency became fully accepted. The issuance of a new parallel currency would simplify the management of the money supply. However, as long as old national currencies continued to circulate, the public would have to put up with dual pricing. Eventually, the authorities should replace the old currencies. To accelerate this process, the union authorities could arrange for taxes to be payable in the new currency, use it exclusively in their accounts, offer quotes in it (e.g., forward rates) and, with greatest effect, could have all central banks offer a small discount on it in order to chase away the old currencies.

d. Exchange rates and intervention rules. The determining factor for the success of a fixed exchange-rate arrangement is the durability of the arrangement as perceived by the public. Exchange rates are intercurrency prices only on the surface. Fundamentally, they express purchasing command and, hence, embody all the factors determining: the demand for and the supply of money, wage and productivity trends and the balance-of-payments position (current and capital accounts). A fixed exchange-rate arrangement is credible in the long run to the extent that it is justified by these factors.

Exchange rates can be fixed in relation to each other by means of a parity grid. Their actual values should then not depart from the central rates. Another way would be to fix the central rates in terms of a numeraire, say the Arab dinar or any other Arab currency basket, and allow them to move together only in relation to the change in the rate of this union currency against the SDR or any set of foreign currencies, or to allow them to move at the same percentage rate.

This would eventually mean intra-union fixity and extra-union floating. There is a definite advantage to floating against the outside world in relation to a basket of foreign currencies representative of, say, Arab imports or in relation to the SDR. The overall balance-of-payments position of the Arab countries, together with their import pattern, would allow them to take advantage of flexibility *vis-à-vis* the outside world. It would also free some of them from their exclusive link to the dollar, hardly justified by trade or capital movements.

The weights of the various foreign currencies in the basket would depend on the objectives of the prospective Arab monetary union. These weights would vary according to whether the Arab states wished to stabilise the value of their imports, their current account balance, income, employment or even their terms of trade. It would take us far afield to offer a technical solution for the attainment of these various objectives.[40]

In practice, and as an interim arrangement, the Arab states might choose to stabilise their currencies around certain central rates and to narrow the deviation margins over time. These central rates would be fixed either directly in relation to the SDR or in relation to the Arab dinar which, in turn, would have a central rate with respect to the SDR or to another such numeraire. The other alternative, the parity grid, implies different intervention obligations: once the margin is crossed, the obligation to intervene with immediately available and unlimited funds arises at once and falls on all countries. The question arises as to access to the reserve pool and to extra intervention funds and as to the settlement of the resulting balances.

In the author's opinion, the first method, i.e., the central numeraire, is preferable. It would identify the deviating currency and hence fix the obligation to intervene. It would also enhance the numeraire function of the Arab dinar and give impetus to its development. Again, the deviation from the central rates must not exceed a given margin; if it does, either the union authority or the relevant central bank should intervene. The intervention medium may be either a reserve currency or the deviating currency in question. The difference mainly concerns access to sources of funds and the arrangements in force for co-operative intra-union swaps.

Interim arrangements must establish clear procedures for modifying the central rates. In devising formulae for setting and adjusting these rates and in outlining the intervention procedures, the structure of the foreign exchange market in which the currencies are traded and its competitive characteristics must be fully taken into account. If the union currencies are not to be traded in a competitive market and if their value does not have to stabilise around a certain numeraire, then most of these considerations become irrelevant. In this case, the union authority posts the rates in terms of the numeraire, preferably the intervention medium, and makes sure that all central banks abide by these central rates.

e. Operation of the reserve pool. The reserve pool should be viewed as a short-term operational modality leading up to an Arab fund for financing payments imbalances. The pool would receive deposits initially in reserve currencies and would be administered by the union. The operation of a reserve pool involves certain legal, institutional and economic issues. Briefly, the first issue concerns ownership, i.e., whether the funds are owned by the pool or owned by the depositor and merely managed by the pool. The second issue concerns investment of reserves by the pool with the attendant questions of risk-sharing, earnings and distribution of expenses. The third issue pertains to the conditions of access to the reserve pool and the procedures for lending to deficit countries. The fourth issue is that of liquidating intervention balances and setting up procedures for settling intra-union payments imbalances via reserve transfers, transfers of other securities or, under certain conditions, prescribed amounts of a member's own currency.

These are all short-term issues. In the long run, the reserve pool must be integrated within an Arab monetary fund whose purpose would be to extend medium-term finance and issue the union currency, e.g., the dinar, against national currency transfers. This would involve union liquidity control and might call for interim designation limits for various countries. The existing Arab Monetary Fund could be gradually charged with these functions and transformed into a supra-national central bank.

f. Monetary co-ordination. In the initial stages, the union should facilitate the co-ordination of monetary policies among members. Later, it should enforce a common policy covering many areas.

In the area of monetary control, the union would have to streamline its reserve requirements across the domain, standardise procedures for discounting and last-resort lending and centralise its open market operations, though specific national central banks might be charged with implementing these operations.

In the circumstances of the Arab world, aggregate money-supply targets should be more effective than interest-rate targets, due to the under-development of the financial markets and the likely use, at least for a time, of independent credit policies. Moreover, because of the size of Arab investments abroad, interest-rate targets cannot be as easily implemented as aggregate money-supply targets.

In setting the money supply targets, the union must be conscious of the uneven demand for money among the various countries and of the manner in which aggregate increases or decreases in money supply will diffuse themselves across the union. Specifically, the domain and degree of security market integration would determine whether only aggregate measures are needed or whether these must be supplemented by country-specific actions. This will be further explored in Part C below.

In the area of banking structure, uniform banking regulations and methods of control must be sought. While this would largely involve the streamlining and restructuring of legislation, in a fundamental sense, banking structures would evolve in the context of the on-going market integration across the union. Both foreign and domestic banking should come under union control and, to the extent possible, non-bank financial intermediaries must be subject to the same rules as commercial banks in order to ensure monetary control at the source.

As concerns external capital movements, the union should have the final word on foreign borrowing, the floating of foreign securities and bank borrowing from foreign branches. Reserve requirements on so-called 'solicited deposits' should be imposed.

Finally, the integration of security markets across the union is a major requirement for a successful monetary union. At this point, it should be stressed that a major task of any monetary union is the promotion and enhancement of market integration. By creating a currency area, standardising banking regulations and diffusing government securities across the union, the monetary authorities would be making a direct contribution to market integration.

g. Fiscal co-ordination. It would be realistic to assume that the relevant question is not how to lodge fiscal prerogatives with the union authorities, but rather what degree of fiscal centralisation is necessary for a successful monetary union. The distribution of fiscal responsibility will be multi-layered in a monetary union, with certain fiscal responsibilities assigned to union bodies or brought under union co-ordination and others, perhaps most, remaining under the control of the member countries.

The case for centralising the two major tools of fiscal policy, i.e., redistribution and stabilisation measures, is convincing. Fiscal measures have spillover effects from one country to another; borrowing creates burdens over time or across the union which are bound to affect the union's welfare; the cost of borrowing declines as volume increases and government security markets should therefore draw on union-wide resources; tax regulations on security holdings, trading and capital gains crucially affect the operation of the money and capital markets. But all of this should be taken by a union as a normative model rather than as an agenda for action.

In a monetary union, it is the level of government expenditure, the size of the tax levy, the financing of the public debt and the redistributive fiscal transfers which fluctuate with the volume of monetary assets. As was stressed in Part f above, monetary policy in the Arab world depends considerably on net fiscal spending which in turn is largely determined by oil revenues and inter-Arab aid flows.

h. Economic policy co-ordination. The guiding analytical principle behind economic policy co-ordination is to bring in line the levels of excess aggregate demand and the determinants of the cost structure (wages and productivity) across the union. Furthermore, this co-ordination should aim at facilitating full resource mobility and increasing intra-union trade. While some of the measures in this respect would be encompassed by fiscal, monetary and banking co-ordination, it is useful to highlight some particular aspects of such co-ordination in the Arab world.

(1) The component of aggregate demand of the greatest instrumental value is the level of investment in each country. The establishment of an Arab investment bank is an idea worth exploring. Already, there are many Arab institutions active in the field of project financing throughout the region. To distinguish itself from other institutions, the proposed Arab investment bank might aim at public sector financing, co-financing arrangements, and, under certain conditions, programme lending to the Arab countries. This would bridge the growth gap between these countries.

(2) To encourage resource mobility, member countries might co-ordinate the establishment of liberal residence regulations for Arab labourers, set up recruitment offices for labour, standardise and co-ordinate tax laws and carry out vocational training programmes for their labour forces. For individual countries, however, the reduction of wage differentials which would result from such mobility could have inflationary and output implications requiring careful treatment.

(3) The transformation of the union domain into one customs zone is essential for the development of inter-Arab trade. A substantial volume of trade is a primary condition for the viability of monetary unions. The establishment of an Arab payments and clearance facility within the AMF, or independently, would go far to facilitate inter-Arab trade. This payments facility could come into operation very early, before the integration of security markets had reached a satisfactory stage.

i. Net transfer of resources in a union. The operation of a monetary union brings about the transfer of resources from deficit to surplus countries through the intra-union balance of payments (current account). This process is slow but sure. When the goods and services markets are integrated, the flow of goods and of the factors of production redistribute resources and productive capacity across the union. This transfer of wealth cannot be dissipated by fiscal counter-measures because, with a substantial degree of market integration, interest-rate differentials would not exist long enough to produce country-specific results. The operation of transfers through the balance on current account can only allow regional targeting in the short run. Hence, a union has to accept responsibility for normative transfers of resources to poor subregions, if not on ethical grounds, then at least on the grounds of generalising economic benefits. In the EMS, this fact has been duly recognised and the European Monetary Fund (EMF) is expected to assume increasing responsibilities in this regard.

For the Arab region, such a normative redistribution of wealth is all the more desirable. The poor Arab regions at this time in history are the more populated, potentially well-endowed regions. A measure of redistribution in their favour would be a direct contribution to the region's overall well-being. Furthermore, transfers are an investment for the future generations of the net donors inasmuch as the duration of their relative income surplus is finite and should not, for the future, be confined to their own territory. For these reasons, the political jealousies associated with net transfers of resources in other monetary unions should be less acute in the Arab region by reason of enlightened self-interest over the long run.

3. The Structure of Authority in a Monetary Union. It would be instructive to draw up the structure of the union monetary authority along functional lines. The control of monetary instruments, i.e., open market operations, reserve policies and the discount window, must be lodged with the union authority. Moreover, the union authority would have control of the currency mint and retain the exclusive right to issue liabilities with the power of legal tender against itself. That is, the union authority would have full control over all the elements of high-powered money.

The union would also have control of the reserve pool and would conduct, or at least supervise, all open market operations on the foreign exchange markets. The union central bank would also be the principal agent of governments in international operations.

As far as banking supervision goes, the union authority must have the final word on banking regulations and should supervise and coordinate bank examinations. The union authority should extend over both domestic and foreign banks.

To the extent that credit policies affect the money markets and entail financing obligations, they should come under union control.[41] Interest ceiling regulations and other asset and liability regulations should fall within the jurisdiction of the union authority.

The question arises as to whether the central banks of the member countries should give way to the union bank or continue to exist under its umbrella. It is argued that given the differences in their regulations and customs and because of their sheer familiarity with the terrain, the old central banks should continue to exist. Decentralisation, it is said, is a beneficial check on the inexorable advance of bureaucracy at the centre. In the author's view, the question does not turn on the continuation or discontinuation of the old central banks, but rather on their functional role in the new monetary structure. The old central banks may be allowed to continue, provided they act as agents and executive arms of the union authority.

The organisation of this authority would normally require three types of operative bodies: a political body in the form of a board of governors to set general policy guidelines; an executive board which would meet regularly to supervise the execution of monetary policy and instruct its various actions; and a central staff of bank personnel, headed by a managing director. The main functional divisions of such a central authority would be research and statistics, foreign operations, bank supervision, union affairs, and finance and administrative services. Both the US Federal Reserve System and the European Monetary System might serve as good organisational models.

C. The Role of Security Market Integration in a Monetary Union

The role of security markets in determining the success or failure of monetary unions and deepening the integration process cannot be over-emphasised. It is particularly appropriate to address this topic in the context of the Arab region since integrated Arab security markets will be of crucial importance to the Arab surplus countries.

1. Basic Concepts and Definitions. Following Scitovsky (1969) and P.R. Allen (1976), the distinction is made between two essential concepts: the domain of integration and the degree of integration. The domain of integration is delimited by the geographical distribution of security ownership across the union. The domain of integration directly covers a given security but also extends indirectly across the domain of other substitutable securities. The terms 'domain of integration' and 'domain of security integration' shall therefore be used to denote these two domains. Furthermore, the word 'security' denotes not only a government security or a security used in open market operations, but also assets acquired by banks in the process of credit expansion.

The degree of integration is defined in terms of the substitutability of securities; two securities exhibit a high degree of integration if they enjoy a high degree of substitutability. When there is perfect integration, the sale of one security and the purchase of another in different regions will not affect their relative prices.[42] This means in effect that the two securities or markets function as one. Similar definitions of integration apply to currency markets, goods and services markets and factor markets. It is to be emphasised that integration does not depend on direct security-to-security substitution, but can be effected through a third security (or a third market, as explained above).

2. The Importance of Market Integration for the Arab Region. Market integration reduces the differences in the way identical assets, factors and products are treated across the union domain. As such, it is a necessary condition for efficiency.[43] Markets are often characterised by overshooting, rigidities and distortions, all of which may be significantly reduced by a high degree of integration. The effective linkage of security markets with the wider security domain resulting from a high degree of integration rapidly diffuses the impact of monetary action all across the domain of integration. In highly integrated markets, the impact of monetary action reaches beyond the securities directly involved in open market operations (or those purchased by banks) to affect other securities and the commodity and money markets as well.

The result of this, from the point of view of the balance of payments, is to facilitate the financing of the payments deficits and postpone real adjustment in the various Arab countries. However, because of the pervasive impact of monetary action, subregional interest-rate differentials are swiftly eliminated through arbitrage. Hence the monetary authority would be capable of generating an overall impact but not a country-specific impact. While the diffused nature of this impact might frustrate directed monetary action, it would spare monetary authorities the task of collecting a great deal of information on subregions and fine-toning country-specific impacts. A by-product of this is the avoidance of sensitive political conflicts within the union. Given conditions in the Arab region, these aspects may be judged desirable.

As was pointed out earlier, the surplus holders among the Arab countries have a vested interest in the development of security markets in order to extend the domain of their investment opportunities and forestall possible recourse to capital controls in the Arab world. On the other hand, Arab net borrowers would benefit from a high degree of security market integration through their increased ability to mobilise Arab savings and through the likely reduction of their borrowing costs resulting from competitive bidding for securities.

The move towards a monetary union promotes the process of market integration in many ways. These include: the encouragement of branch-banking and the creation of incentives for banks to extend their security and investment activities across the union; the encouragement of financial intermediation through liberalised and uniform regulations in the Arab region; the spread of security-holding throughout the union, the development of effective communications networks; the co-ordination and streamlining of tax laws; and, last but hardly least, the development of a union-wide secondary security market for the securities transacted in the union's open market operations. No less important is the fact that the increased co-ordination of fiscal borrowing necessitated by a monetary union could create a pan-Arab government security market in which both private and public funds might be invested. Specific recommendations for the promotion of market integration may be found in the Sergé Report of the EEC.

The implications of the integration of the Arab security market with foreign security markets, given the size of the Arab countries' foreign security holdings, while distinct from those which have been discussed here, nevertheless merit a careful discussion. It is beyond the scope of this paper, however, to discuss international market integration.

Notes

1. In recent discussions, it has rightly been noted that the fixity of exchange rates is only one of the attributes of a common currency area, the other two crucial elements being perfect convertibility and the fixity of forward exchange rates. (See, for example, R.R. Mundell and Alexander K. Swoboda, *Monetary Problems of the International Economy* [Chicago: University of Chicago Press, 1969], pp. 109 and 110.) In what follows, it is assumed that perfect convertibility always goes together with fixed exchange rates. As far as forward exchange rates are concerned, their constancy will depend on governments strictly maintaining them into the indefinite future and on people's belief that they will do so. This point will be touched upon later, when speculation is discussed.

2. See J.M. Fleming, 'On Exchange-Rate Unification', *Economic Journal*, vol. 81 (September 1971), pp. 469-71 and 486-8.

3. See H.G. Grubel, 'The Theory of Optimum Currency Areas', *Canadian Journal of Economics*, vol. 3 (May 1970), pp. 322 and 323.

4. See F. Hirsch, 'The Political Economics of European Monetary Integration', *The World Today*, vol. 28 (October 1972), pp. 427-30.

5. Hirsch, 'The Political Economics of European Monetary Integration', pp. 428 and 429, and Fleming, 'On Exchange Rate Unification', pp. 478 and 479.

6. See R.A. Mundell, 'Uncommon Arguments for Common Currencies', in Harry G. Johnson and Alexander K. Swoboda (eds.), *The Economies of Common Currencies* (London: 1973).

7. See Y. Ishiyama, 'The Theory of Optimum Currency Areas: A Survey', *International Monetary Fund Staff Papers*, vol. 22 (June 1975).

8. See Jorge Gonzalez del Valle, 'Monetary Integration in Latin America', one of the papers presented at this seminar [pp. 205-24].

9. See Ishiyama, 'The Theory of Optimum Currency Areas: A Survey', and J.H. Williamson, 'Comment on Dr. Lamfalussy's paper', paper presented at the Fourth Congress of the International Economic Association, Budapest, 1974.

10. See Mundell, 'A Theory of Optimum Currency Areas', *American Economic*

Review, vol. 51 (September 1961).

11. Kenen, 'The Theory of Optimum Currency Areas: An Eclectic View', in Mundell and Swoboda (eds.), *Monetary Problems of the International Economy*, pp. 43 and 44.

12. See Fleming, 'On Exchange-Rate Unification'.

13. See Kenen, 'The Theory of Optimum Currency Areas: An Eclectic View'.

14. See McKinnon, 'Optimum Currency Areas', *American Economic Review*, vol. 53 (September 1963).

15. See Fleming, 'On Exchange-Rate Unification'.

16. See McKinnon, 'Optimum Currency Areas'.

17. See, for example, W.M. Cordon, *Monetary Integration*, Princeton Essays in International Finance, no. 93 (Princeton: Princeton University Press, 1972), a revised and extended version of his Frank Graham Memorial lecture, Princeton University, April 1971.

18. McKinnon, 'Optimum Currency Areas', pp. 721–3.

19. See Fleming, 'On Exchange-Rate Unification'.

20. Machlup, *A History of Thought on Economic Integration* (London: Macmillan Press, 1977), chap. 2, p. 18.

21. Machlup takes a similar view. After elaborating on the multi-faceted association between monetary and real exchange, he concludes: 'Hence, an international payments system that allows payments and foreign exchange transactions without restrictions or controls – in short, monetary integration – is an integral part of complete economic integration'. Ibid., p. 20.

22. R.A. Mundell, 'A Theory of Optimum Currency Areas'.

23. R.I. McKinnon, 'Optimum Currency Areas'.

24. P.B. Kenen, 'The Theory of Optimum Currency Areas: An Eclectic View', pp. 43 and 44.

25. James C. Ingram, 'A Proposal for Financial Integration in the Atlantic Community', in United States Congress, Joint Economic Committee, 'Factors Affecting the United States Balance of Payments', a paper presented before the 87th Congress, 2nd session, 1962, and Ingram, 'The Exchange-Rate Question for a United Europe: Internal Flexibility and External Rigidity Versus External Flexibility and Internal Rigidity', in Alexander K. Swoboda (ed.), *Europe and the Evolution of the International Monetary System: Proceedings of the first Conference of the International Center for Monetary and Banking Studies*, International Economics Series, no. 1 (Geneva: The Graduate Institute of International Studies, 1973).

26. Scitovsky, 1967.

27. J.M. Fleming, 'Domestic Financial Policies under Fixed and Under Floating Exchange Rates', International Monetary Fund, *International Monetary Fund Staff Papers*, vol. 9 (November 1962).

28. Gottfried Haberler, 'The International Monetary System: Some Recent Developments and Discussions', in George N. Halm (ed.), *Approaches to Greater Flexibility of Exchange Rates* (Princeton: Princeton University Press, 1970).

29. Maria Von Neumann Whitman, *International and Inter-regional Payments Adjustment: A Synthetic View*, Princeton Essays in International Finance, no. 19 (Princeton: Princeton University Press, 1967).

30. W.M. Cordon, *Monetary Integration*.

31. Whitman, *International and Inter-regional Payments Adjustment: A Synthetic View*.

32. The minimal requirements of monetary integration include a single currency or a set of integrated currencies, a simple union authority and, ideally, an integrated security market.

33. For a detailed discussion, see Ishiyama, 'The Theory of Optimum Currency

Areas: A Survey', pp. 344–59.

34. F. Hirsch, 'The Political Economics of European Monetary Integration', pp. 430 and 431.

35. For details, see Ishiyama, 'The Theory of Optimum Currency Areas: A Survey', pp. 368 and 369.

36. For an interesting sceptical view, see Hirsch, 'The Political Economics of European Monetary Integration'.

37. The concept of market integration will be discussed in detail in Section C of this paper.

38. Polly Reynolds Allen, *Organization and Administration of a Monetary Union*, Princeton Essays in International Finance, no. 38 (Princeton: Princeton University Press, 1976), p. 4.

39. Cordon, *Monetary Integration*.

40. There is a growing literature on optimal pegging arrangements. For example, see W. Branson and L. Katseli-Papaefstratiou, *Exchange-Rate Policy for Developing Countries*, Institute for International Economic Studies, S-106 91 (Stockholm: 1978).

41. It should be pointed out that credit policies which entail financing obligations hamper union market integration by segmenting the financial markets.

42. This does not mean identical prices, nor that all potential buyers and sellers encounter the same prices.

43. Efficiency is not to be confused with a high degree of integration. A high degree of efficiency is not a sufficient condition for integration.

COMMENT*

Abdul Munim Al-Sayyed Ali

Mr Medio begins his part of the paper by analysing the various types of costs incurred by a country joining a fixed exchange-rate area. The most important of these is the loss of one of the basic instruments of economic policy for dealing with serious balance-of-payments disequilibria. He also refers to the cost of surrendering control over the money supply and distinguishes between changes in the money supply resulting from internal as compared with external monetary factors. The author shows how these costs associated with fixed exchange rates depend on the size of the economy, the degree of capital mobility and the trade-off between inflation and employment. He distinguishes between market-based and government-based policies in effecting the adjustment operations dictated by fixed exchange rates. He further refers to the effect of government policy in mitigating the impact of balance-of-payments disequilibria and the way this impact is distributed. He then proceeds to enumerate the benefits that result from joining a fixed exchange-rate area. He lists a number of factors which determine the costs and benefits of fixed exchange rates, the most important being: labour and capital mobility among the countries of the fixed exchange-rate area, local product diversification and the openness of their national economies as measured by the ratio of tradeable goods to total production, the degree of money illusion and the similarity of inflation rates in the countries of the region.

The author turns finally to the question of the degree of integration and harmony prevailing among the economic policies of the participating countries. He distinguishes here between two schools of thought: the 'economic' school and the 'monetary' school. The main point of contention between these schools is whether monetary integration should precede economic integration or follow it. The author expresses certain doubts concerning the soundness of the monetary school, pointing out that the centralisation of monetary and banking policy advocated by this school might tend to exacerbate rather than to correct payments disequilibria and that increased capital and labour mobility might have the same negative effect. What is of concern to us here is the conclusion of the paper in which the author relates all these issues to Arab monetary integration. He concludes, in fact, that the establishment of fixed exchange rates — let alone a common currency

---

* Translated from the Arabic.

among the Arab countries — would probably not be desirable or even conceivable, in view of both of the extreme diversity of their economic, social and political structures and the limited volume of inter-Arab trade. Given this situation, fixing the exchange rates among Arab currencies would not, in Mr Medio's opinion, help to promote inter-Arab trade.

Accordingly, he joins Mr Triffin in proposing the adoption of modest policies aimed at strengthening the mechanisms for balance-of-payments financing and reducing both inflation differentials and exchange-rate fluctuations. He points out, however, that the picture changes when monetary integration is considered with respect to smaller groups of Arab countries with common problems and characteristics, referring here to the Arab oil countries. He believes that these countries can establish a common currency in a more or less gradual manner. The benefits of such a move, in his view, would not reflect themselves so much in trade as in the financial area. These benefits would include a reduction in the cost of financial management, the pooling of information and greater possibilities for innovation. Moreover, the stable purchasing power of the common currency in relation to an important commodity like oil would make this currency an attractive financial asset demanded world-wide along with other international currencies like the dollar and the ECU. Mr Triffin makes the same point in his paper.

Although I concur with the views presented by Mr Medio concerning the costs and benefits of integration, I do not feel he provides us with any new ideas concerning the feasibility of Arab monetary integration. Furthermore, he has confined his paper to a single form of integration which is the establishment of a common currency area. It is my view that the author should have detailed other modalities for achieving a degree of uniformity in the monetary sphere and commented on their feasibility. Such modalities could turn to advantage the general economic features common to all or most of the Arab countries.

In the second part of the paper, Mr Sakbani refers on more than one occasion to the costs and benefits of monetary integration which, according to him, should be studied from a dynamic perspective. His reasoning is that economic integration creates new economic and political structures and institutions. This is why the basic decision is a political one, a matter on which I believe all of us agree. Nevertheless, the author has defined monetary integration according to the same statistical criteria as Machlup employs, i.e., equality between marginal product and/or marginal utility per unit of marginal cost, on the one hand, and the marginal prices of production and consumer goods, on the other. When this equality is achieved, efficiency and social welfare are maxim

The author then says that monetary integration is an effective instrument for achieving economic integration, a view which he claims is similar to Machlup's. However, the statement he quotes from Machlup [note 21, p. 374] does not fully support his argument since it merely refers to monetary integration as an 'integral part' of economic integration. Nevertheless, the author rightly points out that the success or failure of monetary integration is determined by cultural, historical and political ties no less than by economic factors. He then examines the extent to which this applies to the situation in the Arab countries and refers to the marked differences among their economic systems which tend to impede the free movement of the factors of production among them and the development of integrated financial markets.

The author also defines a minimal concept of monetary integration as the establishment of an integrated area with either a single currency or several freely convertible currencies tied together by fixed exchange rates. He stresses the need for a central authority to regulate the money supply. The free movement of capital and stable exchange rates are, according to the author, two essential factors in monetary integration.

Mr Sakbani then takes up the feasibility of monetary integration with its costs and benefits, as discussed in the first part of the paper. One point which he mentions in this regard is that when the oil era is over, the risks associated with accumulations of financial investments abroad might increase considerably. It is not clear just how and where these accumulations are likely to originate, since the surpluses currently being invested abroad are all closely connected with oil and will decrease considerably in the post-oil era. How, then, are financial resources going to accumulate when oil revenues are expected to be spent on Arab economic and social development even before the end of the oil era?

As for the financial implications of monetary integration, the author argues that the loss of control over the money supply would mean that deficit financing could only be accomplished through borrowing and that the integration of the money markets would render financial policies aimed at stabilising particular regions ineffective. However the author does not make clear the reasons for this nor does he show the extent to which this is applicable to those Arab countries seeking monetary integration.

As to the forms or modalities of monetary integration, I would take issue with the author's assertion that a situation of 'dual pricing' would result from the introduction of a parallel currency alongside the domestic currencies. In my opinion, the author fails to justify this assertion. Nor can I agree with him that offering a small discount on the new currency would chase away the old currencies as per Gresham's Law. How would this be possible in a single currency area? Could this realistically lead to the achievement of the desired monetary integration?

With regard to the integration of security markets and its importance to the success of monetary integration, this whole question is linked to the issue of capital mobility. It is not so much related to the substitutability of securities as to the freedom of capital to move from one national market to another. What must not be forgotten is that the surplus oil revenues belong to governments. Therefore, discussion of security markets in the traditional sense lies outside the scope of Arab monetary integration because it is government-held financial surpluses which are the source of nearly all capital flows within the oil-producing Arab countries.

Some of the conclusions reached by the author concerning Arab integration appear to be contradictory. On the one hand, he finds that for the countries of any region to achieve monetary integration, there must be substantial intra-regional trade. On the other hand, he says that the political and economic conditions of the Arab region at this historical juncture appear to favour monetary integration. Still elsewhere, he says that monetary integration primarily involves a political decision which it is up to the Arab countries to make, regardless of their differing economic systems. Perhaps the author would care to clarify his views on these issues.

Finally, a problem common to both parts of the paper is that they do not attempt, except in a very limited way, to show the extent to which their models and the conclusions they derive from them correspond to the realities of the Arab situation.

GENERAL DISCUSSION

1. Mabid Al-Jarhi

Mr Medio considers the conditions elaborated by Mundel for the existence of an 'optimal currency area'. After discussing each condition separately, he concludes that, given the current circumstances, the Arab region does not constitute an optimal currency area. It should be noted, however, that these conditions are outlined in Mundel's work in a very loose manner; some of them, as the author notes, are contradictory, and all still require further theoretical and empirical scrutiny.

A different and perhaps more promising approach has been proposed by Robert Vaubel[1] whereby the cost of monetary integration is assessed as follows:

(a) The accompanying common monetary policy, including inflation-rate harmonisation, could lead, under the Keynesian assumption of persistent trade-offs between unemployment and inflation, to needless unemployment in some member countries and needless inflation in others. However, this Keynesian assumption, better known as the 'Phillips curve', has been seriously questioned;
(b) Governments would lose the freedom to increase their revenues through inflation, specifically, by utilising seigniorage and fiscal drag. However this freedom is another 'Phillips curve' illusion, for it is becoming increasingly difficult to defend inflation as a revenue-raising policy;
(c) The effect of exchange-rate movements on the stability of domestic prices would be either reduced (under exchange-rate stabilisation) or eliminated (under currency unification). Nominal exchange-rate adjustments might prove to be less costly. Also it is noted that international transactors seem to be better equipped to cope with nominal exchange-rate adjustments than are ordinary citizens to cope with changes in domestic price levels.

With regard to this third cost, Vaubel suggests as a measurement the 'revealed' need for real exchange-rate changes in the countries constituting the potential members of a monetary union.

As for the Arab case, it should be interesting to see whether these costs would outweigh the benefits of a monetary union. I might hazard a guess that these costs would be minimal in the Arab world, for exchange-rate policy is of little domestic economic importance to the Arab countries.

Finally, Mr Medio concludes with the curious statement that 'a common currency characterized by stability of purchasing power [with respect to] oil might prove to be an attractive financial asset' [p. 356]. This, to my mind, deserves further elaboration.

As for Mr Sakbani's presentation, I fully agree with his conclusion that the choice between the different modalities of monetary integration is less a question of positive analysis than one of political will.

2. Khair El-Din Haseeb

I believe it would be appropriate to judge the paper before us not so much on the basis of the theoretical issues it raises as by the extent to which it succeeds in shedding light on the subject it was intended to address, namely, the advantages of and obstacles to Arab monetary integration.

I find that neither part of the paper does more than treat the theoretical aspects of monetary integration in a general way without taking up the question of their application in the Arab context. In this connection, I find it puzzling that Mr Medio, who does not discuss the Arab economies at all but confines himself to a brief overview of the major theoretical issues relating to monetary integration, should reach the conclusion he does, namely that the establishment of a fixed exchange rate, to say nothing of a common currency, among the Arab countries as a whole would appear not only undesirable but inconceivable, in the light of the disparate economic, political and social structures of these countries.

Turning to the technical possibilities for monetary unity or monetary integration in the Gulf, already discussed here at length, I would like to make two observations:

(a) Oil, the main resource of the Arab Gulf states, is not just an ordinary economic commodity but rather an 'economic and political' commodity. The Gulf states, especially those of the 'lesser Arab Gulf' so often referred to these days, could never have gained the relative control they have over the price of their oil or the relative and limited control they exercise over its production, indeed, they could not even have become independent to start with, had they not been part of the Arab nation. This Arab nation has always considered the interests and destiny of the Arab Gulf to be one with its own interests and destiny and part of pan-Arab security. It has therefore entered into a series of battles with Western colonialism for the protection of the interests of the Arab nation, including the Gulf, and has paid dearly for it, sometimes with blood. The latest but not the last of these battles was the 1973 October War which was a crucial factor in achieving what gains have been made with regard to oil.

The notion that the Gulf countries, especially those of the 'lesser Gulf', can achieve monetary unity in isolation from the Arab nation is based on purely technical considerations and ignores the question of Gulf security which cannot be achieved except as part of Arab national security generally. The Gulf states could hardly preserve the real value of their oil prices and the safety of their deposits and investments in the West without the full weight and protection of the Arab countries behind them. It would be useful for us all to take careful stock of the potential dangers to Arab investments in the West to which Mr Dajani has referred. Similarly, we would do well to imagine what the West might dare to do after the oil has run out or almost run out and when it has in its possession huge Arab deposits and investments. While the West may be reluctant to venture such bold steps now, anxious as it is for the flow of oil in its direction to continue, this attitude could change radically when the oil supplies begin to dwindle or when alternative energy sources become available. For this reason, assuming it is technically possible for the Gulf states to achieve monetary unity, then the protection of their main resource − oil − and the safeguarding of the investments of this monetary union would make Arab national security imperative, security which the Gulf states by themselves cannot ensure.

Hence it is in the interests of the Gulf states that they have behind them the full weight of the Arab countries, themselves economically, politically and militarily strong and capable. This will only happen when all the Arab countries become aware of their interlocking destinies and can commit themselves to joint Arab development in order to build an independent Arab economy and to provide the basis for Arab national security and the safeguards it requires.

For all these reasons, considerations of long-term and even of medium-term interest require that the Gulf countries and particularly those of the lesser Gulf, if only out of narrow self-interest, think and act from a broad Arab perspective and not from the narrow perspective of the Gulf. Without this radically different way of looking at things, we shall continue to delude ourselves, to deceive our nation and to expose ourselves to the harsh judgement of future generations.

(b) There have been repeated attempts to discuss the Arab Gulf in a narrow and restricted context, excluding both Saudi Arabia and Iraq or just Iraq. In this regard, I would like to stress the following points:

(1) There is a geographical reality which defines the countries of the Arab Gulf and which clearly places Saudi Arabia and Iraq among them;
(2) Certain of those countries, which some observers like to exclude

from the context of regional Arab Gulf co-operation, are right now paying the blood tax for the security of the Gulf and of the Arab islands within it;
(3) The considerations to which I have referred in my first observation apply equally well here and make it in the interest of all the countries of the Gulf, including Saudi Arabia and Iraq, to co-operate with each other.

In conclusion, I would like to emphasise that any partial co-operation among the Gulf countries must be understood and evaluated, whenever possible, in the context of the whole Gulf and, secondly, should operate within the framework of general Arab co-operation, both serving it and benefiting from it.

3. Karim Nashashibi

I, too, would like to relate the discussion of this paper to the Arab world. We have before us two parallel and reinforcing paths towards economic integration.

One is the transfer of oil surpluses to the deficit countries to help them overcome their structural problems and build up their capital stock in a concerted and complementary manner in order to maximise economies of scale and pave the way for economic integration. But I do not see any prospects for this approach developing into monetary integration. The other path is the one which would entail the monetary integration of the Gulf countries and the co-ordination of their exchange-rate policies; for government spending is at the origin of liquidity creation in the oil-producing countries. Spending must be calibrated to the ability of the respective countries to absorb their non-traded goods. With respect to traded goods which, apart from oil, are mostly imports, upward adjustments in the exchange rate have been used to reduce exogenous inflation. However, with the creation of a common currency unit, an appreciation in the value of this joint currency unit would not be appropriate for all the members of the monetary union since their economies exhibit different ratios of imports to traded goods.

Another issue pertains to Saudi Arabia. Since such monetary integration cannot be conceived of without its participation, what are the problems which may emerge from its economic domination of the area given that it has its own set of policy preferences including a reluctance to internationalise its currency?

4. Mohammed Labib Shoukair

The two parts of the paper we have before us seem to be contradictory with regard to the concept of monetary integration. Mr Medio's notion of monetary integration is that of a monetary zone where exchange rates remain stable. Mr Sakbani, on the other hand, accepting what he describes as the prevailing view among economists, states that monetary integration implies a common currency. Furthermore, Mr Sakbani has listed different approaches towards monetary integration but has not attempted to indicate which approach could or should, in practice, be followed.

In this connection, I would like to inquire as to why the payments union formula has been excluded from the listed approaches to monetary integration? In Latin America, for example, the payments union has played an important role, not only as an instrument of monetary co-operation but also as an instrument for moving towards economic integration among certain countries of the region.

One of the conclusions Mr Medio draws is that it would not be feasible, at present, to establish monetary integration among the Arab countries. He defines monetary integration simply as the establishment of a free zone of exchange-rate stability. His arguments for drawing this conclusion are based on the fact that the economies and the socio-political structures of the Arab countries are highly dissimilar. It is not certain, however, whether these dissimilarities would tend to encourage the process of exchange-rate stabilisation or impede it. This kind of *a priori* judgement can hardly be accepted. The error here is one of separating the monetary integration process from the economic integration process. If economic integration were brought into the picture, as I think it should be, it would become clear that both monetary integration and exchange-rate stability are indeed possible and can be fully achieved irrespective of any existing diversity among the Arab economies. Mr Sakbani, on the other hand, arrives at the opposite conclusion, i.e., he advocates establishing Arab monetary integration. The two authors obviously reach contradictory conclusions in this regard.

Mr Sakbani argues that if we wish to effect capital transfers in the region under current conditions, we have to employ the market mechanism. This would seem to apply to private capital movement only. Let us remember, however, that the oil surpluses with which we are concerned are not private but government surpluses. Consequently, the decision here does not depend on market mechanisms but essentially on what Mr Haseeb has emphasised, i.e., the pan-Arab ties among the Arab economies. Moreover, most economic and development activity in the oil countries is in government hands and financed by the state budget. The bulk of the development effort is assumed by the government which makes the national economy a public-sector-oriented economy in terms of the development process. If we take this view and introduce the process of Arab economic development as a means of achieving economic integration, we find that many of the difficulties which arise when we base our thinking on microeconomic analysis disappear.

5. Faika El-Refaie

I would like to refer to two general observations which have been made in this seminar: first, that monetary integration must go hand in hand with economic integration and secondly, that monetary integration cannot be attained at the level of the Arab world as a whole.

I submit that the movement towards economic and monetary integration can be pursued along several fronts, beginning with the Gulf dinar.

Permit me to compare the potential advantages and pitfalls of this proposal. The advantages may be enumerated as follows:

(i) Conditions in the Gulf countries are more favourable than ever for joint activity, as the governments of the region are fully aware of the importance of Gulf unity in various areas. As a first step, joint activity in the monetary field would pave the way for the complete co-ordination of overall economic integration;

(ii) Given the importance of the government sector and its role in the economic development of these countries, joint monetary management would promote the co-ordination of investment policies. This is a necessary and important step on the road to full economic and monetary unity, especially as the productive bases of the economies of the region are weak and the governments concerned are about to embark on a process of large-scale industrialisation;

(iii) If a uniform Arab currency were issued, a new organisation would have to be created and developed to manage it. Further co-ordination of foreign exchange and banking policies would be necessary. Such an experiment could not but prove to be of great benefit to all those interested in effecting the process of integration;

(iv) In fact, the mere existence of a common Arab currency would eventually require the creation of a unified capital market, the enacting of joint economic legislation and the co-ordination of financial policies. Inasmuch as these countries have not yet decided on the orientation of the productive base they wish to develop, economic co-ordination would help them to avoid the mistake of establishing similar industries and thereby misallocating their

financial resources;
(v) The creation of a uniform Arab currency, beginning with the countries of the Gulf, would encourage other countries to adopt it in the future, especially since the Gulf currencies are currently in a strong position because of the reserves backing them up. A common currency would be stronger than any single national currency now in existence. It could thus become a strong international currency, for it would be more readily accepted and stabler than any single domestic currency;
(vi) The creation of a uniform currency could have the general effect of facilitating the flow of capital from the surplus countries to the deficit countries of the Arab world.

As to potential pitfalls, the only major one might be an eventual change in the status of oil as a source of energy, or its depletion, which could lead to conflicting interests among the Gulf countries. While this remains a possibility, the achievement of a monetary unit would serve to reconcile the divergent viewpoints in the interest of the region as a whole.

In discussions of the Gulf currency, it has been suggested that the member countries hold on to their monetary reserves and manage them separately, with the central monetary authority merely keeping records of reserve movements and settling payments between member countries' central banks. This, I believe, would preserve an important degree of national sovereignty in the monetary field.

As for the inclusion of Iraq in the Gulf monetary area, it should be recalled that the proposal to establish this area is based on the existence of similar economic conditions, liberal exchange systems and currency convertibility in the countries of the region. These conditions do not apply to Iraq. If Iraq is to be included despite these differences, then why not include other Arab countries as well?

As regards the deficit countries, co-ordination of exchange-rate policies would be a logical first step towards gradually attaining currency convertibility, in addition to the proposed system for settling payments under AMF management.

Along with the measures already mentioned, a regional institution should be established for the purpose of devising an investment programme for the Arab countries as part of a general strategy for the region.

Finally it is proposed that a 'surplus fund' be created to be used for investments in the Arab countries. This fund could be established within the AMF or, alternatively, the capital of the Arab Fund for Economic and Social Development might be increased so that it could play the role of a regional development bank and not simply that of a lending agency.

6. Jorge Gonzalez del Valle

I am encouraged by Mr Haseeb's pointed and frank comments on this paper to speak up concerning the more general question of the purposes and meaning of economic integration.

I am sure that Latin America could not have moved at all in the field of economic integration 20 years ago had we started with extensive speculation on the rather theoretical questions of costs, benefits, optimal monetary areas, efficiency-oriented alternatives, etc. Perhaps it is fortunate that there did not exist at that time an abundance of economic literature on these questions. In any event, I can assure you that common sense and a strong desire for economic independence from external vested interests were always behind the integration experiments which the Latin American countries decided to push ahead with.

It is true that the accomplishments of Latin America are still very modest in comparison with the optimal models of monetary integration; but the bases for future evolution are there and I have no doubt that we will move ahead, probably without again paying too much attention to theoretical definitions of optimal monetary integration.

I am convinced that the basic decision behind monetary integration is a political one. At the same time, I feel that the main purpose of seminars like this one should be to provide those who take the decision with as much technical (though not necessarily theoretical) support as possible to guide them in the right direction.

7. Alfredo Medio, in Response

Given the limitations of time, I shall confine my comments to one single point. I should like to dispel the impression that I do not favour monetary or indeed economic integration on *a priori* grounds. The contrary is true. What I have tried to convey is primarily the notion that it may not be wise to attempt monetary integration when the economic preconditions for its achievement do not exist. It may indeed prove impossible or, at any rate, harmful to the weaker member countries.

In the specific case of the Arab countries, I am inclined to believe that the most urgent task is to elaborate a development and especially an investment strategy so that the economic conditions of monetary integration might be established.

8. Mahmoud Sakbani, in Response

I shall first take up Mr Ali's comments on my part of the paper.

(a) My reference to the accumulation of oil surpluses after the end of the oil era pertains to the stock of surpluses and not to their flow. Mr Ali's point depends on a flow concept.
(b) The proposition that under full market integration, monetary policy is impotent is fully developed in the paper. The argument turns on the fact that interest-rate differentials do not develop under a high degree of market integration. As to adjustment through the goods and services market, full integration of these markets would leave monetary policy effective only in the short run when the balance of payments was still in the process of adjustment.
(c) My comment on subregions in the Arab world does not imply a normative statement on my part; I am making a reference to facts.
(d) I meant by dual pricing, pricing in two currencies and nothing else.
(e) My remarks about the 'Gresham discount', so to speak, naturally imply absorption of old currencies through replacement.
(f) I find Mr Ali's remark about security market integration representing mere security substitution without mobility puzzling. When I defined such integration, I did so in terms of the substitutability of securities held in different regions. Obviously this implies free mobility. It would seem to me, therefore, that Mr Ali's comment in this respect is not valid.

I turn now to Mr Shoukair's arguments. With reference to the apparent inconsistency between the two parts of the paper, this is really due to the fact that my part and that of Mr Medio were conceived and written independently.

Regarding government ownership of surpluses, I do not believe that it reduces the force of my argument about security markets. The identity of the security holder would seem to me to be irrelevant. The idea of a market organisation is predicated on the observation that one needs to create an alternative to private foreign capital markets in the Arab world.

Finally let me address two general observations which have been made. The first is that the paper deals insufficiently with the Arab context. My paper concerns the modalities and operational aspects of monetary integration. As I developed the various arguments, I did not find it particularly helpful to call these tools, modalities, etc., Arab or non-Arab; I do not believe the use of an adjective either adds to or subtracts from the argument. However, when I found it necessary to comment on a specific Arab situation or to accommodate a specific Arab given, I did so readily and in detail. Secondly, many of the participants here are in favour of a Gulf monetary union or Gulf monetary integration scheme. While I have no objection to this, I do not believe it would serve any useful purpose. The purpose of a monetary union in this area is to mobilise Arab resources, especially the surplus funds, and this cannot be done through a Gulf union. Such a union would be simple enough to achieve but without much point. In this regard, I fully subscribe to the arguments made earlier by Mr El-Imam.

Note

1. Robert Vaubel, *Weltwirtschaftliches Archiv* (1976).

11 THE ROLE OF THE ARAB MONETARY FUND IN ACHIEVING ARAB MONETARY INTEGRATION*

Faik Ali Abdul-Rasool

Introduction

This paper will focus on two issues: first, the prevailing Arab monetary situation and its implications for the role of the AMF; and secondly, future prospects for Arab monetary integration and the role the AMF can play in achieving this objective.

I. The Arab Monetary Situation and the Role of the AMF

A. Balance-of-payments Disequilibria and the Role of the AMF in the Corrective Process

1. The External Payments Imbalance. The economies of the Arab states, regardless of their balance of payments positions or their revenue levels, have certain features in common with developing countries as a whole. All Arab economies can be described as one-product economies based on either agriculture or oil. The agricultural sector suffers from low productivity, insufficient use of technology and fertilisers, under-implementation of resources and a shortage of water. The oil sector operates in relative isolation from the other sectors of the economy: it produces solely to meet the demands of the outside world and employs few local workers. Arab manufacturing industries contribute no more than 8 per cent to the GNP and suffer from low productivity, inefficiency, a lack of technology, limited markets and stiff foreign competition. The other sectors of the economy are similarly situated.

Within this general framework common to the economies of all Arab countries, there is an acute imbalance in the structure of their foreign payments. The Arab world today is divided into two distinct groups. The first of these comprises the oil-producing countries which enjoy balance-of-payments surpluses which accumulate further with each new oil price increase. The countries concerned are Saudi Arabia,

---

* This paper, translated from the Arabic, is a condensed version of the paper originally presented at the Seminar. In particular, a first section dealing with the objectives and lending activities of the AMF has been deleted as these questions are taken up in detail in another seminar paper. Some of the comments referring to the deleted material have nevertheless been retained as they relate directly to the issue of Arab monetary integration [eds.].

The Role of the Arab Monetary Fund 391

Iraq, Kuwait, the UAE, Qatar and Libya. Over the period 1974-9, the combined current account surplus of these countries totalled approximately $220 billion, as shown in Table 11.1.

Table 11.1: Total Current Account Surplus of the Six Arab Surplus Countries (billions of dollars)

Year	1974	1975	1976	1977	1978	1979
Total surplus	43	31	36	34	20	50

Source: Government publications.

The countries of the second group, in direct contrast, suffer from deficits in their balance of payments, as illustrated in Table 11.2. Over the period 1976-8, these deficits totalled about $23 billion.

Table 11.2: Current Account Summary of the Arab Deficit Countries[a] 1976-8 (millions of dollars)

	1976	1977	1978
Commodity exports (f.o.b.)	11032	12222	12899
Commodity imports (f.o.b.)	17007	20536	22442
Balance-of-trade deficit	5966	8314	9543
Invisible exports	4682	5731	7270
Invisible imports	6712	7950	9484
Private transfers	2048	2318	2710
Current account deficit	5956	8215	9047

[a] Including: Algeria, Democratic Yemen, Egypt, Jordan, Mauritania, Morocco, Somalia, Sudan, Syrian Arab Republic, Tunisia and Yemen.
Source: International Monetary Fund, *International Financial Statistics*, vol. 31 (1978).

2. Investment Pattern of Arab Surpluses. Table 11.3 shows that the investable surpluses of the OPEC countries amounted to $273 billion over the period 1974-9. This includes $220 billion from the Arab surplus countries. The sum of $225 billion, equivalent to about 82 per cent of the total surplus accumulated, was invested in the industrialised countries, half of it in the form of bank deposits. The financial outflow to developing countries amounted to $42 billion dollars, or only a little over 15 per cent, while the remainder took the form of loans to the World Bank and IMF totalling $6 billion or about 2 per cent.

Table 11.3: Distribution of OPEC Investments, 1974-9 (billions of dollars)

	1974	1975	1976	1977	1978	1979	Total
Current account surplus of OPEC countries	68	35	40	32	35	68	248
(Of which Arab countries)	(43)	(31)	(36)	(34)	(20)	(56)	(220)
Plus oil sector transfers	−12	−1	−6	−1	−28	−8	−24
Plus net borrowing	2	3	8	10	16	11	50
Net foreign currency available for investment	58	38	42	41	23	71	273
Distributed as follows:							
Investments in the markets of the industrialised countries:							
Bank deposits	30	11	14	13	5	40	113
Short-term government securities	8	—	−2	−1	−1	4	8
Other flows	11	17	21	21	13	21	104
Total	49	28	33	33	17	65	225
IMF and IBRD loans	4	3	3	−1	−6	−2	6
Flows to developing countries	5	7	7	8	7	8	42

Source: IMF, *International Financial Statistics*, vol. 33, no. 5 (May 1980).

It is clear from these data that most of the investments of the Arab surplus countries are placed abroad in Eurodollar or US markets in the form of liquid assets exposed to monetary risks such as inflation and currency fluctuation and the consequent erosion of their purchasing power. Moreover, all these investments, liquid or otherwise, whether invested in financial or real, material assets, remain exposed to non-commercial risks such as nationalisation, freezing, sequestration and confiscation, apart from the hazards associated with war and civil disturbances. This being the case, and given the fact that these assets have accrued specifically as a result of the Arab oil exporters' maintaining production at certain levels to meet the demand for energy in the industrialised countries, these Arab countries are entitled to demand safeguards to protect their monetary assets in the industrialised countries against such risks. The obligation to continue producing enough oil to meet the requirements of the industrialised world should be balanced by a commitment by the industrial countries to guarantee the financial and monetary assets of the oil-producing states against the risks mentioned above. These assets should be accorded preferential

3. *Sources of Deficit Financing and the Role of Arab Funds.* Let us now turn to the financial problems facing the second group of Arab countries, those suffering from deficits in their balance of payments. It has already been stated that the total current account deficits of these countries over the period 1976-8 amounted to about $23 billion. If one adds to this figure the increase in their official reserves totalling about $1.5 billion, the figure for the total amount required for deficit financing over the same period becomes about $24.5 billion dollars. Table 11.4 shows the sources for this financing to have consisted of official transfers ($4.7 billion), direct foreign investments ($1.4 billion), long-term loans ($15.6 billion) and short-term and other financial inflows ($2.9 billion). The Arab deficit countries have thus tended to procure long-term financing, whether in the form of loans, direct investments or official transfers. Short-term loans, such as those extended by the AMF, play a secondary role, accounting for no more than 12 per cent of the total requirements.

Table 11.4: Sources of Deficit Financing for Arab Deficit Countries, 1976-8 (millions of dollars)

	1976	1977	1978	Total 1976-8
Current account deficit	5956	8215	9043	23218
Net change in official reserves	529	536	430	1495
Total	6485	8751	9477	24713
Sources of Financing				
Net official transfers	1144	2083	1508	4735
Net direct foreign investments	405	448	578	1431
Net long-term loans	4035	4768	6801	15604
Net other financial flows	200	1453	591	2944
Total	6484	8752	9478	24715

Source: Government and IMF publications.

This fact raises the controversial question of whether the choice of these sources of financing is made on the basis of the wishes of the Arab deficit countries or on the basis of the availability of funds. I am inclined to think that sources of short-term financing are extremely limited, being restricted chiefly to the Eurodollar market and the IMF.

With the exception of Algeria and to a certain extent Morocco, most Arab deficit countries do not enjoy sufficient credit allowances in the world financial market. Their quotas with the IMF and consequently the credit facilities available to them, especially with regard to the reserve tranche and the first tranche, are not sufficient to meet their financing requirements. Accordingly, the facilities of the AMF should be in great demand in these countries because they would help to bring about a better balance between short-term and long-term sources of finance.

At this point, one might raise the question of the volume of funds flowing from the surplus to the deficit countries. It should first of all be noted that aid from the OPEC member states to the developing countries represents roughly 81 per cent of all financial outflows from these countries, as illustrated in Table 11.5.

Table 11.5: Aid to Developing Countries from Arab OPEC Member States (millions of dollars)

	1974	1975	1976	1977	1978	Total
Aid from OPEC countries	5889	8160	7139	7592	5296	35076
Aid from Arab surplus countries	4479	6370	6696	6648	4553	28528
Ratio of Arab aid to total (%)	76.1	78.1	82.3	87.6	86.0	81.3

Source: Government and OPEC publications.

Table 11.5 indicates that OPEC funds, mainly from the Arab member states, contributed to financing nearly 48 per cent of the requirements of the deficit Arab countries during the period 1976-8. While the requirements of these countries amounted to about $25 billion over this period, funds flowing to them from the OPEC countries amounted to about $12 billion, of which some $7 billion took the form of aid and the remainder the form of commercial loans. It thus becomes clear that capital transfers among the Arab countries during this period, while falling short of meeting total Arab financing requirements, were nevertheless capable of meeting about 50 per cent of them. This clearly shows the important and effective role played by Arab funds in financing the Arab balance-of-payments deficit.

4. The Role of the AMF in Correcting Balance-of-payments Disequilibria

a. The AMF and the Arab surplus countries. The source of the Arab balance-of-payments surplus is oil exports priced and paid for in dollars. Oil prices are agreed upon collectively within OPEC, in accordance with political and economic criteria. According to recent reports, OPEC is expected to reach agreement on an oil pricing formula according to which prices will be adjusted regularly on the basis of inflation indicators in the industrialised countries, the real GNP growth of these countries and the fluctuation of the dollar in relation to a basket of leading currencies. As for setting oil production levels, the determining factors· are the world's need for oil as an energy source and a raw material for industry and the international pressure that this generates. This leads to levels of oil production which may be too high in relation to the absorptive capacity of the producing countries. It is this excess of production and, hence, of revenues that creates the surplus in the balance of payments of the producing countries. These countries could, in theory, reduce their surpluses and readjust their balance of payments by cutting back on production, reducing the real price of their oil or expanding their capacity to absorb the oil revenues. If one considers each of these options, one finds that the Arab oil-producing countries, especially those of the Gulf, would prefer to curtail production. The world at large, however, would suffer an acute energy shortage which might have an immediate effect on world economic growth rates. OPEC has exerted strong pressure on oil prices during the last few years, which has led to a reduction in the real value of oil. Thus, the gap between the price of oil and the cost of alternative forms of energy has widened, encouraging wasteful consumption of oil and an increase in its price on spot markets such as Rotterdam. This has led to higher profits by the multinational companies at the expense of the OPEC countries which have retained low official prices. With regard to the absorptive capacity of the Arab surplus countries, it is common knowledge that, with the exception of Iraq, it is relatively low. These countries are nevertheless making a tremendous effort and adopting expansionary economic policies in order to increase their absorptive capacity. Consequently, the economies of these countries are close to operating beyond the resources available to them. This has resulted, for example, in the increased use of manpower and other resources from other Arab and, especially, non-Arab countries.

Given the fact, then, that the balance-of-payments surpluses of the Arab oil countries are mainly due to external factors beyond their control, the role of the AMF in correcting these disequilibria can only be negligible. Furthermore, since the Arab oil producers are not in need of financing from the Fund, their relationship to it is that of a lender, rather than a borrower. This diminishes the applicability of Article XXVI of the AMF Agreement which stipulates that countries are to pursue corrective policies within programmes agreed upon in co-operation with the Fund.

b. The AMF and the Arab deficit countries. Just as the surplus of the Arab oil-producing countries can be attributed chiefly to external factors, so too is the deficit in the balance of payments of the non-oil-producing Arab countries due in large part to factors beyond their control. Since the mid-1970s, the world as a whole and the industrialised capitalist nations, in particular, have been suffering from the phenomenon of 'stagflation'. This would appear, judging by the experience of the past few years, almost to have become a permanent feature of the economies of these countries, though it has been less acute in some years (e.g., 1976-7) than in others (e.g., 1974-5) and 1979-80). This phenomenon has led to a rise in the rates of inflation exported by these countries to the Arab world and to a reduction in the foreign demand for Arab exports, especially raw materials such as cotton and phosphates. Since the industrialised nations control more than two-thirds of the exports and imports of the Arab deficit countries, any inflation and economic recession experienced by the industrialised nations has a direct impact on Arab trade. An increase in the inflation rate of the industrialised countries leads to higher prices for their exports to the Arab world. Moreover, economic recession in the industrialised nations leads to a reduction in the foreign demand for Arab agricultural exports and primary goods such as cotton, phosphates and textiles. This has a negative effect on the prices of these exports and tends to restrict their quantity and variety. This is presently the case with the Arab countries of the Maghreb which are suffering from the protective measures drawn up by the EEC against their exports, especially textiles. These factors have led to a reduction in the purchasing power of the revenues accruing from Arab exports, slower growth rates and higher import costs. These external influences are reflected directly in the balance of payments of these Arab countries, resulting in higher deficit levels. Apart from these external factors which exert an influence on the deficit, there are also internal factors which have an adverse effect on its size. These elements may, of course, be partly seasonal and the result of such natural factors as climate, rainfall and plant disease, but they are related mainly, in the author's view, to the historical stage through which the Arab economies are passing. All these countries, as has been stated, exhibit the economic characteristics of developing countries, where the infrastructure, productivity base and technology are still in the initial stages of growth. Their development does, in general, require large imports, especially of capital goods and suitable modern technology, alongside the consumer durables necessary to meet local demand. This high level of imports represents a particular burden for these countries which can be expected to remain; for as long as development proceeds, there will be an excess of imports over exports giving rise to a quasi-permanent deficit in their balance of trade.

These external and structural factors which are at the source of the balance-of-payments deficits of these countries considerably limit the corrective role which the AMF can play. Because of the structural nature of this deficit, the corrective process itself produces negative political consequences for these countries and has an adverse effect on their economic growth, a result which runs counter to the strategic objectives of the Arab Development Decade. These objectives include the acceleration of economic growth rates in the less developed Arab countries with a view to narrowing the income gap between them and the other Arab countries.

Moreover, it is generally believed that corrective programmes based on the adoption of deflationary financial and monetary policies would not be effective in correcting or even reducing the balance-of-payments deficit for a number of reasons, the most important of which are:

(1) The limitations of the monetary sector;
(2) The close and direct relationship between the balance-of-payments position and the money supply;
(3) The limited effect of interest rates on investment and savings decisions;
(4) The effects of world interest rates on interest-rate levels in the market-oriented Arab economies;
(5) The link between the prices of exports, such as cotton, and the prices prevailing in world markets and, consequently, the negligible effect of changes in national exchange rates on the stimulation of exports;
(6) Insufficient flexibility in relating import costs to prices on the domestic market owing to the effect of administrative measures, advertising and other factors on current prices;
(7) Most adjustments in Arab exchange rates do not represent the real and effective change in the exchange rates of these currencies and therefore do not reflect the competitive position of exports;
(8) The increase in interest rates aimed at encouraging savings raises investment costs and leads to greater inflationary pressures and a reduction in investment opportunities, thereby impeding national development;
(9) Currency devaluation increases project and import costs, thus increasing inflationary pressures and retarding development;

(10) The narrow tax base and the need for government expenditure on national development, together with the narrowing of income differentials and the promotion of health and cultural services, may make it difficult, from the practical and political points of view, to adopt deflationary financial policies.

B. Disparities in Arab Currency Pegs and their Impact on the Role of the AMF

Under the Bretton Woods system, exchange rates were characterised by relative stability. In the event of economic imbalances in a given country, the exchange rate of its currency was adjusted, with the approval of the IMF, while corrective policies were applied at home, in order to strengthen the competitive position of local industry and thus reduce imports and promote exports. Today, there exists a system of floating rates which are determined in accordance with market forces but which are often subject to speculative pressures. The monetary authorities are not supposed to interfere in the money markets except for the purpose of restricting currency speculation. Nevertheless, 'dirty floating' does take place. Under this system, the developing countries, including those of the Arab world, where no developed money or financial markets exist, have resorted to pegging their currencies to other major currencies. In selecting one major currency over another, the Arab countries have based their choice on political and economic considerations. These considerations reflect, to a certain extent, their economic ties to the major industrialised countries concerned and the volume of trade and capital transactions carried out with them. As a result, Arab currencies have begun to fluctuate to the same degree and in the same directions as the major currencies to which they are pegged. This has resulted in the Arab countries losing control over the movements of their exchange rates and sustaining heavy economic losses, particularly in the oil sector, owing to the sharp fluctuations of the dollar *vis-à-vis* other major currencies. These losses can be summarised as follows:

The exposure of the purchasing power of Arab export revenues, especially from oil, and their reserves of liquid foreign assets, to sharp fluctuations and continuous decline;

The increased risks attending inter-Arab trade and Arab trade with the outside world due to foreign-exchange instability and the difficulty of forecasting future prospects;

The increased risks involved in the terms of trade of Arab exports, especially oil, resulting from the large and continuing increase in import costs caused by the inflation in the major industrialised nations set in motion by the system of floating rates;

Table 11.6: Arab Currency Pegs as at 30 June 1980

Country	Arab currency unit	Per dollar rate	Intermediate currency or currencies
Algeria	Dinar	3.7775	Special currency basket
Bahrain	Dinar	0.377	SDR with a margin of 7.25 per cent
Democratic Yemen	Dinar	0.345395	Dollar
Djibouti	Franc	178.16	Dollar
Egypt	Pound	0.70	Dollar
Iraq	Dinar	0.295314	Dollar
Jordan	Dinar	0.387	SDR
Kuwait	Dinar	0.26701	Special currency basket
Lebanon	Pound	3.408	
Libya	Dinar	0.295314	Dollar
Morocco	Dirham	3.7985	Special currency basket
Oman	Riyal	0.3454	Dollar
Qatar	Riyal	3.64	SDR with a margin of 7.25 per cent
Saudi Arabia	Riyal	3.325	SDR with a margin of 7.25 per cent
Somalia	Shilling	6.2950	Dollar
Sudan	Pound	0.50	Dollar
Syrian Arab Republic	Pound	3.925	Dollar
Tunisia	Dinar	0.398278	Special currency basket
UAE	Dirham	3.701	SDR with a margin of 7.25 per cent
Yemen	Riyal	4.5625	Dollar

Source: Government publications.

Table 11.7: Changes in the Cross-rates of the Gulf Currencies 1978-9

Country	Saudi Arabia	UAE	Bahrain	Qatar
Saudi Arabia	–	−0.29	−0.40	−1.56
UAE	+0.29	–	−0.12	−1.27
Bahrain	+0.41	+0.12	–	−1.16
Oman	+1.58	+1.29	+1.16	–

Source: Government publications.

The relative reduction in the volume of financial flows and foreign investment in the Arab deficit countries;

The instability of Arab export earnings, leading to uncertainties with regard to government revenues and, consequently, fluctuations in both ordinary and developmental spending.

As a result of these negative consequences, some Arab countries have moved to sever their ties with one or another of the major currencies, pegging their currencies instead to a general or specific basket of the major currencies. Saudi Arabia, the UAE and Qatar, for instance, have chosen to peg their local currencies to the SDR basket, while Kuwait and Algeria have devised their own baskets consisting of the major currencies (see Table 11.6). Consequently, fluctuations in the cross-rates among Arab currencies have increased.

There are thus ten Arab countries which have pegged their currencies to the dollar, five to the SDR and four to a basket of major currencies. The pegging of a group of Arab currencies to a specific intermediary currency — as in the case of the Iraqi or Libyan dinar to the dollar — helps to keep their exchange rates in step with the dollar *vis-à-vis* other currencies and thus to stabilise their cross-rates. However, as long as varying margins and different currency pegs are used, the cross-rates of Arab currencies will continue to exhibit more or less large daily fluctuations, depending on the movement of the intermediary currency or currencies in the world money markets. This fact can be illustrated with figures which show that although the countries of the Arab Gulf — Saudi Arabia, the UAE, Qatar and Bahrain — have chosen a single intermediary for their currency and tried hard to co-ordinate their efforts to reduce fluctuations in their cross-rates, they have achieved only limited success. Table 11.7 shows the changes in the exchange rates of these countries' currencies during 1979 as compared with 1978.

The cross-rates of Arab currencies and their exchange rates in relation to foreign currencies will only become stable if they are pegged, with given margins, to a common currency. This could be one of the Arab currencies, the Arab accounting dinar or any basket of currencies. But this pegging would not be completely reliable, as differing Arab monetary and financial policies could generate pressures to alter prevailing rates. There is nothing more indicative of this than the experience of Saudi Arabia, the UAE and Qatar during 1979. Although these countries agreed to use the SDR as a medium for currency valuation and adopted uniform margins for their movements, their relative exchange rates still fluctuated, largely as a result of their monetary and financial policy measures. Disparities in interest rates among these countries, and between them and the world at large, no doubt have a great effect on the level of domestic liquidity and on financial flows both into and out of the area, which is reflected in exchange-rate variations. Therefore, the maintenance of cross-rate stability among Arab currencies would seem to require complete co-ordination of monetary and financial policies. It is not enough to lift restrictions on foreign exchange. This has been tried in the Gulf countries to facilitate business transactions and capital transfers, and their currencies have continued to fluctuate. On the other hand, the currencies of Iraq and Libya, despite the fact that both countries impose restrictions on foreign exchange — whether used for external transactions or capital transfers — and despite the lack of co-ordination in their financial and monetary policies, nevertheless exhibit stable cross-rates. This is, in fact, chiefly the result of their currencies being pegged to a common intermediary currency, the dollar.

Accordingly, the co-ordination of monetary policies and the elimination of foreign exchange controls, though important for achieving exchange-rate stability in the Arab countries, are not fundamental to it. The basic factor for bringing about a stable relationship among Arab exchange rates is the creation of a currency or intermediary accounting unit for valuing all the Arab currencies, with the other two factors lending to this relationship and keeping it stable over a long period. We will attempt in the following section to study the alternatives available in this regard.

II. Future Prospects for AMF Activity

A. The AMF as a Permanent Device for Promoting a Uniform Arab Currency

The author is not proposing the creation of a uniform currency at this time. Although it has been suggested in official and non-official circles alike that a single currency be created for a limited number of Arab states, e.g., the Gulf dinar, this section will confine its analysis and proposals to creating such conditions as may lead to the ultimate creation of a uniform Arab currency for the whole Arab world. The following proposals should be considered:

(1) Standardising the nomenclature and components of Arab currency units;
(2) Reviving the Arab Payments Union;
(3) Standardising Arab currency pegs and margins;
(4) Creating an organisation to manage a portion of the Arab official reserves and to issue the Arab dinar.

1. Standardising the Nomenclature and Components of Arab Currency Units. In this connection, I do not mean to imply the standardisation either of Arab currency values or of their exchange rates relative to each other or to the major foreign currencies, as this may come about at a later stage. Rather, I have in mind the standardisation of the nomenclature of Arab currencies at the local level only, because of the positive psychological and social effect this would have in paving the way towards future monetary unity and in making things easier for the Arab traveller within the Arab world.

There are six currency units in use in the Arab world distributed as follows:

Name of unit	Arab country using it
Dinar	Algeria, Bahrain, Democratic Yemen, Iraq, Kuwait, Libya, Jordan, Tunisia
Riyal	Oman, Qatar, Saudi Arabia, Yemen
Dirham	Morocco, the UAE
Pound	Egypt, Lebanon, Sudan, Syrian Arab Republic
Franc	Djibouti
Shilling	Somalia

As shown in this table, the dinar is used as a currency unit in eight Arab countries, covering the entire geographical area, while the riyal is used in four Gulf countries and the lira in Syria and Lebanon. Morocco and the UAE use the dirham. There are numerous ways of standardising the names of these currencies without standardising their parities, internally or in terms of foreign exchange. Of these methods, the following is one example:

The use of the dinar as a currency unit to be issued by Arab banks and monetary institutions whereby there would be an Arab dinar, a Kuwaiti dinar, an Egyptian dinar, and so on. This dinar might consist of the following currency divisions:
One dinar = 1000 fils
One dinar = 20 dirhams, i.e., one dirham = 50 fils
One dinar = 10 liras, i.e., one lira = 100 fils
One dinar = 5 riyals, i.e., one riyal = 200 fils

2. Reviving the Arab Payments Union. Paragraph E of Article IV of the AMF Agreement provides for 'the settlement of current payments between member States in such a way as to strengthen commercial exchanges'. To this end, paragraph F of Article V stipulates that 'the Fund shall allocate sufficient amounts of its resources, payable in the currencies of member States, to provide the necessary credit facilities for the settlement of current payments among member States, in accordance with terms and conditions to be decided by the Board of Governors. These resources shall be allocated for a special account which the Fund shall open for this purpose'. Paragraph A of Article XIV stipulates that, of each country's capital subscription, 'a proportion of two per cent shall be covered by the national currency of the member State, regardless of its convertibility'. Paragraph B of Article XXV stipulates that the 'interest on a loan extended to a member to finance that part of its overall balance-of-payments deficit arising from trade with the Arab States, excluding oil transactions, shall be on easier terms'. These passages make it clear that the Fund was to assume the role of the Arab Payments Union set up by the Council of Arab Economic Unity in early 1970. At that time, it was agreed to establish the Arab Payments Union with a capital of AAD 15 million. The Union was to settle the debit and credit balances relating to current payments among member states at the end of each quarter, with the net credit and debit balances to be transferred to it. The debtor state would defray half of its debit balance in cash in convertible currencies and the remainder would be considered an interest-free credit facility for a period of one year. If no settlement had been made through account-clearing within the next four accounting periods, this balance would become a debt which would have to be discharged with interest within a year, in convertible currency or through account-clearing. The balances of creditor states would be regarded as constituting an interest-free credit facility of the Arab Payments Union for one year, after which they would be settled with interest in convertible currency in two half-yearly instalments.

Iraq was the only Arab country to ratify the Arab Payments Union agreement. The other countries decided not to proceed with the project. There were many reasons for this, including the fact that some Arab countries enjoy a permanent balance-of-trade surplus *vis-à-vis* other Arab countries. This means that their affiliation to the Union might have deprived them of cash payments for the full value of their exports. There are other countries, too, which make use of bilateral payments agreements, and thus preferred bilateral co-operation to multilateral arrangements. Still other countries found that the volume of their trade with other Arab countries was not sufficient to warrant their joining the Arab Payments Union.

Regardless of the volume of inter-Arab trade or the narrow national interests involved, the revival of the Arab Payments Union is a task for which the AMF is responsible under the terms of its Agreement. It should revive the Union either in the form described above, while attempting to surmount the problems which prevented some countries from joining it, or in a new form consistent with developments in economic thinking and their practical application in such places as Europe and Latin America.

This would necessitate overcoming selfish national interests in favour of the general good by adopting the following measures:

Abandoning the use of foreign currencies as a means of commercial exchange among the Arab countries;
Abandoning the intermediation of foreign banks in settling transactions and eliminating their commission;
Utilising credit facilities, especially in the case of Arab countries with debit accounts;
Strengthening Arab monetary co-operation and laying the groundwork for the creation of an Arab monetary unit.

3. Standardising Arab Currency Pegs and Margins. The previous section came to the conclusion that differences among Arab economic systems and the need to rationalise the use of scarce foreign currency have led to the imposition of foreign exchange controls. These controls have had the effect of reducing the impact of monetary policies on exchange rates. For this reason, it was found that the only way left to bring about the stability of Arab currency exchange rates, relative both to each other and to foreign currencies, was the utilisation of an intermediary currency or a common group of currencies. Although this situation would lead to arrangements similar to those contained in the Bretton Woods agreements effective prior to 1971, what now appears unsuitable for the developed nations is not necessarily so for the developing countries, including those of the Arab world. The developing countries still demand an end to exchange-rate fluctuations and a return to the arrangements effective prior to 1971. The alternative available at the regional level is the formation of an Arab Monetary System on the pattern of the European Monetary System, with due consideration for the special circumstances of the Arab world. One of the chief components of an Arab Monetary System would be the valuation of Arab currencies according to a common basket of currencies.

Ruling out a linkage to the dollar or to any other single major currency, there remain three alternatives for the composition of such a currency basket. The first alternative would be a basket of the major foreign currencies used in commercial exchanges and foreign investment transactions. The second alternative would be a basket based on the SDR.

Considering these two alternatives, the first would have the advantage of making the exchange rates of the Arab currencies move together, neutralising the impact of fluctuations in the major investment currencies on national economies and providing Arab monetary authorities with sufficient flexibility in changing the weights and parities of their currencies. On the other hand, it would peg the exchange rates of domestic currencies to an average of the exchange rates of the major foreign currencies with the result that their movements would still be dependent on fluctuations in the international money markets beyond the control of local monetary authorities. The second alternative, on the other hand, would not permit control over exchange-rate fluctuations in relation to other currencies. Furthermore, the structure and directions of Arab trade do not necessarily reflect the relative weights of the currencies making up the SDR basket. Moreover, the SDR basket also gives supremacy to the dollar by making it the preponderant currency.

The third alternative, which the author believes would represent a step towards Arab monetary integration, would peg Arab currencies to the Arab accounting dinar. This is not a reference to the current Arab accounting dinar provided for in the AMF Agreement and 'strictly pegged' to the SDR, deprived of its Arab identity in all but name and of those distinctive characteristics which it might have lent to the Arab countries and which would have helped to establish it and expand its use. The present method of pegging the AAD makes it no more than the shadow of the SDR, exposed to the fluctuations of market and adminstrative factors having nothing to do with the Arab economies or their management. What is meant is an Arab accounting dinar which the oil producers would demand in return for all or part of their oil sales and which the AMF would issue against receipt of foreign currencies from subscribers in settlement of all or a part of the value of their oil purchases. The exchange rate of this dinar would be determined by the supply of and demand for oil.

4. Joint Management of a Portion of Official Reserves and the Issuance of the Arab Dinar. The AMF should assume the task of issuing the Arab dinar against receipt of foreign currency from the Arab surplus oil-exporting countries or directly from oil consumers. The dinar would derive its strength from the pressure of world demand on the huge oil reserves of the Arab countries while its exchange rate would be fixed in accordance with the supply and demand situation in world financial markets. For this reason, it would not require a basket of currencies for its valuation. Its exchange rate could also be influenced by the demand for the dinar as an official reserve currency. The dinar would, of course, circulate alongside local Arab currencies which would be converted from and into the Arab dinar in accordance with their parities. These would be determined in co-ordination and consultation with the Fund and with other Arab countries on the basis of purely technical rules and regulations. This common link between local currencies and the Arab dinar would undoubtedly represent a major step along the road to monetary unity, as it would simultaneously achieve the following main objectives:

(a) Dissociating the Arab currencies from the major investment currencies and eliminating the effects of their fluctuations on Arab export revenues as well as on domestic monetary, financial and development policies in the Arab world;
(b) Stabilising the cross-rates of Arab currencies by pegging them to a common standard, namely the Arab dinar;
(c) Creating an Arab monetary bloc whereby the exchange rates of the currencies included in it would move jointly in relation to foreign exchange rates;
(d) Bringing about a new means of investment which would help Arab oil-producers expand their investment portfolios, reduce risks and safeguard their purchasing power against the fluctuations of the major investment currencies;
(e) Pooling all or a part of Arab assets or surpluses under the management of the AMF, which would help the Arab countries to exert control over the financial and money markets. They should thus be able to dictate their own lending terms to these markets with respect to both earnings and guarantees, in contrast to the present system where these markets impose their terms on Arab investments. The existence of Arab assets under common management would also give them a monopolistic control over the investment market. This plan would offer each Arab member state the freedom to recover its foreign assets whenever it pleased by simply converting its oil revenues received in Arab dinars into foreign holdings. Thus, the Arab countries which had Arab dinars as a reserve currency would be able to earn interest from the fund, in addition to enjoying the security that would come from investment in a strong currency;
(f) Expanding the use of the local Arab currencies of the oil countries, which would pave the way for their becoming international currencies. The readiness of the AMF to convert these currencies into the Arab dinar would encourage foreign countries to accept them in return for their exports to the oil states. The states exporting these currencies would therefore be able to increase their profits and the returns on their foreign currencies by investing them, instead of using them, as was necessary in the past, to cover their international exchanges. There would not, however, be marked advantages for the Arab oil states as long as their financial markets were closed to non-resident deposits, except for those exchanges being conducted at a given moment in local Arab currencies. However, if these markets were opened up to non-

resident investments and deposits, then local Arab currencies could be held as part of the reserves of foreign countries. Thus these Arab states could become among the world's major centres for intermediary financing;
(g) Facilitating both inter-Arab trade and Arab foreign trade. As for those Arab states which are short of capital, thier affiliation to the fund and the allocation of a quota for them would lead to an increase in their foreign assets corresponding to their quota and, consequently, to an increase in their import capacity;
(h) Increasing the flow of capital to the Arab countries, since the Arab dinar could be expected to enjoy exchange-rate stability whereas the convertible foreign currencies are expected to depreciate. One could thus anticipate a world demand for the Arab dinar as a reserve currency. Since foreign assets denominated in Arab dinars would be directly or indirectly redeposited or reinvested in the oil-producing countries, the consequent increase in liquidity would be reflected in an increased flow of capital to the other Arab countries, especially if the latter provided sufficient guarantees for capital transfers and offered competitive interest rates;
(i) Recycling Arab surpluses to deficit Arab countries, because an increase in the resources of the AMF resulting from larger deposits by the oil exporters would enable it to direct these resources to the Arab countries to finance their balance-of-payments deficits;
(j) Reducing non-commercial risks, because the fund — rather than the Arab countries — would be the direct investor of Arab surpluses, though the oil countries would have claims over the fund equal to the fund's foreign claims. And since the fund would be a legally independent financial institution, the countries receiving Arab investments would not be able to adopt political positions with respect to the Fund's investments, as a reaction to the political positions of the oil states, for example.

B. The AMF as a Joint Arab Institution for the Safeguarding and Repatriation of Arab Funds

1. The Role of the AMF in Safeguarding Expatriate Arab Funds. While in the long run, the Arab world will no doubt be capable of absorbing all the oil revenues, Arab investments are currently facing the problem of a decline in their purchasing power resulting from inflation and currency fluctuations, to say nothing of non-commercial risks. It has already been said that the AMF could confront this situation by issuing the Arab dinar, in exchange for the member countries pooling their reserves under AMF management. In addition, the AMF could urge that, in recognition of the effort being made by the surplus Arab oil states to meet their energy requirements, the developed countries should accord special treatment to the investments of these oil states. The following measures might be contemplated:

(a) The adoption of appropriate safeguards for the protection of the real value of the financial assets of the oil-producing countries, including indexation;
(b) Joint efforts by the recipient governments in the developed countries to preserve the purchasing power of their currencies by having their respective monetary authorities jointly draw up appropriate measures;
(c) The enhancement of investment opportunities for the oil countries in the developed countries through the elimination of tax barriers and other investment restrictions with regard to the following operations:

   (i) The repatriation of convertible currencies,
   (ii) The payment of interest on bank deposits in cash;
   (iii) The holding of attractive debt instruments;
   (iv) The issuance of debt instruments denominated in foreign currencies and the organisation of these operations;
   (v) The purchase and sale of financial securities.

(d) Preferential treatment of the official financial assets of the oil-producing countries with regard to income and capital gains taxes.
(e) Protection of the oil producers' investments in developed countries from non-commercial risks by means of a multilateral agreement under which the developed countries would undertake to adopt measures designed to:

   (i) Guarantee the oil countries against seizure, freezing or any other coercive measure designed to deprive them of their investments or investment earnings;
   (ii) Eliminate unjustifiable restrictions on the rapid conversion of investments and their earnings from the currencies of the recipient states to convertible currencies at exchange rates to be agreed upon.

2. The Role of the AMF in the Repatriation of Arab Surpluses. In the Arab arena, the AMF should co-operate with the relevant Arab institutions at all levels in seeking to channel a larger volume of Arab surpluses towards the Arab deficit countries. Efforts should be directed towards creating an attractive investment climate by encouraging the adoption of the measures listed below, most of which have some bearing on the development of the Arab financial market.

(a) Developing the banking sector. Banking structures and mechanisms should be developed to encourage bank mergers, increase bank capital and consolidate the position of the Arab banks in the international financial markets. An effort should be made to step up interbank co-operation and the exchange of credit information in order to promote confidence with regard to loans, provide mutual facilities and encourage Arab banks to issue deposit certificates which could constitute an important source of medium-term financing. This could be done by the central banks accepting certificates of deposit as one of the components of commercial bank liquidity and encouraging their use by developing secondary markets which would provide liquidity for investors in such certificates. The Arab central banks could also introduce sufficient interest-rate flexibility to enable the commercial banks to utilise bank loans with variable interest rates.

This would increase the volume of loans and make it possible to extend their maturity dates to meet the wishes of borrowers. It would also encourage the issuance and purchase of international securities, denominated in the Arab accounting dinar or in any other convertible Arab currency, provided they are issued by credit-worthy borrowers. Governments could also play an important role in developing the mechanisms of the Arab financial market by issuing government bonds and money orders, so as to finance their budget deficits.

(b) Capital repatriation. The necessary legislation should be enacted with regard to the repatriation of capital, as follows:

(i) The deficit Arab countries should amend their financial, monetary and commercial laws to create a more appropriate climate for the inward flow of Arab capital. Such a climate would include, for example, the freedom to transfer capital and capital earnings, guarantees with regard to the stability of existing legislation, reduced tax levels, etc;
(ii) The capital investments of the surplus Arab countries in the deficit Arab countries should be safeguarded against exchange-rate devaluations and non-commercial risks such as war and civil disturbances. Government financial institutions could be established for this purpose;
(iii) The capital of the Arab Investment Guarantee Institution should be augmented so as to enhance its insurance capability. Furthermore, its by-laws should be modified to permit the extension of its sphere of activity to include all types of direct and indirect investment, in addition to the provision of guarantees for the

settlement of loan and interest payments when they fall due;
(iv) All the Arab countries should be encouraged to adhere to the existing arrangement for the settlement of investment disputes between countries receiving Arab investments and the nationals of other Arab countries;
(v) An Arab arbitration body should be set up to look into court rulings on investment disputes and should be given the power to impose economic and financial sanctions on countries which do not abide by these rulings.

(c) Arab capital movements. A comprehensive Arab agreement on Arab capital movements should be concluded as soon as possible. Such an agreement would guarantee the free movement of capital and encourage its transfer among Arab countries. In addition, all administrative and procedural restrictions on Arab investments imposed by recipient countries should be lifted; these investments should be put on an equal footing with their domestic counterparts.

C. The AMF as a Permanent Forum for Consultation

1. Consultation and Co-ordination through the Meetings of the Central Bank Governors. The governors of Arab central banks normally hold an annual meeting in one of the Arab capitals under the auspices of the League of Arab States or, occasionally, of the Council of Arab Economic Unity. These meetings usually deal with regional and international monetary issues, especially those concerning international financial and monetary institutions. The purpose of these meetings is to make known the positions of the central banks on these issues and to co-ordinate and unify these positions.

Among the most important results of these meetings in the past have been the proposals for the establishment of the Arab Payments Union and the AMF. Since all the Arab central bank governors are also either governors or deputy governors of the AMF, and since the governors of the AMF meet annually, the Fund could serve as a regional forum whereby the governors of the central banks would meet once or twice a year in their capacities as governors or deputy governors of the AMF to exchange views with the aim of adopting a common approach to monetary and financial questions in both the Arab and international spheres. The AMF secretariat should prepare the groundwork for such regular meetings. Technical experts from the central banks could possibly assist in this by organising themselves as a monetary committee which would meet regularly to prepare the groundwork for the meetings of the central bank governors and to consider issues of concern to members of the AMF.

2. *Co-ordination with Regional and International Organisations to Secure the Necessary Financing.* Article VII of the AMF Agreement stipulates that the Fund should co-operate with similar Arab institutions and, when necessary, with its international counterparts in order to achieve its objectives. The article in question stipulates that co-operation with international organisations should occur 'when necessary' and the term used is 'co-operation' as opposed to 'co-ordination' which is used in reference to Arab institutions. The Fund, as represented by its Board of Governors or Board of Directors, is free to determine which forms of co-operation are appropriate and to select the corresponding institutions with which the Fund will co-operate within this legal framework. This clearly grants freedom and flexibility to the Fund to co-operate with similar Arab institutions to achieve its objectives. In this context, the Fund might:

(a) Co-operate within the existing committee for co-ordination between the activities of the Arab League and joint Arab organisations;
(b) Co-operate with the general secretariats of the Council of Arab Economic Unity and the League of Arab States to encourage free trade in the Arab world;
(c) Prepare studies on ways of encouraging free trade in the Arab world, to be submitted to the meetings of the Arab central bank governors;
(d) Offer advice on monetary questions to joint Arab organisations and enterprises, especially on questions concerning the encouragement of the expansion and integration of domestic financial markets and the promotion of the use of the Arab dinar in valuing the assets and liabilities of these organisations;
(e) Endeavour to establish an Arab body for short- and medium-term financing comprising both local Arab banks (in those Arab countries with freely convertible currencies) and joint Arab banks, with a view to providing sufficient resources for financing Arab balance-of-payments deficits. To this end, the AMF could play an important role in mobilising sufficient short- and medium-term financial resources to cover Arab balance-of-payments deficits in accordance with a financial plan aimed at achieving the strategic objectives of the Arab Development Decade;
(f) Co-operate with Arab and regional institutions providing development financing, such as the Arab Fund for Economic and Social Development and the regional development funds in Saudi Arabia, Iraq, Kuwait, the UAE and Libya, in the co-ordination of their long-term financing policies, the mobilisation of their resources and their investment in projects which would help to reduce the structural deficit in Arab payments balances;

(g) Endeavour to reach agreement with international financial and monetary institutions such as the IMF and the World Bank, as well as with regional financial institutions like the OPEC Special Fund and the Islamic Development Bank, in accordance with a pre-arranged plan, to provide the short- and medium-term financial resources necessary to finance Arab balance-of-payments deficits and development projects.

D. The AMF as a Centre for Research, Training and the Preparation of Statistics

Article V of the AMF Agreement stipulates that the Fund should provide technical assistance to the Arab monetary and banking systems in order to achieve its objectives. Article VIII stipulates that the Fund should offer technical assistance and services in the financial and monetary fields to member countries which have concluded economic agreements aimed at establishing a monetary union, as one of the steps towards achieving the Fund's objectives. While its financial facilities may only be of use to the Arab deficit countries, the Fund's provision of technical assistance could extend to all Arab countries, particularly in the following areas:

1. The Preparation and Standardisation of Financial and Monetary Statistics. Arab monetary statistics are presently inadequate because of the multiplicity of their sources, the inconsistencies they exhibit, the non-availability of important information, their imprecision and the different formats in which they are presented. The AMF is required under its articles of agreement to draw up a programme, in co-operation with statistical organisations dealing with monetary and financial matters, to remedy these problems in a way that serves the objectives of the Fund.

2. Training and the Exchange of Expertise. The AMF could, either directly or in co-operation with Arab or international institutions, prepare training courses aimed at improving the efficiency of those working in the monetary organisations of the Arab countries and increasing their understanding of the Arab monetary situation, the possibilities for co-operation and the Fund's role in this sphere. The Fund could also make use of the expertise of its own staff, other Arab expertise at home and abroad, or the expertise available in regional and international institutions, to provide advice in the financial and monetary domain.

3. The Preparation of Monetary and Financial Studies and Reports. The AMF, with its financial resources and flexibility, could play an important part in stimulating research and analysis in the monetary and financial fields to achieve its objective of bringing about Arab monetary co-operation aimed at monetary unity. This would enable it both to improve its own efficiency in providing services and facilities and to raise the technical standards of Arab monetary and banking institutions. To this end, the AMF could undertake the preparation of theoretical and applied studies on such subjects as: the development of Arab financial markets; expanding the use of the Arab dinar, making the Arab currencies inter-convertible; the settlement of current accounts, the co-ordination of monetary and financial policies; the possibilities for attaining monetary union on either the regional or bilateral Arab level; and the standardisation of Arab monetary and banking legislation, regulations and technical terms. In preparing these studies, the Fund could either rely on the expertise of its own staff or commission other Arab experts or institutions to carry out the work.

COMMENT

Rafik Sowellem

It is not surprising that Mr Abdul-Rasool's paper, though basically intended to address the issues of monetary integration, devotes a great deal of attention to the lending functions of the AMF. This is appropriate because of the close relationship between the ability of the AMF to be of service to its members in time of need and its ability to induce them to co-operate with it in its endeavour to promote the cause of Arab economic integration. In this regard, I would like to emphasise the comparisons between IMF and AMF lending policies, which were clearly brought out in Mr Abdul-Rasool's paper. In terms of lending capacity, the AMF certainly occupies a less favourable position, particularly in view of the fact that most of its members' capital subscriptions are in convertible currencies as compared with domestic currencies in the case of the IMF. The AMF is at an even greater disadvantage now that the IMF has increased its loan ceilings.

I would like to state my strong conviction that the success of the AMF in fulfilling its regional objectives will depend primarily on its ability to meet the borrowing needs of its members on appropriate terms. It should aim at committing more of its resources to this end. The Fund is essentially neither an investment bank nor a profit-making institution.

I find myself in agreement with most of Mr Abdul-Rasool's proposals concerning the Fund's lending activities (e.g., the establishment of new outlets increasing the resources of the AMF). However, there is one point on which I differ with him. While his proposal for the establishment of a buffer stock facility similar to that of the IMF is commendable, his suggestion that this take the form of direct acquisition by the AMF of strategic raw materials used in Arab industry and of member countries' export commodities when demand for these is weak, for resale to members at moderate prices when the markets for these products become more active, is to me something completely outside the scope of activity of a regional reserve fund such as the AMF. Nor do I understand, I am afraid, the connection between this and the issuing of an Arab dinar. His proposal is presented in much too general a way to allow proper assessment.

I would like now to turn my attention to the issues raised by monetary integration proper. In this regard, I believe it is useful to recall the distinction made by Mr Williamson between complete and partial monetary integration. I would agree with him that for many reasons, including questions of national sovereignty, complete monetary integration among all Arab countries is at present an unrealistic proposition. This does not mean that complete integration may not be feasible on a subregional basis (e.g., among the Gulf countries). Nevertheless, I believe that it would be more realistic for the AMF to concentrate its attention at this stage on the modalities for partial monetary integration. And here I would single out three specific lines of action.

The first is that of establishing a payments union among Arab countries. This is particularly important, because if such an arrangement included adequate credit facilities for financing regional trade and payments imbalances among Arab countries, it could be very effective in persuading member countries gradually to relax and eventually to lift existing trade and payments restrictions and perhaps restrictions on capital movements as well. The resources that could be made available for this purpose would depend essentially on the methods for settling payments which the participating countries might adopt. If appropriate measures were undertaken, particularly in relation to loan maturity and the interest rates associated with these credit facilities, I believe that substantial resources could be made available and that these would expand even further over time. These resources would be independent of the 2 per cent capital contribution in domestic currencies provided for in the AMF Agreement. A basic framework for an Arab Payments Union has recently been finalised and discussed by a group of experts, a framework which many of us believe answers almost all of the objections levelled against proposals made to establish a similar union among six Arab countries in the 1960s. There are at present six or seven such payments arrangements among developing countries, some of which have been in operation for over 20 years. The experience of these payments unions has clearly shown that they require neither the adoption of exchange controls by all participating countries nor the inter-convertibility of all their currencies. The AMF has invited Arab central banks to send their representatives to a meeting here [Abu Dhabi] on 20 December [1980] to discuss its proposals.

The second line of action I would like to single out relates to what Mr Williamson has referred to as 'capital market integration', a point which Mr Abdul-Rasool also discusses in his paper [p. 409]. This matter has received considerable attention within the AMF over the past year and a half. During this period, the Fund participated with other regional organisations in conducting a survey of existing capital markets in the Arab world. The findings of this survey were analysed by a group of experts and the main shortcomings were found to be related to the inadequate diversification of the investment instruments available to these markets, the lack of secondary markets and of specialised investment and issuing houses, the lack of suitable domestic financial legislation and the almost complete absence of linkages among the domestic capital markets in the Arab countries. In the light of these findings, the Fund has adopted a three-year operational plan based on:

(1) Direct intervention in the domestic markets, aimed at promoting their development through technical assistance, and participation in the establishment of appropriate secondary markets and issuing institutions.
(2) Identifying and implementing the measures needed to foster stronger linkages among existing domestic markets, particularly through the relaxation and eventual abolition of existing restrictions on the re-registration and negotiation in one Arab country of financial papers originating in the capital markets of another.
(3) More active intervention by the AMF and other Arab regional financial institutions, with a view to fostering the growth of a market in first-class securities which would be acceptable at the regional level. This the Fund could do by issuing marketable securities in its own name or on behalf of its members (with or without its guarantee) and by adopting appropriate measures to ensure an active secondary market in these securities. These securities would, of course, most appropriately be denominated in the Arab accounting dinar.

I would also like to mention the participation of the AMF in the recent drafting of an 'Investment Agreement' to be proposed to members of the Arab League. This Agreement seeks to provide adequate guarantees for across-the-border investments against non-commercial risks and to define a minimum standard for tax exemptions and other incentives aimed at promoting a greater flow of capital among Arab countries. The Agreement has recently been approved by the Economic and Social Council of the League of Arab States and is awaiting ratification by member countries.

The third line of action which could be pursued to achieve partial monetary integration is that of exchange-rate co-ordination. This has been strongly emphasised, but to my mind inadequately developed by Mr Abdul-Rasool. This brings us, of course, to the Arab accounting dinar and its method of valuation. The aim here is to reduce the costs and risks of exchange, in order to promote trade and capital flows among Arab countries. In this regard, although one would expect exchange-rate instability to have a negative effect on capital flows, one cannot be entirely certain as to how important such instability is as a factor impeding trade flows, as pointed out by Mr Williamson.

Mr Abdul-Rasool argues that exchange-rate co-ordination would require an agreement among Arab countries on a common intervention currency or a basket of currencies, including agreement on the margins of deviation between market rates and the chosen parity of each member's currency in relation to the numeraire. In addition, he states [p. 401] that exchange-rate stability requires complete co-ordination of monetary and financial policies among the Arab countries. I am not sure how this fits in with the strong doubts he expresses elsewhere in his paper as to the potential effectiveness of monetary and fiscal policies in correcting balance-of-payments disequilibria. Could it be that this would require co-ordination of development plans as well? If so, the task would seem to be even more difficult and its accomplishment an even more remote possibility. But I wonder if this is really necessary?

Mr Abdul-Rasool also refers to the 'cosmetic' nature of the present method of valuing the Arab accounting dinar. However, I must admit that I do not fully understand the alternative method of valuation he proposes. I do not believe that he has succeeded in adequately elaborating the mechanics or the modalities by which the Arab dinar — and not the Arab accounting dinar — would be issued and the way in which its value would be determined by the supply of and demand for Arab oil. Nor do I believe that he has sufficiently justified his claim that his proposal would increase the Arab countries' revenues from oil as well as non-oil exports, promote trade among Arab countries and enhance the ability of non-oil Arab countries to increase their imports.

I must admit, however, that the questions I am raising here may be a reflection more of my lack of knowledge in this field than of any lack of clarity on the part of Mr Abdul-Rasool. I must also concede that the issues relating to the Arab accounting dinar have not as yet received adequate attention within the AMF. The Fund plans to devote serious attention to this subject in 1981 and I am sure our discussions here will be very helpful to the AMF management and staff in their endeavour.

In conclusion, then, I believe it is through a multi-faceted attack on the partial monetary integration front that the AMF can most effectively define its role, over the next three to five years, in promoting Arab economic unity.

GENERAL DISCUSSION

1. Anton Kattan

While I support the idea of linking the exchange rates of Arab currencies to the Arab accounting dinar, I would object to the author's third alternative method for standardising the pegging of Arab currencies which would fix the exchange rate of the AAD in terms of oil supply and demand. Given the state of the world oil market and the nature of price changes, this could mean sudden changes in the exchange rate of the AAD, as well as that of the Arab currencies pegged to it, in relation to other world currencies. This would surely have negative consequences for the economies of the Arab countries. I would be in favour of linking the Arab currencies through the AAD which would be valued according to the external transactions of the Arab countries, despite the possibility of disagreement over the criteria to be used in choosing and weighting the currencies constituting the basket. This idea is similar to the first alternative mentioned in Mr Abdul-Rasool's paper [p. 404].

I also would like to clarify what appears to be a source of confusion when reference is made to freeing the exchange rates of Arab currencies from dependency on fluctuations in the world money markets and gaining control over these exchange rates. The exchange rate is by definition the price of a given currency as against other currencies. If the prices of external currencies change, so must the price of the currency under consideration. Since the present world monetary system is characterised by floating, and hence fluctuating, currencies, what is important for the Arab countries is to reduce the effect of these fluctuations in the major currencies on their economies. The purpose of selecting the AAD basket must therefore be, as Mr Williamson has said, to move as close as possible to achieving stable exchange rates between the Arab currencies and those of their major trading partners.

2. Karim Nashashibi

I would like to ask Mr Sowellem to give us more details on the payments union he mentions since it is the first concrete proposal for promoting some immediate form of economic integration that I have heard of for some time. In particular I would like to know the scope of such a proposal. Would it encompass all commodity trade (including oil, for example) and would it cover all Arab countries or just subgroups of countries?

3. Faik Abdul-Rasool, in Response

With regard to Mr Sowellem's objection to the Fund's directly acquiring and stocking strategic raw materials for the member countries and purchasing their export goods when the prices of these are low in order to resell them when their price rises, on the grounds that this is outside the scope of the Fund's activities, I would like to point out that one of the Fund's main objectives is the preservation of the purchasing power of the member states' export earnings and that by taking such action, the Fund would be addressing this objective and helping to accomplish it. My proposal therefore represents the means by which one of the Fund's objectives could be accomplished. Hence it would not be outside the proper scope of the Fund's activities.

Mr Sowellem also refers to what he regards as a contradiction in my paper, namely with regard to monetary policy where I say that the stability of the cross-rates of Arab currencies requires the total co-ordination of monetary policies while in another part of the paper there is a reference to the ineffectiveness of monetary policies. I would like to point out, in this connection, that the effectiveness of monetary policy varies from one Arab country to another, according to the exchange-rate system in effect. In the case of Iraq and Libya we find that the cross-rates of their currencies have been nearly stable since 1973, although there has been no co-ordination of their monetary policies. On the other hand, we find that in the case of the Gulf countries (Saudi Arabia, Bahrain, Qatar and the UAE), despite their mutual co-operation and co-ordination and the regular consultations among their monetary authorities, the cross-rates of their currencies, as I indicated in my paper, continue to fluctuate.

Concerning the Arab accounting dinar, the important issue is not so much its initial value, for it may be pegged to the SDR, the dollar, the Kuwaiti dinar or the Saudi riyal. What matters is the daily movement of its exchange rate and the need to make it independent of the decisions of foreign monetary authorities and of conditions in the international financial markets which affect the exchange rates of the major currencies. This could be accomplished by adopting the proposal which I detailed in my paper. I suggested that the Arab oil countries make it a condition that they receive, for example, 5 per cent of their oil export revenues in the form of Arab dinars. The Fund would issue this dinar in exchange for the foreign currencies it received from oil importers as well as permit its convertibility into other currencies. The Fund would thus have assets denominated in foreign currencies which it would exchange for commitments on the part of the oil countries as well as other countries wishing to hold the dinar as part of their investment portfolios. In this way, the Fund would have resources available for financing the balance-of-payments deficits of the Arab countries.

In addition, under this proposal the Arab countries could peg their national currencies to the dinar whose exchange rate would be fixed daily according to supply and demand. The demand for the dinar would come from oil importers that would need it to pay a part of the cost of their oil imports from the Arab countries. The demand for the dinar might also be for use in investment portfolios. The supply, on the other hand, would depend on a number of factors, the most important being the availability of sufficient resources for financing the balance-of-payments deficits of the Arab countries. Since the determining factor in the demand for the dinar would be the demand for oil and since one can expect that there will be a shortage of oil, the relative scarcity of the dinar would increase its exchange rate *vis-à-vis* other currencies. This in itself would provide a guarantee for a portion of the oil export revenues. Instead of the Arab states receiving 100 per cent of their revenues in dollars, whose value has been depreciating, they would, under this proposal, receive 5 per cent of these revenues in Arab dinars, whose value *vis-à-vis* other currencies would tend to appreciate.

I hope that I have succeeded in clarifying some of the issues that have been raised and I wish to apologise if I have neglected to respond to other questions.

4. Faika El-Refaie*

I agree with Mr Sowellem that the author's discussion of the Arab dinar was unclear, especially as concerns how the value of the proposed dinar would be determined in the first phase and its link with the supply of and demand for oil. What would the oil countries do with the Arab (non-accounting) dinar proposed by Mr Abdul-Rasool? At one point in his paper he says that the dinar should not be linked to the SDR, but at the same time he states that in the first place what really matters is not how the dinar is pegged but the extent of its fluctuations.

Mr Abdul-Rasool also says that the purpose of the Arab dinar is to bring about a new means of investment which would help the Arab oil countries to expand their investment portfolios, reduce risks and safeguard their purchasing power against fluctuations in the major

---

* Comment received subsequent to the author's response to the discussion of his paper [eds.].

investment currencies. He bases this argument on the AMF Agreement which, he says, stipulates that the Fund is supposed to preserve the real value of members' resources. I would like to point out that this is not stipulated in the Agreement. What is stipulated is that the AMF, whenever requested, should advise the member states with regard to the investment of their monetary resources abroad with the aim of ensuring the preservation of their real value. There is no obligation on the part of members to hand over their earnings in foreign currency to the AMF as Mr Abdul-Rasool suggests.

12 BASIC ECONOMIC AND POLITICAL PREREQUISITES FOR ACHIEVING ARAB MONETARY INTEGRATION*

Fouad Morsi

Introduction

The Dual Meaning of Integration for Developing Countries

The economic structures of the developing countries suffer from a double flaw.

On the one hand, their economies exhibit an incomplete social division of labour, in that the process of separating industry from agriculture has not yet been completed so as to make possible internal integration. No single domestic market has yet been formed from the fragmented markets that exist. The backwardness of these countries stems from a situation of either no growth or slow growth in commodity production. This is compounded by the underdeveloped state of the commodity-money relationship in these economies.

On the other hand, these developing economies — their internal integration still incomplete — suffer from being bound to an underdeveloped international division of labour whereby they specialise in producing raw materials or primary goods for export to the world capitalist market.

The production of such basic goods is the decisive factor, not only in the production cycle but right through the whole social cycle of production: from manufacture, distribution and exchange to consumption. Backward economies thus enter the commodity circuit as exporters to the world market — dependent upon it, rather than as partners sharing in its benefits. While they import from that market most of the manufactured goods they need, they export to it goods which they cannot sell elsewhere. If these countries are to extricate themselves from this vicious cycle, they must first attack the problem at its source by developing their social division of labour and carrying out comprehensive economic and social development. To the extent that these countries succeed in developing their social division of labour internally, so will they develop their position within the international division of labour. In other words, the approach to economic integration for the developing countries must be that of changing their production and distribution structures so as to bring about greater development of

---

* Translated from the Arabic.

their productive forces.

The Relationship between Economic and Monetary Integration

Clearly, this approach stresses the development of production and not merely the liberalisation of trade. Foreign trade is primarily a reflection of the sectoral composition of production, though it does in turn influence it. Nevertheless, the long-term experience of the developing countries shows that foreign trade has not succeeded in being a 'vehicle' for socio-economic development. It is rather trade co-operation that has generally been most successful in creating the prerequisites for development.

It is in this context that the relationship between economic and monetary integration must be determined. As to which comes first, monetary integration, like trade integration, cannot occur except as the culmination of economic integration. This is the structural approach to monetary integration; for money is no more than a means for settling internal and external payments. It is the concrete expression of an exchange of goods. Economic equilibrium is thus a prerequisite for both internal and external monetary equilibrium.[1] Hence, there is no point in discussing monetary integration unless some degree of economic integration has already taken place.

However, steps towards monetary integration may be taken prior to the achievement of economic integration provided the qualitative conditions for such steps exist. Monetary integration — in the broadest sense — may under these circumstances serve as a prelude to economic integration, i.e., the integration of production. Monetary integration could, in other words, create favourable conditions which might hasten the process of economic integration itself.

Money is not neutral in economic relationships. Monetary factors can play a more important role in economic integration than seems to be realised. Thus the attainment of a degree of co-ordination with regard to exchange rates, interest rates, credit terms and conditions for international transactions could lead to a similar degree of co-ordination among the countries concerned, with regard to their economic conditions and policies. While it is true that international economic relations are largely an extension of internal economic relations in each individual country, they inevitably take on a certain life of their own and hence exert considerable influence in turn on each country's internal economic development.

Therefore, not only are the internal and external economic sectors interrelated but so are monetary and economic integration. With this in mind, we turn to the discussion of the basic economic and political prerequisites for achieving Arab monetary integration.

I. Basic Requirements of Arab Monetary Integration

A. The Economic Requirements

To achieve Arab monetary integration, two basic prerequisites must be satisfied: the elimination of Arab economic dependency on the world capitalist system and the elimination of disparities in the rates of growth of different Arab countries; we shall take up each in turn.

1. Eliminating Economic Dependency. Most of the oil countries have either wholly or partially nationalised the oil monopolies. Some have also nationalised foreign trade. Here are two examples of measures taken to eliminate unequal forms of exchange, with the effect of moving the Arab economy towards internal integration. Nevertheless, the current pattern of development through integration with capitalism in all spheres — production, trade, capital and technology — serves to maintain the Arab economy as a whole in a state of dependency. This is what has been, from the beginning, the cause of Arab economic backwardness, dependency and fragmentation. This new dependency is part of the new structure of relations between the Arab countries and the multinational monopolies which constitute the basic structure of modern collective or transnational capitalism. For this reason, the dependency under discussion here is first and foremost an expression of the huge economic and technological gap between the Arab countries and the advanced capitalist countries. This gap takes the form of unequal terms of international exchange. Whereas development planning in the Arab countries may be destroying the old structure of dependency, it is nevertheless giving rise to a new structure of dependency which may be even more oppressive than its predecessor.[2]

The reliance up to now on the export of a single, depletable strategic raw material to ensure Arab socio-economic growth represents an important challenge for the Arab oil countries. After letting great opportunities go by in the years following the oil price explosion, the Arab countries find themselves once again isolated and under strong foreign pressure, indeed subjected more than ever before to fluctuations in the price and value of their oil exports, mainly determined by the advanced industrial countries.[3] The West fears that unless the Arab countries are tied to the capitalist economy (especially the oil sector which has been isolated from the Arab economy), these countries will inevitably move towards economic integration with each other. If such integration were to occur, the industrialisation of the Arab countries would be facilitated, especially given the continuing stagnation of the world capitalist economy.[4]

2. Eliminating Financial Dependency. The question of financial dependency merits treatment independently of the problem of economic dependency; for whatever is gained in the way of liberating the oil sector and incorporating it into the Arab economy is liable to be lost in the financial arena. One may well wonder as to the meaning of monetary integration among the Arab countries, especially the oil states, as long as they are almost totally integrated financially with the world capitalist market.[5] It is common knowledge that this market has come to exhibit some dangerous phenomena foremost among which are: (i) the steady internationalisation of capital, the emergence of multinational capital and, in the 1970s, the creation of international banks; and (ii) the export of capital by the developing countries, albeit one of the later phenomena to develop with monopoly capitalism.

Hence, the world financial market appears in its varied and changing structures, methods and instruments to be the main arena for the Arab countries' struggle for independence – oil and non-oil countries, creditors and debtors alike. As it is, oil money comes out of financial purses in the industrial countries only to go right back into other purses in the same industrial countries,[6] thus remaining well beyond Arab control. Furthermore, the Arab countries are obliged to turn to the world market to borrow money on terms imposed by that market. In the end, the Arab countries will have exchanged depletable material assets for financial assets of fluctuating value and a rate of income limited by the erosion of the purchasing power of these assets.

Much has been written about financial dependency; our treatment will confine itself to illustrating the most important forms of this dependency by means of which the world capitalist economy has become the main beneficiary of oil revenues.

a. The recycling of oil revenues. As has been said, the oil revenues do not leave the world financial market, they are merely recycled. One part is fed immediately into the financial markets controlled by the international banks and another part remains in the oil country in order to finance the state budget and, in particular, ambitious development projects whose execution requires foreign expertise and technology. It is not long, therefore, before these revenues as well are returned to the world market as payment for feasibility studies, imports of technology, etc. A third part of the oil revenues is fed into the Arab financial market – a dependent market – which quickly transfers its assets to the world financial market. The bulk of Arab financial resources thus remains abroad, beyond Arab control. These revenues are invested in public and private bonds, real estate, tourist projects and in the automotive and mining industries.[7] The Arab funds may also take the form of loans to the industrial countries.[8]

b. Joint banking projects. Since the mid-1960s a number of international banks have been created. These represent a financial set-up invented by the multinationals in their strategy to internationalise capital. Through these banks, a financial 'free zone' is created embracing the entire capitalist world. Within this world-wide zone, formidable devices are employed for the recycling of funds. These include bank deposit certificates as a short-term device, lending operations as a medium-term device and international securities as a means of long-term financing. It is this multinational world market which has ended up with the lion's share of Arab oil revenues. Since the early 1970s joint Arab banks have been set up with international capital and directly linked to the international financial market. The danger inherent in these joint banks is that decision-making within them is not in the hands of the Arab capital-holding countries but rather takes place in London, in the case of Kuwait, and in New York, in the case of Saudi Arabia. Arab capital ends up being lent to Arab countries by the international banks in Europe and North America.[9]

This situation has been responsible for retarding the formation of Arab money and capital markets and has made them dependent on the world financial markets, especially the Eurodollar market. Contradictions have emerged in existing Arab financial structures as a result of the lack of integration between the Arab financial sector and the domestic Arab economies, forcing the Arab countries to turn towards the economies of the industrial countries. The Arab countries do not co-ordinate their financial policies even with regard to investment abroad. By holding most of their assets abroad in the form of high-liquidity, short-term investments, the Arab countries have provided the world financial market with the opportunity of controlling those assets.[10] Hence Arab monetary integration and the merger of Arab financial sectors is inconceivable as long as one ignores the state of financial dependency stemming from their present effective integration with the international financial market.

3. Eliminating Monetary Dependency. Admitting that the monetary policy of any country is inseparable from its over-all economic policy, particular consideration must be given to the state of monetary dependency in which the Arab countries find themselves. This dependency is particularly evident in the determination of the type of currency that can be used for the final settlement of payments between the Arab states and other countries.

During the post-Second World War period, the Bretton Woods agreements effectively established the US dollar as the international medium of exchange. This gave American capital an enormous advantage over its rivals. The dollar was turned into a weapon in the struggle for

Basic Economic and Political Prerequisites 427

control of international financial and monetary relations. The issuing of dollars — the local currency of a single country, the United States — amounted, in fact, to the issuing of an international currency by that country. The United States thereupon initiated a policy of issuing unlimited quantities of dollars.[11]

Just as the international monetary system was used to ensure the global domination of the dollar, so was it used as an effective means of blackmailing the developing countries and of solving the capitalist world's problems at their expense. This was accomplished by means of the industrial countries making decisions and taking steps unilaterally to change the exchange rates of their currencies.[12] The International Monetary Fund has promoted the interests of the large industrial countries, particularly the United States, by guaranteeing and diversifying international trade and payments under American hegemony. This it has done by making the dollar the currency of world reserves, by fixing exchange rates while allowing the convertibility of currencies, by providing balance-of-payments support and by permitting rate adjustments in cases of fundamental imbalances. It has stood against competitive devaluations while attempting to remove restrictions on trade and international payments.

The IMF has played only a minor role in aiding developing countries, for it has never been equipped to deal with both development-related deficits and chronic deficits which reflect structural phenomena in the developing countries. Nevertheless, the IMF has been used to sanction a kind of monetary dependency in these countries with respect to the dollar. The United States abolished the post-war international monetary system with its decision in 1971 to suspend the convertibility of dollars into gold. Since March 1973, when the dollar was devalued, the capitalist world has had a system of floating exchange rates. The adoption of the Special Drawing Rights system has meant that currencies are pegged to a basket of currencies in which the dollar itself predominates.

In fact, the international monetary system is a reflection of the world capitalist economy. This system is ailing to such an extent that no cure is expected. The dollar is not the only unhealthy currency; in fact, all capitalist currencies are suffering from instability. The reason for this is that the utter domination of the international monopolies has made available to them vast resources which, given the present state of the world capitalist market, can be transformed into marginal capital to be used in speculation and thus contribute to an inflationary spiral and to the loss of parity among currencies. Such resources may be used in this way before being reinvested in production or used to meet the financial commitments of these monopolies. While the perturbations which have characterised the international monetary system may not have been specifically caused by speculation on the part of the multinational monopolies, the indisputable fact remains that these monopolies are able to transfer huge sums of money across borders. There is no doubt but what such monopolies serve to aggravate the world monetary crisis.[13]

The monetary experience, particularly since the 1970s has shown that the United States, as the world's banker, is neither willing nor able to follow a defined monetary policy. Western Europe suffers from currency fluctuations. Most crises affecting the dollar are preceded by pressures on the European foreign exchange markets and wide fluctuations in the exchange rates of European currencies. Even the new European Monetary System is unlikely to prove capable of solving the problem.

Nevertheless, it is not possible to abandon the dollar. It is still the world currency, owing to the reforms introduced to the international monetary system, the increasing domination of the big international banks in international financing operations, the ability of the international monetary system to extend international credit without restriction and the virtual technological and financial monopoly exercised by the multinationals in the implementation of major projects in both the industrial and the developing countries. There are at present some $900 billion in various currencies circulating on the European foreign-exchange markets, as a result of US balance-of-payments deficits and the expansion of US commercial banks. Of these currencies, some 400 billion are in the form of dollars which, if they were the object of speculation, would bring on a catastrophe which even the IMF could not avert.

For this reason, the crisis of the international monetary system persists, with its negative effects on foreign exchange, trade and finance among countries. The dollar continues to occupy centre stage in the international monetary system while the world is impoverished to the benefit of the United States. And the Arab countries continue to suffer from dependency on the dollar.

Even after the Arab countries achieved independence, their currencies continued to be linked to the sterling zone, the French franc zone or to the dollar. What is new is that this dependency has increased with the burgeoning financial resources of the oil countries. The financial sectors of the Arab countries, particularly Saudi Arabia, Kuwait and the UAE, have been annexed to the world's financial market, subject as it is to multinational capital. Joint Arab-foreign banking institutions have been established to finance commercial, industrial and agricultural activities in the industrial countries. This has occurred to the point where the Arab countries in need of outside financing do not obtain it directly from the Arab countries with balance-of-payments surpluses, but rather through New York or London or through multinational corporations. The forces which propel the Arab world outwards have come to be stronger than those factors which pull it inwards.[14]

Despite all its shortcomings and crises, the international monetary system has shown that it is still capable of drawing off and redistributing Arab oil wealth without bringing on any disastrous consequences for the industrialised world. On the pretext of safeguarding the international monetary system, new ways have been invented to recycle these funds to the industrialised world. A financial network has been built up, closely tied to the Arab world so that Arab funds will be used within the framework of the world monetary and financial circuit and through its institutions. When the IMF created its so-called 'Oil Facility' in 1974, it used Arab funds to finance it. In this way, it obtained additional resources for the countries hit by the rise in the cost of their petroleum imports and suffering from balance-of-payments deficits. The funds received by the IMF were turned into non-negotiable rights which were frozen for periods ranging from three to seven years. These funds amounted to three billion SDRs. In 1975, the finance ministers of the EEC countries met in London and adopted a resolution in support of the plan proposed by the IMF to obtain a $12 billion loan from the Arab oil-producing countries to be offered in the form of a loan to the European industrial countries.

In March 1975, the Gulf countries managed to sever the links between their currencies and the dollar. However, this represented only a partial disassociation from the dollar since these currencies continued to be valued in terms of the SDR, a basket of currencies in which the dollar predominates, accounting for between 30 and 33 per cent of the value of one SDR unit. Experience has demonstrated that it is virtually impossible for any currency to be dissociated from the dollar because of the dollar's status as the primary instrument for international payments. All accounting units in effect in the world, whether SDRs, the European ECUs or Arab accounting dinars are valued, either wholly or partially, in terms of the dollar.

There are many factors which determine the basis for monetary dependency, such as the degree of linkage between a country's national economy and the capitalist market, the importance of its foreign trade in generating national income and the structure of its exports. A number of factors contribute to Arab monetary dependency, in particular, of which the following may be cited:

(a) The money supply in the Arab oil countries depends on fluctuations in oil export prices which are quoted in dollars. Despite attempts to quote these prices in SDRs, the conditions of stagflation in the world economy and the fluctuating exchange rates of the world's major currencies, including the dollar, have made the exchange rates of Arab currencies and their monetary reserves in gold and foreign currencies subject to similar, usually even wider, fluctuations;

(b) The Arab countries still prefer the dollar as an investment currency, whether they are investing in the United States or in the European Common Market countries. The dollar was estimated in October 1978 to account for about 70 per cent of all investments by the OPEC countries. International and especially US banks have played a leading role in recycling oil funds, thereby acquiring a large portion — 38 per cent — of OPEC country deposits;[15]

(c) With the collapse of the Bretton Woods system, there is no longer an international monetary system capable of providing the necessary liquidity for international payments in order to cope with the steadily increasing volume of international exchanges. In the absence of such a system, the IMF as an international institution for providing temporary liquidity has become paralysed. This situation has led to the creation of an international money market to handle the balance-of-payments deficits of the developing countries, as these deficits, far from being of a contingency nature, have become a serious structural phenomenon. The role of the IMF in overseeing international liquidity has in fact changed, this role having been assumed by the international banks, particularly the US banks. The European market has thus become the primary source of international liquidity.[16]

Any discussion of Arab monetary integration which does not address itself specifically to the position of Arab currencies with respect to the dollar and which does not propose to eliminate all forms of monetary dependency on the dollar, has the effect of sanctioning this dependency as it affects Arab integration.

The call for emancipation from the international capitalist market is not a call for isolationism or for boycotting that market. It merely advocates the elimination of unequal exchange at all levels, i.e., production, trade, technology and finance. Monetary dependency is a primary instrument for perpetuating such a system.

4. Eliminating Disparities in Economic Growth Levels. The components of economic integration are established over a long period of time. They can be said to exist when specialisation and co-operation in production have gradually demonstrated the importance, in the long run, of the rational, joint use of resources. The reason for the crisis in Arab economic integration lies in a fundamental reality: the disparities and inequalities in economic growth among the Arab countries. The gaps have actually widened in recent years due to the reliance on a backward pattern of Arab economic integration, i.e., trade liberalisation and the pursuit of a dependent Arab development pattern, namely industrialisation for export.[17]

The principal measure of a society's economic progress is the degree of growth of its productive forces. The basic indicator of the growth of these forces is the average growth of material output. While the phenomenon of backwardness and dependency stemming from fusion with the world market − in accordance with the international capitalist division of labour − prevails in all the Arab countries, they in fact differ in terms of their economic and social structures, the distribution of their productive forces and their economic growth levels. Consequently, they also differ in the ability of their local markets to meet local demand. Contributing to these disparities is the political and economic isolation of these countries from each other. This isolation has been reinforced since the advent of national independence by the prevalence of economic similarities in the areas of agriculture, industry and animal husbandry. Each Arab country has adopted a development strategy oriented towards serving the emerging domestic market. Moreover, since 1973, Arab economic development has been oriented towards large-scale investment and has become directly linked with the world market.

After achieving independence in the 1960s the Arab countries turned in the 1970s to the task of consolidating their sovereignty and building their nation states. With the oil boom and the revenues it brought, the Arab countries were able to implement ambitious local development projects which reinforced these national entities. Many similar projects were established in parallel fashion in different countries. This increased the existing polarisation between the oil and non-oil countries.

In addition to the existing disparities in natural resources, then, new disparities have emerged with respect to financial resources. The growth of the Arab countries is no longer balanced at any level, as a result of the rise in the contribution of oil to the GNP and the disparities in the distribution of income, both regionally and nationally. The rate of labour migration has increased. Both capital and labour have become economic and political weapons. Arab capital has come to represent the three-way collaboration of new political affiliations, new consumption patterns and the transplantation of the value system of the industrialised consumer societies to the oil countries and from there to the non-oil countries. What is even more dangerous is that these national development patterns and growth rates and the constant increase in oil prices have become factors steadily contributing to the seriousness of the differences among both countries and individuals. This has tended to accentuate nationalism.

A distinction has come to be made within the Arab world between oil and non-oil countries, between capital-exporting and labour-exporting countries, between balance-of-payments surplus countries and deficit countries. Whereas the GNP of the Arab world increased in general during the 1970s rising from $35.3 billion in 1970 to $132.1 billion in 1975 and an estimated $236.8 billion in 1980, there remain great disparities among the Arab countries.

There has emerged among the Arab countries what is commonly termed a 'development gap', and a dangerous obstacle to any attempt at Arab integration has arisen, namely the differential in production costs, especially as concerns industrial projects. This differential has the effect of impeding free trade, if not causing the elimination of high-cost projects altogether. A study of the cost structures of single projects would undoubtedly reveal disparities in economic structures, in the relative advantages enjoyed by each Arab country separately, and in their economic, financial, fiscal and monetary policies as well.

The differences in economic growth among Arab countries are directly reflected in their trade and financial relations and in the movements of labour among them. Their trade relations are characterised by restrictions and obstacles impeding exchange and thus preventing integration. Some examples of the factors contributing to this situation are the following:

(a) Differences in monetary systems and in the degree of monetisation of the economy. Before one proceeds to monetary integration, the use of money in transactions must become widespread in every Arab country;
(b) Differences in the banking systems, i.e., the extent to which bank credit methods are applied and credit facilities are used and the degree of stability of the banking system within the national economy;
(c) Disparate foreign exchange systems and differences in the balance-of-payments positions. The relative scarcity of convertible currencies at the disposal of the Arab deficit countries makes them reluctant to remove trade restrictions among themselves. Their pressing needs in this area make them prefer, in the last analysis, those transactions which bring them foreign exchange.

Needless to say, it is assumed that the Arab socio-economic systems can be brought closer to each other despite their obvious differences. As Ahmed Murad has written in an unpublished study: 'The decade of the 1960s witnessed a deep conflict between the capitalist and socialist development trends within the Arab world'. In the 1970s, however,

Table 12.1: GNP of Arab Countries 1970-80

Category of country	1970		1975		1980	
	Billions of dollars	Index (1970=100)	Billions of dollars	Index (1970=100)	Billions of dollars	Index (1970=100)
Oil countries	9.6	100	66.7	694.8	135.1	1407.2
Semi-oil countries	7.7	100	24.9	323.3	47.7	619.4
Non-oil countries	18.0	100	40.5	225.0	54.0	300.0
Total	35.3		132.1		236.8	

Source: Report of the Secretary General of the Council of Arab Economic Unity, presented at the Council's session, Abu Dhabi, December 1978.

this conflict largely abated. The socialist-oriented countries gave greater support than they had before to the private sector and enacted legislation to encourage it. At the same time, the public sector in the capitalist-oriented countries expanded for a number of reasons, primarily the assumption of national control over the oil sector and the increased role played by the public sector in development. The national economies of all Arab countries have thereby become mixed economies with both the private and public sectors participating to varying degrees.[18] The problems associated with differing Arab economic systems have thus been surmounted.

The foreign economic policies of the Arab countries differ in respect of their degree of freedom or restriction. Nevertheless, there has been a considerable narrowing of these differences as a result of the general liberalisation which has become the prevailing climate in the oil region. A country pursuing a liberal foreign-exchange policy may at the same time have a monopoly over its oil revenues and exercise centralised state control over their management, though it may lack the necessary expertise for such purposes. Or, a country applying a policy of currency exchange control may in fact pursue a liberal policy with regard to the movements of trade, finance and individuals. Such phenomena need not, however, constitute an insurmountable obstacle to Arab integration.

Only the disparities in the growth of productive forces would seem to constitute a real stumbling block in the way of economic integration for they would render such integration an unpredictable adventure for the benefit of the stronger party. Therefore, one must begin with the development of the productive forces and with an attempt to narrow the gaps in Arab economic growth as the only way to provide the economic structure capable of integrating all the Arab countries. It is common knowledge that co-operation among the socialist countries of Europe has no deep historical roots. Before the Second World War, there was only a small volume of trade among these countries, constituting between 1 and 15 per cent of their foreign trade. Nevertheless, their subsequent economic, social and political unity propelled them along the path of economic integration. In this way, they acted on a fundamental principle, namely that of closing the gaps in their economic growth levels.

B. The Political Prerequisites

Economic integration is not the simple extension and culmination of the international division of labour, a mere continuation of the process by which economic life in every country is steadily taking on an international character. That process is an objective one taking its own course through the forces of production. Economic integration, on the other hand, is a determined course of action requiring the adoption of a positive attitude by a group of countries in dealing with the future development of their productive forces. It is a conscious process involving all aspects of production and exchange as well as financial and monetary relations among a specific group of countries. These countries, bound by close allegiance and co-operation by virtue of having a homogenous socio-political base, can then strive to secure the proper political and economic conditions for the development of their productive forces in a way more compatible with the interests of the politically dominant classes.

Homogeneity here means that the relationships of production in the integrated economies would be similar. Therefore, economic integration can occur only among a group of states sharing the same socio-economic structure and the same mode of production. Economic integration is a unitary process carried out with respect to both the forces and the relationships of production. For this reason, it depends on the nature of the prevailing relationships of production. These are the primary relationships which subsequently determine all the others. Economic integration, whether arising from a certain internationalisation of the productive forces or based on their joint development in a number of countries, presupposes similar relationships of production corresponding to the nature of these countries' productive forces. Thus the social and economic content of integration is determined, in terms of both its forms and the results it produces, by the nature of the socio-economic system it serves.

With the unification of the socio-political-economic system, in terms of the nature of the prevailing relationships of production, a difficulty arises owing to the fact that each national economy constitutes on its own a stable economic structure with a relatively fixed pattern of specialisation. As a result, a natural contradiction emerges between the tendency for production to take on an international character and the narrowness of the organisational framework of such production in the individual state. This is not to say that the political borders of any country should be eliminated or that any country should give up its national sovereignty. The problem is how to reconcile two phenomena: the continuous internationalisation of production and the preservation of national sovereignty. Economic integration can provide the proper framework for reconciling these two phenomena.

This is where the role of political will comes in as the factor which should resolve the contradiction between the objective trend towards economic internationalisation and the normal framework of political sovereignty. In order to resolve this contradiction to the benefit of integration, there must be some common ground among the political systems concerned,[19] for integration is not likely to take place among substantially dissimilar political systems.

Every experience of economic integration is a historical process in that it takes time for its motivating forces to mature and for its components to be formed. For this reason, integration can only come about gradually. And it is the role played by the political will in this historical process that will be decisive, however strong the objective process itself. In the long run it is objective economic laws which influence political developments and bring about change even in political concepts. Our concern here is the short run during which economic decisions are made. In the short run, it is political factors which exert the decisive influence on economic relations.[20]

The management of the national economy is one of the basic prerogatives of state sovereignty. Once the political will exists to achieve economic integration, it is not difficult to find the necessary structure and the technical instruments. As a political activity, economic integration requires that emphasis be placed on the role of the conscious will in determining society's course. This will is not merely the desire to bring about certain specific changes; it involves devising and deciding upon measures, determining stages and mobilising resources, then launching the execution phase in accordance with the attributes and competence of those in charge of implementation. Lastly, economic integration involves having the authority to offer rewards and impose penalties. The political will required to achieve Arab monetary integration must therefore necessarily imply the will to be free, to develop and to integrate.

1. The Will to be Free. There must exist the political will to be liberated from economic dependency on the world capitalist market and on the United States in particular. Arab dependency on the world capitalist market is not inevitable. Another market, the socialist market, does exist and it has an interest in seeing the Arab countries develop, if for no other reason than to isolate them from the world capitalist market. There are enough newly independent developing countries to constitute a majority in international forums. This majority, which is making itself heard within the United Nations organisations and particularly within the non-aligned group and at UNCTAD conferences, is striving to set up a new world economic order which would put an end to unequal terms of exchange. These countries represent a force to be reckoned with in negotiations and confrontations, a force indispensable to the Arabs. Consequently, given the present circumstances, in which the capitalist countries are witnessing increasing economic difficulties leading them to impose restrictions on international trade and on the movement of money and credit among countries, there must emerge a willingness to co-operate with the Third World and an effort to change the world economic order and the international monetary system which is part of it.

2. The Will to Develop. Not only is the will to develop inseparable from the will to be free; it is its very essence. There must be a determination to develop beyond the current state of backwardness, and this determination must lead to the achievement of liberation from dependency on the world capitalist market and not merely to duplicating this dependency in another form. While it is possible to achieve development on a national scale, the conditions exhibited by the Arab economies are such that development has a better chance of succeeding if it is carried out on a pan-Arab scale. It is no longer possible even for the largest nations to develop their productive forces adequately at the national level: neither the United States nor the Soviet Union can afford to do so. The fact that Cuba has embraced the socialist bloc market across the Caribbean Sea and that Great Britain has looked across the English Channel to join the European Common Market should be a clear warning to the under-developed countries, both large and small, that the days of isolated national development are over. If these countries can integrate, why not the Arab countries which share the additional aspiration of national unity?

3. The Will to Integrate. It should be stressed that the Arab countries have not yet demonstrated the political determination to bring about pan-Arab integration. The decision to take any step towards economic integration is no less significant than a political decision in favour of liberation, whether it is achieved by war or by peaceful means. Economic integration in the sense of forming a unified economic structure among the Arab countries means, in fact, a political decision to sever ties with the world capitalist market and to end the dependency relationships of international integration. Such a decision is still lacking at the Arab level.

Political determination will be lacking as long as the Arab entity is dealt with as a multinational entity and not as a single national entity. As illustrations one might cite: the preponderance of bilateral or multilateral relations; the rivalry between national and pan-Arab bodies, notably in the realm of financing; and decision-making in every area by consensus rather than by majority vote.

The importance of any decision related to economic integration cannot be over-emphasised, for it is the ultimate challenge to the forces of fragmentation, backwardness and dependency. It is not enough for the peoples of the Arab countries to share common interests. There must also be a determination to eradicate all traces of accumulated suspicion and mistrust in the Arab world. Every Arab country must give up the idea of doing everything by itself in isolation from the other Arab countries and a progressive division of labour among the Arab countries must be established, a division which does not stop at avoiding duplication in production but which goes on to build the elements of inter-dependence among Arab countries. The basis for building this inter-dependence, however, should not be related to the present division of the Arab world between capital-exporting countries and labour-exporting countries. With such a division or, more precisely, with this form of inter-dependence, the Arab countries will remain bound to the world capitalist market.

There are two factors favourable to laying the groundwork for Arab monetary integration. The first is that the monetary system is not a purely domestic issue for each country to decide; it is also an international issue concerning, after all, international payments. Hence the concern of all developing countries with developments affecting the international monetary system and the world's major currencies. For this reason, there is an international dimension to every local monetary system. The second factor concerns oil developments which have ushered the Arab nation into the world petroleum and financial markets. These developments constitute a crucial factor in favour of achieving Arab monetary integration in the face of the dollar's uncertain predominance in the world market and in order directly to safeguard Arab interests.

There remains a crucial political consideration which is the support of the masses for all steps of Arab economic integration, particularly those of monetary integration. Such steps are still taken in isolation from the Arab masses and are given an aura of technical complexity within the bureaucratic and technocratic systems which make economic decisions. Therefore, just as the decision to integrate is taken in isolation from the masses, so is the decision not to integrate or to suspend the process of integration. The issue of economic integration has not yet been transformed into a political issue for the Arab peoples to take up with enthusiasm, an issue for which they are prepared to make sacrifices, and one which epitomises their struggle against the forces of dependency, backwardness and fragmentation.

II. Means of Achieving the Prerequisites for Arab Monetary Integration

Providing the basic requirements for Arab monetary integration requires sound national economic development from a pan-Arab perspective. This implies building up a modern, rapid-growth national economy through the integration and assimilation of all sectors, an economy comprising productive forces of its own which will permit it to renew itself. It should be capable of achieving cultural, material and spiritual progress for the overwhelming majority of citizens together with their full participation in the development process. Production must at first be primarily directed towards local markets in order to meet local demand as this represents the basic needs of the vast majority of inhabitants. This implies a change in the pattern of income distribution to make it possible to incorporate this majority into the sphere of the money economy and commodity exchange. Only at this point will the pattern of production be basically tailored to local consumption.

No Arab country can, on its own, master the technology required to produce a wide range of commodities. Nor can any Arab country develop outside the sphere of internatinal economic relations. Therefore, the elimination of disparities required for achieving growth cannot take place in isolation from the nature and extent of Arab participation. Hence, pan-Arab integration seems an appropriate outlet for national development. Setting this development in motion at a pan-Arab level implies:

(a) Expanding demand by raising it from the national to the pan-Arab level, and by carrying out projects in an integrated market which would make it possible to increase production capacity and thereby reduce costs;
(b) Expanding specialisation from a national basis to a pan-Arab one, thereby making it possible to combine the comparative advantages of the Arab countries to match the advantages enjoyed by international enterprises. It should thus be possible to limit discrepancies between local and international production costs.

The result would be a reduction in the economic disparities among the Arab countries, effected by overcoming the present inequality of income distribution and eliminating disparities in economic growth levels. This would be reflected in more comparable levels of labour productivity in the Arab countries and would eventually ensure a more even distribution of income.[21]

The starting point for Arab economic integration is the achievement of self-sustained development in each Arab country so as to make possible the exchange of productive resources and not only the exchange of consumer goods. This would be in conformity with an Arab division of labour based on the basic assumptions of the theory of comparative costs, so that national markets would merge into a single domestic Arab market. Alongside this national development one should arrive at a certain level of joint development for which resources would be allocated in the general budget of each Arab country, in addition to all the resources of the Arab Fund for Economic and Social Development. It should be the objective of this joint development to help narrow the development gaps among the Arab countries. This will necessitate the transfer of real resources from surplus to deficit countries. The growth rates in the most under-developed countries should thereafter be higher, on the average, than in the less underdeveloped ones, thus narrowing the gap between them and increasing the development of productive forces.

All this would create the foundation on which Arab monetary integration could then be built. This integration would still appear to be only a remote possibility. To achieve it in the future we must begin now to establish what can be called an Arab monetary system which would lead to the emergence of an Arab monetary zone as a prelude to Arab monetary integration. This integration should come about gradually, bringing along with it a climate of trust among the Arab countries.

An Arab Monetary System

After the Second World War, a number of ideas were put forward with regard to joint Arab action to achieve monetary co-ordination. These ideas took three forms in the mid-1970s: collective clearing, monetary unification and the granting of monetary facilities.[22] Then there was discussion of an Arab Payments Union, the Arab accounting dinar and the Arab Monetary Fund. Internationally, efforts were underway to: reform the world monetary system; undertake the second revision of the IMF convention; recognise the right of states to float their currencies; reduce the role of gold; and expand the use of SDRs. The Arab countries recognised that the form proposed for the Arab Payments Union was unsuitable given the growth they had achieved and given their emerging financial resources, in particular. At the same time, circumstances were not yet favourable to monetary unity because of the small volume of inter-Arab trade, the emphasis on bilateral economic relations and the limited movement of capital among Arab countries. Finally, agreement was reached to set up an Arab Monetary Fund.[23] The AMF Agreement specified that the activities of the Fund should aim at laying the monetary foundations for Arab economic integration which would hasten the pace of economic development in all member states. The Fund realised that in order to move closer to this goal — quite apart from the possibly long period of time required — it would be necessary to develop the monetary components of economic integration through free trade, joint Arab projects and co-ordination of Arab development plans.[24]

Without doubt, the establishment of the Arab Monetary Fund (discussed in other seminar papers) represented a serious attempt to

Basic Economic and Political Prerequisites 441

cope with the wide fluctuations in the values of international currencies, confront the monetary groupings which have emerged recently in world markets and provide a proper environment for investing Arab funds in an effort to achieve more Arab co-ordination, stimulate Arab trade and cope with the balance-of-payments deficits of certain Arab states. The idea proposed here is to try to develop this initial process into a complete monetary system based on the following principles:

(a) Establishing convertibility among Arab currencies;
(b) Stabilising exchange rates within narrow margins of fluctuation;
(c) Creating additional liquidity to cover current account deficits and structural balance-of-payments deficits; and
(d) Avoiding severe fluctuations in the exchange rates of international currencies.

The Arab Monetary System could be conceived as being dependent for its success on creating a composite Arab currency unit and stabilising exchange rates, with the AMF occupying the central role in the system.

A. A Monetary Unit

The governors of Arab central banks recognised during their 1975 meeting in Baghdad the importance of setting up a uniform Arab currency with an Arab Monetary Fund to control it. However, the debates which ensued differentiated between three types of Arab currencies: accounting, reserve and real. The Fund was set up on the basis that the Arab accounting dinar would be used in valuing both the Fund's capital and the loans it extended. It was stipulated that withdrawal and payment of the sums involved in loans, interest and commissions should be effected in any of the currencies which the Fund might from time to time designate. The Arab accounting dinar was pegged to the SDR on the basis of one dinar's being equivalent to three SDRs.

The Arab accounting dinar is admittedly a fair reflection of the status of the Arab currencies with their different bases for valuation and their dependency on foreign markets and given the differences in the financial policies of the Arab countries. The AAD is also a reflection of the lack of an Arab financial market for Arab investment, the varying degrees of convertibility of the Arab currencies, the dominance of international currencies in inter-Arab trade and the investment of Arab wealth in world markets in hard currencies. Nevertheless, one must reject the idea that the role of the Arab dinar should be restricted to purposes of accounting only, especially since its relationship to the SDR constitutes an indirect link with the dollar. Given the circumstances prevailing since the collapse of the Bretton Woods agreement and with the rise of Arab financial power, the way has been paved for abandoning the SDR and the dollar and for creating an Arab monetary unit comprising a basket of Arab currencies. This unit could gradually acquire the role of a day-to-day currency with each of its functions developing separately in the light of the development of the international role of the Arab economy and of inter-Arab economic relations.

It is proposed to establish a single Arab monetary unit, namely the Arab dinar. This dinar would be based on a basket comprising all Arab currencies, taking into consideration: GNP, the importance of foreign trade, international reserves and Arab foreign trade. The dinar could circulate along with the other Arab currencies and gradually acquire its accepted functions which may be briefly listed as follows:

(1) *As an accounting unit.* The proposed Arab dinar would be well suited to this function inasmuch as it would be used in the valuation of Arab currencies, in fixing their cross-rates and in valuing currency reserves. Hence, the dinar should be used as an indicator of the extent of Arab currency fluctuation.

(2) *As a store of value.* The dinar should be used as one of the assets comprising the Arab countries' monetary reserves, in addition to their shares in the capital of the AMF.

(3) *As a medium of exchange.* Here only the Arab dinar should be used to settle monetary transactions between central banks. To pave the way for this, the facilities and loans of the Arab Monetary Fund should be offered in the form of Arab dinars in order to increase their use among Arab central banks.

As a medium of exchange the dinar should normally have a value which is readily predictable in order to minimise future losses due to fluctuation. It should not be widely used as a medium of exchange except where large sums are involved. This would be the case in international transactions of the Arab Monetary System. The Hambros Bank in London was the first to use an Arab accounting unit in 1974, when it issued a loan quoted in US dollars. It then agreed to fix the value of the loan in terms of a basket of eight Arab currencies. The use of this unit was confined to loans and debts.[25] It is inevitable that the role of the Arab dinar will develop in the future as a means of exchange covering, for example, certain types of payments connected with pilgrimages, tourism and oil.

B. Stabilising Exchange Rates

The European Monetary System recently came into being in order to minimise exchange-rate fluctuations and provide the necessary credit facilities to support the efforts by member states to rectify their balance-of-payments positions. Currency stability in the industrialised countries directly affects economic growth rates and employment. Admittedly, the objective of monetary stability does not take on this degree of importance as far as the developing countries, including the Arab countries, are concerned. Unless they experience a radical change, monetary stability will not benefit the development of their economic infra-structures.

None the less, the Arab countries have much to gain from stabilising their exchange rates, if only as a means of confronting the major international currencies. For this reason the question of monetary stability takes on particular importance. Monetary stability is also important in that it would contribute to economic and monetary stability among the Arab states which would, in turn, provide for balanced growth and reduce economic disparities among them.

The task of stabilising the cross-rates of Arab currencies would be accomplished first by establishing complete convertibility among them, then permitting multilateral settlements and relaxing restrictions on capital movements with a view to eliminating them altogether. The stabilisation of exchange rates would inevitably be accompanied by a system of margins within which some fluctuation would be possible. The European currency 'snake' allows for fluctuations of up to ± 2.25 per cent. The new European system has allowed the two weak currencies in it, namely the Italian lira and the Irish punt to fluctuate up to ± 6 per cent. The realistic fixing of Arab exchange rates through a system of monetary stabilisation would stimulate Arab banks to finance foreign trade and develop the Arab financial market.

C. The Arab Monetary Fund

Like the European Monetary System, the prospective Arab Monetary System should be able to occupy an important position in the world economy. The Arab Monetary Fund would have to occupy the central position in any Arab monetary system. While the Fund represents a more advanced form of monetary co-operation than an Arab Payments Union, it does not aim at unifying Arab currencies in the short run.

Nevertheless, aware of its role in establishing the monetary prerequisites for Arab economic integration, the AMF has tried to establish a system for multilateral settlements. It has also begun a study of the state of financial and money markets in the Arab world with a view to developing them. Reference has already been made to the necessity of using an Arab currency unit in clearing operations between Arab central banks and for a portion of their central monetary reserves. Beyond this, the AMF could expand its functions to become, in the long run, an Arab central bank, thus no longer confining its operations to granting short- and medium-term loans and credit facilities. This could come about if:

(a) The Arab Monetary Fund assumed the function of issuing the Arab currency unit, namely the Arab dinar, as a currency which would gradually acquire the attributes of a national currency;
(b) Every Arab country deposited 20 per cent of its foreign currency and gold reserves with the Arab Monetary Fund in exchange for Arab dinars;
(c) The Fund carried out multilateral clearing operations among member states by opening credit accounts for the central banks and offering earnings to banks with surplus accounts.

It should be noted that to the extent that the AMF acts as a financial intermediary among the Arab countries, within the limit of its financial functions, its operations will have an inflationary effect resulting from the granting of loans and facilities. This effect will be temporary, however, because the increase in regional liquidity will have resulted from borrowed reserves. When the Fund begins to create Arab dinar units, on the other hand, the inflationary effect of this operation will be permanent.

D. Arab Monetary Zone

The Arab Monetary System proposed here could well lead to the emergence of an Arab monetary zone capable of establishing itself within the world economy. The following advantages could be realised in such a monetary zone:

(a) The exchange rates of members' currencies could be stabilised;
(b) Monetary assets could be held in Arab dinars, foreign currencies and gold;
(c) Payments between member states could be settled through the AMF; and
(d) Prices and costs would tend to change at the same rate in all member countries.

The more the monetary zone gained prominence in the world market, the more it would become a zone of monetary stability better able to confront the dollar. A monetary system should be set up which takes into account the enormous changes which are taking place in the state of the world economy. This would not only be to the advantage of the Arab countries but would also lead to international financing mechanisms for the benefit of developing countries. Therefore, the establishment of an Arab monetary system would be an attempt to set up an international system which would ensure greater monetary stability, help to control inflation and provide for greater equity in the creation and distribution of international reserves. It would similarly provide the means for correcting imbalances arising out of temporary surpluses and deficits, thereby encouraging the flow of resources to the developing countries.[26]

The call is increasingly heard for the creation of an international currency to replace the dollar, even if that currency were to be called the 'international dollar'.[27] The European Monetary System is but one attempt to set up a regional monetary system which relies on a new reserve currency, namely the ECU.[28]

Inherent in the proposal to set up an Arab monetary zone are two objectives: the first is to bring about the continuous expansion in the use of the Arab dinar inside and outside the Arab world; the second is to increase the use of Arab currencies in Arab bilateral and international relations. This means that Arab currencies should be brought into international circulation at least among Arab countries. The present Arab situation would seem to make possible the circulation of these currencies, given the reciprocal movement of labour and capital in the Arab region. Under these circumstances one could envisage the establishment of an Arab monetary zone which would make possible a measure of joint control over the money supply. This would presuppose the initiation of the following measures:

(a) Setting up joint Arab bodies at the level of commercial banks and financial institutions which would be oriented towards Arab markets. These institutions could offer financial facilities in the form of credit and loans in local currencies;
(b) Encouraging the use of Arab currencies in Arab financial dealings, not only among Arab countries but with the outside world as well;
(c) Instigating the use of Arab currencies, and later the Arab dinar, as a medium of exchange for Arab oil exported to the world.

It is therefore conceivable that an Arab Monetary System could arise which would constitute a further development of existing Arab monetary co-operation as represented by the AMF. Such a system could lead to the establishment of an Arab monetary zone linked to the resurgence in trade, capital and labour movements. Once this zone was established one could look forward to Arab monetary integration in the form of a monetary union.

Whatever may be the economic bases for integration, political will is the indispensable condition for achieving it. Arab economic integration is a process involving complete emancipation for the whole Arab world. A many-faceted struggle must be waged to form a unified economic structure as a prelude to establishing a single domestic market among the Arab countries. The political decision in favour of Arab economic integration means a decision to eliminate the existing economic integration with the international capitalist market and to link up with the Arab national liberation movement.

Notes

1. Ragnar Nurkse, *International Currency Experience: Lessons of the Inter-War Period* (Geneva: League of Nations, 1944).
2. See Fouad Morsi, *The Crisis of Arab Economic Development* (Baghdad: Manshūrāt al-Naft wal-Tanmiyah, 1979) (in Arabic).
3. See George Corm, 'The Economic Future of the Arab Oil Countries', *Al-Mustaqbal al-'Arabī*, vol. 2, no. 14 (April 1980), pp. 32-45 (in Arabic).
4. See Roberto Alibone (ed.), *Industrialization in the Mediterranean: Capital and Labour Movements* and *The Mediterranean: Politics, Economics, Strategy*; and Galia Saguma, *The Arab World in Search of Itself* (Rome: Instituto Affari Internazionale).
5. Even the Jordanian merchant must use London financial markets to settle his debts with his Iraqi creditors.
6. See George Corm, *The Challenge Facing the Arab Economy: Studies in the Economics of Oil, Finance and Technology* (Beirut: Dār al-Tali'a, 1977), p. 253 (in Arabic).
7. Abdul Hamid Brahimi, *Dimensions of Arab Economic Integration and Prospects for the Future* (Beirut: Centre for Arab Unity Studies, 1980), pp. 356-8 (in Arabic).
8. Ibid., p. 358.
9. Ibid.
10. Hussein Abdallah, 'The Financial Dimensions of Arab Oil Prices', *Al-Mustaqbal al-'Arabī*, vol. 2, no. 14 (April 1980), pp. 55-81 (in Arabic).
11. See A. Stadnichenko, *The Monetary Crisis of Capitalism* (Moscow: 1975).
12. 'Uppsala: the Terra Nova Statement on the International Monetary System and the Third World', *Development Dialogue* (1980), p. 1.
13. See Fouad Morsi, *Problems of the Contemporary International Economy* (Alexandria: 1980) (in Arabic).
14. See Brahimi, *Dimensions of Arab Economic Integration and Prospects for the Future*.
15. See Hussein Abdallah, 'The Financial Dimensions of Arab Oil Prices', *al-Mustaqbal al-'Arabī*, vol. 2, no. 14 (April 1980), pp. 55-81.
16. See Angelo T. Angelopoulos, *Pour une nouvelle politique du développement international* (Paris: Presses Universitaires de Paris, 1976).
17. See Morsi, *The Crisis of Arab Economic Development*, p. 3.
18. See Ahmed Murad, 'Major Characteristics of the Arab Economy in the Seventies', Amman, 1980 (mimeographed study in Arabic).
19. See Nadim Al-Bitar, *From Fragmentation to Unity: Basic Laws Governing Past Unity Experiences* (Beirut: Centre for Arab Unity Studies, 1979) (in Arabic).
20. See J. Szita, *Perspectives for All-European Economic Co-operation* (Budapest: 1977).
21. See Morsi, *The Crisis of Arab Economic Development*.
22. See Hussein Khallaf, 'Arab Monetary Co-operation and the Arab Monetary Fund', *Majallat al-Waḥda al-Iqtiṣādiyya*, vol. 1, no. 1 (April 1975) (in Arabic).

23. Arab Monetary Fund, *Annual Report 1977* (Abu Dhabi: Arab-British Chamber of Commerce, 1977) (in Arabic).

24. Arab Monetary Fund, *Annual Report 1978* (Abu Dhabi: Arab-British Chamber of Commerce, 1978) (in Arabic).

25. See Michael Lelart, 'Euro-Arab Financial Co-operation in the Face of the American Monopoly', *Al-Mustaqbal al-'Arabī*, vol. 3, no. 16 (June 1980) (in Arabic).

26. 'The Scheveningen Report: Towards a New International Development Strategy', *Development Dialogue*, no. 1 (7 March 1980).

27. B. Schmidt, *Théorie unitaire de la monnaie nationale et internationale* (Switzerland: Albeuve, 1975).

28. Paul de Grauwe and Theo Peters, *The European Monetary System: A Step Towards Monetary Stability*, International Economic Research Papers, no. 12 (Leuven, Belgium: Universiteit Leuven, Centrum Voor Economische Studien Katholicke, 1979).

COMMENT*

George Corm

Mr Morsi's paper treats the most important aspects of the subject under discussion. I concur with the author that economic integration is, ordinarily, a prerequisite for the achievement of monetary integration and that the unequal relations currency prevailing between the underdeveloped and the advanced industrial world constitute the major obstacle to the implementation of serious integrative measures among the developing countries. Proceeding from this correct positing of the situation, Mr Morsi concludes that the existence of the will to be liberated from economic dependency and to attain independent, self-sustained development is the crucial and decisive political factor in making possible Arab economic and monetary integration. The last part of the study discusses the most important elements of an eventual Arab Monetary System (the monetary unit, the stabilisation of exchange rates and the Arab Monetary Fund) which would lead in turn to the establishment of an Arab monetary zone.

I shall not discuss Mr Morsi's methodology, as I am in agreement with him as to the consequences of the economic dependency which characterises the Arab states. However, I would like to offer two observations.

1. The wide gap between the economic and technological levels prevailing in the Arab countries and those attained in the advanced industrial countries, including the socialist countries, is the main reason for the Arab countries' dependency and the consequent harmful effects on the efforts towards integration. It is true that relations with the socialist countries are more advantageous than those with the capitalist countries (lower prices and credit facilities at lower interest rates). But the crux of the matter is still the way the developing countries deal with the more advanced nations. The reason for this is that a developing country that is unable to deal adequately with the outside world increases its dependency irrespective of whether it is dealing with the capitalist market or with the states of the socialist bloc. Past experience has shown that the application of a correct and well-developed conception of economic liberalism is the factor which allows for autonomous development regardless of the nature of the economic system adopted by the foreign parties.

2. The economic integration attained among the Comecon countries

* Translated from the Arabic.

cannot be taken as an example to be followed for several reasons. First, there is the political price which had to be paid by some of these countries. Also, there is the lack of flexibility and the many bureaucratic restrictions which characterise the Comecon system and which largely explain the fact that over the past decade, the socialist countries have had to increase their economic ties with the capitalist market. In addition, there has been established an unequal form of integration in favour of the Soviet Union.

Nevertheless, I agree with Mr Morsi that strengthening relations with the socialist countries could help the developing countries in many areas to free themselves of certain aspects of exploitation associated with their dealings with the capitalist market. However, the basic issue, in my opinion, is how to cope with the unequal relationship between the developing countries and the industrially advanced states. Here I agree with Mr Morsi as to the need to work towards improving economic and social conditions within the developing countries as a starting point for any improvement in their position with respect to the international division of labour. It is therefore crucial that the developing countries properly manage their relations with the industrial states so as to gradually make of these relations an instrument of progress instead of a means of enslavement and exploitation. In my opinion, there is no possibility of changing this relationship except by changing the international economic conditions in the developing countries themselves.

In this context, it cannot be denied that the Arab countries, like most of the developing countries, still lack the proper economic perspective, in that they depend excessively on their relations with the more advanced countries (socialist or capitalist) in their attempt to emerge from their state of backwardness. The extent to which these relations have been developed has often not only prevented the development of integrative relations between these countries but has also prevented the mobilisation of available internal resources. One can find in the areas of technology transfer and the management of surplus funds many illustrations of this which have frequently been cited and need not be repeated here. In this connection, I differ with Mr Morsi when he speaks of the Arab development gap that exists between the oil countries on the one hand and the non-oil countries on the other. This kind of gap does not exist. Indeed, the non-oil countries are, in most instances, more advanced than the oil countries. The gap which in fact exists between the Arab oil-exporting countries and the others is merely a financial gap in terms of the resources available for intensifying the already existing relationship of inequality with the industrial countries. The real gap which characterises all the Arab countries is a technological gap with respect to the industrialised states. Arab development policies have not treated this gap, up to now, with the seriousness it deserves because of their almost exclusive dependence on a passive rather than a rational use of modern technology.

This is not the place to discuss the transfer of technology. But I wish to underscore what I perceive to be a strong relationship between this issue and Arab economic integration. The main approach to serious Arab economic integration must be the development of a sufficient awareness on the part of Arab political establishments of this technological gap which cannot be bridged except by joint Arab effort, in place of continued dependence on familiar channels controlled by the multinationals or on the acquisition of ready technology. Accordingly, I would add that the elimination of economic and monetary dependency will only come about through the development of a thorough awareness of technology on the part of Arab officials responsible for economic development programmes. As such, it is incumbent on Arab economists to concern themselves with this matter so essential to ensuring the future of Arab society. For integration, if carried out with the mentality and conditions of technological dependency currently prevailing, will only lead to greater dependency. It is the industrial countries that will reap the benefits of any Arab integrative measures which are not accompanied by similar measures designed to raise the degree of self-sufficiency in production. It is enough to look at the way these countries and their giant corporations have taken advantage of the integrative measures carried out in Latin America.

Concerning the monetary issues raised in the paper, I should like first to refer to Mr Morsi's advocacy of severing the tie between the Arab currencies and the dollar. This step, in my opinion, cannot be taken except under conditions arising from a fundamental reform of the international monetary system. As the author mentions, the dollar continues to play a pivotal role in this system; neither the use of SDRs nor the European 'snake' system, has succeeded in diminishing the dominance of the dollar in the international monetary system. On the contrary, following the demonetisation of gold, the dollar remains more than ever the only measure of monetary value.

In my opinion, the main fault with Arab monetary policies is not the continued use of the dollar in determining exchange rates, it is rather the lack of effective participation by the Arab countries holding substantial assets in foreign currencies in the efforts directed towards the reform of the international monetary system. I am particularly concerned by their lack of participation in efforts aimed at reducing the impact of dollar fluctuations and ending the dominance of the dollar as a measure of value and as the major instrument of international payments by encouraging the use of other currencies in the international monetary system such as the strong European currencies, the Japanese yen, the convertible ruble and some of the Arab currencies themselves. Quite the reverse has occurred as certain Arab countries have worked to maintain the present state of affairs and co-ordinated their policies with the monetary policy of the United States. In addition, they have severely restricted transactions in their national currencies.

From this perspective, Arab monetary integration assumes international dimensions, especially in that any true reform of the international monetary system can only be achieved by excluding the dollar as the only major instrument of payment, replacing it with regional units of account consisting of baskets of the currencies of countries making up various regions. The Arab world, with its financial resources, could become a strong monetary zone with an international monetary and financial position. It is in this context that one can see the importance of the Arab monetary zone described by Mr Morsi in his paper and advocated by the late former Algerian minister of Finance, Mr Abdelmalik Tamam, as early as 1973, in a lecture to the Lebanese Banking Association in Beirut.

In this connection, mention should be made of the committee charged with examining the creation of the Arab accounting dinar. After establishing the basket of Arab currencies which should be used initially in determining the AAD, the committee recommended that the AAD unit should be made equivalent to three SDRs with subsequent modifications permitted in accordance with changes in the Arab currencies comprising the basket. However, the governors of the central banks, when adopting the AMF Agreement, decided on a watered-down version of the AAD. The unit which finally emerged was characterised by the old dependency instead of being an integral dinar based on an Arab currency basket as recommended by the committee. The AMF must therefore work persistently to revive the work of the committee in order to lend the AAD its true dimensions by basing it on a basket of Arab currencies.

Given the need for international monetary reform, Arab monetary integration could well be the appropriate initial move towards overall economic integration especially in that some Arab countries have surplus funds while others are in need of capital. Objective conditions exist which militate for the adoption by the Arab countries of the monetary measures proposed by Mr Morsi. It is hoped that Arab countries will exercise the necessary will to move in the direction of monetary integration.

GENERAL DISCUSSION

1. Abdul Wahid Al-Makhzoumi

Allow me to say that I encountered some difficulty in grasping the precise meaning of subparagraphs (a), (b) and (c) under part I a.3 of the paper [p. 429-30] where the author speaks of the factors contributing to monetary dependency. Are these really factors contributing to a phenomenon or are they not rather the consequences of a situation encompassing complex circumstances and relationships which have crystallised over a long period of time? Furthermore in subparagraph (a) the author says that the money supply in the Arab oil countries depends on fluctuations in the price of oil exports, etc. All the studies and economic models which I have seen attempt to establish government spending as the determining factor for the money supply. Not all revenues from oil exports go directly into local money in many of the oil countries owing to differences in the ways these revenues are dealt with in these countries. In subparagraph (b), Mr Morsi says that the Arab countries prefer the dollar as an investment currency. As I see it, preference signifies a choice among equivalent alternatives, a situation which I do not believe exists. West Germany, Japan and others, in this sense, prefer the dollar even more than the Arab countries do.

Finally, the reference in subparagraph (c) to the international monetary system which emerged following the collapse of the Bretton Woods system might be correct, if, by international monetary system is meant the IMF as a creator of liquidity. However, if this is not what is meant, it is common knowledge that liquidity, in the period following the breakdown of the Bretton Woods agreement was, by virtue of its abundance, a source of grievance and uncertainty.

2. Rainer S. Masera

I wholeheartedly agree with what I understood to be the gist of Mr Morsi's thesis: monetary integration, however complete, does not necessarily bring about economic integration. On the other hand, it can play a very useful and important role in the overall process of economic integration. But I would claim that, on the whole, we have to place the primary emphasis on the process of real economic integration because, after all, we are interested in real, not monetary, variables.

What then, is the best definition of economic integration? I would suggest that an alternative to that provided by Machlup, and cited here by Mr Williamson, might be the following: a highly integrated economy is one which is characterised by the absence of regional problems; if you want to achieve a highly integrated economy, you have to overcome these problems.

How do we define or measure regional problems? An approximate answer is provided by the differences in real wage levels. Note here that we come back to Machlup's regional definition because in a world where all markets function perfectly and where there is free movement of labour and of all other factors, one can only end up with a situation where real wages are approximately the same throughout the area being considered. But, and this is the point I wish to make, while this kind of world where competitive markets work perfectly in a perfectly flexible way may have been relevant some time ago, it is no longer conceivable today; for in our day, certain sectors are inevitably characterised by rigidities. These arise because of the great importance of the government sector, because trade unions play a significant role and because multinational corporations have implicitly introduced certain rigidities into the workings of the overall mechanism of market allocations. If one relies on purely market forces in order to solve regional problems one may end up in a painful situation. I might refer, in this regard, to the experience of my own country, Italy. Italy has had monetary integration for over a hundred years and yet it remains a dual economy; the problem of national integration has still to be solved.

From this, I would tend to conclude that economic integration does to some extent require centralised development policies. These are necessary to cope with external diseconomies in the less developed regions. The free movement of labour may not solve these problems. Indeed poor regions may become poorer in the process.

I therefore submit that in order to overcome the problems of economic integration as previously defined, one needs effective aid not only to help maintain real wage differentials but also to overcome external diseconomies. What is required, therefore, is a centralised process. This process should rely on market forces, but with intervention to overcome difficulties associated with external diseconomies. An organisation similar to the one described by Mr del Valle or to the European Investment Bank may be required for this purpose. It should accompany the measures being taken to initiate the process of monetary integration.

3. Samir Makdisi

A careful reading of Mr Morsi's paper shows the connections between monetary and economic integration to be closer than what might appear from certain statements contained within it, e.g., that monetary integration is the culmination of economic integration. Such statements give the impression that the two processes are successive rather than simultaneous though, I would immediately add, Mr Morsi does state in his paper that under certain conditions the process of monetary integration could proceed in advance of full economic integration.

Let me illustrate my point by reference to one of the factors which Mr Morsi cites as having impeded Arab economic integration, namely existing disparities in the level of development of the Arab countries. I fully agree and would add in this connection another factor, namely disparities in the economic policies pursued by the Arab countries; for these have, in my view, also tended to retard the process of closer economic co-operation.

Returning to the question of disparities in levels of development, Mr Morsi points out that one way to overcome them would be to increase the resources of the Arab Fund for Economic and Social Development (AFESD) so that it could play a much more active role in Arab development. Indeed he suggests that each Arab country should contribute a certain portion of its budgetary resources to the AFESD.

Extending this view, one can say that Mr Morsi is advocating a much more active role for the AFESD — and for the Arab Monetary Fund, for that matter — as inter-Arab financial intermediaries, as well as the extensive development of the Arab financial markets. This is one form of partial monetary integration: capital market integration, to which reference was made earlier in the seminar. Perhaps, then, one should no longer view economic and monetary integration as successive steps (i.e., monetary integration as a culmination of economic integration). Rather we should regard moves towards economic and monetary integration as being mutually reinforcing.

4. Rifaat El-Mahgoub

Mr Morsi's paper is a synthesis of all the various factors — historical, economic and political — which influence the process of integration. It also offers realistic solutions to the problems facing such a process.

Looking at the historical factors, Mr Morsi has shown us how traditional thinking has culminated in integration between the advanced and the under-developed worlds and how this integration has benefited industrialised Europe at the expense of the undeveloped countries. We in the Arab world understand this type of integration since we have been suffering from it for a long time. As we pave the way for a new type of integration, especially in the monetary sphere, we must therefore not forget the lessons of the past.

We must learn from these lessons by defining, prior to the establishment of monetary integration, the purposes it is to serve. There should be no disagreement here as to these purposes, namely economic development and economic independence. Any integration which fails to take these purposes into account will never go beyond providing a framework for the further binding of the Arab region as a whole to a particular monetary zone, namely that of the dollar. Such a development should not be permitted to take place. Since the objective of monetary integration is to serve economic integration, it must conform to the requirements of the integration process at each of its successive stages. Monetary integration should accompany economic integration, neither preceding it nor lagging behind it, otherwise, it will merely create difficulties and delays in the economic integration process.

Mr Morsi refers to political factors associated with the process of economic integration and considers that this process can only occur within a uniform political and social framework. In designing the process of economic integration we must therefore not rely exclusively on economic factors but take into consideration the relevant political factors as well so that every Arab country will come to realise that it can benefit from the integration process.

Of the economic factors which have to be considered when contemplating economic integration, Mr Morsi refers first to the disparities in the economic systems of the Arab countries. Here he reaches a conclusion which seems to me somewhat extreme, namely, that we have moved beyond the state of disparate economic systems. The author may mean that differences between the Arab economic systems have narrowed because in the oil countries where oil proceeds are centralised in the hands of the government, the public sector has become dominant and also because the public-sector-oriented Arab countries have been implementing more liberal policies. Despite such developments, I believe that existing disparities among the economic systems of the Arab countries continue to act as an obstacle to the economic integration process. The author refers secondly to the disparate growth of the forces of production in the Arab countries, which prohibits the process of integration. But the logical extension of this argument is that we should postpone integration until we have achieved an acceptable degree of growth in productive forces. In my view we can utilise existing differences in the growth of productive forces in order to facilitate economic integration, provided it is viewed in the context of the whole Arab world.

5. Karim Nashashibi

Both Mr Makdisi and Mr Morsi have touched upon what I wish to say but I will try to put it differently. As we all know, the basic imbalance in the Arab world is the existence of very poor countries alongside other countries which are flush with oil revenues in search of foreign placements and diversification. Any discourse about economic integration in the Arab world must address itself to this imbalance. The question is what type of economic processes or modalities can be devised to make it attractive for oil-producing countries to invest in and help the non-oil countries. In this respect how will Mr Morsi's Arab dinar which, as I understand it, merely creates liquidity for the deficit countries, reduce this imbalance?

6. Rafik Sowellem

I would first like to express my agreement with Mr Morsi that Arab economic integration is essentially aimed at bringing an end to economic and monetary dependency by developing the productive capabilities of the Arab countries within an expanded regional market. However, I would like to add that my own concept of Arab economic integration envisages the need to avoid all forms of economic dependency, whether in relation to the Western capitalist countries, the Eastern socialist countries or any other outside group.

Secondly, I would appreciate some clarification from Mr Morsi as to what he means by his assertion under the heading 'Political Prerequisites' that economic integration must, in order to occur, include countries with a homogeneous political and social base. Does this mean that in order to achieve integration, the Arab countries must have the same political systems and consequently that their economic systems must be either capitalist or socialist? I think such an interpretation is restrictive and would have the effect of dissipating the energies of the Arab nationalist forces by diverting them from their effort to establish economic unity, for the achievement of which objective conditions do exist. It would involve them in disputes over ideological concepts which are irrelevant to the prerequisites and modalities of monetary and economic integration as the only path to achieving development and closing the gaps in the economic levels among participating Arab countries.

Thirdly, can Mr Morsi tell us what is the basis for valuing the accounting rouble which is used for settling payments among the countries of the socialist bloc? I believe it is valued in terms of a basket of Western currencies or gold.

7. Faris Bingaradi

Mr Morsi has pointed out three prerequisites for achieving monetary integration which I consider defeatist.

The first is related to the theory of dependency. This theory is most interesting and has been discussed intensively — especially by certain pioneer thinkers in Latin America — in connection with economic development as it regards the relationship between the centre and the periphery. However, to my mind, this theory has its pitfalls if taken too far because it leads one to see things only in this framework and thus all our economic ills can be attributed to dependency. But most importantly, the solution is seen to be a simple one: the theory requires the abolition of dependency relationship; otherwise no solution is possible.

What is crucial for us is not so much to enumerate the ways Arab economies are dependent on external factors, as this has been dealt with extensively in the literature, but to discuss ways of ending this relationship of dependency in a constructive and realistic manner and to explain the alternatives that we should seek.

It is true that Arab trade depends upon the markets of the OECD for as much as 75 per cent of total exports and imports. It is also true that we are technologically dependent upon the West and that the surplus funds of the oil countries as well as the reserves of the non-oil countries are invested in the West or deposited with Western monetary institutions. No study, not even the one under discussion, has shown us how to do away with such dependency and what to expect or how to proceed after that. Are we to stop exporting oil and, if so, can we? The size of Arab exports requires that they be directed to the Western markets as no other market could absorb them, to say nothing of the strategic nature of such exports which makes even a reduction in their level impossible.

We all know of the pitfalls associated with the transfer of technology from the West in any of its forms, but have we thought of a method for developing our own and what kind of development we might expect?

As far as financial dependency is concerned, I agree with what Mr Corm has said but would like to ask if we have supplied the oil surplus countries with an alternative they could follow in addition to pointing out the pitfalls involved in what they are doing now? To talk of abolishing a dependent structure is not enough. It is more important to analyse how to do away with it and the implications of such a move.

Concerning the second prerequisite, political determination, the author argues for the establishment of homogeneity, i.e., a uniform socio-economic structure and a uniform mode of production. This prerequisite reflects the author's political philosophy and, as Mr Sowellem mentioned earlier, its accomplishment is a very remote possibility. Such homogeneity, according to the author, would lead to economic integration, which in turn is a prerequisite for monetary integration. Hence, if it cannot be accomplished, a dead end is reached. This brings me to the relationship between monetary integration and economic unity. I believe monetary integration can take place between a number of countries without the objective of unity being necessarily contemplated, at least as a short-term objective. By contrast, economic unity relates directly to a number of political objectives which must be taken into account.

We have done everything but take an objective and rational look at the economic and political situation in the Arab world, yet we are trying to infer from our discussions the theoretical measures and even the practical measures necessary for achieving the objective of Arab monetary integration. Are the Arab countries really seeking monetary integration and with what purpose in mind, given the numerous unsuccessful attempts to establish co-ordination in the past?

If they are, then I cannot but feel disappointed, for instead of objectively examining the political and economic situation of the Arab countries with all its present constraints, the discussions here seem to reflect primarily the political convictions of individual participants as to what should be done to achieve economic integration or economic unity among countries that are not necessarily seeking it.

The focus of the discussion has been the surplus oil revenues and how they came to exist, but there should also be an analysis of existing deficits and the reasons for their emergence. Why should a mere transfer of resources solve the problems of the deficitory countries, which we all know are complex and structural? If such transfers take place, then what level should they attain and for how long? Is it possible under such circumstances to achieve any co-ordination at all, let alone integration? What role should the Arab financial markets play, which monetary instruments should be developed to attract the surplus funds and how?

These major issues do not seem to have been sufficiently examined.

8. Mabid Ali Al-Jarni

Mr Morsi defines the relationship between economic and monetary integration by saying that the latter is the culmination of the former, calling this the structural approach to monetary integration. He offers as evidence that economic balance is a condition for monetary balance. Perhaps he has in mind the Walras Law which equates a surplus demand for money with a surplus supply of commodities.

Clearly, the Walras Law means that the balance of each market is interlinked with the balance of the other markets and that the balance of the money market is a reflection of the balance of the commodity markets. It does not mean that economic balance is a condition for monetary balance, for economic balance means the balance of all markets, including the money market. In other words, the achievement of the former is a condition for the achievement of the latter. Regardless of the way one interprets the Walras Law, I do not see the relevance of this law to the relationship between economic and monetary integration.

Despite Mr Morsi's insistence that monetary integration is the culmination of economic integration, he states that 'monetary integration could, in other words, create favorable conditions which might hasten the advent of economic integration itself'. Indeed, he opposes the idea of the neutrality of money, asserting that 'monetary factors can play a more important role in economic integration than seems to be realized' [p. 423].

Clearly, there is a contradiction between his original claim that economic integration is a condition for monetary integration and the view I have just cited concerning the importance of monetary integration as a first step towards economic integration, and the non-neutrality of money. In my opinion, this contradiciton demands an explanation.

Mr Morsi sets down the 'basic prerequisites' for monetary integration which can be summarised as two economic requirements — the elimination of economic dependency in all its forms and the elimination of the gap in growth rates — and one political requirement, namely the political determination to achieve freedom, development and integration.

I interpret the term 'basic prerequisites' to mean that if these are not fulfilled, monetary integration cannot be achieved. If this interpretation is correct then what have been classified as 'prerequisites' are not really so. However beneficial it might be to eliminate all forms of dependency and close the gap in growth rates, monetary integration does not in itself require that these conditions be fulfilled. As far as ending economic dependency is concerned, there is no reason why a monetary union cannot exist among the colonies or possessions of a colonialist state. This has actually happened, as we have seen, in West Africa. The important thing is that in a situation of dependency most, if not all, of the benefits of monetary integration may accrue to the colonisers rather than to the colonised.

It should nevertheless be taken into account that monetary integration, if well designed and well applied, can be one of the best ways to end or reduce dependency. Some of the participants have mentioned that monetary integration enhances the ability of the member countries to deal with the outside world as a group and improves their negotiating and bargaining position *vis-à-vis* other economic blocs.

With regard to eliminating the gap in economic growth rates, monetary integration can take place and has actually taken place among countries with different growth rates. Indeed, in the opinion of certain economists, different growth rates can be more conducive to the flow of resources among the participating countries, thereby increasing the degree of integration of their markets. It is also important to note that monetary integration can be instrumental, when accompanied by the necessary financial policies, in narrowing the gap in growth rates. These policies are inevitably more effective when applied in the context of monetary integration.

As for the political prerequisites, I agree entirely with Mr Morsi as to their necessity; for a country's decision to join a monetary union is a political decision requiring political will. In this connection I am afraid that the emphasis on economic integration as a prelude to monetary integration may encourage those lacking in political will to attribute the results of their failure to achieve integration to technical obstacles, whereas the fault lies with political will or rather the lack of it.

The approach to monetary integration presented by the author at the end of his paper closely resembles the European Monetary System; for it involves a basket of Arab currencies and a system for stabilising exchange rates as well as provisions for convertibility and for a reserve fund. There is one addition, which is the payments union.

In this regard, I prefer an alternative to the European experience, beginning with a parallel currency. It does not matter whether it is a basket of currencies or an oil-based currency (i.e., one whose value is fixed in terms of oil), provided that a clear plan is established and timed to correspond with the transition from the parallel currency to the single currency.

9. Fouad Morsi, in Response

I am certainly pleased with the discussion that has taken place, in its sweet and bitter aspects both. Had I not aroused some controversy, I would have considered my presentation a failure. I therefore thank all the discussants for their points of view concerning my paper.

I would say that the subject which has most preoccupied the participants in these discussions is monetary integration as it relates to economic integration. I shall therefore begin with this fundamental subject and summarise briefly what I said earlier, which is that there is no point in talking about monetary integration before talking about economic integration. Economic integration comes first but this in no way means that monetary integration cannot come about until economic integration has been completed. What it does mean is that monetary integration is implicit in the extent or degree of economic integration that is achieved. The two processes can begin together. Hence, the measures of which I have spoken and which I consider essential are not, for the most part, quantitative measures which must be fully implemented all at once. It is sufficient in each case to initiate the process towards the contemplated objective. For example, with regard to dependency, its complete elimination is not necessary in order to begin the process of economic integration and then monetary integration. Such an approach only serves to place this issue in a narrow mechanical context which is unacceptable when discussing social, economic and political issues. What is important is that the objective process be set in motion so that its effect will be felt in the future. What I am saying is a confirmation of the points raised by Mr Makdisi. I have taken advantage of the discussions here to pose the question of monetary integration always in terms of its relationship to economic integration, even if priority is to be given to economic integration. Otherwise, any discussion of monetary integration would be inconceivable.

With regard to the issues raised by a number of my colleagues concerning the question of integration, I find myself obliged to deal with some of them in detail. Mr Masera's remarks were very useful and can be applied to the situation in the underdeveloped countries. If we only pay attention to market questions, as he so rightly says, we will not be able to arrive at satisfactory results for the underdeveloped countries which have not yet completed the formation of their domestic markets. These markets reflect the state of underdevelopment of these countries and cannot constitute the point of departure for dealing with the problem of economic integration. Therefore, the issues pertaining to the free movement of labour, capital and to the disparities existing in wages all require special treatment with regard to the underdeveloped countries, including the Arab countries.

The crucial issue of economic integration in relation to dependency has been raised by Messrs Corm and Sowellem, among others. Naturally, dependency must be ended, irrespective of whether it relates to the capitalist or to the socialist countries. If unequal relationships should emerge between the socialist countries and the Arab countries, this form of dependency must also be rejected.

As for disparities in economic growth levels among the Arab countries, the differences in their economic policies, as referred to by Mr Makdisi, and the role which can be played by specially-allocated financial credits, whether within the budget of each country individually or in a joint community budget, these are important matters which should be given attention. I believe the Arab summit conference to take place this month [November 1980] will take them up.

As for disparities in the growth of productive forces and in economic and social systems, the under-developed countries cannot be as neatly divided into capitalist and socialist systems as the developed countries. The under-developed countries must develop and must eliminate dependency by developing their own socio-economic systems which resemble neither the traditional capitalist nor the traditional socialist systems. They are systems whose evolution should be guided by innovative steps which are still to be carefully and scientifically determined. The traditional classifications applicable to the developed countries are not, therefore, applicable. What concerns me with regard to the Arab countries is that there be a convergence in their economic, political and social systems and, consequently, a will to work together. This is what I refer to in my paper as the will to integrate, which requires that we overcome the existing legacy of doubt, suspicion and lack of confidence.

As for the problem of monetary dependency, Mr Corm has said that it is difficult to sever the tie with the dollar. This is perfectly true but I nevertheless consider such a step, either now or in the near future, to be a necessary condition for integration. Otherwise, nothing can be achieved. I reject the attitude which says all or nothing; what concerns me is that we work to set in motion the objective process which will ultimately yield the desired results.

Mr Makhzoumi raises a point concerning what I have called the 'factors' of monetary dependency. Actually, what I spoke of were the factors contributing to the phenomenon of monetary dependency as it relates to the Arab countries. As to my reference to the money supply within the Arab oil countries and the extent to which it is dependent on fluctuating oil prices, it is common knowledge that the main reason for the fluctuations is the fact that the Arab monetary systems are tied to the dollar which is the currency in which oil is valued. Hence, the fluctuations occur essentially outside and are imported into these countries. The reference to stagnation is also clear. It might be added that difficulties arise not only because the dollar is used to price oil but also in connection with the utilisation of oil revenues for investment abroad. As to the preference of the Arab countries for the dollar as an investment currency, this phenomenon should be clearly recognised. I have cited figures relating to all the OPEC countries. Seventy per cent of their investments are in dollars. The preference of most oil countries for the dollar as an investment currency is obvious. As for the third phenomenon, relating to international liquidity, the Arab countries are now helping with their oil money to supply the international market with an essential part of its liquidity. It is this liquidity which is later provided to the countries of the under-developed world through international banks and other banks, whether these take the form of consortiums or other forms. Dependency is clearly illustrated, then, in the three phenomena which I have mentioned.

Mr Bengaradi describes my analysis as defeatist. While we may differ among ourselves as to terms, I really wish we could agree on our diagnosis of the existing situation. If there were agreement on the description of the Arab situation, then you could call my analysis defeatist. We should identify the essentials of the Arab phenomenon. Other speakers (e.g., Mr Dajani and Mr Al-Sagban) have hardly presented an optimistic picture of prevailing Arab economic relationships. I, too, have merely identified objectively the existing reality of the Arab economy. The question of whether or not I am defeatist does little to alter this reality. Do the existing trends in the Arab economies give rise to an optimistic picture, or does my analysis convey a more accurate picture of existing reality? If Arab economic trends were indeed as one might wish them to be, then we would have no need to discuss economic integration and how to achieve it.

As for the accounting rouble, I cannot claim to know a great deal about the Comecon system. I studied this subject once in 1973 or 1974 and have not gone back to it since. Therefore, I am not familiar with more recent developments in the Comecon monetary system. What Mr Sowellem may have in mind is the pricing system applicable to transactions among the countries of the Comecon: in fact, it borrows certain feature of the pricing system applied by capitalist industrialised countries, while introducing appropriate modifications. As far as the rouble is concerned, I know that it is convertible and that it is valued in terms of gold. However, it is really an accounting currency used for the settlement of accounts through a specialised bank jointly managed by the Comecon countries.

Mr Nashashibi raises the question of the fundamental imbalance in the Arab world between the poor countries and the rich countries and of how the poor countries can work to attract investments. Can they do this by means of the dollar? Or through market mechanisms? In fact, the problem as posed is a very real one and is at the heart of efforts to establish Arab monetary integration, not to mention the effort to arrive at joint monetary and financial arrangements among the Arab countries. I am concerned by the fact that some of my colleagues have spoken at length about the possibility of establishing monetary integration in the Gulf, for this implies that a group of rich countries would join together to solve their − relatively limited − problems. Then the poor or deficit group of countries would join together and this would lead to a widening of the gap in the Arab world and among the Arab economies. Mr Haseeb has remarked on the inappropriateness of such a course of action and pointed out the need to adopt a programme which would join the Arab countries together as a whole. I recognise that the Arab countries have since 1973 taken many measures aimed at attracting investments, i.e., attracting the Arab surpluses, but it must be recognised that the magnetic force of the international financial market is much stronger and that consequently Arab investments continue to be directed to the international financial market. How is it possible to attract these surpluses to the poor or deficit countries? This is a question not likely to be resolved by any single response or single measure. Rather, the solution will come out of the attempt to cope with the problems of monetary, financial and economic integration as a whole. No single step will suffice and I think that the example offered by Egypt's experience in attracting Arab funds in the period from 1973 to 1977 is a compelling one. Nevertheless, Arab funds accounted for only about 14 per cent of all the funds which entered Egypt under the open door policy during that period. This proportion has not increased since then. It is true that the proportion of these investment funds originating in Europe and America was extremely modest, amounting to 4.5 per cent and 7.5 per cent, respectively, but the Arab portion was small as well. In the end, the investors who took most advantage of the new set of investment laws were Egyptian, as local investments comprised about 60 per cent of the total.

10. Abderrahim Omrana*

I must say that I came away from reading Mr Morsi's paper with the feeling that Arab economic unity was nothing but a mirage. Given the many different views, political options and economic systems operating in the Arab countries, the economic and political conditions for Arab integration, as described by the author, would seem to be impossible to achieve, at least in the short run.

How, then, can we arrive at a way out of this dilemma? I think we must go back to two important points:

First, it should be recognised that the economic groupings which now exist in other regions of the world, whatever form they may take, came about without necessarily following the same political and economic pattern. It is true that these groupings have not achieved all their objectives, but they are constantly evolving and building their unity in a dynamic, parallel fashion.

Secondly, we must take into consideration the obstacles which stand in the way of achieving integration. By these I mean the diversity of

---

* This comment was made subsequent to the author's response to the discussion of his paper [eds.].

geographical and structural conditions and the disparities in growth levels. Therefore, I think the only way to achieve integration is to effect it at the regional level, i.e., to establish co-ordination between existing regional groupings in order eventually to bring about overall Arab economic integration.

I regret that Mr Morsi did not give more attention to this point which I consider vital to the issue at hand.

LIST OF PARTICIPANTS

Dr Faik Ali Abdul-Rasool, General Director at the Central Bank of Iraq, Baghdad, Iraq

Dr Abdul Munim Al-Sayyed Ali, Chairman, Economics Department, Al-Mustansiriyah University, Baghdad, Iraq

Dr Rattan J. Bhatia, Deputy Director, African Department, International Monetary Fund, Washington D.C., USA

Dr Faris Bingaradi, Economist, Arab Monetary Fund, Abu Dhabi, UAE

Mr Isselmou Ould Boye, General Director of Foreign Affairs, Central Bank of Mauritania, Nouakchott, Mauritania

Mr Burhan Dajani, Secretary General, Union of Chambers of Commerce, Industry and Agriculture for Arab Countries, Beirut, Lebanon

Prof. Carlos F. Diaz-Alejandro, Professor of Economics, Yale University, New Haven, Connecticut, USA

Dr John W. Gunter, Consultant, Washington, D.C., USA

Dr Khair El-Din Haseeb, Director General, Centre for Arab Unity Studies, Beirut, Lebanon

Dr Jawad Hashim, President, Arab Monetary Fund, Abu Dhabi, UAE

Dr Izzadin Ibrahim Hassan, Acting Director of Research and Statistics, Arab Monetary Fund, Abu Dhabi, UAE

Mr Adel Hussein, Centre for Arab Unity Studies, Beirut, Lebanon

Dr Mohamed Mahmoud El-Imam, Assistant to the President, Arab Monetary Fund, Abu Dhabi, UAE

Dr Shaker M. Issa, Assistant Director, Research and Statistics Department, UAE Currency Board, Abu Dhabi, UAE

List of Participants

Dr Mabid Ali Al-Jarhi, Economist, Arab Monetary Fund, Abu Dhabi, UAE

Mr Anton Kattan, Assistant Economist, Arab Monetary Fund, Abu Dhabi, UAE

Mr Mohammed Salim Al-Kawari, Member, Board of Trustees, Centre for Arab Unity Studies, Doha, Qatar

Dr Abdul W. Khayata, President, Deputy Chairman, Central Bank of Oman, Muscat, Oman

Dr Amer J. Khayatt, Consultant, London, England

Dr Rifaat El-Mahgoub, Chairman, Economics Department, Cairo University, Cairo, Egypt

Mr Majed Mohammad Al-Majed, Director General, Qatar Monetary Agency, Doha, Qatar

Dr Samir Makdisi, Professor of Economics, American University of Beirut, Beirut, Lebanon

Mr Abdul Wahid Al-Makhzoumi, Senior Economist, Arab Monetary Fund, Abu Dhabi, UAE

Dr Rainer S. Masera, Director, Research Department, International Division, Banca d'Italia, Rome, Italy

Mr Alfredo Medio, Economic Affairs Officer, Money, Finance and Development Division, United Nations Conference on Trade and Development, Palais des Nations, Geneva, Switzerland

Dr Fouad Morsi, Professor of Economics, Alexandria University, Cairo, Egypt

Dr Karim Nashashibi, International Monetary Fund, Washington D.C., USA

Dr Abderrahim Omrana, Deputy Director General, Centre Africain d'Etudes Monétaires, Dakar, Senegal

Dr Faika El-Refaie, Senior Economist, Arab Monetary Fund, Abu Dhabi, UAE

List of Participants 469

Dr Salvatore Rossi, Economist, Research Department, Banca d'Italia, Rome, Italy

Dr Abdul Aal Al-Sagban, Economic Affairs Bureau, Revolutionary Command Council, Baghdad, Iraq

Dr Mahmoud Sakbani, Chief, Monetary Unit, United Nations Conference on Trade and Development, Palais des Nations, Geneva, Switzerland

Dr N.A. Sarma, Economic Adviser, UAE Currency Board, Abu Dhabi, UAE

Dr A. Shakour Shaalan, Director, Middle Eastern Department, International Monetary Fund, Washington, D.C., USA

Dr Salah Al-Shaikhly, Regional Director, United Nations Development Programme, New York, N.Y., USA

Dr Mohammed Labih Shoukair, The Economic Adviser to the Arab Monetary Fund, Abu Dhabi, UAE

Dr Rafik Sowellem, Economic Adviser, Arab Monetary Fund, Abu Dhabi, UAE

Prof. Robert Triffin, Institut de Recherches Economiques, Université Catholique de Louvain, Brussels, Belgium

Prof. Jorge Gonzalez del Valle, Director, Centro de Estudios Monetarios Latinoamericanos, Mexico City, Mexico

Prof. John Williamson, Departamento de Economia, Pontificia Universidade Catolica do Rio de Janeiro, Rio de Janeiro, Brazil

INDEX

Abu Dhabi 79
Algeria 105, 113, 114, 115, 125, 126, 128, 133, 299, 300, 301, 302, 305, 308, 310, 394, 399, 400.
All Saints' Day Manifesto 14, 23, 24.
AMF (Arab Monetary Fund): balance of payments and 155-69, 390-8; capital transfers and 79; consultation and 410-12; currency pegging and 398-401, 404-5; currency unification and 401-7; deficit countries and 318, 323; establishment of 180, 440-1; foreign investments and 407-10; guarantees of 160, 188, 193, 199; IMF and 179-82, 412, 414 interest rates and 162, 164-5; lending of 160, 162-9 *passim*, 188, 189, 202, 317, 322, 414; monetary development and 443-4; objectives of 152-78, 179, 180, 188, 200; payments union and 402-4, 443; policies, application of 163-9; research by 412-13; Reserve Fund of 163; resources of 158-62, 182, 183, 191-3, 196-201 *passim*, 325, 420; statistics prepared by 412; trade and 157, 174-6; training by 412; Trust Fund of 163; *et passim*
Ammam Financial Market 130
Andean Finance Corporation 214
Andean Group 15
Andean Reserve Fund 213, 214, 216, 222, 225, 230, 231
Arab Accounting Dinar 171, 173, 405, 416, 417, 418, 441-2, 451 see *also* Arab dinar
Arab Common Market 167, 174, 177, 178, 309
Arab Company for Trading Shares 130
Arab countries: economic dependence of, 424-30, 448, 450, 452, 457, 459, 461, 463 economic development, untied funds and 80-1; economic disparities between 430-4, 439, 449-50, 454, 455, 461, 462, 463; economic systems, divergences between 99, 103; loans to poorer 75-6, 77-9, 80-1, 94
Arab Development Decade 161, 168, 411
Arab Development Fund 168
Arab dinar 401-7, 411, 414, 417, 420-1, 442, 444, 445, 456 see *also* Arab Accounting Dinar
Arab Economic Unity Agreement 177, 178, 309
Arab Fund for Economic and Social Development 93, 152, 161, 162, 170; 189, 325, 439, 454
Arab Investment Guarantee Institution 409-10
Arab League 92, 102, 152, 191, 411, 416
Arab Monetary System 440-6
Arab Monetary Zone 444-6, 451
Arab Summit Conference 192, 200
Arab Trade and Transit Agreement, 100
Arab unity 194, 195
Arusha Document 139

Bahrain 35, 104, 105, 117, 122, 126, 128, 129, 300, 301, 302, 305, 308; currency of 98, 106, 133, 399 *et passim*
Balance of payments 29, 57, 62-3, 240-2, 252, 263, 310-17, 393-4 *et passim*
Banco d'Italia 244
Bank for International Set lements 43, 68, 263
Bank of Egypt 77
Banks 13, 37, 40, 112, 138, 198, 202; Arab, 87-8, 116, 117, 120, 125, 126, 130-2, 147, 197, 198, 202, 409, 426, 441; Arab-foreign 78, 87; capital flows and 77-8, 328; role of 130-2; *et passim*
BCEAO (Banque Centrale des Etates de l'Afrique Occidental 269-82 *passim*, 286-91 *passim*, 294
Belgium 244, 248, 249, 250

470

Index 471

Benin 269, 279, 280
Bolivia 214
Brandt Commission Report 43
Brazil 219, 227
Bretton Woods Agreement 43, 46, 48, 50, 58, 181, 349, 398, 404 *et passim*
Bundesbank 244

Capital, movement of 11, 12, 14, 15, 21, 23, 24, 32, 135, 148, 349, 351-2; Arab countries 309, 317-23, 325, 383, 386, 394, 409, 410 *et passim*
Capital markets 104, 105, 125-30 *passim*, 415-16, 426, 428; integration of 14-15, 19-20, 23, 24, 415, 416, 454
Caribbean Community Multilateral Clearing Facility 206, 222, 223, 291-2
Cartegena Treaty 214
Central America 217-21; monetary union 207
Central American Clearing House 206, 213, 217, 218, 219, 220, 221, 223, 230
Central American Common Market 205, 212, 228, 229
Central American Monetary Agreement 218, 220
Central American Monetary Council 213, 218, 219, 220-1, 229
Central American Monetary Stabilisation Fund 213-4, 216-21 *passim*, 225, 230
Central American Payments Union 228, 229
'Central American Peso' 210
Centre for Arab Studies 92
CFA franc 271, 287, 288, 291
Colombia 214, 217, 219, 223
Conference of Ministers of Foreign and Economic Affairs 192
'Consols' 54
Council of Arab Economic Unity 91, 93, 102, 152, 161, 167, 168, 177, 178, 191, 200, 403, 410, 411
Credit: control of 116-17, 118, 120
Credit and Savings Bank 131
Credit expansion, domestic (DCE) 14, 19, 22, 25 *see also* Loans

Currency pegs 105, 133, 134, 142-3, 149-50, 172, 191, 398-401, 404-5, 418, 420 *et passim*, *see also* Exchange rates
Currency unification 12, 85-6, 94-5, 172,-3, 195, 327-8, 350, 356, 364-5, 385-6, 401-7, 441 *see also* Arab dinar *and* Gulf countries, common currency in
Customs unions 28, 30

Dahomy 271
Debre, Michel 68
Democratic Yemen 79, 108, 110, 112, 114, 129, 133, 299, 300, 301, 302, 305, 308, 310, 399
Denmark 244, 247, 248, 249
Deutschmark 46, 62, 244, 247
Djibouti 300, 301, 302, 308, 399
Dollar: Arabic currencies, severing of from 450, 451, 462; ECU and 51-4; exchange rate 40-2 *passim*, 52-4 *passim*, 244, 247, 249; international monetary system and 66-7, 426-9, 445, 450; SDR and 34, 42, 43, 172; *et passim*, *see also under* ECU
Dominican Republic, 219

East African Community 35
Economic integration: Arab; benefits of 331, capital flows and 80, institutions for 93, 94, monetary integration and 29, 36, 93-4, 96, 100, 101, 195, 198, 199, 385-6, 387, policy co-ordination and 121-3, politics and 98-9, 187, 434-8; general discussion; concepts of 11-15, definition of 25, 452-3, developing countries, meaning of for 422-3, monetary integration and 12, 289, 291-2, 293, 339, 342, 357, 423, 448, 453-4, 458-9, 460-1; *et passim*, *see also* Monetary inetgration
ECU: Arab countries and 57, 255; central banks and 51; credit and 237-42 *passim*, 259; definition of 48; dollar and 51-4, 243, 244, 254, 264; exchange rates and 49, 234-6; issues, increase of 69; OPEC countries and 255; parallel currency 53, 265; recycling and

254-5; use of outside EEC 52, 254-5; *see also* EMS
Ecuador 214
EEC (European Economic Community): common agricultural policy 243; Monetary Committee 241, 242, 251, 258; nature of 28; *see also* ECU, EMS
EFTA (European Free Trade Association) 56
Egypt 74-5, 82, 99-101 *passim*, 108, 110, 112-14 *passim*, 116, 118, 121, 125, 126-8 *passim*, 133, 139-40, 144, 145, 148, 300-2 *passim*, 305, 308, 310, 314, 399 *et passim*
EMS (European Monetary System): balance of payments and 240-2, 252, 263; construction of 233-43; credit mechanisms 233, 237-42, 259; dollar and 253-4, 259; ECUs and 48-56, 234; exchange rates 48, 50, 233, 234-7, 243-50 *passim*, 253-4, 258, 263, 267; future of 250-5, 259; IMF and 61; international monetary system and 253-5; nature of 48-51, 60-1, 66; operation of 243-50; origins of 233; poorer states help for 233, 234, 242-3; *see also* ECU
Ethier-Bloomfield proposal 258
Eurobonds 52
Eurocurrency 52, 68
Europa 23
European Investment Bank 453
European Monetary Co-operation Fund (EMCF) 50-1, 171, 237, 238, 240, 263
European Monetary Fund 51, 60, 197, 233-4, 237, 250-3
European Payments Union 13, 21, 33-4, 70
European Unit of Account (EAU) 234, 235
Exchange controls 13, 15, 16, 20, 36, 37
Exchange costs 15, 19, 358
Exchange rates: Arab countries 97, 104-11 *passim*, 146, 171, 172, 174, 363, 399, 400, 406, 419, 442-3; and monetary policy 132-7; 145-6, co-ordination of 97, 105, 145, 355-6, 365-7, 384, 416-17, policies for 104-5, 132-7, 141-3, *et passim*; general discussion; co-ordination of 13-14, 19, 21, 24, 25, 37, 66, fixing of 12, floating 14, 16, risks 15-16, stability of 62, trade and 16, 352-3, unification of 31, 349-55 *passim*

FECOM 69
Financial development 127-30, 169, 409
Financial integration 169-71
Financial intermediaries 125-7, 136, 138, 147
Fiscal co-ordination 368-9
France: franc 46, 234-5, 248, 249, 258, 271; WAMU and 269, 271, 272, 273, 274, 286-9, 290, 293-4
Friedman, Milton 32, 55

General Agreement on Tariffs and Trade (GATT) 177
Germany 234-6 *passim*, 244, 247, 248, 249, 258, 261; Deutschmark 46, 62, 244, 247
Giscard d'Estaing 262
Gold 40-6 *passim*, 66; demonetisation of 83, 450; monetisation of 69-70; revaluation of 45, *et passim*
Goods, movement of 32
Gresham's Law 378
Guinea 269
Gulf countries: common currency in 29, 82-5, 94-5, 337, 385-6; dollar and 429; monetary integration 29-30, 35, 37-8, 56, 67, 70, 326-7, 337, 382-3, 389, 415, 463-4
Gulf Fund in Support of Egypt 76, 79

Hirsch, F 361

IMF (International Monetary Fund) 21, 58, 76; AMF and 179-82, 412, 414; articles, amendment of 39, 46, 47, 55, 65; credit from 40, 41, 42, 44, 45, 55; criticisms of 139; developing countries, aid to 427; dollar and 427; effectiveness of 64; establishment

Index 473

of 180; industrial countries benefits from 427; objectives of 179; Oil Facility 161, 163, 429; policies of 144; *et passim*
Inflation 32, 33, 37, 120, 265, 266, 354-5, 380, 396 *et passim*; world (1970s) 40-3
Interest rates 14, 35, 118, 120, 121, 135, 136, 347, 348, 351-2 *et passim*
International Bank for Reconstruction and Development (IBRD) 177, 180, 189
Investment 19, 23, 28, 36, 88-90, 119, 123, 132 *see also* Oil revenues
Iran 77, 101
Iraq 80, 91, 99, 105-7, 114, 115, 126, 128, 129, 300, 301, 302, 305, 308, 311, 314, 317, 391, 395, 399, 400, 401, 403, 419
Ireland 243, 248
Islamic Bank 88, 412
Italy 33, 50, 243, 244, 245, 248, 249, 261, 268, 453
Ivory Coast 269, 271, 279, 280, 281, 288

Japan 248, 343
Joint Defence Council 168
Jordan 88, 99, 107, 110, 114, 117, 118, 119, 125, 126, 128, 130, 131, 133, 300, 301, 302, 305, 308, 311, 399

Keynsianism 13, 14, 17, 25
Korea 343
Kuwait 35, 74, 79, 104, 105, 106, 115, 125, 126, 128, 129, 130, 131, 133, 300, 301, 302, 305, 308, 311, 314, 317, 319, 391, 399, 400, 426 *et passim*

Labour, movement of 11, 32, 91, 97-8, 111, 115, 122, 148, 309, 348, 350-1, 356, 362 *et passim*
Latin America: balance of payments support 212-17, 219, 220-1, 225, 228; clearing and payments arrangements 206-12, 225; dollar and 206, 210, 229, 230, economic integration, origin of 205-6; exchange controls 211; funds, recycling of 338; monetary union 207; reserves of 213-15; trade 211, 212, 222, 225, 226, 227; *see also* Central America
Latin American Economic System (SELA) 227, 231
Latin American Export Bank (BLADEX) 217, 221, 338-9
Latin American Free Trade Association (LAFTA) 205, 206, 207, 208, 212, 213, 214, 215, 217, 222, 223, 228, 230
Latin American Monetary Fund 230
League of Arab States 82, 410, 411, 416
Lebanon 82, 89, 107, 110, 117, 125-33 *passim*, 300, 301, 303, 305, 308, 399
Libya 99, 105-7, 115, 125, 126, 128, 300, 301, 303, 306, 308, 311, 391, 399, 400, 401, 419
Loans: tied 88-90; united 73-81, 87, 94, 141

MacDougall Report 242, 267
Mali 269
Marjolin Report 254
Mauritania 107, 110, 269, 292-3, 300, 301, 303, 306, 308, 312
Mexico 217, 219, 223
Monetarism 14, 17, 25
Monetary co-ordination 19, 22, 24-5, 26 *see also* Monetary integration
Monetary expansion, co-ordination of 35
Monetary integration: Arab countries; AMF and 171-4, 183, 187, 191, common currency 149, cost-benefit analysis 29-30, 346-56, 361-2, 380, dependency and 424-30, feasibility of 56-8, 61, 358-61, 377, 381-3, 414-15, financial surpluses and 323-9, 335, forms of 440, modalities of 363, 378, phasing of 364, policy issues 364-70, politics and 81-2, 86, 194-5, 344, 359, 360, 377, 379, 381, 445-6, 457-8, 460, requirements for, 424-40, 457-8, 459, 460, *see also under* Gulf countries; general discussion; authority, structure of 370-1, benefits of 16, 17, centralisation strategy 31-2, common currency

and 25, 28, concepts 11-15, co-ordination strategy 31, costs of 16-17, currency unification and 96, 98, definition 25, 28, 191, economic integration and 12, 289, 291-2, 293, 339, 342, 357, 378, 423, 448, 453-4, 458-9, 460-1, forms of 23-4, minimal concept of 357-8, nationalism and 18, objectives of 15-20, 36, partial 13-15, 18, 20-5, 28-9, 454, political dimension of 17, 18, 25, 343, production and 29
Monetary policy 113-21, 134-7, 367-8
Monetary system, world: disorder in 39-46; reforms of 46-7, 54-6, 61-5, 68-9, 436-7, 450, 451
'Money illusion' 354, 358, 362
Money supply 13, 113, 114, 115, 118, 131, 140, 347, 367-8, 352 et passim
Morocco 107-8, 110, 114, 118, 119, 125, 126, 128, 131, 133, 143, 300, 301, 303, 306, 308, 312, 394, 399

Netherlands 248
Niger 269, 271, 279, 280

OAPEC 161, 167
OECD (Organisation for Economic Cooperation and Development) 19, 457
Oil revenues: capitalists' benefit from 425, 426; investment of 64, 73, 77, 89, 101-2, 141, 195, 334-5, 341-2, 382, 391-3, 457, 462; recycling of 170, 255, 338, 425, 429, 430; surpluses, problems and risks of 62-3, 156, 360, 378, 382, 388, 392-3, 407-10
Oman 35, 133, 300, 301, 303, 306, 308, 399
OPEC (Organisation of Petroleum Exporting Countries) 255, 392, 412
'Optimum currency areas' 47, 361

Parallel currencies 14, 22-3, 24, 25, 53, 57, 67, 265, 365, 378-9
Payment unions 13, 18, 20, 24, 33-4, 36, 37, 384; Arab countries 34, 87, 384, 402-4, 410, 415, 418-19, 440
Peru 214
Phillips curve 265, 347, 380
Polak, J.J. 56
Pound (sterling) 46
Production 29, 76, 100, 102, 333

Qatar 35, 104, 105, 122, 303, 306, 308, 314, 319, 391, 399, 400; currency of 98, 106, 300, 301

Reserve pooling 13, 19, 20-1, 24, 367
Reserves, world: composition of 55, 64; increases in 40-6, 55, 66; regional shares of 43-6
Rouble 451, 456, 463

'Santa Domingo Agreement' 213, 214, 215, 230
Saudi Arabia 74, 99, 128, 130, 306, 312, 317, 319, 390-1, 399; currency of 105, 106, 133, 399, 400; monetary union with other states 35, 37, 383; money supply 115, 118, 119, 120, 121, 130; trade 104, 300, 301, 303, 308, 314, 426; et passim
Savings 120, 121, 127, 132, 136, 147
Schmidt, Helmut 262
SDR: as international currency 69; balance of payments deficits and 64-5; distribution of 44, 45, 47; role of 63-4; world reserves and, 40-5 passim, 55, 56 et passim
Security market integration 371-3; Arab countries 362, 368, 372-3, 379, 388
SELA (Latin American Economic System) 227, 231
Senegal 269, 271, 279, 280, 281, 288
Serge Report 373
Smithsonian Agreement 182
'Snake', the 14, 21, 24, 50, 234, 239, 443 see also EMS
Socialist countries 108, 448-9, 461
Somalia 108, 110, 300, 301, 303, 306, 308, 312, 399
Sudan 79, 88, 108, 110, 112, 114, 118, 120, 121, 133, 300, 301, 304, 307, 313, 399

Switzerland 248
Syria 80, 82, 99, 108, 110-14, *passim*, 118, 125, 133, 300, 301, 304, 307, 308, 313, 399

Technology 450, 457
Tindemans Report 254
Togo 269, 271, 279, 280
Trade 29, 30, 31, 100-1, 112, 113, 116; foreign 67, 100, 140, 299, 396; institutions financing 87-8, 95; inter-Arab 67, 88, 89, 96, 97, 100, 140, 141, 174, 299-309, 331-4, 338, 344, 411, 417; liberalisation of and the financial system 111-13, 127; regimes of 104-13, 146, 309, *et passim*
Tunisia 107-8, 110, 114, 118, 119, 125, 126, 133, 300, 301, 304, 307, 308, 313, 399

UAE (United Arab Emirates) 35, 37, 56, 98, 104-6 *passim*, 122, 133, 300, 301, 304, 308, 314, 319, 391, 399, 400 *et passim*
UNCTAD (United Nations Conference on Trade and Development) 189, 436
Unemployment 17, 33, 265, 266, 380 *et passim*
United Kingdom 33, 248
United States of America: balance of payments deficit 52-3; Federal Reserve System 84, 247; gold and 46; inflation 62; reserves of 45, 53; *see also* Dollar
Upper Volta 269, 279, 280, 281

Venezuela 214, 217, 219
Volcker, President 247

Wages 17, 25, 33, 266, 354, 453
WAMU (West African Monetary Union): Arab countries, significance of to 282-3, 288-9; background to 269-73; benefits of 287-9, 290; economic data on members 279-80; economic integration and 282-4; operation of 273-6, 278-82; origins of 269; revision of 276-82
Werner Report 12, 24, 358
World Bank 56, 76, 141, 412

Yemen 107, 110, 114, 117, 118, 128, 133, 300, 301, 304, 307, 308, 313, 399 *see also* Democratic Yemen
Yen 34, 46, 62, 451